THE DYSKOLOS OF MENANDER

THE
DYSKOLOS
OF MENANDER

EDITED BY
E. W. HANDLEY

HARVARD UNIVERSITY PRESS
CAMBRIDGE, MASSACHUSETTS
1965

First published in U.S.A. in 1965 by
Harvard University Press, Cambridge, Massachusetts
© E. W. Handley, 1965
Printed in Great Britain by
Robert Cunningham & Sons Ltd, Alva

Contents

Acknowledgements

For help and encouragement in the writing of this book, my first thanks must go to my London colleagues, for it began from the Seminar whose results appeared in the Bulletin of the Institute of Classical Studies, vol. 6, 1959. But I am especially indebted to Professors T. B. L. Webster and A. M. Webster (A. M. Dale) for continuous discussion and improvement of my typescript as it grew, and to Professor E. G. Turner, who shared in reading and criticizing the nascent commentary and part of the Introduction; Dr J. A. Willis has often put both his learning and his library at my disposal. But I am also more grateful than detailed acknowledgements can show to many others, for discussions, letters, and copies of their published work on the play, among whom I must mention particularly Professor Hugh Lloyd-Jones. Naturally, no-one but myself is responsible for the use made here of the advice and information which has been given so freely. As the work progressed, criticism and interpretation of the text proceeded rapidly in many parts of the world; I have used it as fully as I could, both in writing the commentary, and still more in what has been a long process of pruning and revision. It could well have been longer; and among many things for which I have to thank Messrs Methuen is their patience; I can speak with admiration of the care and skill shown by Messrs Robert Cunningham and Sons in printing from a typescript which was often far from straightforward. Professor B. R. Rees gave me great pleasure, and has done the reader great service, in offering himself for the task of proof-reading the text: he has added to my gratitude by helping me with the Introduction also, and by reading the whole book in page-proof. For other corrections and improvements made in proof, I am extremely grateful to Dr Michael Coffey and Dr Holger Thesleff, and (once again) to A. M. Dale, Hugh Lloyd-Jones and T. B. L. Webster. It hardly needs to be added that the errors and inconsistencies which remain are my fault: I hope, as one does, that they are not unusually numerous or troublesome.

Abbreviations, etc.

I hope that most of the abbreviations in this book will be clear or familiar; the lists in the revised (1925-40) edition of Liddell and Scott's *Greek-English Lexicon* (=LSJ) may help readers who are concerned with any which are not. Articles in learned journals are often cited in short form without title (e.g. W. G. Arnott, CQ 1957.188-98), though I have sometimes expanded the form of reference as standard in L'Année Philologique (e.g. 'Class. World', not 'CW'). L'Année Philologique, from vol. 28 onwards, but essentially from vol. 30 (Bibliographie de l'année 1959), 1960, should be consulted for work on the *Dyskolos*; a list of editions appears below at the end of Introd. III, and a note on some editorial conventions of the present work immediately precedes the text of the play.

For other plays by Menander, I quote as a rule from Koerte (see below); fragments of Greek comic poets other than Menander are quoted where possible from Kock, *Comicorum Atticorum Fragmenta* (=K), and where possible with transliterated titles (though the transliterated title does not necessarily reflect my own opinion of the correct original form); papyrus fragments of drama are quoted where possible from D. L. Page, *Greek Literary Papyri* (1941; 3rd edn. 1950); I have occasionally consulted the recent edition of the fragments of Attic Comedy by J. M. Edmonds. Sometimes, when restorations and doubtful readings in a text were immaterial to the matter in hand, I have discarded the apparatus of brackets and dotted letters provided by my source, as with Menander, *Heros* 42f, quoted in the Commentary on 39-40; on other occasions, it has seemed prudent to call special attention to the state of the text, as with *Perikeiromene* 424f, quoted on 144. For quotations from Latin Comedies, see Additional Note at the end of Introd. I; on works of art illustrating comedy, see Introd. II.3.

The following special abbreviations are used for some frequently quoted works:

Koerte I³   *Menandri quae supersunt: pars prior.* Ed. A. Koerte, Leipzig, Teubner, 1938; repr. with addenda, 1955.

Koerte II   *Menandri quae supersunt: pars altera.* Ed. A. Koerte, with revisions and addenda by A. Thierfelder, 1953; repr. with further addenda and corrections, 1959.

Denniston, *Particles*   *The Greek Particles*, by J. D. Denniston: Oxford, 1934; 2nd edn., with revisions and addenda by K. J. Dover, 1954.

KG I ⎫
KG II ⎭   *Ausführliche Grammatik d. griechischen Sprache*, von R. Kühner. Zweiter Teil, dritte Auflage, in zwei Bänden. Revised by B. Gerth, Hanover and Leipzig, 1898 (I); 1904 (II).

NT Gramm.   *A Greek Grammar of the New Testament*, etc., by F. Blass and A. Debrunner: a translation and revision of the ninth-tenth German edition ... by Robert W. Funk, Cambridge and Chicago, 1961.

Schwyzer I ⎫
Schwyzer II ⎭   *Griechische Grammatik*, von Eduard Schwyzer, München, C. H. Beck (=*Handbuch der Altertumswissenschaft* II.i.1-2), 1953 (reprint of I); 1950 (II, ed. A. Debrunner).

Webster, *SM*:   *Studies in Menander*, by T. B. L. Webster, Manchester, 1950; 2nd edn., with an appendix (pp. 220-34), 1960.

Webster, *LGC*:   *Studies in Later Greek Comedy*, by T. B. L. Webster, Manchester, 1953.

Bieber, *HT*² ⎫
Webster, *GTP* ⎪
    MNC ⎬   See Introd. II.3
   MOMC ⎭

INTRODUCTION

I

Menander and the *Dyskolos*

'Menander, son of Diopeithes, of the Kephisian deme, was born in the archonship of Sosigenes': that is, in the Athenian year 342/1 B.C. The year 321, in which he produced his first play, the *Orge*, happens to mark the centenary of Aristophanes' *Peace*; the *Dyskolos*, produced in 316, is separated from the *Plutus* of 388 by nearly three-quarters of a century, or rather more than two generations. These three dates in Menander's life are among those generally accepted, though each is the subject of learned dispute; if we think of him first as a writer of Greek comedy, they are useful to place him in relation to the Greek comic dramatist whose work is most fully preserved and best known.[1]

In the interval between the fifth-century plays of Aristophanes and the years in which Menander grew up, the world as seen from Athens changed widely; and in literature, Comedy transformed itself, turning away from the poetic fantasy and satirical attack with which it treated public issues and prominent men towards an interest in the private affairs of fictional ordinary people; in doing so, it ceased to be topical and became universal, the recognizable prototype of much modern light drama. What we know of the development suggests evolution rather than sudden transition: Aristotle could trace its beginnings to Crates, in the generation before Aristophanes (*Poetics* 1449 b); the drama of everyday life in its most admired ancient form, that of Menander, was still to appear in the thirty years after Aristotle's death, which preceded the production of the *Orge* by some few months. Menander died in 292/1 or a neighbouring year. Provided we do not

---

[1] Texts bearing on Menander's life and works appear in the second volume of the Teubner edition by Koerte-Thierfelder, to which the reader will be referred: the quotation which opens this section is from *IG* 14.1184 (Koerte II, Testimonia, 3). For discussion and dating, see especially Jacoby, *F Gr Hist*, vol. 2 D, pp. 734ff; Koerte, *RE* 'Menandros' 15.1 (1931) 707ff; Webster, *SM* 103-8; for problems arising from the Athenian archon lists and other chronological evidence for the period, see Meritt, Hesperia 26 (1957) 53-54 and A. E. Samuel, *Ptolemaic Chronology* 16ff (=Münchener Beiträge, Heft 43, 1962), with references there given; on the evidence of the *Dyskolos* didascalia, see the Commentary, p. 123f below.

make too much of the date-lines (for poets' lives and literary fashions both cross them), 321 is a convenient boundary between the so-called New Comedy of Menander and his contemporaries and successors, and the Middle Comedy whose later developments were 'modern' to Aristotle. The name Middle Comedy is perhaps best reserved for plays written before 321 and after the death of Aristophanes in the mid-380's; though often one may wish rather to speak of the fifth century as opposed to the fourth: Aristophanes' later plays look both forward and back.

Alongside changes in subjects and attitude, comedy of the fourth century in general shows changes of style and form. Its language tends to the plainness of simple prose or ordinary conversation, losing much of the stylistic variety and the lively scurrilities which characterize Old Comedy as we know it best, from the fifth-century plays of Aristophanes; lyrics become sparse; the chorus declines to a band of interlude performers taking no part in the dialogue; the formal patterns of *agon, parabasis*, and scenes alternating with lyric, in strings or in pairs and groups, have all given way by Menander's time to a structure whose essential parts are what we call 'acts': that is, sequences of scenes forming more or less coherent units of composition, and marked off from each other by choral interludes which are indicated in copies of the plays by the note *XOPOY* (as one might write CHORUS in English); the *Dyskolos* has five such 'acts', and it is probable that for Menander that number was the rule. In costume, there is little room for decorative elaboration, as with Aristophanes' Wasp-chorus, or his Hoopoe and birds in the *Birds*; the grossness of Old Comedy modifies towards decency; the range of masks worn by the players develops to include standard types suitable for a comedy of manners.[1]

One reason for recalling the earlier history of Comedy, however briefly, is to orientate ourselves; another is that Menander and his audiences must themselves have been strongly aware of

---

[1] On the history of Greek Comedy in the period 400-321, see Webster, *LGC*, 1-97; and on the evidence from vases, terracottas, etc., *MOMC*, Introd., pp. 1-12. A classic essay on the character of Middle Comedy by Meineke appears in his *Frag. Com. Graec.* vol. 1 (1839); an admirable encyclopaedic survey by Koerte is in *RE* 'Komödie' 11.1 (1921) 1256-66. On acts and act-divisions there is much debate: since the *Dyskolos* is still the only fully preserved Menander in Greek, a minimal statement might be that the other remains of him are consistent with the 'five-act' pattern of composition and do not warrant the assumption of any other. On costumes and masks in the *Dyskolos*, see below, Introd. II.3.

the past. The aspiring comic poet in Athens wrote in the hope of achieving a production at one of the two major dramatic festivals held in the city, knowing that his own qualities would be measured not only against his contemporary competitors, but by the standards of a long and distinguished tradition. In the fourth century, apart from what they might read or see performed on lesser occasions, Athenians could see five comedies in each year they attended the Lenaea, and five at the City Dionysia; for the year 339 B.C. we have a record of an old play revived at the Dionysia, and it is probable that by 311 such revivals were regular: new and old plays were part of the same great occasion.[1] The *Dyskolos* proves to have many points of contact with our limited knowledge of comedy in the two preceding generations; though not always easily made out, they deserve special emphasis precisely because we are working with a minute fraction of Middle Comedy texts. Although it is unclear what fact lies behind the tradition which associates Menander with Alexis, who was writing in Athens at least as early as the 350's, it can hardly have arisen unless someone who knew something of both recognized a particular affinity in their work, and gave Alexis the credit for inspiring Menander.[2] Though the picture they give is necessarily far from complete, parallels between Menander and other comic poets can show something of what Athenian audiences expected as familiar or conventional in Comedy, and how far their taste for the familiar was satisfied. In allowing for the considerable force of comic tradition in his work, we must also remember what Menander rejected or modified. For example, the first half of the fourth century saw a major development in plays with plots and characters from myth; the type persists in the latter half of the century, though with a marked decline in popularity, but to Menander it was evidently uncongenial. Again,

[1] *IG* 2². 2318, col. xii; *ib.*2323 a: cf. Pickard-Cambridge, *Festivals*, 125. For evidence of fourth-century productions at the Peiraeus and other Attic theatres outside Athens, see Vitucci, Dioniso 7 (1939) 210ff, and Pickard-Cambridge, *op. cit.* 40ff.

[2] Anon. *de com.*, 15 (p. 9 Kaibel) says of Menander: συνδιατρίψας δὲ τὰ πολλὰ Ἀλέξιδι ὑπὸ τούτου δοκεῖ παιδευθῆναι; the Suda, s.v. Ἄλεξις says γέγονε δὲ πάτρως Μενάνδρου: Koerte II, Test. 2 and 5. If Alexis really lived to be 106, he could still have been writing in the early 270's after Menander's death (cf. Alex., *Hypobolimaios* 244 K), but their lives in any case have a long overlap. For dates of Alexis' plays, often debatable, see Webster, CQ n.s. 2 (1952) 13ff: where chronology is no obstacle, resemblances between the two poets could have arisen from influence in either direction. For ancient research into literary 'borrowings' by Menander, cf. Koerte II, Test. 51, and the introductory note to the frgg. of *Deisidaimon*.

if we take the *mageiros* or cook-caterer as a type who is relatively well documented in the remains of later Greek Comedy, Menander's treatment of Sikon in the *Dyskolos* can be quoted both to show him using a popular stock figure and to provide evidence that he rehandles the motifs associated with it with a carefully calculated choice.[1]

A second important aspect of Menander's comedy appears when we remember that he is also in some sense heir to the traditions of tragic drama. Broadly speaking, the influence of Tragedy came to Menander in three ways: most obviously, perhaps, as part of his inheritance from earlier comic writers, in that Attic Comedy perennially borrowed language, themes and dramatic technique from serious drama, and often what was originally taken over for satirical mockery stayed on and was redeveloped as part of the comic poets' own stock-in-trade (for example, recognition scenes, in which rings or other tokens are found to reveal a character's true parentage): in particular mythological comedy, by translating heroic myth into its own kind of everyday reality, seems to have provided a bridge between serious drama about legendary heroes and light drama about fictional ordinary people. Secondly, literary studies of tragedy, as of comedy, by Aristotle and others presented Menander, his contemporaries, and the more educated members of their audiences, with informed dramatic theory and criticism; thirdly, and not least important, Menander and his audiences experienced Tragedy directly by reading their classics and seeing them restaged alongside modern work: it is perhaps mildly amusing, but certainly not ridiculous, to find a charcoal-burner quoting myth as seen in tragedy as part of his case in an argument with a shepherd (Men., *Epitr.* 149ff). In general, we have to recognize the influence of tragedy on Menander's plot-construction and character-drawing; in detail, our evidence goes beyond verbal echoes of known plays, and quotations that are simply part of one character's remarks to another; it extends to the subtler form of reminiscence in which a comic scene is given overtones by echoing a famous incident in tragedy, or by following a tragic pattern of structure, language, or metre, which in performance could be emphasized by voice,

[1] Mythological Comedy: see Webster (quoted p. 5, n. 2) p. 23, and *LGC* 82ff. The alternative title for Menander's *Achaioi* given by P.Oxy.27.2462 shows that it was *not* a mythological play, as some have supposed. Sikon: see especially on 393, 489-98, 889, 946-53.

gesture, and staging. So in the *Dyskolos* at 690ff, when the stricken Knemon is brought out from his house on a couch or bed, the situation which the comic plot has created gains in depth from the echo in stage spectacle, and perhaps in language, of the situation of a stricken hero in tragedy: the audience is to realize that the major crisis of Knemon's life is at hand, and the comparison which the dramatist suggests helps to bring this realization about.[1]

Menander grew up in an Athens dominated by Macedon: Philip's victory at Chaeronea came in 338, when he was about four years old. In autumn 322 (some few months before Menander made his début with the *Orge*), the Athenian-inspired revolt which followed on Alexander's death was crushed in battles on land and sea, and a Macedonian garrison occupied the harbour-fort of Munychia at the Peiraeus; Demosthenes, Hyperides and others who had advocated rebellion were condemned as traitors and hunted to their deaths; Aristotle had left Athens for Chalcis, where he died in refuge against the vindictiveness of the anti-Macedonian party. A new revolution following on the death of Antipater in 319 was in turn fought down by his son Cassander, and early in 317 Cassander established Demetrius of Phalerum as governor of Athens. The preceding spring had seen the theatre packed for a notorious treason trial, to which Phocion and some of his associates were brought for condemnation, and soon afterwards they were executed: as the tide of events turned, outright resistance, reasoned compromise, and willing collaboration were alike disastrous to their less fortunate adherents. Demetrius had been both fortunate and skilful; a man of many talents, he brought to the government of Athens a political and social programme informed by the philosophy of the Peripatetic school, at whose head now stood Aristotle's successor, Theophrastus. Theophrastus could count both Demetrius and Menander among his pupils, and if the date we have accepted for the *Dyskolos* is correct, it was produced during the first winter of the new governor's administration.[2]

[1] See Webster's chapter on 'Menander and earlier Greek Drama' in *SM*, 153-94, and his paper 'Fourth century Tragedy and the *Poetics*' in Hermes 82 (1954) 294ff; for possible tragic reminiscences in the *Dyskolos*, see e.g. on 189, 269ff, 574ff; for metrical effects, Introd. IV.1, at p. 59.

[2] On the events of these years, see especially Ferguson, *Hellenistic Athens*, Ch. 1 (pp. 1-37); on Demetrius of Phalerum and his writings, Ferguson, Chapter 2; F.

Demetrius, born about 350, was perhaps some eight years older than Menander. The two men are linked by education, and perhaps already by the friendship which bade fair to involve Menander in the overthrow of Demetrius ten years later[1]; it is therefore tempting to wonder whether the *Dyskolos* was in any sense influenced by the ideas of the new regime, or by the context of events in which it was produced. Menander is of course no Aristophanes, and what can be seen of the general trend of comedy in the years which separate them does not encourage us to expect political or personal references to be prominent. Nevertheless, direct satirical allusion in the old tradition is still possible in the later fourth century; there are signs of it in the *Orge* and in other plays of Menander which are reasonably dated early; the absence of anything immediately comparable in the *Dyskolos* is therefore striking enough to note, though it may be due to chance or a change in the author's mood rather than to the new political climate. Historical events of the near or remoter past sometimes appear in New Comedy as part of the background of its characters' lives, and may therefore introduce an element of political or social commentary, as when 'the war and the troubles in Corinth' are part of Glykera's past in the *Perikeiromene* (5f, cf. 282ff). But again, whether significantly or not, the *Dyskolos* gives no occasion for relating its characters' lives to events outside the play. Perhaps the nearest thing to a pointed historical allusion is the passage of Knemon's major speech in which he contrasts his own ideal of life with the way of the world, where the evils of trials, imprisonment and war arise, according to Knemon, because men seek selfish gain and will not be content with a moderate living (743-5). The thought is wide enough to be of general application, but has enough relevance to the events of the immediate past to strike home: some of the audience must have seen Phocion on trial.[2] But however vividly Menander intended it to do so, his basic point is an ethical and not a political

Wehrli, *Schule des Aristoteles* iv (1949); and Erich Bayer, *Demetrios Phalereus der Athener*, Tübinger Beiträge 36, 1941. Menander and Theophrastus: Koerte II, Test. 7.

[1] The source is Diog. Laert. 5.79 = Koerte II, Test. 8.

[2] See the Commentary ad loc., and for discussion in relation to the trial of Phocion, F. della Corte, Maia 1960.83ff. The *Dyskolos* is briefly considered in relation to its historical background by Momigliano, Riv. Storica Italiana 1959.326ff; on contemporary allusions in Menander and other fourth-century comic poets, see Webster, *SM* 103ff, and *LGC* 37ff, 100ff.

one; and unless we are prepared to account politically for the lack of more direct references to personalities and current events (never, it seems, an important element in Menander's comedy), we have to ask in more general terms whether the thought and moral tone of the play are politically inspired. Here, apart from the difficulty in the terms of the question, there are manifold problems in the evidence which can be brought to bear on it. The study of Menander in relation to Greek philosophy, and especially that of Aristotle and his followers, reveals that the words and actions of the dramatic characters are sometimes strongly coloured by what was the more advanced thought of the age; Menander can be shown to owe to his education not only much of the literary doctrine which helped him to arrive at a particular kind of comedy, but also the keen observation of human qualities and the careful discrimination of ethical values which give the characteristically serious tone beneath the light-hearted surface. But the affiliation of ideas between Theophrastus, Demetrius and Menander (to say nothing of Aristotle in the background) is perhaps rarely to be traced with schematic precision. Apart from the difficulties of disputed chronology and incomplete information (in any event the originator of an idea is not necessarily the first to give it wide currency), it is easier in the nature of the case to establish community of views between contemporaries than to establish influence from A to B; and points made in a drama have not necessarily the same value as when they appear as part of a philosophic treatise or a political programme. Thus, to take an example, Knemon's denunciation of extravagance in sacrifice at *Dyskolos* 447ff can be claimed to have contemporary point from its kinship with the doctrines of Theophrastus, *On Piety* and with the moralizing tone of Demetrius' sumptuary laws. But its potential value as philosophic or political propaganda is affected both by the character and situation of the speaker – a disagreeable old recluse disturbed by visitors to the shrine next door – and by the audience's memory of variations on the same theme in other dramatic contexts. Menander gives circulation to the philosophic coinage of his day, and some of it he thought highly valuable, but he is neither a systematic philosopher nor a professional politician. If, as is probable enough, he found much in the ideals of the new regime of which he approved, it is pertinent to note from what reference he makes to Demetrius' legislation, that the activities of the governor do not seem to have earned Menander's unqualified approval.[1] It seems best to accept the serious content of Menander as a function of his attempt to give ordinary human affairs depth and contemporary interest through the medium of light drama; his tone is not that of a purveyor of officially approved attitudes, but rather that of a detached yet sympathetic observer of his fellow men's thoughts and deeds.

If Menander ever expounded his views of drama in detail, we have no record of the fact; but among the stories told of him there is one which at least gives a lead to what he thought important. According to Plutarch (*Moralia* 347 E), a friend is said to have remarked 'Well, Menander, the festival's nearly here, and you haven't composed your comedy, have you?' 'Composed my comedy?', replied Menander, 'I most certainly have: I have my treatment of the theme worked out – I just have to set the lines to it.' Designing the play was the vital and difficult part; once that was done, the dialogue would follow.[2] One should not of course go too far in deducing a literary doctrine from what is after all a neat and possibly half-ironical way out of a friendly social challenge; but there is a recognizable core of truth in the

---

[1] Webster, SM 119f, referring to *Kekryphalos*, frg. 238 (272 K), with Plautus, *Aulularia* 475ff and 504 (see p. 12, n. 2), and *Bacchides* 912; on Menander and philosophy, see SM 195-219 and SM² 234; on Peripatetic ideas and the *Dyskolos*, see W. Schmid, RhM 1959.157-82 and 263-6; on *Dysk.* and Theophrastus, P. Steinmetz, RhM 1960.185-91; and, most recently, K. Gaiser's remarks in O. Rieth, *Die Kunst Menanders in den 'Adelphen' des Terenz* (1964), p. 146 and n.

[2] νὴ τοὺς θεοὺς ἔγωγε πεποίηκα τὴν κωμῳδίαν. ᾠκονόμηται γὰρ ἡ διάθεσις, δεῖ δ' αὐτῇ τὰ στιχίδια ἐπᾶσαι. The point is not that the dialogue is of no consequence (one need only read some to discover that that is not the case), but that it is secondary to the design. The kinship of this view with Aristotle's treatment of μῦθος / σύστασις τῶν πραγμάτων in the *Poetics* needs no stress. A commentator on Horace, *Ars Poetica* 311 gives the gist of Menander's remark in saying *Menander cum fabulam disposuisset, etiamsi nondum uersibus adornasset, dicebat tamen se complesse*; but this generalized version changes the musical metaphor given by ἐπᾶσαι (lit. 'sing in accompaniment'); in my own translation it is possibly overworked. διάθεσις is apparently intended to refer to the plot *qua* plan of composition, not *qua* story or subject: it should not be replaced by ὑπόθεσις as is done in the text printed in Koerte II, Test. 11.

Wilamowitz, *Das Schiedsgericht* (*Epitrepontes*), 119, quotes the story to begin his discussion of 'The Art of Menander'. It could be fictional, as such anecdotes commonly are; but a likely source of personal reminiscences of Menander is his contemporary Lynceus of Samos, who may be the ultimate source here, as Wilamowitz suggests, whether it came from one of his books περὶ Μενάνδρου (Koerte II, Test. 50), or from another work.

remark, which may well have helped to make it memorable in the first place.

In being virtually complete, the *Dyskolos* offers an admirable illustration of this concept of comedy: a play planned as a whole, to progress from beginning through dramatic climax to light-hearted conclusion, with its detail taking a place in the main design and contributing to it. By some modern standards of dramaturgy, this is an unpopular quality; when narration or commentary attempts to bring it out in an ancient play, one is apt to feel either that the obvious is being laboured at length, or that the conclusions drawn from the text are too calculatedly academic to be real in terms of the dramatist's own practical intentions: but it is the general fate of commentators to follow with labour where original writers go by genius. A good example of detailed planning in the *Dyskolos* will present itself later when we consider how Menander brings out the rustic setting of the play through the words of the text (Introd. II.1), and the Commentary will attempt to point out others; here it is perhaps useful to call attention to one striking general feature of the design.

The central feature of the *Dyskolos* is the character who gives it its title, Knemon, the 'Angry Old Man', the misanthrope. We see him on stage for roughly a quarter of the time the play would take to act, over half of this in two scenes which come late on – the predominantly serious scene of Act IV, from 691 to about 760, which brings the climax of dramatic interest, and the scene in Act V from 909 onwards, where a situation from earlier in the play is taken up and refashioned to provide a finale of lively comic revel. For much of the time, Knemon remains in the background, dominating the play through what we hear of him from others, until his long scene in Act IV brings the moment for him to reveal himself, and in revaluing his way of life to resolve most of the dramatic tension which has been built up around and about him; with that, the pattern of the plot is worked out almost to completion.[1] The main line of the action begins from, and follows, the attempts of young Sostratos to approach Knemon for consent to marry his daughter, and it is through the lover's story, complicated and diversified by the presence of unreliable

[1] For details of Knemon's part, see Introd. II.2; for a view of the ending of the play in relation to the main design, see the Commentary under 729-39 (end of note), 867ff (end of note), and 880-958 (iii).

helpers and unexpected allies, that the portrait of Knemon is built up: the audience sees him as he is seen by different characters, whose reactions to Knemon are intended, in different proportions, to reveal both him and them.[1] This example of a central character portrayed to a high degree by indirect means finds an interesting contrast in a close dramatic relation of Knemon's, the self-centred old miser Euclio of Plautus, *Aulularia*; to make the point by arithmetic, Euclio is on stage for something over half, and possibly near to three-quarters of the time the play would take to act, calculating approximately from the incomplete Latin text: he and his affairs are largely in the foreground, and the lover's story, analogous to that of Sostratos in the *Dyskolos*, is correspondingly made to recede. Since the Greek original of the *Aulularia* was almost undeniably a play by Menander, it seems hard to avoid the conclusion that the two plays were seen by the author as complementary variations in the study of a similar central character – not of course exclusively, but at least to some extent consciously.[2]

From Antiquity onwards, Menander has been much praised for his realism: the unaffected naturalness of his language, the

---

[1] For example, in Act I, basic facts about Knemon are given by Pan in the prologue speech; we then see him through the eyes of a badly frightened slave whom he has chased off his land, and can observe the reactions of Sostratos and Chaireas to what they hear of him (81-146); then we have Sostratos confronted with Knemon, and learn more of the old man from seeing and hearing him ourselves (147-88); a little more is added by what we see and hear of his daughter (189-206); the act ends with a portrait of Knemon as he appears to the slave next door (220ff). One aspect of the dramatist's problem is of course to engage dramatic interest and sympathy for a character who is by nature static, withdrawn, and uncongenial: for discussion of the type in Greek and other literature, see Penelope Photiades, Chron. d'Égypte 34 (1959) no. 68, pp. 305ff, and Claire Préaux, *ib.* 327ff. Comparison and contrast heighten the effect of the portrait: the young countryman Gorgias is in some ways akin to the old countryman Knemon, for instance in his devotion to work and his instinctive dislike of strangers; the lightly-drawn figure of Sostratos' father Kallippides is largely Knemon's opposite.

[2] On P. *Aul.* and other Latin adaptations from Greek Comedy, see Additional Note, pp. 17-19; the far-reaching differences of theme, treatment and emphasis in the two plays should not be allowed to obscure the many common features which emerge from the detailed comparison which the rediscovery of the *Dyskolos* makes possible. It is credible that the original of *Aul.* was close to and later than *Dysk.* in date, but the evidence available does not allow the two productions to be related with chronological precision: if *Aul.* 504 is accepted as a reference to *gynaikonomoi* under Demetrius of Phalerum, the limits of date for its original are 317-07; but see Fraenkel, *Plautinisches im Plautus*, 137ff (=*Elem. Plaut.* 130ff; cf. 413) and Claude Wehrli, Mus. Helv. 19 (1962) 33-38.

likeness of his characters to real people, the true portrait he gives of life in fourth-century Athens.[1] After what has been said already, it is perhaps not necessary to spend long in remarking that realism is a relative term, and that Menander's realism is not only the product of acute observation, but of a refined art working in a traditional medium. His subjects, while less limited than one might believe from those who listen too closely to Ovid's assertion that 'there is no play of Menander's without love', are chosen and treated with a regard for the conventions of civilized high comedy: so far as we know, Menander excluded from his plays a whole range of grave events and permanent misfortunes (such as murder and distressing illness) to which real human beings are unfortunately prone; nor, as a rule, does he indulge in realistic detail purely for realistic detail's sake: his plays are plays and not documentary records.[2] We may judge his characters to be drawn with acute psychological insight, yet he is not, as a modern dramatist might be, concerned to explore the inner depths of their personalities; his analysis of character is ethical rather than psychological, and it is striking in the *Dyskolos* that Knemon's major speech of self-revelation leaves the old man's emotions almost entirely to the audience's imagination.[3] Menander's Greek can still appeal to modern critics, as it did to ancient ones, by its air of aptness to character and situation, and its

---

[1] See especially two recent papers by Claire Préaux, *Ménandre et la société Athénienne*, Chron. d'Égypte 32 (1957) no. 63, 84-100; and *Les fonctions du droit dans la comédie nouvelle*, *ib.* 35 (1960) no. 69, 222-39. Legrand (tr. Loeb), *The New Greek Comedy*, Ch. V (206ff), ranges widely round the topic of realism, mixing useful with misleading and outdated information; on some conventions of representation in Menander's theatre, see Introd. II and works there quoted; on some conventions of language, S. Zini, *Il linguaggio dei personaggi nelle commedie di M.*, Firenze, 1938.

[2] Ovid: *Tristia* 2.369f = Koerte II, Test. 35; his epigrammatic summary of Menander's themes by characters at *Amores* 1.15.17f (*Ib.*, Test. 34) is similarly misleading when elevated beyond the status its context provides. Conventions of comedy: 'Comedy treats of private affairs and does not involve danger' (κωμῳδία ἐστὶν ἰδιωτικῶν πραγμάτων ἀκίνδυνος περιοχή) according to a definition known principally from its quotation by the grammarian Diomedes, and deriving in all probability from Theophrastus: Diom., *Gram. Lat.* I, p. 488 Keil = Kaibel, *CGF* I, p. 57, cf. Cantarella, *Aristofane* I, under B.75 (p. 89), Webster *LGC* 113f. A good summary introduction to some ancient and modern theories of comedy appears in Duckworth, *Nature of Roman Comedy*, 305ff. '... not documentary records': see, for instance, the Commentary on 842-4.

[3] *Dysk.* 708-47: Knemon expounds the principles on which he has acted and the decision he has reached: he does not say what are and have been his more personal feelings about himself and those near to him, and what we learn otherwise is probably far less than would have satisfied a modern dramatist with as serious an interest in the character.

range of effects from seriousness and high emotion to easy colloquial familiarity: from it, one seems to hear real people speaking; yet one suspects that Menander would not have dissented
strongly from the modern dramatist who argued that 'it is not the
purpose of dialogue to reproduce conversation naturalistically but
rather, in the guise of conversation, to supply conversation's
deficiencies – to be amusing where conversation is dull, to be
economic where conversation is wasteful, to be articulate and
lucid where conversation is mumbling or obscure'.[1] The mirror
in which Menander is said to reflect life filters, concentrates,
and sometimes distorts the impression it receives; often, we may
think, it thereby shows more than the superficial truth; but if we
expect it to reflect life in too literal a sense, the result will not be
gratification.[2]

The rediscovery of the *Dyskolos* in the 1950's adds one more
chapter to a story already rich in material for a study in historical
paradox. Menander's dramatic career began with successes
which rivals must have envied. The *Orge*, produced in the year
of his twentieth birthday, appears to have won first prize at the
Lenean festival, where five years later the *Dyskolos* was also
placed first; victory at the Dionysia came in the following year,
with a play of unknown title: for such honours others worked
longer and in vain. There were less pleasant occasions. In 312,
it seems, a play of Menander's came last at the Dionysia, his
Heniochos; by 302/1, when he wrote the *Imbrioi* for a Dionysiac
production which had to be cancelled, the number of his plays
could be reckoned in the 70's; by the time of his death ten years
later, he had written over a hundred; he was awarded first
prizes eight times in all – an eminently creditable but not spec-
tacular total.[3] If satisfaction depended on winning the first,
disappointment must have been frequent in a dramatic career
of some 30 years: Aulus Gellius (17.4) has a story of Menander

---

[1] Charles Morgan, *Dialogue in Novels and Plays* (Hermon Ould Memorial Lecture,
1953; publ. 1954), p. 7.

[2] 'omnem uitae imaginem expressit' says Quintilian in recommending the study
of Menander to the young orator, *Inst. Or.* 10.1.69 = Koerte II, Test. 38. This and
similar pronouncements by ancient critics and those who echo their views are prone
to need qualification in our own age, when drama on the stage and the cinema screen
has set different standards of realism.

[3] See above, p. 3, n. 1; apart from the *Dyskolos* didascalia, the texts immediately
relevant here are Koerte II, Test. 1, 2, 14, 23-24, 27-28.

meeting one of his principal rivals, and saying 'Do tell me, Philemon – don't you blush when you beat me?'[1] But competitive success, however welcome, was not an infallible test of merit and esteem. Soon after his death, perhaps within his lifetime, Menander was honoured by a statue commissioned from Kephisodotos and Timarchos, the sons of Praxiteles, and set up in the Theatre of Dionysus; only its base now survives.[2] A more enduring monument came with the praises of later writers and critics generally, who were to reverse what seemed to some the unjust verdict of Menander's own contemporaries. 'What is the good of an educated man going to the theatre' asks Plutarch 'except to see Menander?'; for Quintilian, Menander's brilliance makes all other writers in the same genre seem dim; and there were others who shared these opinions, both before Quintilian's time and after.[3] For all that, zealots for the purity of Classical Attic could deplore Menander's use of words not found in the most approved authors, and question his value as a model for correct composition.[4] Performances still took place well into Roman Imperial times; copies continued to be made in the fifth and sixth centuries A.D.; but if we attempt to trace the survival of the plays through those who show direct knowledge of them, we lose the trail in the sixth century or the early seventh.[5] From then until rediscovery begins to transform the situation, in the later nineteenth century, Menander was virtually a lost author. His influence on modern western drama has been considerable, but

---

[1] The remark may well be fictional; but see above, p. 10, n. 2.

[2] This work, which was seen by Pausanias, is probably the ultimate source of many later likenesses, including the well-known relief in Rome of Menander with comic masks (Lateran Museum 487: Bieber HT², figs. 317 a-c; Webster, MNC, no. IS 10). By the second century A.D., the theatre seems to have abounded in statues of poets 'mostly of the less distinguished': Pausanias 1.21.1 = Koerte II, Test. 19.

[3] Plutarch, Comp. Ar. et Men., Moralia 854 B; Quintilian, Inst. Or. 10.1.69 (=Koerte II, Test. 41 and 38); for discussion, see RE 'Menandros' 714ff; and on some aspects of ancient criticism of Menander, A. Garzya, Riv. Fil. Ist. Class. 1959.237-52, and F. Quadlbauer, Wiener Studien 1960 (=Festschr. J. Mewaldt) 40-82.

[4] 'What Aristophanes gained in the schools, Menander lost' according to Koerte, RE 'Menandros', 717; but see Quadlbauer (quoted n. 3) pp. 70ff. For criticisms of Menander from Phrynichus and Pollux, see Koerte II, Test. 46-47.

[5] Cf. Koerte II, p. 13, and Cantarella, Dioniso 17 (1954) 22-37. The fragments from St Catherine on Sinai now in Leningrad were part of a codex dated to the fourth century A.D. which was apparently dismembered in the eighth century and re-used for writing a Syriac text: Koerte I, p. xvii; Cantarella, p. 23. For evidence of performances (perhaps continuing as late as the sixth century A.D.), see Webster, AJA 1962.333ff; for literary reminiscences of the Dyskolos, see Photiades, quoted p. 12, n. 2 and J.-M. Jacques, Bull. Ass. Budé, 1959.200-15.

came almost exclusively though the Latin adaptations of his work by Plautus and Terence, more fortunate in their survival; of Menander in Greek, all that was known directly came from quotations and excerpts preserved by other authors for the sake of their memorable moral sentiments, their antiquarian or linguistic interest, and for a variety of other reasons, few of which have much to do with the qualities of the plays as drama.[1] Texts bearing on Menander, quotations, and adaptations in Latin were thus for long the total stock of evidence available to those who wished to study him. The most substantial accession to this material so far was brought by the Cairo Codex, discovered in 1905 and published in 1907 by its discoverer, G. Lefèbvre. This preserves large parts of *Epitrepontes*, *Perikeiromene* and *Samia*, as well as the opening scene of *Heros* and some lesser items – a bulk of text exceeding that of the *Dyskolos*, but with many damaged lines and no single play nearly as complete. There followed both increased appreciation, and – perhaps inevitably – disappointment.[2] First reactions to the publication of the *Dyskolos* were somewhat similarly mixed, and it would not be surprising if the same happened again when (as may be expected with confidence), some more substantial new texts become available.[3] For many

[1] Latin adaptations: see Additional Note below. The preface to Koerte II, written in 1943, traces the earlier history of the 'quoted' fragments, beginning from Hugo Grotius (1616) and Johannes Clericus (1709).

[2] The progress of rediscovery from fragments of ancient copies is admirably outlined by K. J. Dover, in M. Platnauer (ed.) *Fifty Years of Classical Scholarship* (1954) 105-8.

Appreciation: I mention three shorter studies in English, by Gomme, *Essays in Greek History and Literature* (1937) 249-95; by Murray, *Aristophanes* (1933) 221-63; and by Post, *From Homer to Menander* (1951) 214-44. Disappointment: e.g. Angus, in *Cambridge Ancient History*, vii (1928) 224ff; W. W. Tarn, in his *Hellenistic Civilization*, expresses still stronger feelings: 'It is usual to praise (Menander) without stint . . . But to the writer he and his imitators seem about the dreariest desert in literature.' (3rd ed., 1952, p. 273).

[3] Since the *Dyskolos* was published, some fragments ascribed to the *Misogynes* of Menander have appeared in Antinoopolis Papyri, vol. 2, no. 55, and are appended in Mette, *Dyskolos*[2]; but reliable report has it that discoveries of new text have considerably outrun publication. A good bibliography of the first spate of work on the *Dyskolos* by J. T. McDonough, Jr., appeared in Class. World 53 (1960) 277-80, 296-8; if considered opinions of the Cairo plays are any guide, widely different views of the merits of the *Dyskolos* are likely to be expressed long after the initial impact of the discovery has been forgotten. As this edition went to press, the discovery of some 400 lines of the *Sikyonios* (? *Sikyonioi*) was announced at the Académie des Inscriptions in Paris by Professor André Bataille, and their publication is eagerly awaited ('The Times', 'The Guardian', 22.vi.63). See further A. Dain, 'La survie de Ménandre', Maia 1963.278-309, and the Addenda below, p. 305f.

reasons, not least because of the singular and still growing history of the recovery of Menander's works, the study of him is, and is likely to remain, one of some technical complexity, in which broad critical generalizations are not easily made, and once made are prone to prove fragile. The *Dyskolos* may be commended as an attractive, well-made play, essentially light-hearted, but with a blend of deeper human insight and sympathy. To claim that it is a great play by universal standards would be extravagant; nor, as a single relatively early work, should we expect it to show all of Menander's most admired qualities to their best advantage; it does however offer an opportunity to readers and audiences which has been lacking for centuries, to recognize, and appreciate if they will, a virtually complete work in its original language by the supreme ancient writer, and in some sense the originator, of a highly fruitful form of civilized literature.

ADDITIONAL NOTE: LATIN ADAPTATIONS
FROM MENANDER

(i) Latin *fabulae palliatae*, or plays adapted from Greek Comedy, are of prime importance in the study of Menander, but the use of evidence derived from them presents many problems. For general discussion and a wide selection of bibliography, see Webster, *SM* and *LGC*, and Duckworth, *Nature of Roman Comedy* (1952), especially 52ff, 59ff, 202ff; for a contrasting approach, see Beare, *Roman Stage*[2] (1955). Ch. 15 of Duckworth's book (pp. 396-433) gives a most useful survey of the influence of Plautus and Terence (and hence in part Menander) upon modern European Comedy. Fraenkel's *Plautinisches im Plautus* (1922), which is basic to the study of Plautine adaptation, appeared in 1960 in an Italian version with additional notes, under the title *Elementi Plautini in Plauto*.

(ii) The following eight plays by Plautus and Terence may be accepted as based on Menander; the Greek title is given in brackets:

a) Plautus, *Aulularia* (*Apistos* or another); *Bacchides* (*Dis Exapaton*); *Cistellaria* (*Synaristosai*); *Stichus* (*First Adelphoi*);

b) Terence, *Andria* (*Andria*, with additions from *Perinthia*); *Heauton Timorumenos* (same title); *Eunuchus* (*Eunouchos*, with additions from *Kolax*); *Adelphoe* (*Second Adelphoi*, with a scene based on Diphilus, *Synapothnescontes*.)

The original of P. *Aul.* is confirmed as Menandrean by the strong affinities between it and the *Dyskolos*; for detailed discussion following on the rediscovery of the *Dyskolos*, see Kraus, Serta Philologica Aenipontana 7-8 (1962) 185-90, and Ludwig, Philologus 1961.44-71 and 247-62.

(iii) Terence's *Phormio* and *Hecyra* are based on plays by Apollodorus, a younger poet much influenced by Menander; Plautus' *Mercator*, *Mostellaria* and *Trinummus* derive from Philemon; *Casina*, *Rudens* and (probably) the fragmentary *Vidularia* are from Diphilus; *Asinaria* from an otherwise unknown Demophilus. For the remaining 10 Plautine plays, we have less satisfactory evidence, but a reasonable case can be made for recognizing Menander's hand, or marked Menandrean influence, in the Greek originals of *Poenulus* (*Karchedonios*; but possibly from Alexis), *Curculio*, and *Pseudolus*; in the rest, though likenesses to Menander are sometimes observable, the balance of probability is against an ascription of the original to him, sometimes decisively so.

(iv) Since very little of the adapted plays has survived in Greek, the possibilities of direct comparison between original and adaptation are extremely limited. The Latin authors' methods can however be shown to vary in all gradations from literal translation to free composition, sometimes on the basis of another Greek source, sometimes independently; Terence seems in general to have remained closer to the letter and spirit of his originals than Plautus, though some of their differences undoubtedly arise from selecting originals of different kinds.

(v) Accordingly, the status of parallels from these plays quoted in this edition also varies widely: where valid, they may be evidence for a similar expression or scene in another play by Menander; they may represent a Greek original by another author; or they may be no more than coincidences between writers of the same genre in different languages: obviously, one can often not be sure which. I have attempted to provide a selection which may be informative in reading the *Dyskolos*, but am naturally not concerned to pursue their implications for the interpretation of the Latin plays; and I have thought it reasonable to refer to P. *Aul.*, T. *Phormio*, etc., without constantly reminding the reader of the Greek original (where known), or the likelihood (where calculable) that the Latin version reflects it.

(vi) Additional evidence of the same kind comes from fragments of plays by Plautus and other Latin comic poets, with (of course) the added complications which arise from dealing with fragments. I have quoted Plautine fragments from Lindsay's Oxford Classical Text, and those of others from Ribbeck, *Comicorum Romanorum Fragmenta*[3] (1898).

II

The *Dyskolos* in the Theatre

I: STAGING, SCENERY, SETTING

Pickard-Cambridge, *Theatre of D.*, Ch. iv (pp. 134-74); Webster, *Gk Theatre Production*, Ch. i, esp. 20-28, and (on the *Dyskolos*) Proc. Class. Ass. 1960.17ff, and Bull. Rylands Library 1962.235ff. On the Nymphaeum at Phyle and its surroundings, see F. Brommer, *RE* 'Pan', Suppl. 8 (1956) 993f, who quotes the archaeological reports; J. G. Frazer, *Pausanias' Descr. of Greece* ii.421ff; *Guide Bleu*, Grèce; H. Herter, RhM 1959.96; P. J. Photiades, G. & R. 1958.108ff; L. Robert, C. R. de l'Acad. des Inscriptions 1961 (pub. 1962), 179.

Although we cannot hope to reconstruct the first performance of an ancient play in detail, our understanding of the text remains incomplete if we ignore the theatrical conditions in which the author worked, or equate them uncritically with modern practice in one place or another. For all who wrote Attic drama, a general standard of practice was set by the conditions of production in the Theatre of Dionysus at Athens and the conventions which grew up there; for Menander, this means the theatre as it stood after the extensive rebuilding credited to Lycurgus. Since at least the major part of the work is likely to have been completed while Lycurgus was in charge of Athens' finances (ca. 338-326 B.C.), Menander can hardly have known the earlier theatre except as a childhood memory, and though much in the history of the building is disputed, it seems not to have undergone any other substantial alteration until after his death.

We may therefore use what is known of the 'Lycurgan' period of the theatre to form an idea of the environment in which Menander expected his *Dyskolos* to be performed. The following paragraphs offer an outline. Against this background, it seems useful to consider the dramatic setting as presented in the play itself, and to note how that presentation relates to the design as a whole and to the real place in which the action is supposed to happen.

For the present purpose, Menander's stage may be thought of

as a space about 66 feet wide, framed by colonnaded wings which gave a depth of some 15 feet. It communicated, probably by a low step or steps, with a circular orchestra, again of about 66 feet across: there the chorus still held its place. Actors could enter from either side past the wings; between them, the main block of the stage building provided three doors, a large centre one and two flanking. Its architecture (which is very differently reconstructed) must have given at least some features of background common to all kinds of plays, but hangings and painted panels were used to add to the decorative effect, and it is a fair presumption that they also served to provide different scenic arrangements (for instance by masking doors not in use), and could be modified or changed to suggest different kinds of set. We should not however expect great elaboration in a large open-air theatre, nor prolonged intervals for changes of scene between plays within the limited time of the dramatic festivals.

One thinks of a street in Athens or some other town as the natural background for a New Comedy, and certainly at a later period a standard comic set consisted of painted 'urban' scenery.[1] Such a background could hardly have been acceptable for comedies where the action took place out of town, and for these it may have been the practice to set the scene as for tragedies played in remote places (like *Ajax* and *Philoctetes*), or as for satyr plays, with whatever individual variations the available resources allowed. At all events, Menander was not averse to a change from urban surroundings. Apart from the *Dyskolos*, plays set in the Attic countryside include *Heautontimoroumenos* ('at Halai', frg. 127) and *Heros* ('at Ptelea', 22); at the beginning of *Leucadia* (frg. 258), the scene is set at the temple of Apollo on the cliffs of Leucas, from which Sappho was supposed to have thrown herself for love of Phaon. The more individual character a setting had, the more need to augment what could be shown in the theatre through the words of the text. The *Dyskolos*, by virtue of its completeness, shows well what care Menander took to

---

[1] See Webster's discussion of Vitruvius 5.6.9. in connection with the wall paintings of the cubiculum of P. Fannius Synistor's villa at Boscoreale: *GTP* 26f and pl. 23; Pickard-Cambridge 225ff and plates (Webster, *MNC*, no. NP 49; *Monuments illustrating Tragedy* . . . , nos. NP 25-27; Bieber, *HT*[2], figs. 471-4 and text). The use of the three doors to represent two houses with a central shrine is well known from Plautus, *Aulularia* and *Curculio*; the *Dyskolos* now clearly confirms the view that this was a standard arrangement in New Comedy.

create the background he required in the audience's imagination. The place of the action is to be Phyle in Attica: Pan says so in the opening lines. In the theatre it is obvious at once who the speaker is (though presently he will mention his name); the central door from which he enters is a shrine of Pan and the Nymphs, but no nondescript one: 'it belongs', we are to think, 'to the people of Phyle and those who can farm the rocks here—a most distinguished shrine.' Already we know the setting and something of its character. The prologue speech is to give the essential information, in this as in other respects; the rest will appear as the play goes on.

On the left, as the audience sees it, is the door of Knemon's farmhouse, where he lives a life of morose isolation, alone but for his daughter and the old slave woman, Simiche; his wife has left him and now lives in the house on the right of the shrine, with Gorgias, her son by a former marriage, and their one slave, Daos – a household of three, barely supported by Gorgias' small farm.[1]

Inside the shrine, the Nymphs have their spring, and there is room for a sacrifice and celebration; this the audience cannot see, and does not need to be told: it will be accepted when necessary (197ff and later *passim*). By one of the house-doors – let us say Knemon's – Apollo Agyieus is represented by his altar or emblem, a familiar object which matters only when it is referred to (see 659 and n.). Behind Knemon's door, again invisible but imagined, is his yard with its well (first mentioned 191), and its dung-heap (584f).

Off stage right, the road, bordered by trees (395f), goes past Kallippides' large estate, where young Sostratos is with his family for the hunting; then on 'down to Cholargos', and so to Athens.[2] Off stage left, it goes up the valley past Knemon's land, and Gorgias' much smaller holding nearby.[3] From near his house, Knemon can be pointed out 'up on the ridge there collecting wild pears' (99ff); below it and nearer to hand, a thicket is supposed to be visible, where Pyrrhias says he escaped from the

---

[1] 'Left' and 'right' are given here and later from the audience's viewpoint, on the assumption (to be discussed in the Commentary) that ἐπὶ δεξιά in 5 refers to Pan's own right. Only Knemon is referred to by name; at this stage Menander has more important things to tell the audience than the characters' names, and declines to burden the speech with them.

[2] 33, 39ff; cf. on 216f and 393.   [3] 5, 23ff, 162f, 351f and context.

old man after a hill-and-dale chase of what seemed like nearly two miles (117ff). The isolation of the place is brought to mind not only by direct reference, as in Daos' words at 222ff, but more often and more effectively by indirect means: it is reflected, for instance, in the hostility to strangers which is shown in violent form by the misanthrope Knemon, but also present in the reactions of Daos and Gorgias to Sostratos; Sostratos arrives there 'by chance' while hunting some way from home[1]; when the shrine is visited by his mother, who 'goes all round the district sacrificing', her advance guard arrives sorely tried by the journey, and the main party is late.[2] The hard rocky landscape figured in Pan's first sentence; it reappears conspicuously in the portrait of the farmer's life there – a typically Attic 'battle with the rocks' among wild thyme and sage, with the dry-walling to attend to for a change, a battle which is nearly too much for Sostratos, as an active young man who is unused to it.[3]

Apart from his audience in the Theatre of Dionysus and those who would see the play restaged elsewhere, Menander could probably expect a considerable reading public. In making the play convey its own scenery and atmosphere through the words, he may have had readers in mind as well as the conditions imposed by relatively simple standards of production; but we shall be disappointed if we look for passages of picturesque description, or expect the setting to be as fully mapped out as it might be in a novel. The most striking feature of the verbal scene-painting is one with a less obvious appeal – the extreme economy and regard for dramatic relevance with which it is done. Once the action begins, the portrait of Phyle is built up gradually and naturalistically, by a method similar to that of the character portraits; like them, it is also carefully integrated with the whole design, so that details which appear at first hearing to be no more than casual touches of realism generally prove to have been selected to serve other purposes as well. A good example is Pyrrhias' phrase about Knemon 'up on the ridge there, collecting wild pears'. This helps to portray the setting, as we noted; but there are two other points of immediate importance in the context: it matters that Pyrrhias should see Knemon at a distance before they meet, and that he should see him doing something which will naturally

[1] 43; cf. 70ff, 131ff, 266f.
[2] 262f, 393-426, 430ff.
[3] 603ff, 376-7, 522-45.

provoke the reaction 'wretched old peasant'. Presently the ridge will become the scene of the two-mile chase; and, by a neat stroke of comedy, the pears will become missiles hurled by Knemon when his fury has exhausted everything else (120f). When Knemon appears, we learn that he works on the ridge because working the lower part of his land by the public road is more than his misanthropy can bear (162-6): in other words, in order to be inaccessible, he farms uneconomically. The original vivid detail of Knemon at work is thus made to lead up to the point that his hardships and poverty, unlike those of Gorgias, arise not from circumstance but by his own misguided choice; this emerges with full emphasis when Gorgias remarks to Sostratos on the extraordinary behaviour of the old man: he owns a valuable farm ('worth about two talents'), but insists on working it alone, with no help from neighbours, hired labour, or slaves.[1]

The imagined setting goes beyond the physical limitations of the theatre, as we have seen; but it sometimes compromises with them. For instance, Knemon's house in the theatre must be literally next door to the shrine; accordingly Menander makes dramatic capital of the fact, as at 10ff, 442ff and 663. The lands of Knemon and Gorgias need to be off stage on the same side, so that characters may come and go that way without seeming to meet those who arrive from further off; accordingly, the plot makes a point of having the two work close by each other, and the audience must accept the result that while Knemon's house is on the same side as his land, the house of Gorgias is not (see on 24f).

Another kind of compromise is imposed by the nature of the real place which lends its identity to the dramatic scene. To an Athenian audience, the real Phyle was a district of the north-western borderland of Attica, a journey of some thirteen miles from town, remote among mountains. Some presumably knew the place personally from service in the fort there, or from travelling the pass through Parnes which it guarded, the most direct of the three ancient routes to Thebes and Delphi; others may have lived or worked in the district, or visited it for the hunting, like Menander's Sostratos – but anyone who knew or knew of Phyle as more than a name could well have known some-

[1] 327ff. On the scale of values in the play, see under 842-4. The same careful exploitation of detail is evident in the picture of self-imposed poverty presented by Knemon's domestic life: for an example, see on 584; and in general cf. Webster, *Proc. Class. Ass.* 1960.19f.

thing of its celebrated Nymphaeum. It is a cave in the side of a gorge, with a high and narrow entrance framed in an angle of cliff; all round and opposite there is steep rock, breaking into patches of scree and rough scrubby slope with scattered low trees; one arrives by scrambling precipitously down the mountainside from above, or by a sharp ascent from the torrent-bed below, having reached it from a place where the crags on the side facing the cave relent enough to allow a way down.[1] Secluded by nature from the ancient village of Phyle and from the main branches of the pass, this forbidding valley is an ideal place for the home of an imaginary misanthrope; but for dramatic purposes the cave must become a wayside shrine like any other, where people can come and go without climbing, which can have houses built next to it, and where, at any rate notionally, a family party with music and dancing can be held.[2] We need not ask whether the gorge was ever in fact inhabited, what sort of cultivation can have gone on there, or what sort of road or track ever led through. The eye accustomed to the documentary realism of the cinema may regard Menander's Phyle as a creation of fancy; but the standards to be adopted are those of artistic representation, not literal or would-be literal record. If patterns were needed for the tree-bordered country road, the narrow lonely valley, cultivation among the rocks, thyme, sage, pear-trees and so on, the district of Phyle could still offer them: its likeness in the play is (and presumably was) acceptable as a generalized one made to fit the author's dramatic requirements; it can seem realistic without being topographically real.

2: NUMBER OF ACTORS AND THEIR RÔLES

See in general Pickard-Cambridge, *Festivals*, pp. 137-53; and on the *Dyskolos*, G. P. Goold, Phoenix 1959 at pp. 144-50; J. G. Griffith, CQ 1960.113-17.

A modern production of the *Dyskolos* is likely to give each

---

[1] Bingen, *Dyscolos*[2], has a photograph of the gorge looking down it south-west towards the ridge of Harma, with the entrance to the cave in the left foreground. I am grateful to Professor Eugene Vanderpool for help in finding my way there. The site owes its rediscovery to Dodwell, who gives an amusing account of his visit: *Tour through Greece*, i.505-7.

[2] It will not do to say, after Herter, that the shrine of the play must be some other local Nymphaeum. Numerous dedications found at the cave bear witness to its identity and show that it was a place of some repute; Pan calls the shrine of the play ἱερὸν ἐπιφανὲς πάνυ.

speaking part to a different actor; it will then need twelve (or thirteen if Sostratos' mother is to speak at 430ff); and yet others will probably play the walk-on parts, like Parthenis (432) and Myrrhine (709).

Evidence of several kinds, including the structure of the plays themselves, forbids us from assuming such luxury of casting in the ancient Greek theatre, and various combinations of parts in the *Dyskolos* have been proposed. For example Mette, in his edition, presents a scheme for six actors: 1. Knemon, Kallippides, and (probably) Pan; 2. Sostratos; 3. Chaireas and Gorgias; 4. Pyrrhias and Getas; 5. Daos and Sikon; 6. Knemon's daughter, Simiche (and Sostratos' mother?). This has the attraction of grouping the rôles approximately by type, but does not constitute proof that the play was written with six actors in mind, or performed by six at its première. After much dispute, there still seems good ground for the common view that three actors normally shared the speaking parts, with extras to walk on for them at need in scenes where they were silent, as well as to take other non-speaking parts; and of course with changes of dramatic rôle which by most modern standards seem unnatural; but modern standards do not necessarily apply to an ancient performance, in which masks and relatively simple costumes made changes easier and gave a wide scope to a skilful dramatist with a small, highly-trained cast. None the less, critics who accept this view in principle differ in their readiness to admit the use of additional speakers in special circumstances. In working out a minimal scheme of casting, Goold shows that the *Dyskolos* can practicably be performed throughout by three speaking actors; this is odd, if the poet could depend on having assistance from others, and it remains true that we have no certain evidence of a scene in Menander which demands the presence of four speakers or more.[1] On the other hand, there is evidence (not always as straightforward as it seems) that small parts in Comedy might be spoken by extras. Griffith's paper presents schemes of casting for three actors and for four (both with assistance for certain small parts) which illustrate some of the possibilities if the limita-

---

[1] Pickard-Cambridge, 152f, is unsatisfactory on this point; cf. Koerte, *RE* 'Menandros' 15.1 (1931) 755f – both probably too ready to admit more than three actors on grounds of practical convenience and dramatic plausibility. Emphatic opposition to the 'three actor rule' has recently been expressed by K. Schneider, *RE* ὑποκριτής, Suppl. 8 (1956) 190-3.

tion to three principals is not strictly applied. It seems obvious that any competent dramatist must have written with his potential resources in mind; it is perhaps less clear how far the original plan was followed in practice. It may have been modified if an extra 'unofficial' actor was available, or if the proposed allocation of rôles did not suit a particular cast: when we learn from Aristotle that the tragic actor Theodoros 'would never let anyone come on stage before him' (i.e. insisted on speaking the opening lines), it seems to follow that poets for whom he acted could not rely on having their own scheme of casting carried out.[1]

The following notes attempt to outline the main possibilities and problems of 'three actor' casting in the *Dyskolos*, and are in close concord with Goold, who suggests, perhaps rightly, that the protagonist Aristodemos took the part here assigned to 'Actor B', and the tritagonist that of 'Actor A'; I have preferred to label them in order of appearance.

ACT I (including prologue speech), 1-232:

Actor A: Pan, 1-49; Pyrrhias, 81-146; Knemon's daughter, 189-206; at 212 speaks for her from inside the stage-building, then reappears as Pyrrhias, 214-17.

Actor B: Chaireas, 50-134; Knemon, 153-78 (his approach is announced at 143); Daos, 206-32.

Actor C: Sostratos, 50-217 (off stage 203-11).

134-46: damage to our copies leaves some points obscure, but B's exit as Chaireas after 134 seems beyond reasonable doubt from the words of the text. Pyrrhias takes flight to the shrine on seeing Knemon approach. My own arrangement of the text puts his final remark in 146; but perhaps it comes a moment earlier at 144, as Goold and others would have it.

189-212: Griffith and others give the daughter's few lines to a supernumerary actor, thus simplifying the staging; the outline given follows Goold and Webster (*SM*[2] 225f). Pyrrhias' words at 216-17 show that he is supposed to have overheard 181ff; this effect can be secured if an extra non-speaking player takes over the costume and mask from A and is seen at the shrine door. Similarly, at 212, an extra can appear as the daughter at Knemon's door to take the pitcher from Sostratos, while A speaks her two words from within.

[1] Aristotle, *Politics* 1336 b 28: cf. Pickard-Cambridge, 136.

ACT II, 233-426

Actor A: Gorgias, 233-381; Sikon, 393-426.

Actor B: continues as Daos, 233-378.

Actor C: continues as Sostratos, 259-392 (seen approaching 255); Getas, 402-26.

Pyrrhias is wrongly introduced by ed. pr. and others at 301f. There is no trace of his presence after Act I, and the context itself gives adequate proof that it is Daos who interrupts Sostratos. A and C not only change costumes and masks, but re-enter from the opposite side. Their movements are perhaps fully covered by Sostratos' exit monologue and Sikon's opening speech; but time can be gained for both by a pause after 392 when the stage is empty, with the appropriate comic effect of sheep noises off. B could take Sikon or Getas in this Act, but not later without giving up the part of Knemon.

ACT III, 427-619

More complex; with three principal actors some sharing of the same rôle is necessary.

Actor A: continues as Sikon to 521; Simiche, 574-96; resumes as Gorgias, 611-19 (his approach announced, 607f).

Actor B: resumes as Knemon for three appearances between 427 and 514, and 588-601; takes over Sostratos from C for 522-73 and 611-19 (Sostratos' approach announced, 607).

Actor C: continues as Getas.

430-41: If, with OCT and others, we accept Ritchie's assignment of a part to Sostratos' mother, it can be taken by A, who is not then needed as Sikon till 487. The procession in any case requires extras, perhaps six or more. If Plangon is allowed the cry τάλαν in 438, as Webster suggests (*SM*² 228), it may be spoken by the extra who represents her, or, in the general confusion, by A or C.

487-521: Getas may well appear with Sikon on the stage and witness the scene between him and Knemon (cf. 891), but (as Griffith rightly notes) there is no justification for making him speak in it at 515f or elsewhere.

574-96: If Simiche's part is given to a supernumerary, as in Griffith's 'three-actor' scheme, C can retain his part as Sostratos in this Act. He is not needed as Getas for 487-521 (see above), and can hand over Getas' part from 546-619 to A. (C cannot take over Simiche either here or in Act V (874).) But the outline given follows Goold in dividing Sostratos' rôle. In his major speech at 522-45 he is supposed to show the effects of a morning's hot sun and hard work, and any difference in the new actor's manner would be acceptable, if it was not actually exploited. Sostratos has been off stage since 392; it is interesting, but possibly irrelevant to the change of actor, that he neatly reintroduces himself on entering at 522. When C speaks for him again at 666, he has had time to restore himself with rest and food (cf. 779f).[1]

607-19: Daos is present, played by an extra. Griffith brings in a 'parachoregema' for Gorgias: in his 'three-actor' scheme, A is Getas here and C is Sostratos; but B is then free after 601.

ACT IV, 620-783

Actor A: resumes as Sikon, 621-65, and as Gorgias, 691-783.

Actor B: takes over Simiche from A, 620-38; resumes as Knemon, 691-ca. 760; Kallippides, 775-80.

Actor C: takes over Gorgias from A for 635-8; cries out off stage as Knemon's daughter (cf. 648-9); returns to Sostratos, 666-783.

620-38: Sostratos goes from the shrine to Knemon's house at 637-8; he does not speak and can be played by an extra. Griffith, as in Act III, gives Simiche's part to a supernumerary, and brings in a 'parachoregema' for Gorgias at 635-8. This avoids the transfer of Simiche's rôle, and allows C to appear as Sostratos at 637-8; but B is once again free to take over Gorgias for a few moments.

691-783: Extras are needed for Knemon's daughter (enters 691) and perhaps for Simiche; certainly for Myrrhine (enters between 702 and 708): they go off at about 760.

ACT V, 784-969

Actor A: continues as Gorgias to 873; resumes as Sikon, 891-end.

Actor B: continues as Kallippides to 860; retains Simiche's part from Act IV, 874-84; resumes as Knemon, 909-end.

---

[1] Ar. *Plutus* 'could well be acted by three actors only, if the part of Ploutos were divided between two actors with different masks – the one representing him before, the other after his restoration to health' (Pickard-Cambridge, 151; cf. my remarks in CQ 1953, p. 60). I am unhappy with Goold's argument that the exchange with Getas at 551ff helps to emphasize Sostratos' identity to the audience.

Actor C: continues as Sostratos to 873; resumes as Getas, 879-end.

866-8: Extras again appear as Knemon's daughter and wife.

873-84: C has a quick change between entering the shrine as Sostratos after 873 and appearing from it as Getas at 879. Griffith as before brings in a supernumerary for Simiche, declining to give the part to B.

959: Donax is presumably a slave of Kallippides' household, played by an extra, as when he appeared previously in the procession at 430-41. The same applies to Syros if we accept the conjecture which introduces his name.

Griffith gives approximate figures for the length of each part and for the individual actors' rôles as he divides them. Taking these as a basis, the above scheme gives Actor A 382 lines; B has 289, and C 298. If (with consequences which I have tried to indicate) we assume that a supernumerary actor was available for the parts of Knemon's daughter and Simiche, he would have some 40 lines to speak, relieving A of about 23 (10 + 13), and B of about 17; this pair of parts (and that of Sostratos' mother?) might perhaps be done by a boy in his 'teens with theatrical interests or ambitions.

3: COSTUMES AND MASKS

(i) Three kinds of evidence are used when we try to form an impression of Menander's characters as contemporary audiences saw them. They are (a) the texts of the plays; (b) works of art representing actors, masks, etc.; and (c) other objects and texts which bear on the interpretation of both, principally the catalogue of comic masks compiled by Julius Pollux in the second century A.D. for his *Onomasticon* (4.143ff).

In quoting (b) for the purposes of this edition, I have taken as standard the reference numbers given by Webster in his two recently published catalogues of comic monuments, namely *Monuments illustrating Old and Middle Comedy* (=*MOMC*), and *Monuments illustrating New Comedy* (=*MNC*); these works place all that is said of the monuments here very greatly in their debt, and will readily give the reader much fuller information than my own remarks can or need provide.

Three contrasting approaches to the topic of costumes and masks are presented by Bieber, *History of the Greek and Roman*

Theater[2] (=HT[2]: see especially Chapters vii, viii, and xi);
Pickard-Cambridge, *Festivals*, Ch. iv (pp. 175-238); and Webster,
Greek Theatre Production (=GTP: see especially 73ff, together with
the introductions to *MOMC* and *MNC*; and Hesperia 1960,
pp. 269ff, on the monuments closest to Menander in date).
On the problems of identifying the masks worn by characters in
the plays, see Webster, *The masks of Greek Comedy* (=Bull. Rylands
Library 32 (1949) 97ff), together with Pickard-Cambridge, 210ff,
and Bieber, 105; on the *Dyskolos*, see especially Webster, SM[2]223f,
and for other suggestions, G. P. Goold, Phoenix 1959.150ff.

(ii) Any account of costumes and masks as used by Menander
must make some important reservations. Dramatic monuments
which are securely dated to the later fourth or early third century
are few, and fewer still are of certain Attic origin; their direct
evidence needs to be assessed and supplemented by earlier and
later monuments from Attica and other parts of the Greek and
Greco-Roman world. What makes an idea of Menander's
practice attainable is, firstly, the general uniformity in theatrical
matters which can be shown to exist between Athens (as the
chief centre of New Comedy) and other places where it was
written and performed; and, secondly, the high probability that
many of the numerous New Comedy monuments later than
Menander reflect practices which were already standard in his
lifetime, the most creative period of that genre. Equally, statements about costumes and masks in New Comedy by Pollux
and other ancient authorities require careful assessment against
the evidence of the monuments and that of the plays if ana-
chronisms and other confusions are to be eliminated; nor are the
plays themselves always unequivocal: for instance, the dramatist
may refer, as in matters of staging, to something which is not
visible but to be imagined (such as a particular facial expression);
and he may fail to refer to what is visible if the audience are
supposed to take it for granted. The following general remarks
(greatly, but I hope not grossly, simpler than the evidence) are
offered as a preface to a list of possible illustrations for the characters of the *Dyskolos*.

Costume in New Comedy appears essentially to be that of
ordinary everyday wear, but, like the characters themselves, it
is subject to the special values and conventions of the stage. Both

sexes, slave and free, normally wear varieties of the tunic-like *chiton*; over it may be worn a *himation* – a length of material which can be variously draped and pinned to form a wrap – or one of the different sorts of cloak or mantle; accessories such as hats, shoes, sticks, scarves and aprons are worn or carried as appropriate. The padding and obscenity of the traditional comic costume – a legacy of its origins in fertility cult – can be seen from the monuments to be tending towards decency in the third quarter of the fourth century, and probably became obsolete in the period 325/300.

A simple *chiton* of knee-length or near is worn by male slaves and the humbler sort of free men, such as the class of parasites or 'hangers-on' to which Chaireas in the *Dyskolos* is generally believed to belong. For work in the country, a jerkin of leather or skin (particularly goatskin) could be worn, the *diphthera*; hence in drama it can be the badge of the rustic, if need be of the rustic in town. The shorter *chiton* is also normal for soldiers, and apparently for other active young men: Sostratos in the *Dyskolos* presumably wears it since he is in the country to hunt. Old men generally, and young men dressed for the town, wear a *chiton* of calf or ankle length; full length clothes are worn by women, in styles ranging from high fashion to the simple girded *chiton* worn without an overgarment by young slave-girls.

The status, activity, and sometimes the character of the wearer may be reflected in the style of his dress, and by elaboration or lack of it; and the dramatist may call attention through the dialogue to what people are wearing if he wishes to make a special point of it. The soldier's normal costume, for example, includes his military cloak (*chlamys*), and cap (*causia*); he may appear carrying weapons or other equipment. In the country setting of the *Dyskolos*, Sostratos is conspicuous as a rich young man from town because his overgarment is a *chlanis* (257 n.); in the *Georgos* 'the man in the *tribonion*' – a much humbler sort of cloak – is a phrase used to mean 'the poor man' (132f). Of course, appearances may be deceptive; and if, as Menander often does, a dramatist wishes to show that there is more to a character than meets the eye, costume is among the means which can be used to create a first impression which will later be modified.

From Pollux (4.119ff) and elsewhere it appears that attempts were made by ancient scholars to classify comic costumes by colour, and colours are present in some of the monuments. It may be that in Menander's time some of the usage of everyday life had become stereotyped into dramatic convention: for instance, Pollux says that parasites wear black or grey 'except for white in the *Sikyonios*' (*sc.* 'of Menander' or 'of Alexis'?) 'when the parasite is going to marry'. If a colour code existed, it could no doubt have been exploited by dramatists in the same way as other variations in dress, but it remains unclear how many of the individual pieces of information we have are reliable, and how many of them reflect actual practice in Menander's own day.

Masks were of course taken for granted by Greek audiences, who did not expect the actor's expression to aid the impact of the words, and were prepared to have speaking parts shared out between actors as the production required. The style of acting developed by generations of masked players in a large open-air theatre would probably seem exuberant, to say the least, if it could be recreated on a modern indoor stage; just so, the realistic stage acting of our own day does not necessarily suit the still more realistic world of the cinema. In spite of much work on the subject, it remains hard to say precisely how far conventions in the design and use of masks were fixed in Menander's day; but it seems likely that the main types at least were far enough fixed to suggest a basis of characterization for both dramatist and audience. A good dramatist and an intelligent audience were nevertheless not prevented from recognizing that a character typified by his mask admits a variety of treatment ranging from conventionality within the type to an individuality which goes against superficial appearances. Thus the Gorgias of the *Dyskolos* may well have been indistinguishable in appearance as well as in name from the young countrymen of the *Heros* and the *Georgos*, to say nothing of other young rustics elsewhere; we may call such characters stock types if we remember that an important part of Menander's dramatic achievement lies in differentiating the detail of characters and situations which are superficially familiar. If there is any literal truth in the famous portrait of Menander looking at one of the standard masks, apparently in search of inspiration, it is fair to comment that a standard may be both a pattern and a measure of difference.[1]

---

[1] See above, p. 15, n. 2, and below under (iii) (*d*); for the type of portrait cf. Webster, *MOMC*, no. AS 1, with references there given.

(iii) The following notes on possible illustrations for the characters of the *Dyskolos* are based on suggestions made by Webster: they give brief particulars of some type-examples for each character, where possible quoting some accessible plates, but do not attempt to explore the full range of possible choices from the known material. The allocation of the male masks depends partly on the assumption that their variant styles of hairdressing had a conventional significance in relating and distinguishing households. Thus the household of Kallippides is placed within the 'wavy-haired' series of masks, and contrasted thereby with Knemon on the one hand, and Gorgias and Daos on the other. Monuments which illustrate this distinction include the Delos mosaic quoted below for Pan, and the relief from Pompeii quoted for Sostratos.[1]

(*a*) PAN – The mask is known in two types, a young beardless and a bearded one.

(*i*) *Young beardless*: fragment of a Gnathia skyphos in Oxford (Beazley), 350/25 B.C.: Webster, *MOMC*, under no. GV 3, and JHS 71 (1951), plate xlv (a); cf. *MNC*, no. TJ 1, a silver cup from Tarentum (now lost), found with coins of 315-272 B.C.: Nachod, Römische Mitteilungen 33 (1918), plates 7-8.

(*ii*) *Bearded*: mosaic in Delos, early 2nd cent. B.C.: Webster, *MNC*, no. DM 1; coloured illustration in Chamonard, *Délos XIV*, pl. vi. See also *MOMC*, no. GV 4, a Gnathia oenochoe in Sèvres, 350/25.

The Pan mask appears with others, mostly recognizable as standard comic types, on the Tarentine silver cup and in the Delos mosaic: the cup is relevant here for Daos, Getas and Kore, and the mosaic for Kallippides, Sostratos, Getas, Daos. Webster suggests the beardless Pan for the *Dyskolos*, but an old and rather mild version of the bearded type would suit, for the prologue speech looks back some 16 years into the past and emphasizes the youth of the younger characters. For Pan in dramatic costume, it is perhaps relevant to mention Webster, *Monuments illustrating Tragedy* ... (1962), no. AV 37, an Attic rf. covered cup in Leningrad, 370/60 B.C., on which he is seen wearing a shaggy loincloth.

[1] See Webster, *GTP* 92ff, and for more evidence, *Masks of Greek Comedy*, 13ff (=107ff). Goold's use of the same principle brings in some variations: e.g. that Knemon's mask should match that of Gorgias since he is to adopt him, and that Pyrrhias should be treated independently as a 'protactic' character.

(*b*) GORGIAS – He is placed by type as the Rustic Youth (ἄγροικος), no. 14 in Pollux' catalogue as numbered by Webster, according to which he has a dark complexion, thick lips, a snub nose, and a crown of hair (στεφάνη). His costume is the *diphthera*. If it is right that the features suggested cowardliness and sensuality, Gorgias departs from the type, like the young rustics of *Heros* and *Georgos*: cf. Webster, *GTP* 79f, and below on 257.

Mask: Terracotta brazier from Delos, 2nd century B.C.: Webster, *MNC*, no. AV 25; Marcadé, Bull. Corr. Hellenique 1952, p. 623, fig. 25 (left). Silver cup from Boscoreale in the Louvre, 1st cent. A.D., *MNC*, no. NJ 2. See further *MNC*, p. 18. The mask illustrated by Bieber, *HT*², fig. 384, and Pickard-Cambridge, *Festivals*, fig. 117 (among others) is of very doubtful relevance, and probably of modern manufacture: Rumpf, Ἀρχ. Ἐφ. 1953/4, vol. 2, p. 124.

(*c*) DAOS – Webster suggests 'Leading Slave' (ἡγεμὼν θεράπων), Pollux no. 22, described as having a roll of red hair, raised brows, and a frown; but as the faithful old family servant (*Dysk.* 26f), Daos may have appeared in an old version of the mask akin to Pollux no. 21, the white-haired 'Old Slave' mask (πάππος), which Pollux says is the mark of the freedman: this is suggested by Goold. Costume: *diphthera*, as for Daos and Syriskos in *Epitr.* (53f). On the typology of slave-masks, see Webster, *MNC*, pp. 5-14, where early examples are quoted, and in Jahrbuch deutsch. Arch. Inst. 1961, 100-10.

'*Leading slave*', *no. 22*: terracotta statuette of slave with child in Taranto, 3rd cent. B.C.: Webster, *MNC*, no. TT 2; Bieber, *HT*², fig. 400. For the mask, see the Tarentine silver cup and the Delos mosaic quoted above for Pan; and cf. *MNC*, no. ZT 18 = Bieber *HT*², fig. 389.

'*Old slave*', *no. 21*: terracotta statuette from Myrina in Athens, 2nd cent. B.C.: Webster, *MNC*, no. MT 27; Bieber, *HT*², fig. 396; Pickard-Cambridge, *Festivals*, fig. 128. Painting in Pompeii, Casa del Centenario, 1st cent. A.D.: *MNC*, no. NP 27 = *Festivals*, fig. 99. Old slave, leading slave and girl piper appear in a painting in Naples from Herculaneum, 1st cent. A.D.: Webster, *MNC*, no. NP 45; Bieber, *HT*², fig. 328.

(*d*) KALLIPPIDES – 'Wavy-haired old man' (πρεσβύτης μακροπώγων καὶ ἐπισείων), Pollux no. 4, according to whom he has a crown of hair, long full beard, brows not raised, and is sluggish in expression. If the features suggested 'a normally calm old man,

who may be subject to fits of anger' (Webster, *GTP* 76), Kallippides suits the type well: generally mild and benevolent, he is
neither soft nor automatically compliant, as appears clearly
from 776-96. A forerunner in Middle Comedy is perhaps to be
seen in Webster-Trendall 'Type L', as worn by the character
named Philotimides on an Apulian bell-krater in Milan, dated
to 400/375: Trendall, *Phlyax Vases*, no. 42 and Plate II; Bieber,
HT², fig. 509.

Examples: relief in Naples, quoted below for Sostratos; mask in the
Delos mosaic, quoted above for Pan; Menander relief, Webster, *MNC*,
nos. AS 6 and IS 10; Bieber, *HT²*, figs. 316, 317 a. See further *MNC*,
p. 16.

(*e*) SOSTRATOS – 'Second youth with wavy hair' (δεύτερος
ἐπίσειστος), Pollux no. 16: more delicate than the first *episeistos*
(the soldier), and has fair hair.

Marble relief in Naples from Pompeii, 1st cent. A.D.: Webster,
MNC, no. NS 25, and *Gk Theatre Production*, plate 24 (a); Bieber, *HT²*,
fig. 324; Pickard-Cambridge, *Festivals*, fig. 94. On the right is the
young man, accompanied by a girl piper and supported by his slave
(no. 27, type of Getas); on the left, 'wavy-haired old man' (no. 4,
type of Kallippides) restrains 'leading old man' (no. 3). For young
man and slave, cf. Webster, *MNC*, no. BT 1 and plate I a, a terracotta
group in Thebes from Halai in Boeotia, 335-280 B.C.; for the young
man's mask, cf. *MOMC*, no. GV 9 (350/25 B.C.) = *Gk Theatre Production*,
plate 11 (e); and the Delos mosaic quoted above for Pan.

Costume: short (knee-length) *chiton* (370 n.); cf. the group from
Halai quoted above, and *MNC*, no. MT 3.

(*f*) GETAS, PYRRHIAS (and other male slaves of Kallippides'
household: cf. on 959) – Getas should wear the mask of the
'wavy-haired leading slave' (ἡγεμὼν ἐπίσειστος), Pollux no. 27.
He and Pyrrhias may have been differentiated by older and
younger versions of the same mask (see above on Daos); but
they never meet, and Pyrrhias may have been differentiated by
dress as a huntsman. Donax and Syros (?) are too minor and too
obviously attached to the household for it to matter greatly how
(if at all) their masks were different.

Examples: Delos mosaic and Tarentine cup (quoted for Pan); relief
in Naples (quoted for Sostratos). Webster, *MNC* p. 7, mentions among
other early instances a terracotta mask in Athens from the Agora,
dated to the end of the fourth century, no. AT 5.

(g) CHAIREAS – 'parasite' according to the list of *dramatis personae*; as a 'helpful friend' (cf. *Dysk.* 56f), he should wear the mask of the *kolax* rather than one of the other types available for this class: Pollux no. 17.

Examples: terracotta statuette in Athens, from Myrina, 2nd cent. B.C.: Webster, *MNC*, no. MT 18. MT 19 is similar, but with the 'parasite' mask (Pollux no. 18), and is illustrated by Bieber, *HT²*, fig. 372, and Pickard-Cambridge, *Festivals*, fig. 120. For the *kolax* mask, cf. a terracotta head from the Agora, 3rd/2nd cent. B.C., Webster, *MNC*, no. AT 4; *ib.*, no. UT 15 (= *Later Greek Comedy*, plate 4 (b)); and no. IS 14 (bottom left in Bieber, *HT²*, fig. 564, and Pickard-Cambridge, *Festivals*, fig. 160).

(h) SIKON – as a cook, presumably wears the *maison* mask, Pollux no. 25. The origin of the name was disputed in antiquity (Athenaeus 14.659): see most recently Pickard-Cambridge, *Dithyramb²* (1962), 181f, where Webster quotes an Apulian vase of ca. 380-370 B.C. as evidence for the earliest traceable history of the mask (Trendall, *Phlyax Vases*, no. 35; see 954 n., under (a)). Examples contemporary or near-contemporary with Menander are noted in *MNC*, p. 7, including no. BT 2, a mask in Thebes from Halai in Boeotia, 335-280 B.C.: Pickard-Cambridge, *Festivals*, fig. 91.

Terracotta statuette in Berlin from Megara, late third to early second century B.C.: Webster, *MNC*, no. XT 8 (with a replica); Bieber, *HT²*, fig. 156; Pickard-Cambridge, *Festivals*, fig. 81. Cf. *MNC*, no. TT 1 (=*HT²*, fig. 155).

(i) KNEMON – Webster attractively suggests a mask classified by himself and Trendall as AA, a variant of Middle Comedy Type A, both of which appear to persist in a few examples dated later than 325 B.C., and are possibly included in Pollux no. 6, the 'wedge-bearded old man' (σφηνοπώγων), who, according to Pollux, has receding hair, raised brows, and a sharp chin: he is 'a somewhat cross-grained character' (ὑποδύστροπος). This mask, apparently unusual and old-fashioned by New Comedy standards, could have been chosen to emphasize the point that Knemon is an unusual and old-fashioned character; it is imaginable that the type was already associated with the misanthrope through Antiphanes' play *Timon* (Kock, vol. 2, p. 100: cf. the Commentary on line 6). If not the *diphthera*, Knemon may have worn a knee-length *chiton*, unlike Kallippides and other old men in New Comedy: it would go with the mask suggested, and suit the image of poverty and toil which his way of life presents.

Type A: Pollux' 'receding hair and raised brows' – not always present – are clear in Trendall, *Phlyax Vases*, no. 148, an Apulian crater in Leiden dated ca. 340-20 B.C.: cf. Webster, *GTP*, plate 11 (c). Webster, *MOMC*, no. KT 8, lists a terracotta head in Cyprus, found with coins dated 317-311 B.C.

Type AA: (distinguished from A by fuller hair and longer beard): Trendall, *Phlyax Vases*, no. 165 and plate VI c, an Apulian pelike in Warsaw dated ca. 350-340; Webster, *MNC*, no. AT 1, a terracotta mask from the Agora, dated early third century.

(*j*) MYRRHINE, Knemon's wife (and Kallippides' wife): probably (respectively) Pollux no. 31 'Garrulous woman' (λεκτική), and no. 32 'Curly-haired' (οὔλη). Note: (a) apropos of no. 31, that Knemon quarrelled with his wife day and night, *Dysk.* 17ff; (b) that both ladies have grown up children and are thus middle-aged, but not necessarily old.

No. 31: 'hair round the head, fairly smooth; straight brows, white complexion': recognized in a terracotta statuette in Berlin, from Capua: Webster, *MNC*, no. NT 12; Bieber, *HT²*, fig. 353. For her Middle Comedy prototype, cf. *MOMC*, under nos. AT 76-77 and ST 16.

No. 32 (perhaps a variant introduced for plays needing two wives): terracotta mask in Geneva from Corneto 'probably 2nd cent B.C.': Webster, *MNC*, no. IT 26; cf. IS 35 (=Simon, *Comicae Tabellae*, pl. XII.1).

(*k*) KORE, Knemon's daughter (and Sostratos' sister): Pollux no. 33 'smoothed and parted hair, straight dark brows, pale complexion'. Long-haired and short-haired forms are known for New Comedy, as earlier.

(*i*) *Long hair* (K.'s daughter?): Webster, *MNC*, no. CT 1, terracotta statuette of an actor holding the mask, and draped as for a female part (Corinth, 250 B.C.); perhaps compare the mask of NP 48 (Bieber, *HT²*, fig. 760, who interprets as Andromeda).

(*ii*) *Short hair* (S.'s sister?): terracotta mask from a tomb in Egypt, dated late 4th-early third cent. B.C.: Webster, *MNC*, no. ET 3 and plate I (g); cf. TJ 1 (quoted above for Pan), and perhaps NT 28, an elegantly dressed terracotta statuette described by Bieber as a courtesan, *HT²*, fig. 548 b.

(*l*) SIMICHE – 'Little housekeeper' (οἰκουρὸν γρᾴδιον), Pollux no. 30 'snub-nosed, with two teeth in each jaw'.

The mask is one of three on the terracotta brazier from Delos quoted above for Gorgias: Webster, *MNC*, no. AV 25 and plate II a. Cf. *ib.*, no. FT 2, illustrated in *Later Greek Comedy*, pl. 4 c, and UT 84 (=Bieber, *HT*², fig. 351).

For her dramatic ancestry as a nurse, cf. Webster, *MOMC*, under AT 8 and p. 10 (AT 8 a =Bieber, *HT*², fig. 185; Pickard-Cambridge, *Festivals*, fig. 85); for her tragic counterpart, cf. Webster, *Monuments illustrating Tragedy* . . . , no. NP 34; Bieber, *HT*², fig. 591; Pickard-Cambridge, *Festivals*, fig. 70.

(*m*) FEMALE SLAVES OF KALLIPPIDES' HOUSEHOLD (430ff)

Pollux distinguishes between those who serve respectable women (no. 43) and those who serve hetairai (no. 44). No. 43 is not identified among monuments of the Hellenistic period, but perhaps to be seen in a marble mask from Pompeii in Naples, 1st cent. A.D.: Webster, *MNC*, no. NS 13; Bieber, *HT*², fig. 356; Pickard-Cambridge, *Festivals*, fig. 152. For no. 44, cf. Webster, *MNC*, no. TT 13, a terracotta mask in Munich from Apulia, probably early 2nd cent. B.C.; Bieber, *HT*², fig. 367 (left). Parthenis, if a professional music-girl, may have worn Pollux no. 39 'Little blooming hetaira', as (e.g.) in the painting from Herculaneum quoted above for Daos: see the Commentary under 880.

III

The text: its sources and constitution

The text of the *Dyskolos* depends very largely on the single manuscript to which it owes its survival as a play. Since this was
published, small fragments of two other ancient copies have
been recognized; some 40 lines or parts of lines previously known
from quotations now fall into place as supplementary authorities
for the text, and are augmented by other quotations and reminiscences of the play which, for lack of other evidence, could not
be recognized as such until we had a copy from which to identify
them. Since textual problems constantly arise in any study of
the *Dyskolos*, it seems useful here to survey the material from which
critics work.

H Oxford, Bodleian Library, Gr. Class. g 49 (P), containing
parts of vv. 139-50 and 169-74: a fragment of a vellum codex,
measuring 56 × 90 mm., from Hermopolis in Egypt. It was first
published by Grenfell and Hunt in *Mélanges Nicole* (Geneva,
1905) 220-2, under the heading 'Fragment of a Comedy', and
tentatively dated in the fourth century A.D.; Blass had suggested
that the author might be Menander. The content was first
recognized by C. H. Roberts, who is to republish the fragment in
the Bodleian Record. Both sides are rubbed and discoloured,
especially the verso, and on some points judgement must await
the republication. I give readings provisionally with the aid of
corrections to the first editors' transcript communicated by Mr
Roberts, and of a photograph for whose loan I am most grateful. Cf. Turner, BICS 1959.63 and Lloyd-Jones' Oxford Text of
1960.

O Two minute scraps of papyrus from Oxyrhynchus (which
now appear in Oxyrhynchus Papyri, vol. 27, no. 2467): they contain ends of vv. 263-72 and 283-90; late second century A.D.
Readings and other information were provided for me by E. G.
Turner, by whom the fragments were first identified.

P Papyrus Bodmer IV, in the library of Dr Martin Bodmer at Le Grand Cologny near Geneva, containing the *Dyskolos* virtually complete, preceded by hypothesis, didascalia and dramatis personae; the place and circumstances of its discovery remain unknown; its date, from the handwriting, is to be placed in the latter half of the third century A.D., perhaps as late as the early fourth century. P consists of 21 pages (i.e. ten leaves and the first side of an eleventh), measuring originally ca. 275 × 130 mm., from a codex which evidently contained a collection of plays by Menander. The first publication, by Victor Martin, is also the *editio princeps* of the play; dated Cologny-Genève, 1958, it became generally available in mid-March 1959, and was accompanied by a complete set of photographs, at a reduced scale, from which the reports of readings in this edition are checked or derived.[1]

Losses of text: P is generally well preserved, but damage to the tops and outer edges of leaves has affected groups of lines at more or less regular intervals, depriving them of middles, beginnings and ends; the eighth leaf (plates 15-16 of ed. pr.) is some 30 mm. shorter than the rest, and has apparently lost a few lines entirely from its top: see the commentary under 649 and 703-7. Where P is damaged, other sources occasionally make good the loss, for example at 805ff; for the most part restoration depends upon conjecture, simple and certain where the damage is slight and the context is clear; more complex and more doubtful according as the context fails to give a clear lead to what is missing, as it commonly does when the damage is relatively great or when textual corruption is present.

Editions which restore freely, as this one does, are obliged to adopt supplements of widely differing probability, some of which can only claim to illustrate what Menander may conceivably have written, not to restore what he wrote. There are some con-

---

[1] Many proposed corrections to the transcript given in ed. pr. have been published in later editions of the play, and are to be found scattered widely through the papers and books devoted to it. Most are based on the photographs, some derive from the original manuscript or have been checked against it, including two lists published by Harsh in Gnomon 1959.577ff, and Turner in BICS 1959.61ff. Where a reading seems open to reasonable doubt, I have printed dots under letters in the text, and sometimes added notes or ascriptions of credit in the *apparatus criticus* and the commentary. For palaeographical description of P, see Martin's remarks in his introduction to ed. pr. and in Scriptorium 1960.3ff; H. Juhnke, Hermes 89 (1961) 122-7; and, most recently, J.-M. Jacques, ed. Dysk., 45ff. On the date of P, see especially Turner, *loc. cit.*; Kraus, *Dyskolos*, p. 10; and Bingen, *Dyskolos²*, x.

spicuous advantages in having a continuous text; but the reader must be prepared for constant reminders on the printed page and from remarks in the notes that its appearance of solidity may be mere illusion.[1]

Distinction of hands: One page of P is in a handwriting different from that of the others, namely the first side of the tenth leaf (plate 19 of ed. pr.), containing vv. 850-87. Speakers' names (usually abbreviated) appear at intervals throughout the play, written in the margins and (twice) above the line; some of these, and some corrections to the copy, show certain variations in style from the writing of the adjacent text, and here too the possibility of distinguishing different hands has been raised. The first editor, however, has reaffirmed his view that, except for the page mentioned, the whole of P is in the same handwriting; however this may be, and whatever is the explanation of the odd page, there is nothing to show clearly that a second original was anywhere employed, or that any long interval elapsed between writing the text and making such alterations and additions as were made.[2]

In this edition P refers to the papyrus throughout, irrespective of the odd page; the symbols P[1] and P[2] are used to distinguish successive states of the copy and do not imply any distinction of hand.

Corrections: P's corrections are sporadic and trivial, most if not all of them repairs (or attempted repairs) to blunders of copying; it is not clear that any are conscious textual emendations, still less that the copyist had a second source to hand.

Accordingly this edition often takes them for granted without

[1] Supplements by nature profess to restore not only the author's words but the damaged copy itself; hence, if the space available for them is restricted, they must fit it within the limits allowable for the writing in question. Many proposed supplements to the *Dyskolos* do not. Of course P may be corrupt where damaged (as at 142 and perhaps 450); but to supplement on the hypothesis that it is, is usually an expedient of desperation: for examples, see the text adopted at 49, 445 and 839.

[2] V. Martin: Scriptorium 1960.3ff. In cramped or unusual situations, with the angle of the pen perhaps altered, variations in handwriting may be expected; the cursiveness found in speakers' names, etc., differs only in degree from the cursiveness which P's normal hand sometimes shows in copying the text. As Martin notes, this itself varies in appearance with the state of the writer's pen, and does so suddenly when he changes or sharpens it. Hence one can sometimes say precisely at what stage of copying speakers' names and corrections were written: e.g. at 813 the prefaced speaker's name is written with the same thick point as the preceding lines; the writer then goes on with a finer one. Jean Martin, ed. Dysk., pp. 4, 28, is among those who take a less sanguine view of the homogeneity of P.

comment; the critical notes call attention to some where points of textual interest arise (e.g. at 95 and 788) or where P's corrected mistake contributes a useful illustration of the writer's habits as a copyist (e.g. omission: 99, 173, 204 et al.).[1]

It is convenient to mention here two apparent variants (hyp. 6, and 128), and two glosses (113, 944), all presumably inherited from the original, as the gloss at 944 certainly was. H has a correction in 148; O offers a variant (or gloss?) in 284.

Orthography; accents and other aids to reading: P's orthography is in general good, but shows certain common phonetic deviations: e.g. interchange of ι and ει (very frequently), of ε and αι, and of ο and ω. Iota in long diphthongs (iota adscript) is commonly but not systematically present: e.g. οχλωι 7, but οχλω 8; it is sometimes wrongly added: e.g. κατ᾽ ηλλαγηι hyp. 9.

Accents and breathings are rare except in certain sections of the text, e.g. 50-149; but even then they are not systematically applied, and sometimes wrongly; breathings may appear in the middle of a compound, as in ανόσιε 108.

Elision is frequent, but not always marked by diastole; sometimes the diastole appears in compound words (e.g. κατ᾽ ηλλαγηι quoted above), between double consonants (ματ᾽τω, 549), and after the negative (ουκ᾽, ουχ᾽). *Scriptio plena* is usual at changes of speaker, but otherwise alternates irregularly with elision.[2]

Punctuation, rare, irregular and unreliable, is by single high point; for the dicolon or double point, see below under *Distribution of Parts*.

These and other minor details sometimes enter into a textual decision, and I have tried to note them where they appear to. In recording P's orthography, as with its corrections, the critical notes are selective, perhaps too generously so, but are rarely hospitable to the interchange of ι and ει. In spelling the verb ποιῶ/ποῶ, P is inconsistent. I follow it where the variable syllable is *anceps*, but print -οι- regardless of P where it scans long, and -ο- likewise where it scans short.

[1] The corrections in P are not all satisfactorily recorded in printed sources; failing an inspection of the manuscript, the reader who wishes for the fullest possible information will naturally consult the photographs on this matter as on others.

[2] It is a common current practice to print dramatic texts without marking elision at the changes of speaker. We can only guess whether in performance actors clipped each others' words or were allowed to let the metre limp; my own guess is for the former alternative.

Distribution of Parts: For evidence and discussion of ancient practice in Greek dramatic texts, see E. G. Turner, *Athenian Books*... (1952), p. 7, and P. Oxy. 27.2458, Introduction; J. Andrieu, *Le Dialogue Antique* (1954), esp. 258ff; E. J. Jory, BICS 1963.65ff; and especially J. C. B. Lowe, BICS 1962.27-42. On the *Dyskolos*, see F. Stoessl, *Personenwechsel*... (Sitzb. Öst. Ak., ph.-hist. Kl., 234.5, 1960), and M. Pope, Acta Classica 3 (1960) 40ff.

(*a*) *Paragraphus and dicolon*: In P, the words of different speakers are distinguished by paragraphus and dicolon. The paragraphus (—) is inset at the left below verses in which or after which a change of speaker occurs; the dicolon (:) stands at the end of each speaker's part, whether within the verse or at the end of it. For example, at 54ff we have:

σκώπτεις· ἐγὼ δέ, Χαιρέα, κακῶς ἔχω:
ἀλλ' οὐκ ἀπιστῶ: διόπερ ἥκω παραλαβὼν
σὲ πρὸς τὸ πρᾶγμα, κτλ.

Sometimes, as here, the correct division between the speakers is obvious from the words themselves and the context; since it is often far from obvious, the value of the notation in P is an issue of some importance.

It is likely, on historical and other grounds, that part-division has been present in the text of the *Dyskolos* since the first copies were made. It appears in H and O, as well as in P, and can be traced as a normal feature of Greek dramatic texts back to the early third century B.C., the time of our earliest surviving copies – or rather, fragments of copies – the earliest of which, on a high dating, could have been written within Menander's own lifetime; but they are in any case close enough to give a fair impression of Athenian books in his day.[1] From the first, the paragraphus

---

[1] Cf. Turner, *Athenian Books*... loc. cit.; Lowe, p. 34f and notes, mentions the relevant fragments: they include P. Hibeh 6, 300/280 B.C. (=Com. Anon., Page, *Lit. Pap.* 63); P. Heid. 184 and other frgg. of the same roll, 280/40 B.C. (probably Philemon; but cf. Page, *Lit. Pap.*, under no. 64); P. Hamb. 120, third cent. B.C.; possibly Menander (=frg. d 951); and P. Vind. 29811 (Oellacher, *Mitteilungen*... III.22), unidentified comedy: in Koerte's view 'perhaps the earliest comic papyrus we have', Archiv für Papyrusforschung 14 (1941) 119. On H, see app. crit. and commentary to 139-50, noting that the presence of traces of paragraphi is doubtful, and that no example of a dicolon at the end of a verse is preserved; I am unclear about the end of 170, which H preserves in very poor condition. O has only verse-ends, where there are dicola in agreement with P.

appears as the regular sign of part-division, and was apparently basic to the system. In conjunction with it, dicola mark changes of speaker within the verse, as in P, but in texts earlier than the Christian era they are not normally written at verse-end; an alternative to the medial dicolon is a short blank space within the verse, as for instance in P. Heid.184 (see p. 44, n. 1). That is to say, the paragraphus itself is taken to give sufficient indication where changes of speaker occur only at verse-end; when a verse is divided one or more times between speakers, the words them-selves are left to show whether the end of it runs on into the next verse or not. This ambiguity, in practice not a serious one, is avoided by writing dicola at verse-ends, as in P and later practice generally (though they are strictly necessary only when there is also a medial division); it is also avoidable by beginning each speaker's part on a new line from the left, and treating it as a whole verse.[1]

Ambiguity also arises if spaces or dicola appear otherwise, whether accidentally or not. Spaces may appear (as they some-times do in P) by irregular writing, or from a tendency to separate words, and – more particularly – to mark pauses and breaks in a speech by spacing, as for example in P. Oxy.211 (1st-2nd cent. A.D.: *Perikeiromene*), and in the British Museum Herondas papyrus.[2] The single point, which is normally a mark of punctuation, sometimes does duty for the dicolon in indicating a change of speaker; the dicolon itself is not wholly specialized as a sign of part-division, but is sometimes written where there is a break within a speech, characteristically where the speaker changes direction: e.g. from direct address to soliloquy, or from addressing one person to addressing another. Once again, these ambiguities and confusions of practice were probably not desperately serious to readers who followed the words with patience and intelligence; but the less clearly and regularly a text is set out, the more likely a copyist of it is to misplace part-divisions or ignore them; some-times, as in P. Oxy.211, we find the copyist's work supplemented

---

[1] Andrieu, *Dial. Antique* 262 quotes S. *Ichneutai* 199 as set out in P. Oxy. 1174, end of the 2nd century A.D. One might expect this convention to be more widespread, for it has obvious practical advantages, but in many passages of comedy it would be wasteful of space and give an irregular column of script. See Lowe, pp. 33-35, where evidence for some other variant conventions will also be found.

[2] Cf. Headlam-Knox, *Herondas*, lxii n. 4: of the blank spaces 'only about fifty per cent. have any value, as marking a change of sense, a change of speaker, or a stop'.

and revised by a corrector, not always rightly. Add, among other possibilities, that dicola may be omitted, not clearly distinguished from neighbouring letters, confused with the single point or other lectional signs, and mistaken for iota, and the presence of manifest errors in P becomes not only explicable but venial.[1]

The commonest fault in P's part-division seems to be the loss of dicola, sometimes for obvious palaeographical reasons, from places where the text and the writing convention demand their presence; the fact that they can much more rarely be shown to be misplaced or interpolated suggests that in the main we are dealing with an inherited system corrupted by simple transcriptional faults, and not one which has been imposed or extensively modified by some incompetent person. I quote a selection of examples:

(i) *dicola omitted*: (within the verse) 774, 956; (at verse-end) 624, 779.

(ii) *dicola transcribed as iota*: 945 ($\mu\epsilon\mu\nu\eta\sigma o\iota = \mu\epsilon\mu\nu\eta\sigma o$:); 639 ($\delta\iota o\nu\nu\sigma o\nu\iota = \delta\iota o\nu\nu\sigma o\nu$:?: if so, dicolon at a change of direction – see below); compare 594, where some transcribe]ω: from P, and others]$\omega\iota$.

(iii) *dicola wrongly added, misplaced*: 361 (:$o\iota\lambda\epsilon\gamma\epsilon\iota\sigma$:), 766 (for single point? – an erroneous one if so: cf. 54 $\sigma\kappa\omega\pi\tau\epsilon\iota\sigma$: P[1]); 140 $\eta\delta\iota\kappa\eta$:$\kappa\alpha$ P[1] (cf. 436 $\epsilon\upsilon\tau\rho$:$\epsilon\pi\eta$); 906.

(iv) *dicola at a change of direction in a speech*: 177 (cf. 213 end); 638 (after $\delta\epsilon\upsilon\rho$'); 639 ($\delta\iota o\nu\nu\sigma o\nu\iota = \delta\iota o\nu\nu\sigma o\nu$:?); 926 (after $\sigma\iota\mu\iota\kappa\eta$) and 927 (after $\theta\epsilon o\iota$).[2]

The paragraphus, in the transmission of the *Dyskolos* at least, appears to have been a less equivocal object; it is however sometimes manifestly omitted (83, 343) and omitted together with dicolon at 359 and 954, not to mention less certain cases. I

---

[1] It is not unfair to note that the transcript of ed. pr. is sometimes at fault in reproducing P's changes of speaker, and that expert opinion at large cannot always agree whether the copyist in fact wrote a dicolon or not: e.g. at 594, to be mentioned below.

[2] On this phenomenon in the Cairo codex of Menander, see Koerte I[3], p. xii, and Jensen, *Menandri reliquiae*, p. xii; and cf. Andrieu, pp. 251, 259, 264; Lowe, p. 33. It is debatable whether dicola at such places arise from a recurrent type of error, from a writing convention in which the dicolon was not fully specialized as a sign of part-division, or from a stage in the textual transmission in which the dicolon was only used to mark certain kinds of pause or break. The distinction, though of interest for the history of punctuation, would be hard to sustain as a point of great critical consequence: what matters is that the phenomenon itself should be recognized.

know of no completely satisfactory instance of wrong addition in this text, but assume it at 438 and 896, where see the commentary.

In general then, the position seems to be that the part-divisions in P are legitimately used, together with the words it preserves, as primary evidence of Menander's intentions. Fallible though the notation is, it can reasonably claim the benefit of any textual doubt over the division of parts; since however it is by nature prone to a wide variety of textual accident and confusion, serious suspicion will attach to any version of the text which does violence to the words, whether by emendation or otherwise, in order to save the paragraphi and dicola.

(b) *The identification of speakers*: If parts were distinguished in the dramatic texts of Menander's day, common sense would suggest that the speakers were at least occasionally identified: by the poet, as a mnemonic for the purposes of production, and hence perhaps in the text as it circulated. If full labelling were thought useful in anything approximating to a production script or a prompt copy, it could no doubt have been provided; but our limited information about theatrical production in fourth century Athens throws no light on the physical characteristics of the texts used.[1]

Whatever the requirements of ancient production may have been (and in this a modern 'common sense' view is often an unreliable guide), what is known of dramatic texts in the six centuries which separate P from Menander's own copy of the *Dyskolos* suggests that ancient readers were rarely given more generous guidance to the identity of the speakers than the intermittent labelling of parts which P provides: they may well have been fortunate to have as much. An early example of a text with parts extensively labelled by abbreviated names is the Berlin fragment of Euripides, *Telephus*, of the second century A.D.; in the 1st/2nd century, the Oxyrhynchus *Perikeiromene* fragment has names added intermittently, probably by a contemporary hand, in the course of revising the copy; if we go back to dramatic texts earlier than the Christian era (where admittedly the material is much less extensive), the evidence for names or other methods of labelling parts disappears almost to vanishing point, as has

---

[1] Students of the Elizabethan theatre are more fortunate: Mr K. J. Palmer refers me to Sir W. W. Greg, *Dramatic documents from the Elizabethan playhouse* (1931).

47

recently been made clear by Lowe (p. 34f).[1] It therefore seems unlikely that the intermittent identifications of speakers in P are relics of a full or substantially fuller system of labelling; but if the evidence of the earliest surviving copies of drama offers no satisfactory verification for the view that they derive from or are contemporary with the author, it still does not seem adequate to eliminate the possibility *ab initio*. Essentially, a circulated copy of an ancient play seems to have been a bare record of the words, but certain other information, such as the *XOPOY* which marks choral performances (as in the *Dyskolos* after 232, 426, 619, 783), and very occasional 'stage-directions' (as αὐλεῖ in the *Dyskolos* after 879) was apparently accepted and transmitted with the text from the first; and it is not impossible to think that identifications of speaker were sometimes treated similarly, though as accessories to the text, they may well have been freely discarded or modified, where present, by those who made or owned copies, like the general class of marginalia in which they are possibly to be reckoned.[2] However this may be, the evidence for the antiquity of P's identifications of speakers (as opposed to the distinction of the parts themselves) inspires no confidence that we are dealing with authentic Menandrean material.

In P itself, some of the identifications of speaker appear to be related to the prefatory list of *dramatis personae*; but the nature of the relationship is not clear; the list itself shows no reliable signs of very early origin, and some of not very perceptive modification. The distribution of the names is neither so casual as to suggest that the corpus of them has grown up from random marginal jottings by readers, nor so systematic as to suggest the rigid application of a principle. If there is in them a nucleus of material which derives from Menander, or from someone who remembered a production which preserved his intentions, we cannot hope to isolate it; losses and accretions of names may have obscured any design on the part of the person originally responsible for them, but we gain nothing by postulating widespread textual accidents

---

[1] *Telephus*, P. Berol. 9908 (BKT 5.2.64; cf. BICS, Suppl. 5, 1957); *Perikeiromene*, P. Oxy. 211, referred to above; Lowe, p. 41, n. 51, gives corrections to Andrieu.

[2] Cf. Lowe, p. 36. *XOPOY* is already present in the earliest surviving dramatic texts (e.g. P. Vind. 29811, mentioned p. 44 n. 1); the list of instances from papyri given in CQ 1953, p. 58 n. 3, may now be augmented from the *Dyskolos*, *Sikyonios*, and *Misoumenos* of Menander (Turner: cf. p. 305); and from P. Hibeh 184, ca. 270/40 B.C., a tragic fragment with *XOPOY ΜΕΛΟΣ*. On αὐλεῖ see ad loc.

to suit; perhaps the most plausible explanation of the names as they stand is that they derive either wholly or largely from an attempt to clarify the text for reading which was not carried out with full scholarly determination.[1]

If that is indeed the position, in following P's assignations of parts, we may well obtain no more than a partial reconstruction of some ancient reading of the text, based upon the words and the part-divisions as they stood at the time. The strongest case for overriding an explicit attribution in P (though it is not in my view decisive) has been made apropos of 430-41, where see the commentary. We have freqently to supplement P's silence, and sometimes to wonder what it portends: for instance at 365, does P genuinely mark Daos' first intervention into the discussion, or has he already spoken at 363? The result in practice, aggravated by losses of text and confusion of the part-divisions, is a degree of uncertainty about the author's intentions which, in the absence of better evidence, is likely to persist; it is a doubtful consolation that many ancient readers were no better off.

General character of P's text: While so many textual problems are disputed, and so little comparative evidence is available, it is bound to be difficult to form a clear picture of P's quality as a source of the text. None the less, one principal feature of P can be disengaged from controversy: it abounds in errors of the kind commonly produced by careless copying. Some of these, as we have noted, are already corrected in P; many were observed and successfully remedied in the *editio princeps*; subsequent work has added to the quota by demonstrating the presence of simple errors where the text had been allowed to stand or had been treated as if suffering from some graver malady. The following notes take a number of conjectural corrections for granted, but may serve as an introduction to some typical situations in the text as we have it.

Errors of *omission* are particularly frequent. It is not clear that P ever omits whole verses, though that fault has sometimes been

[1] See Victor Martin, Scriptorium 1960 at pp. 6ff, Stoessl and Pope, quoted at the beginning of this discussion. Stoessl's interesting attempt to arrange the dialogue by giving a maximal theoretical value to P's part-distribution requires a high degree of improbable hypothesis for its support, and if acceptable in principle, would require us to think that the tradition is more trustworthy in this matter than in preserving Menander's words, where it is lamentably faulty.

suspected, for instance at 726/7; but short words, single letters, and groups of them are constantly passed over in the copying process; in particular, the repetition or near-repetition of a letter or group in close sequence causes the sequence to be reduced by the phenomenon known as haplography: e.g. τελευτηκοτοσ for τετελευτηκότος 14, and μεγακον for μέγα κακόν 877. Some characteristic specimens of this class of error are: 143 καὶ before πάρεστι omitted by P¹; 292 πραμθανάτων P¹ for πρᾶγμα θανάτων; 311 νύμφαι P¹ for αἱ Νύμφαι; 775 απολειμ᾽ for ἀπολέλειμμ᾽; 860 χρηματοσ for χρὴ πράγματος. See above under *Corrections*.

Addition: (i) by dittography, the opposite of haplography: e.g. 314 εισεισοι P¹ for εἴ σοι; 610 αγειννυν for ἄγει νῦν; 663 αλλ᾽ υποτατοσ for ἀλυπότατος; apparently associated with other textual troubles at 445, 788, 817; cf. on 350. This error is recurrent with parts of οὗτος/ὅδε, where, perhaps sometimes confused by the presence of variants or corrections, the copyist produces such readings as 173 τουτοτι for τουτί; 185 τοτουτουδ᾽ for τὸ τοῦδ᾽ or τούτου δ᾽; 814 ταυταυτ᾽ for ταῦτ᾽.¹

(ii) by incorporating variants, etc. (see above): 26 θεναμα is a compound of θ᾽ἕνα and θ᾽ἅμα; 635 (extent of addition uncertain); 944 (gloss added to end of line); 958.

(iii) by mistaken insertion of the article and of particles (two classes of words often found omitted in P): 151 τουσθεουσ; 372 τοπλειστον P¹; 769 τηστυχ[ησ; 18 καιτοπολυ (καί added rather than τό: but see ad loc., and cf. 520, 920); 745 δ᾽ην P¹, cf. 736 ταδ᾽αλλα for τἄλλα (possibly by dittography).

Transposition: (i) anagrammatic: e.g. 43 παραλαβοντ᾽ for παραβαλόντ᾽; 58 οτι for τις P¹; 536 κηλωναειμε for κηλώνειά με; 605 σκαφο(ν) for σφάκον (cf. 914).

(ii) of whole words: e.g. τις, τι: 105, 288, 397; 365 γαρδη for δὴ γάρ; 834 μικραπολλα for πολλὰ μικρά.

---

¹ The usage of ὅδε and οὗτος in Later Greek is different from that of Menander: *NTGramm.* §289. The combination of a careless copyist and an original with corrections and other added material can have serious results when it leads to the loss of genuine text, as seems to have happened at 817 and possibly elsewhere. It should perhaps be stressed that even where simple error and not deep corruption is manifestly present, textual ambiguity will persist if the context and the author's usage do not show decisively which of two or more possible mistakes has been made. The less formally an author writes, the more scope there is for such minor ambiguities to remain unresolved; hence they are relatively frequent in this and other texts of comedy, but more often an irritant to the reader than a serious obstacle to his comprehension.

Substitution: (i) words and word-endings affected by context: e.g. hyp. 10 ερων from hyp. 4 for ἔχειν (?); 156 λιθινουσ for λίθους by influence of λιθίνων in 159; 372 ημερασ for ἡμᾶς by influence of τήμερον; hyp. 3 τροπουσμονουσ P¹ for τρόπους μόνος; 577 βουλομενουτουδεσποτου for βουλομένη τοῦ δεσπότου.

(ii) words, especially parts of the verb, replaced by synonyms or other variants of analogous function. Later Greek forms have sometimes replaced those used by Menander; sometimes a variant, or a note intended to clarify the text, appears to have invaded it; some such errors may have arisen from writing with a hazy idea of the sense in mind rather than an exact image of the words to be copied. Errors with verbs: e.g. 15 λαμβανοντος for λαβόντος; 62 αυξάνει for αὔξει; 418 αποβαιη for ἀποβῇ; 420 ποιησωμεν for ποῶμεν or ποήσω; 780 ποησω for ποῶ; 785 προσεδοκουν P¹ for προσεδόκων; 950 βρεχεισα for βραχεῖσα. Variants known from P itself illustrate this class of error in other varieties and at an earlier stage: hyp. 6 ποει/λεγοι; 26 θ'ένα/θ'ἄμα; 128 πρακτικώτατον/ -τερον. Cf. 284 in O (ευπορεισ in textu; ευτυχεισ s.v.); and see further under *Graver corruption*.

Misreading: (i) Certain confusions of letters appear to have arisen from their similarity in the script of P's original or an earlier copy. For example: (*a*) π/τ/γ (in the form г): 74 τοτ' for ποτ' P¹, cf. 16, 531; 379 παρ- for γάρ(?); 423 ανεσπογ' for ἄνες ποτ'(?). Note also the interchange ττ/π by haplography and dittography: e.g. 466 απει for ἄπτει; 699 πταιδευειν for παιδεύειν. (*b*) ε/θ/ο/σ (in the form c): 796 εατερον P¹ for θάτερον; 409 θυσοντοσ for θυσοντεσ; 38 εχειν P¹ for σχεῖν, cf. 910 ευτηρει, 965 ευνησθεντεσ. These errors, like εκπεσων for εἰσπεσών (if right) in 641, could have arisen from misreading a large formal book hand, as Victor Martin has argued (Scriptorium 1960.14f); they need not necessarily have done so. (*c*) στ/τ, σθ/θ: this interchange could most easily have happened from misreading a hand in which the cross-stroke of τ and θ tended to begin with a curve: cf. van Groningen, *Étude Critique*, on 12. Examples include 121 εστι P¹ for ἔτι; 239 απετησ for ἀπέστης; 296 αδικησθεισ for ἀδικηθείς; 343 εθ' for ἐσθ'.

(ii) While any presumption about the handwriting of P's original must be made with caution, there is reasonably good evidence to suggest that on occasion at least it was liable to be more cursive than that of P. The unintelligible ιοθι corrected to πωσ in 95 has been convincingly explained by Turner as a mis-reading of a rapidly written group of letters (BICS 1959.63, with diagram); some other places where the same phenomenon may possibly have given difficulty are 133 επεντερ P¹ for ἐπείπερ; 250 τουτω for τοῦτον; 345 διατελει for διαλέγει; 730 κακωσοιονεχω P¹ for κακῶς ἴσως ἔχω; 809 end (see ad loc.); 910 μη for ἤν. Confusion over certain final syllables may further entitle us to suppose that abbreviation appeared in the original more often than it does in P: e.g. 76 τοιουτ᾽ for τοιοῦτον (if right); 902 πινουσ᾽, εστ᾽ for πίνουσιν, ἐστίν; 483 λαβων for λάβω; cf. 773 ορων for ὁρῶ.¹

Graver corruption: (i) Although a high proportion of ortho-graphical and other superficial errors can reasonably be attri-buted to P itself, one should perhaps beware of thinking too highly of the textual character of its original. P is on any account a highly uncritical copy, and could have taken over such errors as well as making them; it may well be that some corruptions are to be recognized as the product of one simple mistake super-imposed upon another: e.g. 211 καθοσαι P for κάθησαι by way of καθεσαι (cf. 441); 376 ετιγαροικοδομησω P for ἐποικοδομήσω γάρ by way of ετιοικοδομησωγαρ; 955 τυπτε P, for τί ποτε by way of τιπτε. If this is so, we need to guard against the manifold and often legitimate attractions of technical simplicity in judging emendations of this text; in the last two passages mentioned the technically simpler corrections ἔτ᾽ οἰκοδομήσω γὰρ and τύπτετε do not seem to produce convincing results.

(ii) Something has been said already of variants, corrections and notes already present in the text when P was written, and of errors arising from following the sense rather than the words. Since the traces of all these are commonly obscured by successive processes of copying, the fact that they appear at all may be a sign that the tradition behind P was more defective than it seems from the surface.

(iii) An important issue on which critics differ sharply is the evidence provided by quotations of deep corruption in P: the most significant in this respect is the quotation of 797-812 pre-served in Stobaeus. On the view taken in this edition, major divergencies between P and the quoting sources (e.g. 802 μήτε P:

¹ Cf. van Groningen, *op. cit.*, on 76. Abbreviation in P, apart from σκαφō 605, is confined to the marginal speakers' names and the prolegomena: heading, *ΑΡΙΣΤΟΦΑΝ ΓΡΑΜΜΑΤΙ* [.]; didasc., αρχοντ (=ἄρχοντος), αντιεπιγραφετ᾽ (=-εται); dram. pers. δραματ (=δράματος), αδελ/(=ἀδελφός), κνημων (=Κνήμωνος).

τί ἄν Stob.) have arisen at some stage in the process of quotation and are not due to a disturbance of the direct transmission which P represents. If we suppose the opposite, we shall conclude that sometimes at least the text represented by P has been subject to interpolation or interference of a kind which cannot be explained in terms of transcriptional accident or causal error; we may therefore be more ready to disbelieve P's text where dissatisfied with it, and the less confident that the answers to its problems are within reach.

(iv) In many passages where grave critical dissatisfaction is felt, damage to the papyrus brings an incalculable factor into the diagnosis of error. It may be that some of these passages are gravely corrupt as well as damaged, but they obviously offer no reliable guide to the quality of the copy.

As the evidence stands, it is clear that any overall estimate of P's text must be put tentatively: my own impression is that beneath the heavy layer of superficial corruption there is to be recognized the descendant of a relatively pure or reasonably well purified copy,[1] certainly some way further from Menander's own than we are ever likely to know, but by no means the monster of depravity one might fear from the sheer bulk of the conjectures which the text has attracted. However this may be (and new evidence could change one's opinion radically), errors of whatever kind revealed by undeniable defects of sense or metre are common enough in P to make textual corruption a very real possibility whenever a difficulty or anomaly presents itself. On the other hand, one must be prepared to learn something new from 960-odd lines of largely new Greek text: the acknowledged fallibility of P does not absolve critics from trying to preserve as much of the truth as it contains, even when the temptation to smooth their own and their readers' path with a stroke of the pen is extreme. In deciding what Menander is or is not likely to have written in this play, the scope for legitimate difference of opinion is still wide: for this and other reasons it has seemed necessary in this edition to give on the printed pages a fairly full account of the constitution of the text, and to quote in the commentary at least a selection of alternative critical treatments of it.

---

[1] The ancient prolegomena in P give dim glimpses of scholarly concern with the *Dyskolos*, but the effect on the text of the work of Aristophanes of Byzantium and other scholars interested in Menander cannot now be measured: for some records of their work, see Koerte II, Test. 50ff.

Except in very minor matters, I have consistently noted differences from one other edition, the Oxford Classical Text of 1960 by Hugh Lloyd-Jones[1]; the *editio princeps* by Victor Martin is frequently (but far from exhaustively) mentioned, since, apart from its intrinsic merits and defects, it has inevitably been the starting point of much later work. For the rest, it will be seen that my references are highly and personally selective, intended to illustrate some of the possibilities available, not to portray the present state of critical opinion. The reader who wishes to explore further may make useful preliminary soundings in van Groningen's *Étude Critique*, which valiantly attempted to assess the work available by June 1960; but he will naturally not expect to gain a complete picture of what has been suggested from anywhere but the original publications themselves. The following list gives brief particulars of editions of the *Dyskolos* which have already appeared[2]:

Jean Bingen, Leiden, E. J. Brill, ed. 1, 1960; ed. 2, 1964 (Textus minores, xxvi): critical edition; the Introd. of ed. 2 includes a useful bibliography.

Carlo Diano, Padova, Editrice Antenore, 1960 (Univ. di Padova, Proagones: Testi, i): critical edn. with Ital. trans.

Otto Foss, København, Gyldendal, 1960: text with Danish notes.

Carlo Gallavotti, Napoli, Edizioni Glaux, 1959: critical edn. with free version in Ital.

B. A. van Groningen (*a*) *Étude critique du Texte*, Amsterdam, N. V. Noord-Hollandsche Uitgevers Maatschappij, 1960 (Verhandelingen der k. Nederlandse Akad. van Wetenschappen, Afd. Letterkunde, N.R. lxvii.3): text with critical comm. in French.

(*b*) Leiden, E. J. Brill, 1960 (Gr. en Lat. Schrijvers met Aantekeningen, lxvi): text with brief notes in Dutch.

Jean-Marie Jacques, Paris, Soc. d'Édition 'Les Belles Lettres', 1963 (Coll. Budé): critical edn. with Fr. trans., introd., and short selective comments.

---

[1] Often, for brevity, cited in the form 'OCT (———)' – the bracket containing an acknowledgement of the conjecture in question. I am particularly grateful to have seen this text from its earliest stage of proof, and often differ from it, where I do, with grave doubts.

[2] Jacques' edition became available in January 1964, while this book was in course of production, and Bingen's second edition in March. I am grateful for the opportunity to include some references to them, brief and sparing though these are.

Wilhelm Koch, Münster i. Westf., Aschendorff, 1960: text (after ed. pr.) with brief German notes.

Walther Kraus (*a*) Wien, Hermann Böhlaus Nachf., 1960 (Sitzb. Öst. Ak., phil.-hist. Kl. 234.4): text with app. crit. and critical comm. in German.

(*b*) Zürich, Artemis-Verlag, 1960 (Lebendige Antike): text with German trans.

H. Lloyd-Jones, Oxford, Clarendon Press, 1960 (Oxford Classical Texts): critical edn.; includes *Index verborum*.

Jean Martin, Paris, Presses Univ. de France, 1961 (Collection Érasme): critical edn. with French comm.

Victor Martin, Cologny-Genève, Bibliothèque Bodmer, 1958 (Papyrus Bodmer iv): the *editio princeps*, with facsimile, transcript, text, and translations into Eng., Fr., and German.

Benedetto Marzullo, Torino, Giulio Einaudi, 1959: text with Ital. trans. and brief critical comments.

Hans Joachim Mette, Göttingen, Vandenhoeck & Ruprecht, ed. 1, 1960; ed. 2, 1961: critical edn. Ed. 2 has supplements to the indexes of Koerte II.

N. B. Sphyroeras, Athens, Papyros, 1959: text (after ed. pr.), with Modern Greek version, introd., and brief notes.

F. Stoessl, Paderborn, Schöningh: text, 1961; 'Erläuterungen', 1963.

Max Treu, München, Ernst Heimeran, 1960 (Tusculum-Bücherei): text with app. crit. and German comm.; parallel verse translation.

IV

Metre

On this topic, D. S. Raven, *Greek Metre: an introduction* (1962), gives concise, modern and most welcome guidance. The following account of the three metres of the *Dyskolos* is intended firstly to describe Menander's general practice in using them; and secondly to present certain metrical problems which are more conveniently treated together in one place than separately as they arise in the play.

J. W. White's *Verse of Greek Comedy* (1912) took account of 826 metrically intact lines of Menander from the plays preserved in the Cairo codex; though now seriously out of date, it contains much useful information, especially for technical comparison between Menander and Aristophanes.[1] Some later special studies of Menander's verse are quoted in Franca Perusino's paper 'Tecnica e stile nel tetrametro trocaico di Menandro' (Riv. di Cult. Class. e Med. 4 (1962) 45ff) – an admirable presentation of the facts relevant to Section II below. Many of the points raised in Section I are discussed at length by J. Descroix, *Le trimètre iambique* (1931); on some different contemporary approaches to Greek Metre in general, see A. M. Dale, 'Greek Metric, 1936-1957' in Lustrum 2 (1957) 5ff.

I: IAMBIC TRIMETER

This metre is overwhelmingly predominant in our remains of Menander. In it are written the first three acts of the *Dyskolos*, and about half each of the last two: that is, about five-sixths of the play if we count numbers of lines, less if we reckon that the trochaic and iambic tetrameters of Acts IV and V took longer to deliver.

$$- - \overset{,}{\smile} - \mid - - \smile - \mid - - \smile -$$

Example 1   ὦ δυστυχής, ὦ δυστυχής, ὦ δυστυχής   [574]

---

[1] White's detailed study of 'The iambic trimeter in Menander' appeared in Class. Phil. 1909.139ff. In the course of it, he criticized several kinds of metrical error and improbability in restorations to plays in the Cairo codex – often rightly; but they recur in work on the *Dyskolos*.

Example 2 ᴗ _ ᴗ _ |ᴗ _ ᴗ _|ᴗ _ ᴗ _
Example 2 ἐρῶν ἀπῆλθες εὐθύς: εὐθύς: ὡς ταχύ   [52]

These two lines illustrate the basic pattern at its simplest. Adding letters and numbers for ease of reference, we may write it as follows:

	1					2					3		
A	B	C	D		A	B	C	D		A	B	C′	D′
ᴗ	_	ᴗ	_		ᴗ	_	ᴗ	_		ᴗ	_	ᴗ	_

A = anceps; B, D and D′ = long; C and C′ = short. The anceps element is by nature indeterminate between long and short, so that unless any special restriction operates, it admits syllables of either quantity. Where a naturally short syllable appears at D′, as in Example 2, it counts as long by virtue of its final position in the metrical unit, and should preferably be marked long in scansion, as is done throughout this book.[1]

Comic trimeters are in general freer than those of Tragedy. Menander, in common with other comic poets, admits two shorts in place of any element except the last two; but never or very rarely consecutively.[2]

Two further lines may serve as illustrations:

Example 3 ᴗᴗ _ ᴗ ᴗ _|ᴗ _ ᴗᴗ _ |ᴗ _ _ ᴗ _
Example 3 διὰ τοὺς παριόντας, ἀλλ᾽ ἐπὶ τοὺς λόφους ἄνω   [165]

Substitution of two shorts for A and C produces the pattern traditionally described as 'anapaest': aaB, ccD.

Example 4 _ ᴗ ᴗ ᴗ _| _ _ ᴗᴗᴗ ᴗᴗ|ᴗ _ ᴗ _
Example 4 ἐνθάδε γεωργεῖν, ἱερὸν ἐπιφανὲς πάνυ   [4]

Resolution of the longs B and D into two shorts produces 'dactyls' if long anceps precedes; otherwise 'tribrachs'. The second metron is AbbCdd with long anceps; or, in the traditional nomenclature, 'dactyl + tribrach'.

Caesura (in the sense of a break between words after 2 A or 2 C) is usual but often absent, as in Comedy generally; nor does

---

[1] I am grateful to A. M. Dale for this treatment of the final element, and for much other advice in metrical matters.

[2] On the last point, see Note C, p. 70f. In the verse-ending καὶ θυλάκιον at Ar. *Frogs* 1203, two shorts appear either for C′ or for D′. The anomaly is acceptable in its context as part of a metrical joke, but does not justify apparent instances in less specialized situations: e.g. χοιρίδιον at the end of Ar. *Ach.* 777 in MSS other than R (χοιριδι[in Π); cf. *Dysk.* 156 in P.

Porson's law against the final cretic apply: i.e. comic poets admit a break between words after 3 A when long:

$$\smile \_ \quad \smile \_ \mid \_ \quad \_ \quad \smile \_ \mid \_ \quad \_ \smile \_$$

Example 5   πατρὸς γεωργοῦντος ταλάντων κτήματα   [40]

'Break between words' as used here does not necessarily imply a pause in the sense, but does mean something different from the spacing in a writing convention like our own. In Greek many short words (such as the article, prepositions, enclitics and particles) form groups with the main units of meaning in their sentences; and by common poetic practice, based no doubt on normal pronunciation, the intervals in such sequences of words as ὁ παῖς δέ, εἶδόν γέ πως, καὶ ταῦτα are inadequate to provide a normal caesura; conversely, if an undesirable metrical break falls within such a sequence, the degree of cohesion present is capable of bridging it: the group in practice behaves almost indistinguishably from a single word. Thus, metrically speaking, *Dyskolos* 3 and 376 contain only three 'words' each (Φυλασίων καὶ-τῶν-δυναμένων τὰς-πέτρας, τὴν-αἱμασιὰν ἐποικοδομήσω-γὰρ τέως); neither line has caesura; the first one breaks Porson's Law, the second does not.[1]

The basic pattern of iambic verse (as of trochaic) provides only for single short syllables. Where consecutive shorts were admitted in such metres by resolution or substitution, their disposition between words was evidently felt to be highly critical to the rhythm by all poets who wrote to strict metrical standards. Here again comic writers are less restricted: for instance, they treat more sequences containing common short words as word-groups, and admit them more freely. Menander's practice, though still liberal by tragic standards, is generally recognized to be more regular than that of Aristophanes and others. It may be stated in outline as follows:

(i) Where two shorts stand for a long (B or D), they normally fall within the same word, as in Example 4, or within the same word-group, as in 215 ἔσται κατὰ τρόπον (preposition and noun: a recurrent phrase). This does not apply to 1 B: e.g. 199 ἔνδον ἐνοχλεῖν.

(ii) Where two shorts stand for A or C, both they and the

---

[1] This paragraph and the next are much indebted to Maas, *Gr. Metrik* §§135ff and 110f (see Note A, *ad init.*).

following long normally fall within the same word or word-group, as in Example 3. This does not apply to 1 A: e.g. 529 χρόνον εἶτα.[1]

The movement of the verse derives not only from the pattern of syllables and their disposition in words and word-groups, but from free variation in the placing of pauses in the sense and changes from one speaker to another; the total effect obviously depends also on the sequence of sounds and the manner and pace of delivery. In spite of these reservations, one can sometimes speak of the contribution of metrical pattern to meaning. Perhaps the most striking 'special effect' of metre in Menander's trimeters is his version of a traditional comic technique – that of adopting tragic standards of resolution and caesura in situations of high emotion, as he does conspicuously in the recognition scene of *Perikeiromene* (349ff); but in the *Dyskolos* only momentarily, and as a minor overtone, as at 189 and 620. The effect of metrical freedom in a genre which is naturally free is harder to isolate: for example in 450, one might expect an actor to exploit the unusual concentration of short syllables to add pace and pepper to Knemon's irritable discourse, and one might suppose that the poet intended this; but if so, the cue is given essentially by the context, not by any inherent quality of the pattern.

II: TROCHAIC TETRAMETER CATALECTIC
(708-783)

_ ◡ _ _| _ ◡ _ _ || _ ◡ _ ◡| _ ◡ _

Example 6 Γοργίας ἔργον ποήσας ἀνδρὸς εὐγενεστάτου   [723]

◡ ◡ ◡ ◡ ◡ _| _ ◡ _ _ || _ ◡ _ _| _ ◡ _

Example 7 ἕτερον ἑτέρῳ τῶν ἁπάντων ἂν γενέσθαι· τοῦτο δὴ   [721]

Example 6 illustrates the basic pattern, which may be written as for the iambic trimeter:

		1				2				3				4	
B	C	D	A	B	C	D	A	B	C	D	A	B	C'	D'
_	◡	_	◡̲	_	◡	_	◡̲	_	◡	_	◡̲	_	◡	_

---

[1] Deviations from the norm, however we define it, are called respectively 'divided resolutions' and 'split anapaests'. More precise formulation depends partly on what collocations of words we accept as groups for this purpose, partly on how far we trust our texts, partly on what other factors we recognize. Hence the whole topic has a long history of dispute and enjoys a wide measure of current controversy. See Notes A and B.

Median diaeresis (break between words after 2 A), is observed to a high degree by Menander, who occasionally allows the break to be obscured, but seems never to ignore it: that is, it occasionally falls after a prepositive word (ἀλλά‖, οὐδ'ὡς‖), or before a postpositive (‖ἄν, ‖γὰρ, ‖ἐστι); elision, though not common after 2 A, is not avoided there (e.g. *Dysk.* 726, 731); there may be strong neighbouring punctuation, as at *Perik.* 107 εἰς τὸ προσδοκᾶν ἔχουσι ‖ πῶς. In comparable tetrameters in Aristophanes, median diaeresis is ignored (i.e. the second metron ends within a word) on average once in seven verses.[1] Like other comic poets, Menander does not observe the 'Porson-Havet' law: that is, he does not avoid a break between words after 1 A or 3 A when long (Example 7).

B and D resolve, producing 'anapaests' where long anceps follows, otherwise 'tribrachs': in Example 7 the first metron is bbCddA with long anceps.[2] The two shorts produced by resolution normally fall within one word or word-group; it generally includes the following syllable, but the anceps is occasionally detached in 1 and 3, as at *Dysk.* 779 and 773 (see Note B). Substitution of two shorts for A and C is found very rarely, as in Aristophanes; it is possibly to be accepted once in *Dysk.* (774: see Note D).

The trochaic tetrameter appears in the *Dyskolos* as a vehicle both of serious discourse and of rapidly alternating dialogue; some possible reasons for the choice of the metre are considered in the Commentary.

---

[1] For details here and later see White and Perusino, quoted p. 56. M. *Thyroros* frg. 208.3, if sound, would be abnormal (ὀλιγοστ-| ούς); but cf. Thierfelder's note in Koerte II. The certain aberrant cases are reduced in number if we allow that in Menander the diaeresis is sometimes anticipated or postponed by one syllable, but they offer a doubtful basis for generalization. *Dysk.* 752 is restored by ed. pr. and others with a questionable diaeresis between οὐδὲ and ἕν; Gallavotti writes [τὴν | παῖδα γ]οῦν (761) and οἴ-| ον (731). Restorations and conjectures naturally cannot be trusted to do more than illustrate the metrical doctrines of their authors.

[2] Some 75 examples of the resolution dd give a ratio of approximately 5:1 in favour of long anceps following; this is probably high enough to indicate a definite rhythmic preference. In Aristophanes, again with some 75 examples, the ratio is 3:2; in Euripides, with 46 examples, it is 5:3 (Dale, Glotta 1958.104). In the second metron, the pattern — ∪ ∪ ∪ ∪‖ is admitted six times by Euripides; but not at all by Aesch. or Soph., and very rarely by Ar. and Menander – a factor to be considered in the restoration of *Birds* 285 and *Dysk.* 713; in M. the examples are *Sam.* 205 and *Perik.* 102 as against 22 + with long anceps. [These figures do not take account of the troch. tetr. of *Sikyonios*, which seem to support the argument. Cf. p. 305f.]

III: IAMBIC TETRAMETER CATALECTIC
(880-958)

$$\_ \_ \cup \_ \mid \cup \_\cup\_ \Vert \cup \_ \cup \cup \cup \mid \cup \_\_$$
Example 8   ἄλλος δὲ χερσὶν εὔιον γέροντα πολιὸν ἤδη   [946]

$$\_ \ \cup\cup\cup \ \_ \mid \_\_ \ \ \cup \_\mid\_ \Vert \cup\cup\cup \ \_\mid\cup \_ \ \_$$
Example 9   μὴ καταλαβὼν ἡμᾶς καθαίρῃ: θόρυβός ἐστιν ἔνδον   [901]

The basic pattern may be written as follows:

1				2				3				4		
A	B	C	D	A	B	C	D	A	B	C	D	A′	B′	D′
⏑	_	⏑	_	⏑	_	⏑	_	⏑	_	⏑	_	⏑	_	_

Notation: ABCD and D′ as above; in the last metron A′ is short and B′ long: neither varies.[1]

The normal line in the *Dyskolos* has either (*a*) median diaeresis, as marked in Example 8; or (*b*) caesura after 3 A, as marked in Example 9. The two types are approximately equal in frequency. Both breaks are occasionally obscured, like the diaeresis of the trochaic tetrameters (*a*) 904 εἰ δ'‖ἔσται; (*b*) 881 πέμπουσ'‖ἐνθαδί, 886 ἀλλὰ‖ (or ἀλλ'‖α-?), 957 χόρευε‖ δὴ σύ. But at 895, P gives evidence of a line without either break; if it is valid, the rule is not absolute, and the examples of 'obscured break' are less cogent. See Note E.

B and D resolve, producing 'dactyls' if long anceps precedes; otherwise 'tribrachs'. The shorts produced by resolution normally fall within the same word or word-group: 905 ἔργον ὑπενεγκεῖν is an exception at 1 B, as in the trimeter (Note B). Substitution of two shorts for A and C is nowhere verifiably present, although some treat the text so as to admit it (Note D).

Differences from Aristophanes are striking. In 69 'recitative' tetrameters from the *parodoi* of *Lysistrata* and *Plutus*, median diaeresis is ignored (i.e. the second metron ends within a word)

---

[1] The catalectic iambic close is variously analysed and described; here we need only consider it as a set traditional pattern. Two shorts replace A′ at Ar. *Thes.* 547 in the proper name Πηνελόπην – an isolated anomaly.

No other example of this metre is so far known from Menander, and analysis is hampered by its relatively limited extent and the defects of the papyrus. Two classes of iambic tetrameters in Aristophanes may usefully be compared: those described by White as 'recitative', of which he reckons 156 lines; and the 'melodramatic', of which he reckons 362. The lack of a parallel in Menander for the iambic septenarii of Latin Comedy has now been made good; this, however, is no occasion to exploit it.

only 5 times, 1 in 13.8[1]; for the much freer 'melodramatic' tetrameters, the figure is 1 in 4.3; the type of line represented by
Example 9 (caesura after 3 A), although prominent among those
without diaeresis, is still very far from the status it has in the
Dyskolos. In the 'recitative' tetrameters, resolution is extremely
sparing: there are five instances in the 69 lines quoted; White
notes 11 in 156, and two of substitution, both open to doubt.
The 'melodramatic' tetrameters have a lower average of resolution than Menander's lines, though this is in some sense offset by
moderately free substitution (66 instances in 362 lines); but in
the *Dyskolos* resolution is more heavily concentrated in the third
metron, where it probably appeared in something between a
quarter and a third of the total number of lines, and predominates
in the two patterns illustrated by Examples 8 and 9.[2]

The smooth and elevated writing at the close of the party
narrative (943ff) is apparently matched in the metre, where
resolution is sparse and median diaeresis predominates. The
preceding passage with its lively action, beginning from 911,
is marked by rapid interchange between speakers, freer resolution, and a predominance of lines with caesura after 3 A. It seems
not unreasonable, in view of the control provided by 880-910,
to see some correlation between the change of emphasis in the
metre and the change in tone; but the metre unfortunately does
not reveal what (if anything) happened to alter the manner of
performance.

---

[1] *Lys.* 350-81; *Plut.* 253-89: the two longest runs of lines of this class, and probably
the best comparison; for more details, see White, whose figure for the 156 lines is
1 in 7.8. 156 (not 155) appears as White's true total from the references he gives.

[2] That is to say, 3 D resolved in lines with median diaeresis, 3 B after caesura: not,
perhaps a surprising tendency; but well marked enough to be noted as characteristic.
This text prints 24 lines with third metron resolutions, of which some are subject to
textual doubt and should only count metrically with reservations. On this basis,
however, only 923, 940 and 957 fall outside the two types, in that they overrun
diaeresis but resolve 3 D; 913 and 918 resolve both halves of the metron after diaeresis.

The shape of the verse probably also makes itself felt in the second metron, where,
in conformity with Aristophanes' tendency to avoid resolution before diaeresis
(White, p. 64), D appears only to be resolved in lines which overrun: 883, 890, 919,
924 (conj.), 958 (if τὰ κακά); perhaps therefore not ἐστρωννύετο‖, conjectured in 943.
White's remark apropos of Aristophanes that the metrical form of the melodramatic
tetrameter 'differs in no material particular from the trimeter of dialogue' should be
treated with reserve.

NOTE A

'SPLIT ANAPAESTS' IN THE TRIMETER

(a‖a, c‖c; aa‖, cc‖)

White, *VGC* §§ 116-22, with 160-2 on Menander (cf. Class. Phil. 1909.150-7); Descroix, *Trim. iambique*, 210-21; Maas, *Gr. Metrik* (1923¹; 1927²; 1929³) §§ 111, 135ff (=*Greek Metre*, tr. H. Lloyd-Jones (1962), same references). Among later work, see especially W. G. Arnott, CQ 1957.188-98; and on the *Dyskolos* M. Coccia, in *Menandrea* (Univ. di Genova, Ist. di Fil. Class., 1960) 159-94.

(i) The rule given above (p. 58f under (ii)) is a positive counterpart of Maas's rule against instances of the kind κλέψαντα: ποίαν αὐλητρίδα (Ar. *Wasps* 1369), and ἄρχομεν, ὑμεῖς δ' οἱ θεοί (*Birds* 1226), in which a word or group of shape (. . .) ‿ ‿, (. . .) ‿ ‿ ‿ ends between or after the two short syllables arising from substitution. Both formulations treat these as abnormal; in Greek Comedy as a whole, Maas reckons approximately one instance per 700 lines, accepting one from Menander as attested without textual objection (*Trophonios*, frg. 397.3). Both accept as normal at the beginning of the line such collocations of words as σύ, τάλαινα . . . (*Heros* 69) and ὁδόν. ἀλλ' ἐγώ . . . (*Epitr.* 384) in which the anapaestic pattern is broken by a pause, but the positive formulation discriminates against them in other positions; the negative one does not. In fact, though Menander admits such 'anapaests' as in φέρε δεῦρο, πολὺ μᾶλλον, πρὸς ἔμ' ἦλθες, ἔτυχ' ἑσπέρας at places other than 1 A, almost all the cases are consistent with the view that the words involved rank as groups, with a connection derived either from a close relationship in sense, as in the first two, or elision, as in the last two; and instances in which the pattern is broken (except at 1 A) seem to be exceptional rather than normal in his practice: cf. *Perik.* 184, at 2 A ἐντεῦθεν εἶ: τυχόν· ἀλλά . . . , and with it *Dysk.* 358 (2 A) μὰ Δί', ἀλλά . . . , and 96, where λ[έγειν. ἄφε]ς. ἕστηκεν is tentatively suggested in OCT. There is perhaps no strong objection to the extension to other places in the line of a licence clearly established at the beginning; but the 'break' in τυχόν· ἀλλά and μὰ Δί', ἀλλά which punctuation conveniently indicates may be more apparent than real (cf. 'Perhaps; but . . .'; 'No – but . . .'). An example such as Ar. *Lys.* 731 οὐκ εἶ πάλιν: ἀλλ' ἥξω (with change of speaker) has some claim to be separated as a more striking anomaly.

However this may be, it seems clear that for this purpose comic poets treat words scanning ‿ and ‿ ‿ with some freedom. Arnott, p. 189 (after White) gives a useful classification of those which are capable of beginning an 'anapaest'; the following selection from the *Dyskolos* gives instances which are generally accepted as 'normal', ignoring the commonest cases such as article or preposition with noun or other associated word: (*a*) 152, at 1 C: τί γάρ ἄν τις, cf. 304 (1 A). (*b*) 212, at 1 C: φέρε δεῦρο, cf. βλέπε δεῦρ' Sam. 97 (2 C). (*c*) 406, at 1 C: τί δ' ἐγ[(suppl. ἐγ[ώ, ἐγ[ωγε vel sim.). The intrusion of a particle into the phrase does not create a break, cf. (*g*). (*d*) 452, at 2 A: ὅτι ἔστ' ἄβρωτα. (*e*) 609, at 2 A: ἐκ τοῦ τόπου τ[ιν]ές εἰσιν. τινες enclitic, but followed by another. (*f*) 835, at 1 C: νὴ τὸν Δία τὸν μέγιστον. Oaths of this type seem to have been treated as single expressions (e.g. Sam. 296, *Epitr.* 183); but the behaviour of the group νὴ Δία (νὴ τὸν Δία) is a little more puzzling: see Note D under (i). (*g*) 846 at 3 A: τὸ δὲ χωρίον, cf. τὸ δὲ νῦν 541 (1 C). (*h*) 872, at 2 C: τίς ὁ λῆρος, cf. *Perik.* 198 (1 C).

(ii) Instances involving longer words are usually more debatable. Some are reasonably justified by the presence of elision at the 'break', though such cases are rare in Menander (cf. *Perik.* 58, frg. 620.10); for others, several lines of approach are open, not necessarily distinct; one may say that the words involved are treated as a word-group and are not phonetically distinct; or that the apparently broken rhythm receives cohesion from its metrical position; failing that, one may consider whether special justification is forthcoming from the context, or whether we have simply an unexplained anomaly. Coccia gives a full survey of proposed departures from the norm in the *Dyskolos*; the following notes briefly examine what seem to be the critical cases, ignoring many produced by pure conjecture. Two cautionary points may be made in advance: that analogies from other poets, while they certainly carry some weight, need not be binding; and that in a source as careless as P the possibility of chance corruption is a strong one: cf. 38, where we get ἐπιμέλειαν σχεῖν from P², but ἐπιμέλειαν ἔχειν from P¹, with an abnormal break at 3 A. On the other hand, it will be seen that most of the examples discussed stand at 2 C, with the break Bc‖cD (. . .) after caesura – a fact from which they may derive some collective support.

(*a*) 176, at 2 C: οἰκοδομῆσατ' ἐάν   (-τεεαν P)
     205, at 2 C: λ[ήψ]ομ' ἐάν

– both adopted by ed. pr. and others. In spite of the elision, ἄν should be read, as many recognize. P's evidence for ἐάν is of negligible value, especially since both verbs end in -ε/-αι. Cf. *Epitr.* frg. 9, quoted both as οὐθὲν πέπονθας δεινόν, ἄν μὴ προσποίῃ and (incorrectly) as οὐδὲν κακὸν πέπονθας, ἐὰν μὴ προσποίῃ.

(*b*) 187, at 2 C: πολλὰ δ' ἄν ἡμέρᾳ μιᾷ (P), defended by some in this form as a coherent word-group (cf. (*f*) below), or as πολλὰ δ' ἐν ἡμέρᾳ μιᾷ (Eitrem): the next words are correctly read as γένοιτ' ἄν— ἀλλὰ . . ., though P may have written γενοιτοαναλλα· with a stop. Either δ' or ἄν may be interpolated; I assume the former. Cf. *Perik.* 278 οὐκ ἄν δύναιντο δ' ἄν ἐξελεῖν νεοττιάν (δ' ανεξελειν cod.), where Croenert and others delete αν and Sudhaus δ'. πόλλ' ἐν ed. pr., followed by OCT and others, but ἐν is linguistically unnecessary.

(c) 230, at 2 C: καὶ γὰρ προσιόντας τούσδε παιανιστάς τινας (P), adopted in this edition (after Lond.) and elsewhere: abnormal, perhaps because a metrically inconvenient word was accommodated to a standard pattern of phrase; hardly a phonetic group, unless we are prepared to extend the concept almost indefinitely, but for the rhythm note 678 (2 C) τοῦ δὲ πεπληγμένου κάτω (τοδε P). The correption παιανιστάς is not in itself a valid objection to the text; a similar line is Ar. *Wasps* 1369, quoted at the beginning of this Note (cf. Arnott, p. 191 and n. 2). The most plausible emendation is πανιστάς (van Groningen, Lloyd-Jones); for further discussion, see Coccia, 185f, and the Commentary ad loc.

(d) 242, at 2 C: μηδὲ τὸ τούτου δύσκολον (P), adopted by ed. pr. and others, and defended as a coherent group with the prepositive μηδέ (Gallavotti); but the δέ seems linguistically otiose, and is probably therefore interpolated, as happens elsewhere in P. But see Note B under (b) on p. 67f.

(e) 251, at 2 A: ἀναγκάσειέ τις εἰς τὸ βελτι[(P), adopted by ed. pr. and others, and defended as a coherent group; but less plausibly than *Perik.* 236 (1 C) εἰ μέν τι τοιοῦτ' ἦν, ὦ Πολέμων, οἷόν φατε. There the vocative ὦ could well be interpolated; but where the indef. is interlaced with other words a better case for postulating a group can be made: cf. *Perik.* 151 δοκ]εῖς λέγειν μοι, Δᾶέ, τι πάλιν, a third metron BCddA in trochaics. ἀναγκάσαι τις OCT (Lloyd-Jones) seems all but certain, and is well supported.

(f) 256, at 1 C: ωσπερανειπον P; ὥσπερ ἂν εἶπον Gallavotti and others, as a coherent group, but the context suggests that ἄν is better absent, and it may have arisen by conflation of a variant ὡσάν with ὥσπερ: ed. pr. deletes it. ὡς ἀνεῖπον Arnott; ὡς ἂν εἶπον Diano, but ὅπερ ἄν may be better if ἄν is thought desirable.

(g) 356, at 2 C: οὓς ζῶσι. σὲ δ' [ἂν ἄγον]τ' ἴδη ed. pr., with some followers. Cf. the passages discussed by Arnott, p. 190f, including Ar. *Wasps* 1369. Failing more serious corruption, I prefer to suppose, with OCT (Lloyd-Jones) and others, that ἄν has been transposed: σὲ δ' ἄγοντ' ἂν ἴδη. For ἄν (⏑) wandering and causing metrical trouble, cf. *Epitr.* 280, and note also (b) above.

(h) 358, at 1 C: νῦν ἐστιν ἐκεῖ
694, at 2 C: τοιοῦτόν ἐστιν ἐρημία
– both adopted by ed. pr. and others from P, and perhaps supported by *Epitr.* 172: see under (j) below. But ἐστ' is widely and rightly preferred, since the presence or absence of final -ι(ν) in P is of negligible consequence. Cf. Arnott, p. 191, quoting with approval Radermacher's note on Ar. *Frogs* 1220. A similar case is *Epitr.* 170: φησίν, 'ἀρέσκει' at 2 C; see also the Commentary on ἀφίησιν, *Dysk.* 111.

(i) 414: κομψῷ γε νεανίσκῳ: περικρούειν πέδας ed. pr. and others from P. The scansion νεανίσκῳ is just conceivable (cf. Arnott, p. 192);

but περικρούειν 'insolito more produci videtur' (ed. pr.). Given κομψῷ νεανίσκῳ γε the passage may be dismissed.

(*j*) 568: ἄξιον ἰδεῖν τιν'. ἀλλὰ γύναια ταῦτά μοι (P), followed in this edition and elsewhere. Some take it that the prepositive ἀλλὰ coheres with the word following: so Gallavotti and Coccia. But preferably scan γύναῖα with correption: οὔκ ἐστι δίκαιον is similarly postulated by Koerte in *Epitr.* 172, to avoid ABc‖cD in the first metron. ἄξιον ἰδεῖν. ἀλλὰ ⟨τὰ⟩ γ. (Maas et al.) is adopted by OCT and others; but the absence of the article is not indefensible, and τινα is welcome in the context. See further ad loc.

(*k*) 817, at 3 A: πόριζε πόριζε δή ed. pr., from a textually uncertain situation in P, with slight support from Ar. *Thes.* 1184 and *Frogs* 1393, on which see Arnott, p. 193 n. 7. This and similar anomalies introduced with little or no warrant from the papyrus have probably been influential in preserving and producing others. Unless the case in their favour can be better made out, perhaps with the aid of new texts, the greatest caution still seems necessary in dealing with what are at best rarities. The only safe criteria come from textually unshakable examples preserved by the direct tradition of surviving copies; quotations, which are prone to be garbled in many ways, may sometimes give seriously misleading evidence: for instance in *Plokion*, frg. 342, and in frg. 727, where some see 'split anapaests', it is not clear from the sources what Menander in fact wrote. This is said with due respect for Koerte's remark in Archiv für Papyrusforschung 14 (1941) 121: in preparing his second volume, with the quoted fragments, he was inclined to wonder if Menander's avoidance of 'split anapaests' was as consistent as he had earlier supposed. If, as many hold, it is imprudent to emend purely because a particular rhythm is supposed to have been objectionable to a particular poet, it is equally so to generalize what may be isolated exceptions into normal practice.

NOTE B

'DIVIDED RESOLUTIONS'

(b‖b, d‖d)

(i) in iambics: White, *VGC* §§ 103-6 and 111-12, with 150-5 on Menander (cf. Class. Phil. 1909.142-9), and 170-85 on the tetrameter in Aristophanes; Descroix, 155-94; Maas, quoted Note A, §§110, 135ff; among recent discussions, see Fraenkel in *Festschr. G. Jachmann* (1959) at pp. 20ff. (ii) in trochaics: White, *VGC* §§248-9, 262-3; Dale and Perusino, quoted Note D and p. 56.

(i) *Iambic trimeter*: When preceded by short anceps or short, bb and dd behave in many cases analogously to aa and cc; when they belong to different 'words' in the grammatical sense, the pattern is normally

(to take dd), either (. . .)C‖d⋮d . . . (as in *Dysk.* 45 (2 D) τὰ κεφάλαια·
τὰ καθ' ἕκαστα δέ) or ‖Cd⋮d . . . (as in 125 ἡμᾶς: τυχὸν ἴσως . . .), and the
'break' occurs within what is recognizably a group, either from the
nature of the components (article + noun, preposition + noun, etc.) or
from its appearance as a recurrent phrase, like τυχὸν ἴσως; the 'break'
may also be bridged by an enclitic or other postpositive following, or
by elision. The abnormal cases, as with 'anapaests' involve a pause
in the sense (except at 1 B) or a polysyllable (i.e. (. . .)BCd‖d. . .);
the latter sometimes arises in Aristophanes with set phrases (e.g.
αὐτίκα μάλ', *Knights* 746), or where elision is present; the relative
strictness of these limits, which is sometimes overlooked, has recently
been emphasized by Fraenkel; and Menander's practice, as in some
other matters, might be described as similar but less adventurous.
The break Ab‖b after long anceps is recurrent in Menander in the
first metron; rare but securely attested in the second with prepositives
(e.g. ἀλλά); in the third metron, as throughout Attic drama, the break
b‖b is scrupulously avoided both after long anceps and after short.
The incidence of breaks *after* resolution (bb‖, dd‖), while not so carefully controlled as the break after aa and cc, is to some extent affected
by the special characteristics of the three metra – particular freedom
at line beginning, regular incidence of caesura in the second metron,
particular restriction of the third: the same characteristics, in fact,
which show themselves in tables of the distribution of consecutive
shorts of whatever kind throughout the line. These remarks may be
amplified by some illustrations:

(*a*) First metron, beginning ⌣ ⌣ ⌣: for pause in the sense, cf. Ar. *Ach.*
1023 πόθεν: ἀπὸ Φυλῆς . . . A long syllable usually follows in this situation (i.e. aa‖B, not ⌣b‖b). Normal in the *Dyskolos* are 544 διὰ] τί μὲν
οὐκ ἔχω; 537 μόλις ἀνακύπτοντ'; 552 ἐμὲ τίς: ἐγώ; at 203 τίς ἂν ἐμὲ (P),
I prefer unemphatic με with Lloyd-Jones (OCT), but on linguistic
grounds. Cf. on 388 and 480.

– beginning ‒ ⌣ ⌣: at 144, I assume αὐτός: ὑπάγω, βέλτιστε on the
basis of α]ὐτός: ὑπόμεινον δι' ἐμέ at *Fab. Inc.* 25. So well marked a pause
is unusual: for normal cases, see e.g. *Dysk.* 82, 134, 296, 305, 522, 807.

– 1 D: note 257 ὁ τὴν χλανίδ' ἔχων (closely coherent group with
elision); similarly 629 οὗτος καλά γ' ἐπόησε; 827 οὐκ οἶδ' ὅτι λέγεις,
cf. Ar. *Eccl.* 989. At *Epitr.* 544, we have γύναι, πόθεν ἔχεις . . .

(*b*) Second metron, bb after short anceps: normal is, e.g., 212 δεῦρο:
τί ποτ' ἐβούλεθ'. At *Heros* 69 σύ, τάλαινα: τί: φ[αν]ερῶς depends on
conjecture.

– after long anceps: 386 μηδὲν ὑπό; 476 οὐδὲ κοχλίαν (cf. *Eunouchos*,
frg. 162.1). Add 568, if we read ἀλλὰ ⟨τὰ⟩ γύναια, which would be
supported by *Perik.* 272 ἀλλὰ τί φέρω νῦν. These instances may arise by
analogy from the first metron; if however we are to treat the words
involved as groups, they may support similar cases with 'split ana-

paests': see Note A (ii) (*d*). For οὐδέν/μηδέν, etc., cohering with a following word, cf. Descroix, loc. cit. and p. 331.

– 2 D: note, e.g., 112 ἀλλά σ' ὁ Ποσειδῶν; 813 Σώστραθ'· ἃ συνελεξάμην; 356 (conj.) ζῶσι. σὲ δ' ἄγοντ'; *Phasma* 30 ὑπὲρ ἐμ[οῦ.

(*c*) Third metron: Where resolution is present, the third metron most commonly has a break after the anceps, in Menander as elsewhere; and the line generally ends with a word or word-group of shape bbC′D′: e.g. *Dysk.* 12 αὐτῷ μεταμέλει; 325 ... ἡμᾶς: ὁ χαλεπός; 124 οἶόν ἐστι· κατέδεται. Possible variants are e.g. *Epitr.* 73 καὶ δικαίως: λέγε: λέγω; 85 'Δᾶος;' 'τί γάρ;' ἐγώ; 300 σοῦ παρούσης: πέρυσι, ναί.

The third metron may also be occupied by a word or group beginning at 3 A or earlier, though single words of the required shape are not particularly common in themselves and are – not surprisingly – rare as line endings. See for example *Dysk.* 41 ἀστικὸν τῇ διατριβῇ; 100 ἐπὶ τοῦ λοφιδίου; *Fab. Inc.* 40 τ]ὰ γεγονότα, cf. *Methe*, frg. 264.6 γίνεται τὸ κατὰ λόγον; *Dis Exapaton*, frg. 109 προκατέλαβες (probably); *Misogynes*, frg. 276.15 μηδὲν ἀντιπαρατιθείς; *Halieus*, frg. 18 καὶ δυσδιάθετον, cf. frg. 680.3. Within the same category fall the line-endings ἔχεις κοιτίδα τινά; (*Epitr.* 205) and μὰ τοὺς δώδεκα θεούς (*Sam.* 91, *Kolax* 116), a word-group being formed in the first instance by a noun and enclitic, and in the second by a set phrase.

A small collection of lines can be made with a clear (or relatively clear) break of the type (...)Abb‖C′D′, but it seems not to have been a rhythm favoured by Menander: e.g. τὸν πατέρα πατὴρ S. *OT* 1496; τὴν κεφαλὴν κόρακος ἔχων Ar. *Wasps* 43 (cf. 45); αὐλητρίδα λαβέ Nikostratos, *Pseudostigmatias* 26 K; καὶ πότε βάδην Sosipater, *Katapseudomenos* 1 K.50 (cf. perhaps *Sam.* 16 καθ' ὃν δ' ἦν χρόνον ἐγὼ). Ephippos, *Empole* 7 K.1 should probably end ὦ μειράκιον, ἡ.

The ending ‖bC′D′ seems to have been particularly objectionable, as at the similar close of the trochaic tetrameter. Word-groups of the type ὁ χαλεπός (*Dysk.* 325, quoted above) do not of course constitute exceptions; and Menander admits σφόδρ' ὀλίγους (*Hypobolimaios*, frg. 416.6), and ὁ δὲ τότε μὲν – in which the short words are presumably treated as a group – at *Epitr.* 87. I mention four apparent exceptions: Ar. *Ach.* 830 τὰ χοιρίδι' ἀπέδου has elision, but was simply and perhaps rightly emended by Elmsley; in Alexis, *Eretrikos* 84 K, the first verse, ending δῆμος ἀφύαι, is corrupt; in [Philemon] 164 K, the ending οὐ δίδωσι γὰρ ὁ λέγων depends on conjecture; in Com. Anon., Page, *Lit. Pap.* 65.44, the line τί γάρ ἐστιν ἡμῖν τῶν φίλων μεῖζον ἀγαθόν; is easily normalized by transposition, but should perhaps be accepted as a special case: the speaker seems to use μεῖζον ἀγαθόν as an ironical substitute for μεῖζον κακόν.

These considerations are of obvious importance for the treatment of those lines in the *Dyskolos* which are damaged or corrupt at the end. For instance, in 251, given εἰς τὸ βελτι[......]ν from P, we may say that metrical probability strongly favours a supplement like εἰς τὸ βέλτι[ον φρονεῖ]ν against εἰς τὸ βέλτι[ον ἂν ἄγει]ν vel sim.; at 156, the conjecture ὃ λιθίνους gives a normal rhythm, while ἐκεκτῆτο· λιθίνους is sufficiently improbable to be discounted on metrical grounds alone. Cf. L. Strzelecki, Eos 1961.263ff.

Iambic tetrameter: Perusino, op. cit., announces a forthcoming detailed study; the following notes supplement what has been said of resolution above, p. 61f.

905, 1 B: ἔργον ὑπενεγκεῖν: cf. Ar. *Knights* 422 ὥσπερ ἀκαλήφας. The ending λαθεῖν μόνον ἐπιθύμει (-θυμου P, ut vid.) has given anxiety both on linguistic and metrical grounds: προθυμοῦ Fraenkel. White, *VGC*, p. 64, notes for this division only Ar. *Knights* 893, *Clouds* 1056 and 1440: the closest of the three is the first, ἵνα σ' ἀποπνίξῃ. By the sense, μόνον should go with λαθεῖν rather than the word after it, but I doubt if this argument should be pressed, and retain ed. pr.'s text with OCT and others.

919, 2 D: τίνα τρόπον, a set phrase: τρόπον τίν' is easy but unnecessary.

923, 955: The first line certainly, and the second possibly, involves a break after initial Abb, for which there are very few parallels in tetrameters: λεπάσιν, ἐχίνοις Archippos, *Ichthyes* 24 K, καθάπερ ὀπωρίζοντες ἂν com. inc. 766 K; for long anceps, cf. perhaps Ar. *Lys.* 1316 (melic) ἀλλ' ἄγε κόμαν.

(ii) *Trochaic tetrameter*: The tendency to avoid a break between words *after* resolution is more strongly marked in Menander's iambic tetrameters than in his trimeters, and more strongly marked in his trochaic tetrameters than in either; but the possible occasions for such a break are limited both by the structure of the verse and by the freedom with which words scanning ‿ ‿ are treated in comic practice as single units with what follows them. Given regular diaeresis, the position (...)Cdd‖A can only arise at the end of the first and third metra, and there it occasionally does. As Dale has remarked (Glotta 1958.104), it is a universal rule of Attic drama that the fourth metron, if resolved, must be ‖bbC′D′ in one word (or, in Comedy, one word-group: e.g. ἔνεκ' ἐμοῦ Perik. 136, τὸ γεγονός Sam. 257); accordingly, the position (...)Abb‖C is only possible between the first and second metra, as in E.*HF* 863 οἳ' ἐγὼ στάδια δραμοῦμαι. A pause in the sense after a disyllable bb or dd could give the effect of a break, as in E.*IA* 859 τίνος; ἐμὸς μὲν οὐχί, but the nearest Menander comes to this effect is perhaps Sam. 267 εἰ δ' ἐλήφθη τότε π[άρ]ο̣ξ[υ]ς̣; compare Dysk. 718. Since however the number of resolutions available for examination is still not very large, it is hard to say whether great significance attaches to the absence of precise parallels for the two Euripidean lines quoted.

bb and dd are divided from each other only within word-groups: e.g. *Dysk.* 717 (3 B) τὸν ἐπικουρήσοντ' ἀεί; 718 (1 D) ἀλλὰ μὰ τὸν

Ἥφαιστον; 774 (2 D) πά-νυ μὲν οὖν. On *Perik.* 151, see Note A under (ii) (*e*). At *Dysk.* 752 the text is treated in this edition and generally so as to admit οὐδὲ ἐν ἔτι: cf. *Perik.* 129 ὅτι πάρει 'μηδὲν ἔτι τούτων'; and *Dysk.* 386, discussed above under (*b*) on p. 67f. Bingen, with οὐδὲν ἔτι τοιούτων, and Mette (οὐδὲν ἔτι τοιοῦτο) give versions which avoid this; the former is preferred by Perusino. At 713, the conjecture ἡμάρτανον ὅτι is metrically unacceptable, since it introduces (*a*) an anomalous diaeresis (see above, p. 60 and n. 2); and (*b*) a divided resolution in the form (...)Cd‖dA.

NOTE C

CONSECUTIVE SUBSTITUTION AND RESOLUTION IN THE TRIMETER

(aabb, bbcc, etc.)

White, *VGC* §§125, 165 (cf. *Class. Phil.* 1909.159f); Descroix, 224-32; H. J. Newiger, *Hermes* 1961.175-84, with further references; L. Strzelecki, *Eos* 1961.261ff.

The apparent examples are not many, and all are debatable; those in Menander perhaps especially so. Four passages in the *Dyskolos* call for mention:

(i) 496, first metron: ἐκάλεσ' ἱέρειαν ed. pr. and others, following P. ἱέρειαν ἐκάλεσ' Dale and Maas, to avoid the sequence AbbccD ('tribrach + anapaest'), or aabbCD ('proceleusmatic'); but, on the evidence quoted ad loc., we should scan the word for 'priestess' with short penult., giving AbbCdd, and may prefer to spell it ἱερέαν.

(ii) 541, second metron: P gives ǀἐάσ-ομεν· ὅ τε ǀΔᾶος i.e. ABccdd ('proceleusmatic'), with support from the sources at *Georgos* 84 and *Heautontim.*, frg. 129 (on which see Thierfelder's remark in Koerte II). But (apart from the consideration that the quoted fragment may be incomplete), all three passages admit extremely simple corrections; here ἐῶμεν (ed. pr.) avoids the unattractive parallelism with τηρήσομεν at the end of the previous line; it is technically justified by P's behaviour at 780 and elsewhere, and has found general approval. ἐάσομ' (Gallavotti) suits the context less well: if we delete τε the result is a divided resolution (Note B).

(iii) 528, first metron: ἢ καὶ πλέον, ἐπεκείμην Hommel and Mette, for P's †εγαιπλειον† or †ειγαιπλειον†. Neither the sense obtained nor the alteration itself seem especially attractive, and the conjecture has not proved popular (it is abandoned in Mette[2], where the text is obelized).

(iv) 388, first metron: †μεταυτου† πατρὸς ἀγρίου (P), could yield μετὰ τοῦ πατρός, ἀγρίου – a treatment hardly more attractive than that of (iii).

These instances in which P gives *some* warrant for 'proceleusmatic' or 'anapaest following resolution' add little to those previously available for metrical discussion, and do not encourage the construction of others by conjecture: e.g. 95 Σώ]στρατ', ἀπολο[ύμεθα: λέγε] δέ πως φυλακτικῶς and 516 ... νὴ Δί' ἐφ' ὁποτέραν θύραν – the latter unnecessary, and objectionable on other grounds.

NOTE D

SUBSTITUTION IN TETRAMETERS

(aa, cc)

(i) *Trochaic*: White, *VGC* §§205, 250, 264; among later discussions, see especially Dale, Glotta 1958.102ff, Lustrum 1957.40; and Perusino (quoted p. 56) 55ff.

At *Dyskolos* 774, P gives:

ἐστὶ σοῦ πατήρ: πάνυ μὲν οὖν: νὴ Δία, πλούσιος γ[

This line apparently has a third metron in the form BccDA. 'Dactyls' in trochaic tetrameters have provoked much controversy. They are undeniably present in Epicharmus (including the fragments recently published in Oxyrhynchus Papyri, vol. 25); Attic Tragedy and Comedy both occasionally admit them in the special case of proper names (e.g. E. *IA* 882 εἰς ἄρ' 'Ιφιγένειαν; *Or.* 1535 σύγγονόν τ' ἐμὴν Πυλάδην τε); otherwise our evidence from drama is limited to a very few passages of Aristophanes and Menander which, by their rarity, merit the closest examination. There are three possible parallels for the line we are discussing: Ar. *Ach.* 318 τὴν κεφάλην ἔχων λέγειν; *Wasps* 496 ταῖς ἀφύαις ἤδυσμά τι; and M. *Perik.* 150 πορνίδιον τρισάθλιον. These, as Dale and Perusino rightly maintain, cannot realistically be eliminated by 'emendation'; but in all three the anomalous short syllables are accommodated within a word (or group) of shape BccD, a consideration which has been stressed by Dale.

Nevertheless, if νὴ Δία κάμὲ is acceptable as an initial trochaic metron in Ar. *Knights* 319, and νὴ Δία, καὶ γενήσομαι as the close of an iambic trimeter in Menander, *Orge*, frg. 303.5, it is not completely clear that we should discriminate against νὴ Δία, πλούσιος γ[∪ – on grounds of word-division. I incline therefore, with ed. pr., Kraus, OCT and others to preserve P's words as they stand. μὰ Δία (Barigazzi) offers a way out which some have taken, but is hardly justified from the appearance of oaths with μά at 151 and 639, where see nn.

Two complications must be considered, for they may mean that our problem is illusory. Firstly, the end is lost, and we do not know that P had γ' ἀνήρ, γέρων or an expression of similar metrical shape. Accordingly, in avoiding what is at best a great rarity, Lond. assumed πλούσιος γ[ε in P and suggested πλούσιός γε, νὴ Δία; Goold (Phoenix

1959, 152ff) would write νὴ Δί', ἀλλὰ πλούσιος on the assumption that the γ[is part of a *nota personae* for Gorgias (cf. γε[= Getas, to the right of 901). Secondly, though instances could be multiplied in favour of the view that νὴ Δία, νὴ τὸν Δία etc. may be treated in comic verse as if closely cohering with the following word, the explanation of this, if we exclude formulaic phrases like νὴ τὸν Δία τὸν μέγιστον, is less than obvious: apart from the passages quoted above, it may need to include (e.g.) Ar. *Frogs* 285 νὴ τὸν Δία· καὶ μὴν . . . ('split anapaest'; apparently strong pause), and *Lys.* 24 καὶ νὴ Δία παχύ ('divided resolution', if textually sound). Was dĭă (whether as the acc. of Zeus or otherwise) invariably pronounced and scanned as two shorts? The two syllables dĭă appear very occasionally where a single long is strongly demanded by the metrical context, and the scansion dyā has been invoked (cf. Maas, *Gk. Metre* §120; Dale, *Lyric Metres of Greek Drama* 25 n. 1; emphatic opposition is expressed by Fraenkel, in *Festschr. G. Jachmann*, 1959, at p. 30). With νὴ Δία κἀμὲ in Ar. *Knights* 319, as in other passages where a single short would remove an anomaly, Dindorf reduced νὴ Δία to _ ◡ by invoking the doubtfully attested form νηδί or νὴ Δί (the evidence for it is available from Stephanus-Dindorf, s.v. Ζεύς). If this procedure, and the hypothetical scansion dyă (which could have wider application) seem equally uncongenial, we are left to explain or remove the anomalies involved individually as best we can: that is the procedure which criticism has followed in dealing with our passage of the *Dyskolos*.

At 729, the ending μειράκιον δ', ἐὰν ἐγώ (adopted by ed. pr.) is unsatisfactory on linguistic grounds, and the δ' must be deleted; nor is it clear that a 'dactyl' pattern should be admitted at *Sam.* 203, or restored at *Perik.* 111. Proposals by ed. pr. and later critics to introduce further examples of dactyls into the *Dyskolos* are noted and rightly dismissed by Perusino and Goold: since, apart from the present doubtful case at *Dysk.* 774, the only dependable instance in Menander is *Perik.* 150, one should demand very strong compulsion from the context before propagating others. See Addenda, p. 305f.

(ii) *Iambic*: White, *VGC* §§172, 177, 185 on Aristophanes; on the *Dyskolos*, Coccia (quoted Note A) 192ff, and Goold, quoted in (i) above.

The instances present in P need not detain us long. 911, seriously defective, and possibly spurious, ends παιδίον οἴχομ' οἴμοι; 930, also defective, ends παιδίον οὐδ' ὁ κρατήρ, where the word παιδίον, uncongenial to the context, has attracted well-founded suspicion on other than metrical grounds; 924]ποδῶν τὸ μῆκος εκαστον (P) requires εκαστον to be corrected to ἑκατόν for the sake of the sense, as was done by ed. pr.; moreover, all three ostensible 'anapaests' are divided between words in ways which would cause the gravest metrical doubt even if they appeared in Aristophanes' tetrameters (White, as is his practice, counts as divided between words such instances as παρὰ σοῦ, *Frogs* 939).

The fact that Aristophanes (and others) admit substitution in iambic tetrameters cannot be pressed with great force in favour of introducing instances conjecturally in the *Dyskolos*, since in other respects (e.g. diaeresis), Menander's practice can be shown to be markedly different. One might in theory claim that substitution in this metre was an occasional licence of Menander's, as in trochaic tetrameters; but it would be a little odd if the only instances had disappeared by accident. Two much disputed lines deserve special mention, 943 and 949: their problems are considered in the Commentary. In a third line (924, mentioned above), the beginning can be, but need not be, supplemented with an expression of shape ⏑ ⏑ —. Unless new evidence clarifies the position, the text can only be treated so as to admit substitution with grave risk of error.

NOTE E

Dyskolos 895

τύπτειν ἀναστάς: οὐδ᾽ ἀναστῆναί ‹γ᾽ ἄν›, ὡς ἐγῷμαι

So the line is printed in this edition, on the common assumption that ἀναστῆναι is sound and a single short missing after it. The line then has neither median diaeresis nor caesura after 3 A, its pattern being similar to that of Ar. *Lys.* 268:

ὅσαι τὸ πρᾶγμα τοῦτ᾽ ἐνεστήσαντο καὶ μετῆλθον.

Other parallels can be cited from Aristophanes, but his practice with this metre is different enough from Menander's to make their support doubtful; the best analogy in the *Dyskolos* itself is a line with obscured break after 3 A, namely 957:

ἤδη σε: τί ποήσω: χόρευε δὴ σύ: φέρετε, κρεῖττον.

ἀναστῆν᾽, as in Thierfelder's ἀναστῆν᾽ αὐτός, would give a break with elision as in 881; but elision of the aor. infin. in -ναι is abnormal in Menander (cf. Koerte on *Perik.* 153, where he reluctantly accepts μ]εταστῆν᾽). ἀναστῆναι then, is probably after all what Menander wrote; the sense admits several alternatives for the syllable following.

If 936 were undoubtedly to be articulated]αγκας οὐδὲ τὴν[, as is often assumed, it might be claimed as further support; for we should have a clear break after 2 A (as after ἀναστάς), and none (or a minimal one) after 2 D or 3 A, within the word-group introduced by the definite article. But nothing can be determined from so small and ambiguous a piece.

THE DYSKOLOS OF MENANDER

P   = Papyrus Bodmer IV, on which this edition is based. On this and subsidiary sources, see above, pp. 40ff.

[ ]   Square brackets indicate places where text is lost by damage and restored by conjectural supplement. Losses and omissions restored from subsidiary sources are indicated by the signs ⌊ ⌋.

τισ
.. σ
..]σ[7-8]   Dots under letters indicate that they are doubtfully read; doubtful traces of letters are also indicated by dots alone, especially in the critical notes; inside square brackets, dots or figures give an estimate of the space available for supplements.

⟨ ⟩   Pointed brackets enclose conjectural additions to the text (but I have avoided using them within words).

(Σω.)   Speakers' names within round brackets are supplied editorially. The ancient evidence for the arrangement of parts is discussed above, pp. 44ff; the paragraphus and dicolon used to distinguish them are often referred to or transcribed in the critical notes.

plerique
et al.   Where a supplement or emendation has been proposed by several scholars independently, I credit it to 'plerique', or add 'et al.' to the name or names mentioned (but the absence of 'et al.' does not guarantee that a particular suggestion was advanced solely by those named).

Lond.
Sydn.
Ha.   'Lond.' refers to joint contributions by several scholars to E. G. Turner's paper 'Emendations to Menander's Dyskolos', in BICS 6 (1959) 61ff. 'Sydn.' similarly refers to J. H. Quincey and others, 'Notes on the Dyskolos of Menander' (Australian Humanities Research Council, Occasional Paper, No. 2, 1959); 'Ha.' refers to suggestions of my own not included as 'Lond.' or 'plerique'.

ed. pr.   The first edition of the play, by Victor Martin. To it should be credited all supplements and corrections adopted in this text without attribution.

ΑΡΙΣΤΟΦΑΝΟΥΣ ΓΡΑΜΜΑΤΙΚΟΥ Η ΥΠΟΘΕΣΙΣ

"Εχων θυγατέρα δύσκολος μητρὸς μόνην
ἔγημεν ἔχουσαν υἱόν· ἀπελείφθη τάχος
διὰ τοὺς τρόπους, μόνος δ' ἐπ' ἀγρῶν διετέλει.
τῆς παρθένου δὲ Σώστρατος σφοδρῶς ἐρῶν
προσῆλθεν αἰτῶν· ἀντέπιφθ' ὁ δύσκολος.　　　　　5
τὸν ἀδελφὸν αὐτῆς ἔπιθεν. οὐκ εἶχ' ὅ τι λέγοι
ἐκεῖνος· ἐμπεσὼν δὲ Κνήμων εἰς φρέαρ
τὸν Σώστρατον βοηθὸν εἶχε διὰ τάχους.
κατηλλάγη μὲν τῇ γυναικί, τὴν κόρην
τούτῳ δ' ἐδίδου γυναῖκα κατὰ νόμους ἔχειν·　　　10
τούτου δ' ἀδελφὴν λαμβάνει τῷ Γοργίᾳ,
τῷ τῆς γυναικὸς παιδί, πρᾶος γενόμενος.

5 Cf. Hesych. (I.184 Latte) ἀντέπιπτεν· ἐναντιοῦτο

ΑΡΙΣΤΟΦΑΝ ΓΡΑΜΜΑΤΙ[.] P; vide praef. p. 52 n.　2 ετημεν P　3 μονουσ P¹
5 ἀντέπιφθ' Mayer, Pfeiffer: αντετιφθ' P　6 ἔπιθεν Diano, Lond.: επειθεν P　λεγοι P
in marg.: ποει P in textu　9 κατ'ηλλαγηι P, vide praef. p. 43　10 τηγυναικα P　ἔχειν
Lloyd-Jones: ερων P　11 τούτου ed. pr.: τουτω P

Ἐδίδαξεν εἰς Λήναια ἐπὶ Δημογένους ἄρχοντος καὶ ἐνίκα· ὑπεκρίνατο
Ἀριστόδημος Σκαρφεύς· ἀντεπιγράφεται Μισάνθρωπος.

1 Δημογένους ed. pr.: διδυμογενης P　2 Σκαρφεύς ed. pr.: σκαφευσ P

ΤΑ ΤΟΥ ΔΡΑΜΑΤΟΣ ΠΡΟΣΩΠΑ

Πάν	ὁ θεός	Δᾶος	
Χαιρέας	ὁ παράσιτος	Γοργίας	ὁ ἐκ μ[η]τρὸς
			ἀδελφ[ός
Σώστρατος	ὁ ἐρασθείς	Σίκων	μάγειρος
Πυρρίας	ὁ δοῦλος	Γέτας	ὁ δοῦλο[ς
Κνήμων	ὁ πατήρ	Σιμίχη	γραῦς
Παρθένος	θυγάτηρ	Καλλιππίδης	π[α]τὴρ τοῦ
	Κνήμωνος		Σωστράτ[ου

5

2 παν ex πανθεοσ P; post δαοσ litterae αδελ/ aut deletae aut evanidae 3-4 ante σωστρατοσ β, ante πυρριασ α add. P², quasi ad immutandum ordinem personarum 5 Σιμίχη Marzullo et al.: σιμικη P, ut solet 6 κνημων P, vide praef. p. 52 n.

ΔΥΣΚΟΛΟΣ

(ΠΑΝ)

Τῆς Ἀττικῆς νομίζετ' εἶναι τὸν τόπον
Φυλήν, τὸ νυμφαῖον δ' ὅθεν προέρχομαι
Φυλασίων καὶ τῶν δυναμένων τὰς πέτρας
ἐνθάδε γεωργεῖν, ἱερὸν ἐπιφανὲς πάνυ.
τὸν ἀγρὸν δὲ τὸν [ἐ]πὶ δεξί' οἰκεῖ τουτονὶ   5
Κνήμων, ἀπάνθρωπός τις ἄνθρωπος σφόδρα
καὶ δύσκολος πρὸς ἅπαντας οὐ χαίρων τ' ὄχλῳ—
ὄχλῳ λέγω; ζ[ῶ]ν οὗτος ἐπιεικῶς χρόνον
πολὺν λελάληκεν ἡδέως ἐν τῷ βίῳ
οὐδενί, προσηγόρευκε πρότερος δ' οὐδένα   10
πλὴν ἐξ ἀνάγκης γειτνιῶν παριών τ' ἐμὲ
τὸν Πᾶνα· καὶ τοῦτ' εὐθὺς αὐτῷ μεταμέλει,
εὖ οἶδ'. ὅμως οὖν τῷ τρόπῳ τοιοῦτος ὢν
χήραν γυναῖκ' ἔγημε, τετελευτηκότος
αὐτῇ νεωστὶ τοῦ λαβόντος τὸ πρότερον   15
υἷόν τε καταλελειμμένου μικροῦ τότε.
ταύτῃ ζυγομαχῶν οὐ μόνον τὰς ἡμέρας,
ἐπιλαμβάνων δὲ τὸ πολὺ τῆς νυκτὸς μέρος
ἔζη κακῶς· θυγάτριον αὐτῷ γίνεται·
ἔτι μᾶλλον. ὡς δ' ἦν τὸ κακὸν οἷον οὐθὲν ἂν   20
ἕτερον γένοιθ', ὁ βίος τ' ἐπίπονος καὶ πικρός,
ἀπῆλθε πρὸς τὸν υἷον ἡ γυνὴ πάλιν
τὸν πρότερον αὐτῇ γενόμενον. χωρίδιον
τούτῳ δ' ὑπάρχον ἦν τι μικρὸν ἐνθαδὶ
ἐν γειτόνων, οὗ διατρέφει νυνὶ κακῶς   25
τὴν μητέρ', αὐτόν, πιστὸν οἰκέτην θ' ἕνα
πατρῷον. ἤδη δ' ἐστὶ μειρακύλλιον
ὁ παῖς ὑπὲρ τὴν ἡλικίαν τὸν νοῦν ἔχων·
προάγει γὰρ ἡ τῶν πραγμάτων ἐμπειρία.
ὁ γέρων δ' ἔχων τὴν θυγατέρ' αὐτὸς ζῇ μόνος   30

1-3 (... Φυλασίων) cit. Harpocrat. s.v. Φυλή, p. 183, 11; 1-2 (... Φυλήν) citant
Schol. Ar. Ach. 1023 et alii: frg. 115

tit. ΔΥΣΚΟΛΟ[Σ praebet P   7 ed. pr.: απαντασ·υ P   10 οὐδενί Diano, Lloyd-Jones:
ουδεν P   11 εξαγαγκεισ P¹   12 τοῦτ' plerique: τουστ' P   14-15 ed. pr.: τελευτηκοτοσ,
τουλαμβανοντοσ   16 τότε plerique: ποτε P   18 ed. pr.: δεκαιτο P   26 αὐτόν ed.
pr.: αυτον P   θ'ἕνα plerique: θεναμα P

καὶ γραῦν θεράπαιναν, ξυλοφορῶν σκάπτων τ', ἀε[ὶ
πονῶν, ἀπὸ τούτων ἀρξάμενος τῶν γειτόνων
καὶ τῆς γυναικὸς μέχρι Χολαργέων κάτω
μισῶν ἐφεξῆς πάντας. ἡ δὲ παρθένος
γέγονεν ὁμοία τῇ τροφῇ τις, οὐδὲ ἐν   35
εἰδυῖα φλαῦρον. τὰς δὲ συντρόφους ἐμοὶ
Νύμφας κολακεύουσ' ἐπιμελῶς τιμῶσά τε
πέπεικεν αὐτῆς ἐπιμέλειαν σχεῖν τινα
ἡμᾶς· νεανίσκον τε καὶ μάλ' εὐπόρου
πατ[ρ]ός, γεωργοῦντος ταλάντων κτήματα   40
ἐντα]ῦθα πολλῶν, ἀστικὸν τῇ διατριβῇ,
ἥκο]ντ' ἐπὶ θήραν μετὰ κυνηγέτου τινὸς
φίλο]υ, κατὰ τύχην παραβαλόντ' εἰς τὸν τόπον
αὐτῇ]ς ἔχειν πως ἐνθεαστικῶς ποῶ.
ταῦτ'] ἐστὶ τὰ κεφάλαια· τὰ καθ' ἕκαστα δὲ   45
ὄψεσ]θ' ἐὰν βούλησθε· βουλήθητε δέ.
καὶ γὰ]ρ προσιόνθ' ὁρᾶν δοκῶ μοι τουτονὶ
τὸν ἐρῶντα τόν τε συγκ[υνηγέτη]ν ἅμα
αὐτοῖς ὑπὲρ τούτων τι σ[υγκοινουμ]ένους.

ΧΑΙΡΕΑΣ

τί φῄς; ἰδὼν ἐνταῦθα παῖδ' ἐλευθέραν   50
τὰς πλησίον Νύμφας στεφ[ανο]ῦσαν, Σώστρατε,
ἐρῶν ἀπῆλθες εὐθύς;

ΣΩΣΤΡΑΤΟΣ
                                            εὐθ[ύς].
(Χα.)   ὡς ταχύ.
ἢ τοῦτ' ἐβεβούλευσ' ἐξιών, ἐρᾷ[ν] τινος;
(Σω.) σκώπτεις· ἐγὼ δέ, Χαιρέα, κακῶς ἔχω.
(Χα.) ἀλλ' οὐκ ἀπιστῶ.   55
(Σω.)   διόπερ ἥκω παραλαβὼν

50, 52 (omisso v. 51) cit. Ammonius p. 62 Valckenaer: frg. 120

31 σκαπτοντ'αι.[P 36 φλαρουν P 38 εχειν P¹ 41-47 ed. pr. 43 φίλο]υ multis
displicet παραβαλόντ' ed. pr.: -λαβ- P 46 βουλεσθε P 48 locus conclamatus:
συγκ[υνηγέτη]ν Ha., Quincey et al. (-ετοῦνθ]' ed. pr.): συν.[7-9].αμα P 49 ed. pr.,
longiore fortasse supplemento: τισσ[7 +]ενουσ P 50-51 ed. pr. ἔνθεν γε πᾶς δ'ἐλευθερῶν
Ammon. (scil. ἐλευθερῶν pro ἐλευθέραν ἐρῶν; ἐνθένδε coni. Valckenaer) 51 πλησιας P¹
52 suppl. plerique (scil. ευθ[υσ:]ώσταχυ·) (ἐλευθ-)ερῶν ἀπῆλθες εὐθὺς ὡς ταχύ Ammon.
53 ἐβεβούλευσ' plerique: εβουλευσ' P 54 σκωπτεισ· ex σκωπτεισ: P

σὲ πρὸς τὸ πρᾶγμα, καὶ φίλον καὶ πρακτικὸν
κρίνας μάλιστα.

(Χα.)   πρὸς τὰ τοιαῦτα, Σώστρατε,
οὕτως ἔχω· παραλαμβάνει τις τῶν φίλων
ἐρῶν ἑταίρας· εὐθὺς ἁρπάσας φέρω,
μεθύω, κατακάω, λόγον ὅλως οὐκ ἀνέχομαι·   60
πρὶν ἐξετάσαι γὰρ ἥτις ἐστί, δεῖ τυχεῖν.
τὸ μὲν βραδύνειν γὰρ τὸν ἔρωτ' αὔξει πολύ,
ἐν τῷ ταχέως δ' ἔνεστι παύσασθαι ταχύ.
γάμον λέγει τις καὶ κόρην ἐλευθέραν·
ἕτερός τίς εἰμ' ἐνταῦθα· πυνθάνομαι γένος,   65
βίον, τρόπους· εἰς πάντα τὸν λοιπὸν χρόνον
μνείαν γὰρ ἤδη τῷ φίλῳ καταλείπομαι
ὅσ' ἂν διοικήσω περὶ ταῦτα.

(Σω.)   καὶ μάλ' εὖ,
οὐ πάνυ δ' ἀρεσκόντως ἐμοί.

(Χα.)   καὶ νῦν γε δεῖ
ταῦτα διακοῦσαι πρῶτον ἡμᾶς.   70

(Σω.)   ὄρθριον
τὸν Πυρρίαν τὸν συγκυνηγὸν οἴκοθεν
ἐγὼ πέπομφα.

(Χα.)   πρὸς τίν' ;
(Σω.)   αὐτῷ τῷ πατρὶ
ἐντευξόμενον τῆς παιδός, ἢ τῷ κυρίῳ
τῆς οἰκίας, ὅστις ποτ' ἐστίν.

(Χα.)   Ἡράκλεις·
οἷον λέγεις.   75

(Σω.)   ἥμαρτον· οὐ γὰρ οἰκέτῃ
ἥρμοστ' ἴσως τὸ τοιοῦτον. ἀλλ' οὐ ῥᾴδιον
ἐρῶντα συνιδεῖν ἐστι τί ποτε συμφέρει.
καὶ τὴν διατριβὴν ἥτις ἔστ' αὐτοῦ πάλαι
τεθαύμακ'. εἰρήκειν γὰρ εὐθὺς οἴκαδε
αὐτῷ παρεῖναι πυθομένῳ τἀνταῦθά μοι.   80

ΠΥΡΡΙΑΣ

πάρες, φυλάττου, πᾶς ἄπελθ' ἐκ τοῦ μέσου.
μαίνεθ' ὁ διώκων, μαίνεται.

(Σω.)   τί τοῦτο, παῖ;

---

56 καιαπρακτικον P   58 οτι pro τισ P¹   61 διτυχεῖν P¹   62 αὔξει ed. pr.: αυξάνει P
67 μι ante μνείαν del. P² ut vid.   68 ὅσ' ἂν Ha.: ὡσαν P   69 αρεσκόντοσ P¹ (-οσ fort.
ex -ογ)   74 όστιστοτ' P¹   76 τοιοῦτον ed. pr.: τοιουτ' P   79 δε pro γαρ P¹

(Πυ.)   φεύγετε.

(Σω.)   τί ἐστι;

(Πυ.)   βάλλομαι βώλοις, λίθοις·
ἀπόλωλα.

(Σω.)   βάλλει; ποῖ, κακόδαιμον;

(Πυ.)   οὐκέτι
ἴσως διώκει.   85

(Σω.)   μὰ Δί'.

(Πυ.)   ἐγὼ δ' ᾤμην.

(Σω.)   τί δὲ
λέγεις;

(Πυ.)   ἀπαλλαγῶμεν, ἱκετεύω σε.

(Σω.)   ποῖ;

(Πυ.)   ἀπὸ τῆς θύρας ἐντεῦθεν ὡς πορρωτάτω.
'Οδύνης γὰρ ὑὸς ἢ κακοδαιμονῶν τις ἢ
μελαγχολῶν ἄνθρωπος οἰκῶ[ν ἐνθάδ]ε
τὴν οἰκίαν, πρὸς ὅν μ' ἔπεμψ[ας—ὦ θεοί   90
μεγάλου κακοῦ· τοὺς δακτύλους [κατέαξα γὰρ
σχεδόν τι προσπταίων ἅπα[ντας.

(Σω.)   μαίνετ' ἢ
ἐλθών τι πεπαρῴνηκε δεῦ[ρο;

(Χα.)   παραφρονῶν
εὔδηλός ἐστι.

(Πυ.)   νὴ Δί' ἐξώλ[ης ἄρα,
Σώ]στρατ', ἀπολο[ίμην. ἔχε] δέ πως φυλακτικῶς.   95
ἀλλ' οὐ δύναμαι λ[έγειν, προ]σέστηκεν δέ μοι
τὸ πνεῦμα. κόψας [τὴν θύ]ραν τῆς οἰκίας
τὸν κύριον ζητεῖν [ἔφ]ην. προσῆλθέ μοι
γραῦς τις κακοδαίμων· ᾳ[ὐτ]όθεν δ' οὗ νῦν λέγων
ἔστηκ', ἔδειξεν αὐ[τὸ]ν ἐπὶ τοῦ λοφιδίου   100

---

83 paragrapho caret P 85 τιδ'αι P¹ 88 κακοδαιμονῶν ed. pr.: κακοδαίμων P
89 ἄνθρωπος Ha.: ἀν- P, sequente οἰκω[suppl. ed. pr.:]ε vel]ει P 90 ἔπεμψ[ας
ed. pr., ὦ θεοί Page 91 Barigazzi et al., collato Liban., Decl. 27.18 92 ἅπα[ντας ed. pr.:
ἅπα[P (Σω.) Ha., Jacques; μαίνετ' ἢ Webster, qui (Χα.) praemisit (paragr. sub
versu P) 93 Lond., Mette, nisi quod (Σω.) παραφρονῶν maluerunt (paragr. sub
versu P) 94 (Πυ.) Barrett et al. (paragr. sub v. et post εστι dicolon P) suppl. Ha.
(olim μὲν οὖν) 95 ἀπολο[ίμην Kraus et al., ἔχε Winnington-Ingram et al. δεπωσ P²,
δ'ειοθι P¹, ut vid. 96 ed. pr.:]σεστηκεν P 97 ed. pr. (]ρασ P¹) 98 χητειψ[P¹
ἔφ]ην plerique 99 γρασκακοδαίμων P¹

ἐκεῖ περιφθειρόμενον, ἀχράδας ἢ πολὺν
κύφων᾽ ἑαυτῷ συλλέγονθ᾽.

Χα.   ὡς ὀργίλως.
(Πυ.) τί, ὦ μακάρι᾽; ἐγὼ μὲν εἰς τὸ χωρίον
ἐμβὰς ἐπορευόμην πρὸς αὐτόν. καὶ πάνυ
πόρρωθεν, εἶναί τις φιλάνθρωπος σφόδρα   105
ἐπιδέξιός τε βουλόμενος, προσεῖπα· καὶ
"ἥκω τι", φημί, "πρός σε, πάτερ, ἰδεῖν τί σε
σπεύδων ὑπὲρ σοῦ πρᾶγμ᾽." ‹ὁ δ᾽› εὐθύς, "ἀνόσιε
ἄνθρωπε," φησίν, "εἰς τὸ χωρίον δέ μου
ἥκεις ‹σὺ› τί μαθών;" βῶλον αἴρεταί τινα·   110
ταύτην ἀφίησ᾽ εἰς τὸ πρόσωπον αὐτό μου.

Χα.   ἐς κόρακας.
(Πυ.)   ἐν ὅσῳ δ᾽ "ἀλλά σ᾽ ὁ Ποσειδῶν" λέγων
κατέμυσα, χάρακα λαμβάνει πάλιν τινά·
ταύτῃ μ᾽ ἐκάθαιρε, "σοὶ δὲ κἀμοὶ πρᾶγμα τί
ἔστιν;" λέγων, "τὴν δημοσίαν οὐκ οἶσθ᾽ ὁδόν;",   115
ὀξύτατον ἀναβοῶν τι.

Χα.   μαινόμενον λέγεις
τελέως γεωργόν.
(Πυ.)   τὸ δὲ πέρας· φεύγοντα γὰρ
δεδίωχ᾽ ἴσως με στάδια πέντε καὶ δέκα,
περὶ τὸν λόφον πρώτιστον, εἶθ᾽ οὕτω κάτω
εἰς τὸ δασὺ τοῦτο, σφενδονῶν βώλοις, λίθοις,   120
ταῖς ἀχράσιν ὡς οὐκ εἶχεν οὐδὲν ἀλλ᾽ ἔτι,
ἀνήμερόν τι πρᾶγμα, τελέως ἀνόσιος
γέρων. ἱκετεύω σ᾽, ἄπιτε.
(Σω.)   δειλίαν λέγεις.
(Πυ.) οὐκ ἴστε τὸ κακὸν οἷόν ἐστι· κατέδεται
ἡμᾶς.   125
Χα.   τυχὸν ἴσως ὠδυνημένος τι νῦν

---

101 Cf. Hesych. περιφθείρεται· τὰς φθεῖρας συλλέγει, quod si huc spectat falso dici
uidetur
102 Cf. Hesych. s.v. κύφων . . . τάσσεται δὲ καὶ ἐπὶ πάντων τῶν δυσχερῶν καὶ ὀλεθρίων;
similia proferunt Photius, I. 362 Naber, et alii, quibus praeter notum Archilochi
locum (frg. 178 Bergk, 50 Lasserre-Bonnard) et noster subesse potest
112 ἐς κόρακας: cf. Zenob. 3.76, item Miller, *Mélanges*, 356 (=Men., frg. 971 Kock)

101 dist. Ha., Thierfelder et al. αχράδασ·ἡ P   102 κύφων᾽ Gallavotti et al.: κυφῶν᾽ P
Χα]ιρ in marg. sinist. P (Lond.)   105 ed. pr.: εἶναιφιλάνθρωπόστισ P   108 plerique:
πραγμα· ευθὺσ P   109 ανθρωπ᾽ ex ανθρώπωνπε P² 110 Kassel, Page   111 αφίησιν P²
112 ἐς plerique: ἦσ P   113 μαστιγγα in marg. dext. P   114 Ha.: ἐκάθαιρεταύτην P
118 δεδίωχ᾽ Thierfelder et al.: -ωκ᾽ P   125 ed. pr.: τυχῶν, ουδυνωμένοσ (ex -μένωσ) P

τετύχηκε· διόπερ ἀναβαλέσθαι μοι δοκεῖ
αὐτῷ προσελθεῖν, Σώστρατ'. εὖ τοῦτ' ἴσθ', ὅτι
πρὸς πάντα πράγματ' ἐστὶ πρακτικώτερον
εὐκαιρία.

Πυ.   νοῦν ἔχεθ'.

(Χα.)   ὑπέρπικρον δέ τι
ἔστιν πένης γεωργός, οὐχ οὗτος μόνος,   130
σχεδὸν δ' ἅπαντες. ἀλλ' ἕωθεν αὔριον
ἐγὼ πρόσειμ' αὐτῷ μόνος, τὴν οἰκίαν
ἐπείπερ οἶδα· νῦν δ' ἀπελθὼν οἴκαδε
καὶ σὺ διάτριβε. τοῦτο δ' ἕξει κατὰ τρόπον.

(Πυ.) πράττωμεν οὕτως.   135

Σω.   πρόφασιν οὗτος ἄσμενος
εἴληφεν. εὐθὺς φανερὸς ἦν οὐχ ἡδέως
μετ' ἐμοῦ βαδίζων, οὐδὲ δοκιμάζων πάνυ
τὴν ἐπιβολ]ὴν τὴν τοῦ γάμου. κακὸν δέ σε
κακῶς ἅπ]αντες ἀπολέσειαν οἱ θεοί,
μαστιγία.   140

(Πυ.)   τί] δ'ˌ ἠδίκηκα, Σώστρατε;
(Σω.) ἔκλεπτες] εἰς τὸ χωρίον τι δηλαδὴ
ἐλθών.]

(Πυ.)   ἔκλ]επτον;
(Σω.)   ἀλλ ἐμαστίγου σέ τις
οὐδὲν ἀδικ]οῦντα;

(Πυ.)   καὶ πάρεστί γ' οὑτοσί.
(Σω.) αὐτός;
(Πυ.)   ὑπάγω, ˌβέλτιστε· σὺ δὲ τούτῳ λάλει.
(Σω.) οὐκ ἄ[ν] δυνˌαίμην· ἀπίθανός τίς εἰμ' ἀεὶ   145
ἐν τῷ λαλεῖν. ποῖον λέγει[ς σύ;

139-50 Accedit H, de quo vide praef., p. 40; incertiora quaedam in commentario
citantur

128 πρακτικώτατον P¹, litteras ερον s.l. add. P²   130 εστι P   133 επεντερ P¹
135 πράττωμεν ed. pr.: -ομεν P   136 post εἴληφεν dist. Fraenkel et al., post εὐθὺς P
138 ed. pr.: 8-9]ὴν P   139 ed. pr.   140 μαστιγία plerique]δ' vel]σ' H:]ε P
ηδίκη:κα P¹ dicolon ad fin. habet P: deest H   141-2 suppl. dubitanter Lloyd-Jones
141 6-7]....στοχωριορ[H   142 2-3]....εκλεπτον: H: 8-9]ερον: P   143 (Πυ.) plerique;
sic H ut vid.   καὶ om. P¹   παρεστιγε P: παρεστιψ H paragraphum sub v. habet H, ut vid.;
dicolon post ἀδικοῦντα habent HP, et ad fin. P, ubi H deest   144 (Σω.) αὐτός; (Πυ.)
ὑπάγω Ha., Jacques: αυτοσυπαγωβελτιστε H; paragraphum habere videtur, interpunc-
tionem nullam, sed lacera post αυτοσ membrana, post τουτω[deficit: βελτιστε—λαλει:
P   145 (Σω.) plerique; sic H, ut vid.   146 λέγει[ς σύ Lond. et al.

(Πυ.)   τουτο]νί.
(Σω.)   οὐ πάνυ φιλάνθρωπον βλ[έπειν μ]οι φαίνεται,
        μὰ τὸν Δί'. ὡς δ' ἐσπούδακ'. ἐπ[ανά]ξω βραχὺ
        ἀπὸ τῆς θύρας· βέλτιον. ἀλλὰ κ[αὶ β]οᾷ
        μόνος βαδίζων· οὐχ ὑγιαίνειν μ[οι] δοκεῖ.   150
        δέδοικα μέντοι, μὰ τὸν Ἀπόλλω καὶ θεούς,
        αὐτόν· τί γὰρ ἄν τις μὴ οὐχὶ τἀληθῆ λέγοι;

ΚΝΗΜΩΝ
        εἶτ' οὐ μακάριος ἦν ὁ Περσεὺς κατὰ δύο
        τρόπους ἐκεῖνος, ὅτι πετηνὸς ἐγένετο
        κοὐδενὶ συνήντα τῶν βαδιζόντων χαμαί,   155
        εἶθ' ὅτι τοιοῦτο κτῆμ' ἐκέκτηθ' ᾧ λίθους
        ἅπαντας ἐπόει τοὺς ἐνοχλοῦντας; ὅπερ ἐμοὶ
        νυνὶ γένοιτ'. οὐδὲν γὰρ ἀφθονώτερον
        λιθίνων γένοιτ' <ἄν> ἀνδριάντων πανταχοῦ.
        νῦν δ' οὐ βιωτόν ἐστι, μὰ τὸν Ἀσκληπιόν.   160
        λαλοῦσ' ἐπεμβαίνοντες εἰς τὸ χωρίον
        ἤδη. παρ' αὐτὴν τὴν ὁδὸν γάρ, νὴ Δία,
        εἴωθα διατρίβειν, ὃς οὐδ' ἐργάζομαι
        τοιοῦτο τὸ μέρος χωρίου, πέφευγα δὲ
        διὰ τοὺς παριόντας. ἀλλ' ἐπὶ τοὺς λόφους ἄνω   165
        ἤδη διώκουσ'. ὦ πολυπληθείας ὄχλου.
        οἴμοι· πάλιν τις οὑτοσὶ πρὸς ταῖς θύραις
        ἕστηκεν ἡμῶν.

Σω.   ἆρα τυπτήσει γ' ἐμέ;
Κν.   ἐρημίας οὐκ ἔστιν οὐδαμοῦ τυχεῖν,
        οὐδ' ἂν ἀπάγξασθαί τις ἐπιθυμῶν τύχῃ.   170
Σω.   ἐμοὶ χαλεπαίνεις; περιμένω, πάτερ, τινὰ
        ἐνταῦθα· συνεθέμην γάρ.
(Κν.)   οὐκ ἐγὼ 'λεγον;
        τουτὶ στοὰν νενομίκατ' ἢ τὸ τοῦ λεώ;

153-66 Loci memoriam servat Aelianus, *Ep. Rust.* 14
159 ἀνδριάντων: cf. Bekker, *Anecd.* 82.11: frg. 126. Vide etiam ad v. 677.
169-74 Frustula horum versuum continet H

146 *(Πυ.)* Ha., τουτο]νί ed. pr. paragraphum sub v. habent et H, ut vid., et P; post
]νι, ubi H deest, dicolon habet P 147 *(Σω.)* ed. pr. βλ[έπειν plerique 148 ωσδ'
P: ωσ H²: ουδ' H¹ ἐπ[ανά]ξω Turner 149 post θύρας dist. H κ[αὶ Rees et al., β]οᾷ
ed. pr.: αλλα.[2-3]οᾶι P 151 ed. pr.: καιτουσθεουσ P 156 ed. pr.: εκεκτητοωιλιθινουσ
P 159 ed. pr. 167 τισ ex τοι vel τοσ P πρὸς ed. pr.: προ P 168 τυπτήσει ed. pr.:
τυπησεισ P γ'ἐμέ Gallavotti, Lond.: γεμε P 171 χαλεπαίνεις van Groningen: -ει P
173 τουτὶ στοὰν ed. pr.: τουτοτιστοα P ητουλεω P¹

85

πρὸς τὰς ἐμὰς θύρας ἐὰν ἰδεῖν τινα
βούλησθε, συντάττεσθε πάντα παντελῶς   175
καὶ θῶκον οἰκοδομήσατ', ἂν ἔχητε νοῦν,
μᾶλλον δὲ καὶ συνέδριον. ὦ τάλας ἐγώ·
ἐπηρεασμὸς τὸ κακὸν εἶναί μοι δοκεῖ.

Σω.   οὐ τοῦ τυχόντος, ὡς ἐμοὶ δοκεῖ, πόνου
τουτὶ τὸ πρᾶγμά <γ >, ἀλλὰ συντονωτέρου·   180
πρόδηλόν ἐστιν. ἆρ' ἐγὼ πορεύσομαι
ἐπὶ τὸν Γέταν τὸν τοῦ πατρός; νὴ τοὺς θεούς,
ἔγωγ'. ἔχει <τι> διάπυρον καὶ πραγμάτων
ἔμπειρός ἐστι παντοδαπῶν· τὸ δύσκολον
τὸ τοῦδ' ἐκεῖνος <πᾶν> ἀπώσετ', οἶδ' ἐγώ.   185
τὸ μὲν χρόνον γὰρ ἐμποεῖν τῷ πράγματι
ἀποδοκιμάζω· πόλλ' ἂν ἡμέρᾳ μιᾷ
γένοιτ' ἄν—ἀλλὰ τὴν θύραν πέπληχέ τις.

ΚΟΡΗ

οἴμοι τάλαινα τῶν ἐμῶν ἐγὼ κακῶν.
τί νῦν ποήσω; τὸν κάδον γὰρ ἡ τροφὸς   190
ἱμῶσ' ἀφῆκεν εἰς τὸ φρέαρ.

Σω.   ὦ Ζεῦ πάτερ
καὶ Φοῖβε Παιάν, ὦ Διοσκούρω φίλ[ω,
κάλλους ἀμάχου.

(Κο.)   θερμὸν <δ'> ὕδωρ πρ[οσέταξέ μοι
ποιεῖν ὁ πάππας ἐξιών.

(Σω.)   ἄνδρε[ς, τί δρῶ;
(Κο.)   ἐὰν δὲ τοῦτ' αἴσθητ', ἀπολεῖ κακ[ὴν κακῶς   195
παίων ἐκείνην. οὐ σχολὴ μάτ[ην λαλεῖν·
ὦ φίλταται Νύμφαι, παρ' ὑμῶν λη[πτέον.
αἰσχύνομαι μέν, εἴ τινες θύουσ' ἄ[ρα
ἔνδον, ἐνοχλεῖν—

(Σω.)   ἀλλ' ἂν ἐμοὶ δ[ῷς ἣν ἔχεις
βάψας ἐγώ σοι τ[ὴν χύτραν ἥξ]ω φέρων.   200

---

176 -σατ', ἂν plerique: -σατεεαν P   177 dicolon post συνέδριον habet P   180 Page et
al.: πραγμααλλα P   183 τι add. plerique   184 εστι Lond.: -τιν P   185 τὸ τοῦδ' Diano,
Thierfelder et al.: τοτουτουδ' P   πᾶν add. Diano ἀπώσετ' ed. pr.: -αιτ' P   187 Ha.:
πολλαδ'αν P   188 post αλλα dist. P ut vid.   189 η κορη θυγατηρ κνημ̄ in marg.
sinist. P   193 καλουσ P δ' add. plerique πρ[οσέταξε ed. pr., μοι Kraus et al.   194
παπασ P, sicut alias τί δρῶ Barrett, Hagenmayer   195 ed. pr. τουτουτοεσθητ' P
196 incertum utrum εκεινην: an εκεινην' habeat P suppl. Gallavotti, Georgoulis
197 Barrett   198 θύουσ' ed. pr.: θυοσ P ἄ[ρα Eitrem, Turner   199 δ[ῶς plerique (fort.
δω[P) ἣν ἔχεις Foss   200 ed. pr.

(Κο.)　ναὶ πρὸς θεῶν ἀ[νύσας γ'.]

(Σω.)　　　　　　　　ἐλευθερίως γέ πως
ἄγροικός ἐστιν, ὦ [πολυτί]μητοι θεοί.
τίς ἄν με σώσαι δ[αιμό]νων;

(Κο.)　　　　　　　　τάλαιν' ἐγώ,
τίς ἐψόφηκεν; ἆρ' ὁ [πά]ππας ἔρχεται;
ἔπειτα πληγὰς λ[ήψ]ομ', ἄν με καταλάβῃ　　　　205
ἔξω.

ΔΑΟΣ

　　διατρίβω σοι διακονῶν πάλαι
ἐνταῦθ'· ὁ δὲ σκάπτει μόνος. πορευτέον
πρὸς ἐκεῖνόν ἐστιν. ὦ κάκιστ' ἀπολουμένη
Πενία, τί σ' ἡ[μ]εῖς τηλικοῦτ' ἐφεύρομεν;
τί τοσοῦτον ἡμῖν ἐνδελεχῶς οὕτω χρόνον　　　210
ἔνδον κάθησαι καὶ συνοικεῖς;

(Σω.)　　　　　　　　λάμβανε
τηνδί.

(Κο.)　　φέρε δεῦρο.

Δα.　　　　　　τί ποτ' ἐβούλεθ' οὑτοσὶ
ἄνθρωπος;

(Σω.)　　　ἔρρωσ', ἐπιμελοῦ τε τοῦ πατρός.
οἴμοι κακοδαίμων.

Πυ.　　　　　　παῦε θρηνῶν, Σώστρατε.
ἔσται κατὰ τρόπον.　　　　　　　　　　　215

(Σω.)　　　　κατὰ τρόπον τί;

(Πυ.)　　　　　　　　μὴ φοβοῦ.
ἀλλ' ὅπερ ἔμελλες ἄρτι τὸν Γέταν λαβὼν
ἐπάνηκ', ἐκείνῳ πᾶν τὸ πρᾶγμ' εἰπὼν σαφῶς.

Δα.　　τουτὶ τὸ κακὸν τί ποτ' ἐστίν; ὡς οὔ μοι πάνυ
τὸ πρᾶγμ' ἀρέσκει. μειράκιον διακονεῖ
κόρῃ· πονηρόν. ἀλλά σ', ὦ Κνήμων, κακὸν　　　220
κακῶς ἅπαντες ἀπολέσειαν οἱ θεοί.
ἄκακον κόρην μόνην ἀφεὶς ἐν ἐρημίᾳ
ἐᾷς φυλακὴν οὐδεμίαν ὡς προκειμένην

201 Webster (paragr. sub v. P)　202 suppl. ed. pr.　203 με Lloyd-Jones: εμε P
δ[αιμό]νων Barrett　204 τισεθηκεν P¹ [πα]πασ P, solita orthographia　205 suppl.
ed. pr. ἄν plerique: εαν P　207 σκεπτει P¹, σκαπτει P² ut vid.　211 καθοσαι P
213 (Σω.) Kassel, Lond. (213 ανθρωπος: — πατρος: 214 οιμοι κακοδαιμων: P)
218 τουτὶ ed. pr.: τουτοτι P　223 προκειμένην Bingen, Meertens, Webster: προκενην P

ποιούμενος. τουτὶ καταμανθάνων ἴσως
οὗτος προσερρύη, νομίζων ὡσπερεὶ
ἔρμαιον. οὐ μὴν ἀλλὰ τἀδελφῷ γε δεῖ   225
αὐτῆς φράσαι με τὴν ταχίστην ταῦθ', ἵνα
ἐν ἐπιμελείᾳ τῆς κόρης γενώμεθα.
ἤδη δὲ τοῦτ' ἐλθὼν ποήσειν μοι δοκῶ.
καὶ γὰρ προσιόντας τούσδε παιανιστάς τινας   230
εἰς τὸν τόπον δεῦρ' ὑποβεβρεγμένους ὁρῶ,
οἷς μὴ 'νοχλεῖν εὔκαιρον εἶναί μοι δοκεῖ.

ΧΟΡΟΥ

ΓΟΡΓΙΑΣ

    οὕτω παρέργως δ', εἰπέ μοι, τῷ πράγματι
    φαύλως τ' ἐχρήσω;
Δα.   πῶς;
(Γο.)   ἔδει σε νὴ Δία
τὸν τῇ κόρῃ προσιόντα <τόνδ',> ὅστις ποτ' ἦν,   235
ἰδεῖν τότ' εὐθύς, τοῦτο τοῦ λοιποῦ χρόνου
εἰπεῖν θ' ὅπως μηδείς ποτ' αὐτὸν ὄψεται
ποιοῦντα· νυνὶ δ' ὥσπερ ἀλλοτρίου τινὸς
πράγματος ἀπέστης. οὐκ ἔνεστ' ἴσως φυγεῖν
οἰκειότητα, Δᾶ'. ἀδελφῆς ἔτι μέλει   240
ἐμῇ[ς]. ὁ πατὴρ ἀλλότριος εἶναι βούλεται
αὐ[τ]ῆς πρὸς ἡμᾶς; μὴ τὸ τούτου δύσκολον
μ[ι]μώμεθ' ἡμεῖς. ἂν γὰρ αἰσχύνῃ τινὶ
αὕτη] περιπέσῃ, τοῦτο κἀμοὶ γίνεται
ὄνειδο]ς· ὁ γὰρ ἔξωθεν οὐ τὸν αἴτιον   245
ὅστις] ποτ' ἐστὶν οἶδεν, ἀλλὰ τὸ γεγονός.
ὑπάγωμε]ν.
(Δα.)   ὦ τᾶν, τὸν γέροντα, Γοργία,
δέδοικ'· ἐ]ὰν γὰρ τῇ θύρᾳ προσιόντα με
λάβῃ, κρ]εμᾷ παραχρῆμα.
Γο.   δυσχρήστως γέ πως
ἔχει· ζυ]γομαχῶν τοῦτον οὔθ' ὅτῳ τρόπῳ   250

239-40 (οὐκ ἔνεστ'.... Δᾶ') cit. Schol. Eur. *Andr.* 975: frg. 122

224 καταμαθανων P 226 τἀδελφῷ ed. pr.: αδελ- P 230 versus metri causa suspectus, sane dubius 235 Lloyd-Jones et al. 236 τότ' ed. pr.: τουτ' P 239 απετησ P ἔνεστί σοι Schol. Eur., cod. M 240 ἔτι μέλει Ha., Robertson: επιμελει P 241 Lloyd-Jones: ειμη[.] P 242 μὴ plerique: μηδε P 244 Lloyd-Jones, Lond. (αὐτὴ ed. pr.) 245-6 ed. pr. 247 suppl. Lond.:]ν: vel fort.]ι: P 248 ed. pr. 249 λάβῃ Roberts, κρ]εμᾷ plerique 250 suppl. ed. pr., dist. Bingen τοῦτον ed. pr.: τουτω P

ΔΥΣΚΟΛΟΣ

ἀναγκάσαι τις εἰς τὸ βέλτι[ον φρονεῖ]ν
οὔτ' ἂν μεταπείσαι νουθετῶν ο[ἷ' ἂν φίλο]ς·
ἀλλ' ἐμποδὼν τῷ μὲν βιάσασθαι [τὸν ν]όμον
ἔχει μεθ' αὑτοῦ, τῷ δὲ πεῖσαι τὸν τρ[όπο]ν.

Δα.   ἔπισχε μικρόν· οὐ μάτην γὰρ ἥκ[ομ]εν   255
       ἀλλ' ὥσπερ εἶπον ἔρχετ' ἀνακάμψας πάλιν.

Γο.   ὁ τὴν χλανίδ' ἔχων οὗτός ἐστιν ὃν λέγεις;
(Δα.)   οὗτος.
(Γο.)   κακοῦργος εὐθὺς ἀπὸ τοῦ βλέμματος.

Σω.   τὸν μὲν Γέταν οὐκ ἔνδον ὄντα κατέλ[α]βον,
       μέλλουσα δ' ἡ μήτηρ θεῷ θύειν τινὶ   260
       οὐκ οἶδ' ὅτῳ—ποεῖ δὲ τοῦθ' ὁσημέραι,
       περιέρχεται θύουσα τὸν δῆμον κύκλῳ
       ἅπαντ'—ἀπέσταλκ' αὐτὸν αὐτόθεν τινὰ
       μισθωσόμενον μάγειρον. ἐρρῶσθαι δὲ τῇ
       θυσίᾳ φράσας ἥκω πάλιν πρὸς τἀνθάδε.   265
       καί μοι δοκῶ τοὺς περιπάτους τούτους ἀφεὶς
       αὐτὸς διαλέξασθ' ὑπὲρ ἐμαυτοῦ. τὴν θύραν
       κόψω δ', ἵν' ᾖ μοι μηδὲ βουλεύσασθ' ἔτι.

Γο.   μειράκιον, ἐθελήσαις ἂν ὑπομεῖναι λόγον
       σπουδαιότερόν μου;   270
(Σω.)   καὶ μάλ' ἡδέως· λέγε.
(Γο.)   εἶναι νομίζω πᾶσιν ἀνθρώποις ἐγώ,
       τοῖς τ' εὐτυχοῦσιν τοῖς τε πράττουσιν κακῶς,
       πέρας τι τούτου καὶ μεταλλαγήν τινα·
       καὶ τῷ μὲν εὐτυχοῦντι μέχρι τούτου μένειν
       τὰ πράγματ' εὐθενοῦντ' ἀεὶ τὰ τοῦ βίου,   275
       ὅσον ἂν χρόνον φέρειν δύνηται τὴν τύχην
       μηδὲν ποήσας ἄδικον· εἰς δὲ τοῦθ' ὅταν
       ἔλθῃ προαχθεὶς τοῖς ἀγαθοῖς, ἐνταῦθά που
       τὴν μεταβολὴν τὴν εἰς τὸ χεῖρον λαμβάνει.
       τοῖς δ' ἐνδεῶς πράττουσιν, ἂν μηδὲν κακὸν   280
       ποιῶσιν ἀποροῦντες, φέρωσι δ' εὐγενῶς

263-72, 283-90: horum versuum frustula continet O (vid. p. 40). Vv. 284-7 exstant
apud Stobaeum, *Ecl.* 3.22.19 (=frg. 250, vv. 8-11: vide comm.)

251 ἀναγκάσαι Lloyd-Jones: -σειε P   βέλτι[ον ed. pr., φρονεῖ]ν Kraus   252 suppl.
dubitanter Ha.   253-4 ed. pr. μετ'αυτου P   255 ἔπισχε μικρόν plerique: επισχεσμικρον
P   256 ed. pr.: ωσπερανειπον P   257 ὁ ed. pr.: ου P   266 καίμοι Winnington-Ingram:
καμοι P   270 ηδωσ P   273 τούτου Mette, Winnington-Ingram et al.: τουτο P
281 φέρωσι Lond.: -σιν P

τὸν δαίμον', εἰς πίστιν ποτ' ἐλθόντας χρόνῳ,
βελτίον' εἶναι μερίδα προσδοκᾶν τινα.
τί οὖν λέγω; μήτ' αὐτός, εἰ σφόδρ' εὐπορεῖς,
πίστευε τούτῳ, μήτε τῶν πτωχῶν πάλιν   285
ἡμῶν καταφρόνει· τοῦ διευτυχεῖν δ' ἀεὶ
πάρεχε σεαυτὸν τοῖς ὁρῶσιν ἄξιον.

Σω.   ἄτοπον δέ σοί τι φαίνομαι νυνὶ ποεῖν;
(Γο.) ἔργον δοκεῖς μοι φαῦλον ἐζηλωκέναι,
πείσειν νομίζων ἐξαμαρτεῖν παρθένον   290
ἐλευθέραν ἢ καιρὸν ἐπιτηρῶν τινα
κατεργάσεσθαι πρᾶγμα θανάτων ἄξιον
πολλῶν.

(Σω.)   Ἄπολλον.
(Γο.)   οὐ δίκαιόν ἐστι γοῦν
τὴν σὴν σχολὴν τοῖς ἀσχολουμένοις κακὸν
ἡμῖν γενέσθαι. τῶν δ' ἀπάντων ἴσθ' ὅτι   295
πτωχὸς ἀδικηθεὶς ἐστι δυσκολώτατον.
πρῶτον μέν ἐστ' ἐλεεινός, εἶτα λαμβά[νει
οὐκ εἰς ἀδικίαν ὅσα πέπονθ', ἀλλ' εἰς [ὕβριν.

Σω.   μειράκιον, οὕτως εὐτυχοίης, βραχ[ύ τί μου
ἄκουσον.   300
(Δα.)   εὖ γε, δέσποθ', οὕτω πολλά [μοι
ἀγαθὰ γένοιτο.
(Σω.)   καὶ σύ γ' ὁ λαλῶν πρ[όσεχε δή.
κόρην τιν' εἶδο[ν ἐνθαδί· τ]αύτης ἐρῶ.
εἰ τοῦτ' ἀδίκημ' [εἴρηκ]ας, ἠδίκηκ' ἴσως.
τί γὰρ ἄν τις εἴποι; π[λὴν π]ορεύομ' ἐνθάδε
οὐχὶ πρὸς ἐκείνη[ν, βο]ύλομαι δ' αὐτῆς ἰδεῖν 305
τὸν πατέρ'. ἐγὼ γά[ρ], ὢν ἐλεύθερος, βίον
ἱκανὸν ἔχων, ἕτοιμός εἰμι λαμβάνειν
αὐτὴν ἄπροικον, πίστιν ἐπιθεὶς διατελεῖν
στέργων. ἐπὶ κακῷ δ' εἰ προσελήλυθ' ἐνθάδε,

294 ἀσχολουμένοις: cf. Sud. s.v. ἄσχολος; Bekker, Anecd. 457.18: frg. 828

284 μήδ' ap. Stob., ubi correxerat Meineke ευπορεις P, O in textu: ευτυχεισ O supra
versum 286 τουδ' ευτυχεῖν ap. Stob. 287 σαυτον P; item ap. Stob., ubi corr. Gesner
288 σοί τι vel σοι τί plerique: τισοι P 289 εξηλ- P 292 πραμθανάτων P¹ 296 -ησθεισ
P 298 plerique 299 plerique 300 (Δα.) plerique (ακουσον: 301 αγ-γενοιτο:
P) μοι Harsh, Sydn. 301 ed. pr. αγαθον P¹ 302 ἐνθαδί plerique 303 Lloyd-
Jones, Sydn. et al. αδικημα[P², ηδικ- P¹ 304 Sandbach, van Groningen

ἢ βουλόμενος ὑμῶν ‹τι› κακοτεχνεῖν λάθρα,   310
οὗτός μ᾽ ὁ Πάν, μειράκιον, αἱ Νύμφαι θ᾽ ἅμα
ἀπόπληκτον αὐτοῦ πλησίον τῆς οἰκίας
ἤδη ποήσειαν. τετάραγμ᾽, ‹εὖ› ἴσθ᾽ ὅτι,
οὐδὲ μετρίως, εἴ σοι τοιοῦτος φαίνομαι.

Γο.   ἀλλ᾽ εἴ τι κἀγὼ τοῦ δέοντος σφοδρότερον   315
εἴρηκα, μηδὲν τοῦτο λυπείτω σ᾽ ἔτι.
ἅμα γὰρ μεταπείθεις ταῦτα καὶ φίλον μ᾽ ἔχεις.
οὐκ ἀλλότριος δ᾽ ὤν, ἀλλ᾽ ἀδελφὸς τῆς κόρης
ὁμομήτριος, βέλτιστε, ταῦτά σοι λέγω.

Σω.   καὶ χρήσιμός γ᾽ εἶ νὴ Δί᾽ εἰς τὰ λοιπά μοι.   320
(Γο.)   τί χρήσιμος;
(Σω.)   γεννικὸν ὁρῶ σε τῷ τρόπῳ.
(Γο.)   οὐ πρόφασιν εἰπὼν βούλομ᾽ ἀποπέμψαι κενήν,
τὰ δ᾽ ὄντα πράγματ᾽ ἐμφανίσαι· ταύτῃ πατὴρ
ἔσθ᾽ οἷος οὐδεὶς γέγονεν οὔτε τῶν πάλαι
ἄνθρωπος οὔτε τῶν καθ᾽ ἡμᾶς.   325
(Σω.)   ὁ χαλεπός;
σχεδὸν οἶδ᾽.
(Γο.)   ὑπερβολή τίς ἐστι τοῦ κακοῦ.
τούτῳ ταλάντων ἔστ᾽ ἴσως τουτὶ δυεῖν
τὸ κτῆμα. τοῦτ᾽ αὐτὸς γεωργῶν διατελεῖ
μόνος, συνεργόν δ᾽ οὐδέν᾽ ἀνθρώπων ἔχων,
οὐκ οἰκέτην οἰκεῖον, οὐκ ἐκ τοῦ τόπου   330
μισθωτόν, οὐχὶ γείτον᾽, ἀλλ᾽ αὐτὸς μόνος.
ἥδιστόν ἐστ᾽ αὐτῷ γὰρ ἀνθρώπων ὁρᾶν
οὐδένα· μεθ᾽ αὑτοῦ τὴν κόρην ἐργάζεται
ἔχων τὰ πολλά· προσλαλεῖ ταύτῃ μόνῃ,
ἑτέρῳ δὲ τοῦτ᾽ οὐκ ἂν ποήσαι ῥᾳδίως.   335
τότε φησὶν ἐκδώσειν ἐκείνην, ἡνίκ᾽ ἂν
ὁμότροπον αὐτῷ νυμφίον λάβῃ.
(Σω.)   λέγεις
οὐδέποτε.
(Γο.)   μὴ δὴ πράγματ᾽, ὦ βέλτιστ᾽, ἔχε·
μάτην γὰρ ἕξεις. τοὺς δ᾽ ἀναγκαίους ἔα
ἡμᾶς φέρειν ταῦθ᾽, οἷς δίδωσιν ἡ τύχη.   340

---

310 τι add. plerique 311 αἱ om. P¹ 313 Bingen, Ha. et al. 314 εισεισοιτοιουτο
P¹ 315 αλλετι P 317 αιμαγαρ P 324 ed. pr.: ουδεεισ P 326 ἐστι Lond.: -τιν P
329 ανθρωπον P 337 νυμφ᾽ον P 338 ουδεποτ᾽ει P 340 διδωσειν (vix -εῖν) P

(Σω.) πρὸς τῶν θεῶν οὐπώποτ' ἠράσθης τινός,
μειράκιον;
(Γο.)   οὐδ' ἔξεστί μοι, βέλτιστε.
(Σω.)   πῶς;
τίς ἐσθ' ὁ κωλύων;
(Γο.)   ὁ τῶν ὄντων κακῶν
λογισμός, ἀνάπαυσιν διδοὺς οὐδ' ἡντινοῦν.
(Σω.) οὔ μοι δοκεῖς· ἀπειρότερον γοῦν διαλέγει   345
πε[ρὶ τ]αῦτ'. ἀποστῆναι κελεύεις μ'· οὐκέτι
τοῦτ' ἔσ]τιν ἐπ' ἐμοί, τῷ θεῷ δέ.
(Γο.)   τοιγαροῦν
οὐδὲ]ν ἀδικεῖς ἡμᾶς, μάτην δὲ κακοπαθεῖς.
(Σω.) οὐκ ἂν λά]βοιμι τὴν κόρην;
(Γο.)   οὐκ ἂν λάβοις·
ὄψει σὺ ν]ῦν, ἂν συνακολουθήσας ἐμοὶ   350
ἐκεῖσε] παράγῃς· πλησίον γὰρ τὴν νάπην
ἐργάζε]θ' ἡμῶν.
(Σω.)   πῶς;
(Γο.)   λόγον τιν' ἐμβαλῶ
εἰκῇ περὶ] γάμου τῆς κόρης· τὸ τοιοῦτο γὰρ
ἴδοιμι κἂ]ν αὐτὸς γενόμενον ἄσμενος·
εὐθὺς μαχεῖται πᾶσι, λοιδ[ορούμενο]ς   355
εἰς τοὺς βίους οὓς ζῶσι· σὲ δ' [ἄγον]τ' <ἂν> ἴδῃ
σχολὴν τρυφῶντά τ', οὐδ' ὁρ[ῶν ἀν]έξεται.
Σω.   νῦν ἐστ' ἐκεῖ;
(Γο.)   μὰ Δί', ἀλλὰ μ[ικρ]ὸν ὕστερον
ἔξεισιν ἦν εἴωθεν.
(Σω.)   ὦ τᾶν, τὴν κόρην
ἄγων μεθ' αὑτοῦ, φῄς;   360
(Γο.)   ὅπως ἂν τοῦτό γε
τύχῃ.

341, 345: Cf. Aristaen., *Ep.* 2.17 [p. 168 Hercher] ἀλλ' οὐπώποτε ἠράσθης ἀφ' ὧν λέγεις
. . . σφόδρα γοῦν ἀπειρότερον διαλέγῃ (ἀπειρότατα Hercher)

343 τισεθ'ου P post κωλύων dicolon habet P; paragraphus deest 345 διαλέγει Browning (cf. Aristaen. loc. cit.): διατελεῖ P 346 τ]αῦτ' Barrett, Lond. et al. 347 ed.
pr. 348 οὐδὲ]ν plerique ἀδικεῖς ed. pr.: -ειτ' P 349 οὐκ ἂν Post, van Groningen
et al. 350 rest. Post (εἴσει vel ὄψει): 7]ηνασυνκ- P (συνακ- ed. pr.) 351 ἐκεῖσε
Webster παράγῃς Lloyd-Jones: παρατησ P 352 ἐργάζε]θ' plerique εμβαλωι P 353 εἰκῇ
Barrett, Winnington-Ingram 354 Blake, Post 355 ed. pr. 356 Kraus, Lloyd-
Jones: [5-6]τ' ἴδηι P 357 ὁρ]ῶν plerique 358 ἐστ' Lloyd-Jones, Lond. et al.: εστιν P
μ[ικρ]ὸν plerique 359 ἴωθεν P¹ (Σω.) ὦ τᾶν ed. pr.: οταν P, ubi desunt et paragraphus
et dicolon 360 μεταυτου P

(Σω.)   βαδίζειν <εἴμ᾽> ἔτοιμος οἷ λέγεις.
              ἀλλ᾽, ἀντιβολῶ, συναγώνισαί μοι.
(Γο.)   τίνα τρόπον;
(Σω.)   ὅντινα τρόπον; προάγωμεν οἷ λέγεις.
(Δα.)   τί οὖν;
        ἐργαζομένοις ἡμῖν παρεστήξεις ἔχων
        χλανίδα;   365
(Σω.)   τί δὴ γὰρ οὐχί;
Δα.   ταῖς βώλοις βαλεῖ
        εὐθύς σ᾽, ἀποκαλεῖ τ᾽ ὄλεθρον ἀργόν. ἀλλὰ δεῖ
        σκάπτειν μεθ᾽ ἡμῶν σ᾽. εἰ τύχοι γὰρ τοῦτ᾽ ἰδών,
        ἴσως ἂν ὑπομείνειε καὶ παρὰ σοῦ τινα
        λόγον, νομίσας αὐτουργὸν εἶναι τῷ βίῳ
        πένηθ᾽.   370
(Σω.)   ἔτοιμος πάντα πειθαρχεῖν· ἄγε.
Γο.   τί κακοπαθεῖν σαυτὸν βιάζῃ;
Δα.   βούλομαι
        ὡς πλεῖστον ἡμᾶς ἐργάσασθαι τήμερον,
        τοῦτόν τε τὴν ὀσφῦν ἀπορρήξανθ᾽ ἅμα
        παύσασθ᾽ ἐνοχλοῦνθ᾽ ἡμῖν προσιόντα τ᾽ ἐνθάδε.
Σω.   ἔκφερε δίκελλαν.   375
(Δα.)   τὴν παρ᾽ ἐμοῦ λαβὼν ἴθι.
        τὴν αἱμασιὰν ἐποικοδομήσω γὰρ τέως
        ἐγώ· ποιητέον δὲ καὶ τοῦτ᾽ ἐστί.
(Σω.)   δός.
        ἀπέσωσας.
(Δα.)   ὑπάγω, τρόφιμ᾽· ἐκεῖ διώκετε.
(Σω.)   οὕτως ἔχω γάρ· ἀποθανεῖν ἤδη με δεῖ
        ἢ ζῆν ἔχοντα τὴν κόρην.   380
(Γο.)   εἴπερ λέγεις
        ἃ φρονεῖς, ἐπιτύχοις.
(Σω.)   ὦ πολυτίμητοι θεοί·
        οἷς ἀποτρέπεις νυνὶ γὰρ ὡς οἴει με σύ,
        τούτοις παρώξυμμ᾽ εἰς τὸ πρᾶγμα διπλασίως.

---

376 Cf. Liban., *Decl.* 27.21 τὴν αἱμασιὰν οἰκοδομήσας

361 εἴμ᾽ add. ed. pr. ετοιμοσ:οιλεγεισ: P 363 (Δα.) Post (Gorgiae trib. ed. pr.)
365 δὴ γὰρ Ha.: γαρδη P βαλλει P 371 paragrapho caret P 372 ωστοπλειστον P¹
ἡμᾶς ed. pr.: ημερασ P 376 ἐποικοδομήσω γὰρ Barrett, Turner et al.: ετιγαροικ- P
377-8 εστιν P ἀπέσωσας Sostrato trib. ed. pr. (377: δοσ: 378 α̲π̲ε̲σ̲ω̲σ̲ασυ·παγω) 379 γάρ·
ἀποθανεῖν Lloyd-Jones: παραποθανειν P 383 παροξ- P

93

εἰ μὴ γὰρ ἐν γυναιξίν ἐστιν ἡ κόρη
τεθραμμένη, μηδ' οἶδε τῶν ἐν τῷ βίῳ　　　　　　385
τούτων κακῶν μηδὲν ὑπὸ τηθίδος τινὸς
δεδιξαμένη μαίας τ', ἐλευθερίως δέ πως
μετὰ πατρὸς ἀγρίου μισοπονήρου τῷ τρόπῳ,
πῶς οὐκ ἐπιτυχεῖν ἐστι ταύτης μακάριον;
ἀλλ' ἡ δίκελλ' ἄγει τάλαντα τέτταρα　　　　　　390
αὕτη· προαπολεῖ μ'. οὐ μαλακιστέον δ' ὅμως,
ἐπείπερ ἦργμαι καταπονεῖν τὸ πρᾶγμ' ἅπαξ.

ΣΙΚΩΝ

τουτὶ τὸ πρόβατόν ἐστιν οὐ τὸ τυχὸν καλόν.
ἄπαγ' εἰς τὸ βάραθρον. ἂν μὲν αἰρόμενος φέρω
μετέωρον, ἔχεται τῷ στόματι θαλλοῦ κράδης,　　395
κατεσθίει τὰ θρῖ', ἀποσπᾷ δ' εἰς βίαν·
ἐὰν δ' ἀφῇ χαμαί τις, οὐ προέρχεται,
τοὐναντίον δὲ γέγονε· κατακέκομμ' ἐ[γὼ
ὁ μάγειρος ὑπὸ τούτου νεωλκῶν τὴν ὁδ[όν.
ἀλλ' ἐστὶν εὐτυχῶς τὸ νυμφαῖον τοδ[ί,　　　　400
οὗ θύσομεν. τὸν Πᾶνα χαίρειν. παῖ Γέ[τα,
τοσοῦτ' ἀπολείπῃ;

(ΓΕΤΑΣ)

　　　　　　　　τεττάρων γὰρ φορ[τίον
ὄνων συνέδησαν αἱ κάκιστ' ἀπολο[ύμεναι
φέρειν γυναῖκές μοι.

(Σικ.)　　　　　πολύς τις ἔρ[χεται
ὄχλος, ὡς ἔοι[κε. στρ]ώματ' ἀδιήγηθ' ὅσα　　405
φέρεις.

(Γε.)　　　τί δ' ἐγὼ[γε;]

(Σικ.)　　　　　　　ταῦτ' ἐπέρεισον δεῦρ'.

(Γε.)　　　　　　　　　　　　　ἰδού.

ἐὰν ἴδῃ γὰρ ἐνύ[πνιο]ν τὸν Πᾶνα τὸν
Παιανιοῖ, τού[τ]ῳ βαδιούμεθ', οἶδ' ὅτι,
θύσοντες εὐθύς.

(Σικ.)　　　　[τ]ίς δ' ἑόρακεν ἐνύπνιον;

387 δεδιξαμένη Bingen: δεδεισαμενη P　388 μετὰ πατρὸς ed. pr.: μεταυτουπατροσ P
389 ἐστι plerique: -τιν P　390 post αὕτη dist. Page　προαπολεῖ Kraus, Maas: προσ-
P　393 σικων μαγ´ in marg. sinist. P　394 βαραθμον P　395 post μετέωρον dist.
plerique　396 εἰς van Groningen et al.: εσ P　397 ed. pr.: αφηιτισχαμαι P　398
δὲ γέγονε Blake: δ'ηγαγον P　399 νεολκων P　400 τοδ[ί plerique　401-5 ed. pr.
403 -σαν. ακακιστ'απολ.[P (fort. απολυ[)　406 ἐπέρεισον Bingen, Quincey; cetera ed.
pr.: φερεισ:τιδ'εγω[4-5]ερεισονταυταδευροϊδου: P　407-8 ed. pr.: ανιδη—τονπανατε
| τονπαιανιοι—βαζιουμεθ' P　409 ed. pr.: θυσοντοσευθυσ[..]ιδ'εωρακεν P (scil. [:τ]ιδ')

(Γε.) ἄνθρωπε, μή με κόφθ'.   410
(Σικ.)   ὅμως εἶπον, Γέτα·
τίς εἶδεν;
(Γε.)   ἡ κεκτημένη.
(Σικ.)   τί πρὸς θεῶν;
(Γε.) ἀπολεῖς· ἐδόκει τὸν Πᾶνα—
(Σικ.)   τουτονὶ λέγεις;
(Γε.) τοῦτον.
(Σικ.)   τί ποιεῖν;
(Γε.)   τῷ τροφίμῳ τῷ Σωστράτῳ—
(Σικ.) κομψῷ νεανίσκῳ γε—
(Γε.)   περικρούειν πέδας.
(Σικ.) Ἄπολλον.   415
(Γε.)   εἶτα δόντα διφθέραν τε καὶ
δίκελλαν ⟨ἐν⟩ τοῦ πλησίον τῷ χωρίῳ
σκάπτειν κελεύειν.
(Σικ.)   ἄτοπον.
(Γε.)   ἀλλὰ θύομεν
διὰ τοῦθ', ἵν' εἰς βέλτιον ἀποβῇ τὸ φοβερόν.
Σικ. μεμάθηκα. πάλιν αἴρου δὲ ταυτὶ καὶ φέρε
εἴσω. ποῶμεν στιβάδας ἔνδον εὐτρεπεῖς   420
καὶ τἄλλ' ἕτοιμα· μηδὲν ἐπικωλυέτω
θύειν γ', ἐπὰν ἔλθωσιν, ἀλλ' ἀγαθῇ τύχῃ.
καὶ τὰς ὀφρῦς ἄνες ποτ', ὦ τρισάθλιε·
ἐγώ σε χορτάσω κατὰ τρόπον τήμερον.
Γε. ἐπαινέτης οὖν εἰμι σοῦ καὶ τῆς τέχνης   425
ἔγωγ' ἀεί ποτ', οὐχὶ πιστεύω δ' ὅμως.

ΧΟΡΟΥ

Κν. γραῦ, τὴν θύραν κλείσασ' ἄνοιγε μηδενί,
ἕως ἂν ἔλθω δεῦρ' ἐγὼ πάλιν· σκότους
ἔσται δὲ τοῦτο παντελῶς, ὡς οἴομαι.
Γε. Πλαγγών, πορεύου θᾶττον· ἤδη τεθυκέναι   430
ἡμᾶς ἔδει.

423 Cf. Aelian., *Ep. Rust.* 15 λῦσον δὲ καὶ τὴν ὀφρῦν

410 με ed. pr.: μοι P 412 απολεισ' P 414 νεανίσκῳ γε plerique: γενε- P παιδασ P
415 δ'ονταδιαφθεραν P 416 ἐν add. ed. pr. τοῦ Lond.: τω P 418 ed. pr.: αποβαιη P
420 ed. pr.: ποιησωμεν P 422 θύειν Lond. et al.: θυσειν P 423 ἄνες ποτ' Kassel,
Szemerényi et al.: ανεσπογ' (fort. ανεσποτ') P 429 οιμαι P

Κν.   τουτὶ τὸ κακὸν τί βούλεται;
     ὄχλος τις· ἄπαγ' ἐς κόρακας.
(Γε.)   αὔλει, Παρθενί,
Πανός· σιωπῇ, φασί, τούτῳ τῷ θεῷ
οὐ δεῖ προσιέναι.
(Σικ.)   νὴ Δί', ἀπεσώθητέ γε.
ὦ 'Ηράκλεις, ἀηδίας. καθήμεθα   435
χρόνον τοσοῦτον περιμένοντες, εὐτρεπῆ
ἅπαντα δ' ἡμῖν ἐστι.
(Γε.)   ναὶ μὰ τὸν Δία.
τὸ γοῦν πρόβατον—μικροῦ τέθνηκε γὰρ τάλαν—
οὐ περιμενεῖ τὴν σὴν σχολήν. ἀλλ' εἴσιτε,
κανᾶ πρόχειρα, χέρνιβας, θυλήματα   440
ποιεῖτε. ποῖ κέχηνας, ἐμβρόντητε σύ;
Κν.   κακοὶ κακῶς ἀπόλοισθε. ποιοῦσίν γέ με
ἀργόν· καταλιπεῖν γὰρ μόνην τὴν οἰκίαν
οὐκ ἂν δυναίμην. αἱ δὲ Νύμφαι μοι κακὸν
ἀ[εὶ] παροικοῦσ', ὥστε μοι δοκῶ πάλιν   445
με]ϝοικοδομήσειν, καταβαλὼν τὴν οἰκίαν,
ἐντ]εῦθεν. ὡς θύουσι δ' οἱ τοιχωρύχοι
κοίϝϝας φέρονται, σταμνί', οὐχὶ τῶν θεῶν
ἕνεϝκ', ἀλλ' ἑαυτῶν. ὁ λιβανωτὸς εὐσεβὲς
καὶ τὸϝ πόπανον· τοῦτ' ἔλαβεν ὁ θεὸς ἐπὶ τὸ πῦρ 450
ἅπαϝν ἐπιτεθέν· οἱ δὲ τὴν ὀσφῦν ἄκραν
καὶϝ τὴν χολήν, ὅτι ἔστ' ἄβρωτα, τοῖς θεοῖς
ἐπιθέντες αὐτοὶ τἄλλα ϝϝαταπίνοϝυσι. γραῦ,
ἄνοιγε θᾶττον τὴν θύραν· [τηρητέ]ον
ἐστὶν γὰρ ἡμῖν τἄνδον, ὡ[ς ἐμοὶ] δοκεῖ.   455
(Γε.)   τὸ λεβήτιον, φής, ἐπιλέλη[σθ]ε; παντελῶς

433-4 σιωπῇ ... προσιέναι cit. Schol. Ar. Lys. 2, Sud. s.v. Πανικῷ δείματι: frg. 121
447-53 ὡς θύουσι ... καταπίνουσι cit. Athenaeus 4.146 e; 449-51 ὁ λιβανωτός ... ἄπαν
τεθέν (sic) cit. Porphyrius De abstinentia p. 147 Nauck²; versuum 451-3 memoriam
servant Clem. Alex., Stromata 7.6, Et. Gen., s.v. ἱερὸν ὀστοῦν. His subsidiis olim consti-
tutum est frg. 117.

432 ἐς plerique: εισ P 434 δεῖν Schol. Ar., Sud. (Σικ.) ed. pr. (ου—προσιεναι:)
436 ευτρ:επη P 437 (Γε.) ed. pr. (απαντα—εστι:) 438 τάλαν ed. pr.: ταλαιν' P
Getae contin. Ha.; post γαρ dicolon, et paragr. sub versu habet P 440 προχρεια P
441 κεχονασ P 445 Lloyd-Jones: α[.].αρπαροικουσ P, velut α[ι]ϝαρπαρ-, α[.]χαρπαρ-
446-7 ed. pr. 447 τοιχωρυκοι P 448 ed. pr.: κοίτας φέροντες Ath.:]αιφεροντα P
449 εαυτον P εὐσεβὴς Porph. 450 3-4]ποπανον P, ubi τὸ fortasse deerat 451 τεθέν
Porph. 452 ὀστέα τὰ ἄβρωτα Clem. 453 ἐπιτιθέντες ... τὰ ἄλλα ἀναλίσκουσι Clem.
θύσαντες Et. Gen. 454 Lond. et al. 455 ed. pr. 456 ἐπιλέλη[σθ]ε Zuntz: -λη[..]αι P

ἀποκραιπαλᾶτε. καὶ τί νῦν ποιή[σ]ομεν;
ἐνοχλητέον τοῖς γειτνιῶσι τῷ θεῷ
ἔσθ᾽, ὡς ἔοικε. παιδίον. μὰ τοὺς θεούς,
θεραπαινίδια γὰρ ἀθλιώτερ᾽ οὐδαμοῦ   460
οἶμαι τρέφεσθαι. παῖδες. οὐδὲν ἄλλο πλὴν
κινητιᾶν ἐπίσταται—παῖδες, κ[α]λῶ—
καὶ διαβαλεῖν ἐὰν ἴδη τις. παιδίον.
τουτὶ τὸ κακὸν ‹τί› ἐστι; παῖδες. οὐδὲ εἷς
ἔστ᾽ ἔνδον. ἠήν, προστρέχειν τις φαίνεται.   465

Κν.   τί τῆς θύρας ἅπτει, τρισάθλι᾽, εἰπέ μοι,
     ἄνθρωπε;

(Γε.)   μὴ δάκῃς.

(Κν.)   ἐγώ σε, νὴ Δία,
     καὶ κατέδομαί γε ζῶντα.

(Γε.)   μὴ πρὸς ‹τῶν› θεῶν.

(Κν.)   ἐμοὶ γάρ ἐστι συμβόλαιον, ἀνόσιε,
     καὶ σοί τι;   470

(Γε.)   συμβόλαιον οὐδέν. τοιγαροῦν
     προσελήλυθ᾽ οὐ χρέος σ᾽ ἀπαιτῶν, οὐδ᾽ ἔχων
     κλητῆρας, ἀλλ᾽ αἰτησόμενος λεβήτιον.

(Κν.)   λεβήτιον;

(Γε.)   λεβήτιον.

(Κν.)   μαστιγία,
     θύειν με βοῦς οἴει ποεῖν τε ταῦθ᾽ ἅπερ
     ὑμεῖς ποεῖτ᾽;   475

(Γε.)   οὐδὲ κοχλίαν ἔγωγέ σε.
     ἀλλ᾽ εὐτύχει, βέλτιστε. κόψαι τὴν θύραν
     ἐκέλευσαν αἱ γυναῖκες αἰτῆσαί τέ με·
     ἐπόησα τοῦτ᾽· οὐκ ἔστι· πάλιν ἀπαγγελῶ
     ἐλθὼν ἐκείναις. ὦ πολυτίμητοι θεοί·
     ἔχις πολιὸς ἄνθρωπός ἐστιν οὑτοσί.   480

(Κν.)   ἀνδροφόνα θηρί᾽· εὐθὺς ὥσπερ πρὸς φίλον
     κόπτουσιν. ἂν ὑμῶν προσιόντα τῇ θύρᾳ

472f λεβήτιον Cf. Cramer, *Anecd. Oxon.* iii.273, 8: frg. 866

458 τοιγιτνιωσι P   462 επιστανται P   κ[α]λῶ ed. pr.: κ[α]λοι P (cf. 912)   464 τί
add. ed. pr.   465 ἠήν ed. pr.: ην P   466 ἅπτει Barigazzi, Szemerényi et al.: απει P
467 (Γε.) μὴ δάκῃς Ha., Post, Stoessl: dicolon post ἄνθρωπε non habet P   468 ed.
pr.   473 ed. pr.: λεβοιτιον bis P; post alterum non habet dicolon   474 τε ed. pr.:
δε P   476 κομψαι P   477 τέ με plerique: τ᾽εμε P   478 ἀπαγγελῶ ed. pr.: -λλω P
482 κο- ex ψο- P   ὑμῶν ed. pr.: ημων P

λάβω τιν᾽, ἂν μὴ πᾶσι τοῖς ἐν τῷ τόπῳ
παράδειγμα ποιήσω, νομίζεθ᾽ ἕνα τινὰ
ὁρᾶν με τῶν πολλῶν. ὁ νῦν οὐκ οἶδ᾽ ὅπως   485
διευτύχηκεν οὗτος, ὅστις ἦν ποτε.

Σικ.   κάκιστ᾽ ἀπόλοι᾽. ἐλοιδορεῖτό σοι; τυχὸν
ᾔτεις καταφανῶς. οὐκ ἐπίστανταί τινες
ποεῖν τὸ τοιοῦθ᾽· εὕρηκ᾽ ἐγὼ τούτου τέχνην.
διακονῶ γὰρ μυρίοις ἐν τῇ πόλει,   490
τούτων τ᾽ ἐνοχλῶ τοῖς γείτοσιν καὶ λαμβάνω
σκεύη παρ᾽ ἁπάντων. δεῖ γὰρ εἶναι κολακικὸν
τὸν δεόμενόν του. πρεσβύτερός τις τ[ῇ] θύρᾳ
ὑπακήκο᾽· εὐθὺς πατέρα καὶ πάππα[ν καλῶ.
γραῦς, μητέρ᾽. ἂν τῶν διὰ μέσου τ[ις ᾖ γυνή,   495
ἐκάλεσ᾽ ἱερέαν. ἂν θεράπων, [γενναῖον ἢ
βέλτιστον. ὑμεῖς δ᾽ <οἳ> κρεμάνη[νσθ᾽ ἄξιοι—
ὦ τῆς ἀμαθίας—᾽παιδίον, παῖ[δες᾽ φατέ.
ἐγὼ—πρόελθε, πατρίδιον—σὲ β[ούλομαι.

Κν.   πάλιν αὖ σύ;   500
(Σικ.)   π[αῖ, τί το]ῦτ᾽;
(Κν.)   ἐρεθίζεις μ᾽ ὡσπερεὶ
ἐπίτηδες. οὐκ [εἴρη]κά σοι πρὸς τὴν θύραν
μὴ προσιέναι; [τὸ]ν ἱμάντα δός, γραῦ.
(Σικ.)   μηδαμῶς·
ἀλλ᾽ ἄφες.
(Κν.)   ἄφε[ς;]
(Σικ.)   βέλτιστε, ναὶ πρὸς <τῶν> θεῶν.
(Κν.)   ἧκε πάλιν.
(Σικ.)   ὁ Ποσειδῶν σε—
(Κν.)   καὶ λαλεῖς ἔτι;

---

489 εὕρηκ᾽ . . . τέχνην cit. Ammonius p. 61 Valckenaer: frg. 125

483 λάβω ed. pr.: -ων P   485 ουραν P   487 ελυδωρειτο P   488 καταφανῶς Dodds, Ha.: καταφαγ᾽ωσ P   489 τοιουθ᾽ ed. pr.: τοιουτον P εὑρηκὸς κἀγὼ Ammon. 416 τ᾽ Barigazzi, Thierfelder et al.: τι P γειτοσι P   492 παρ᾽ ἁπάντων Sandbach et al.: παραπαντων P 494-6 Loci rationem inter primos explicaverunt Dale, Lloyd-Jones, Thierfelder 494 πατέρα Dale, Ll.-J., Th.: πατερ P suppl. Ll.-J., Th.: παπα[P, solita orthographia 495 γραασ P μητέρ᾽ Dale, Ll.-J., Th.: μητερ P suppl. Ll.-J. et al. (τις ἦν γυνή ed. pr.) 496 ἱερέαν Ha.: ἱερειαν P suppl. Dale 497 δ᾽<οἳ> Lloyd-Jones: δε P suppl. Ll.-J., παῖ[δες᾽ Winnington-Ingram, φατέ Lloyd-Jones 499 β[ούλομαι Barrett 500 suppl. dubitanter Ha. (]ντο P) 501-2 ed. pr. 503 τῶν add. ed. pr.; partes dist. Diano, Stoessl, Zuntz, secundum P ut vid. (αλλ᾽ αφεσ: αφε[.]: βελτιστε—θεων: incertiore tamen post αφε[.] dicolo)

98

(Σικ.) χυτρόγαυλο[ν] αἰτησόμενος ἦλθον.   505

(Κν.)   οὐκ ἔχω

οὔτε χυτρό[γ]αυλον οὔτε πέλεκυν οὔθ᾽ ἅλας

οὔτ᾽ ὄξος οὔτ᾽ ἄλλ᾽ οὐδέν· ἀλλ᾽ εἴρηχ᾽ ἁπλῶς

μὴ προσι[έ]ναι μοι πᾶσι τοῖς ἐν τῷ τόπῳ.

(Σικ.) ἐμοὶ μὲν οὐκ εἴρηκας.

(Κν.)   ἀλλὰ νῦν λέγω.

(Σικ.) ναί, σὺν κακῷ γ᾽. οὐδ᾽ ὁπόθεν ἄν τις, εἰπέ μοι,   510

ἐλθὼν λάβοι φράσαις ἄν;

(Κν.)   οὐκ ἐγὼ 'λεγον;

ἔτι μοι λαλήσεις;

(Σικ.)   χαῖρε πόλλ᾽.

(Κν.)   οὐ βούλομαι

χαίρειν παρ᾽ ὑμῶν οὐδενός.

(Σικ.)   μὴ χαῖρε δή.

(Κν.) ὦ τῶν ἀνηκέστων κακῶν.

(Σικ.)   καλῶς γέ με

βεβωλοκόπηκεν. οἷόν ἐστ᾽ ἐπιδεξίως   515

αἰτεῖν· διαφέρει, νὴ Δί᾽. ἐφ᾽ ἑτέραν θύραν

ἔλθῃ τις; ἀλλ᾽ εἰ σφαιρομαχοῦσ᾽ ἐν τῷ τόπῳ

οὕτως ἑτοίμως, χαλεπόν. ἆρά γ᾽ ἐστί μοι

κράτιστον ὀπτᾶν τὰ κρέα πάντα; φαίνεται.

ἔστιν δέ μοι λοπάς τις. ἐρρῶσθαι λέγω   520

Φυλασίοις· τοῖς οὖσι τούτοις χρήσομαι.

Σω. ὅστις ἀπορεῖ κακῶν, ἐπὶ Φυλὴν ἐλθέτω

κυνηγετῶν. ὦ τρισκακοδαίμων, ὡς ἔχω

ὀσφῦν, μετάφρενον, τὸν τράχηλον, ἑνὶ λόγῳ

ὅλον τὸ σῶμ᾽. εὐθὺς γὰρ ἐμπεσὼν πολὺς   525

νεανίας ἐγώ τις, ἐξαίρων ἄνω

σφόδρα τὴν δίκελλαν, ὡς ἂν ἐργάτης βαθύς,

505-7 Cf. Choerobosc., *in Theodos.* i.259.16 Hilgard, ubi e Menandro citantur verba
οὐκ ἔχω οὔθ᾽ ἅλας οὔτ᾽ ὄξος οὔτ᾽ ὀρίγανον: frg. 671
514-15 καλῶς . . . βεβωλοκόπηκεν cit. Aldus Manutius, *Horti Adonidis* p. 234a, auctore
Aelio, π.ἐγκλινομένων λέξεων : cf. Bekker, *Anecd.* iii.115.14. quae verba olim Aristophani
tribuebantur: Ar., frg. dub. 57 Demiańczuk, 913 a Edmonds
527 βαθύς: cf. Sud. s.v.: βαθύς·ἀντὶ τοῦ πονηρός· οὕτως Μένανδρος: frg. 830

505 ed. pr.: αιτουμενοσ P   507 οὔτ᾽ ὄξος οὔτ᾽ ὀρίγανον Choerob. loc. cit.   510 ναί
ed. pr.: νη P οὐδ᾽ Barigazzi et al.: ονθ᾽ P¹, ουκ ut vid. P²   514 γε om. Ael.   516 ἐφ᾽
ἑτέραν plerique: εφαιτεραν P   517 εντοπωι P, το s.v. addito   518-19 dist. Ha., Quincey,
Shipp   520 ed. pr.: εστιδεμοικαι P   521 ed. pr.: φυλασιτοισουσι P   523 κυνηγετῶν
Quincey: -ησων P τρισκακοδαίμων, ὡς Willis et al.: -δαιμονωσ P   527 βαθύς ed. pr.:
βαθυ P

ἐπὶ πλέον ἐπεκείμην φιλοπόνως, οὐ πολὺν
χρόνον· εἶτα καὶ μετεστρεφόμην τι, πηνίκα
ὁ γέρων πρόσεισι τὴν κόρην ἄγων ἅμα   530
σκοπούμενος. καὶ νὴ Δί᾽ ἐλαβόμην τότε
τῆς ὀσφύος λάθρᾳ τὸ πρῶτον. ὡς μακρὸν
ἦν παντελῶς δὲ τοῦτο, λορδοῦν ἠρχόμην,
ἀπεξυλούμην ἀτρέμα δ᾽. οὐδεὶς ἤρχετο·
ὁ δ᾽ ἥλιος κατέκα᾽, ἑώρα τ᾽ ἐμβλέπων   535
ὁ Γοργίας ὥσπερ τὰ κηλώνειά με
μόλις ἀνακύπτοντ᾽, εἶθ᾽ ὅλῳ τῷ σώματι
πάλιν κατακύπτοντ᾽. "οὐ δοκεῖ μοι νῦν", ἔφη,
"ἥξειν ἐκεῖνος, μειράκιον." "τί οὖν", ἐγὼ
εὐθύς, "πῶμεν;" "αὔριον τηρήσομεν   540
α[ὐ]τόν, τὸ δὲ νῦν ἐῶμεν." ὅ τε Δᾶος παρῆν
ἐπὶ] τὴν σκαπάνην διάδοχος. ἡ πρώτη μὲν οὖν
ἔφο]δος τοιαύτη γέγονεν. ἥκω δ᾽ ἐνθάδε,
διὰ] τί μὲν οὐκ ἔχω λέγειν, μὰ τοὺς θεούς,
ἕλκ]ει δέ μ᾽ αὐτόματον τὸ πρᾶγμ᾽ εἰς τὸν τόπον.   545

(Γε.)   τί τὸ κακ]όν; οἴει χεῖρας ἑξήκοντά με,
ἄνθρ]ωπ᾽, ἔχειν; τοὺς ἄνθρακάς σοι ζωπυρῶ,
ἔπο]μαι, πελανοὺς φέρω, κατατέμνω σπλάγχν᾽, ἅμα
μάττω, περιφέρω ταῦ[τα, τηρῶ το]υτονὶ
ὑπὸ τοῦ καπνοῦ τυφλὸς [γεγονώ]ς· τούτοις ὄνος   550
ἄγειν δοκῶ μοι τὴν ἑορτή[ν.

Σω.   π]αῖ Γέτα.
Γε.   ἐμὲ τίς;
(Σω.)   ἐγώ.
(Γε.)   σὺ δ᾽ εἶ τίς;
(Σω.)   οὐχ [ὁρᾷ]ς;
(Γε.)   ὁρῶ·
τρόφιμος.
(Σω.)   τί ποιεῖτ᾽ ἐνθάδ᾽; [εἰ]πέ μοι.

---

536 ὥσπερ τὰ κηλώνεια : cf. Liban., *Decl.* 27.25

528 ἐπὶ πλέον Ha.: εγαιπλειον, deinde επαικ- P   531 τότε Ha.: ποτε P   534 δ᾽εουδ᾽εισηρ-
χετο P   536 ed. pr.: τακηλωναειμε P   541 ἐῶμεν ed. pr.: εασομεν P   542 Lloyd-Jones
543 plerique   544 ed. pr.   545 Barrett, Lond.   546-7 suppl. plerique   547 εχων
P[1] ἄνθρακάς σοι ed. pr.: -κασοι P   548 ἔπο]μαι Turner, πελανοὺς Ha. (πελανὸν φύρω
Bingen): 4]μαι·πολυνωφερω· P   549 ταῦ[τα ed. pr., cetera Lloyd-Jones   550 suppl.
ed. pr. ὄνος Barrett, Ha. et al.: ολοσ P   551 ed. pr.   post γετα dicolon non habet P
552 ed. pr.: συδετισ P

(Γε.)   τί γάρ;
τεθύκαμεν ἄρτι καὶ παρασκευάζομεν
ἄριστον ὑμῖν.   555
(Σω.)   ἐνθάδ' ἡ μήτηρ;
(Γε.)   πάλαι.
(Σω.) ὁ πατὴρ δέ;
(Γε.)   προσδοκῶμεν· ἀ[λ]λὰ πάραγε σύ.
(Σω.) μικρὸν διαδραμών ‹γ' ›. ἐνθαδὶ τρ[ό]πον τινὰ
γέγον' οὐκ ἄκαιρος ἡ θυσία. παραλήψομαι
τὸ μειράκιον τουτί, παρελθὼν ὡς ἔχω,
καὶ τὸν θεράποντ' αὐτοῦ· κεκοινωνηκότες   560
ἱερῶν γὰρ εἰς τὰ λοιπὰ χρησιμώτεροι
ἡμῖν ἔσονται σύμμαχοι πρὸς τὸν γάμον.
(Γε.) τί φής; ἐπ' ἄριστόν τινας παραλαμβάνειν
μέλλεις πορευθείς; ἕνεκ' ἐμοῦ τρισχίλιοι
γένοισθ'. ἐγὼ μὲν γὰρ πάλαι τοῦτ' οἶδ', ὅτι   565
οὐ γεύσομ' οὐδενός· πόθεν γάρ; συνάγετε
πάντας. καλὸν γὰρ τεθύκαθ' ἱερεῖον, πάνυ
ἄξιον ἰδεῖν τιν'. ἀλλὰ γύναια ταῦτά μοι,
ἔχει γὰρ ἀστείως, μεταδοίη γ' ἄν τινος;
οὐδ' ἄν, μὰ τὴν Δήμητρ', ἁλὸς πικροῦ.   570
(Σω.)   καλῶς
ἔσται, Γέτα, τὸ τήμερον. μαντεύσομαι
τοῦτ' αὐτός, ὦ Πάν. ἀλλὰ μὴν προσεύξομαι
ἀεὶ παριών σοι καὶ φιλανθρωπεύσομαι.

ΣΙΜΙΧΗ
ὦ δυστυχής, ὦ δυστυχής, ὦ δυστυχής.
(Γε.) ἄπαγ' εἰς τὸ βάραθρον· τοῦ γέροντός τις γυνὴ   575
προελήλυθεν.
(Σιμ.)   τί πείσομαι; τὸν γὰρ κάδον
ἐκ τοῦ φρέατος βουλομένη τοῦ δεσπότου
εἴ πως δυναίμην ἐξελεῖν αὐτὴ λάθρᾳ,
ἀνῆψα τὴν δίκελλαν ἀσθενεῖ τινι
καλῳδίῳ σαπρῷ, διερράγη τέ μοι   580

---

574 De formula loquendi ὦ δυστυχής agit Choeroboscus, in Theodos. i.176 Hilgard,
qui aut hunc versum aut v. 919 citavisse videtur. Vide comm.

557 γ' add. Stoessl et al. dist. Thierfelder 558 θυσιαν P 561 χρησιμωτεραι P
568 versus suspectus 572 προσεύξομαι Winnington-Ingram et al.:-χομαι P 574 σιμικη
γραυσ in marg. sinist. P, solita orthographia; vid. comm. p. 126. 577 βουλομένη
plerique: -νου P 579 ανηψα P² (Lond.): ενηψα P¹

τοῦτ᾽ εὐθύς—

(Γε.)   ὀρθῶς.

(Σιμ.)   ἐνσέσεικά τ᾽ ἀθλία

καὶ τὴν δίκελλαν εἰς τὸ φρέαρ μετὰ τοῦ κάδου.

(Γε.) ῥῖψαι τὸ λοιπόν σοι σεαυτὴν ἔστ᾽ ἔτι.

(Σιμ.) ὁ δ᾽ ἀπὸ τύχης κόπρον τιν᾽ ἔνδον κειμένην

μέλλων μεταφέρειν περιτρέχων ταύτην πάλαι   585

ζητεῖ βοᾷ τε, καὶ ψοφεῖ γε τὴν θύραν.

Γε. φεῦγ᾽, ὦ πονηρά, φεῦγ᾽—ἀποκτενεῖ σε—γραῦ·

μᾶλλον δ᾽ ἀμύνου.

Κν.   ποῦστιν ἡ τοιχωρύχος;

(Σιμ.) ἄκουσα, δέσποτ᾽, ἐνέβαλον.

(Κν.)   βάδιζε δὴ

εἴσω.   590

(Σιμ.)   τί ποιεῖν δ᾽, εἰπέ μοι, μέλλεις;

(Κν.)   ἐγώ;

δήσας καθιμήσω σε.

(Σιμ.)   μὴ δῆτ᾽, ὦ τάλαν.

(Γε.) ταὐτῷ γε τούτῳ σχοινίῳ νὴ τοὺς θεοὺς

κράτιστον, εἴπερ ἐστὶ παντελῶς σαπρόν.

(Σιμ.) τὸν Δᾶον ἐκ τῶν γειτόνων ἐγὼ [καλ]ῶ.

(Κν.) Δᾶον καλεῖς, ἀνόσι᾽ ἀνειρηκυῖα [γραῦ;   595

οὐ σοὶ λέγω; θᾶττον βάδιζ᾽ εἴσω. [τάλας

ἐγώ, τάλας ἐρημίας τῆς νῦν, [τάλας

ὡς οὐδὲ εἷς. καταβήσομ᾽ εἰ[ς τὸ φρέαρ· τί γὰρ

ἔτ᾽ ἔστιν ἄλλ᾽;

(Γε.)   ἡμεῖς ποριοῦ[μεν ἁρπάγην

καὶ σχοινίον.   600

(Κν.)   κακὸν κάκ[ιστά σ᾽ οἱ θεοὶ

ἅπαντες ἀπολέσειαν εἴ τί μ[οι λαλεῖς.

(Γε.) καὶ μάλα δικ[αίως. εἰσ]πεπήδηκεν πάλιν.

ὦ τρισκακοδαί[μων οὗ]τος· οἷον ζῇ βίον.

τοῦτ᾽ ἔστιν εἰλικρ[ινῶς] γεωργὸς Ἀττικός·

---

581 *(Γε.)* ed. pr.: nec sub versu paragraphum habet P, nec post ὀρθῶς dicolon; post εὐθύς dicolon incertius   584 ὁ δ᾽ plerique: οιδ᾽ P   585 ed. pr.: μελλοντων P 592-3 Getae trib. Webster: post ταλαν 591 aut deest dicolon aut evanuit   593 ἐστὶ plerique: -τιν P   594 ed. pr.:]ω: (vix]ωι) P   595 ἀνειρηκυῖα plerique: ανηρεικυια P   γραῦ Treweek, Webster   596-7 Winnington-Ingram (597 τησ ante ερημιασ P: deleverat ed. pr.)   598 Ha.   599 ἔτ᾽ Ha.: ειτ᾽—αλλο: P suppl. Shipp et al.   600 Gallavotti, Page   601 Fraenkel   602 *(Γε.)* κ.μ.δ. plerique (601 απαντεσ) δικ[αίως ed. pr., εισ]- plerique   603-5 ed. pr.

πέτραις μαχόμ[εν]ος θύμα φερούσαις καὶ σφάκον   605
ὀδύνας ἐπίστα[τ', ο]ὐδὲν ἀγαθὸν λαμβάνων.
ἀλλ' ὁ τρόφιμος [γ]ὰρ οὑτοσὶ προσέρχεται
ἄγων μεθ' α[ὑτ]οῦ τοὺς ἐπικλήτους. ἐργάται
ἐκ τοῦ τόπου τ[ιν]ές εἰσιν· ὦ τῆς ἀτοπίας.
οὗτος τί τούτους δεῦρ' ἄγει νῦν; ἢ πόθεν   610
γεγονὼς συνήθης;

Σω.   οὐκ ἂν ἐπιτρέψαιμί σοι
ἄλλως ποῆσαι. "πάντ' ἔχομεν"· ὦ Ἡράκλεις,
τουτὶ δ' ἀπαρνεῖται τίς ἀνθρώπων ὅλως,
ἐλθεῖν ἐπ' ἄριστον συνήθους τεθυκότος;
εἰμὶ γάρ, ἀκριβῶς ἴσθι, σοὶ πάλαι φίλος,   615
πρὶν ἰδεῖν. λαβὼν ταῦτ' εἰσένεγκε, Δᾶε, σύ,
εἶθ' ἧκε.

Γο.   μηδαμῶς μόνην τὴν μητέρα
οἴκοι καταλείπων, ἀλλ' ἐκείνης ἐπιμελοῦ
ὧν ἂν δέηται· ταχὺ δὲ κἀγὼ παρέσομαι.

ΧΟΡΟΥ

Σιμ.   τίς ἂν βοηθήσειεν; ὦ τάλαιν' ἐγώ.   620
τίς ἂν βοηθήσειεν;

Σικ.   Ἡράκλεις ἄναξ.
ἐάσαθ' ἡμᾶς, πρὸς θεῶν καὶ δαιμόνων,
σπονδὰς ποῆσαι. λοιδορεῖσθε, τύπτετε,
οἰμώζετ'. ὦ τῆς οἰκίας τῆς ἐκτόπου.

(Σιμ.)   ὁ δεσπότης ἐν τῷ φρέατι.   625
Σικ.   πῶς;
(Σιμ.)   ὅπως;
ἵνα τὴν δίκελλαν ἐξέλοι καὶ τὸν κάδον
κατέβαινε κᾆτ' ὤλισθ' ἄνωθεν, ὥστε καὶ
πέπτωκεν.

(Σικ.)   οὐ γὰρ ὁ χαλεπὸς γέρων; σφόδρα
οὗτος καλά γ' ἐπόησε, νὴ τὸν οὐρανόν.
ὦ φιλτάτη γραῦ, νῦν σὸν ἔργον ἐστί.   630
(Σιμ.)   πῶς;

---

605 σκαφō P   606 ἐπίστα[τ' Turner et al.   607-9 ed. pr.   610 αγεινννν P   611 γονωσ P
612 dist. Ha. ((Γο.) πάντ' ἔχομεν. (Σω.) ὦ 'Η. Webster)   616 ειδειν P.   rest. Gallavotti:
ταυταδ'εισενεγκεδεσυ P   620 σιμικη in mg. sinist. P   624 dicolon post ἐκτόπου non
habet P   627 κατωλισθ' P   628 post γέρων dist. Sandbach et al.   σφοδραῖ P

(Σικ.) ὅλμον τιν' ἢ λίθον τιν' ἢ τοιοῦτό τι
       ἄνωθεν ἔνσεισον λαβοῦσα.
(Σιμ.)   φίλτατε,
       κατάβα.
(Σικ.)   Πόσειδον, ἵνα τὸ τοῦ λόγου πάθω,
       ἐν τῷ φρέατι κυνὶ μάχωμαι; μηδαμῶς.
(Σιμ.) ὦ Γοργία, ποῦ γῆς ποτ' εἶ;   635
(Γο.)   ποῦ γῆς ἐγώ;
       τί ἐστι, Σιμίχη;
(Σιμ.)   τί γάρ; πάλιν λέγω,
       ὁ δεσπότης ἐν τῷ φρέατι.
Γο.   Σώστρατε,
       ἔξελθε δεῦρ'. ἡγοῦ, βάδιζ' εἴσω ταχύ.
Σικ.   εἰσὶν θεοί, μὰ τὸν Διόνυσον· οὐ δίδως
       λεβήτιον θύουσιν, ἱερόσυλε σύ,   640
       ἀλλὰ φθονεῖς; ἔκπιθι τὸ φρέαρ εἰσπεσών,
       ἵ]να μηδ' ὕδατος ἔχῃς μεταδοῦναι μηδενί.
       νυ]νὶ μὲν αἱ Νύμφαι τετιμωρημέναι
       εἴσ'α]ὐτὸν ὑπὲρ ἐμοῦ δικαίως. οὐδὲ εἷς
       μά┐γειρον ἀδικήσας ἀθῷος διέφυγεν.   645
       ἱερο┐πρεπής πώς ἐστιν ἡμῶν ἡ τέχνη·
       ἀλλ' εἰ]ς τραπεζοποιὸν ὅτι βούλει πόει.
       ἀλλ' ἆ]ρα μὴ τέθνηκε; πάππαν φίλτατον
       κλαί]ουσ' ἀποιμώζει τις. οὐδὲν τοῦτό γε   649
         650-653

       †δηλονοθικαθ[
       οὕτως ἀνιμήσ[ουσιν· ὦ καλῆς θέας.   655
       τὴν ὄψιν αὐτοῦ τίν[α γὰρ ἐκ τούτων, τίνα
       οἴεσθ' ἔσεσθαι, πρὸς θεῶν, βεβ[ρεγ]μένου,

634 Cf. Zenob. iii.45 (Paroemiographi Graeci i.68 Leutsch-Schneidewin), Greg.
Cypr. (cod. Mosq.) iii.16 (ibid. ii.111) cum adnotationibus editorum.
644 (οὐδὲ εἷς . . .)-646 cit. Athenaeus 9.383 f: frg. 118

633 (Σικ.) ed. pr. καταβαϊποσιδον sine paragrapho P, item λογ ex του, ut vid. 634 post
μάχωμαι dicolon del. P² ut vid. 635 γῆς ποτ' εἶ; (Γο.) ed. pr.: τισποτει: (fort. ποτ'
ει:) P; paragr. sub versu ποῦ γῆς ἐγώ; ed. pr.: πουποτ'εμιγησεγω P 636 Σιμίχη
Marzullo et al.: σιμικη P, ut solet. 638 verba ἡγοῦ . . . ταχύ Gorgiae con-
tinuant Diano, Kassel, Ritchie, et al. (εξελθεδευρ':—ταχυ:) 639 διονυσονι P
641 εἰσπεσών Arnott: εκ- P 642-4 ed. pr. 645 ἀθῷος Ath.: αθωιωσ P 647 Webster
648 ἀλλ' Peek et al., ἆ]ρα ed. pr. παπαν P 649 κλαί]ουσ' (vel κλάουσ') Lond., Roberts
650-3 summo folio abscisso lacunam quattuor versuum indicavit ed. pr. 654 fort.
δῆλον ὅτι καθ[(ed. pr.) vel δηλονότι, κᾆθ[' 655-6 suppl. exempli gratia Ha. (656 τιν[
Barrett, sed vestigia incertiora) 657 εσεσθε P βεβ[ρεγ]μένου Barrett

τρέμοντος; ἀστείαν ἐγὼ μέν. ἡδέως
ἴδοιμ᾽ ἄν, ἄνδρες, νὴ τὸν Ἀπόλλω τουτονί.
ὑμεῖς δ᾽ ὑπὲρ τούτων, γυναῖκες, σπένδετε,   660
εὔχεσθε τὸν γέροντα σωθῆναι κακῶς,
ἀνάπηρον ὄντα, χωλόν· οὕτω γίνεται
ἀλυπότατος γὰρ τῷδε γείτων τ[ῷ] θεῷ
καὶ τοῖς ἀεὶ θύουσιν. ἐπιμελὲς δέ μοι
τοῦτ᾽ ἐστίν, ἄν τις ἆρα μισθώσητ᾽ ἐμέ.   665
(Σω.) ἄνδρες, μὰ τὴν Δήμητρα, μὰ τὸν Ἀσκληπιόν,
μὰ τοὺς θεούς, οὐπώποτ᾽ ἐν τὠμῷ βίῳ
εὐκαιρότερον ἄνθρωπον ἀποπεπνιγμένον
ἑόρακα μικροῦ· τῆς γλυκείας διατριβῆς.
ὁ Γοργίας γάρ, ὡς τάχιστ᾽ εἰσήλθομεν,   670
εὐθὺς κατεπήδησ᾽ εἰς τὸ φρέαρ, ἐγὼ δὲ καὶ
ἡ παῖς ἄνωθεν οὐδὲν ἐποοῦμεν· τί γὰρ
ἐμέλλομεν; πλὴν ἡ μὲν αὐτῆς τὰς τρίχας
ἔτιλλ᾽, ἔκλα᾽, ἔτυπτε τὸ στῆθος σφόδρα·
ἐγὼ δ᾽ ὁ χρυσοῦς, ὡσπερεί, νὴ τοὺς θεούς,   675
τροφὸς παρεστώς, ἐδεόμην γε μὴ ποεῖν
ταῦθ᾽, ἱκέτευον ἐμβλέπων ἀγάλματι
οὐ τῷ τυχόντι. τοῦ δὲ πεπληγμένου κάτω
ἔμελεν ἔλαττον ἤ τινός μοι, πλὴν ἀεὶ
ἕλκειν ἐκεῖνον, τοῦτ᾽ ἐνώχλει μοι σφόδρα·   680
μικροῦ γε νὴ Δί᾽ αὐτὸν εἰσαπολώλεκα.
τὸ σχοινίον γὰρ, ἐμβλέπων τῇ παρθένῳ,
ἀφῆκ᾽ ἴσως τρίς. ἀλλ᾽ ὁ Γοργίας Ἄτλας
ἦν οὐχ ὁ τυχών· ἀντεῖχε καὶ μόλις ποτὲ
ἀνενήνοχ᾽ αὐτόν. ὡς ἐκεῖνος ἐξέβη,   685
δεῦρ᾽ ἐξελήλυθ᾽. οὐ γὰρ ἐδυνάμην ἔ[τ]ι
κατέχειν ἐμαυτόν, ἀλλὰ μικροῦ [τὴν κόρην
ἐφίλουν προσιών· οὕτω σφόδρ᾽ ἐ[νθεαστικῶς
ἐρῶ. παρασκευάζομαι δὴ—τὴν θ[ύραν
ψοφοῦσιν. ὦ Ζεῦ σῶτερ, ἐκτόπου θ[έας.   690

677 ἀγάλματι: huc respicit fortasse grammaticus ap. Bekker, *Anecd.* 82.9ff (frg. 126);
cf. 159.

658 dist. Barrett 661 ευχεσθαι P 663 αλύποτατος plerique: αλλ'υποτατοσ P τ[ῷ]
θεῷ Ha., Roberts et al. 664 καιτουσ P 668 αποπενιγμενον P 669 εωρακα P 678 τϲῦ
ed. pr.: το P 679 ἔμελεν ed. pr.: εμελλον P 680 ενοχλι P 683 ϊσωτριϲ P
684 αντειχηκαμολισ P 687 ed. pr. 688 προσϊον P suppl. Turner et al. 689-90
ed. pr.

Γο.   βούλει τι, Κνήμων; εἰπέ μοι.
(Κν.)   τί [βούλομαι;
φαύλως ἔχω.
(Γο.)   θάρρει.
(Κν.)   τεθάρ[ρηκ'· οὐκέτι
ὑμῖν ἐνοχλήσει τὸν ἐπίλοιπον γὰ[ρ χρόνον
Κνήμων.
(Γο.)   τοιοῦτόν ἐστ' ἐρημία κ[ακόν.
ὁρᾷς; ἀκαρὴς νῦν παραπόλωλας ἀ₍ρτίως.   695
τηρούμενον δὴ τηλικοῦτον τῷ βίῳ
ἤδη καταζῆν δεῖ.
(Κν.)   χαλεπῶς μέν, οἶδ' ὅτι,
ἔχω. κάλεσον δέ, Γοργία, τὴν μητέρα.
(Γο.)   ὡς ἔνι μάλιστα. τὰ κακὰ παιδεύειν μόνα
ἐπίσταθ' ἡμᾶς, ὡς ἔοικε.   700
(Κν.)   θυγάτριον,
βούλει μ' ἀναστῆσαι λαβοῦσα;
Σω.   μακάριε
ἄνθρωπε.
(Κν.)   τί παρέστηκας ἐνταῦθ', ἄθλι₍ε;

.   .   .   .   703-7
                              ]εσοισ ἐβουλόμην
                    Μυρ]ρίνη καὶ Γοργία,
ε.[   ]ον προειλόμην   710
οὐχὶ σω.[. . . .]. . .[.].οὐδ' ἂν εἷς δύναιτό με
τοῦτο με[τα]πεῖσαί τις ὑμῶν, ἀλλὰ συγχωρήσετε.
ἐν δ' ἴσω[ς] ἥμαρτον, ὅστις τῶν ἁπάντων ᾠόμην

---

691 βούλει. . . μοι cit. Choerobosc., in Theodos. ii.330.6 Hilgard, idem iterum
ii.175.25: frg. 677
695 cit. Et. Gen. (Miller, Mél. p. 18)=Et. Magn. 45.23; eadem Et. Gud. p. 62.22
de Stefani: frg. 686 a
703-7 huc fortasse pertinet versus sine fabulae nomine citatus a Stobaeo, Ecl. 4.53.5:
ἡδύ γ' ἀποθνήσκειν ὅτῳ ζῆν μὴ πάρεσθ' ὡς βούλεται (frg. 647); confer Dyscoli verba apud
Liban., Decl. 26.30: εἰ οὖν δεῖ με λυπούμενον ζῆν, μὴ ζῆν μοι βέλτιον.

691 Szemerényi   692 τεθάρ[ρηκ' Barrett, οὐκέτι ed. pr.   693 γὰ[ρ Mette et al. χρόνον
ed. pr.   694 ἐστ' plerique: εστιν P suppl. ed. pr.   695 νῦν om. Etymologica
699 (Γο.) Gallavotti (698 paragr. sub versu et fort. ad fin. dicolon habet P) παιδευειν
P   700 (Κν.) Gallavotti: nec paragraphum nec dicolon habet P   702 fin. suppl.
ed. pr., sed lectio incertior   703-7 summo folio deperdito lacunam statuit ed. pr.
708 fort. μ]έσοις (ed. pr.)   709 ed. pr.   710 ει₍[, ερ[vel sim.   711 ουχ' ισω.[P:
fort. οὐχὶ σωθ[ῆναι (ed. pr.), δ]ίκ[α]ι[ο]ν (Quincey), sed vestigia imprimis incerta
713 ὅστις Winnington-Ingram: οτι P ωμην P

αὐτὸς αὐ[τά]ρκης τις εἶναι καὶ δεήσεσθ' οὐδενός.
νῦν δ' [ἰ]δὼν ὀξεῖαν οὖσαν ἄσκοπόν τε τοῦ βίου   715
τὴν τε[λ]ευτήν, εὗρον οὐκ εὖ τοῦτο γινώσκων τότε.
δεῖ γὰρ [εἶ]ναι καὶ παρεῖναι τὸν ἐπικουρήσοντ' ἀεί.
ἀλλὰ μὰ τὸν Ἥφαιστον—οὕτω σφόδρα διεφθάρμην ἐγὼ
τοὺς βίους ὁρῶν ἑκάστους, τοὺς λογισμοὺς ὃν τρόπον
πρὸς τὸ κερδαίνειν ἔχουσιν—οὐδέν' εὔνουν ᾠόμην   720
ἕτερον ἑτέρῳ τῶν ἁπάντων ἂν γενέσθαι· τοῦτο δὴ
ἐμποδὼν ἦν μοι. μόλις δὲ πεῖραν εἷς δέδωκε νῦν
Γοργίας, ἔργον ποήσας ἀνδρὸς εὐγενεστάτου.
τὸν γὰρ οὐκ ἐῶντά τ' αὐτὸν προσιέναι τῇ μῇ θύρᾳ,
οὐ βοηθήσαντά τ' αὐτῷ πώποτ' εἰς οὐδὲν μέρος,   725
οὐ προσειπόντ', οὐ λαλήσανθ' ἡδέως, σέσωχ' ὅμως·
ὅπερ ἂν ἄλλος, καὶ δικαίως, "οὐκ ἐᾷς με προσιέναι,
οὐ προσέρχομ'· οὐδὲν ἡμῖν γέγονας αὐτὸς χρήσιμος,
οὐδ' ἐγώ σοι νῦν." τί δ' ἐστί, μειράκιον; ἐάν ‹τ'› ἐγὼ
ἀποθάνω νῦν—οἴομαι δέ, καὶ κακῶς ἴσως ἔχω—   730
ἄν τε περιῶ που, ποοῦμαί σ' ὑόν, ἅ τ' ἔχων τυγχάνω
πάντα σαυτοῦ νόμισον εἶναι. τήνδε σοι παρεγγυῶ,
ἄνδρα ‹τ'› αὐτῇ πόρισον· εἰ γὰρ καὶ σφόδρ' ὑγιαίνοιμ' ἐγώ,
αὐτὸς οὐ δυνήσομ' εὑρεῖν· οὐ γὰρ ἀρέσει μοί ποτε
οὐδὲ εἷς. ἀλλ' ἐμὲ μέν, ‹ἂν ζῶ,› ζῆν ἐᾶθ' ὡς βούλομαι·   735
τἄλλα πρᾶττ' αὐτὸς παραλαβών· νοῦν ἔχεις σὺν τοῖς θεοῖς,
κηδεμὼν ‹τ'› εἶ τῆς ἀδελφῆς, εἰκότως· τοῦ κτήματος
ἐπιδίδου ‹σὺ› προῖκα τοὐμοῦ διαμετρήσας ἥμισυ,
τ[ὸ] δ' ἕτερον λαβὼν διοίκει κἀμὲ καὶ τὴν μητέρα.
ἀλλὰ κα]τάκλινόν με, θύγατερ· τῶν ἀναγκαίων λέγειν   740
πλείον'] οὐκ ἀνδρὸς νομίζω, πλὴν ἐκεῖνό γ' ἴσθι, παῖ·
περὶ ἐ]μοῦ γὰρ βούλομ' εἰπεῖν ὀλίγα σοι καὶ τοῦ τρόπου.
εἰ τοιοῦτ]οι πάντες ἦσαν, οὔτε τὰ δικαστήρια

---

714 δεησεθ' P   715 [ἰ]δων plerique ἄσκοπον ed. pr.: ασκαπτον P   716 ed. pr.: ουκευτο P   717 plerique: καπαρειναι P   718 ed. pr.: σφοδραεφθαρμην P   722 εἷς δέδωκε plerique: εισδ- P   724 ἐῶντά τ' Gallavotti, Ha., Page: εωντ' P τῇ μῇ Maas: τη P   725 βοηθήσαντά τ' ed. pr.: βοηθησαντ' P   727 Dale et al.: αλλωσ P   728 χρησμοσ P   729 post νῦν dist. Dale, Lloyd-Jones et al. μειράκιον; ἐάν τ' plerique: μειρακιον δ'εαν P   730 ισωσ P²: οιον P¹   731 που, ποοῦμαι Diano: τουμαι P τ'εχεον (vix χ'εχεον) P   732 σοι ed. pr.: συ P   733 τ' add. Ha. ὑγιαίνοιμ' Kraus, Lond.: υπαινειν P   735 ουδ'εισ P ἂν ζῶ add. Zuntz ('fort. ἦν ζῶ' Ha.)   736 τἄλλα πρᾶττ' ed. pr.: ταδ'αλλαπρατ' P   737 τ' add. ed. pr.   738 σὺ add. Lloyd-Jones πρυκα P   739 τ[.]δ' potius quam τ[.]θ' P (Turner)   740 ἀλλὰ Fraenkel τῶν ἀναγκαίων Ha. (Jean Martin): τωνδ'αν- P   741 suppl. Kraus et al. (πλείον ed. pr.) ἐκεῖνό γ'ἴσθι ed. pr.: εκεινοσιθι P   742-3 suppl. Shipp et al.   742 ὀλίγα σοι ed. pr.: σοιολιγα P

    ἦν ἄν, ο]ὕθ' αὑτοὺς ἀπῆγον εἰς τὰ δεσμωτήρια,

    οὔτε π]όλεμος ἦν, ἔχων δ' ἂν μέτρι' ἕκαστος ἠγάπα. 745

    ἀ[λ]λ' ἴσως ταῦτ' ἔστ' ἀρεστὰ μᾶλλον· οὕτω πράττετε.

    ἐκποδὼν ὑμῖν ⟨ὁ⟩ χαλεπὸς δύσκολός τ' ἔσται γέρων.

Γο. ἀλλὰ δέχομαι ταῦτα πάντα. δεῖ δὲ μετὰ σοῦ νυμφίον

    ὡς τάχισθ' εὑρεῖν ⟨τιν'⟩ ἡμᾶς τῇ κόρῃ, σοὶ συνδοκοῦν.

Κν. οὗτος, εἴρηχ' ὅσ' ἐφρόνουν σοι· μὴ 'νόχλει, πρὸς τῶν θεῶν. 750

Γο. βούλεται γὰρ ἐντυχεῖν σοι—

(Κν.)   μηδαμῶς, πρὸς τῶν θεῶν.

(Γο.) τὴν κόρην αἰτῶν τις ⟨οὗτος⟩—

(Κν.)   οὐδὲ ἓν ἔτι μοι μέλει.

(Γο.) ὅ ⟨σε⟩ συνεκσώσας.

(Κν.)   ὁ ποῖος;

(Γο.)   οὑτοσί· πρόελθε σύ.

(Κν.) ἐπικέκαυται μέν· γεωργός ἐστι;

(Σω.)   καὶ μάλ', ὦ πάτερ.

(Κν.) οὐ τρυφῶν οὐδ' οἷος ἀργὸς περιπατεῖν τὴν ἡμέραν; 755

    ......] ... ενοσ .. [

    † ...] . δίδου· πόει τοῦ[τ'

    εἰσκ]υκλεῖτ' εἴσω με.

(Γο.)   καὶ . [

    ἐπιμ]ελοῦ τούτου. τὸ λο[ιπόν ἐστιν ἡμῖν ἐγγυᾶν

    τὴν] ἀδελφήν. 760

(Σω.)   ἐπανα[9-11] ... [

    οὐ[δ]ὲν ὁ πατὴρ ἀντερεῖ [μοι.

(Γο.)   τοιγαρ]οῦν ἔγωγέ σ[ο]ι

    ἐγγυῶ, δίδωμι, πάντων [τὴν κόρη]ν ἐναντίον

---

744 ed. pr.:]υτ' αυτοσ P, ανηγον ut vid. P¹ 745 ed. pr.: δ' ante ην del. P² 746 post
μᾶλλον dist. Diano, Sydn. et al. 747 ed. pr. 748 [Γοργι]' in marg. sinist. P (Turner)
749 ed. pr. 750 θεων[, 751 θεων sine dicolo P; personarum notas huc pertinere
agnovit Stoessl (Κν. μηδαμῶς ... Γο. τὴν κόρην ed. pr. et al.) 752 οὗτος add. Ha.
οὐδὲ ἓν ed. pr.: ουδεν P 753 σε add. et οὑτοσί ... σύ totum Gorgiae dedit ed. pr.
(ουτοσϊ: προελθεσυ:); hinc usque ad v. 761 partium distributio incertior 754 (Κν.)
ἐπικέκαυται ... ed. pr., (Σω.) καὶ ... πάτερ Ha. (επικ— — εστι:—πατερ:) 755 (Κν.)
Lloyd-Jones et al.: ima margine folii ad init. versus abscissa nulla exstant paragraphi
vestigia; ad fin. ημεραν[756] . γένος ψ.[, vel fort.].ειεν ὃς τα[,] ... ἑνὸς τα[P:
alii alia legunt. 757 fort. προ]σδίδου πόει ⟨τε⟩ του[τ (Barrett); sed ab initio versus
aliquid deesse potest, sicut infra v. 763 758 εἰσκ]υκλεῖτ' plerique (Γο.) ed. pr. (με:)
fort. καὶ δ[ὴ (Barrett) 759 ἐπιμ]ελοῦ, τὸ λο[ιπόν ed. pr.; cetera ex. gr. suppl. Diano;
Gorgiae contin. Ha. (τουτου:) 760 τὴν] ed. pr. (Σω.) Lond. et al. (αδελφην:)
761 μοι ed. pr. (Γο.) Lond. et al. (ου[δ]εν) τοιγαρ]οῦν Quincey 762 Quincey

<ὥστ᾽> ἐνεγκεῖν ὅσα δίκαιόν ἐστι πλ[ή]ρη, Σώστρατε.
οὐ πεπλασμένῳ γὰρ ἤθει πρὸς τὸ πρᾶγμ᾽ ἐλήλυθ[ας,
ἀλλ᾽ ἁπλῶς, καὶ πάντα ποιεῖν ἠξίωσας τοῦ γάμου   765
ἕνεκα· τρυφερὸς ὢν δίκελλαν ἔλαβες, ἔσκαψας, πονε[ῖν
ἠθέλησας. ἐν δὲ τούτῳ τῷ μέρει μάλιστ᾽ ἀνὴρ
δείκνυτ᾽, ἐξισοῦν ἑαυτὸν ὅστις ὑπομένει τινὶ
εὐπορῶν πένητι· καὶ γὰρ μεταβολὰς οὗτος τύχ[ης
ἐγκρατῶς οἴσει. δέδωκας πεῖραν ἱκανὴν τοῦ τρόπ[ου·   770
διαμένοις μόνον τοιοῦτος.
(Σω.)   πολὺ μὲν οὖν κρείττω[ν ἔτι.
ἀλλ᾽ ἐπαινεῖν αὐτόν ἐστι φορτικόν <τι> πρᾶγμ᾽ ἴσως.
εἰς καλὸν δ᾽ ὁρῶ παρόντα τὸν πατέρα.
(Γο.)   Καλλιππίδ[ης
ἐστὶ σοῦ πατήρ;
(Σω.)   πάνυ μὲν οὖν.
(Γο.)   νὴ Δία, πλούσιός γ[᾽ ἀνήρ,
<καὶ> δικαίως <γ᾽, ὢν> γεωργὸς ἄμαχος.   775

ΚΑΛΛΙΠΠΙΔΗΣ
                                    ἀπολέλειμμ᾽ ἴσως.
καταβεβρωκότες γὰρ ἤδη τὸ πρόβατον φροῦδοι πάλαι
εἰσὶν εἰς ἀγρόν.
Γο.   Πόσειδον, ὀξυπείνως πως ἔχει.
αὐτίκ᾽ αὐτῷ ταῦτ᾽ ἐροῦμεν;
(Σω.)   πρῶτον ἀριστησάτω·
πραότερος ἔσται.
(Καλλ.)   τί τοῦτο, Σώστρατ᾽; ἠριστήκατε;
(Σω.) ἀλλὰ καὶ σοὶ παραλέλειπται· πάραγε.   780
(Καλλ.)   τοῦτο δὴ ποῶ.
Γο.   εἰσιὼν οὕτω λαλήσεις, εἴ τι βούλει, τῷ πατρὶ
κατὰ μόνας.
(Σω.)   ἔνδον περιμενεῖς, οὐ γάρ;

778f Cf. Aelian., *Ep. Rust.* 15 καὶ ἐμπιὼν καὶ κοινωνήσας σπονδῶν ἔσῃ τι καὶ πραότερος.

763 versus vixdum sanatus. ὥστ᾽ add. Ha. ὅσα ed. pr.: οσ P πλ[ή]ρη Barigazzi et al.,
sed lectio imprimis dubia; potius fortasse πι[..].η legendum   766 dist. plerique:
τρυφεροσων:—ελαβεσ᾽ εσκαψασ᾽ P   768 ed. pr.: εξισουν (ν ex σ) αιαυτονοτισ P   769 ed.
pr.: μεταβολησουτοστηστυχ[P   771 ἔτι Bingen, Kassel   772 ἐστι Lond.: -τιν P τι
add. ed. pr.   773 ed. pr.: τ᾽ορων, καλλιπιδ[P   774 suppl. plerique post πατήρ dicolon non habet P   775 init. rest. ed. pr.: δικαιοσγεωργοσ P ἀπολέλειμμ᾽ plerique:
απολειμ᾽ P   777 ed. pr.:καταβεβρωκοτεδητοπροβατον P   779 πρατεροσ P; post ἠριστήκατε
dicolon non habet   780 παρελ- ut vid. P¹ ποῶ ed. pr.: ποησω P   781 οὕτω Fraenkel,
λαλήσεις Ha.: αυτωλαλειειτιβουλεισ P

(Γο.)   οὐκ ἐξέρχομ[αι
    ἔνδοθεν.
(Σω.)   μικρὸν διαλιπὼν παρακαλῶ τοίνυν ⟨σ'⟩ ἐγώ.

ΧΟΡΟΥ

Σω.   οὐχ ὡς ἐβουλόμην ἅπαντά μοι, πάτερ,
       οὐδ' ὡς προσεδόκων γίνεται παρὰ σοῦ.   785
(Καλλ.)   τί δὲ
       οὐ συγκεχώρηχ'; ἧς ἐρᾷς σε λαμβάνειν
       καὶ βούλομαι καί φημι δεῖν.
(Σω.)   οὔ μοι δοκεῖς.
(Καλλ.) νὴ τοὺς θεοὺς ἔγωγε, γινώσκων ὅ[τι
       νέῳ γάμος βέβαιος οὗτος γίνετ[αι,
       ἐὰν δι' ἔρωτα τοῦτο συμπεισθῇ ποε[ῖν.   790
(Σω.)   ἔπειτ' ἐγὼ μὲν τὴν ἀδελφὴν λήψ[ομαι
       τὴν τοῦ νεανίσκου, νομίζων ἄ[ξιον
       ἡμῶν ἐκεῖνον; πῶς δὲ τοῦτο νῦ[ν σὺ φῄς,
       οὐκ ἀντιδώσειν τὴν ἐμήν;
(Καλλ.)   αἰσχρὸν λέγει[ς.
       νύμφην γὰρ ἅμα καὶ νυμφίον πτωχοὺς λαβεῖν   795
       οὐ βούλομ', ἱκανὸν δ' ἐστὶν ἡμῖν θάτερον.
(Σω.)   περὶ χρημάτων λαλεῖς, ἀβεβαίου πράγματος.
       εἰ μὲν γὰρ οἶσθα ταῦτα παραμενοῦντά σοι
       εἰς πάντα τὸν χρόνον, φύλαττε, μηδενὶ
       τούτου μεταδιδούς· ὧν δὲ μὴ σὺ κύριος   800
       εἶ, μηδὲ σαυτοῦ, τῆς τύχης δὲ πάντ' ἔχεις,
       μή τι φθονοίης, ὦ πάτερ, τούτων τινί.
       αὕτη γὰρ ἄλλῳ, τυχὸν ἀναξίῳ τινί,
       ἀφελομένη σοῦ ταῦτα προσθήσει πάλιν.
       διόπερ ἐγώ σέ φημι δεῖν⌋ ὅσον χρόνον   805

797-812 cit. Stobaeus, *Ecl.* 3.16.14: frg. 116

782 ed. pr.: εξερχει[vel εξερχετ[P   783 ed. pr.   785-6 προσεδοκουν P¹ dist. Ha.
788 εγωγ'εγιγινωσκων (vel -ετιγιν-) P¹; εγι del. et τοῦτο s.v. add. P²   ὅ[τι plerique:
ο[, α[, ε[P   790 τουτοσσυν- P   ποεῖν ed. pr.: πονε[P, ν e corr. ut vid.   791-3 suppl.
ed. pr.   796 ed. pr.: εστινεατερον:ημιν P¹; θατερον P², θ s.v. addito   798 οισθασ P¹
παραμενοῦντα Stob.: περι- P   800 τουτου P: ἄλλῳ Stob. ὡνδεμησυ P: αὐτὸς ὢν δὲ Stob.
(ὧν δὲ Mᵈ)   801 εἰ δὲ μὴ σεαυτοῦ Stob. (sic S MᵈA¹: οὐ superascr. A²: εἰ μὴ δὲ
σαυτοῦ Meineke)   802 μή τι Barigazzi, Page et al.: μητε P: τί ἂν Stob.   803 αὕτη P:
αὐτὴ Stob. (correxerat Blaydes)   804 παρελομένη Stob. ταυταπροσθησει P (Gallavotti),
vix cum Stobaeo πάντα προσθήσει; sed lacero folio lectio incertior

εἶ κύριος, χρῆσθαί σε γͺενναίως, πάτερ,
αὐτόν, ἐπικουρεῖνͺ πᾶσιν, εὐπόρους ͺποεῖν
ὡͺς ἂν δύνῃ πλείστουͺς διὰ σαυτοῦ. τοῦτο γͺὰρ
ἀθάνατον ͺἐστι,ͺ κἄν ποτε πταίσας τύχῃͺς,
ἐκεῖθεν ἔσται τͺαὐτὸ τοͺῦτό σοι πάλιν.   810
πολλῷ δὲ κρεῖττόν ἐστιν ἐμφανὴς φίλος
ἢ πλοῦτος ἀφανής, ὃν σὺ κατορύξας ἔχεις.

Καλλ.   οἶσθ' οἷόν ἐστι, Σώστραθ'· ἃ συνελεξάμην
οὐ συγκατορύξω ταῦτ' ἐμαυτῷ· πῶς γὰρ ἄν;
σὰ δ' ἐστί. βούλει περιποήσασθαί τινα   815
φίλον; δοκιμάσας πρᾶττε τοῦτ' ἀγαθῇ τύχῃ.
τί μοι λέγεις γνώμας; βάδιζε, ⟨νοῦν ἔχεις·⟩
δίδου, μεταδίδου. συμπέπεισμαι πάντα σοι.

(Σω.)   ἑκών;
(Καλλ.)   ἑκών, εὖ ἴσθι· μηδὲν τοῦτό σε
ταραττέτω.   820

(Σω.)   τὸν Γοργίαν τοίνυν καλῶ.
Γο.   ἐπακήκο' ὑμῶν ἐξιὼν πρὸς τῇ θύρᾳ
ἅπαντας οὓς εἰρήκατ' ἐξ ἀρχῆς λόγους.
τί οὖν; ἐγώ ⟨σε⟩, Σώστρατ', εἶναι μὲν φίλον
ὑπολαμβάνω σπουδαῖον ἀγαπῶ τ' ἐκτόπως.
μείζω δ' ἐμαυτοῦ πράγματ' οὔτε βούλομαι   825
οὔτ' ἂν δυναίμην, μὰ Δία, βουληθεὶς φέρειν.

(Σω.)   οὐκ οἶδ' ὅ τι λέγεις.
(Γο.)   τὴν ἀδελφὴν τὴν ἐμὴν
δίδωμί σοι γυναῖκα· τὴν δὲ σὴν λαβεῖν
καλῶς ἔχει μοι.

(Σω.)   πῶς καλῶς;
(Γο.)   οὐχ ἡδύ μοι
εἶναι τρυφαίνειν ἀλλοτρίοις πόνοις δοκεῖ,   830
συλλεξάμενον δ' αὐτόν.

(Σω.)   φλυαρεῖς, Γοργία.
οὐκ ἄξιον κρίνεις σεαυτὸν τοῦ γάμου;

(Γο.)   ἐμαυτὸν εἶναι κέκρικ' ἐκείνης ἄξιον,

---

806 πατηρ P 809 αθανατον [5-6] P (scil. [εστιν]) πταίσας τύχης Stob.: incertum est
an eadem habuerit P (πτοιμ.τυχη[vel sim. legunt plerique) 811 πολλω P: πολλῶν
Stob. (correxerat Gesner) κρειττον Stob.: κριττων P, ει supra ι addito. 813 οἷον
Mette: οιοσ P 814 ed. pr.: ταυταυτ' P 817 rest. ex. gr. Ha.: πορι ζεπορι ζβαδιζε P,
πορι ζ ante βαδι ζε deleto 819 (Σω.) ἑκών; ed. pr.: διδου—σοι | εκων: εκωνευ- P
822 απαντασουειρ- P 823 ed. pr. 830 δοκεῖ plerique: δοκω P

MENANΔPOY

λαβεῖν δὲ πολλὰ μίκρ' ἔχοντ' οὐκ ἄξιον.

Καλλ. νὴ τὸν Δία τὸν μέγιστον, εὐγενῶς γέ πως   835
π[ερίεργ]ος εἶ.

(Γο.)   πῶς;

(Καλλ.)   οὐκ ἔχων βούλει δοκεῖν
ἔχειν.] ἐπειδὴ συμπεπεισμένον μ' ὁρᾷς—
αὐτῷ δ]ὲ τούτῳ μ' ἀναπέπεικας διπλασίως—
μὴ φεῦγ' <ἔτ'>] ὧν πένης <τις> ἀπόπληκτός θ' ἅμα
ὅσ' ὁ γάμο]ς ὑποδείκνυσιν εἰς σωτηρίαν.   840

(Γο.) νικᾷς· τ]ὸ λοιπόν ἐστιν ἡμῖν ἐγγυᾶν.

(Καλλ.) ἀλλ' ἐγγυῶ παίδων ἐπ' ἀρότῳ γνησίων
τὴν θυγατέρ' ἤδη, μειράκιόν, σοι, προῖκά τε
δίδωμ' ἐπ' αὐτῇ τρία τάλαντ'.

(Γο.)   ἐγὼ δέ γε
ἔχω τάλαντον προῖκα τῆς ἑτέρας.   845

(Καλλ.)   ἔχεις
μηδ' αὖ σὺ λίαν;

(Γο.)   ἀλλ' ἔχω.

(Καλλ.)   τὸ δὲ χωρίον
κέκτησ' ὅλον σύ, Γοργία. τὴν μητέρα
ἤδη σὺ δεῦρο τήν τ' ἀδελφὴν μετάγαγε
πρὸς τὰς γυναῖκας τὰς παρ' ἡμῖν.

(Γο.)   ἀλλὰ χρή.

(Σω.) τὴν νύκτα [ταύτην ἐνθάδ' εὐφρανούμεθα   850
πάντες μέγ[οντες· αὔριον δὲ το]ὺς γάμους
ποήσομεν. κ[αὶ τὸν] γέροντα, [Γορ]γία,
κομίσατε δε[ῦ]ρ'· ἕξει τὰ δ[έον]τ' ἐνταῦθ' ἴσω[ς
μ]ᾶλλον παρ' ἡμῖν.

(Γο.)   οὐκ ἐθ[ελ]ήσει, Σώστρατε.

(Σω.) σύμπεισον αὐτόν.   855

(Γο.)   ἂν δύνωμ[αι].

(Σω.)   δεῖ πότον

---

849 ἀλλὰ χρὴ: cf. Hesych. s.v. (I, p. 110 Latte): frg. 820

834 πολλὰ μίκρ' ed. pr.: μικραπολλα P   836-41 supplementa incertiora   836 Gallavotti
837 ἔχειν ed. pr.: 5-6]επειδη P   838-40 sic ex. gr. Webster, nisi quod 838 αὐτῷ suppl.
Post 838 τουτω P   839 5-6]ων P   841 νικᾷς ex. gr. Lloyd-Jones, τ]ὸ λοιπὸν ed.
pr. ἐστιν ἡμῖν plerique: ημινεστιν P (—σωτηριαν:—εγγυαν:)   846 (Καλλ.) ed. pr.: post
ἔχω dicolon non habet P   850-1 exempli gratia suppleti   850 ταύτην ἐνθάδ' ed. pr.,
εὐφρανούμεθα Ha.   851-5 ed. pr.   854 εθ[ελ]ησεισ P

112

ἡμῶν γενέσθαι, παππία, νυνὶ [κ]αλόν,
καὶ τῶν γυναικῶν παννυχίδα.

Καλλ.)   τοὐναντίον
πίοντ᾽ ἐκεῖναι, παννυχιοῦμεν, οἶδ᾽ ὅτι,
ἡμεῖς. παράγων δ᾽ ὑμῖν ἑτοιμάσω τι τῶν
προὔργου.   860

Σω.   πόει τοῦτ᾽. οὐδενὸς χρὴ πράγματος
τὸν εὖ φρονοῦνθ᾽ ὅλως ἀπογνῶναί ποτε.
ἁλωτὰ γίνετ᾽ ἐπιμελείᾳ καὶ πόνῳ
ἅπαντ᾽· ἐγὼ τούτου παράδειγμα νῦν φέρω.
ἐν ἡμέρᾳ μιᾷ κατείργασμαι γάμον
⟨ὃν⟩ οὐδ᾽ ἂν εἷς ποτ᾽ ᾤετ᾽ ἀνθρώπων ὅλως. 865

Γο. προάγετε δὴ θᾶττόν ποθ᾽ ὑμεῖς.

Σω.   δεῦτε δή·
μῆτερ, δέχου ταύτας. ὁ Κνήμων δ᾽ οὐδέπω;

Γο.) ὃς ἱκέτευεν ἐξαγαγεῖν τὴν γραῦν ἔτι,
ἵν᾽ ᾖ τελέως μόνος καθ᾽ αὑτόν;

Σω.)   ὦ τρόπου
ἀμάχου.   870

Γο.)   τοιοῦτος.

Σω.)   ἀλλὰ πολλὰ χαιρέτω.
ἡμεῖς δ᾽ ἴωμεν.

Γο.)   Σώστραθ᾽, ὑπεραισχύνομαι
γυναιξὶν ἐν ταὐτῷ—

Σω.)   τίς ὁ λῆρος; οὐ πρόει;
οἰκεῖα ταῦτ᾽ ἤδη νομίζειν πάντα δεῖ.

Σιμ. ἄπειμι, νὴ τὴν Ἄρτεμιν, κἀγώ. μόνος
ἐνταῦθα κατακείσει· τάλας σὺ τοῦ τρόπου. 875
πρὸς τὸν θεόν σε βουλομένων [τούτων ἄγειν
ἀντεῖπας. ἔσται μέγα κακὸν πάλιν [τί σοι,
νὴ τὼ θεώ, ⟨καὶ⟩ μεῖζον ἢ νῦν. εὖ πά[θοις.

Γε. ἐγὼ προσελθὼν ὄψομαι δεῦρ᾽ [ὡς ἔχω.
       α ὐ λ ε ῖ

860-3 οὐδενὸς . . . ἅπαντα cit. Stobaeus, Ecl. 3.29.45-46: frg. 119

856 παπια P νυνὶ [κ]αλόν plerique 860 χρὴ πράγματος Stob.: χρηματοσ P 861 φρονοῦνθ᾽
P: ποιοῦνθ᾽ Stob., ubi πονοῦνθ᾽ coni. Grotius 863 τούτου ed. pr.: τουτο P 865 ed.
pr. 866 προαγεδη P 867 μητερα P 870 (Γο.) τοιοῦτος. (Σω.) ἀλλὰ . . . plerique
(αμαχου: τοιουτοσαλλα) 872 γυναιξι P 873 οἰκεῖα ed. pr.: ουκ᾽εια P 874 σιμικρ᾽ in
marg. sinist. P 875 εντ αυτα et fort. ταλατρυτου P 876 ed. pr. 877 μεγακον P suppl.
Page, Webster 878 καὶ add. Blake, Lloyd-Jones suppl. ed. pr. 879 suppl. Ha.
(ὡς ἔχει ed. pr.)

τί μοι προσαυλεῖς, ἄθλι' οὗτος; οὐδέπω σχολή [μοι.   880
πρὸς τὸν κακῶς ἔχοντα πέμπουσ' ἐνθαδί μ'· ἐπίσ[χες.

Σιμ.   καὶ παρακαθήσθω γ' εἰσιὼν αὐτῷ τις ἄλλος ὑμῶ[ν.
ἐγὼ δ' ἀποστέλλουσα τροφίμην βούλομαι λαλῆ[σαι
ταύτῃ, προσειπεῖν, ἀσπάσασθαι.

(Γε.)   νοῦν ἔχεις· βάδ[ιζε.
τοῦτον δὲ θεραπεύσω τέως ἐγώ. πάλαι δ[έδοκται   885
τ[οῦτο]ν λαβε[ῖν] τὸν καιρόν, ἀλλὰ διαπον[εῖν τι χρὴ νῦν.
              ]εσει καὶ τῶν β[
ο]ὔπω δυνησ[   ]ι. μάγειρε
Σίκων, πρόελ[θε δ]ευρό μ[ο]ι [σὺ θᾶττ]ον. ὦ Πόσειδον·
οἵαν ἔχειν οἶμ[αι δι]ατριβήν.   890

(Σικ.)   σύ μ[ε κα]λεῖς;
(Γε.)   ἔγωγε.
τιμωρίαν [βούλ]ει λαβεῖν ὧν ἀρτίως ἔπασχες;

(Σικ.) ἐγὼ δ' ἔπασχ[ον ἀ]ρτίως; οὐ λαικάσει φλυαρῶν;
(Γε.)   ὁ δύσκολος [γέρ]ων καθεύδει μόνος.
(Σικ.)   ἔχει δὲ <δὴ> πῶς;
(Γε.)   οὐ παντάπ[ασ]ιν ἀθλίως.
(Σικ.)   οὐκ ἂν δύναιτό γ' ἡμᾶς
τύπτειν ἀναστάς;   895
(Γε.)   οὐδ' ἀναστῆναι <γ' ἄν>, ὡς ἐγῷμαι.
(Σικ.) ὡς ἡδὺ πρᾶγμά μοι λέγεις. αἰτήσομ' εἰσιών τι·
ἔξω γὰρ ἔσται τῶν φρενῶν.

(Γε.)   <τί δ' ἄν,> τὸ δεῖνα, πρῶτον
ἔξω προελκύσωμεν αὐτόν, εἶτα θέντες αὐτοῦ
κόπτωμεν οὕτω τὰς θύρας, αἰτῶμεν, ἐπιφλέγωμεν;
ἔσται τις ἡδονή, λέγω.   900
(Σικ.)   τὸν Γοργίαν δέδοικα
μὴ καταλαβὼν ἡμᾶς καθαίρῃ.

Γε.   θόρυβός ἐστιν ἔνδον,
πίνουσιν· οὐκ αἰσθήσετ' οὐδείς. τὸ δ' ὅλον ἐστὶν ἡμῖν
ἄνθρωπος ἡμερωτέος· κηδεύομεν γὰρ αὐτῷ,

880-1 plerique   882-4 ed. pr.   882 σιμικ / P   883 βουλομαλαλη[P   885 Thierfelder   886 τ[οῦτο]ν λαβε[ῖν plerique διαπον[εῖν Barigazzi, cetera Ha.   889 ed. pr. 890 οἶμ[αι Barigazzi et al.   891-2 ed. pr.   893 [γέρ]ων Barrett, Lond. et al. δὴ add. ed. pr.   894-7 partium distributio incerta   894 (Γε.) ed. pr.   (893 πωσ[P) 895 γ'ἄν add. Barigazzi, Ha.   896 ην P¹   897 ἔξω ... τῶν φ. Siconi contin. ed. pr. (896 ωσ—τι:) τί δ'ἄν add. Ha. τοδινα P   898 προελκύσωμεν Thierfelder: προσ- P αὐτοῦ ed. pr.: αυτον P   900 εσταιστισ P   902 ed. pr.: πινουσ', ἐστ' P   903 Kassel: ημερωτεροσ P

οἰκεῖος ἡμῖν γίνετ'· εἰ δ' ἔσται τοιοῦτος ἀεί,
ἔργον ὑπενεγκεῖν.   905

(Σικ.)   πῶς γὰρ οὔ;
(Γε.)   λαθεῖν μόνον ἐπιθύμει
αὐτὸν φέρων δεῦρ' εἰς τὸ πρόσθεν· πρόαγε δὴ σύ.
(Σικ.)   μικρὸν
πρόσμεινον, ἱκετεύω σε· μή με καταλιπὼν ἀπέλθῃς.
καὶ μὴ ψόφει, πρὸς τῶν θεῶν.
(Γε.)   ἀλλ' οὐ ψοφῶ, μὰ τὴν Γῆν.
εἰς δεξιάν.
(Σικ.)   ἰδού.
(Γε.)   θὲς αὐτοῦ. νῦν ὁ καιρός· εἶέν.
ἐγὼ προάξω πρότερος—ἤν—καὶ τὸν ῥυθμὸν σὺ τήρει.   910
⟨παῖ⟩, παιδίον, παῖδες ⟨καλῶ⟩, παῖ, παῖδες.
(Κν.)   οἴχομ', οἴμοι.
(Γε.)   παῖδες καλῶ, παῖ, παιδίον, ⟨παῖ,⟩ παῖδες.
(Κν.)   οἴχομ', οἴμοι.
(Γε.)   τίς οὗτος; ἐντεῦθέν τις εἶ;
(Κν.)   δηλονότι. σὺ δὲ τί βούλει;
(Γε.)   λέβητας αἰτοῦμαι παρ' ὑμῶν καὶ σκάφας.
(Κν.)   τίς ἄν με
στήσειεν ὀρθόν;   915
(Γε.)   ἔστιν ὑμῖν, ἔστιν ὡς ἀληθῶς.
καὶ τρίποδας ἑπτὰ καὶ τραπέζας δώδεκ'· ἀλλά, παῖδες,
τοῖς ἔνδον εἰσαγγείλατε· σπεύδω γάρ.
(Κν.)   οὐδὲν ἔστιν.
(Γε.)   οὐκ ἔστιν;
(Κν.)   ⟨οὐκ⟩ ἀκήκοας μυριάκις;
(Γε.)   ἀποτρέχω δή.
Κν.   ὦ δυστυχὴς ἐγώ· τίνα τρόπον ἐνθαδὶ προήχθην;

---

919 ὦ δυστυχὴς: vid. ad v. 574

904 ειδ'εισται P ἀεί Page: ααιει ut vid. P   905 ἐπιθύμει ed. pr.: επιθυμου (vix -ει) P 906 δὴ σύ ed. pr.: συδη P   (Σικ.) μικρόν Diano, Merkelbach: αυτον—μικρον: P   909 post ἰδού (ειδου) dicolon non habet P. hinc usque ad 958 partium distributio saepius incerta est   910 ην ed. pr.: μη P   ευτηρει P   911 παῖ, καλῶ add. ed. pr.   παῖ, παῖδες Barigazzi, Lond.: παιπαιδιον P   (Κν.) ed. pr.: nec paragraphum nec dicola habet P   912 ed. pr.: καλοι P, ubi desunt et paragraphus et dicola   913 (Γε.) Merkelbach, Sandbach (912, vid. supra; 913 τισ—ει: sed post βουλει dicolon nullum) δηλονότι ed. pr.: λονοτι P, antecedente duarum litterarum spatio (cf. 931)   914 σκάφας Ha.: σφακον P   917 εἰσαγγείλατε Lond., Page: αγγειλατε P   918 οὐκ add. ed. pr. μυριακις P   919 προήχθην ed. pr.: προϊχθην P

τίς μ' εἰ]ς τὸ πρόσθε κατατέθηκεν;   920

(Σικ.)   ἄπαγε δὴ σύ. καὶ δή·
παῖ, παι]δίον, γυναῖκες, ἄνδρες, παῖ θυρωρέ.

(Κν.)   μαίνει,
ἄνθρ]ωπε; τὴν θύραν κατάξεις.

(Σικ.)   δάπιδας ἐννέ' ἡμῖν
χρήσα]τε.

(Κν.)   πόθεν;

(Σικ.)   καὶ παραπέτασμα βαρβαρικὸν ὑφαντὸν
λινοῦν,] ποδῶν τὸ μῆκος ἑκατόν.

(Κν.)   εἴθε μοι γένοιτο
ἱμάς] τ̣[ο]θεν. γραῦ· ποῦστιν ‹ἡ› γραῦς;   925

(Σικ.)   ἐφ' ἑτέραν βαδίζω
θύραν.

(Κν.)   ἀπαλλάγητε δή. γραῦ Σιμίχη. κακόν σε
κακῶς ἅπαντες ἀπολέσειαν οἱ θεοί. τί βούλει;

(Γε.)   κρατῆρα βούλομαι λαβεῖν χαλκοῦν μέγαν.

(Κν.)   τίς ἄν με
στήσειεν ὀρθόν;

(Σικ.)   ἔστιν ὑμῖν, ἔστιν ὡς ἀληθῶς
τὸ παραπέτασμα, παππία.   930

(Κν.)   μὰ τὸν Δί'.

(Γε.)   οὐδ' ὁ κρατήρ;

(Κν.)   τὴν Σιμίχην ἀποκτενῶ.

(Σικ.)   κάθευδε μή ‹τι› γρύζων.
φεύγεις ὄχλον, μισεῖς γυναῖκας, οὐκ ἐᾷς κομίζειν
εἰς ταὐτὸ τοῖς θύουσι σαυτόν· πάντα ταῦτ' ἀνέξει.
οὐδεὶς βοηθός σοι πάρεστι· πρῖε σαυτὸν αὑτοῦ.
ἄκουε δ' ἐξῆς πάντα . . . . . [. . . .] . . . [935
. . . .]αγκασουδετην[7-9] . [.] . [. . . .].
. . . .].ον αἱ γυναῖκες. [6-7] παρ' ὑμῶν

---

920 suppl. Ha., Page κατατέθηκεν Gallavotti, Ha.: κατεθηκεν P (Σικ.) ἄπαγε Mette et al. (-θηκεν:) δὴ σύ ed. pr.: δηκαισυ P 921-2 suppl. ed. pr. 923 Barrett 924-5 supplementa incertiora 924 suppl. Ha. εκατον P 925 ἱμάς Gallavotti, cetera ed. pr. 926-7 θυραν:—σιμικη:—| κακως—θεοι:—βουλει: P Σιμίχη Marzullo et al. σε Lloyd-Jones: δε P 930 παραπεπτασμαπαπια P μὰ τὸν Δί' Fraenkel, Quincey: παιδιον P (Γε.) οὐδ' ὁ κρατήρ; Kraus: post κρατηρ, sed non post παιδιον dicolon habet P 931 Σιμίχην Marzullo et al.: σιμικην P καθευθε P τι add. ed. pr.: post μη spatium vacuum reliquit P (cf. 913), post γρυζων dicolon habet, ut vid., postea deletum 932 μισεῖς γυναῖκας ed. pr.: γυναικασμισεισ P 934 πάρεστι plerique: -τιν P αὑτοῦ plerique: αυτοι P 935 paragr. sub versu habet P; post πάντα, fort. γαρ,]τιϛ[
(Roberts)

τῇ σῇ γυν]αικὶ τῇ τε παιδὶ [περιβ]ολαὶ τὸ πρῶτον
καὶ δεξιώ]ματ'. οὐκ ἀηδὴς διατρ[ι]βή τις αὐτῶν.
μικ]ρ[ὸν δ'] ἄνωθεν· ηὐτρέπιζον συμπόσιον ἐγώ τι   940
τοῖς ἀνδράσιν τούτοις. ἀκούεις; μὴ κάθευδε.

(Κν.)   μὴ γάρ;
οἴμοι.

(Σικ.)   <τί φῄς;> βούλει παρεῖναι; πρόσε[χε] κα̣ὶ̣ τὰ λοιπά.
σπουδὴ γὰρ ἦν· ἐστρώννυον [χα]μαιστιβεῖς τραπέζας
ἔγωγε· τοῦτο γὰρ ποεῖν ἐμοὶ προσῆκ', ἀκούεις;
μάγειρος ὢν γὰρ τυγχάνω, μέμνησο.   945

(Γε.)   μαλακὸς ἀνήρ.

(Σικ.) ἄλλος δὲ χερσὶν εὔιον γέροντα πολιὸν ἤδη
ἔκλινε κοῖλον εἰς κύτος, μειγνύς τε νᾶμα Νυμφῶν
ἐδεξιοῦτ' αὐτοῖς κύκλῳ καὶ ταῖς γυναιξὶν ἄλλος.
ἦν δ' ὥσπερ εἰ ψάμμον φοροίης· ταῦτα μανθάνεις σύ;
καί τις βραχεῖσα προσπόλων εὐήλικος προσώπου   950
ἄνθος κατεσκιασμένη χορεῖον εἰσέβαινε
ῥυθμὸν μετ' αἰσχύνης ὁμοῦ μέλλουσα <καὶ> τρέμουσα·
ἄλλη δὲ συγκαθῆπτε ταύτῃ χεῖρα κἀχόρευεν.

(Γε.) ὦ πρᾶγμα πάνδεινον παθών, χόρευε, συνεπίβαινε.

(Κν.) τί ποτε, τί βούλεσθ', ἄθλιοι;   955

(Γε.)   μᾶλλον <σὺ> συνεπίβαινε.
ἄγροικος εἶ.

(Κν.)   μὴ πρὸς θεῶν.

(Γε.)   οὐκοῦν φέρωμεν εἴσω
ἤδη σε.

(Κν.)   τί ποήσω;

(Γε.)   χόρευε δὴ σύ.

(Κν.)   φέρετε, κρεῖττον
ἴσως ὑπομένειν ἐστὶ τἀκεῖ.

(Γε.)   νοῦν ἔχεις· κρατοῦμεν.

938 init. suppl. ed. pr. [περιβ]ολαὶ Quincey   939 init. Kraus   940 init. Bingen,
Marzullo (μικρόν γ' Diano) συμποσιν P   942 τί φῄς ex. gr. add. Ha.   943 uersus vix
sanatus: ἐστρώννυον ed. pr., χαμαιστιβεῖς Dale, Quincey: εστρωννυν .. [1-2]μαιστιβασ P
(fort. -νυντι̣[, νυνγχ[)   944 ἐμοὶ ed. pr.: εμε P   ad fin. verba τὸν Διόνυσον add. P, glos-
sema ad v. 946 pertinens   945 (Γε.) μαλακὸς ἀνήρ plerique (μαγειροσ—μεμνησοι (pro
μεμνησο: ut vid.) P; incertum est an ad fin. dicolon olim habuerit)   947 μιγνυσ
P   948 ἐδεξιοῦτ' ed. pr.: εδεξιουν P   949 Lond.: ωσπερεισαμμον P   950 βραχεῖσα
Lond.: βρεχ- P   952 ed. pr.   953 ἄλλη δὲ ed. pr.: αλλ'ηδη P   955 (Κν.) τί ποτε τί
ed. pr.: τυπτετι P deinde βουλεισθ' (v. 954 et paragrapho caret et dicolo; 955 τυπτετι
— αθλιοι:) (Γε.) plerique σὺ add. ed. pr.   956 (Γε.) plerique: post θεῶν dicolon non
habet P   957 (Κν.) τί ποήσω; ed. pr., (Γε.) χόρευε ... plerique: ηδη—συ: P   958 τἀκεῖ
ed. pr.: κεικακα P, τα supra κει addito κρατοῦμεν plerique: κρατου P

ὦ καλλίνικοι· παῖ Δόναξ, Σίκων, Σύρε,
αἴρεσθε τοῦτον, εἰσφέρετε. φύλαττε δὴ   960
σεαυτόν, ὡς ἐάν σε παρακινοῦντά τι
λάβωμεν αὖτις, οὐδὲ μετρίως, ἴσθ᾿ ὅτι,
χρησόμεθά σοι τὸ τηνικαῦτ᾿. ἀλλ᾿ ἐκδότω
στεφάνους τις ἡμῖν, δᾷδα.

(Σικ.)   τουτονὶ λαβέ.
(Γε.)   εἶέν· συνησθέντες κατηγωνισμένοις   965
ἡμῖν τὸν ἐργώδη γέροντα, φιλοφρόνως
μειράκια, παῖδες, ἄνδρες ἐπικροτήσατε.
ἡ δ᾿ εὐπάτειρα φιλόγελώς τε παρθένος
Νίκη μεθ᾿ ἡμῶν εὐμενὴς ἔποιτ᾿ ἀεί.

ΜΕΝΑΝΔΡΟΥ
ΔΥΣΚΟΛΟΣ

968-9:   eadem fabulae clausula et alias utitur poeta: vide comm.

959 Σύρε Maas: συγε P   960 εἰσφέρετε Barigazzi et al.: εσ- P   963 Lond., Thierfelder:
τοτηνικαδωεκδοτω P (τηνικα ut vid. P²)   965 (Γε.) εἶέν Diano, Marzullo et al. (στεφανουσ
—δαιδα:—λαβε) ευνησθεντεσ P

COMMENTARY

[Square brackets in the commentary enclose references, textual comments, and certain sections of detailed discussion which I have chosen to present as ancillary to the main body of the notes.]

Hypothesis, didascalia, dramatis personae

A metrical summary of the plot, a notice of the first production, and a list of characters in order of appearance – these occupy p. 19 (*IΘ*) of the papyrus as originally numbered, the text under its title following from the top of p. 20; they raise a number of problems which are not in themselves uninteresting, but contribute little to the study of the play apart from the evidence for its date in the didascalia.

All three components of the prefatory page are familiar from later copies of ancient drama, but this is the earliest example so far known of a play complete with a form of preface. The earlier history of the material is a matter for conjecture; it may derive (with or without modifications) from a uniform collection of plays by Menander, but no firm date can be offered either for the constitution of the 'preface' as such or for the composition of the component parts. The next play in the Bodmer codex is said to begin without prefatory material or title, and short of holding the copyist himself responsible for the change in practice, we must presume that his original, for whatever reason, was not provided with these aids to the reader: cf. V. Martin, Scriptorium 14 (1960) p. 3 n. 2. In the Cairo codex, the *Heros*, headed [Η]Ρ[ΩΣ Μ]ΕΝΑΝΔΡΟΥ, has a similar hypothesis and a list of characters, but no didascalia. The present heading may have been composed in the form Ἀριστοφάνους γραμματικοῦ ὑπόθεσις, as Pfeiffer and others have suggested, but here, as in the list of dramatis personae, the original form cannot be established with confidence.

Hypothesis: 12 iambic trimeters in a style based on Menander's, but with faults of expression, metre, and factual accuracy which effectively discredit their ascription to so eminent a scholar and so great an admirer of Menander as Aristophanes of Byzantium. Neither the presence of A.'s name nor the evidence of Alexandrian scholarship in the didascalia can tell us anything about the date of the verses, which may fall well within the Christian era. It is possible, indeed likely, that this hypothesis, and that of the *Heros* are survivors of a twelve-line series by one or more authors: pertinent analogies include the ten-line hypotheses to Aristophanes (these too have tended to be fathered on A. of Byzantium, as is the metrical hypothesis to Sophocles, *OT*), and the twelve-line *periochae* to Terence, whose author is named as C. Sulpicius Apollinaris. περιοχαὶ τῶν Μενάνδρου δραμάτων were written, according to the Suda, by one Sellios, and it is tempting to think of him as a writer in this genre; but unless the notice of him there under Ὅμηρος Σέλλιος is confused or misleading, his work was in prose, and

Koerte would therefore associate him with the prose hypotheses preserved in P. Oxy.1235 (ed. Menand. I³, p. LXIV). Such a prose hypothesis may well have been the immediate source of the present verses, as of the didascalia following; the unknown poetaster displays little, if any, sign of personal acquaintance with the play. See further E. G. Turner in *Proc. of the 9th International Congress of Papyrology, Oslo, 1958* (published 1962), and in Oxyrhynchus Papyri, vol. 27, on no. 2455; Kraus and Jean Martin in their editions of *Dysk.*, and R. Cantarella, Rendiconti Ist. Lombardo 93 (1959) 77ff; for some earlier relevant work, see Coulon's note to Ar. *Ach.*, hyp. II, adding Leo, *Plaut. Forsch.*², 21f; C. R. Opitz, Leipziger Studien 6 (1883) 193-316; and Zuntz, *Political plays of Eur.*, 129ff.

1 δύσκολος: this key word, provided by the play's title, is naturally introduced at once.

μητρὸς μόνην: 'motherless'. μόνος with separative gen. (as e.g. at E. *Med.* 52) seems to be a usage of high poetry discordant with the pseudo-Menandrean style, as is the scansion of ἀγρῶν in 3 and the form ἔπιθεν (if right) in 6.

Knemon's daughter is wrongly represented as the child of a previous marriage, in spite of Menander's clear statement of the situation in the prologue speech at 13ff. Similar slips follow, and are found in other metrical hypotheses (e.g. *Heros*, Ar. *Peace*); there is therefore little to be said for conjectures and interpretations designed to bring the hypothesis into line with the play and to mitigate the defects of what was evidently a poor composition. μέν, ἦν Bingen, Pfeiffer; adopted in OCT and elsewhere.

2-3 ἔγημεν gives a 'split anapaest', easily removed by reading ἔγημ'; but metrical orthodoxy is not to be expected in verse of this kind: see e.g. Ar. *Wasps*, hyp. II, 1 and 4, and on Menander's practice, Introd., IV, Note A. The scansion ἀγρῶν (which would have been acceptable in iambics of tragic style) is likewise un-Menandrean: 414 n. ἔγημ' ἐν' Gallavotti.

ἀπελείφθη: see on 22.

μόνος ... διετέλει: cf. 328f.

5 αἰτῶν: see 752 n. ἀντέπιπτε 'opposed him' is no doubt the right reading, whether or not the entry in Hesychius comes from here; ἀντέτυφθ' (ed. pr.) assumes that ἀντιτύπτω can be used in this sense.

6 ἔπιθεν: a form of the aor. appropriate to a tragic or other high poetic manner; it strikes a false note in this style. αὖτις ἔπειθεν ed. pr., adopted by OCT *et al.*; but αὐτῆς is welcome, and less well placed if we transpose to αὐτῆς τὸν ἀδελφὸν ἔπειθεν with Barigazzi and Mette.

οὐκ εἶχ' ὅτι λέγοι apparently means that Gorgias 'did not know what to say' to Knemon on Sostratos' behalf, and may reflect the purport of his remarks at 352ff and elsewhere in Act II. ποεῖ is accepted by ed. pr. and others in spite of the odd indicative. The author might have known and used the form ποοῖ (Degani: cf. Schwyzer I.796 A.1); ποῆ Mayer, Jacques.

8-11 It is in fact Gorgias who rescues Knemon, with Sostratos' not very efficient help (670-85); Knemon sends for his wife when he thinks he is near death, but (at least in the extant text) shows little concern to make up their quarrel (698, cf. 709 and on 739); and he takes no part in either of the betrothals (761ff, 842ff).

10 δέ late in the sentence, as commonly in Menander (10 n.).

ἔχειν: a conjecture which restores normal Greek for P's impossible ερων, which should probably be recognized, with Lloyd-Jones, as a blunder introduced from v. 4 above, and not treated as a miscopying of ἐρᾶν (ed. pr.), ἐκών (Georgoulis, Kerschensteiner), or whatever else. Cf. *Perik*.10f for the idiom; for the textual fault assumed, see Introd. III, p. 51, and Fraenkel on A. *Ag.* 1216 (iii.559).

12 cf. 779 πραότερος ἔσται, said by Sostratos of Kallippides; and 903 ἄνθρωπος ἡμερώτερος (so P, wrongly), said by Getas of Knemon.

Didascalia: This learned notice no doubt derives ultimately from material compiled in Alexandria in the third century B.C. on the basis of official Athenian production records; it may owe its present form to Aristophanes of Byzantium; it may therefore have had a long history of association with the text. We cannot say how long, since a collection of prose hypotheses could have preserved the information for an indefinite period before its addition to an ancestor of our copy of the play. See especially Cantarella, Kraus and Turner, quoted above, p. 122, with further remarks by Cantarella in *Menandrea* (Univ. di Genova, Ist. di Fil. Class., 1960) pp. 55ff.

ἐδίδαξεν: of the poet 'producing' the play 'at' the festival; the aorist, as in ὑπεκρίνατο, simply records the event; the imperfect ἐνίκα ('was the victor in the contest') describes the state of affairs, a use of the tense familiar from inscriptional records: e.g. *IG* 2² 2318, 2319-23, reproduced by Pickard-Cambridge, *Festivals*, 106ff.

ἐπὶ Δημογένους ἄρχοντος: 317/16 B.C., the Lenean festival being held in the year 316 of our reckoning, in the month which corresponds approximately to January.

The date is not completely certain, though widely and rightly accepted as highly probable. It is obtained by a technically satisfying correction of P's διδυμογενησ (as Kraus observes, διδυ- could be produced from δη-, and the ending from -γεν, or -γεν̄ with a sign of abbreviation); it is (I believe) satisfactorily reconciled with the statement in the *Marmor Parium* that Menander's first victory at Athens came ἄρχοντος Δημοκλείδου (316/15 B.C.) by adopting the common assumption that the reference there is to the City Dionysia (text in Jacoby, *F Gr Hist* 239 B 14; Koerte II, Test. 24). The play, although wholly acceptable as a work of the year 317/16, offers no precise verification of that date, having no precisely datable contemporary allusions.

On the evidence so far available, no alternative correction of the text appears to be warranted; if unconvinced by this one, our choice should be to reserve judgement and obelize, as does Lloyd-Jones in OCT. For discussion and further references, see Cantarella, opp. cit., and Introd. I, pp. 3 n. 1, 7 ff.

Ἀριστόδημος Σκαρφεύς: the protagonist, not otherwise known; perhaps so called to distinguish him from the famous tragic actor Aristodemos, whose family came from Metapontum (O'Connor, *Chapters in the History of Actors* . . . (Chicago, 1908), no. 62.) Skarphe (Skarpheia), a town near Thermopylae, should probably be accepted as his home district, as for two near contemporaries, the actor Lykon (O'Connor, no. 319), and the poet Philodamos (Powell, *Collectanea Alexandrina*, 165ff; Oldfather in *RE* 19.2 (1938) 2442f): if so, we have his name in its Attic form. σκαφενσ is retained by Gallavotti, and by Jean Martin and others (after Koumanoudis); but the actor is markedly less likely to have been called 'digger' or to have taken his name from Skaphai in Boeotia.

ἀντεπιγράφεται Μισάνθρωπος: 'it is alternatively entitled M.'. The passive, and this technical sense of the compound, are not recorded in LSJ, but cf. under ἐπιγράφω II.2. The alternative title was not previously known, and its origin is a subject of speculation: see Cantarella's paper in Rend. Ist. Lomb., referred to above.

Dramatis Personae: This list shows signs of modification by the writer of P, and may have suffered other changes in the course of copying and revision since it was first compiled; I have however preferred to print it in all essentials as it stands, and not in a hypothetical earlier form. It apparently gives all the speaking characters in order of appearance, ignoring others, whether they are mentioned by name or not (e.g. Parthenis, 432) – 'apparently', because if we give a speaking part to Sostratos' mother or one of her maids at 430-41, we must assume that the list is incomplete, whether in compilation or by textual accident: see ad loc.

Knemon's daughter is nameless, as in the play: i.e. the list (as I believe, correctly) does not identify her with the Myrrhine of 709. Simiche's name is spelt with a kappa, consistently with the (incorrect) spelling elsewhere in P.

The article in Πὰν ὁ θεός was very likely added by the writer of P himself, who may have done the same elsewhere; he also seems to have wanted the entries for Sostratos and Pyrrhias to be transposed – wrongly, and for reasons which remain mysterious; it is clear from the arrangement of the entries on the page that he failed to allow adequately for the layout of the material, but not clear (*pace* Jean Martin, ed. Dysk., p. 28) that he added any of it from another copy of the play.

The ultimate origin of the list remains uncertain, like that of the marginal speakers' names in P, with which it has obvious analogies of function (to help the reader) and of form (e.g. $\Sigma i\kappa\omega\nu$ $\mu\acute{a}\gamma\epsilon\iota\rho\sigma s$); perhaps in both there is a core of authentic Menandrean material: see Introd. III, pp. 47ff. Yet whether or not Menander had copies of his play made with a list of characters prefixed, one should beware of supposing that its present form is of great antiquity: apart from the possibility of minor changes by the writer of P and earlier copyists, some of the appended descriptions look more like annotation for annotation's sake than serious attempts to convey useful information – especially, perhaps, that of Gorgias, which could be clear only to those who knew enough to make it unnecessary. In describing Chaireas as 'the parasite', the list classifies him by dramatic type – correctly, to judge by his rôle in the play, but without a clear verbal clue from the text, unless the damaged line 48 can be satisfactorily supplemented so as to admit one. No great general knowledge of Greek comedy would be necessary for a reader or copyist to add this description; but if – as I think likely – Menander left Chaireas' status to be taken for granted, one might prefer to think that the source was a scholarly prose summary such as we have envisaged in discussing the verse hypothesis and the didascalia; although the other descriptions appear more readily from the words of the play, the same possibility is open for them.

$\Pi\grave{a}\nu$ $\acute{o}$ $\theta\epsilon\acute{o}s$: $\pi\alpha\nu\theta\epsilon\omega\sigma$ was first written as one word, then $\theta\epsilon\omega\sigma$ deleted; in $\omega\theta\epsilon\omega\sigma$ at the top of the parallel column, the article looks like a subsequent addition. Cf. $"H\rho\omega s$ $\theta\epsilon\acute{o}s$ (the only description present in the list for *Heros*).

$X\alpha\iota\rho\acute{e}as$ $\acute{o}$ $\pi\alpha\rho\acute{a}\sigma\iota\tau\sigma s$: see on 48.

$\Sigma\acute{\omega}\sigma\tau\rho\alpha\tau\sigma s$ $\acute{o}$ $\acute{e}\rho\alpha\sigma\theta\epsilon\acute{\iota}s$: 'the man who fell in love'; but $\tau\grave{o}\nu$ $\acute{e}\rho\hat{\omega}\nu\tau\alpha$ in 48. For β and α added with the intention of indicating a change of order, Turner compares P. Hamburg 133, line 2, and P. Oxy. 9, col. 2.15, col. 4.15-16.

$\Pi\upsilon\rho\rho\acute{\iota}as$ $\acute{o}$ $\deltaο\hat{\upsilon}\lambda\sigma s$: cf. 76.

$\Pi\alpha\rho\theta\acute{e}\nu\sigma s$ $\theta\upsilon\gamma\acute{a}\tau\eta\rho$ $K\nu\acute{\eta}\mu\omega\nu\sigma s$: cf. 189 marg. η $\kappa\sigma\rho\eta$ $\theta\upsilon\gamma\alpha\tau\eta\rho$ $\kappa\nu\eta\mu'$.

$\Delta\hat{a}\sigma s$: one expects $\acute{o}$ $\deltaο\hat{\upsilon}\lambda\sigma s$, but that is not a good reading of P, where $\alpha\delta\epsilon\lambda/$ ($=\acute{a}\delta\epsilon\lambda\phi\acute{o}s$) was probably written by confusion with the next entry.

$\Gamma\sigma\rho\gamma\acute{\iota}as$, $\kappa\tau\lambda$.: cf. 318f.

$\Sigma\acute{\iota}\kappa\omega\nu$ $\mu\acute{a}\gamma\epsilon\iota\rho\sigma s$: cf. 888f $\mu\acute{a}\gamma\epsilon\iota\rho\epsilon$ $\Sigma\acute{\iota}\kappa\omega\nu$; 393 marg. ($\sigma\iota\kappa\omega\nu$ $\mu\alpha\gamma/$), 419 marg. ($\sigma\iota\kappa\omega\nu$ $\mu\alpha\gamma\epsilon\iota\rho/$).

$\Sigma\iota\mu\acute{\iota}\chi\eta$ $\gamma\rho\alpha\hat{\upsilon}s$: cf. 926. P consistently spells the name with a kappa

THE DYSKOLOS

(in the text, 636, 926, 931; in the margin, σιμικη γραυσ 574: cf. at 620, 874, 882). This form, although unexpected and otherwise unknown, is attributed to Menander by OCT *et al.*, following ed. pr. For instances of Σιμίχη and its variant Σιμμίχη see Pape, *Wörterbuch d. gr. Eigennamen* under these names; Szemerényi further refers me to *IG* 12.2, 287 B 17 (Delos, 249 B.C.), and *ib.* 161 B 23 ἀνέθηκε Σιμίχη Μυκονία (280 B.C.). On the formation, see Headlam-Knox on Herondas 1.6 and Chantraine, *Formation des noms* 404; on the spelling with -κ- in P, cf. Mayser, *Gramm. d. gr. Papyri*, I.i.171.

Καλλιππίδης, κτλ.: cf. 773f.

Act I (1-232)

1-49 Prologue speech. Enter Pan. He sets the scene, briefly introduces the principal characters, and reveals the situation from which the action begins. See Introd. II.1 'Staging, scenery, setting'; on Pan's costume and mask, see Introd. II.3 at p. 34.

Exposition speeches of this kind are used in wide variety in Later Greek Comedy to supplement what the poet tells his audience in dramatic scenes. They occur either at the beginning of the play, as here, or after an opening scene, as in *Heros, Perikeiromene* and elsewhere. If not a known divinity, like Pan, the speaker may be a special prologue figure, like Agnoia 'Ignorance' in *Perikeiromene*, who represents the motive force of the dramatic action; or alternatively a character, like the young man in Plautus, *Mercator*; if the play has a mythical plot, the speaker can be both divine and a character, like Mercury in *Amphitruo*.

The ancestors of these speeches in fifth-century comedy show that Menander and his contemporaries were working with a long tradition behind them. Like many comic traditions, it was nourished by the continuous influence of Tragedy, especially Euripidean tragedy; and as a divine prologue figure Pan includes among his forbears in Attic drama not only Kalligeneia in Aristophanes, *Second Thesmophoriazusae* (335 K), but Aphrodite in Euripides, *Hippolytus*, and the other divine prologue figures of the tragic stage.

The tradition was naturally modified by up-to-date literary theory and by the poets' own personal achievements and tastes. Three outstanding features of the *Dyskolos* prologue speech are the deliberate economy of detail, the neat strokes of character-portraiture, and the appropriateness of the speaker to the play: already Menander shows qualities which are characteristic of him.

[F. Stoessl, *RE* 'Prologos' 23.1 (1957) 632-41 and 23.2 (1959) 2312-2440 gives a very full recent survey of the topic.]

1f τῆς Ἀττικῆς ... Φυλήν: as commonly in classical idiom, the genitive, with the article, precedes and denotes geographical area; the place name follows without the article: ὁ δὲ στρατὸς ... ἀφίκετο τῆς Ἀττικῆς ἐς Οἰνόην, Thuc. 2.18.1. Later Greek standardized the reverse order, ἐν Ταρσῷ τῆς Κιλικίας *NT Acts* 22.3. [Schwyzer II.113f.]

νομίζετε: cf. Heniochos 5 K, 7f τηνδὶ δὲ τὴν σκηνὴν ἐκεῖ | σκηνὴν ὁρᾶν θεωρικὴν νομίζετε. The audience is addressed directly, as again at 45ff, and by Agnoia in *Perik.* (7f, 47ff); see also *Phasma* 19f, and on 194 below. Menander here uses with restraint a simple and traditional device of the comic poet to engage interest in his exposition.

127

Among the fifth-century examples are Cratinus, *Ploutoi* (Page, *Lit. Pap.* 38: ?430 B.C.: chorus); Ar. *Wasps* 71ff (a character); and Philyllios, *Herakles* 8 K (410/400?: a personified figure, Dorpia).

The construction should be taken to continue with τὸ νυμφαῖον δέ ... ('... and suppose that the shrine ...', etc.). [Kraus, who prefers to understand ἐστί and not εἶναι, prints a colon after Φυλήν; the fact that P also has a stop there is of no moment: its punctuation generally is of little critical consequence (cf. Introd. III, p. 43), and in this sentence it also has stops after προέρχομαι, Φυλασίων, γεωργεῖν and πάνυ.]

2 ὅθεν προέρχομαι: cf. P. *Aul.* 2f: ego Lar sum familiaris ex hac familia | *unde exeuntem* me aspexistis.

3f Φυλασίων ... γεωργεῖν: in naming the shrine as that of 'the people of Phyle and those who can farm the rocks here', Pan is made to stress the identity of the place and at once to give a material fact of its character – hard country, lived in by hard-working farmers like Knemon. He introduces a recurrent motif of the play: see especially 603ff, and cf. Introd. II.1, p. 23.

The phrase follows the formal pattern familiar from Ἀθηναίων καὶ τῶν συμμάχων and the like (this is a cliché which Socrates is made to play with at Plato, *Meno* 94 d). We have, however, not a legal definition of identity or ownership, but a mildly humorous echo of one; and in it the καί need not imply that 'Phylasians' and 'farmers' are somehow two separate classes of people, like 'Athenians' and 'allies': it is best taken as explicative, introducing an amplification of Φυλασίων either in the sense 'and in general' (i.e. including non-native farmers), or as 'and in particular' (i.e. the farmers of the community have a special proprietary interest in the shrine). Cf. Denniston, *Particles* 291; KG II.247; Gudeman on Aristotle, *Poetics* 1448 a 11; Verdenius, Mnemosyne 1954.38.

Φυλασίων has no article, being (like Ἀθηναίων) an ethnic adjective, used as the name of a particular people: cf. 521. Numerous examples are given by Gildersleeve, *Syntax of Attic Greek* II.230f.

4 ἱερὸν ἐπιφανὲς πάνυ: a 'most notable' or 'most distinguished' shrine – complimentary, perhaps, but with a basis in fact: cf. Introd. II.1, p. 25 n. 2.

5 τὸν ἀγρὸν ... τὸν ἐπὶ δεξιά: Knemon's ἀγρός is his 'farm' – that is, his house, represented by one of the side doors of the stage-building, and his land nearby which is imagined. But is ἐπὶ δεξιά stage right (as I assume with ed. pr. and others) or spectators' right (OCT *et al.*, after Quincey)? In performance a gesture at τουτονί makes this clear.

The straightforward view that Pan, who has just come out of the shrine, must mean his own right is balanced by the consideration that he is a prologue speaker explaining the setting to the spectators, and might be expected to point to the right as they see it, perhaps even turning as he does so. Two other points about staging fail, I believe, to settle the matter decisively:

(i) At 909, Sikon and Getas carry out their plan to bring Knemon from his house asleep on a bed, and one of them (presumably Getas) cries 'to the right'. Quincey reasonably holds that the old man is to be brought to the centre of the stage or near it, and not deposited at the side. This means, if both conspirators are facing front, that Knemon's door is stage left and spectators' right: but are they both facing front? If not (and either or both might well not be facing front as they move the bed), the command could equally well cover a movement from the opposite side towards the centre: the text does not reveal how Menander envisaged the action.

(ii) Wing entrances in the Theatre of Dionysus are generally thought to have had a conventional significance based on its real topography (e.g. Peiraeus to the spectators' right), though the evidence, particularly for plays set outside Athens, is less than clear: see W. Beare, CQ 32 (1938) 205-10 (= *Roman Stage*, Appendix B), and Pickard-Cambridge, *Theatre of D.*, 234ff. In the *Dyskolos*, there is country all round, and no town or harbour; but we can say that the entrance on Knemon's side is from his land and Gorgias's, quite close by in the valley, while that on the side of Gorgias' house is from Athens (ultimately) and places on the way (for references, see Introd. II.1, p. 22 and notes). On the view taken in this edition, the 'near' side, that of the 'country' activities, will have been on the audience's left in the Theatre of Dionysus, and the 'further' side, that from which the strangers arrive, will have been on the audience's right. Stage directions will be given in the commentary accordingly; but again there seems no way to verify the assumption that Menander envisaged his play in the same way: we may in fact have left and right reversed.

5ff Pan now introduces the characters, beginning with Knemon, who is the only one named. No characters' names are given in the prologue speeches of *Perik.*, *CF*, and *Phasma*, so far as they are preserved; one name is neatly introduced in *Georgos* 16 and *Plokion*, frg. 333. Some of Plautus' prologue speeches follow the same practices: e.g. *Aul.* 1-39, *Merc.* 1-110, and *Rud.* 1-82 – adapted respectively from Menander, Philemon, and Diphilus. Here it is obvious that Menander wishes to avoid all unnecessary and confusing detail; and names, which modern audiences tend to seek avidly in their printed programmes, are something for which his audience can wait: see 45f and note, and on 24f and 889.

6 ἀπάνθρωπός τις ἄνθρωπος σφόδρα: 'a positive hermit' – but the verbal echo of the Greek gives a touch of rhetorical colour to emphasize one of Knemon's leading characteristics. As an angry old man, he is one of a long line of leading characters in Comedy; as a misanthrope in particular he belongs to a tradition which seems to have grown from satirical portraiture of the historical fifth-century misanthrope Timon: note especially Pherekrates, *Agrioi* (420 B.C.), with Plato, *Prot.* 327 d on its chorus; and Phrynichos, *Monotropos* (414 B.C.), frg. 18 K, where the hermit says: ... ζῶ δὲ Τίμωνος βίον | ἄγαμον, ἄδουλον, ὀξύθυμον, ἀπρόσοδον, | ἀγέλαστον, ἀδιάλεκτον, ἰδιογνώμονα. A *Timon* was written by the Middle Comedy poet Antiphanes; the one surviving quotation (206 K) touches on a theme which appears (among its other occurrences) in the *Dyskolos* (447-54, where see n.). The word ἀπάνθρωπος is specifically associated with Timon in a passage of Menander the Rhetorician quoted by Kraus (*Rhet. Graeci*, III, p. 397 Spengel) ἀπάνθρωπος ἐπικληθήσομαι ὥσπερ τὸν Τίμωνά φασι. Reminiscences of the *Dyskolos* and its hero in later writers (a selection of them is quoted in the notes to the text and in the commentary) show how Menander's Knemon added himself to the tradition. For general discussion of the 'misanthrope-theme' and ideas related to it, see Schmid, quoted Introd. I, p. 10 n. 1, and Photiades and Préaux, *ib.*, p. 12 n. 1.

7 οὐ χαίρων: 'disliking'; the words go closely together, as in οὐκ ἐθέλων 'unwilling', etc. Three approximately parallel expressions, all negative in character, the last containing a negative, are connected by καί and τε. Cf. *Epitr.* 598 ἀτυχὴς γεγονὼς καὶ σκαιὸς ἀγνώμων τ' ἀνήρ and Denniston, *Particles* 500; and for οὐ ... τε, see on 724ff: it is a mistake to delete the τε with Treu.

Knemon's sullen taciturnity, which Pan is about to describe, is a characteristic of the self-willed man in Theophrastus, *Char.* 15: ἡ δὲ αὐθάδειά ἐστιν ἀπήνεια ὁμιλίας ἐν λόγοις: cf. Aristotle, *Eth. Eud.* 1233 b 35; *Magn. Mor.* 1192 b 31 ὅ τε γὰρ αὐθάδης τοιοῦτός ἐστιν οἷος μηθενὶ ἐντυχεῖν μηδὲ διαλεγῆναι; and for δύσκολος as an extreme in disagreeability and unfriendliness, see *Eth. Nic.* 1108 a 26ff.

8ff 'Do I say "crowd"? He's lived a pretty long time, and not willingly spoken to anyone all his life, never given anyone a greeting ...' The speaker questions, and then corrects his statement with a stronger one, the figure of speech known technically as ἐπιδιόρθωσις, and exemplified in Dem., *de cor.* (18).130 ὀψὲ γάρ ποτε—ὀψὲ λέγω; χθὲς μὲν οὖν καὶ πρώην. The form of the sentence, once recognized, makes it highly likely that Menander wrote λελάληκεν ... οὐδενί and not λελάληκεν ... οὐδέν (ed. pr. and others, with P) as the 'correction' of οὐ χαίρων τ'ὄχλῳ: cf. Kassel, Gnomon 1961.135. Knemon echoes this description of his behaviour at 726; the opposite of it is portrayed in Pyrrhias' story of his approach to Knemon at 104ff: wishing to be polite, he took care to speak first and hailed him from a distance. In fact, as we learn later, Knemon makes one exception to his rule of silence – his daughter (334f).

8 ἐπιεικῶς, like Eng. 'fairly', is commonly a limiting qualification, though in colloquial usage it is sometimes emphatic: at Plato, *Gorgias* 485 e, Jowett (though with disapproval from Dodds, ad loc.) translates πρὸς σὲ ἐπιεικῶς ἔχω φιλικῶς by '. . . very well inclined towards you'. Knemon is not *very* old (at least he is still distinctly vigorous) – probably a conventional 6o-odd, like the name-character of *Heautontimoroumenos* (frg. 127 = T. *Heaut.* 62f).

9 ἡδέως: 'willingly', 'gladly', cf. 270, 658; here with a negative, as e.g. at 726 and Diphilos, *Zographos* 43 K. 13f οὐδὲν ἡδέως | ποιεῖ γὰρ οὗτος, ἀλλ᾽ ὅσον νόμου χάριν 'he does nothing with a will, but just for form's sake'. E. G. Turner remarks: 'The adverb is a commonplace in later writing, especially when the writer asks a favour and offers to do anything desired in return: e.g. P. Cairo Zenon V 59843 (260/40 B.C.) καλῶς οὖν ποιήσεις γράφων ἡμῖν περὶ ὧν χρείαν ἔχῃς τῶν ἐνταῦθα· ἡδέως γάρ σοι πάντα ποιήσομεν.'

10 προσηγόρευκε πρότερος δ᾽ οὐδένα: connecting particles which normally stand second in word-order are commonly postponed by Menander (as by other authors) when the preceding words form a short closely coherent group: e.g. in *Dysk.*, τὸ νυμφαῖον δ(έ) 2; οὐ χαίρων τ(ε) 7; ἐπὶ κακῷ δ(έ) 309. But like other authors of later Greek comedy, Menander goes further in this than prose writers normally do. With the present example, compare 233 οὕτω παρέργως δ(έ), and 26 πιστὸν οἰκέτην τ(ε); more striking instances are at 24 χωρίδιον τούτῳ δ(έ), and (e.g.) *Sam.* 45 εἰποῦσ᾽ ἐκείνη δ(έ); *CF* 77 σὺ πάντα δ᾽ [εἴσει]; and *Perik.* 292 τὸν Δᾶον εἰσπέμπω δὲ δηλώσονθ᾽, ὅτι; τε is unusually late at *Dysk.* 237, and δέ in P. Didot I.32f (Koerte I³, p. 144). Not all the common particles behave with such freedom; but γάρ is in general still freer in its placing (see on 66-68). The explanation is probably not to be seen in metrical necessity, but in a desire for a realistic, colloquial effect.

11ff '. . . except that, as he lives next door and passes by, he's bound to greet me – Pan; and at once he's sorry he's spoken, I'm quite sure.'

προσηγόρευκε governs ἐμὲ τὸν Πᾶνα and is qualified by ἐξ ἀνάγκης and the two participles γειτνιῶν and παριών, which are closely coupled by τε, the second supplementing the sense of the first: on this use of τε see KG II.241f.

Pan is recognizable visually from his costume and mask; his identity is now made completely clear from the text at a point where clarity is helpful, for Menander is exploiting a custom of the Pan-cult which his audience could presumably be expected to remember, especially if gently prompted. 'One should not, they say, approach this god in silence' (433f, where see note): a grudging τὸν Πᾶνα χαίρειν or the like when occasion takes him past the shrine is supposed to be the one concession Knemon makes in his rule of not speaking first.

Aelian, *Ep. Rust.* 16, recalls the passage, but uses the idea differently: τὸν Πᾶνα ἀσπάζομαί τε καὶ προσαγορεύω παριὼν μόνον, θύω δὲ οὐδέν.

12 τοῦτ' ...μεταμέλει: cf. Ar. *Clouds* 1114 οἶμαι δὲ σοὶ ταῦτα μεταμελήσειν. μέλει and μεταμέλει both occur with things, particularly neuter pronouns, as subject. [τοῦδ' ed. pr.]

13 εὖ οἶδα, εὖ ἴσθι and variants scan with hiatus in Attic drama: for examples and discussion, see A. C. Moorhouse, CQ 1962.239ff.

15f τοῦ λαβόντος τὸ πρότερον: 'her previous husband'. The two perfect participles τετελευτηκότος and καταλελειμμένου describe the state of affairs at the time of the marriage (τότε). By now (ἤδη, 27), the child is grown up. [P's ποτε: cf. Introd. III, p. 51.]

17 ζυγομαχῶν: ζυγομαχεῖν, 'to fight with one's yokefellow', is perhaps particularly in point of fighting with a wife; Menander uses it of fighting with one's own weakness in *Heniochos*, frg. 177, and of fighting against Fortune in frg. 637; see also 250 below, and n. there.

18 'he took up the best part of the night': δέ after οὐ μόνον, as in frg. 250.4 (conj.), 622.8; τὸ πολύ, with or without μέρος, is 'the great part', equivalent to 'the greater' (or 'the greatest') part, as in τὸ πολὺ τοῦ βίου Plato, *Rep.* 405 b (see further Stephanus-Dindorf, s.v. πολύς, at col. 1419f); τῆς νυκτός, balancing the plural τὰς ἡμέρας, as it were 'all his days and most of every night'.

[P's interpolated line is otherwise cured by deleting τό, as in OCT (Lloyd-Jones), or τῆς (Diano, referring to KG I.606 (g)); but the article is welcome in both cases, and the deletion of καί gives a line with a more probable rhythm.]

19f T. *Adel.* 866ff seems to reproduce a similar context from Menander's *Second Adelphoi* (866 translates *Adel.* II, frg. 11): ego ille agrestis saeuos tristis parcus truculentus tenax | duxi uxorem: quam ibi miseriam uidi! nati filii, | alia cura. A daughter, who will one day need a dowry, can be considered a particularly heavy burden: χαλεπόν γε θυγάτηρ κτῆμα καὶ δυσδιάθετον *Halieus*, frg. 18; cf. *Anepsioi*, frg. 54.

Note the short, unconnected statements: 'asyndeton is characteristic of Menander's style, especially in narrative passages', remarks Capps on *Epitr.* 74 (33 of his numbering). Demetrius, *de elocutione* 193f contrasts Menander in this respect with Philemon, distinguishing the disjointed or acting style from the connected or reading style, and quoting as an illustration from Menander the line which appears (with part of its context) as frg. 685 in Koerte II: ὑπεδεξάμην, ἔτικτον, ἐκτρέφω, φιλῶ (ἐδεξάμην ... φίλε cod.).

22 ἀπῆλθε ... πάλιν: i.e. she left her husband and passed out of his legal guardianship into the care of her son (though Menander, in sketching the background, does not say when this took place, or what would have happened if she had needed legal protection while Gorgias was too young to give it). The technical term for a wife leaving her husband is ἀπολείπειν, as at Dem. 30.4 and elsewhere (a recently published instance is in P. Oxy. 27.2464, col. ii): cf. hyp. 2, where it appears in the passive, of the husband, and *Epitr.* 610, frg. 823. The legal background to Knemon's family relationships is considered below under 729-39, where it is of especial importance to the interpretation.

23f χωρίδιον, diminutive from χωρίον 'plot of land'; -ίδιον as in *Philadelphoi*, frg. 436, and similarly οἰκίδιον Ar. *Cl.* 92, M. *Perik.* 199; but -ίδιον e.g. in λοφίδιον, θεραπαινίδια, 100 and 460 below. [No simple rule seems to account for this variation: see Arnott, CQ 1957, p. 194 n. 3; and earlier Chantraine, *Formation des noms*, 69; Schwyzer I.471.]

ὑπάρχον ἦν, as in Lysias 13.91 ἀφείλετο ἃ ἦν ὑπάρχοντα ἐκείνῳ ἀγαθά. The periphrasis (present ptcp. with a form of εἶναι) possibly gives a shade more emphasis than the simple tense ('he was the owner of a small plot'). [On later developments of the construction, cf. *NTGramm.* §353.]

24f ἐνθαδὶ ἐν γειτόνων: 'here in the neighbourhood' (=hic uiciniae, T. *Phorm.* 95) – by origin an elliptical phrase like ἐν Ἅιδου and English 'at George's': τὸ χωρίον τὸ ἐν γειτόνων μοι, Dem. 53.10, ἐν γειτόνων δ'οἰκοῦσα *Perik.* 27, and similarly elsewhere; ἐν τῶν γειτόνων *Phasma* 13; τὸν Δᾶον ἐκ τῶν γ. . . . καλῶ *Dysk*.594. [Schwyzer II.120 convincingly rejects the view that such phrases developed from local genitives with added prepositions.]

Gorgias' house is represented by the door in the stage building on the opposite side from Knemon's (i.e. audience's right), and Pan possibly points to it: but the house identifies itself from 206 onwards – the actor who enters from it there is manifestly the single faithful old slave of a poor household from the moment one sees and hears him; that effect is prepared for by the information given in the present context. It first becomes clear at 232 that Gorgias' land is reached by the wing entrance on Knemon's side, when the slave goes off that way to find his master; their names do not appear till the beginning of the next Act (240, 247); the fact that Gorgias' land is close by Knemon's comes in when relevant at 350ff.

25 κακῶς: 'barely enough'. τὰ κακῶς τρέφοντα χωρὶ' ἀνδρείους ποιεῖ (*Anepsioi*, frg. 57): Gorgias' hard life has given him discretion beyond his years (28); both this and the less congenial aspects of his rustic upbringing will be brought out in the play.

26 θ'ἕνα is more pointed than the θ'ἅμα preferred by ed. pr.: P's θεναμα combines the two readings (Introd. III, p. 51, under 'Substitution (ii)'). The 'single faithful slave of his father's' is a further sign that Gorgias' household is not well off; similarly in T. *Adel.*, the

133

widowed Sostrata is left with one slave, Geta, who supports her and her daughter (479ff).

'Rarely, τε couples the last two units of an otherwise asyndetic series', Denniston, *Particles* 501. The reflexive αὐτόν is deferred from its natural place at the head of the series in favour of the more pointed collocation διατρέφει τὴν μητέρα: emendation to αὐτοῦ with OCT (Lloyd-Jones, after αὐτοῦ Photiades) appears to be unnecessary.

29 προάγει: 'brings on', 'matures', as Xen. *Cyr.* 1.4.4: προῆγεν αὐτὸν ὁ χρόνος . . . εἰς ὥραν τοῦ πρόσηβον γενέσθαι. The line is possibly better taken as a general statement about Gorgias ('Experience of life's hardships makes him mature') than as a general statement about mankind ('Experience of hardship matures us', ed. pr.): i.e. understand αὐτόν rather than an indefinite object. In either case the intention is to sum up Gorgias in terms of a readily understood commonplace before going on to Knemon.

Sententious reflections are a feature of Menander's prologues, according to Theon, *Progymnasmata* (II, p. 91 Spengel), who refers to the *Dardanos* (frg. 96) and the *Xenologos* (frg. 294), and criticizes this method of rounding off sections of the narrative as a device of the dramatic poets to win applause. Cf. *Perik.* 49f διὰ γὰρ θεοῦ καὶ τὸ κακὸν εἰς ἀγαθὸν ῥέπει | γινόμενον; P. *Cist.* 193f, *Truc.* 16f; E. *Tro.* 26f, *El.* 37f. [The passage of Theon is reprinted by Koerte under frgg. 96 and 294: see further Leo, *Plaut. Forsch.*[2] 223, Lindsay on P. *Capt.* 44-45.]

30 αὐτὸς . . . μόνος: 'on his own', as at 331, but here separated by the verb with which the phrase belongs; the whole complex is enfolded within the larger unit ἔχων τὴν θυγατέρα καὶ γραῦν θεράπαιναν. For similar departures from normal or 'logical' word-order, see under 223ff below.

31f Jean Martin well compares T. *Heaut.* 67ff: numquam tam mane egredior neque tam uesperi | domum reuortor quin te in fundo conspicer | fodere aut arare aut aliquid ferre denique.

33 μεχρὶ Χολαργέων κάτω: cf. πρὸς Μελίτην ἄνω Dem., *Conon* (54).7. 'Right down to Cholargos' means down the road for a good ten miles, if the ancient village is rightly located at the foot of Mount Aigaleos, near modern Néa Lióssia, shortly before the road from the Phyle pass crosses the Kephissos on its way to Athens. The name of the people, Χολαργεῖς, stands for the place-name, as often. [The site of this deme (to which, incidentally, Pericles belonged) is still debated, but see B. D. Meritt, Hesperia 1940.53f; A. Philippson, *Gr. Landschaften* I.3 (1952) 1001; and A. Kirsten, *Der gegenwärtige Stand der att. Demenforschung*, in Atti del III Congresso di Epigrafia Greca e Latina (Rome, 1959) 155-72 – a reference I owe to Dr V. L. Ehrenberg. See also Robert, quoted Introd. II.1, p. 20.]

Plautus, inc. fab. iii reads 'gannit odiosus omni totae familiae', perhaps just close enough to this context to raise the question whether it came from his *Dyscolus*; but on the one known fragment, cf. on 198ff.

34ff The girl is a paragon of untainted virtue; later, Menander illustrates her modesty (198), her open and free manner (201), and her concern for the other members of the household, Simiche (195f), and Knemon (648ff, cf. 740); Sostratos is made to reflect on the advantages of her secluded upbringing with a fierce and upright father, away from the bad influence of older women (384ff). Cf. Longus, *Daphnis and Chloe* 1.13 νέα κόρη καὶ ἐν ἀγροικίᾳ τεθραμμένη καὶ οὐδὲ ἄλλου λέγοντος ἀκούσασα τὸ τοῦ ἔρωτος ὄνομα; Fraenkel refers me to Turpilius, *Paedium* 157 R³: neque mirum: educta, ut par est, expars malitiis, metuens sui. [In 35, γέγον' ἀνομοία OCT (Lewis) inverts the sense of the passage.]

35 οὐδὲ ἕν: often more emphatic than οὐδέν, but in any case a useful metrical variant; the scansion with hiatus is regular in comedy of all periods: Cratinus 302 K, Ar. *Frogs* 927, etc. [Cf. Moorhouse, quoted 13 n.]

37ff κολακεύουσα: unusually, in a good sense, as the following words show 'cultivating the Nymphs' favour with thoughtful reverence'. The context is very close to P. *Aul.* 23ff, where the Lar says of Euclio's daughter: ea mihi cottidie | aut ture aut uino aut aliqui semper supplicat, | dat mihi coronas. (cf. *Dysk.* 51) eius honoris gratia | feci thensaurum ut hic reperiret Euclio, | quo illam facilius nuptum, si uellet, daret.

In both plays, the god is moved by the character of the worshipper and her simple, constant attentions; here, as later when Knemon denounces extravagance in sacrifice, Menander presents a view which agrees with Theophrastus' pronouncement that the gods favour simple offerings, and regard the character of the giver rather than the magnificence of the gift (see on 447-54). Pan, like the Lar, sets in motion a chain of events which will lead to the girl's marriage, and at the same time to the discomfiture of her disagreeable father; and in this he has the Nymphs as allies. The gods are thus a factor in the course of the action, and they are recalled to the audience by the presence of their shrine, and by the characters' references to them; they add 'atmosphere' to the play, and coherence to its structure, but they do not, except in a very limited sense, make it into a religious play, or one dominated by the divine: as Jean Martin puts it (ed. Dysk., p. 182) 'à partir du moment où il est question de morale, le dieu s'efface devant l'homme' – this specifically of Pan in relation to Knemon.

Reward of piety (and its reverse) is a recurrent motif in New Comedy: for examples and discussion, see Webster, *SM* 198ff, and *LGC* 159f on Diphilus' original of P. *Rudens*. [38 αὐτῆς ed. pr.: KG I.559 A.8 is rightly quoted in favour of αὐτῆς; P has no breathing.]

THE DYSKOLOS

39ff Pan piles on the remaining facts as he leads up to the essential statement that he has made the young man fall in love.

39-40 τε (also printed here by Gallavotti, by OCT and by Jacques) is very easily but not certainly rightly corrected to δέ with ed. pr. τε as a sentence connection ('and so', 'and accordingly') appears to be avoided by the best writers of fourth century Attic (see Denniston, *Particles* 497ff); but here the sense is suitable, and the sentence itself is hardly a model of elegance. A slightly easier example is *Heros* 42f ἀλλὰ τὠμῷ δεσπότῃ | εἴρηχ᾽, ὑπέσχηταί τ᾽ ἐμοὶ συνοικιεῖν | αὐτήν ... : cf. also *Thesauros*, frg. 199; *Dysk.* 541, 580.

καὶ μάλ᾽ εὐπόρου πατρός: καὶ μάλα is used similarly to μάλα. Kallippides' estate, 'worth many talents', contrasts with Knemon's, worth 'about two talents' (327f), and with Gorgias' humble χωρίδιον (23). On the scale of values, see below under 842-4.

[41-47 This passage is the first of a series in which lines have lost their beginnings through damage to P, and supplements of them are judged for length according to the theoretical line of the left hand edge of the column of verses; in placing it by projection from the preserved part, the more certain supplements (here 41 ἐντα]ῦθα and 47 καὶ γὰ]ρ) give a check on the rest: e.g. in 42 a participle of a verb of motion is called for by the context, and ἥκοντα appears to suit the space available (if not also the sense) better than the alternatives ἐλθόντα and ἰόντα which some have preferred. Cf. Introd. III, p. 41f.]

41f ἀστικὸν τῇ διατριβῇ: 'a townsman'; διατριβή here is probably 'way of life'. As a fashionable young man, Sostratos naturally goes hunting, and we are to assume that he has come to his father's country estate especially for that (cf. 522f). Pausanias 1.32 says that wild boars and bears could be hunted on Parnes; from the *Dyskolos* we hear nothing of this dangerous game.

42-43 μετὰ κυνηγέτου τινὸς φίλου: Eng. 'with a hunting friend'. With this text we assume that Chaireas is the person referred to; φίλου is taken to function as a noun in apposition to κυνηγέτου. For ἥκοντα, compare *Heros*, frg. 8 νῦν δὲ τοῖς ἐξ ἄστεως | κυνηγέταις ἥκουσι περιηγήσομαι τὰς ἀχράδας ('Now I will take the huntsmen from town round the pear-trees'). The sequence ἥκοντ᾽ ... παραβαλόντ᾽ distinguishes Sostratos' hunting expedition in general from the accidental incident which was a consequence of it – his arrival 'by chance' in the neighbourhood of the shrine. The Greek need not imply that Chaireas was present then; and from the opening scene, where he is being told what happened, it is clear that he was not; hence I print a comma after φίλου. For the type of apposition assumed, see KG I.271f; Schwyzer II.176; Gildersleeve, *Syntax of Attic Greek* II.199f; and for the participles in asyndeton, cf. KG II.103f.

[On this view, the mention of Chaireas as a hunting friend paves the way for the reference to him as Sostratos' συγκυνηγέτης in 48; but it remains odd that he is associated so prominently with the hunting. This notion gives him a relationship with Sostratos, and accounts for his presence in Phyle; but in the play itself we hear Sostratos speak of the slave Pyrrhias as his συγκυνηγός, and gather that Pyrrhias *was* out with him on the day in question, for he is supposed to have been sent back to see Knemon at his house early on the next day, the day in which the play's action takes place (70ff, cf. 90). The difficulty is not wholly countered by saying that it is more apparent in the study than on the stage, but we may note (*a*) that Chaireas' true nature will be clarified very soon when he appears; (*b*) that Pyrrhias is adequately introduced to the audience by 70-76; and (*c*) that in other respects the professedly summary exposition given by the prologue speech is supplemented and modified as the play goes on: e.g. Knemon is a hard-working farmer, but not in fact the poor man one might suppose him to be: cf. above on 39-40, and on 8ff, 24f.

OCT and others adopt no supplement to 43. Many suppose that the κυνηγέτης referred to is Pyrrhias, but this approach seems to create insuperable difficulties with 48, where see n. καί πο]υ Diano (with ἐλθό]ψτ' in 42), but μετὰ κυνηγέτου τινός seems flat without a qualifying word. αὐτο]ῦ ... εἰς τὸν τόπον (Barigazzi) may be acceptable Greek (see, e.g., Sharpley on Ar. *Peace* 1269) but is open to the same objection; ἄλλο]υ Peek; δούλο]υ Webster; alii alia.]

44 'I made him fall rapturously in love with her': cf. especially 191ff (when Sostratos sees the girl again), 381ff, 675ff; and on the sudden thrill of passion, Webster, *SM* 64.

ἐνθεαστικῶς ἔχειν is appropriate of someone possessed by love; cf. LSJ s.v. ἔνθεος. For the gen. αὐτῆς, compare Plato, *Smp.* 222 c ἐρωτικῶς ἔχειν τοῦ Σωκράτους. [αὐτῆς is welcome in the context; but the traces of ink before εχειν in P, though reconcilable with]σ (Turner), are untypical enough of any letter to make restoration problematical, and OCT leaves the place blank. I do not find an attractive alternative. Jean Martin, from autopsy, suggests that there are traces of punctuation rather than part of a letter before εχειν; but then the αὐτῆς] which he prints is inconveniently long.]

45-46 'These are the essentials; the details you shall see, if you like; and please like!'

Plautus and Terence also on occasion warn their audiences not to expect too much in advance: P. *Trin.* 16f, *Vid.* 10f (fragmentary), T. *Adel.* 22ff: dehinc ne exspectetis argumentum fabulae, | senes qui primi uenient i partem aperient, | in agendo partem ostendent. These passages, although primarily relevant to Roman conditions, may reflect a recurrent feature of the brief prologue. See Addenda, p. 305f.

The problems of exposition in comedy are among those dealt with by Antiphanes, *Poiesis* 191 K. Prologue speeches vary widely in conception and scale. The 'long-winded god' as prologue speaker is deplored in a comic prologue of unknown authorship, Page, *Lit. Pap.* 60, of which lines 2-10 read as follows (Page's text and translation): 'Many there are, I know, who diligently try to tell their story's beginning – how it came into being at the start – then the second stage; who add both the causes and the proofs of this: for the sake of which they are bound to make a lengthy, tiresome speech, to an audience half-asleep, giving the clearest information and setting every detail forth ...'

Perhaps Menander applied to his prologue the method recommended by Aristotle for the composition of a plot. Whether it is original or not, one should sketch the story in general terms before developing it (*Poetics* 1455 b): τούς τε λόγους καὶ τοὺς πεποιημένους δεῖ καὶ αὐτὸν ποιοῦντα ἐκτίθεσθαι καθόλου, εἶθ' οὕτως ἐπεισοδιοῦν καὶ παρατείνειν (he then illustrates from Eur. *IT*) μετὰ ταῦτα δὲ ἤδη ὑποθέντα τὰ ὀνόματα ἐπεισοδιοῦν. On the relative unimportance of names, cf. 1451 b 12ff in regard to Comedy, and see under 5ff above; on Menander's idea of composition in general, see Introd. I, p. 10ff.

[46 Perhaps another verb at the beginning, but there seems nothing more likely. βουλήθητε, picking up ἐὰν βούλησθε, is too good a turn of phrase to be emended on the ground that the imperative is an unexpected form: cf. 905. ἐὰν βούλησθ'· ἐβούληθητε δέ Sandbach. βουλήθητε δή Treu.]

47-49 Pan prepares to return to the shrine, announcing the arrival of the characters who open the play. The form in which he does so is conventional: see e.g. E. *Hip.* 51ff, P. *Aul.* 37ff; and for καὶ γάρ in this situation, E. *Phaethon* 58 (=753.10 N²); Ar. *Peace*, 232, 1208; *Dysk.* 230 below, with n. there.

48 συγκυνηγέτην 'hunting companion' is here hesitantly supplied as the missing description of Chaireas, a 'helpful friend' according to Sostratos' remark about him at 56f, 'the parasite' according to the list of *dramatis personae* in P, which describes him, I believe rightly, by dramatic type. For συγκυνηγέτης, see especially Aeschines, *in Ctes.* (3).255 πότερον οἱ συγκυνηγέται ἢ οἱ συγγυμνασταὶ αὐτοῦ, ὅτ' ἦν ἐν ἡλικίᾳ; and Liban. *Decl.* 27.25 συμπότης εἰμί σοι, συστρατιώτης, συγκυνηγέτης; noting also E. *IT* 709 (Orestes to Pylades) ὦ συγκυναγὲ καὶ συνεκτραφεὶς ἐμοί. Libanius, who echoes the *Dyskolos* elsewhere in *Decl.* 27, could have recalled the word from here, but the possibility is too slight to count much: cf. on 91-2.

[The strongest argument in favour of this treatment of the text, a variant of that given in ed. pr., is that the expression τὸν ἐρῶντα τόν τε (x) ἅμα requires (x), like τὸν ἐρῶντα, to be a description recognizable from what has gone before; (x) must therefore refer to the κυνηγέτης of 42, who must accordingly be Chaireas. Serious objections are seen in the paradox of exposition which results, that the συγκυνηγέτης of the prologue is not the same person as the συγκυνηγός of the play: for these, see on 42-43; on Chaireas *qua* parasite, see under 57ff; on the list of *dramatis personae*, see above, pp. 124ff.

OCT and other edd. adopt no supplement; many are offered, and some printed in texts, by those who identify the κυνηγέτης of 42 as Pyrrhias and require a word other than 'hunting companion' to describe Chaireas: they may be classed as (*a*) attempts to find a suitable synonym for 'parasite', prompted partly by ὁ παράσιτος in the list of *dramatis personae*: e.g. τόν τε συγκ[λίτην βάδη]ν ἅμα (Bingen); (*b*) attempts to find some other word descriptive of Chaireas: e.g. τόν τε συνακ[ολουθήσανθ]' ἅμα (Turner, who refers to 350 for the corruption he assumes.) None of the solutions arrived at on these lines appear to take adequate account of the limitations imposed by the pattern τὸν ἐρῶντα τόν τε (x) ἅμα, and some introduce improbabilities of language and/or palaeography: συνκ[, not συνπ[, συνγ[etc. is almost certainly the reading of P. More adventurous hypotheses (grave corruption or interpolation; the prologue written for another version of the play) remain without verification, except in the sense that the text is not so far satisfyingly restored.]

49 '. . . talking to each other about this.' The verb συγκοινόομαι is probably to be accepted in a similar sense at Thuc. 8.75, and the pres. ptcp. is admirably suited to the context here, but it is inconveniently, if not impossibly, long for the space available if correctly written in P: perhaps σ[υγκινομ]ενους vel sim. was what the copyist wrote. [σ[υννοουμ]ένους Fraenkel (perhaps compare E. *Or.* 634); αὐτοὺς . . . σ[υμβαλουμ]ένους Jean Martin ('qui apporteront eux-mêmes des précisions à ce sujet'); Rees suggests σ[ημειουμ]ένους; alii alia.]

50-80 Opening scene: Sostratos and Chaireas enter in conversation. Sostratos is evidently supposed to have pointed out the place of his romantic meeting with Knemon's daughter; Chaireas at first reacts with bland detachment, but cannot decline the chance to parade his expertise in arranging love-affairs for friends. Sostratos gives more details, and we learn that he has already sent the slave Pyrrhias to see Knemon, and is worried at the lack of results.

51 'garlanding the Nymphs' suggests putting garlands on statues of them. Pan and the Nymphs could have been represented outside the stage-Nymphaeum by scene-painting or otherwise, but it is doubtful if Menander's audience needed this aid to imagination. [In 50, OCT, after Maas, adopts ἐνθένδε for P's ἐνταυθα from the quotation in Ammonius as emended by Valckenaer – a long shot, but possibly a true one. For the sense 'hereabouts', cf. Bluck on Plato, *Meno* 83 a 4.]

52 '... you came away in love with her at first sight?' ἐρῶν goes closely with ἀπῆλθες: cf. frg. 568.6 ἕτερος ... οὐδὲν πέπονθεν, ἀλλ' ἀπῆλθε καταγελῶν | ἕτερος δ' ἀπόλωλε. For Chaireas' comment, cf. 102 ὡς ὀργίλως.

53 ἢ τοῦτ' ἐβεβούλευσ' ἐξιών: 'had you decided when you set out?' [ἢ or ἦ (Kraus)? – P has no accent.]

54f The lover naturally wishes to be taken seriously, and tacitly accepts the reassurance (such as it is) of Chaireas' 'I can well believe it.' Cf. *Heros* 39 (Daos) Γέτα, καταγελᾶς; (Getas) μὰ τὸν Ἀπόλλω, and for remarks in similar form, see Ar. *Frogs* 58, *Plut.* 973; slaves joke more boisterously at the expense of their lovesick young masters in the opening scenes of P. *Curc.* and *Pseud.*

57ff *The part of Chaireas*: (i) The list of *dramatis personae* calls him ὁ παράσιτος. His name apparently gave no clear clue to his nature, for it is not otherwise known as a parasite name, and is given by Menander to young men in *Fab. Inc.* and *Koneiazomenai*, and to an old man in *CF*. Nor, it seems, is there a clear verbal clue in the text, unless we are prepared to introduce one at 48. In the theatre, such a character could have been recognized by his mask, and possibly also by costume (Introd. II.3, pp. 33, 37(g)); but Menander spends little time before giving him a speech which characterizes him beyond doubt; and it is probably from this, rather than from any other possible source, that the description in the *dramatis personae* ultimately derives. He emerges not simply as a friend with a helpful gift for affairs who happens to be with Sostratos in the country, but as a member of the class who make friendship a profession, cultivating their social superiors for their own advantage (for instance, earning dinners by praising a man's wit and enduring his insults): in fact a 'sponger' or 'hanger-on' of the kind known variously in Antiquity as 'parasite' and *kolax* or 'flatterer'. Doric comedy had such a figure, known from Epicharmus' play 'Hope or Wealth' (34-35 Kaibel), and probably recalled in the standard 'Sicilian parasite' mask (cf. Webster, *GTP* 82, *MNC* 21); in Attic comedy, the type goes back at least to the chorus of Eupolis, *Kolakes*, of 421 B.C., though the name 'parasite' as a special name for it appears to be a fourth-century innovation, possibly by Alexis, as has been argued by Arnott (BICS 1959.78). In Menander, the traditional type of boon companion and cadger is well represented by the Gelasimus of P. *Stichus* (from *First Adelphoi*); but there is also, as already in Middle Comedy (e.g. Antiphanes, *Progonoi* 195 K), a younger, more active figure in the rôle of lover's confidential *aide*, like Chaireas here (who shows no interest in food and drink), and Gnathon in *Kolax* (see especially T. *Eun.* 232ff). See further Webster, *SM* 75, *LGC* 65: Athenaeus 6.235 f and following is the source of some of the most relevant texts, including Timokles, *Drakontion* 8 K, of which vv. 6f read: ἐρᾷς, συνεραστὴς ἀπροφάσιστος γίνεται· | πράττεις τι, πράξει συμπαρὼν ὅ τι ἂν δέῃ 'If you are in love, he joins in to help with a will; if you've something to do he'll be with you and do what's needed.' For the rich young man accompanied by a parasite on a hunting trip, cf. Astylos and Gnathon in Longus, *Daphnis and Chloe* 4.10ff.

(ii) Chaireas' rôle, therefore, like that of Sikon the cook, is partly to be seen as a standard turn of the comic stage (cf. Introd. I, p. 6 with n. 1). Like Sikon at 489ff, Chaireas boasts of his expertise, and in both cases it comes to nothing. But Menander is not prepared to spread himself far simply in order to gratify anyone's taste for the familiar: both the cook and the parasite are integral to the design of the play, and the traditional humour they bring with them is deployed with conspicuous economy – an instance of what *can* happen is the parasite-speech of 45 lines quoted from Nikolaos (frg. 1 K.) Although Chaireas drops out of the play after 134, his disappearance is acceptably motivated, and he is not expected to return. He has served his dramatic purpose in the exposition, and begun the trials of Sostratos, who started out (as we may think already) by depending too much on the prospect of help, and parts from his fair-weather friend in a mood of angry disillusionment (135ff).

(iii) The form of the speech: Chaireas gives two instances of love-affairs (with *hetaira* and with free-born girl), and says what he does in each case. This kind of self-description, like the character himself, is traditional; both it and the syntactical construction which goes with it are extensively paralleled in comedy, and recur with Sikon the cook at 493ff. The parataxis παραλαμβάνει ... φέρω ..., where a less lively style might use a condition ('If he ... then I') is seen in a parallel form in the lines of Timokles quoted above under (i). Punctuation in such sentences is problematical, since the proposition with which they begin may usually be interpreted either as a statement or as a question (Does he ...? Then I ...); and in the present passage some prefer to read interrogatively the words παραλαμβάνει ... ἑταίρας and γάμον ... ἐλευθέραν. [Cf. KG II.233f; *NTGramm.* §494; on speeches of self-description, see Eduard Fraenkel, *de med. et nov. com. quaestiones selectae* (Göttingen, 1912), 76ff.]

57 τοιαῦτα scans with its first syllable short by correption, as commonly: see on παιανιστάς τινας in 230.

58-63 Violent passion calls for violent action. Chaireas' method is the common one of going in revel to the girl's door (like Phaedromus in P. *Curc.*, for example), and threatening to burn it down with his torch if not let in to carry her off. See Headlam-Knox on Herondas 2.34-37 for a full array of references.

58f παραλαμβάνει: *sc.* ἐμέ, the object understood from the context, as with κατακάω in 60.

59f For the string of verbs, cf. 547-9; for κατακάω see above. The parasite in Antiphanes, *Progonoi* 195 K says he is 'an earthquake at crowbarring doors, and a cricket at jumping in.'

62 αὔξει: the shorter form αὔξω continues in use in Attic and Hellenistic Greek alongside αὐξάνω: e.g. in Comedy, A. *Ach.* 227, Philemon 148 K. In P the commoner form has replaced the rarer one: cf. Introd. III, p. 51 under 'Substitution (ii)'.

63 'In (acting) quickly there is quick relief': ἐν τῷ ταχέως is a striking illustration of the ease with which the Greek article forms the equivalent of a noun: cf. Plato, *Laws* 667 c (Truth gives to learning) τὴν ... ὀρθότητα καὶ τὴν ὠφέλειαν καὶ τὸ εὖ καὶ τὸ καλῶς.

64-68 A marriage contract is permanent: therefore careful enquiries are needed. The theme is developed in frg. 581 by a father with a daughter to betroth; cf. also frg. 580. βίον (66) is the financial status of the proposed in-laws: cf. 306f βίον ἱκανὸν ἔχων.

66-68 'for I am leaving my friend with all my arrangements in the case as a permanent record for the future.'

εἰς πάντα τὸν λοιπὸν χρόνον: cf. Isocrates, *Busiris* (11).10 ᾠήθη δεῖν καὶ τῆς ἀρετῆς τῆς αὐτοῦ μνημεῖον εἰς ἅπαντα τὸν χρόνον καταλιπεῖν.

γάρ is deferred to 7th place in the sentence (i.e. εἰς πάντα τὸν λοιπὸν χρόνον forms a single unit of expression, and γάρ takes second place in the next unit). It is in general less rigorously treated in respect of word-order than δέ and other connecting particles: cf. 10 n., and Denniston, *Particles* 95ff. The conversational style of later comedy provides such parallels as τοὺς ἐν τῇ πόλει | μάρτυρας ἔχω γάρ Philemon, *Pareision* 60 K, and τὸν μὲν ἀπράγμονα | καὶ κοῦφον ἐξαπατᾶν γάρ ἐστι δεσπότην | φλύαρος, M. *Perinthia* 13ff.

ὅσ' ἂν διοικήσω: with the text as here emended, the arrangements themselves are said to constitute a 'reminder' or 'record': cf. Plato, *Phaedrus* 233 a οὐκ ἐξ ὧν ἂν εὖ πάθωσι ταῦτα εἰκὸς ἐλάττω τὴν φιλίαν αὐτοῖς ποιῆσαι, ἀλλὰ ταῦτα μνημεῖα καταλειφθῆναι τῶν μελλόντων ἔσεσθαι – but in such expressions, concord of number and gender may be absent, as here: KG I.62f; on the tense of the subj., see KG I.187f. [ὡς ἂν is accepted from P by ed. pr., OCT and generally; but it leaves διοικήσω without a direct object, and seems to me improbable either in reference to the manner of the transaction (so Kraus, among others, quoting Plato, *Smp.* 181 a: cf. Jebb on S. *Ai.* 1369) or as an indefinite temporal (Diano, referring to KG II.445, 447-8: cf. LSJ s.v. ὡς A. d).]

68f καὶ μάλ' εὖ: understand λέγεις, as often with εὖγε: 'Very good, but not very satisfying to me.' Chaireas does not accept the reproach implied: 'Even in your case we must begin by hearing all about it.' [On οὐ πάνυ 'not at all', 'not very', see H. Thesleff, *Studies on Intensification* ... 76ff (Soc. Sci. Fennica, Comm. Hum. Litt. XXI.1, 1954).]

70ff ὄρθριον τὸν Πυρρίαν . . . πέπομφα: so far the scene has been largely concerned to display the lover and his parasite to the audience; it now turns to the exposition proper, as at P. *Curc.* 67: nunc hinc parasitum in Cariam misi meum – in *Curc.*, the rôles of slave and parasite are reversed. If the view here taken of the prologue speech is right, this is the first the audience hears of Pyrrhias: see on 42-43 and 48. Sostratos' statement that he has sent the slave to see the girl's father, or the master of the house, confirms that he is serious about marrying her: hence Chaireas' exclamation of shocked surprise. Cf. 136ff.

75-77 Sostratos realizes that he may have been tactless ('that was not something that suited a slave'); here, as later, he is conscious of his own situation, and capable of seeing himself as others may see him: cf. on 522-45. [ἥμαρτον need not be interpreted as a question, with OCT; ἥρμοστ' is probably acceptable as pluperfect passive (cf. εἰρήκειν 78), though it is apparently a novel use of the verb; some prefer to read ἥρμοττ' (Kamerbeek). τὸ τοιοῦτό γ' OCT (Page), but see van Groningen ad loc., and Introd. III, p. 52.]

78ff πάλαι τεθαύμακα: 'I am very surprised (and have been for some time) . . .' εἰρήκειν . . . τἀνταῦθά μοι: 'My instructions to him were to find out the situation there and report home to me at once.'

81 Enter Pyrrhias at a run, as slaves and others with news constantly do in comedy; he comes from the audience's left, the direction of Knemon's land. A prototype of this scene is the entry of Amphitheos in A. *Ach.* 176ff, who, like Pyrrhias, has been sped on his way by pursuit, and was threatened with shouts and stones by the infuriated rustics of the chorus. The comic effect, and the suspense, are heightened by the cries to clear the way, the breathlessness (96f), and the general note of alarm: all this is familiar, but two neat individual touches are that the hunted man has himself just been described as a hunter (71), and that he stubs his toes on the rocks of Phyle (91f). At the same time, throughout the scene, Menander is building up his portrait of Knemon, and preparing the audience for his first entry at 153. [Running slave: for examples and discussion, see Webster, *LGC* 92f, Duckworth, *Nature of Roman Comedy* 106f, and the indexes of both works, s.v.]

πάρες: 'let me pass', as e.g. in Com. Anon., Page, *Lit. Pap.* 48.7 εὐλάβει, βέλτιστε· πρὸς θεῶν, πάρες.

πᾶς ἄπελθ' ἐκ τοῦ μέσου: 'get out of the way everybody', a colloquial use of the second person imperative which appears at A. *Ach.* 204 τῇδε πᾶς ἕπου δίωκε, and several times elsewhere.

82 Cf. *Epitr.* 558-9 ὑπομαίνεθ' οὗτος, νὴ τὸν Ἀπόλλω, μαίνεται, | μεμάνητ' ἀληθῶς, μαίνεται, νὴ τοὺς θεούς.

83 φεύγετε . . . **86** ἀπαλλαγῶμεν . . . **87** ἀπὸ τῆς θύρας, κτλ: Knemon is made out to be a man possessed, whose house should be avoided for fear of evil. In P. *Most.*, Tranio tells Theopropides to flee from the 'haunted house' in very similar terms (460, 512, 527, etc.). [Treu assigns τί ἐστι to Chaireas.]

βώλοις, λίθοις: cf. 120. The vivid asyndeton in both passages is not unnaturally replaced with connectives in the flatter style of prose adaptations: e.g. Aelian, *Ep. Rust.* 14: βάλλω τοὺς εἰσφοιτῶντας εἰς τὸ χωρίον καὶ βώλοις καὶ λίθοις.

84 ποῖ: understand φέρει or φεύγεις. ποῖ σύ; ποῖ, μαστιγία; *Sam.* 109, cf. 225, 237; ποῖ σύ, ποῖ; answered by ...πρὸς τὴν ἀσφάλειαν, Com. Anon., Page, *Lit. Pap.* 48.13f.

[**85** Eitrem, van Groningen and others read οὐκέτι ἴσως διώκει as a question. τί δαί Gallavotti, after P¹. Confusion of δαί with δέ etc. by copyists makes it hard to be sure of the incidence of the word, but since it is not so far known to be Menandrean, P²'s correction to δέ (which is linguistically acceptable) is much better adopted. Cf. Page on E. *Med.* 339, and Bluck on Plato, *Meno* 71 c 4.]

88-95 Pyrrhias tries to make the others understand that there is evil abroad; they think he has run wild, perhaps that he has gone mad. The general sense of the passage emerges, though not without difficulty, from what is preserved in P; but damage to the ends of 89-94 leaves ambiguities which mean that nothing more than a specimen restoration can be offered, and OCT leaves the text unrestored. The alternatives mentioned in the notes below do not exhaust the range of suggestions and possibilities.

88-91 'For some son of Woe, some man with the evil eye on him, or the black bile, living here in the house, the man you sent me to see – Gods above, it's something terrible!' In this version of the text, Pyrrhias' breathless excitement and desire to impress are supposed to lead him from a grandiloquent beginning to an incoherent conclusion. In 88-89, Ὀδύνης ... ἄνθρωπος is interpreted as a tricolon based on the form described by Fraenkel on A. *Ag.* 55f: i.e. τις goes with all three expressions; ἄνθρωπος is taken to be common to the last two, P's rough breathing being disregarded. After two attempts at a plainer description of Knemon, the slave breaks off and groans at the pain of his feet. [A main verb, which this version lacks, can be found in different ways: commonly, as in OCT, ἄνθρωπος is accepted and ἐστί understood; since]ει and not]ε is a possible reading at the end of 89, τυγχάν]ει (Barrett) or another verb may be thought to have stood there, since μεγάλου κακοῦ in 91 may be a dependent gen. and not an exclamatory one, ἦρξέ μοι (Ha.) vel sim. could be imagined as the end of 90; perhaps – though the tense would be odd – the verb ἦν has been lost by omission or corruption in 88 (κακοδαίμων ⟨ἦν⟩ Gallavotti; ἦν, κακοδαιμονῶν Diano). The possibilities of ᾠκῶ[ν for οἰκῶ[ν (with crasis as in ᾠκότριψ, Ar. *Thes.* 426), and of πρὸς ἤν for πρὸς ὄν are offered respectively by ed. pr. and by Maas and others: without further exploration, it becomes clear that several or many ways of writing the sentence can be devised; what Menander in fact wrote we cannot determine without further evidence.]

88 Ὀδύνης . . . υός looks as if it anticipates such Biblical phrases as ὁ υἱὸς τῆς ἀπωλείας (=The Antichrist), 2 *Thess.* 2.3; in these, however, the influence of Hebrew appears to be paramount (see, e.g., *NTGramm.* §162 (6)); in true Greek usage the genealogical metaphor was probably always felt to be alive, even in its more fanciful developments: hence Ὀδύνης is appropriately printed with a capital letter and taken as a personification. Examples are: Κόρον, ῞Υβριος υἱόν in an oracle quoted by Hdt. 8.77; ἐγὼ δ᾽ ἐμαυτὸν παῖδα τῆς τύχης νέμων, κτλ. S. *OT* 1080ff; Διόνυσος, υἱὸς Σταμνίου Ar. *Frogs* 22 ('D., son of Winejar'); from later Greek, (Palladas) *Anth. Pal.* 9.394, quoted by Gigante: Χρυσέ, πάτερ κολάκων, ὀδύνης καὶ φροντίδος υἱέ. Cf. also P. *Epid.* 673: apage illum a me! nam ille quidem Vulcani irati est filius, with Duckworth's note ad loc. [Detailed discussions include S. Boscherini, Stud. Ital. Fil. Class. 1959.247ff, and S. Eitrem, Symb. Osl. 1959.132f.]

κακοδαιμονῶν: lit. 'possessed by an evil spirit', cf. κακοδαιμονᾶς Ar. *Plut.* 372, and δαιμονῶντας E. *Pho.* 888. In spite of P's accent, ed. pr.'s conjecture seems best.

89 μελαγχολῶν: 'melancholy-mad' (LSJ), cf. *Sam.* 218; for 'black bile' and madness, cf. *Epitr.* 560f χολὴ | μέλαινα προσπέπτωκεν ἢ τοιοῦτό τι, and Sedgwick on P. *Amph.* 727; a similar expression is χολάω, *Epitr.* 217 and elsewhere.

οἰκῶν, κτλ.: cf. *Heros* 21f ποιμὴν γὰρ ἦν Τίβειος οἰκῶν ἐνθαδὶ | Πτελέασι. The article (i.e. a form of crasis) is not necessarily to be expected: cf. Headlam-Knox on Herondas 6.52: ὁ δ᾽ ἕτερος ἐγγὺς τῆς συνοικίης οἰκέων | τῆς Ἑρμοδώρου . . . | ἦν μέν κοτ᾽, ἦν τις . . . [P's ἄνθρωπος (if significant at all) may have come from an attempt to find a definite antecedent for πρὸς ὄν. It does not suggest that the line ended with a verb; it may mean that there should be a stop before οἰκῶ[ν, as in OCT. Crasis of ὁ οἰ-: cf. Schwyzer I.401.]

90 πρὸς ὄν μ᾽ ἔπεμψας: cf. 70-74. πρὸς ἤν (Maas *et al.*) makes the sentence run more smoothly. For the break in thought assumed in this text, cf. *Sam.* 109-12, perhaps *Fab. Inc.* 19f. [ἔπεμπ[ες OCT (Page), and others. Ἡράκλεις Arnott. αἴτιος (ed. pr.), ἄξιος (Browning *et al.*) and ἵνα τύχω (Kamerbeek) illustrate other ways of accounting for the following genitive.]

91 μέγα κακόν (like Lat. *magnum malum*) is an expression constantly on the lips of slaves to refer to the pains, punishments and other troubles they meet or fear: cf. Simiche at 877, ἔσται μέγα κακὸν πάλιν [τί σοι '. . . something else dreadful on the way', and see on 99ff.

91-96 The text continues to be uncertain, and with it the assignment of parts (on this topic, see Introd. III, p. 44ff). OCT adopts no restorations; as before, and as usually where blocks of lines are damaged, the text given in this edition is a specimen, and variant possibilities of restoring it are by no means exhausted in the notes.

Three leading assumptions are made: that πεπαρῴνηκε in 93 refers to Pyrrhias; that 94f contains a strong denial by him that he is or has been acting abnormally; and that 95f sees his story off to an incoherent start: as appears at once, he can tell a good tale, and he is possibly supposed to be exploiting his alarm and breathlessness to impress his listeners all the more.

91-92 The reference is to stumbling over the rocks (προσπταίων) while being chased by Knemon (117ff) – a point which would be well taken by those who knew their upland Attica.

[To complete the sense, a verb meaning 'break' or 'bruise' is needed: not ἔαξα uncompounded (ed. pr.); perhaps κατέαξα, with the slight chance that Libanius preserves the right word in *Decl.* 27.18 τὸ μοσχίον εἴ ποτε ἐσκίρτησε, κατέαξα λίθοις αὐτοῦ τῶν ποδῶν (cf. on 114 below). Otherwise, e.g., συνέτριψα γὰρ (Shipp). P marks change of speaker in or at the end of 92; in spite of P's breathing, I take ἄπα[ντας to be certain, and the sense there to be complete; τοὺς ἐμούς (ed. pr.), τῶν ποδῶν (Oguse) and other continuations are possible. Many alternatives exist for μαίνετ' ἤ (e.g. ἆρ' ὁ παῖς Lloyd-Jones; Ἡράκλεις Ha., with interrog. τί in 93; πεύσομαι or ὄψομαι Quincey, Shipp, comparing 879).]

92-95 SO. 'Is he mad, or did he come here and do something crazy?' CH. 'It's obvious he's out of his mind.' PY. 'I'll be utterly damned if I did, Sostratos.'

93f παροινέω means not only to misbehave when drunk but to misbehave as if drunk: see *CF* 41; τὸ σὸν πάροινον is said of Polemon's cutting off Glykera's hair in *Perik.* (444, cf. 410). At 138ff Sostratos again suspects that Pyrrhias has done something wrong, still unable to credit Knemon's spontaneous nastiness. Chaireas follows the lead he is given.

[P omits the iota in πεπαρῴνηκε, producing a small crop of violent emendations by ed. pr. (ἐλθών τι πάλλων ἧκε) and others. Change of speaker is indicated in or at the end of 93; a participle describing Pyrrhias (or a finite verb, cf. *Heros* 1-3) seems most likely; Jean Martin, filling in the line with δηλαδή, leaves Chaireas to say εὔδηλός ἐστι alone.]

94f Pyrrhias' denial: cf. 140, 142 (ἔκλεπτον;); and Xanthias in Ar. *Frogs* 612ff καὶ μὴν νὴ Δία, | εἰ πώποτ' ἦλθον δεῦρ' ἐθέλω τεθνηκέναι, | ἢ 'κλεψα τῶν σῶν ἄξιόν τι καὶ τριχός. For the oath as assumed here, see Ar. *Lys.* 933 'Don't deceive me ...' answered by νὴ Δί', ἀπολοίμην ἄρα;

146

Euboulos, *Chrysilla* 117 K εἶτ' ἐγὼ κακῶς ποτε | ἐρῶ γυναῖκας; νὴ Δί'
ἀπολοίμην ἄρα; for a fuller form, e.g. *Dysk.* 309-13, *Epitr.* 704f.

[Ed. pr., disregarding the paragraphi in P, continues Pyrrhias to
εὐδηλός ἐστι (of which the subject is supposed to be Knemon); then
(Σω.) ἔξω τ[ῶν φρενῶν.; and 95 *(Πυ.)* Σώ]στρατ' ἀπολο[ύμεθ'· ἔχειν] δὲ
δεῖ φυλακτικῶς. If ἀπολο[ύμεθ', with elision, the only likely sequel on
metrical grounds is a long syllable or a resolved long (◡ ◡); if
ἀπολο[ύμεθα without elision, the sequel must be a long (Introd. IV,
Notes A, B and C). Other parts of ἀπόλλυμι have been considered:
e.g. ἀπολε[ῖ σε (Shipp), ἀπόλω[λα (Ha.).]

95f ἔχε δέ πως φυλακτικῶς: 'But be on the look-out', cf. 777 ὀξυπείνως
πως ἔχει. I take it that Pyrrhias says this as a preface to his story,
somewhat after the fashion of Tranio at P. *Most.* 472ff as he prepares
to tell the story of the haunted house: circumspicedum numquis
est | sermonem nostrum qui aucupet ... circumspice etiam. (cf. on
83). If so, the implication is 'If you don't believe me, mind he doesn't
catch us here while I explain.' But (*a*) ἀλλ' οὐ δύναμαι λέγειν seems to
several critics to be the beginning of a reply; and (*b*) the absence of a
more explicit introduction to the story (e.g. a command to tell it) is
singular. Hence *(Σω.)* λέγε] δέ πως φυλακτικῶς. *(Πυ.)* ἀλλ' οὐ δύναμαι, κτλ.
(Blake) may be nearer the truth.

[P has no sign of a change of speaker (traces of a paragraphus
would probably be visible in spite of the damage at the beginning of
the line if the copyist originally wrote one there). On P's reading
after the gap in 95, see Introd. III, p. 51f under 'Misreading (ii)';
above δε, there is probably to be seen not a upsilon, but a diastole
crossed through to delete it.]

96-97 ἀλλ' οὐ δύναμαι λέγειν, κτλ.: cf. E. *Ion* 336 ἄκουε δὴ τὸν μῦθον. -
ἀλλ' αἰδούμεθα; for ἀλλά in continuous speech, see further Denniston,
Particles 7f, who quotes among other passages E. *Med.* 1051ff τολμητέον
τάδ'. ἀλλὰ τῆς ἐμῆς κάκης, | τὸ καὶ προσέσθαι μαλθακοὺς λόγους φρενί. |
χωρεῖτε, παῖδες ... This highly dramatic reference to breathlessness
is interesting in contrast with the beginning of the Guard's speech
in S. *Ant.* (223ff); similar, perhaps, but much more fully developed,
is the parasite's exploitation of his tiredness and hunger before telling
his tale in P. *Curc.*, 309ff: tenebrae oboriuntur, genua inedia succidunt,
etc.

προσέστηκεν: 'is pushed up', 'checked', for which ed. pr. refers to
Aristotle, *Problems* II.38 (870 a 32ff), and I.41 (864 a 13). Similarly
μόλις λαλοῦντα καὶ τὸ πνεῦμ' ἔχοντ' ἄνω M. *Halieus*, frg. 23.

[λ[αλεῖν Quincey. It is of course quite uncertain that P's]σέστηκεν
derives from a compound, but the presence of the breathing does not
prove the contrary: in 98, P has προσῆλθε, and in 108 ἀνόσιε. OCT,
adopting no restoration, has 'fort. λ[έγειν. ἄφε]ς.' in the app. crit.

(cf. Introd. IV, Note A, at p. 63). If 95 is treated on the lines proposed by Blake (see above), an attractive possibility is *(Πv.)* ἀλλ' οὐ δύναμαι. *(Σω.)* λ[έγ' εὐθύ]ς. *(Πv.)* ἔστηκεν δέ μοι (van Groningen, after Roberts). 98: "τὸν κύριον ζητεῖτ[' " ἔφ]ην Bingen, Mette; Jean Martin finds 7['beaucoup plus vraisemblable' as the reading of P.]

99ff The 'wretched old woman' is Simiche, the γραῦς θεράπαινα of whom we heard from Pan, 31.

Tr. '. . . and from where I stand talking now, she pointed him out wandering round on the ridge there, the miserable old man, gathering himself wild pears – or something ghastly.' On the dramatic relevance of this detail, see Introd. II.1, pp. 22, 23f.

περιφθειρόμενον: cf. Lycurgus, *in Leocr.* 40, of the aged and infirm after Athens' defeat at Chaeronea: καθ' ὅλην τὴν πόλιν τότ' ἐπὶ γήρως. ὁδῷ περιφθειρομένους, διπλᾶ τὰ ἱμάτια ἐμπεπορπημένους '. . . wandering about wretchedly at death's very door with their clothes pinned up double'. In both passages there is a second participle in apposition. The passive of φθείρω and of some of its compounds is not uncommon in the sense 'go', with an overtone of anger, or other emotional colour: e.g. θᾶττον εἰσφθαρῆθι σύ ('get in quickly, damn you'); and ἀποφθαρεὶς ἐκ τῆς πόλεως ('clearing out of Athens' – to sign on as a mercenary), *Sam.* 229, 282.

The ἀχράς (syn. ἄχερδος) is a wild pear (*Pirus amygdaliformis*, Villars), with spiny branches and astringent fruit, called ἀχράς like the tree: see Gow on Theocr. 7.120, 24.89f; for the wild pear as a feature of rural Attica (where it may now be seen growing, in the district of Phyle and elsewhere), see *Heros*, frg. 8, quoted on 42-43. Schmid, RhM 1959 at p. 161, points out that Timon the Misanthrope is said to have crippled himself in a fall from a pear-tree: Schol. Ar. *Lys.* 808, and other sources, quoting Neanthes (Jacoby, *F Gr Hist* 84 F 35).

πολὺν κύφωνα, on the view taken here, is to be recognized as a phrase parallel to μέγα κακόν; Thierfelder interprets it admirably by translating 'magnam malam crucem'. For the form of the idiom assumed, see Theopompus 63 K ὥς μοι δοκεῖν | εἶναι τὸ πρόθυρον τοῦτο βασανιστήριον, | τὴν δ' οἰκίαν ζητρεῖον ἢ κακὸν μέγα '. . . and the house a place of torture or something horrible'; and Antiphanes, *Tyrrhenos* 211 K θρᾶτταν ἢ ψῆττάν τιν' ἢ | μύραιναν ἢ κακόν τί μοι δώσει μέγα | θαλάττιον. '. . . or a *muraena* or some dreadful sea-creature'. κύφων (or κυφών? – see below) has, like Lat. *crux*, a well-documented literal meaning as an instrument of punishment (see LSJ, s.v., where the equivalent 'pillory' is offered); the extension of sense to 'object causing pain', hence 'pain', 'trouble' or 'something generally unpleasant' is well paralleled in Greek by ἀγχόνη (*a*) as 'noose', in the sense of 'rope for hanging': Semonides 1.18 and elsewhere; cf. Fraenkel on A. *Ag.* 1008ff; (*b*) idiomatically, ταῦτα δῆτ' οὐκ ἀγχόνη; (roughly 'Isn't that murder?') Ar. *Ach.* 125; cf. Aeschines, *False Embassy* (2).38

τοῦτο δὲ ἦν ἄρα ἀγχόνη καὶ λύπη τούτῳ. Finally, the use of πολύς as an intensive may be seen as similar to that in the phrase πολλὴ ἀνάγκη. Attempts to interpret the expression in a more literal sense (e.g. 'collecting a pile of wood', ed. pr.; 'collecting a large amount of wood to build a pillory for himself' Lloyd-Jones, and similarly Jean Martin and others) seem to me far from convincing.

[Hesychius and Photius, quoted in the notes below the text, at least give a lead to good counsel on πολὺν κύφωνα; but on περιφθειρόμενον Hesychius does nothing but darken it: his bizarre explanation has long been felt to depend on some passage of Comedy, and possibly this is the passage. For the possibility of misleading or erroneous lexical entries, etc., see below under 472f, 527f, 531-4; the present instance is responsible for the translation 'ridding his pear-trees of blight' ('en train d'épouiller ses poiriers') in ed. pr.; but in any case is τὰς φθεῖρας συλλέγει supposed to refer to collecting lice or collecting pine-cones (see LSJ s.v. φθείρ)?

Lloyd-Jones, printing περιφθειρόμενον ἀχράδας, ἢ πολύν, κτλ. in OCT, describes the verses as 'obscuri' and suggests that the sense must be 'prowling round the pears, curse him', with ἢ ... συλλέγοντα as an expression tantamount to a wish (CR 1959.184): i.e. 'I wish he were collecting wood for a pillory'. This gives improbable syntax; the fact that ἢ πολύς is a known collocation of words is (I believe) a false lead to interpretation, as is P's stop after ἀχράδας. P offers no accent on ἢ; its accent κυφῶν', preserved by ed. pr., OCT et al., adds to the evidence for κυφών as opposed to the form κύφων, which is here preferred and which is standard in dictionaries (see Schol. Ar. Plut. 606). It is possible that the variation represents a distinction between different senses of the word, either a genuine one of pronunciation or a theoretical one of the grammarians – if so, it is a nice point how the sense here postulated was treated or pronounced.]

102f The comment ὡς ὀργίλως is provoked by the slave's highly coloured language; he brushes it aside and continues. The speaker was probably identified as Chaireas in P (for this is the likeliest reading and interpretation of the damaged marginal *nota personae*): if so, rightly – as in 112, 116f, 125ff. He seems to be trying to live up to his reputation as a helpful friend by words rather than by deeds. Cf. ὡς ταχύ, 52. Kraus notes *quid tam iracundu's?* at P. *Sti.* 321, said by Gelasimus the parasite to Pinacium the slave.

τί, ὦ μακάριε;: see on βέλτιστε in 144. Hiatus after interrog. τί is common in Comedy, but probably not admitted after indef. τι: see under 247ff.

[Some edd., including OCT, follow ed. pr. in attributing ὡς ὀργίλως to Sostratos; OCT continues (against P) with Χα. τί ⟨δ'⟩, ὦ μακάριε; (Πυ.) ἐγὼ μέν ... (Lloyd-Jones). The marginal *nota personae* is hardly Σωσ]τρ, possibly Πυ]ρρ, referring to 103.]

104ff Pyrrhias' polite approach: see above under 8ff. Greeting someone from a distance is a characteristic of the ἄρεσκος in Theophrastus, *Char.* 5; for ἐπιδέξιος cf. Aristotle, *Eth. Nic.* 1128 a 17 τοῦ δ' ἐπιδεξίου ἐστὶ τοιαῦτα λέγειν καὶ ἀκούειν οἷα τῷ ἐπιεικεῖ καὶ ἐλευθερίῳ ἁρμόττει.

106f προσεῖπα· καὶ | "ἥκω . . . : 'run-on' of this kind is not uncommon in M., e.g. *Sam.* 43f βάδιζε καὶ | σπεῦδ'; see 114 and on 407f.

107-8 ' "I've come to you about something sir," I said " – I'm anxious for your sake to see you about a thing." '

Pyrrhias' attempt at the civilized man's casual politeness has provoked doubts about the text from many (including myself): for the repetition of τι . . . σε, the construction of the accusatives, and the word-order all make one hesitate. But ἥκω τι gives acceptable idiomatic Greek with τι in its limiting sense of 'about something' (i.e. 'for some reason', 'for some purpose'); and ἰδεῖν . . . πρᾶγμα may be taken as an expansion of the first part of the remark: i.e. σπεύδων, qualified by ὑπὲρ σοῦ , governs ἰδεῖν, which has σε as direct object and πρᾶγμά τι as qualification. Similar in sense is T. *Andr., ex. alt.* 1 (= 982), quoted by Jean Martin: est de tua re quod ego agere tecum uolo. Alternatively, after Thierfelder, who was among the first defenders of the text, 'uenio ob quandam rem ad te, tua causa operam dans, ut certam rem intellegas': i.e. σπεύδων with acc. + inf., and πρᾶγμά τι as direct object of ἰδεῖν ('look at', 'look into').

τι . . . τι πρᾶγμα: compare (*a*) Plato, *Prot.* 310 e: αὐτὰ ταῦτα . . . ἥκω παρὰ σέ; (*b*) Lucian, *Philops.* 39 δέομαι γὰρ αὐτῷ τι συγγενέσθαι, and see further Jebb on S. *OT* 788, Schwyzer II.77 under (ζ) and (θ).

[Dr J. A. Willis refers me to two further passages of *Protagoras* in which the same idiom should probably be recognized: (*a*) 316 b: ὦ Πρωταγόρα, πρὸς σέ τι ἤλθομεν ἐγώ τε καὶ Ἱπποκράτης οὗτος; (*b*) 314 e: Πρωταγόραν γάρ τι δεόμενοι ἰδεῖν ἤλθομεν. In both, τι is the reading of BTW, printed by Bekker in (*a*) and approved by Orelli in both; in both τοι, which is quoted from certain of the *recentiores*, has attracted critical favour generally (e.g. Burnet, Nestle, Croiset and Bodin.) Cf. also *Perik.* 39f, reading ἰδ[εῖν with Sudhaus and τι with cod.]

πάτερ as a mark of respect, as e.g. at 171; cf. 493f.

ἰδεῖν 'see' (i.e. 'interview', 'meet'): cf. 305n.

For examples of repetitions involving pronouns and indef. τι, see KG I.660, 665 A.3, and cf. on 805f; for the word-order, cf. on 223ff.

[†ιδειντισε† OCT; ἰδεῖν σ' ἔτι Eitrem, leaving the first τι far from πρᾶγμα (and why ἔτι?); others think that the end of 107 may derive from an infin. in -ισαι: e.g. πατρίδιον, κτίσαι Maas, adopting πατρίδιον from Barber. 'Possibly ἥκω δέ', I suggested in BICS 1959.65, referring for 'inceptive' δέ to Denniston, *Particles* 170-2. τινα . . . πράγματ' (ed. pr.) is essentially a means to remove hiatus from 108, which is better done otherwise. κευθύς Eitrem, quoted by van Groningen.]

109f 'And what was the idea of coming on to my land?' – but in the Greek Knemon puts first what concerns him most. For the δέ cf. Denniston, *Particles* 174f; for the deferred interrogative, cf. 114, Ar. *Lys.* 599 σὺ δὲ δὴ τί μαθὼν οὐκ ἀποθνῄσκεις; and in general, G. Thomson, CQ 33 (1939) 147ff.

[Numerous alternative corrections exist. Ed. pr. adds σύ after τί μαθών, but it comes better after ἥκεις; and from there it could have been lost very easily by haplography (*HKEIΣΣYTI-*): cf. Introd. III, p. 50. Kassel would treat the first part of the sentence as an exclamation, punctuating after ἥκεις σύ, with τί μαθών; as a separate question. βῶλόν ‹θ᾽ἅμ᾽› Diano, ‹καὶ› βῶλον Fraenkel.]

[**111** ἀφίησιν (P) has found supporters, among them Gallavotti, Kraus, and Jean Martin: cf. Kassel, Gnomon 1961.135, quoting Maas, RhM 68 (1913) 357. But the reading cannot be trusted as evidence for the quantity ῑ in Menander, any more than ἐστὶν ἐκεῖ and the like can be trusted as evidence of 'split anapaests': cf. Introd. IV, p. 65 under (*h*). At *Epitr.* 754 most editors (including Jensen, Koerte and Wilamowitz) adopt Lefèbvre's ἀφίεσο, which involves a choice between a 'split anapaest' and a short iota. The minority (including van Leeuwen) is right in accepting ἀφεῖσο (αφεισο ex αφεεσο cod.); in spite of LSJ, this is a perfect imperative, like πέπαυσο at *Sam.* 135, not 'plpf. 2 sg.']

112 ἐς κόρακας is invariable in this set phrase, although Menander elsewhere uses εἰς: cf. Wilamowitz, *Schiedsgericht*, p. 53; Jackson, *Marginalia Scaenica* 82. Chaireas presumably means 'To hell with him', or 'To hell with that', not 'To hell with you' (for telling such a tale). Cf. on ἄπαγ᾽ εἰς τὸ βάραθρον in 394.

ἀλλά σ᾽ ὁ Ποσειδῶν, sc. ἀπόλεσειεν: cf. 504. [Here and elsewhere P spells the god's name with -ι-, not -ει-: 504, 633, 777, 889.]

113 κατέμυσα: the upsilon is presumably short; for this treatment of the first metron, see on 496. The aorist, of a single rapid action, is the appropriate tense.

πάλιν 'in turn', introduces the second of a related series of actions (taking hold of the stake, after picking up the clod and hurling it), and it is followed by τὸ δὲ πέρας (117), as at *Epitr.* 568-71. It is not clear what the χάραξ was supposed to be: a piece of one of the pear trees, a tree-prop, a fence-post, or (as I should like to think), a rustic equivalent of the old man's βακτηρία with which Menander has endowed his hero: he may be supposed to be carrying it still at 168. Cf. Gow on Theocr. 4.49. [The marginal gloss μάστιγγα in P is apparently an attempt at explanation based on Sostratos' reference to the incident in 142; χάραξ can hardly *mean* 'whip', but the fact that it could be explained as 'whip' may bear on the text of the following line. See LSJ s.v., and Pritchett, Hesperia 1956.305f.]

114 ταύτῃ μ' ἐκάθαιρε: 'he set about me with it'. This emended text assumes καθαίρω as 'beat', 'strike': cf. 901, and Theocr. 5.119, with Gow's note. There is a similar colloquial use of πλύνω 'wash' to mean 'abuse': cf. Eng. 'dress down'. The emendation is prompted by the reference back to the incident at 142 and 168 (?), by P's gloss μάστιγγα (see above), and by the behaviour of the misanthropes in Lucian, *Timon* 48 and Libanius, *Decl.* 27.18: (*a*) Lucian: (*Timon*) πλὴν ἀλλὰ πρόσιθι· καί σε φιλοφρονήσομαι τῇ δικέλλῃ. (*Philiades*) ἄνθρωποι, κατέαγα τοῦ κρανίου ὑπὸ τοῦ ἀχαρίστου, διότι τὰ συμφέροντα ἐνουθέτουν αὐτόν. (*b*) Libanius: καὶ ὁ κύων εἰ σαίνει με προσιόντα, τῇ σκαπάνῃ συνθραύω.

[Taking P's ἐκάθαιρε ταύτην, we can hardly say that it means 'hit my head' with ed. pr.; the idea that Knemon was 'cleaning' the stake of earth or twigs has been advanced more than once, and is adopted by Jean Martin, but seems singularly weak in the context (why is Knemon suddenly so deliberate, or Pyrrhias so specific?); ἐκάθαιρε ταύτῃ (Sydn.) leaves the verb without an object; ἐκάθαιρε †ταύτην† OCT. The imperfect is, I suppose, descriptive rather than conative.]

114f σοὶ δὲ κἀμοὶ πρᾶγμα τί ἔστιν; as γεωμετρικῇ δὲ καὶ σοὶ πρᾶγμα τί; 'What have you to do with Geometry?' Nicomachos, *Eileithuia* 1 K.24. The corresponding Latin is *quid tibi mecumst rei?* P. *Men.* 323, 494, cf. T. *Adel.* 177; for a variant, cf. *Dysk.* 469f. [cf. *NTGramm.* § 127.]

116f 'This farmer of yours must be completely out of his mind'. Cf. Ar. *Plut.* 992 λέγεις ἐρῶντ' ἄνθρωπον ἐκνομιώτατα, quoted with other passages by Headlam-Knox on Herondas 6.95.

117 τὸ δὲ πέρας, elliptically, like 'to cut a long story short', the verb notionally present being λέξω, ἄκουέ μου vel sim. γάρ resumes the narrative (or as Jean Martin puts it 'répond à l'attente ainsi provoquée'): cf. Denniston, *Particles* 58f, noting Dem. 56.10, *Georgos* 49f, and *Dysk.* 942f.

118ff The perfect δεδίωχα, if rightly read, stresses the result of the action, not merely its occurrence '... and then on (εἶθ' οὕτω) down into this thicket (and here I am)': cf. on 627f. Fifteen stades is just under 1¾ miles; ἴσως with a numeral 'about', as for instance at 327. On the scene suggested, see Introd. II.1 at p. 22ff. [The form δεδίωχα is warranted by Hyperides, *Lyc.* 16, and accordingly to be preferred; on P's spelling, cf. above, p. 126 (on σιμικη in the list of *dramatis personae*). Shipp suggests ἐδίωκ' as 'the natural tense'.]

120f 'clods, stones, his pears' – the pears are those referred to in 101. Prose adaptations flatten the effect: e.g. Aelian, *Ep. Rust.* 13 βάλλεις οὖν ἡμᾶς ταῖς βώλοις καὶ ταῖς ἀχράσι: cf. 83 n.

122f ἀνήμερόν τι πρᾶγμα: compare English 'a nasty piece of work'. Greek similarly admits πρᾶγμα, κτῆμα, χρῆμα and other neuters as predicates of masc. or fem. nouns, or in apposition to them, as here.

See on 449f, and cf. Euboulos 117 K ... (γυναῖκας) ... πάντων ἄριστον
κτημάτων. εἰ δ᾽ ἐγένετο | κακὴ γυνὴ Μήδεια, Πηνελόπη δέ γε | μέγα πρᾶγμα.
[Ed. pr. wrongly takes ἀνήμερόν τι πρᾶγμα ... γέρων as a complete
sentence, attributing it to Sostratos, against P; Bingen and Marzullo
make Chaireas the speaker: so OCT. Jean Martin and Jacques agree
with them in punctuating with a stop after ἔτι, but leave the words
with Pyrrhias.]

123 δειλίαν λέγεις: cf. on 116f.

124f κατέδεται ἡμᾶς: cf. 467f.

125 'Perhaps he's thoroughly upset about something just now.'
τετύχηκε of a past event with present consequences, as e.g. Metagenes,
Aurai 1 K: ἱερεὺς γὰρ ὢν τετύχηκα. Perfect forms of ὀδυνάω are not
quoted from elsewhere, and ὠδυνημένος is doubtful here.
[τυχὸν ἴσως seems certain. If we prefer ὀδυνώμενος, which is perhaps
closer to P, a syllable must be presumed missing: e.g. ἀλλ᾽ ὀδυνώμενος
Dale; ὅδ᾽ ὀδυνώμενος Kraus, Zuntz; ὑποδυνώμενος (not recorded),
Quincey, Treweek.]

127ff 'Take my word for it, the secret of success in everything is
timing the approach'. Kraus compares T. Heaut. 364f: in tempore ad
eam ueni, quod rerum omniumst | primum. Chaireas covers his
retreat with a wise-sounding platitude, and a promise to see Knemon
himself 'first thing in the morning'. His impression of Knemon contains a measure of truth, like Getas' fuller portrait of the old man as
a typical Attic farmer at 603ff; but as the play will make clear, the
poverty arises from choice not circumstance, and the sharp temper
is not only rooted in the soil. 'It'll be all right', he says (134); Sostratos' reaction, though coloured by impatience and disappointment,
is essentially just: in another context the advice might have been
reasonable; as it is, the facile readiness to sum up the situation in his
own interest is an apt sign of the shallowness of Chaireas' own character.

128 πρακτικώτερον: εὐκαιρία (in a word 'tact', as Arnott translates it)
is the 'more effective' plan – more effective than ἀκαιρία, by an implication which can sometimes be felt in the common use of κάλλιον,
χεῖρον, βέλτιον (149), etc. The alternative reading πρακτικώτατον,
adopted by ed. pr., is more obvious and less likely to be right. Cf.
Neil on Ar. Knights 83-84, Holzinger on Plut. 67.

129 νοῦν ἔχετε: cf. ἱκετεύω σ᾽, ἄπιτε, 123; but this is quite likely not
another imperative: i.e. Pyrrhias (illogically) calls both sensible,
breaking in to approve the turn the discussion has taken, and hoping
it will go that way. Cf. on νενομίκατε in 173.
ὑπέρπικρον: 'exceedingly sharp in temper', LSJ on A. PV 944, the
only instance of the compound quoted.

132f τὴν οἰκίαν ἐπείπερ οἶδα: a nice touch, implying that his journey has not been wasted. ἐπείπερ as in 392.

133f καὶ σύ, 'you in your turn': as Webster suggests, the meaning is brought out by 'Now I will go home and stay there, and so should you.' Cf. Headlam-Knox on Herondas 2.65.

The presumption from the sense that this is Chaireas' exit-line is reinforced by the reactions of the others. Pyrrhias leaps in to agree, as if the topic were closed; Sostratos comments as he hardly could have done if Chaireas were still present, then turns in fury on his other unhelpful helper, 138. In spite of (ὧ) βέλτιστε in 144, which some take as a sign of his presence, Chaireas has no part to play in the following dialogue. After what he has just said, any further intervention would be dramatically pointless; the stage needs to be cleared of Sostratos' companions, for he is to face Knemon alone; and in leaving after 134, the actor who played Chaireas has a convenient interval to change and enter as Knemon (see Introd. II.2).

135 πράττωμεν οὕτως: 'Let's do as you say': compare οὕτω ποίει . . . εἰ βούλει at Plato, Smp. 214 d, and Knemon's οὕτω πράττετε 'Do as you like', in 746 below. Sostratos is presumably too angry to answer at once, and the slave presumptuously speaks for him.

135f 'That's an excuse, and he's glad to have found it.' Ed. pr. quotes CF 50 πρόφασιν εἴληφ' ἀσμένως | πρὸς αὐτόν; note also προφάσεις εὐλόγους εἰλήφεσαν, Dem. de Cor. (18).152.

εὐθύς: 'from the very beginning'.

[**138** τὴν προσβολ]ὴν Diano; βουλὴν ἐμ]ὴν Page; OCT adopts no restoration.]

139-50 The accession of H solves some textual problems; others remain, and are complicated by uncertainties of part-division, and sometimes reading, in both copies.

[Pending republication of H, I remark here on some doubtful details. 139: traces of ink at the top of the fragment may represent]ᾳπολ[(Mette). 140:]δ̓ Turner;]σ̓, preferred in OCT, is in accord with the restoration of ed. pr. 141: the traces of letters at the beginning appear unhelpful: before στοχωριογ[, probably the expected ει, before that, Mette would read [ἐλθὼν γὰ]ρ. 142: possibly 2-3] . . .: εκλεπτον:. Before ἔκλεπτον, OCT records . . .] . [.]λ[.]', but everything here seems too uncertain to give a lead to conjecture. 144: OCT reports dicola before βέλτιστε in H, and (with others) after βέλτιστε in P; I am not clear about either. After αὐτός, where H is damaged, the spacing of the letters does not suggest that a dicolon was present, but does not exclude the possibility. Traces of speakers' names in the margin at 143 and 145 appear to support the attribution of καὶ πάρεστί γ̓, κτλ. to Pyrrhias, and οὐκ ἂν δυναίμην, κτλ. to Sostratos (Roberts).

Under 143 and 144, as under 146, I seem to see traces of paragraphi; but cf. Turner, BICS 1959.60.]

Recriminations between master and slave are cut short by the arrival of Knemon. 143 'Yes, and here he is': Pyrrhias (who must be the speaker) is supposed to see Knemon coming from some little distance away, as is clear from 147-52. With the text here given, I assume that Sostratos' reaction is of alarm mixed with incredulity. Pyrrhias will not face the enemy again, and retreats to the shrine, speaking τουτονί in 146 from its door (cf. Introd. II.2). Confronted with Knemon, Sostratos holds his ground till 149, then he too withdraws a little. The delayed entrance of Knemon, as well as adding a final touch of dramatic suspense, is used to characterize both speakers. Two classic examples of this kind of 'build-up' are especially instructive: E. *Cycl.* 193-202 (entry of the Cyclops), and S. *Phil.* 201-219 (entry of Philoctetes).

[**140** According to P, Sostratos continues at the beginning, for there is no dicolon at the end of 139, nor any stop. If so, what he said is quite uncertain. If not a vocative, like μαστιγία, perhaps an exclamation should be supplied: e.g. τῆς μωρίας Lond.]

[**141-2** Here restored *exempli gratia*; other suggestions and possibilities are numerous.]εις in 141 may be a verb-ending: e.g. ἐκακοτέχν]εις Blake, comparing 310; OCT leaves the place blank. *(Σω.)* ἐμβὰς σύ γ'] εἰς . . . . . *(Πυ.)* ἀλλ' οὐκ ἔκλεπτον (Lond.); this and some other ideas assume change of speaker after δηλαδή, against P.]

142 'But someone beat you, you say?' referring back to Pyrrhias' story at 114. Cf. 487.

144 αὐτός: cf. *Perik.* 424f *(Δω.)* καὶ μὴν ἔμελλεν ἐξιέναι δ[ὴ χὠ πατήρ.] | *(Πο.)* αὐτός; τί γὰρ πάθῃ τις; (The source is P. Oxy. 211, which has <u>και</u>—αυτος·—τις:). For αὐτός as an independent remark, cf. Ar. *Clouds* 219. [Bingen has this punctuation also, without the change of speaker in ed. 1, with it in ed. 2. So strong a pause after initial _ ◡ is unusual: Introd. IV, Note B, at p. 67.]

ὑπάγω, βέλτιστε: cf. ὑπάγω, τρόφιμε 378 and n. Holding that Pyrrhias is the speaker, I take the tone of βέλτιστε to be like that of 476, Getas to Knemon. Both slaves have suffered a rebuff, and their formal politeness conveys a hint of self-righteous reproach. ὦ βέλτιστε, ὦ ἀγαθέ and the like have a wide range of function according to context, a point well made apropos of Plato by E. Brunius-Nilsson, *ΔΑΙΜΟΝΙΕ*, 110, 112. Cf. on 496f, 503.

There seems to be no parallel in comedy for this use of βέλτιστε from a slave to his master; hence many would arrange or interpret the text differently. But Pyrrhias is something different from the ordinary household slave. He is the young man's hunting companion, now promoted to confidential agent; he speaks freely of and to his

betters, brusquely dismissing a comment from Chaireas on his strong
language about Knemon (103), breaking in to influence a decision
(129, 135), and dispensing advice to Sostratos with all the assurance
of a well-meaning friend (214ff). To him, Sostratos is not τρόφιμος
(contrast Getas at 553); nor does he call him δέσποτα, but elsewhere
only addresses him by name (95, 140, 214).

145 οὐκ ἂν δυναίμην ... λαλεῖν: when he has a chance to speak to
Knemon, Sostratos can do no better than offer a feeble excuse for
being there at all, 171f. This incident gives what is perhaps the strongest
proof that he is the speaker here. Later on, circumstances lead him to
resolve to do better, as indeed he does, though not in the way he
intended: 266ff.

[**144-5** appear in widely different arrangements, of which the following are specimens. OCT, continuing from 143 with Pyrrhias, has
... αὐτός. ὑπάγω, βέλτιστε. κτλ.; Oguse, again continuing with Pyrrhias,
suggests αὐτὸς ὑπάγω, βέλτιστε ('Quant à moi, je m'en vais ...'). But
αὐτός is to be distinguished from what precedes on the evidence of
P's dicolon after οὑτοσί, and I am not clear that it can well be taken
with what follows in the sense of a personal pronoun antithetic to σύ.
In the first publication of H, Grenfell and Hunt assumed the word-
division ὕπαγ' ὦ βέλτιστε, and some have followed them. ὕπαγε ('Come
on') could well be right; but ὑπάγω is slightly favoured by H (no sign
of elision) and by *Dysk*. 378 in P; it gives a useful cue for Pyrrhias'
retreat. *(Σω.)* αὐτὸς ὕπαγ', ὦ βέλτιστε. *(Πυ.)* σὺ δὲ τούτῳ λάλει Lond.;
... αὐτός. *(Χα.)* ὕπαγ', ὦ βέλτιστε. *(Σω.)* σὺ δὲ τούτῳ λάλει Kraus,
according to whom Chaireas also speaks 145f. The δέ does not favour,
though it does not exclude, the assumption of a change of speaker
after βέλτιστε, or indeed before it; Chaireas is not an acceptable
speaker for 145f, and on other grounds should leave after 134. Gallavotti would have Sostratos speak 144 (αὐτὸς ὕπαγ', ὦ βέλτιστε, σὺ δὲ
τούτῳ λάλει) and Pyrrhias 145f; I owe to discussion with Goold the
idea that Pyrrhias may say ὕπαγ', ὦ βέλτιστε to the advancing Knemon.]

146 'Who do you mean?' 'This man here.' Like the audience,
Sostratos has not seen Knemon before, and might well turn to look
at him with some surprise. For ποῖος, see on 753; on Knemon's costume
and mask, cf. Introd. II.3, p. 37, under (i).
[*(Πυ.)* ποῖον λέγει[ς σὺ τουτο]νί; Lond. *et al.*, assuming loss of a
dicolon; OCT, continuing with Sostratos, accepts ποῖον λέγει[ν δεῖ
τουτο]νί from ed. pr.; alii alia. Bingen, ed. 2, arrives independently at
the arrangement here given: cf. 144. His name should be added to the
app. crit.]

147-8 φιλάνθρωπον: the common limiting acc. with βλέπω, 'He
doesn't look at all friendly ...' βλ[έπων ed. pr.; but the infin. is required by the sense.

ὡς δ' ἐσπούδακ': 'and what a hurry he's in' – a sign of mental agitation, see 150. Jean Martin, adopting ὡς from H², prefers to interpret 'Comme il a l'air sévère', with Kamerbeek and others. The verb has both senses, but given ὡς δ', the former seems slightly preferable; compare Euphron, *Synepheboi* 10 K: ... καὶ γὰρ οὑτοσὶ | προσέρχεθ' ὁ γέρων. ὡς δὲ καὶ γλίσχρον βλέπει.

148f ἐπανάξω: 'I'll retreat', intrans., as e.g. Xen. *Cyr.* 4.1.3; βραχύ as *Georg.* 32f βραχὺ ... μεταστῶμεν 'Let's move away a bit'. With βέλτιον the verb is understood (ἔσται, ἂν εἴη vel sim.) as at 592f ταὐτῷ γε τούτῳ σχοινίῳ ... κράτιστον; cf. Ar. *Thes.* 773-4 τί δ' ἄν, εἰ ταδί ... διαρρίπτοιμι; βέλτιον πολύ. [ἔτ[' ἀφέ]ξω Barigazzi; alii alia.]

149f 'What's more, he's shouting...': for ἀλλὰ καί cf. Denniston, *Particles* 21f. Cf. 116 ὀξύτατον ἀναβοῶν τι; Knemon strides along shouting still, although he has lost his quarry. οὐχ ὑγιαίνειν κτλ. is a euphemistic way of saying 'He must be mad', as e.g. Plato, *Lysis* 205 a, quoted by Jean Martin: οὐχ ὑγιαίνει ... ἀλλὰ ληρεῖ τε καὶ μαίνεται. Contrast Pyrrhias' more violent reaction, 83ff.

[ἀλλὰ γ[ὰρ ed. pr.; alii alia. The trace of a letter before the gap suits κ[rather than γ[; ρ[or ι[would be suitable; μ[ὴν, ν[ῦν and other possibilities are less likely. ἀλλ' Ἄρ[η β]οᾷ OCT (Lloyd-Jones) is perhaps more likely in an elevated style than in the present context: cf. A. *Ag.* 48.]

151 μὰ τὸν Ἀπόλλω καὶ θεούς: so ed. pr., following P. According to the accepted rule for Classical Greek, μά is used to strengthen a positive protest (as opposed to its regular use in denials) only when preceded by the affirmative particle ναί (νή): for example, Ar. *Knights* 338 (Κλ.) οὐκ αὖ μ' ἐάσεις; (Ἀλ.) μὰ Δία. (Κλ.) ναὶ μὰ Δία. (Ἀλ.) μὰ τὸν Ποσειδῶ 'Won't you let me?' 'No, by Zeus' 'Yes you will, by Zeus' 'No I won't, by Poseidon.' Here it seems that the tone of the protesting assertion is set by μέντοι, and we have an anticipation of the affirmative μά already recognized in Later Greek. See further on 639 εἰσὶν θεοί, μὰ τὸν Διόνυσον. [At P.*Capt.* 880 (for what it is worth) μὰ τὸν Ἀπόλλω gives a positive reply, not a negative one as at *Most.* 973: ναὶ τὸν Ἀ. is conjectured by Thesleff. It seems doubtful if the oath can be taken with οὐχ ὑγιαίνειν ... δοκεῖ (Fraenkel, in CR 1959 at p. 184), or justified by the quasi-negatival nature of the verb δέδοικα: so van Groningen, cf. Thesleff, *Yes and No in Plautus and Terence*, 51 n. 3 (Soc. Sci. Fennica, Comm. Hum. Litt. XXVI.3, 1960); νή (Barrett, Shipp) is adopted in OCT.]

For the oath by Apollo and the gods, see *Epitr.* 224, 631; it could be restored at *Sam.* 94.

152 μὴ οὐχί: the meaning required is 'Why not tell the truth?' (more literally, perhaps 'Why tell anything but the truth?'): i.e. why not admit to being very frightened? The nearest available parallel

seems to be Plato, *Philebus* 12 d πῶς γὰρ ἡδονή γε ἡδονῇ μὴ οὐχ ὁμοιότατον ἂν εἴη; 'for how could one pleasure help being most like another?', where Bury defended the text, following Goodwin (*Moods and Tenses*, p. 93), but doubts continue to be raised (e.g. Hackforth, *Plato's Examination of Pleasure*, p. 15 n. 2). The appearance of similar questions with οὐ at E. *IA* 1423 and with οὐχί at Ar. *Plut.* 252 (τί γὰρ ἄν τις οὐχὶ πρὸς σὲ τἀληθῆ λέγοι;) certainly prompt one to consider deleting μή, as is done in OCT and elsewhere (Fraenkel, cf. Lond.), and similarly in the *Philebus* passage (Badham). Greek usage does however admit an apparently gratuitous second negative in the presence of a quasi-negatival interrogative: cf. Plato, *Tht.* 153 a (quoted by Bury): τίς οὖν ἄν... δύναιτο... μὴ οὐ καταγέλαστος γενέσθαι; On balance, the μὴ οὐχί seems more likely to be due to the author than to textual corruption. The scansion μὴ οὐ by synizesis is normal, and common to Comedy and Tragedy.

153-68 Knemon's soliloquy: he wishes he had Perseus' winged sandals to escape from earth, and the Gorgon's head to turn nuisances to stone. He would certainly use it, for as it is he can't work his land for people pestering him. And now another!

The speech is refashioned by Aelian to provide the main material for *Ep. Rust.* 14 (Knemon to Kallippides!); seen side by side, original and adaptation throw some new light on Aelian's literary technique; twice, perhaps, we gain a little help with the text of the *Dyskolos* (156, 159; 164?).

153-9 'Well, wasn't Perseus lucky...?' The note of anger, sarcasm or contempt commonly conveyed by εἶτα at the beginning of a speech is well represented here: cf. LSJ s.v. By dramatic type, Knemon is a traditional character (6 n.); it is attractive to think that part of the audience's pleasure in what they have heard of him already is pleasure in the familiar, and that the point is reinforced by his physical appearance, wearing an old-fashioned mask; now Menander introduces him with a form of harangue to match, for which writers of Middle Comedy provide apt parallels: cf. Antiphanes, *Misoponeros* 159 K (which has a point of contact with *Dysk.* 384ff); Amphis, *Athamas* 1 K and *Erithoi* 17 K (εἶτ' οὐχὶ χρυσοῦν ἐστι πρᾶγμ' ἐρημία;); Alexis, *Daktylios* 43 K and *Mandragorizomene* 141 K. The sardonic use of a mythological commonplace is seen again in Menander himself, frg. 718: 'Well, aren't they right to paint Prometheus pegged to the rocks, with a lamp and nothing else good? He did what I think all the gods hate him for – made women...'; similar is Aristophon, *Pythagoristes* 11 K: εἶτ' οὐ δικαίως ἔστ' ἀπεψηφισμένος | ὑπὸ τῶν θεῶν τῶν δώδεκ' εἰκότως τ' Ἔρως; | ἐτάραττε κἀκείνους γὰρ ἐμβάλλων στάσεις, | ὅτ' ἦν μετ' αὐτῶν (accordingly, the speaker goes on to say, the Gods exiled Love to earth, cutting his wings off to keep him there, and giving them to Nike.).

As the old man turns to his present situation, 160ff, there emerge through the torrent of feeling some of the details about him which go to make up the portrait of his character: cf. Introd. I, p. 12 n. 1, and II.1, p. 23f.

When Knemon implies that he would outdo Perseus in turning people to stone (158f), an element of hyperbole is introduced which recalls one of Plautus' favourite forms of monologue opening: e.g. *Ba.* 925ff, where the pattern is 'They say the Atreidae did a great deed in storming Troy: this was nothing to the way I shall carry my master by storm.' On the very different and typically Plautine style of these passages, see Fraenkel, *Plautinisches im Plautus* 8ff (=*Elem. Plautini*, 7ff).

[154: possibly punctuate with an additional question mark after ἐκεῖνος, as in OCT, instead of continuing to 157. Aelian, *loc. cit.*, has ὅτι τε πτηνὸς ἦν καὶ οὐδενὶ συνήντα; τε πτηνὸς for πετηνὸς has been offered in a text of *Dyskolos*, where it does not scan. 156: (τοῦ κτήματος ἐκείνου) ᾧ τοὺς συναντῶντας ἐποίει λίθους Aelian, gives slight support to ed. pr.'s ᾧ λίθους; λιθινους (P) may have come from λιθίνων in 159 (Introd. III, p. 51 under 'Substitution (i)'). Alternatively, ὁ λιθίνους (Gallavotti *et al.*): cf. Introd. IV, p. 57 n. 2, and p. 68f under (*c*). 159: the addition of ἄν is so obviously right that it hardly needs the 'support' of Aelian's οὐδὲν ἂν ἦν ἀφθονώτερον λιθίνων ἀνδριάντων.]

158f 'Stone statues would be the commonest thing everywhere': πανταχοῦ has its normal meaning, unaffected by the cancelling negatives in οὐδὲν ἀφθονώτερον. Contrast οὐ πανταχοῦ 'not at all', Plato, *Parm.* 128 b.

160 νῦν 'as it is', turning from the hypothetical situation to the real. νυνί, 158, is 'right now'.

οὐ βιωτόν ἐστι: 'It's unendurable' (i.e. 'life's unliveable'). Cf. Dem. *Meid.* (21).120 οὐ γὰρ ἦν μοι δήπου βιωτὸν τοῦτο ποιήσαντι; Xen. *Hell.* 2.3.50 τοῦτο οὐ βιωτὸν ἡγησάμενος. The phrase is immediately explained by the following sentence in asyndeton.

161f The plural λαλοῦσι (like διώκουσι in 166) refers of course to the visit of Pyrrhias, 103ff: to the misanthrope one visitor is a crowd.

ἐπεμβαίνοντες εἰς: LSJ quote one example of this combination of prepositions, E. *IT* 649.

ἤδη is much better taken with what precedes it than with what follows; the text is punctuated accordingly, after Webster and others. Cf. 166. [P gives no help; ed. pr. puts a stop after χωρίον.]

162ff Knemon offers, then rejects, an ironical explanation of the trespassing he suffers: 'I suppose I'm in the habit of spending my time right along the roadside. Why, I don't even work that piece of farmland – such land too – I've abandoned it because of the passers-by!' This manner of expression (hypophora) is most readily paralleled from the orators, though by no means confined to them. [OCT *et al.* punctuate παρ᾽ αὐτήν . . . διατρίβειν as a question, and ὃς οὐδὲ . . . παριόντας as a statement in answer, which perhaps makes the form easier to grasp; but γὰρ νὴ Δία does not suggest an interrogative tone.]

For the ironic γάρ, see e.g. *Perinthia* 13f (*Daos*) τέχνην ἐγώ; ('What me, a trick?') (*Laches*) ναί, Δᾶε, τὸν μὲν ἀπράγμονα | καὶ κοῦφον ἐξαπατᾶν γάρ ἐστι δεσπότην | φλύαρος. ('Yes, Daos' – then, quoting his own words back at him (frg. 1 b) – 'Of course, it's child's play to cheat a casual, easy going master.') For νὴ Δία underlining the irony of the false suggestion, see e.g. Dem., *False Embassy* (19).222 ἀλλὰ διὰ τί σοῦ κατηγορῶ; συκοφαντῶ νὴ Δία, ἵν᾽ ἀργύριον λαβῶ παρὰ σοῦ.

ὃς οὐδέ adds a strong, even scornful refutation, as e.g. E. *Suppl.* 523 πόλεμον δὲ τοῦτον οὐκ ἐγὼ καθίσταμαι | ὃς οὐδὲ σὺν τοῖσδ᾽ ἦλθον εἰς Κάδμου χθόνα: cf. Dem. *de Cor.* (18).312, and ὅς at *Dysk.* 868.

Aelian, *loc. cit.*, paraphrases with καὶ τοῦ χωρίου τὸ παρὰ τὴν ὁδὸν ἀργὸν εἴασα καὶ τοῦτό μοι τῆς γῆς χῆρόν ἐστι καρπῶν, where τὸ παρὰ τὴν ὁδὸν μέρος is possibly to be read with cod. A, now supported by Menander. τοιοῦτο τὸ μέρος χωρίου, which is retained in this edition with ed. pr. and others, has attracted textual suspicion, and, with support from Aelian, τουτὶ τὸ μέρος ⟨τοῦ⟩ χωρίου (Lond., followed in OCT) and similar emendations are proposed.

τοιοῦτο τὸ μέρος χωρίου is nevertheless probably what Menander wrote. τοιοῦτο in predicative position is acceptable in a sense equivalent to τοῦτο τὸ μέρος τοιοῦτο ὄν, as Kamerbeek points out: so at Dem., *First Philippic* (4).22 τηλικαύτην ἀποχρῆν οἶμαι τὴν δύναμιν is equivalent to 'I think the force mentioned, though small, is sufficient'; this is quoted with other examples by Gildersleeve, *Syntax of Attic Greek* II.292. An allusion to the quality of the lower land which he has abandoned, as opposed to the ridges where he works, is nicely in point as part of the portrayal of Knemon's extraordinary agriculture (Introd. II.1, p. 23f). The lack of the article with χωρίου is perhaps more disturbing, but two explanations appear to be open: χωρίου may be generic, as it is taken here, 'that piece of farmland' rather than 'that piece of my farm': so in *Naukleros*, frg. 287 εἴ τις πατρῷαν παραλαβὼν | γῆν καταφάγοι expresses generically the idea of a man devouring his inheritance, τὰ πατρῷα; cf. frg. 716 εἷς ἐστι δοῦλος οἰκίας ὁ δεσπότης 'the one real slave in a household is its master', ὁ δεσπότης τῆς οἰκίας. Alternatively, χωρίου may be specific, but lack the article as a term of familiar reference (such as terms for one's relations, etc.: 883 n.), though the obvious parallels are set prepositional phrases: ἀφ᾽ ὑπερῴου ('from upstairs', *Sam.* 17), ἐξ ἀγροῦ, ἐν γειτόνων etc. The apparent parallel in Anaxandrides, *Aischra* 6 K τὰ μὲν διανεκῆ σώματος μέρη 'the full-length pieces of carcass' should be treated with reserve, since the language of the fragment explicitly recalls the elevated style of Timotheos.

165 ἐπὶ τοὺς λόφους ἄνω: adverb amplifying a prepositional phrase, as μεχρὶ Χολαργέων κάτω 33, ἐπὶ τοῦ λοφιδίου ἐκεῖ 100f, etc.

166 ὢ πολυπληθείας ὄχλου: the first gen. is exclamatory, the second defining, *lit.* 'What a multitude of a crowd!'

167f It is best to take the remark as a statement 'Oh! and now here's someone standing at my door', with τις indef. as at Ar. *Birds* 1121 ἀλλ' οὑτοσὶ τρέχει τις Ἀλφειὸν πνέων. Ed. pr., with some followers, prints a question with τίς. For πάλιν, cf. on 113.

168 Sostratos remembers what happened to Pyrrhias; perhaps Knemon is still carrying his χάραξ (113). τυπτήσει third person is called for, not second person with P, since the remark must be to himself; the emphatic pronoun, rather than γέ με (ed. pr., OCT *et al.*) seems preferable, perhaps not necessary: 'Will he actually hit *me*?'

169ff Not even a quiet place to hang yourself: ἐρημία is a key word in relation to Knemon, cf. 222, 597, 694. The proverb on which Knemon's admirably Knemonic turn of phrase seems to be based is quoted, with apologies, by the Paidagogos in *Phasma* 40ff; cf. LSJ s.v. χέζω and Ar. *Eccl.* 320. Liban., *Decl.* 26.4 possibly recalls the passage: ἐλθὼν ἂν εἰς ἐρημίαν ἐπί τι δένδρον ἀπηγχόμην καθ' ἡσυχίαν.

Knemon speaks at Sostratos rather than to him. With the text as printed in 171, 'Is it me you're angry with?' is the defensive prelude to the white lie with which Sostratos accounts for his presence, unable to face the old man. χαλεπαίνει is unlikely as 2nd person passive; as third person active it could be a remark by Sostratos to himself (ed. pr. *et al.*), or a question to himself, as 168 (OCT).

συνεθέμην γάρ: cf. frg. inc. 951, 15f.

172 οὐκ ἐγὼ 'λεγον; approximately 'What did I tell you?', *lit.* 'Wasn't I saying (that)?', as e.g. in 511, *Misoumenos* 19; Sostratos' talk of meeting someone (yet another stranger!) is seized on by Knemon as confirmation of what he has just been saying, and he breaks out with sarcastic instructions to use his frontage as a public meeting-place.

173 'Do you take this for a stoa or the assembly-place?' I retain, with some doubts, the text and punctuation of ed. pr.

τουτί: 'this place here', as ταυτί at Ar. *Knights* 99, for instance; it is no doubt said with a gesture, and may have been all the more amusing if the actor swept in the colonnaded *skene* and part of the auditorium; such an allusion to the realities of the theatre is not unthinkable in Menander (758 n.).

νενομίκατε: the perfect with present meaning ('consider', 'treat as', 'take for') appears several times in Menander and in fourth century prose: Chantraine, *Parfait Grec* 147, quotes Plato, *Sophist* 227 b and Lycurgus *in Leocr.* 75. For the plural, used in talking to (or at) one person, but including his real or imagined associates, cf. 129 n., 482ff, 621ff.

τὸ τοῦ λεώ is a phrase of common type, but unknown meaning: I am not clear that anything is gained by emending it to τι τοῦ λεώ with Lloyd-Jones (OCT) or otherwise. The type is that of τὸ τοῦ Πανός 'Pan's cave', Ar. *Lys.* 911; for more examples, see Headlam-Knox on Herondas 5.52, and for developments of it in the *koine*, Mayser, *Gram. d. gr. Pap.* II.1 (1926) 7. Outside poetry, the word λεώς is of severely restricted use in Attic (see e.g. van Leeuwen on Ar. *Wasps* 186); this phrase, if right, is therefore hardly likely to be a new creation of Menander's, and should be a colloquial way of referring to something well-known, and prone, like a stoa, to be crowded or surrounded with crowds. The idea that it means 'assembly-place' (i.e. the Pnyx) is developed by Monaco, Stud. Ital. Fil. Class. 1959.240; Koumanoudis, Platon 1959.91 would write Λεώ and assume that the reference is to the Leokoreion. More evidence is needed. ἢ λεωφόρον Dale, Fraenkel, Post.

[Since the text and interpretation of the following lines are also in dispute, it is perhaps worth noting that νενομίκατε could be claimed to be an imperative parallel to those which follow – with support from the textual tradition of Aristophanes at *Ach.* 133 and *Wasps* 415 but against the grammarian Herodian, who adduces the former passage as evidence for the ending -ετε (not -ατε). The imper. εὕρηκε is quoted from Later Comedy, Nausikrates, frg. 1 Demiańczuk = 3A Edmonds. Cf. Schwyzer I.799.]

174ff 'If you want to come and meet anyone at my door, get everything properly organized and build a seat, if you've any sense – better still, build a council-room.'

By this interpretation, πρὸς τὰς ἐμὰς θύρας is to be taken with ἰδεῖν; the acc. is accepted in the view that ἰδεῖν in its sense 'see = meet' (107, 234, 305 n.) is capable of implying motion to. Similarly συμμιγνύναι εἰς Xen. *Anab.* 6.3.24, and συναντᾶν εἰς (see LSJ s.v.); for πρός compare ὥσπερ πρὸς φίλον κόπτουσιν, 481; and (of a place of rendezvous) ἀναμενῶ σε πρὸς τοὔλαιον frg. 700. [KG I.543f.]

συντάττεσθε πάντα παντελῶς goes one better on Sostratos' conventional συνεθέμην γάρ, and leads Knemon to his sarcastic suggestion of suitable amenities. Cf. Dem. 24.27 πάντα συνταξάμενοι καὶ οὐδὲν ἐκ ταὐτομάτου τούτων ἔπραττον; *Fab. Inc.* 62 ἐ[π' ἐμ]ὲ ταῦτα συνετάξασθ' ἄρα.

οἰκοδομήσατε suggests that θῶκος and συνέδριον are something more than a bench and a place to sit and talk in: contrast Plato, *Prot.* 317 d συνέδριον κατασκευάσωμεν, ἵνα καθεζόμενοι διαλέγησθε, which is quoted by Kraus. θῶκος is possibly a stone seat ('siège d' honneur' ed. pr.), a special throne for the president of the imaginary Council.

[οἰκοδομήσατ' ἐὰν ed. pr.: see Introd. III, at p. 64 under (*a*) on the

'split anapaest' involved: otherwise the text and interpretation given
here are in agreement with ed. pr. Attempts to take πρὸς τὰς ἐμὰς
θύρας with συντάττεσθε produce versions which strike me as markedly
less probable: e.g. Kraus, πρὸς τὰς ἐμὰς θύρας, ἐὰν ἰδεῖν τινα | βούλησθε,
συντάττεσθε; πάντα παντελῶς· | καὶ . . . . Lloyd-Jones in OCT prints
πρὸς τὰς ἐμὰς θύρας, ἐὰν ἰδεῖν τινα | βούλησθε, συντάττεσθ' ἀπαντᾶν;
παντελῶς | καὶ θᾶκον οἰκοδομήσετ', ἂν ἔχητε νοῦν . . .]

177f ὦ τάλας ἐγώ: Knemon continues (so Lond. *et al.*), now speaking
to himself as he goes in; hence the sudden change from outwardly
expressed fury to the inner feeling that all the world is against him.
Cf. 442ff, 514, 596ff. These passages help to foreshadow the theme
and tone of his major speech at 713ff.

ἐπηρεασμός: 'spite', in a word, is defined by Aristotle, *Rhet.* 1378 b
17ff as interference with the plans of others not to gain anything
oneself but merely to disconcert them. Cope (vol. 2, p. 15f) has a
useful discussion.

[P's dicolon after συνέδριον may have been intended to mark the
strong break in the speech: Introd. III, 45, 46 and n. 2. Ed. pr. gives
ὦ τάλας . . . δοκεῖ to Sostratos, and has found supporters, among them
Schmid, RhM 1959 at pp. 171, 264; but P rightly labels 179 with
Sostratos' abbreviated name. The introduction of Pyrrhias to speak
179 οὐ τοῦ τυχόντος . . . 181 πρόδηλόν ἐστιν (ed. pr. and others) is a
consequence of the foregoing decision which involves further improbabilities: Kraus offers a defence of it.]

179ff Sostratos reflects that his situation requires more than ordinary
effort – and thinks of someone else to make it for him.

[**180** ἔστ' ἀλλὰ ed. pr.; ἦν ἀλλὰ Maas; alii alia. Hardly μάλλὰ in spite
of its palaeographical attractions.]

181 πρόδηλόν ἐστιν: ed. pr. compares *Perinthia* 2f κληματίδ]ας ἔξεισιν
φέρων . . . καὶ πῦρ· πρόδηλον.

183 ἔχει τι διάπυρον: cf. *Perik.*233 ἔχεις τι πρὸς πολιορκίαν σὺ χρήσιμον.
Getas, in colloquial English, is red-hot, full of bright ideas: cf. P. *Epid.*
673, quoted above on 88, where the cunning Epidicus is described
as 'a son of angry Fire'; and in general θερμός and *calidus*; for discussion and further references, see particularly Schmid, RhM 1959.180,
who, in rejecting ed. pr.'s ἔχει νοῦν διάπυρον, is rightly hesitant to see
a philosophical reference here in the association of thought (or mind)
and fire. Getas' inventiveness in fact plays no part till Act V: see
under 880-958 (iii). [ἔχει τὸ διάπυρον Eitrem.]

185 τὸ τοῦδ': ὅδε in Greek drama normally indicates someone
physically present (including the speaker himself); but is used by
Menander to refer to someone immediately present in mind: see on
234ff. There is little to choose between this reading and τούτου δ'

(ed. pr., OCT *et al.*); P appears to conflate both (Introd. III, p. 50 under 'Addition').

[ὡς ἀπώσετ' ed. pr.; ⟨τάχος⟩ ἀπώσετ' OCT (Lloyd-Jones); the future seems preferable to P's apparent optative, which is accommodated (e.g.) by ⟨τάχ' ἂν⟩ ἀπώσαιτ' (Kraus, Mette, Page).]

186f χρόνον ἐμποεῖν: 'to introduce delay', as Dem. 23.93.

ἡμέρα μιᾶ: cf. *Karchedonios*, frg. 228 ἔργον ἐκ πολλοῦ χρόνου | ἄνοιαν ἡμέρα μεταστῆσαι μιᾶ ; S. *Ant.* 14; E. *HF* 510. [In frg. 544 ἔργον ἐστί, Φανία, | μακρὰν συνήθειαν βραχεῖ λῦσαι χρόνῳ should probably be read with Gataker.] Cf. KG II.445f. With P's δέ deleted, the thought introduced by τὸ μὲν χρόνον γάρ ... is developed in the following short sentence in asyndeton, but never answered by an antithesis, for the unexpected noise of the door interrupts it. Cf. 198f. The idea that 'much can happen in a day' is appropriately echoed in Sostratos' words at 864f, when the day's course has brought his love-affair to a happy ending.

[πόλλ' ἐν ed. pr., followed by OCT *et al.*; πολλὰ δ' ἂν ... γένοιτ' ἄναλλα Gallavotti: see further Introd. IV, p. 64, under (*b*).]

188 τὴν θύραν πέπληχέ τις (with variants) is a conventional formula of someone coming out of a house, as at *Epitr.* 586. It should not be taken to imply that real or stage doors opened outwards, and were knocked to warn anyone who happened to be passing by; this ancient and persistent view is well refuted by Beare, *Roman Stage*, App. G; cf. A. M. Dale, JHS 1957.206, and Webster, Bull. Rylands Library 1962.257f. But what precisely it means to say that someone 'has struck the door' is less than clear; perhaps the reference is to some manner of pushing it aside to go through, probably to unfastening it; at all events 'bang' or 'rattle' is a less misleading equivalent than 'knock': an equivalent in Tragedy is E. *Helen* 858ff ἐκβαίνει δόμων | ἡ θεσπιῳδὸς Θεονόη· κτυπεῖ δόμος | κλήθρων λυθέντων. Phrases with ψοφέω (for example τίς ἐψόφηκεν; 204) may refer to any noise made by a door, including the creak of pivots or hinges for which ancient doors were notorious. See further Christina Dedoussi, 'Studies in Comedy' (repr. from Hellenika, 1964), 6ff.

189 Cf. οἳ 'γὼ τάλαινα συμφορᾶς κακῆς A. *Pers.* 445; οἴμοι τῶν ἐμῶν ἐγὼ κακῶν E. *Pho.* 373; here, as in the second quotation, pronoun and possessive adjective stand together and reinforce each other. The gen. with τάλας, μέλεος, τλήμων etc. is analogous to that with verbs of emotion (e.g. ἀλγέω), and usually described as causal.

The elevated tone is appropriate for a moment of high emotion, and brings with it, as commonly, a hint of tragic style in the strictness of the metre. Possibly the figure of the lamenting girl carrying her pot to get water is intended to recall the situation of the Euripidean Electra (E. *El.* 54ff, 112ff); a similar, but much clearer, case is the recall of the suicide of Ajax in Alcesimarchus' preparations for suicide in P. *Cist.* (639ff). See on 201f, and cf. Introd. I, p. 6f.

The first appearance of the girl also introduces the accident at the well which leads to the complication and ultimate resolution of the plot. Sostratos, who first saw her yesterday, is quite overcome by this fresh sight of her irresistible beauty. See 44 n., and on his threefold invocation of the gods, see under 666-90. The problems of staging this scene with a limited cast are considered in Introd. II.2.

190 The κάδος, which in English one naturally calls '(well-) bucket', is a round jar with two handles, of pottery (as Knemon's would presumably be) or of bronze. Its loss is a domestic calamity because he is too mean to own a spare, or a hook and a good rope to get it out (575ff, 595ff, 625ff). Simiche, who was 'a wretched old woman' to Pyrrhias (99), is 'Nurse' to the girl, whose evident affection for her is an endearing trait of a lightly drawn character. [κάδος: see D. A. Amyx, Hesperia 1958.186ff and plate 47; Sparkes and Talcott, *Pots and Pans of Classical Athens* (American School, Agora Picture Book, No. 1), figs. 27, 30; Webster, Bull. Rylands Library 1962.256.]

193f Knemon said that he must have his hot bath when he came home from work in the evening; his unexpected return makes no difference. The idealized rustic of Tibullus 1.10.41f has a wife who sees to this for him, as well as a son who shares his work as a shepherd (cf. Knemon and his daughter, *Dysk.* 333f). [The text is variously restored. Since θερμόν alone may mean 'hot water', it is possible that P's ὕδωρ is an explanatory note which has intruded into the text: θερμὸν ⟨δὲ⟩ πρ[οσέταξ' εὐπρεπές Barrett. Perhaps the words have suffered transposition: e.g. θερμὸν πρ[οσέταξ' αὐτὴν ὕδωρ ed. pr. (ἡμῖν for αὐτὴν Quincey), but a connecting particle seems desirable. Here as elsewhere in the play (and at *Misoumenos* 15), the spelling πάππας (short a) seems preferable to the παπας of the copies (long a); so also in the derivative παππίας. Cf. Schwyzer I.315, 422. Edd. are divided over the point: OCT follows P.]

194 ἄνδρες (which seems certain to be the right restoration) is addressed to the audience, as at 659, 666; cf. 967; see further under 'allocutiones spectatorum' in the index of *Notabilia varia* in Koerte II. The rest of the line cannot be restored with confidence. [For τί δρῶ; cf. Ar. *Thes.* 70, 925, and τί δράσω; *Sam.* 223; numerous alternatives are offered, including ἄνδρε[ς φίλοι (Fraenkel *et al.*: cf. ἄνδρες γλυκύτατοι *Titthe*, frg. 396); ἄνδρε[s, τί φῶ; Page; less likely is (e.g.) ἄνδρε[s, καλή. ed. pr.]

195f 'He'll beat her to death as a criminal.' Ed. pr.'s idiomatic restoration of κακὴν κακῶς is generally rejected on the ground that the girl would not speak of the old woman as κακή, being fond of her; but it may be hypercritical to do so, for (*a*) the girl can be thinking of the situation from Knemon's viewpoint; and (*b*) it is not clear that in this combination the adj. always has separate descriptive force. Cf. E. *Cycl.* 268f . . . ἢ κακῶς οὗτοι κακοὶ | οἱ παῖδες ἀπόλοινθ᾽, οὓς μάλιστ᾽ ἐγὼ φιλῶ '(If I am lying), may these children whom I love dearly die a villain's death', and see also Ar. *Knights* 189f. [κακ[ῶς πάνυ plerique, adopted in OCT; κάκ[ιστα δὴ (vel. sim.) alii; hardly κακ[ῶς ἐμέ (Jean Martin).]

196 'No time to waste in talking'. The restoration (and the identity of the speaker) are again uncertain.

[No paragraphus in P; the dicolon, if present, may have been intended to mark the break in the speech, as, e.g., at 177. ματ[suggests an oath: οὐ σχολὴ μὰ τ[ὼ θεώ ed. pr., continuing with the girl; μὰ τ[οὺς θεούς OCT (Kassel) or μὰ τ[ὸν Δία (Barigazzi) are suitable supplements if Sostratos is introduced as the speaker (cf. on 201f). 197: λ[ήψομαι ed. pr., but cf. 458f.]

198ff αἰσχύνομαι expresses appropriate modesty and reverence: it would be wrong, she feels, to disturb anyone actually making an offering simply in order to get her water. Sostratos does not stop to weigh the proprieties; for him, respect for the gods can sometimes go too far (259ff).

The one quotation of the Plautine (or pseudo-Plautine) *Dyscolus* reads: 'uirgo sum: nondum didici nupta uerba dicere'. If the play was based on Menander's, this is a possible context for it, assuming (as is not unreasonable) that the scene was treated with some freedom. For discussion, see T. Mantero, in *Menandrea* (Univ. di Genova, Ist. di Fil. Class., 1960), 125ff, and L. Strzelecki, Giorn. Ital. di Filologia 1959.305-8. A more interesting comparison is the scene in P. *Rudens*, 414ff, where Ampelisca gets water from the slave Sceparnio – distinguished as it is from the present one by its lively comic by-play. The date of Diphilus' original of the *Rudens* is uncertain (see Webster, *LGC* 154); but if, as is likely, it was written later than the *Dyskolos*, it is possible that Diphilus had this scene of his rival in mind.

198 ἄρα late in the sentence. Turner, punctuating after it, as does OCT, compares *Epitr.* 336 ἂν συναρέσῃ σοι τοὐμὸν ἐνθύμημ᾽ ἄρα; but θύουσ᾽ ἄρα ἔνδον could well belong together. Cf. πλὴν ἔν τι τῶν πάντων ἀδύνατον ἦν ἄρα | εὑρεῖν, frg. 622.5f; and see further Denniston, *Particles* 41f; Dodds on Plato, *Gorgias* 486 e 6.

[ἄ[μα Barigazzi, Kraus *et al.*]

199f 'But if you give me the pot you're holding, I'll dip it in the spring for you and bring it back here.'

With this text, the relative clause ἣν ἔχεις anticipates the noun it refers to, as at S. *Ant.* 404 ταύτην γ᾽ ἰδὼν θάπτουσαν ὃν σὺ τὸν νεκρὸν | ἀπεῖπας; and at Plato, *Rep.* 477 c εἰ ἄρα μανθάνεις ὃ βούλομαι λέγειν τὸ εἶδος; these examples are quoted with others in KG II.420, A.1. Simpler instances, in which a demonstrative pronoun is present as well as or instead of a noun, are διὰ ταύτην ἣν λέγω τὴν δωρεάν Phoenikides, 4 K.9; ὃν ἔχω τοῦτον Archedikos, *Thesauros* 3 K.6, and ἀφεὶς ἃ φλυαρεῖς ταῦτα M. *Samia* 313.

[τὴν χύτραν is likely to be right either in 200 (where Jacques thinks of τ[ὴν ὑδρίαν), or at the end of 199, but nothing else is certain. 199: possibly δ[ῶς, αὐτίκα (Shipp); several critics suggest δοῦναι ᾽θέλῃς (or θέλῃς): OCT adopts the latter. If we have δ[ῶς τὴν χύτραν in 199, 200 is less easily supplemented: τ[αχὺ πλέαν ἤ]ξω, Gallavotti, followed by Jean Martin.]

201f 'Oh, please yes, and be quick': cf. P. *Rud.* 438f, from the context referred to above: sc. cedo mi urnam. AM. cape. | propera, amabo, ecferre. sc. manta, iam hic ero, uoluptas mea.

ἀνύσας is a recurrent idiom in Aristophanes, known in later comedy from Anaxilas, 37 K, but not so far from Menander. ἄ[νθρωπε (Kraus, Winnington-Ingram) is among the likelier alternatives, but it would not necessarily be a sign of ἀγροικία in the girl to address Sostratos in that way, for she does not know his name: cf. Wilamowitz on *Epitr.* 270 (his line 229).

Sostratos' comment, in paraphrase, means 'She may be a simple country girl, but she has the poise and the frankness of the truly civilized'; a remark in similar form is made by Kallippides of Gorgias at 835f. It is prompted, no doubt, by her reaction to his offer, straightforward and earnest, but brusque; but it has wider implications: Sostratos recognizes already the ideal which he will later admire in her (384ff); the audience, if they see anything of Electra in Knemon's daughter, may reflect all the more readily that a life of primitive simplicity does not necessarily enslave the spirit of the person who lives it (see 189 n.).

ὦ πολυτίμητοι θεοί is a strong expression, used by men elsewhere in Menander (*Dysk.* 381, 479; *Fab. Inc.* 56; *Deisidaimon*, frg. 97; frg. 718.5), as it is at Ar. *Wasps* 1001; as Barigazzi and others have observed, it should on that ground be spoken by Sostratos, in accordance with P's part-division, and not ascribed to the girl, as some do after ed. pr. It is less clear to which of the neighbouring sentences the phrase should belong, partly because 203 is not certainly restored; and I take it, somewhat doubtfully, with the former.

Proprieties in invoking the gods were sometimes strict. In Attic, women but not men swore by τὼ θεώ (meaning Demeter and Kore). Accordingly, in Aristophanes, a woman disguised as a man can give away her sex by using the wrong oath (*Eccl.* 155ff: see the commentators there and on *Ach.* 905). Euripides' kinsman in *Thesmophoriazusae* tries harder, but makes a slip which seems to prove two points of usage: disguised as a woman, he produces what Aristophanes

must have intended as an amusing hybrid, the expression ὦ πολυτιμήτω
θεώ (594).

[Ed. pr.'s version of the text does not respect the part-divisions in P,
and is otherwise unsatisfactory. P has, in detail, 200 βαψας—[—]—φερων:
201 ναι—[—]—πως, dicolon presumably in the gap; 202, no paragraphus,
single point after εστιν; 203 τισ—[—]νων: ταλαιν' εγω. I follow Lond. in
holding that the arrangement is correct. OCT, leaving 201 unrestored,
differs from the part-division adopted here in giving to Knemon's
daughter all from 202 ὦ πολυτίμητοι θεοί to 206 ἔξω.]

203 τίς ἄν με, as e.g. at 914, 928; P offers (and many accept) the
unwanted emphasis of τίς ἄν ἐμέ. The cry of despair comes with
startling suddenness, presumably at the moment when Sostratos
takes his eyes off the girl and moves to go into the shrine; similarly
οἴμοι κακοδαίμων, the moment after he has said good-bye to her, 214;
in P. *Curc.*, 'iamne ego relinquor? pulchre, Palinure occidi' is said by
Phaedromus the moment after Planesium has left him (214).

The girl's cry, τάλαιν' ἐγώ, is prompted by the noise of Daos coming
out of Gorgias' house (188 n.). Without stopping to think, she flies to
the fear uppermost in her mind ('Father's coming'), and runs from
somewhere near the centre of the stage back to her own door. The
echo of mood between τίς ἄν με σῶσαι κτλ. and τάλαιν' ἐγώ is presumably
a deliberate comic effect, not unlike that at 521f, Φυλασίοις ... ἐπὶ
Φυλήν ... For the misinterpretation of a 'noise off', cf. P. *Aul.* 243f.

[τ[ῶν πό]νων (ed. pr.), spoken by Sostratos, could refer to the
troubles or pangs of love (cf. frg. 722, λαβέ με σύμβουλον πόνων, says
a slave to his worried young master); but δ[seems a shade more
suitable than τ[for the minute trace of a letter before the gap: δ[' ἐκ
πό]νων Mette. Lloyd-Jones, who assigns the whole line to the girl,
compares *Epitr.* 535: τίς ἄν θεῶν τάλαιναν ἐλεήσειέ με;]

205f ἔπειτα: the 'then' corresponds to Eng. 'now': 'Now I shall
catch it, if he finds me outside'. Cf. *Perinthia* 4 (Here he comes with
brushwood and a light) ... ἔπειτα κατακαύσει με ('Next thing, he'll
burn me up'). Knemon's fierceness here must be measured by the
standards of a society in which respectable women and girls did not
normally go out alone, much less talk to young strangers: for some
references, see Headlam-Knox on Herondas 1.37 and 56. Even so,
he is not stern enough in Daos' eyes, 218ff.

206-11 Enter Daos from Gorgias' house, talking, as he leaves it, to
Gorgias' mother: he has been helping her at home 'for ages', and
must now go and join his master in the fields. His brief address to
Poverty serves several purposes at once: in vivid terms, it underlines
the character of the slave and the household he works for (see under
24f); it prepares the way for an important development of the 'Poverty'
theme in the scene between Gorgias and Sostratos which is to come,

271ff; it allows time to elapse while Sostratos is supposed to be fetching water, and makes possible the change of rôles which is necessary if the play is to be performed by three actors without a speaking 'extra' to help them (Introd. II.2). [205 λ[ήψ]ομ' ἐὰν ed. pr. and others, with P: cf. Introd. IV, p. 64, under (a).]

207   ὁ δέ: 'he' is the master of the house, as at 584.

208ff   'Accursed Poverty', as at Ar. *Plut.* 456. The image of Poverty staying in the house like an unwanted old woman is a traditional one, well represented in Theognis 351ff; in the *Plutus*, she appears on the stage looking like a cross between a tragic fury and the fraudulent barmaid next door, or something equally low, and announces herself as Πενία . . . ἢ σφῶν συνοικῶ πόλλ' ἔτη (415-37). In the *Georgos* of Menander (77f), she is thought of as a stubborn, self-willed animal: παύσασθε πενίᾳ μαχόμενοι | δυσνουθετήτῳ θηρίῳ καὶ δυσκόλῳ (compare *Dysk.* 249ff, of Knemon).

[See, with special reference to Ar. *Plut.*, H. J. Newiger, *Metapher und Allegorie: Studien zu Aristophanes*, 155ff (Zetemata, Heft 16, 1957).]

209   'Why do we find you so great a burden?': τηλικοῦτο, neuter predicate of a feminine; cf. on 122f.

210f   τοσοῦτον . . . ἐνδελεχῶς οὕτω χρόνον: 'so long and so continuously'. ἔνδον κάθησαι suits the image of poverty as an old woman: see above, and under 205f.

211f   Sostratos comes out to find the girl gone, like Sceparnio in P. *Rud.* 458-84. 'Bring it here' is said from the house door, or from just inside it; Sostratos does so, while Daos watches and comments disapprovingly from the other side of the stage. P distinguishes the parts correctly, labelling Daos' words with his name.

τί ποτ' ἐβούλετο: 'What was he after . . .?' The tense shows that the first thought in the slave's suspicious mind is of the young stranger's motive for coming to the neighbourhood at all; in a moment he will reflect on what he sees Sostratos doing, and come to a pessimistic but not unnatural conclusion. For the imperfect, see *Fab. Inc.* 60-62; for the slave's judgement of human nature, compare Sosias' misunderstanding of Glykera's motives in *Perik.* (179ff; cf. 37ff). [τί ποτε βούλεθ' οὑτοσὶ . . . Szemerényi, adopted in OCT and elsewhere; P has τιποτ' εβουλετο, with the verb in *scriptio plena*.]

213   'Goodbye, and take care of your father', a polite, conventional leave-taking – not without its humour in the circumstances. ἔρρωσο (Lat. *uale*), with a second verb coupled to it by τε (cf. *Perik.* 50f); ἐπιμελοῦ in the same sense as at 618. Similar phrases are commonplace at the close of letters: e.g. ἐπιμελοῦ δὲ καὶ σαυτοῦ ὅπως ὑγιαίνῃς

P. Petrie II.xi.(1) (260 B.C.); ἀσπάζου πάντας τοὺς σοὺς καὶ σεαυτοῦ ἐπιμελοῦ ἵν' ὑγιαίνῃς. ἔρρωσο P. Oxy. 4.745 (1 A.D.).

214 Sostratos' despair: see on 203. Pyrrhias reappears from the shrine, and tries to cheer his master up. Since he ran away from the approach of Knemon at or just after 144, he may have been seen peering from the door from time to time, represented by an extra non-speaking actor wearing the costume and mask: unless Menander has forgotten himself, Pyrrhias is supposed to have overheard Sostratos' resolve to call in Getas (181ff), of which he is about to remind him. See Introd. II.2.

215 'How do you mean, "all right"?': τί as, e.g., in 321 τί χρήσιμος; but here the expression echoed from the other speaker precedes the interrogative which questions it. The same idiom with other parts of speech is seen in E. *Alc.* 807 (τί ζῶσιν;), and M. *Samia* 159 (τί καί;).

216f ὅπερ ἔμελλες ἄρτι: 'as you were going to do just now' (181ff): ποιεῖν/ποιήσειν is left unexpressed; the whole clause is loosely in apposition to the sentence, as with ὅπερ εἶπον and similar phrases.

τὸν Γέταν ... σαφῶς: 'tell Getas the whole story, and come back here with him'. λαβών, as commonly, is timeless and goes closely with the main verb; only εἰπών refers to a prior action. Cf. on 616f.

Sostratos, accompanied by Pyrrhias, goes off home; they walk past Daos, standing in the background near Gorgias' door, and go off by the way they came on, spectators' right; 233 exit Daos, crossing the stage, to the left; he is going to find Gorgias on his land. They meet Sostratos coming from the opposite side to their own when they return, 255ff.

218f 'How very little I like it!': the negative in an exclamation looks odd from the point of view of English; but compare, for example, Amphis, *Dexidemides* 13 K ὦ Πλάτων, | ὡς οὐδὲν οἶσθα πλὴν σκυθρωπάζειν μόνον '... how totally ignorant you are, except for looking solemn'; M., frg. 644 ὦ γῆρας βαρύ, | ὡς οὐδὲν ἀγαθόν, δυσχερῆ δὲ πόλλ' ἔχεις.

220 πονηρόν: 'a bad business', commenting on the statement of what he has just seen. Cf. *Heros* 17, *Perik.* 200.

223ff 'An innocent girl – you abandon her, leave her alone in a lonely place, like an outcast child, with no thought of protecting her.'
ἄκακον: cf. *Heros* 19. The idea of the sentence is that Knemon's treatment of the girl is tantamount to exposing her as a baby; that emerges not only from μόνην ἀφεὶς ἐν ἐρημίᾳ but from the notion that Sostratos thinks of her as 'a lucky find' (226; cf. *Epitr.* 108 and context). Hence the neat correction ὡς προκειμένην has strong claims to correctness over ὡς προσῆκον ἦν (Barber, Winnington-Ingram *et al.*), which is adopted in OCT and elsewhere; for προκεῖσθαι 'to lie abandoned' in this connotation, see e.g. Hdt. 1.111; Post compares Ar.

Thes. 1033 and sees a reference to Andromeda (AJP 1961.96f). The acc. is still governed by ἀφεὶς ... ἐᾶς, although part of another phrase has intervened; similarly at Ar. *Eccl.* 1049, the transmitted text (rightly preserved by Coulon) is αὕτη σὺ ποῖ παραβᾶσα τόνδε τὸν νόμον | ἕλκεις ... ; 'Here you, where are you dragging him off to, against the law?', τόνδε ... ἕλκεις being interlaced with παραβᾶσα ... τὸν νόμον; at E. *Hec.* 1224f we have καὶ μὴν τρέφων μὲν ὥς σε παῖδ᾽ ἔχρην τρέφειν | σώσας τε τὸν ἐμόν ... '... if you had spared my son and brought him up, as you should have done ...'. A related phenomenon of word order is that known as hyperbaton, in which one part of a unit of expression is delayed by the speaker in such a way that another unit is enfolded completely within the first, as for instance at *Dysk.* 30f ὁ γέρων δ᾽ ἔχων τὴν θυγατέρ᾽ αὐτὸς ζῇ μόνος | καὶ γραῦν θεράπαιναν, ξυλοφορῶν σκάπτων τ᾽ ... where αὐτὸς μόνος enfolds ζῇ, and is itself enfolded by the larger unit ἔχων τὴν θυγατέρα καὶ γραῦν θεράπαιναν; then the speaker passes on to develop his main idea in a string of participles. In naturalistic writing like Menander's, there is a strong presumption that such departures from 'logical' word-order are intended to reflect what happened in the language of everyday use; sometimes, as here and at 234-8, the speaker is patently angry or upset, and the disturbance of his thoughts appears to be reflected in the disturbed sequence of their expression. For general discussion and references, see KG II.600ff, Schwyzer II.697f, *NTGramm.* §477 (1); Denniston, *Greek Prose Style*, 47ff; and J. H. Kells, 'Hyperbaton in Sophocles' CR 1961.188ff. [ὥσπερ πρὸς κένην ed. pr. ('sans plus de précaution que si la maison était vide'); alii alia.]

225 προσερρύη: perhaps 'slipped along here quickly' – the implication being of speed, stealth, or both.

226f οὐ μὴν ἀλλὰ ... γε: 'But anyway, I must tell her brother ...'. For the crasis of τἀδελφῷ cf. τἀδικεῖν = τῷ ἀδικεῖν *Epitr.* 181.

τὴν ταχίστην, sc. ὁδόν, 'as quickly as I can'.

228 Cf. Gorgias' remarks at 239ff.

230-2 καὶ γὰρ ...: see on 47-49, adding for τούσδε (e.g.) E. *Alc.* 24, *Ion* 78f, Ar. *Eccl.* 41f and 27ff: ἀλλ᾽ ὁρῶ τονδὶ λύχνον | προσιόντα· φέρε νῦν ἐπαναχωρήσω πάλιν | μὴ καί τις ὢν ἀνὴρ ὁ προσιὼν τυγχάνῃ.

The introduction of the chorus follows a pattern which is repeated with variations elsewhere in Menander: *Epitr.* 33ff.

> ἴωμεν· ὡς καὶ μειρακυλλίων ὄχλος
> εἰς τὸν τόπον τις ἔρχεθ᾽ ὑποβεβρεγμένων
> οἷς μὴ 'νοχλεῖν εὔκαιρον εἶναί μοι δοκεῖ.

In *Perikeiromene*, 71-76, the chorus is introduced as follows: 'Slaves! – here come a crowd of tipsy young men. I congratulate my mistress: she's bringing the girl to our house – that's what it is to be a mother.

I must find my master; it seems to me the moment for him to come here as quick as he can.' Traces of similar situations are recognizable in two Latin plays adapted from Menander, at P. *Bacchides* 107, and at T. *Heaut.* 168ff (see Duckworth, *Nature of Roman Comedy*, 99f for a brief discussion and further references). The repetitiveness need cause no surprise; the closing lines of the play are a clear indication that Menander was sometimes mechanical over details. Moreover, the pattern itself is a traditional one, and can be traced through Middle Comedy back to Classical Tragedy. In Aristophanes, choruses usually require, and get, a more elaborate introduction (e.g. *Wasps* 214-29); but analogies for the pattern in different dramatic situations are legion, e.g. *Eccl.* 27ff, quoted above, and 279ff. The most relevant passage from a Middle Comedy poet is Alexis, *Kouris* 107 K: 'For (καὶ γάρ) I see a crowd of men coming to a revel – all the best people collect here. I hope I don't meet you at night alone when your dancing has gone well: I should never get away with my cloak without growing wings.' From Tragedy, E. *Pho.* 193ff has been cited in this connection by Fraenkel (*de med. et nov. com.*, 71): (Go into the house and stay in your room) ὄχλος γάρ, ὡς ταραγμὸς εἰσῆλθεν πόλιν | χωρεῖ γυναικῶν πρὸς δόμους τυραννικούς, | φιλόψογον δὲ χρῆμα θηλειῶν ἔφυ, κτλ.; compare also *Alope*, frg. 105 'I see a band of athletes coming here after their morning run is over'; *Hippolytus* 51ff, *Cyclops* 32ff.

παιανιστάς τινας: 'a band of paean-singers'. P's reading is here retained, with Gallavotti, Kraus, Lond., and others. The scansion presumed is τούσδὲ παιᾶν-, with 'split anapaest' and correption. On metrical and other grounds the text must be judged doubtful, but the presumption that it is corrupt falls short of certainty. The conjecture πανιστάς, 'followers of Pan' is preferred in OCT and widely. The following notes attempt to explore the issues involved in the decision.

(i) *Metre and Prosody*: A similar verse, also much debated, is Ar. *Wasps* 1369, scanning ... κλέψᾰντᾰ: ποῖᾱν αὐλητρίδᾱ; but in Menander, who is generally stricter in metrical practice than Aristophanes, there seems to be no satisfying parallel yet known. Cf. Introd. IV, Note A, where at p. 65 under (c) it is suggested that the abnormal 'split anapaest' may have arisen from the accommodation of a metrically inconvenient word to a standard pattern of phrase ('I see . . . coming here').

The word παιανιστάς must scan with its first syllable short if it is to appear at all in this metre; παιάνιξαν is similarly treated at Bacchylides 17.129; cf. also Παιήονα in a paean by Limenios: Powell, *Coll. Alex.* 149, v. 18. Correption of this kind is especially familiar in Attic Comedy from τοιοῦτος, ποιεῖν and the name Πειραιεύς, three cases in which Menander certainly admits it; it rests on a feature of pronunciation which is sometimes reflected in the spelling of our copies of literary texts and of inscriptions contemporary with their com-

position, as in ποιεῖν/ποεῖν; though predominant by comic practice
in certain common words and their cognates, it is not exclusively
confined to them. The appearance of παιανιστάς therefore, is not in
itself valid evidence that the text is corrupt; nor is it surprising that
so exceptional a situation should not recur elsewhere in our remains of
Menander. [For other possible instances of corruption in Menander,
see *Epitr.* 172 (δίκαῖον), with Koerte's note; *Dysk.* 496 (perhaps ἱέρειαν,
with P), 568 (γύναῖα); and frg. 788, ὡράῖζεθ᾽, with Schwyzer I.265f,
and Hilberg, *Wiener Studien*, 1891.172-4. On the phonetics of correption, see Schwyzer I.236; for further examples and discussion of
comic practice, see White, *Verse of Greek Comedy*, §§801-2; Starkie on
Ar. *Wasps* 40; Descroix, *Trim. Iambique*, 24; and Fraenkel, in *Festschr.
G. Jachmann* (1959), 27, on κολοῖάρχους in Ar. *Birds* 1212. See p. 305f.]

(ii) *The character of the chorus*: If considerations of metre and prosody
are not decisive against the transmitted text, neither is the identity it
provides for the chorus; for though we know too little to verify the
presence of 'paean-singers' in the play, we equally know too little of
the comic chorus in the period to presume against them on grounds of
dramatic appropriateness or otherwise.

παιανισταί are not known as such from fourth-century Attica or
earlier. When the word appears, it is a title of members of musical
guilds attached to religious cults: the cult of Sarapis in Egypt, and in
Imperial Rome; and the cult of Asklepios at Mounychia. These facts
are of doubtful relevance to Menander: since the paean was a flourish-
ing form of composition in his lifetime, there can be no *a priori* objection
to the existence of people called παιανισταί at the date of the *Dyskolos*;
on the other hand, the known Greco-Egyptian associations of the
word cast an air of suspicion on its appearance in P (cf. on βραχεῖσα
in 950).

If, in spite of these doubts, we believe that Menander chose to
describe the chorus as 'paean-singers', he can hardly have done so
without intending them to sing something recognizable as a paean
– if so, presumably a slight and light-hearted one, for this is Comedy,
and they enter in revel 'a little drunk', like the choruses of *Epitr.* and
Perik. Nevertheless their words, whether specially composed for the
occasion or not, do not appear as part of the text; and their rôle is of
no discernible consequence to the action. After this introduction,
which gives them their character, we hear no more of them, and cannot
say if any effort was made to sustain it. As is usual in New Comedy,
the word ΧΟΡΟΥ is written into the text in token of the choral performance; like the fuller form ΧΟΡΟΥ ΜΕΛΟΣ, from which it presumably derived, it leaves the reader free to imagine, and the poet
free to provide, a wide range of possible interludes. Nor is anything
said to explain the presence of 'paean-singers' in Phyle: perhaps the
more realistically-minded members of the audience were supposed

to think of them passing through on their way to perform at Delphi or elsewhere. A chorus of 'followers of Pan' might seem more appropriate to the play; but with that in mind, one must note that their arrival anticipates that of the cook and slave at 393 and the sacrifice party at 430ff – perhaps unfortunately so.

[*Paeans*: Smyth, *Greek Melic Poets*, xxxviff; von Blumenthal, *RE* 'Paian', 18.2 (1942) 2345ff; A. E. Harvey, CQ 1955.172f. παιανισταί *in the cult of of Sarapis*: in Egypt, Preisigke, *Sammelbuch d. gr. Urkunden*, I.1743, 5803 (Demetrius of Phalerum wrote paeans to Sarapis during his residence in Egypt: Diog. Laert. 5.76 = Dem., frg. 68 Wehrli); in Rome, *IG* 14.1084 (146 A.D., cf. *ib.* 1059); in the cult of Asklepios at Mounychia, *SIG*³ 1110 (212 A.D.). ΧΟΡΟΥ: cf. Introd. III, p. 48 n. 2. *Chorus in Later Comedy*: Webster, *SM* 181ff, *LGC* 58ff, with further references; relief from the Athenian Agora, 350/25 B.C. = Bieber, *HT*², fig. 181; Webster, *MOMC*, no. AS 3; cf. *ib.* AS 4. '*Followers of Pan*': ed. pr. printed καὶ γὰρ προσιόντας πανιαστὰς νῦν τινας, quoting in support of πανιαστὰς *IG* 12 (1).155.75 (Rhodes; saec. ii B.C.), and *IGRom.* 4.1680; and – of necessity – rewriting the line in order to accommodate the word. Πανιστάς for παιανιστάς (van Groningen, Lloyd-Jones) is a conjecture of attractive technical simplicity (cf. Jacques, Bull. Ass. Budé 1960.420); it assumes an unrecorded form, though one which is adequately paralleled: see for instance under ἀγαθοδαιμονισταί/-ιασταί in LSJ. The search for other possible identities for the chorus appears unprofitable: Παιονίδας Diano.]

232 μὴ 'νοχλεῖν = μὴ ἐνοχλεῖν: cf. 750 and on 949.

Act II (233-426)

233-392 Daos returns with Gorgias. They are still considering what can be done, when Sostratos reappears – alone, and at last determined to act for himself. Gorgias stops him on his way to Knemon's door, and tries to warn him off from what seems, in Gorgias' eyes, to be an attempt at seduction or worse. Sostratos convinces him that he has the most honourable intentions, and though Gorgias can hold out no hope that Knemon will agree to a proposal to marry his daughter, they decide that Sostratos shall come and work on the land for a spell, to meet Knemon and see what the prospects are.

The analogy in conception (and sometimes in detail) between the earlier part of this Act and the opening of T. *Eun.* 'Act V' (817-922) is well presented by W. Görler, Philologus 1961.299-307; it throws an interesting light on Menander's capacity for varied treatments of similar themes and situations.

233f 'But were you really so casual about it, so feeble?' Daos has told his story, only to be reprimanded for not doing better. The reference back with which the Act opens helps the audience to grasp the new situation, and secures a degree of continuity after the break: compare, for instance, *Epitr.* 243ff, and 50ff above, where Chaireas' opening remark confirms that he has just heard the story which the audience know already from Pan. Gorgias knows that they have no right to intervene in his half-sister's affairs, but insists that kinship brings a duty to do so; he is facing the prospect of an unpleasant interview with Knemon (247ff). Daos' idea (which proves correct) was that they would catch the young stranger coming back to the house again (256): the slave's limited, practical outlook is contrasted with that of his master. All this emerges by implication as much as by direct statement; the treatment is deliberately naturalistic, and the motivation for the two characters' entry and their subsequent actions is presented late and with seeming casualness. See on 543-5 and 784ff, and cf. Gomme, *Essays in Greek History and Literature*, 254ff.

The young man's impatience with his would-be helper is a little like that of Sostratos in Act I (135ff); his instant assumption from the slave's story that the stranger is up to no good is comparable with Polemon's leap to the worst conclusion from what he is told about Glykera in *Perik.* (cf. 37ff), but the essentials of character and situation are different: Gorgias' main feeling is no doubt the very proper care for his sister which he stresses, but it is combined with something of the countryman's instinctive dislike for leisured strangers from town (257f), and with a prickly and self-righteous pride born of his life of

175

poverty and hard work: for this, note especially the conclusion of his speech to Sostratos, 293-8.

234ff 'This man who accosted the girl, whoever he was – you should certainly have seen him at once and told him to be sure that no-one ever catches him doing that in the future.'

The word-order is unusual, and has given difficulty. τοῦτο τοῦ λοιποῦ χρόνου belongs with ὄψεται ποιοῦντα, where a calmer speaker might well have put it; instead, it comes first in its clause, and the τε which connects εἰπεῖν to ἰδεῖν is therefore deferred to 6th place: see on 10 and 223ff.

τόνδ’, if rightly restored, is not 'this man here', but 'this man we are talking about', as, e.g., at *Kolax* 111, *CF* 4; for τόνδε . . . τοῦτο cf. perhaps *Epitr.* 163. [προσιόντα γ’ ὅστις δήποτ’ ἦν ed. pr.; προσιόντα τοῦτον ὅστις ἦν Barrett; προσιόντα, Δᾶ’, ὅστις ποτ’ ἦν Eitrem; alii alia.]

ἰδεῖν: 'see = interview', cf. 305 n.; some take the sense to be 'see to = guard against'; ed. pr. interprets as 'see', with the ὅστις clause as an indirect question.

τότ’ εὐθύς: cf. Ar. *Clouds* 1359, 1215; and perhaps 581 below, where P gives τοῦτ’ εὐθύς as here.

ὅπως + future indic. and neg. μή is familiar as a form of exhortation or command in direct speech, where a verb meaning 'see that', 'take care that', is left unexpressed. Here the construction is subordinate to εἰπεῖν; at *Epitr.* 752f a parallel sentence gives what is in effect a halfway stage to subordination: αὖθις δ’ ὅπως μὴ λήψομαί σε, Σμικρίνη, | προπετῆ, λέγω σοι 'Be sure I don't catch you being headstrong again, Smikrines, I tell you.' Somewhat similarly, ὅπως + future is sometimes found as an alternative to the infin. after δεῖ: e.g. Cratinus, *Nemesis* 108 K δεῖ σ’ ὅπως . . . ἀλεκτρυόνος μηδὲν διοίσεις 'You must be just like a hen'.

238f νυνί 'as it is'; ἀπέστης 'you gave up', 'stood aside': cf. 346.

239f ἴσως: 'I suppose', rather than 'perhaps'; see 730 n. Gorgias' stress on the claims of relationship is in direct contrast to the attitude of Knemon. Obligations to the family are a special case of the obligations of φιλία as discussed by Aristotle (see *Eth. Nic.* 1165 a 30ff) and in other ethical writing of the later fourth century: hence – at least in part – derives the interest of New Comedy in exploring the implications of such relationships. Hegio in Terence, *Adelphoe*, is an older man who is shown to take a right view of his duty to his relations in helping the widowed Sostrata and her daughter in their trouble; in the original, Menander's *Second Adelphoi*, he was Sostrata's brother. Cf. especially T. *Adel.* 455ff, 351ff (with Donatus' note on 351), and M. *Adel. II*, frg. 6. [See further Webster, *SM* 204ff, *LGC* 139 (on Philemon), and F. Zucker, *Freundschaftsbewährung i.d. neuen att. Komödie*, Berichte d. sächsischen Akad. d. Wissenschaften, ph.-hist. Kl. 98.1 (1950).]

239: οὐκ ἔνεστί σοι, given by one MS in the quoted version of the text, does not merit the support which some give it.]

240ff 'I am still concerned for my sister. Her father wants to be a stranger to us, does he? Don't let us imitate his misanthropy.' I adopt the text arrived at jointly by Lond. and by Lloyd-Jones, and printed in OCT, except that a colon is there preferred to a question mark in 242.

ἀδελφῆς . . . ἐμῆς (if right) should mean 'I am still concerned for someone who is a sister of mine': i.e. the absence of the article would be abnormal in Menander if the sense were simply 'my sister'. A possible parallel is *Plokion*, frg. 333.6 *(ἵνα . . . ᾖ) εὔγνωστος οὖσ' ἐμὴ γυνὴ | δέσποινα (ἐμε* codd.) 'so that she, as my wife, shall be clearly recognizable as the mistress'; πατὴρ ἐμός πού; in *Misoumenos* 14 is in a paratragic context. Cf. Schwyzer II.202.

ὁ πατήρ . . . βούλεται (whether read interrogatively or not) should be taken as an objection to the preceding statement which is disposed of by μὴ . . . ἡμᾶς: see on 57ff (iii), and on 162ff. The point at issue is essentially one between law and equity (or common humanity). Knemon is within his rights in treating the wife who has left him and her son as complete strangers, if he chooses to do so; nor does Gorgias' relationship to Knemon's daughter give him any legal right to make himself responsible for her; until she marries and passes into the care of her husband, her affairs are solely Knemon's concern. Cf. 253, and on 729-39.

[Different versions of the text are numerous: e.g. P's επιμελει has been thought of as dat. of ἐπιμελής and taken with ἔνεστι; ed. pr. considers ἐπιμελοῦ; Blake suggests οἰκειότητα . . . . ἀδελφῆς· ἐπιμένει. 241: εἰ μὲν ed. pr.; τί μή[ν]; Page; ἡμῖ[ν] Barber, Merkelbach *et al.*; but I doubt if [ν] could have been written in P; ἔμοιγ' Winnington-Ingram. 242: μηδὲ or μὴ δὲ is obtained from P. The former is defended by some as a species of emphatic negative, but not convincingly (e.g. Kraus ad loc.; Barigazzi, Parola del Passato 1959.370); the connective δέ is unwanted but may have been added by a copyist (Introd. III, p. 50, under 'Addition (iii)'); on the 'split anapaest' accepted by those who follow P, see Introd. IV, p. 65 under (d).]

245 ὁ . . . ἔξωθεν: 'the outsider', 'the onlooker'. [ἐπιμελ]ές (Jacques) suits the space available and the sense less well.]

247ff What prompts Daos' violent reaction of fear must surely be a move towards Knemon's house: i.e. Gorgias intends to go and confront him with Daos' story, although, as his next speech shows, he can see no prospect of doing good. ὑπάγωμε]ν ('Let's get on') is supplied as the cue for this movement; it is perhaps a shade long for the space available, but has to match (approximately) the supplements of the following lines, not that of the line above. τί δ' ἐστί]ν (Sandbach) suits the sequel, and may be right: cf. 729 and n. there. OCT does not restore.

[ὅσον ἐστί]ν Bingen. εὖ ἴσθ]ι ed. pr., and suggestions which end with indef. τι (e.g. εἴ πού τ]ι Diano), may be set aside on metrical grounds, since they introduce unwarranted hiatus; on hiatus after indef. τι, see Fraenkel on A. *Ag.* 1115.]

247 ὦ τᾶν ... Γοργία: cf. ὦ τᾶν, Φαίδιμε Com. Anon., Page, *Lit. Pap.* 65.61 (= 22.66 Demiańczuk). There is no reason to suspect P's division of speakers because of the double vocative, much less to emend. [On ὦ τᾶν, see G. Björck, *Das Alpha Impurum* (1950) 275ff.]

248f κρεμᾷ: 'he'll string me up for a whipping', as at *Perik.* 79 (Daos) κρέμασον εὐθύς, εἰ [πλανῶ 'String me straight up if I'm cheating'. [248 ἔα ποτ'·] Gallavotti, with ἴδη κρ]εμᾷ in 249.]

249-52 Text uncertain. With the aid of the following lines, the general sense of the antithesis between compulsion and persuasion is clear, but supplements and interpretations vary widely in detail, as they do in grammatical difficulty; none known to me is wholly straightforward. It may be that there is more serious corruption present than one can tell; but in view of Gorgias' involved manner of speaking at moments of strong feeling elsewhere (234ff, 271ff) we should probably expect something less than economical and lucid perfection.

I take the text given to mean: 'He *is* rather awkward. No-one could compel him to better sense by fighting with him anyhow, nor make him change his mind by giving friendly advice.'

The two leading assumptions are that the opening remark refers to Knemon, and that we have optatives in 251-2 which are main verbs (i.e. ὅτῳ τρόπῳ does not introduce a subordinate clause).

249f For δυσχρήστως γέ πως ἔχει, cf. ὀξυπείνως πως ἔχει, 777. δυσχρηστέω is used of people 'making themselves difficult' by Polybius 27.7.10; the adj. δύσχρηστος is applied to intractable dogs by Xen. *Cyn.* 3.11; the implication may be that Knemon is 'mulish': compare *Georgos* 77f, of Poverty παύσασθε πενίᾳ μαχόμενοι | δυσνουθετήτῳ θηρίῳ καὶ δυσκόλῳ; and Plato, *Laws* 808 d ὁ δὲ παῖς πάντων θηρίων ἐστὶ δυσμεταχειριστότατον. Alternatively, supply a second person of the verb, as ἕξεις OCT (Lloyd-Jones), and take the remark to be made of Daos: 'You will be useless', or 'You will be in trouble'. This *may* suit the known usage of the adverb better: e.g. δυσχρήστως ἔχειν at Plut., *vit. Aem.* 19 (the only instance with ἔχειν) is used of King Perseus' condition while trying to fight a battle after being kicked by a horse: ἔχοντα δυσχρήστως καὶ κωλυόμενον ὑπὸ τῶν φίλων. It is not however so apt to the context: Gorgias is not seriously concerned with the prospects of Daos in a struggle with Knemon, but with the old man himself.

Ed. pr., punctuating after ζυγομαχῶν, translates 'Il est un adversaire pénible'. The Greek, however, seems tautologous if so taken, and in spite of the following demonstrative, which suggests itself as the start of a new sentence, a stop after ἔχει may be better. ζυγομαχῶν is then advanced from its natural place, making a link between the opening statement and the development of it, and providing a welcome parallel to νουθετῶν in 252. The fact that the word is used of Knemon in 17 does not guarantee that it was used of him here; it could be appropriate to the sort of family argument or quarrel Gorgias seems to have in mind, but need not be pressed to mean more than 'fight'.

[Other parts of ἔχειν have been considered, as have other participles ending -γομαχῶν -τομαχῶν: λογομαχῶν ed. pr., in a footnote, commended by Lond., and adopted by Treu; εἴμ' αὐ]τομαχῶν Gallavotti.]

250-2 ὅτῳ τρόπῳ is taken as equivalent to ὁτῳοῦν τρόπῳ or ὅτῳ βούλει τρόπῳ. For ὅστις indefinite, cf. LSJ s.v., IV.2. d; Schwyzer II.216; and Gow on Theocr. 18.25, quoting, *inter alia*, Plato, *Hip. Maj.* 282 d ... ἢ ἄλλος δημιουργὸς ἀφ' ἧστινος τέχνης ' . . . of any craft whatsoever'. In the commentary on Epicharmus, *Odysseus Automolos*, published as P. Oxy. 2429, the phrase ἢ ὅτι is explained as ἢ τὸ τυχόν (frg. 1 (*a*), col. ii.10).

ἀναγκάσαι is corrected from P's αναγκασειε to avoid a 'split anapaest' (Introd. IV, p. 65 under (*e*)). For the assumed construction with εἰς, see e.g. Thuc. 1.23. τις is taken to be understood from here with the parallel verb μεταπεῖσαι, and ἄν from there with this verb. ἄν is not uncommonly left unexpressed in the second of two parallel clauses, but very rarely unexpressed in the first; some indeed deny the possibility of this altogether. See, however, KG I.248f, quoting Aeschines, *in Ctes.* (3).217 οὔτε τοὺς εἰρημένους ἐν ὑμῖν λόγους ἐμαυτῷ ἀρρήτους εἶναι βουλοίμην, οὔτε τὰ αὐτὰ τούτῳ δημηγορήσας ἐδεξάμην ἂν ζῆν; and Dem. 24.7 οὐχ ὅτι τῶν ὄντων ἀπεστερήμην, ἀλλ' οὐδ' ἂν ἔζων (so Navarre-Orsini (1954); Butcher (OCT) prints ἂν ἀπεστερήμην, ἂν ἀπεστερήθην being added as a variant in one MS).

The ends of 251 and 252 are restored here without confidence. For οἷα cf. *Pseudherakles*, frg. 451.6; for advice to the misanthrope, cf. Lucian, *Timon* 48, quoted on 114, and Aelian, *Ep. Rust.* 15 fin. φίλου ταῦτα παραίνεσις νουθετοῦντος εἰς ἀγαθόν (νοοῦντος codd.: corr. Meineke).

[The general view that ὅτῳ τρόπῳ followed by the optative is a subordinate clause makes it hard to supply a governing verb convincingly, and at the same time to account for the construction of the second οὔτε clause. Ed. pr., for example, has τοῦτον οὔθ' ὅτῳ τρόπῳ | ἀναγκάσειέ τις εἰς τὸ βέλτι[ον ἂν ἄγει]ν | οὔτ' ἂν μεταπεῖσαι νουθετῶν ο[ἶδ' οὐδαμῶ]ς: i.e. οἶδα governs both ὅτῳ τρόπῳ ἀναγκάσειέ τις and the presumed aor. infin. with ἄν (P has no accent). OCT, with μεταπεῖσαι aor. opt., has τοῦτον οὔθ' ὅτῳ τρόπῳ | ἀναγκάσαι τις εἰς τὸ βέλτι[ον ῥέπει]ν | οὔτ' ἂν μεταπεῖσαι νουθετῶν ο[ἶδ' οὐδὲ εἶ]ς (ῥέπειν Kassel, possibly rightly; οἶδ' οὐδὲ εἰς Diano, Maas). On this view, ὅτῳ τρόπῳ has to be understood from the first clause in the second; Winnington-Ingram similarly suggests 251 ποτ' ἄ]ν, and 252 ὁ[ρῶ σαφῶ]ς, two interesting supplements which seem inconveniently short. Kamerbeek attempts to supply a governing verb in 251, but his ἄρ' ἐνῆ]ν is unlikely to be right; it clears the way for ο[ὐδεὶς ὅλω]ς in 252, where, apart from other considerations, something shorter than ed. pr.'s ο[ἶδ' οὐδαμῶ]ς seems to be necessary.

Metrical considerations affect the treatment of 251. As a postpositive, ἄν should not be inserted conjecturally at the beginning, with Barigazzi and Blake (cf. Maas, *Gk Metre* §137); nor, at the end, is anything but βέλτῖον [◡ _] likely (Introd. IV, p. 68f under (c)): i.e. with βέλτῖ[ον ἄν ... we have an improbable rhythm; with βέλτῖ-[ον ◡ ἄ]ν it is not easy to see how the space in P was filled. For possible interpretations of the opt. of 251 if ἄν is neither brought in conjecturally nor held to be understood from 252, see (e.g.) KG I.226 (main clause potential without ἄν); and I.231.A5, quoting, among other debated passages, Plato, *Phaedo* 107 a οὐκ οἶδα εἰς ὀντινά τις ἄλλον καιρὸν ἀναβάλλοιτο.

As alternatives to φρονεῖν or ῥέπειν, other infinitives have been thought of; a participle in parallel with νουθετῶν is possible (e.g. τρέπω]ν Page *et al.*); τροπῆ]ι Gallavotti, but]ι is less attractive than]ν as a reading of P.]

[254 μετ' αὐτοῦ (P) is preferred by Diano *et al.*; for discussion, see van Groningen, *Étude Critique*, ad loc., and cf. *NTGramm.* §283.]

255 ἔπισχε μικρόν: 'wait a minute' – ἔπισχε intrans., as at E. *El.* 758, where see Denniston's note: μικρὸν δ' ἐπίσχες ed. pr. See further under 258.

256 ὥσπερ εἶπον may be taken to refer back, like the opening lines of the scene, to what Daos has already said off stage: see on 233f. Gorgias has admitted that an approach to Knemon is virtually doomed to failure, and the slave, who had dreaded the idea, is relieved that Sostratos has come back as he forecast, and so prevented their return from the fields from being in vain. [P's αν, which could give ὥσπερ ἄν εἶπον ('as I should have said', 'as I should say') offers a possible though less likely sense, and an improbable rhythm: see Introd. IV at p. 65 under (f).]

ἀνακάμψας πάλιν: πάλιν gives the phrase the sense 'turn back again'; cf. *Sam.* 341.

257 ὁ τὴν χλανίδ' ἔχων οὗτος: e.g. 'that smart-looking individual', since there is no simple modern equivalent. χλανίς is a cloak or mantle of fine wool, worn on different occasions by both men and women; it appears here, as in *Orge*, frg. 303, and elsewhere, as elegant wear for a fashionable young man; it was liable therefore to attract attention, or even suspicion, in the depths of the country. Gorgias' own everyday dress is the countryman's *diphthera*, a jerkin for work made of some hide or skin. The difference in dress was of course obvious and natural to Menander's audience; it is emphasized in this way partly to show

in Gorgias the instinctive reaction of the countryman to a stranger
from town, partly because the dramatist wishes to make a point of the
contrast in each of his two young men between superficial appearance
and underlying qualities of character. For the contrast in Gorgias,
see especially 321 and 835f; for further developments with Sostratos'
chlanis, see 364f and 370 n.; and for further consideration of the
appearance of the pair, see Introd. II.3.

258 'It's obvious he's a rogue from the look in his eye'. Görler well
compares T. *Eun.* 834ff. *Pythias*: era mea, tace tace obsecro, saluae
sumus: | habemus hominem ipsum (*Dysk.* 255f) . . . (838) *Pythias*:
uide amabo, si non, quom aspicias, os inpudens | uidetur! non est?
tum quae eius confidentiast! Chaerea, the owner of the *os inpudens*,
may, in Menander's original production, have worn the same mask
as Sostratos, that of the 'Second youth with wavy hair': cf. Webster,
Bull. Rylands Library 1949.121ff.

εὐθύς: 'obviously', 'clearly', of something immediately apparent.
Cf. Aristotle, *Poetics* 1452 a 13 (plots are both simple and complex,
for the actions which they imitate) ὑπάρχουσιν εὐθὺς οὖσαι τοιαῦται 'are
clearly so by nature'; similarly in introducing comparisons, ὥσπερ
εὐθύς, οἷον εὐθύς, 'to take the immediately available instance' (e.g.
Poetics 1449 a 34).

ἀπό 'judging from' as, e.g., Theophr. *Char.* 28.4 εἰδεχθής τις ἀπὸ τοῦ
προσώπου; cf. Theocr. 16.49; Lucian, *Dial. Mort.* 10.8.

For βλέμμα 'look', 'expression', see e.g. E. *HF* 306, Ar. *Plut.* 1022.

259ff Sostratos returns alone: Getas, whom he had gone to fetch,
was out on an errand. Details follow not unnaturally as Sostratos
grumbles to himself about the situation; but it is worth looking ahead
to see the dramatic relevance of a monologue which a less careful
dramatist might have added purely for local colour.

260-4: Getas, we learn, is out because Sostratos' mother is so super-
stitious; she is always sacrificing to some god or other, and has sent
him to get a cook to prepare an offering. Sostratos will therefore carry
on alone. At the end of his scene with Gorgias and Daos, 391f, Sostratos again says that he is determined to see the matter through, and
goes off. 393, enter a cook with a sheep; 401: enter Getas, addressed
by name to introduce him. The audience then can look forward to
what is going to happen, having been told exactly enough in advance
to make sure that they enjoy the situation. 406ff: the mother's immediate motive for sacrificing to Pan of Phyle is that he appeared to her
in a dream about Sostratos. The narrative of the dream shows (to the
audience's superior knowledge) that the two apparently independent
lines of action by Sostratos and his mother were both in fact prompted
by Pan. Sostratos himself does not discover that his family is sacrificing
in Phyle until 551ff; by then Menander is already preparing for

Kallippides' arrival (773), and the closing stages of the action, when the sacrifice will become a celebration party.

262f 'She goes all round the district sacrificing', an excess of super-stitious zeal which is deplored even more strongly by those who have to carry it out, 393-414: cf. Introd. II, p. 23, and on cults at Phyle, A. Milchöfer, text to Curtius-Kaupert, *Karten von Attika* vii-viii (1895) 14, and W. Wrede, Ath. Mitt. 1924 at p. 211.

264f μάγειρον: see on 393.

ἐρρῶσθαι ... τῇ θυσίᾳ φράσας: 'said goodbye to the sacrifice' implies 'told them to carry on without me and good luck to them'; the 'good luck', as in the English idiom, can convey a whole range of feelings, including annoyance and disapproval. Cf. χαίρειν λέγω, and 520f below.

266f καί μοι δοκῶ ... διαλέξασθ' ...: 'I have a good mind to speak for myself'; the final stage of the decision is taken with τὴν θύραν κόψω κτλ. When ἐμοὶ δοκῶ (or δοκῶ μοι) expresses decision or intention, the generally recognized construction is with future infin., as else-where in Menander (*Dysk.* 229, 445f; frg. 654 – unless ἐξακεῖσθαι there is taken as present); Barigazzi, Winnington-Ingram and others accordingly propose to read διαλέξεσθ' here, and may well be right. [Some, but not all critics accept the present as an alternative to the future (e.g. Coulon, but not Starkie at Ar. *Wasps* 177); the aorist, which I am here inclined to preserve with ed. pr. and OCT, is listed as doubtful by LSJ, and is again liable to be emended where found: e.g. Plato, *Euthyd.* 288 c ἐγὼ οὖν μοι δοκῶ καὶ αὐτὸς πάλιν ὑφηγήσασθαι (so codd., followed by Burnet; -εσθαι Heindorf). Middle forms of διαλέγομαι are rare in Attic, the future being found in Isocrates, 12.5 and 112, and the aorist quoted from Aristophanes (frg. 343). See Blaydes on Ar. *Ach.* 994, Starkie on *Wasps* 177, 250; and in general KG I.195ff. κἀμοὶ (with P) seems to give unwanted emphasis: note καμολισ for καὶ μόλις in 684.]

268 '... so that I shan't be able to go on thinking it over': εἶναι = ἐξεῖναι as at 283 below and elsewhere. He is going to Knemon's door when Gorgias interrupts.

269 μειράκιον: the appropriate formal address to a young man: 299, 729, 843 etc.

269ff '... would you listen to something rather serious I have to say?' The polite request in fact warns the audience, as well as Sos-tratos, what sort of speech is to follow. Compare for instance Eur. *Suppl.* 293 (Aithra to Theseus) εἴπω τι, τέκνον, σοί τε καὶ πόλει καλόν; and *Tro.* 903f (Helen to Menelaus) ἔξεστιν οὖν πρὸς ταῦτ' ἀμείψασθαι λόγῳ | ὡς οὐ δικαίως, ἢν θάνω, θανούμεθα;

The speech itself (271-98) falls into three sections, a new direction being given twice by Sostratos' interruptions at 288 and 293. Gorgias' argument is (i) that human prosperity and ill-fortune are finite and variable: an unjust rich man can expect a change for the worse, and an honest poor man a change for the better. Sostratos should therefore act worthily of his position and not despise the poor; (ii) that Sostratos' designs on the girl are dishonourable, if not criminal; (iii) that causing trouble for people who are busy is an unjust misuse of leisure: Sostratos should remember that a poor man unjustly treated is a difficult adversary – 'a gorgeously incoherent attempt at logic' as Post describes it, Am. Journ. Phil. 1959, at p. 410. Sostratos' reply, 302-14, consists of a brief statement of his honourable intentions, a denial on oath that he has anything bad in mind, and an implied reproof to Gorgias for thinking so. Daos stands by, and makes one interjection, 300f, by way of comment on the proceedings. In all this, there is a hint of the formal pattern of a tragic *agon*; the philosophizing young rustic and the honourable young elegant both take themselves very seriously; and the audience, as in the long debate between the two farm labourers in *Epitrepontes*, is expected to react to the paradoxes of the situation with a gentle amusement not inconsistent with sympathy for the characters (*Epitr.* 41-199; note especially 51ff.)

271-87 The idea that a man should remember the uncertainty of human fortune and not overreach himself is found in different forms throughout Greek literature; on its use by Gorgias, cf. Ar. *Rhet.* 1395 a 6: οἱ . . . ἄγροικοι μάλιστα γνωμοτύποι εἰσί. Here (i) the sanction against wrongdoing is not the traditional external force of the gods' jealous anger, but the limit set by one's personal fortune (τύχη 276 = δαίμων 282), which is affected by just and unjust behaviour. For this idea, cf. especially frg. 714, *Epitr.* 735ff (discussed by Webster, *SM* 196f); in considering its background Schmid (RhM 1959.174) aptly refers to Eur., frg. 1073 N²: 'A man who goes his way in good fortune should not suppose that he will always have the same luck (*daimon*). For the god – if one should use the name god – becomes tired of associating with the same people for ever. Mortals' prosperity is itself mortal: those who are proud and trust in the future on the basis of the present find in what happens to them that their fortune proves them wrong.' (ii) The poor man claims respect because he may one day rise in station. Compare Syriskos' claim for fair treatment of the exposed child in *Epitr.* 144ff, and on the positive workings of Fortune and the gods, see Webster, *op. cit.* 198ff. (iii) The special application of the moral rule to just behaviour by the rich to the poor is closely paralleled in *Georgos*, frg. 1 'Whoever it was who wronged you is possessed by an evil genius, because he will perhaps come to know the poverty he has wronged. Even if he is very rich, his insolent pride is insecure: the current of fortune soon changes.' See further Webster, *op. cit.*, 50, 61; and in general compare Sostratos' speech to his father, 797ff.

273 τούτου: the pronoun refers back collectively to the states indicated by the two verbs, 'a sort of limit and change in their condition'. Cf. Thuc. 1.6.6 πυγμῆς καὶ πάλης ἆθλα τίθεται, καὶ διεζωσμένοι τοῦτο δρῶσιν (τοῦτο δρῶσιν ='they box and wrestle'); M. Perik. 282f πολλῶν γεγονότων ἀθλίων ... φορὰ γὰρ γέγονε τούτου νῦν καλή; 277 and 284f below, and on 800. [Ed. pr.'s τούτων has no advantage; P's τοῦτο is favoured by Gallavotti, Jean Martin et al., and may be supported from E. Heracleidae 1, and from Plato, Smp. 175 b ἔθος τι τοῦτ' ἔχει 'this is a sort of habit of his'. But the καί of 274 is against it, and the gen. to clarify πέρας and μεταλλαγήν is desirable.]

274f μένειν ... εὐθενοῦντ' ἀεί: 'remain ever-flourishing'; for μένειν with ptcp. cf. Poseidippos 30 K.

277f εἰς δὲ τοῦθ': i.e. εἰς τὸ ἄδικα ποιεῖν.

προαχθεὶς τοῖς ἀγαθοῖς: 'led on by the good things in his life'.

279 λαμβάνει: λαμβάνειν (ed. pr.) is an easy correction to secure the continuity of the νομίζω construction and is adopted by OCT and others; but it seems possible, and perhaps preferable, to assume that the Oratio Obliqua is allowed to lapse here (cf. 1-5), and immediately resumed when τοῖς δ' ἐνδεῶς πράττουσιν picks up from τῷ μὲν εὐτυχοῦντι, 274: so Mette, Jean Martin et al.

282f '. . . can achieve a position of credit in the course of time, and expect a rather better holding of prosperity.'

Appropriately to the context, the language seems to take colour from the world of finance; Gorgias, one might think, is reaching for language which he hopes will impress the young stranger from town, just as Sostratos himself later brings the technical vocabulary of property to his aid is persuading his father to be generous (797-812). For πίστις Thierfelder aptly compares Dem. 36.44 πίστις ἀφορμὴ τῶν πασῶν ἐστι μεγίστη πρὸς χρηματισμόν 'a good name (i.e. 'good credit' in the commercial sense) is the greatest asset in business'; cf. also 20.25 νυνὶ τῇ πόλει, δυοῖν ἀγαθοῖν ὄντοιν, πλούτου καὶ τοῦ πρὸς ἅπαντας πιστεύεσθαι, ἐστὶ τὸ τῆς πίστεως ὑπάρχον. εἰ δέ τις οἴεται δεῖν ὅτι χρήματ' οὐκ ἔχομεν μηδὲ δόξαν ἔχειν ἡμᾶς χρηστήν, οὐ καλῶς φρονεῖ. For μερίς with technical meaning, see (e.g.) Dem. 42.3 (a holding in a mine); M. Thesauros, frg. 198 has it in the sense of 'tithe' on property, and is otherwise a good example of the figurative use of financial language in Menander. The verbal echo of πίστιν in πίστευε, 285, is presumably deliberate, but does not imply that πίστις is necessarily self-confidence; the speaker has shifted his ground. Cf. κύριος in 800 and 806.

ἐλθόντας: accusative subject of προσδοκᾶν; it could (but of course need not) have been assimilated to the dative required by εἶναι (= ἐξεῖναι as e.g. at 268). Aeschines in Ctes. (3).2 (quoted by KG II.27) shows both constructions: ἵν' ἐξῆν πρῶτον μὲν τῷ πρεσβυτάτῳ τῶν

πολιτῶν ... παρελθόντι ... τῇ πόλει συμβουλεύειν, δεύτερον δ' ἤδη καὶ τῶν
ἄλλων πολιτῶν τὸν βουλόμενον ... γνώμην ἀποφαίνεσθαι.
[A much pondered passage, in which πίστιν has been thought too
puzzling to be sound (e.g. by van Groningen: see his *Étude Critique*
ad loc.). OCT, after Dodds, prints Χρόνῳ, as a personification – too
high a flight of language, I suspect, for this context.]

[284-7 These verses appear as vv. 8-11 in a quotation presented by
Stobaeus, *Ecl.* 3.22.19, under the heading Μενάνδρου; the whole piece
has been taken to be from *Kybernetai* because vv. 5-7 of it appear again
under that title at *Ecl.* 4.51.8: cf. frg. 250, with Koerte's notes. Either,
therefore, Menander used the same lines twice (if so, I should guess
that they were first written for the *Dyskolos*); or else two different
passages have become joined by accident or design since his day: by
accident, if, as ed. pr. suggests, the loss of a heading for the *Dyskolos*
lines has caused them to combine with the preceding extract; by
design if two quotations were deliberately fused, or if the whole was
taken from an interpolated copy of *Kybernetai*.]

284 τί οὖν λέγω; as a preface to the main point, as τί οὖν δὴ λέγω;
Plato, *Epist.* ii, 310 e, and elsewhere.

286f διευτυχεῖν ἀεί: cf. frg. 740.3 πράσσων ἃ βούλει καὶ διευτυχῶν ἀεί.
For the sentiment, cf. especially T. *Adel.* 500ff, presumably from a
similar context in Menander. τοῖς ὁρῶσιν ἄξιον: 'worthy in the eyes
of the world' (as witness of the prosperity).

288 ἄτοπον ... τι: τι indefinite seems slightly preferable to τί interrogative, as printed in OCT and elsewhere. Cf. *Epitr.* 742f; for
ἄτοπον as a euphemism for 'bad', see 417 below.

289 ἐζηλωκέναι: 'to have set your mind on': cf. Dem. *Ol.* ii (2).15
(of Philip) ὁ μὲν δόξης ἐπιθυμεῖ καὶ τοῦτ' ἐζήλωκε.

290ff '... you thought you would persuade an innocent girl to do
wrong, or watch for an opportunity and accomplish a crime worth
death many times over.'
νομίζων with future infin.: cf. Soph. *OT* 551f. It is best taken as
governing both πείσειν and κατεργάσεσθαι, with the phrase καιρὸν
ἐπιτηρῶν absolute, as at Plutarch, *Vit. Publicolae* 17, Polyb. 3.72.7 *al.*
An aorist, not a future, would be expected if the second infin. were
dependent on this phrase, as ed. pr. takes it: Kraus and others accordingly read κατεργάσασθαι and maintain that view.
ἐλευθέραν: cf. 50, 64. There the ἐλευθέραν is added because it is a
question of marriage, for which the girl must be a freeborn Athenian
and not a slave or foreigner; here it is added to underline the gravity
of the charge. Cf. Lysias 13.66 γυναῖκας τοίνυν τῶν πολιτῶν τοιοῦτος ὢν
μοιχεύειν καὶ διαφθείρειν ἐλευθέρας ἐπεχείρησε; and T. *Eun.* 857ff.

θανάτων ἄξιον πολλῶν: cf. Dem., *False Embassy* (19.)16, *Meid.* (21).21, etc. [On crimes against women and their punishment in Attic law, see U. E. Paoli, Aegyptus 32 (1952) 265ff, quoted by Treu.]

Ἄπολλον: cf. 415, *Perik.* 440 etc. The exclamation (obviously) expresses Sostratos' horrified astonishment; the god, as Apollo Apotropaios, is called to witness the situation and avert evil: he is given his full title at Ar. *Birds* 61. Other protectors similarly invoked by characters in Menander include Herakles (*Dysk.* 74, 612 and commonly), Poseidon (*Dysk.* 633, 777 *al.*), Zeus Soter (*Epitr.* 587 *al.*), and Athena (*Kol.* 23).

294 ἀσχολουμένοις: cf. 343f.

296 δυσκολώτατον: cf. *Georgos* 77f, of Poverty, quoted on 208ff above.

297f ἐλεεινός: the poor man calls forth the pity of public opinion, or of a jury trying his case. Athenian litigants (even Socrates: Plato, *Apol.* 23 c) were not slow to call attention to their poverty, or indeed to invite sympathy by other means of playing on the feelings of juries: see for instance Ar. *Wasps* 550ff, esp. 564, and Dem. 57 §§36, 45, 52. Kleainetos in *Georgos* 129ff makes the opposite point – that a poor man is easily treated with disrespect, even if his case is just, and is suspected of taking proceedings purely for gain even when wronged; cf. also Philemon 102 K, arguing that poor men inspire no confidence as public speakers.

λαμβάνει εἰς: cf. Philostr., *Imagines* 2.32 (quoted by LSJ): εἰ ἐς κόρην λαμβάνοιτο 'if it (*sc.* the figure) be taken for a girl'; and see further *NTGramm.* §157, and M., frg. 539.3 (εἰς μέμψιν... λαβεῖν conj. Salmasius).

ὕβριν: i.e. apart from being pitiable, he exaggerates the nature of the wrong, taking it not as injustice but (if we so restore) as 'outrage'. This restoration claims strong support from Aristotle's analysis of different kinds of wrong, which M. follows elsewhere, as Tierney has demonstrated (Proc. Royal Irish Acad. 43 sect c. (1936) 248f; for a brief discussion, see Webster, *SM* 204ff). According to Aristotle: (i) ἀδικήματα occur either δι' ὕβριν or διὰ κακουργίαν (*Pol.* 1295 b 10f *al.*); the former kind are particularly grave, in that they involve αἰσχύνη to the injured party, the wrongdoer's primary motive being not criminal gain, but the wanton pleasure of feeling superior (*Rhet.* 1375 a 13, cf. 1378 b 22ff, the *locus classicus* on *hybris*); (ii) the young and the rich are especially prone to hybristic acts of this kind (*Rhet.* 1378 b 26, cf. 1389 b 7); (iii) ps.-Aristot. *de virt. et vit.* 1251 b 22 says that the μικρόψυχος (the 'mean-spirited' man) is οἷος πάντα τὰ ὀλιγωρήματα καλεῖν ὕβριν καὶ ἀτιμίαν; cf. M. *Adel. II*, frg. 8 (=T. *Adel.* 605ff) ὁ πένης... πάντας αὐτοῦ καταφρονεῖν ὑπολαμβάνει. Gorgias' whole behaviour so far is an illustration of the poor man's readiness to suspect gratuitous insult. [τύχην ed. pr.; βίαν as an alternative to ὕβριν Eitrem;

for Aristotle's treatment of *hybris*, see further Cope on the passages of
Rhet. referred to above (esp. vol. I.268, vol. II.17ff; on this and on
the criminal offence of *hybris* in Attic Law, see J. J. Fraenkel, *Hybris*
(Utrecht, 1941), esp. 52ff, 61ff.]

299 οὕτως εὐτυχοίης: *lit.* 'so may you prosper' (if you do as I ask).
This and similar forms of wish commonly strengthen emphatic requests,
as here: 'I do beg you to listen'. Their other function, corresponding
to English 'So help me . . .', is to strengthen emphatic assertions: as it
were 'So may I prosper' (if I am telling the truth); that is the case in
300f, with the text restored as here: 'Splendid, master, as I hope for
good luck.' So for instance, at *Perik.* 210-13 οὕτως ὄναιο, λέγε . . .
(request), and καὶ γὰρ οἴχεται . . . οὕτω μοι γένοιθ᾽ ἃ βούλομαι (assertion).

βραχύ τι: 'just a word or two', as χάρισαι βραχύ τί μοι 'just do me a
little favour', Ar. *Thes.* 938.

[βραχ[έα μου Webster: cf. Dem. 36.36 βραχέ᾽ ἡμῶν ἀκούσατε and
45.27 μίκρ᾽ ἀκούσατέ μου.]

300f The speaker is certainly Daos, as is generally recognized (but
not in OCT, which follows ed. pr. in restoring πολλά [σοι, and assigning
the part to Pyrrhias: but Pyrrhias has no part in this Act). εὖ γε,
δέσποτα congratulates Gorgias on the effect of his speech, as reflected
in Sostratos' highly conciliatory beginning; the wish-formula, which
must be completed with μοι, then adds emphasis: see above (299 n),
comparing *Epitr.* 349 ὑπέρευγε, νὴ τὸν Ἥλιον. καὶ σύ γ᾽ ὁ λαλῶν πρόσεχε,
said by Sostratos to Daos is *lit.* 'You pay attention too, that man who's
talking . . .', ὁ λαλῶν being used to refer to someone who is a stranger
to the speaker, as σὺ πρότερος ὁ σιωπῶν λέγε at *Epitr.* 63. [Jacques
adopts σοι, punctuating οὕτω . . . γένοιτο as a separate unfinished
sentence. 301 πρ[όσεχέ μοι Gallavotti, Lond. *et al.*]

302ff Sostratos' direct reply contrasts admirably with Gorgias'
approach to him; its disarming sincerity, though certainly not feigned,
is not artless either. For the opening, a good comparison is T. *Andria*
896: ego me amare hanc fateor; si id peccare est, fateor id quoque
(Blake); cf. also Callimachus, *Epigr.* 42.6 εἰ τοῦτ᾽ ἔστ᾽ ἀδίκημ᾽, ἀδικέω
(Kassel); and M., frg. 674 ἤρων γάρ, ἤρων, ὁμολογῶ· καὶ νῦν δ᾽ ἐρῶ; see
further, among many examples of 'concessive' beginnings in defensive
speeches, Syriskos' elaborate concession to Daos at the opening of
his speech in *Epitr.* 118ff, and Tranio's mocking parody of the same
gambit in P. *Most.* 1138ff. Love is of course the lover's excuse for all:
e.g. T. *Eun.* 877: unum hoc scito, contumeliae | me non fecisse causa,
sed amoris; P. *Aul.* 744f (where Euclio and Lyconides are amusingly
at cross purposes) *Euclio*: quid tibi ergo meam me inuito tactiost? |
Lyconides: quia uini uitio atque amoris feci.
[302: or, e.g., εὐπρεπῆ· τ]αύτης (Marzullo); 303: or, e.g. [ἐνόμισ]ας
(Kraus).]

304 τί γὰρ ἄν τις εἴποι; 'What else could one say?' (i.e. 'I don't deny it'); cf. 152 above, frg. inc. 951.11 τί γὰρ ἂν ἄλλο τις λέγειν ἔχοι; πλήν 'except that', introducing a qualifying sentence, as at 673, *Epitr.* 307, *Georgos* 13, frg. 622.5: cf. *NTGramm.* §449. [Alternatives exist (e.g. π[ροσπ]ορεύομ' Webster); but this restoration seems virtually certain.]

305 ἰδεῖν: 'see', in the common English sense of 'meet', 'interview': cf. 107f, 174, 236; LSJ s.v. εἴδω A.1.b. S.'s words amount to the statement: 'I wish to make a formal proposal of marriage' – i.e. he is a freeborn Athenian of adequate means, willing to accept the girl without a dowry (a considerable concession, which was not always accepted: see on 845f); and willing to 'love, honour and cherish' her always. For διατελεῖν στέργων, cf. P. Didot. I (Koerte I³, p. 143), 14ff ἔστ' ἀνδρὶ καὶ γυναικὶ κείμενος νόμος | τῷ μὲν διὰ τέλους ἦν ἔχει στέργειν ἀεί, | τῇ δ' ὅσ' ἂν ἀρέσκῃ τἀνδρί, ταῦτ' αὐτὴν ποεῖν.

310 ὑμῶν with λάθρᾳ, 'behind your backs'; cf. *Sam.* 61f (ἐμοῦ λάθρᾳ), and 577f below.

[ὑμῶν P (Roberts). ἢ βουλόμενός τι κακοτεχνεῖν ὑμῶν λάθρᾳ ed. pr., reading ἡμῶν in P.]

311 οὗτος . . . ὁ Πάν: 'Pan here', cf. 659. The invocation of the god in his presence is a powerful reinforcement of the oath; ed. pr. wrongly emends to οὕτως.

312f ἀπόπληκτον . . . ποήσειαν: ἀπόπληκτος is both literal, as here, of someone paralysed, mentally deranged or struck dumb; and also figurative, as in 839, of someone who behaves as stupidly as if he were so afflicted: cf. παροινέω (93 n.). 'Pan was believed to cause not only panic (Πανικὸν δεῖμα), but also fainting and collapse (Eur. *Med.* 1172 and Σ)' Dodds, *The Greeks and the Irrational*, p. 95 n. 89. Here Pan and the Nymphs are naturally conjoined; between them they have, by repute, such a range of powers to take possession of men as to make the oath a convincingly strong one, and not merely an appropriate one to the speaker's situation and to the design of the play. [See further on 433f; Photiades, Greece & Rome 1958.117 n. 1; Pastorino, in *Menandrea* (Univ. di Genova, Ist. di Fil. Class., 1960), 88 n. 46; and Frazer's note on Ovid, *Fasti* 4.761 (vol. iii, 358ff), to which Dr J. A. Willis refers me.]

313f 'I do assure you, I am very much upset': εὖ ἴσθ' ὅτι parenthetic, as in Philemon 152 K. [This seems a slightly easier and more likely emendation than τετάραγμαι δ', ἴσθ' ὅτι, ed. pr., adopted in OCT, or τετάραγμαί γ', ἴσθ' ὅτι (Page).]

οὐδὲ μετρίως: 'to no small degree', as in *Halieus* frg. 24; 'not at all gently' in 962 below.

Before this conclusion 'there is perhaps a moment's pause' remarks

Turner 'in which Pan gives no sign of disapproval'. The apology for giving a bad impression is so phrased as to convey a reproof to Gorgias for making so grave an accusation so hastily, and it receives a generous reply.

315 κἀγώ: 'I for my part'.

317 μεταπείθεις with double acc., as ταῦτα συμπείθεις με σύ; at *Epitr.* 709, but the με is expressed only in the parallel clause, φίλον μ' ἔχεις.

319 ὁμομήτριος: Eng. 'half-brother' does not distinguish ὁμομήτριοι like Gorgias and his sister from ὁμοπάτριοι like the young man and his sister in *Georgos* (10).

320ff 'What's more, I'll swear you can help me with the next step' 'Help you?' 'I can see you're a man with his heart in the right place' 'It's not that I want to send you away with a worthless excuse . . .'

With ed. pr. and others, I adopt the text and arrangement of speakers of P. To Sostratos, with his mind set on the marriage he is pursuing, a new friend is a potential new ally, and he hastens to recruit him, moved not only by Gorgias' relationship to the girl he loves, but by the spirited temperament which attacked wrong vigorously and met sincere denial with swift reparation. Like his father, he sees an inherent nobility in Gorgias, the counterpart of the ἐλευθεριότης he recognizes in the girl (835f, 201f); Gorgias, who has never been in love himself, completely misses the point of the first broad hint, and responds to the second by saying, in effect, that the situation is hopeless: cf. 338-42. OCT, after Fraenkel, continues with Gorgias after τί χρήσιμος; reading γεννικὸν ὁρῶν σε τῷ τρόπῳ, οὐ πρόφασιν, κτλ.: those who support this arrangement include Jean Martin and Foss.

320 Sostratos recruiting an ally: cf. 558-62. For χρήσιμος cf. Com. Anon. (? Philemon) δύναμαι γενέσθαι χρήσιμος κἀγώ τί σοι | εἰς ταῦτα (= Page, *Lit. Pap.* 64.29: add P. Heid. 184, frg. 2).

321 τί χρήσιμος; cf. on 215.

323-70 What Gorgias says of Knemon here is a major part of the portrait of his character, and of Gorgias' character also. In telling Sostratos about him, he gives the audience facts which would have been hard to present naturalistically by more direct means; he speaks disapprovingly, but with no malice, showing a generosity which will culminate in the 'noble act' of disinterested help that changes Knemon's outlook on life (722ff). Knemon left the stage at 178, and will not reappear till the beginning of Act III at 427; in this Act, as for much of Act I, he is interesting entirely through what we hear said of him. Cf. Introd. I, p. 11f.

325f ὁ χαλεπός; cf. *Epitr.* 720f ὦ, Σμικρίνης | ὁ χαλεπός.
σχεδὸν οἶδα: 'I think I know him'. σχεδόν is 'frequently used to

soften a positive assertion with a sense of modesty, sometimes of irony', LSJ s.v., IV.2. We need not suppose that S. is being ironical, in spite of his previous experience of Knemon.

ὑπερβολή . . . τοῦ κακοῦ: 'You might say he is the very limit of badness' – not merely 'intractable', or 'disagreeable', as Sostratos had described him.

327 ταλάντων δυεῖν: the value involved is discussed below on 842-4. Allowing, as seems necessary, that values in Comedy may be conventionally higher than real values, the estate is still a considerable one, large enough to make it remarkable, indeed absurd, that Knemon works it all alone (Introd. II.1, p. 23f). The Hellenistic form δυεῖν appears also in *Pseudherakles*, frg. 453, where δυοῖν is a variant reading. [Cf. Theophr. *Char.* 2.3 (cod. A); Meisterhans-Schwyzer, *Gramm. d. att. Inschr.* 157, 201 (quoting δυεῖν in inscriptions from 329-229 B.C.); Mayser, *Gramm. d. gr. Papyri* I².2 (1938) 73 n. 1.]

329ff 'He has no helper': the three obvious kinds of help are eliminated: he might have owned a slave, hired help locally, or called in a neighbour. The fact that Knemon takes his daughter to work with him makes Sostratos all the keener to join Gorgias and Daos on the land when that is suggested (359f), but it also shows, more clearly than anything yet, that the misanthrope has a spark of human feeling in him, if only a faint spark. Note the qualification of Pan's words at 8ff.

335 'He would be very reluctant to speak to anyone else'. For τοῦτο ποιεῖν, see on 676f; for οὐ ῥᾳδίως, Headlam-Knox on Herondas 7.69-70.

337f ὁμότροπον αὐτῷ νυμφίον: 'a man like himself to marry her'. Cf. *Perik.* frg. 1 οὕτω ποθεινόν ἐστιν ὁμότροπος φίλος, and see on 355ff.

λέγεις οὐδέποτε: 'that means never'.

338f 'Don't give yourself trouble about it: it will be useless.'

339 ἀναγκαίους: 'relations'; see on 239f.

341ff To the lover his own feelings are supremely important; compare in general Sostratos' impatience with Chaireas and Pyrrhias in the opening scene, and see on 54f, quoting the opening of *Heros*. For a similar situation, one may also compare the fragment printed by Koerte as *Heros* frg. 10 οὐπώποτ' ἠράσθης, Γέτα; | (Γε.) οὐ γὰρ ἐνεπλήσθην (. . . 'No, I never had enough to eat'). Gorgias' lack of imagination over affairs of the heart (of which he has no experience) is matched by Sostratos' lack of imagination when it comes to dealing with an old countryman whose character is outside *his* experience, 364ff.

343f In effect, Gorgias says 'My mind is fully occupied with the troubles I have': i.e. λογισμός 'reasoned calculation' implies an antithesis to passion, τῶν ὄντων κακῶν implies that love would be an added misfortune to poverty.

345f οὔ μοι δοκεῖς: sc. ἐρασθῆναί τινος from 341: 'I shouldn't think you had; at any rate what you say about it suggests inexperience. You tell me to give up . . .'

οὔ μοι δοκεῖς: cf. 787.

[The reminiscence of this passage in Aristaenetus confirms Browning's conjecture, which is adopted in OCT, and thereby settles the textual problem presented by P. I owe my knowledge of it to Sandbach: cf. his remarks in CR 1962, p. 205.]

346f 'That is no longer in my power, but the god's'. S. means Eros; the audience knows, as he does not, that Pan made him fall in love. Cf. P. *Aul.* 737, deus mihi impulsor fuit, is mihi ad illam inlexit, and 742 deos credo uoluisse; *Samia* 286f (Moschion) οὐ γὰρ ἔξεστ', οὐδ' ἐᾷ | ὁ τῆς ἐμῆς νῦν κύριος γνώμης "Ερως. [τόδ' ἐσ]τὶν OCT (Page). Perhaps, with OCT and others, ἀποστῆναι κελεύεις μ' is to be read as a question.]

347f 'Well then, we can't blame you; but you are hurting yourself for nothing': οὐδὲν ἀδικεῖς as, for instance, at *Sam.* 113 οὐδὲν γὰρ ἀδικεῖ Μοσχίων σε 'You have no ground for complaint against M.'; cf. 143 above. Gorgias admits that Sostratos has every right to propose marriage with someone he cannot help loving, but insists once more that it is useless to do so.

[οὐδέ]ν seems much the most satisfactory supplement, though possibly somewhat short for the space: if it were clearly one letter short, one might think that P had ουδεε]ν.]

349-54 Sostratos will not be dissuaded, and Gorgias offers to prove that the case is hopeless by taking him to see Knemon. The sense is relatively clear from the preserved words and the context; but corruption as well as damage makes restoration problematical, and the version of the text given (one of several or many possible) should be treated with due reserve. It agrees with OCT except in 350, which is not there restored.

'No chance of marrying her?' 'No chance. You'll see right now if you come along there with me – he works the valley near us'.

[**349** πῶς ἂν ed. pr., εἰ γὰρ Page.]

350-2 For ὄψει without object expressed, cf. *Perik.* 61, quoted on 879; for νῦν of the immediate future, compare its use with πρόσεισι at *Sam.* 319, 337; πλησίον with gen., as at *Epitr.* 66. [The loss of the verbs in P, no matter how we divide it between damage and corruption, creates ambiguities of structure. At the end must come a remark about Knemon, with its verb in 352. Perhaps ⌣_με]θ' ἡμῶν, after ed. pr.; Webster suggests that παρατησ can be saved at the cost of taking παρὰ τῆς πλησίον γὰρ τὴν νάπην | [διέρχε]θ᾽ ἡμῶν to mean 'he goes through our valley from the next one'. It seems both simpler and safer to take πλησίον ... ἡμῶν together and assume that παρατησ is corrupt: if so, it admits other easy corrections, e.g. παραστῆς Barrett, or παρ᾽ αὐτῆς as Kraus once suggested. 350 almost certainly begins in P with traces of a upsilon. 'fort. ὄψει δ᾽ ἐὰν σ]ύ' OCT (Lloyd-Jones). This, like the suggestion adopted, assumes confusion in the repeated sequence of letters]γνασυν; but if συν is simply a duplicate of σ]γνα, the text could be more seriously deranged. Others see in]γνα(ς) the ending of a verb or participle: e.g. ἐὰν δ᾽ ἐρε]γνᾶς, συνακολουθήσας ἐμοὶ | [γνώσει] παρ᾽ αὐτοῦ Turner, followed by Foss.]

352-4 'I'll raise the subject of the girl's marriage; it's a thing I should be glad to see happen myself.' τὸ τοιοῦτο γάρ ... ἄσμενος is rightly separated from what follows and taken to refer to Gorgias; ed. pr. supplements and punctuates so as to refer it to Knemon, with some followers. [353, possibly ἐγώ (Blake, Kraus); alii alia.]

περὶ γάμου τῆς κόρης is acceptable Greek in reference to the girl's marriage as a general concept (i.e. 'about her marrying'); similarly περὶ φυλακῆς τῆς χώρας Xen. *Mem.* 3.6.10, quoted with other examples by KG I.607; the article should not be expected. Cf. on τοιοῦτο τὸ μέρος χωρίου in 164.

355 μαχεῖται: 'will take it out of everybody': see for instance *Epitr.* 375 μαχοῦμαί σοι τότε 'I'll have it out with you then'; and Theophr. *Char.* 23.8: the braggart is the sort of man to order something expensive in a shop, and then turn on his slave – τῷ παιδὶ μάχεσθαι – for forgetting the money.

355ff Knemon, who will only accept a bridegroom like himself (336f, cf. 734f), thinks that other men's lives are based on false standards: note especially 447ff on true and false piety, and (in his major speech) 719ff, 743ff on self-seeking and disinterestedness. The present passage gives a deliberate hint of the positive side of Knemon's nastiness (if we may so call it), later to be portrayed and examined. [356: P presumably had ἂν ἄγοντ᾽ giving a 'split anapaest'; on this and on 358, cf. Introd. IV p. 65 under (g) and (h).]

357 ... 'he won't even put up with the sight of you' [Not ὁρ[ᾶν, ed. pr., possibly ὁρ[ῶν γ᾽ OCT (Roberts).]

358f ἣν εἴωθεν sc. ὁδόν, 'come out his usual way', the common quasi-cognate acc. with ἰέναι. Knemon indeed sets out, 427, only to turn back because he feels unable to leave the house while a sacrifice is going on next door: the consequences for Sostratos appear at 522ff. [μ[εῖν]ον ed. pr.; μ[ἀλλ]ον Lond.; hardly ἣν εἴωθεν ὥραν (Blake). Gorgias' reference to the girl at 333f justifies ed. pr.'s assumption (against P) that Sostratos is speaking of her here; it is much in point for him to do so, pointless for Gorgias to mention her again.]

359ff Sostratos' eagerness at the prospect of seeing the girl again is met with an unconcerned 'Maybe, maybe not': the contrast in mood and manner between the two young men continues to be brought out. See on 341ff.

ὅπως ἂν ... τύχῃ: *lit.* 'however it happens'; cf. LSJ s.v. τυγχάνω A.3.

[μεθ' αὑτοῦ / μετ' αὐτοῦ: see on 254. P indicates change of speaker after φῄς and τύχῃ, this time rightly.]

363 ὅντινα τρόπον: 'How, you ask?'. ὅστις is commonly used in echoing questions put by τίς; similarly πῶς;/ὅπως; 625. The full form is given by Krobylos, *Pseudhypobolimaios* 5K —ποῖ;— ὅποι μ' ἐρωτᾷς; (Jean Martin).

363ff Daos is rightly identified by P as the speaker of ταῖς βώλοις ... πένηθ', for it follows from the dialogue at 371ff that he was the author of the idea that Sostratos should actually do some work. We should therefore assume, with Post, that he also speaks τί οὖν ... χλανίδα and that P, whether in error or by omission of a speaker's name, has failed to mark his first entry into this conversation. Sostratos quite fails to see that his appearance would be fatal to his chances; Gorgias had the more limited object of demonstrating that Knemon would not hear of a proposal of marriage: it is wholly appropriate for the slave's earthy common sense to take him one jump ahead, with motives of self-interest which are soon disclosed.

365 χλανίδα: see on 257, and below under 370.

τί δὴ γὰρ οὐχί; 'Why ever not?'; cf. Denniston, *Particles* 211, quoting τί δὴ γὰρ οὔ; from E. *Or.* 1602 and Plato, *Parm.* 138 b, 140 e. [So OCT and Jacques: γὰρ δῆτ' ed. pr., and hence generally.]

ταῖς βώλοις: cf. 83, 110, 120. For the article ('the clods on his land'), perhaps compare Ar. *Ach.* 184 ξυνελέγοντο τῶν λίθων 'They collected some stones' (from those on the ground), *Wasps* 199, etc.

366 ἀποκαλεῖν is 'to call someone a name', usually a bad name as here; ὄλεθρον ἀργόν, 'an idle pest' – but perhaps these are two separate terms of abuse, as Shipp suggests.

369 '... thinking that you live the life of a poor independent farmer': i.e. a citizen with his own plot who happens to be helping Gorgias.

τῷ βίῳ: cf. *Epitr.* 590, *Georg.* 66, frg. 594. It is simple, but probably unnecessary, to add σ' after νομίσας with Fraenkel and others, for the pronoun is readily understood from the context. Cf. *Georgos* 59 νομίσας ἑαυτοῦ πατέρα (*sc.* αὐτόν).

370 'I'm prepared to do all you say: come on.' It is attractive to assume that with these words Sostratos removes the offending cloak and folds it over his arm or slings it over his shoulder to carry. In the short *chiton* which he can be presumed to wear underneath it, he is suitably dressed for physical activity and could well be taken for a poor citizen farmer helping Gorgias. Meanwhile the others talk aside; then, with ἔκφερε δίκελλαν 375, he again shows how eager he is to start. If this is right, the action emphasizes the words by providing a visual symbol of Sostratos' readiness to abandon the conventions of his upbringing and work to win the girl he loves. If not, he probably removes the cloak off-stage after 392; for after what has been said about it, he can hardly reappear with it on when he comes from the digging at 522. There are signs in the text which suggest (but do not prove) that his appearance had changed by then. His opening remark about hunting at Phyle would be useful if he were not wearing his cloak, though it is amply justified otherwise; similarly at 552, Getas fails to recognize his young master – partly, no doubt, because the encounter is unexpected and he is blinded by cooking-smoke, as he has just complained; but perhaps also because Sostratos is, as it were, in his shirt-sleeves. It is not untypical of Menander to make his words serve several purposes at once: an example is Daos' short monologue at 208ff. Then, at 559, Sostratos says that he will invite Gorgias and Daos to join the sacrifice, and go 'as I am' (see n.); at 754f he is presented to Knemon as a sunburnt farmer who is no idle waster: he may therefore still not have put the cloak on again. Perhaps he leaves it off-stage, or (better) in the shrine when he goes there at 619; if he is to put it on again, he probably does so before he enters with his father at 784, for in the last Act it is appropriate not only to the atmosphere of weddings and celebrations but to the renewed emphasis on Sostratos' position as the son of a rich man *vis à vis* the poverty of Gorgias.

We have however no hard evidence that Sostratos changed costume at all. Still less likely, I believe, is the view originating with ed. pr. that Sostratos borrows a *diphthera* to dig in, which he returns to Gorgias with the borrowed *dikella* at 616, when he says 'take these things in with you'. It is true that at 415 Sostratos' mother is said to have dreamt that Pan gave her son a leather jerkin and a mattock and told him to dig; but the fact that she also saw Pan putting fetters on him should warn us against taking the dream too literally. In our present context, although a mattock is provided at 375, there is no sign of a *diphthera* being borrowed; at 616, the remark 'take these things in with you' could equally well apply to the tools which Daos and Gorgias are carrying: the mattock is certainly not returned then, for Sostratos must already have given it back to Daos when Daos took over the digging from him (see 541f); and it is at least arguable, as we have seen, that Sostratos is still supposed to be dressed as for digging as late as 754f. But in any case, if Sostratos is really to dress up as a rustic (i.e. in the standard costume of another dramatic type), one would expect the change of costume to be much more neatly prepared for and much more neatly managed than the text as we have it suggests; nor am I clear that dressing up, as opposed to removing his *chlanis*, is suitable to the portrait of Sostratos' character: note especially what is said about him by Gorgias, 764ff. One can show good intentions while getting down to honest work with one's coat off; but to appear as a suitor in borrowed working clothes is perhaps going too far for a young man of such gentlemanly virtue. A good contrast is offered by the disguising of Chaerea in T. *Eun.*

371 σαυτὸν βιάζῃ: cf. *Epitr.* 4f. Gorgias cannot see why the slave wants to inflict a day's work on himself; but Daos has thought faster. Perhaps read αὐτόν, as many have thought; the alternative view, that Gorgias is addressing Sostratos, gives clumsy dialogue and an awkward aside to follow.

373 τὴν ὀσφῦν ἀπορρήξανθ': 'spraining' his lumbar muscles, rather than 'breaking' anything: cf. Xen. *Eq.* 8.6, who says that some people are afraid to ride their horses downhill μὴ ἀπορρηγνύωνται τοὺς ὤμους κατὰ τὰ πρανῆ ἐλαυνόμενοι. Delebecque takes this to mean 'break their shoulders', although, as he points out, a sprain is much the more likely injury; Marchant (Loeb) translates the word by 'put out'. The wish is nearly fulfilled, cf. 531ff.

375 δίκελλαν: 'mattock', see under 525-31.
  τὴν παρ' ἐμοῦ: 'mine', cf. Headlam-Knox on Herondas 1.2; *NTGramm.* §237. It seems clear (*pace* ed. pr. and others) that Daos, not Gorgias says this, and hands over the mattock with the remark that he will build up the dry-wall, for it is Daos who comes to take over the digging when Sostratos gives up, 541f.

[**376** P's ετιγαροικοδομησω apparently shows a corruption in two stages, επ>ετι, then γαρ transposed. ἔτ' οἰκοδομήσω γὰρ ed. pr. Cf. Introd. III, p. 52. Libanius' τὴν αἱμασιάν οἰκοδομήσας is hardly useful.]

377ff *Sostr.* Give it to me. You've saved my life . . . *Daos* I'm off, young master; hurry along to the land. *Sostr.* . . . for this is my position: either I die now, or live with her as my wife.

378 ἀπέσωσας: cf. Lucian, *Dial. Meretr.* 2.4 ἀπέσωσας, ὦ Πάμφιλε· ἀπηγξάμην γὰρ ἄν, εἴ τι τοιοῦτο ἐγένετο; for the ellipse of the object, cf. ἀπολεῖς 412 and n., and in general KG II.561f. Similar is P. *Amph.* 313f. ME. quid si ego illum tractim tangam, ut dormiat? SO. seruaueris, | nam continuas has tris noctes peruigilaui. [ἀπέσωσά σ' Lond., giving the words to Daos. P's dicolon after δός suggests this, but may be erroneous or indicate the strong break in the speech, as in 177. (Δα.) ἀπέσωσας OCT (Lloyd-Jones), with Diano and others.]

ὑπάγω: cf. Ar. *Birds* 1017 ὑπάγοιμι τἄρ' ἄν. This word, which in later
Greek means simply 'go', can imply either 'advance' or 'withdraw'
according to context.

τρόφιμε: *Kolax* 86 *al.* τρόφιμος is the 'young master', the son of the
house; τροφίμη (883), the 'young mistress': Lat. *erilis filius (-a)*. The old
slave, who had worked for Gorgias' father (27), addresses him in-
differently as τρόφιμε and δέσποτα (300), even as ὦ τᾶν (247).

διώκετε: apparently intrans. (see LSJ s.v., III.2), or at least with με
unexpressed; Page suggests δίωκέ με. Possibly punctuate ... ἐκεῖ
διώκετε after Kraus and others. [ὕπαγ', ὦ τρόφιμε would be possible
(cf. 144); but τρόφιμε is the form of address elsewhere in Menander;
nor is ὦ τρ. completely certain in Com. Anon. (?Philemon), Page, *Lit.
Pap.* 64 (2).]

379 Daos goes off left, to the fields. With the text as given here,
Sostratos' οὕτως ἔχω γάρ picks up from ἀπέσωσας, still following his
train of thought in spite of the interruption. Cf. Denniston, *Particles*
63f; *Sam.* 327ff is a good example in Menander. The conjecture is
well recommended by the passages quoted on 378. [παραποθανεῖν is
adopted from P in ed. pr. and generally: cf. παραπόλλυμι, as at 695
below. The word is not certainly to be read in Dio Cassius frg. 102.11
(I, p. 346 Boissevain) and is not quoted from elsewhere.]

381 ἐπιτύχοις: abs. 'succeed'; with gen., 389, 'win her'. Gorgias goes
off left, after Daos; Sostratos speaks his brief monologue, then follows

382 ὡς οἴει με σύ: με, governed by ἀποτρέπεις, is attracted away from
it by the other pronoun: cf. 189 οἴμοι τάλαινα τῶν ἐμῶν ἐγὼ κακῶν.

383 παρώξυμμαι: 'I am driven on'; abs. 'I am excited', *Sam.* 276.

384-9 Sostratos contemplates the blissful good fortune of marrying
a girl who has not been spoilt by female domination, but brought up
ἐλευθερίως by her father, as a young man might have been. Compare
particularly 201f ἐλευθερίως γέ πως | ἄγροικός ἐστιν, and see on 34ff. It
is a favourable (though conventional) trait in the young lover that
he admires the girl's character as well as her beauty.

Once more, as at 355f, it is suggested that there is more to Knemon's
misanthropy than perversity and blind hatred; he hates the bad
(388); and in this, the 'odd man out' of society may after all be right:
if Knemon's unpleasantness and his determination to live minimally
have driven his wife from home and provided his daughter with no
better τρόφος than the maid-of-all-work Simiche, she has at least (we
are reminded) had the simple discipline of a stern father and been
saved from the bad influences which may afflict girls in a more sophisticated household. No doubt this picture of the girl's upbringing is
intended to be set against what Daos has said at 220ff. For the misanthrope as a critic of the bad, compare the tale of Timon, as told (with

a comic twist of logic) by the chorus of women in Ar. *Lys.* 805-20: (812) οὗτος οὖν ὁ Τίμων | . . . | ὤχεθ᾽ ὑπὸ μίσους | πολλὰ καταρασάμενος ἀνδράσι πονηροῖς. | οὕτω κεῖνος ὑμῶν ἀντεμίσει | τοὺς πονηροὺς ἄνδρας ἀεί, | ταῖσι δὲ γυναιξὶν ἦν φίλτατος.

As a criticism of evil influences on children, the passage coincides partly in theme with Antiphanes, *Misoponeros* 159 K, a play which Menander may perhaps have had in mind: 'Well, aren't the Scythians supremely intelligent to give their children mares' and cows' milk to drink from birth? I'll swear they don't call in wicked old hags of nurses, nor tutors for that matter; there's nothing worse than them, except of course a nanny (μαῖα), they're supremely bad . . .' (The *misoponeros* himself appears to be speaking; the words translated by 'except . . . bad' may however have come from a second speaker, as Wilamowitz suggests.)

As elsewhere in the play, Menander brings in briefly and relevantly a topic which might well have been developed on conventional lines for its own sake; nor is the criticism of women's ways out of character for Sostratos, who has already spoken with some scorn of the religious activities of his mother (259ff).

385ff '. . . and knows nothing of the evils of life from the terrors of some old aunt or nanny, but has been brought up honestly by her father . . .'

386 τούτων: the evils that all know of – a normal use of οὗτος and a word-order which is not uncommon: e.g. *Hydria* frg. 401 ἥ τε κατὰ πόλιν | αὕτη τρυφή: see further Gildersleeve, *Syntax of Attic Greek* II.331f, and Meineke, *Frag. Com. Graec.* V, at p. 774. Emendation to τούτῳ, with ed. pr., OCT and some other edd., is therefore needless.

μηδέν with οἶδε, not with the following clause. οἶδα with gen. seems to be confined to high poetry: cf. KG I.370. The metrical break at μηδὲν ὑπὸ is not of a common type: cf. Introd. IV p. 67f under (*b*).

386f τηθίδος τινός . . . μαίας τ᾽: an 'aunt' appears among a list of tiresome relations in *Thyroros*, frg. 208-9, but is not, so far as I know, a traditionally bad influence like the μαῖα. It is however a nice point whether τηθίς τις means precisely 'an aunt' and does not rather apply to any older woman within the family circle. μαῖα likewise should perhaps not be pressed to too precise a sense; translated here by 'nanny' it seems to refer, as in Antiph. 159 (quoted above) to someone called in for the purpose of looking after the girl, but that need not exclude one of her relations. Attempts by ancient and modern lexicographers to classify the senses of such words sometimes seem to stumble over the waywardness of informal usage: cf. τηθία at *Misoumenos* 13, with Koerte's note. On μαῖαι and their like in drama, see H. G. Oeri, *Der Typ der komischen Alten*, 28, 53ff: the obvious example of a 'bad influence' is the Nurse in E. *Hip.*

δεδιξαμένη, from δειδίσσομαι (Att. δεδίττομαι), if right here, is 'frightened', with ὑπό + gen. of the source of the fear; for this sense of the aor., cf. Polyaenus, *Strategemata* 1.12, quoted in Stephanus-Dindorf, s.v. δεδίσκομαι (1): οἱ Βοιωτοί ... τὴν ὄψιν τοῦ πυρὸς ... ἰδόντες ἐδεδίξαντο καὶ πρὸς ἱκεσίαν τῶν Θεσσαλῶν ἐτράποντο. In spite of its use in this and other military contexts and more generally, the word is not inappropriate for fears inflicted on a child: see e.g. *Iliad* 20.200 μὴ δή μ' ἐπέεσί γε νηπύτιον ὣς | ἔλπεο δειδίξεσθαι and Lucian, *Zeuxis* 4 ὡς δεδίξαιτο σὺν παιδιᾷ τὰ βρέφη, in both of which passages the sense is 'frighten' actively. It seems likely, from P's reading and from the context, that Menander used some form of this word; it remains unclear what form.

[δεδισαμένη Gallavotti: cf. δειδισάμενος in Appian, *Bell. Civ.* 5.79, where Nauck conjectured δεδιξάμενος. δεδισσομένη OCT (Lloyd-Jones), with a note suggesting some alternatives; but hardly -σσ- in Menander's Attic. δεδιδαγμένη (ed. pr.) cuts the knot, and some adopt it. On the formation, see Schwyzer I. 710. I am not clear that the entry δεδεῖσαι (or δὲ δεῖσαι?)· φοβῆσαι in Hesychius is any help (Δ 67; vol. I, p. 409 Latte).]

388 'With a father of untamed fierceness and ingrained hatred of evil'. ἄγριος probably implies rough or wild, not merely δύσκολος; it is highly proper to the figure of the misanthrope (Pherekrates, *Agrioi*, referred to on 6 above; Lucian, *Timon* 35, τὸ πάνυ τοῦτο ἄγριον καὶ τραχύ of the mood of Timon) For μισοπόνηρος see above under 384-9. With this text, scan μετὰ πᾰτρὸ̆ς ἄγρῐ-|οῦ the line beginning with two tribrachs (‿bbCdd), as at *Georgos* 61 and elsewhere, for πᾰτρός, with lengthening before τρ would be abnormal in Menander (496 n., 414 n.).

[μετὰ πατρὸς αὐτοῦ OCT (Griffith); πατρὸς μετ' ἀγρίου Post; not μετὰ τοῦ πατρὸς ἀγρίου (the article is in any case unwanted): Introd. IV, Note C. 389: ἐστιν αὐτῆς ed. pr.]

390 ἄγει 'weighs'. 4 Attic talents would be rather more than 2 cwt, 4 Aeginetic talents nearly 3 cwt; Sostratos is in effect saying that the mattock is a carrying load for four men, with an exaggeration which is to be echoed in a moment by Getas, struggling under a load fit for four donkeys, 402f. The number 'four' in both cases is arbitrary: cf. *Arrephoros*, frg. 61, the drunkard waking up with four heads. A character in Sosikrates, *Parakatatheke* 1 K, talks of a fat pale idler used to high living being made to puff and pant by a *dikella* weighing five staters (πεντεστάτηρον). Pollux, the quoting source, gives conflicting equations for the weight, but at maximum it can hardly be more than 8 lb – perhaps a comically lightweight pattern. It is tempting to think that the two plays are somehow related (see e.g. Treu, *ed. Dysk.*, ad loc.), but we know too little to make a connection out. Chremes in T. *Heaut.* comments on the heavy weight of the *rastri* with which

Menedemus is labouring to punish himself (92). On the δίκελλα, see under 525-31.

391 προαπολεῖ μ᾽: 'I shall be dead before I'm done with it'. [προσαπολεῖ (ed. pr., with P) seems to give no acceptable sense, but has found some support.]

392 '. . . now that I've really begun to tackle the business'. καταπονεῖν *lit.* 'reduce by hard work', cf. frg. 526.

The result of Sostratos' forebodings and his resolution will appear from 522ff. As he goes, following the others off left to Gorgias' land, the stage is momentarily empty.

393 Enter right, Sikon the cook, with a sheep. We do not learn his name until much later (perhaps 499; certainly 889); his profession is obvious from the moment he appears with the animal, wearing the *maison* mask appropriate to his status (Introd. II.3), and possibly equipped with the badge of his profession in the shape of a knife (cf. *Samia* 68f, referred to on 440, and P. *Aul.* 417). The sharper-witted members of the audience will guess at once what is happening from what they have heard already (259ff), but before long everybody will join in the enjoyment of a typically comic 'coincidence'.

We should perhaps not ask too closely where Getas had been to hire the cook, since Menander leaves it conveniently vague. The natural answer is 'to Athens', where indeed the cook claims to practise (490): if so, we must allow that for dramatic purposes, a journey of around 25 miles is possible in the time since Sostratos' mother woke up from the dream we shall hear of, and decided to send Getas off. What is clear is that he is coming now from the home of the family, where the womenfolk have loaded his companion (402ff). On the day's time-table, see Webster, Bull. Rylands Library 1962.235ff; on the change of rôles from the previous scene, see Introd. II.2.

μάγειροι, in modern terms, are butchers, cooks and caterers rolled into one: Sikon has brought the meat with him, on the hoof, and will presently kill the animal in sacrifice and prepare the feast to follow. As a dramatic type, the cook seems to be a creation of Middle Comedy; little can be safely said of his ancestors in the age of Aristophanes, though they may well have included the Sikon who lent his name to Aristophanes' lost play *Aiolosikon* (see on 889). Cooks are experts; and like other experts ancient and modern, they can be amusing when they exaggerate their own skill and importance and otherwise impose on any non-experts who happen to be at their mercy, whether as fellow dramatic characters or members of a theatrical audience; most of them, as seen by Comedy, have a dash of sophistry and pretentious-ness: ἀλαζονικὸν δ᾽ ἐστὶ πᾶν τὸ τῶν μαγείρων φῦλον, says Athenaeus (7.290 b).

Sikon has a substantial part in this play. The treatment of him is not unlike that of another popular Middle Comedy type, Chaireas the parasite. The audience gets what it expects and enjoys – some variations on the routine behaviour of stage cooks by way of comic relief – but in moderation, and in such a way that they contribute something to the development and effect of the drama and do not simply hold it up: Sikon could be described as a modernized and sophisticated cook, just as Chaireas could be described as a modernized and sophisticated parasite. He does not, for example, dilate at length on the nature and ancestry of his art (see on 646), or on the miraculous flavour of his dishes (see on 424); he is not a thief, or accused of being one (see e.g. Euphron, *Adelphoi* 1 K; P. *Aul.* 322 *al.*, *Pseud.* 790f, 851f); his own peculiar excellence lies in a new technique of borrowing (for comic cooks, like plumbers in English popular tradition, never seem to have what they need); and it is part of the fun that the technique proves to be lamentably unsuccessful (489ff).

[See Latte, *RE* μάγειρος 14.1 (1928) 393ff; Webster, *SM* and *LGC*, indexes under 'Cooks'; Max Treu,'Ein Komödienmotif in zwei Papyri', *Philologus* 1958.215-39, at pp. 219ff; A. Giannini, Acme 13 (1960) 135-216; Fraenkel, *Elementi Plautini* 408ff; H. Dohm, *Mageiros* (Zetemata, Heft 32, 1964).]

393-4 'A remarkably fine sheep this is! To hell with it!'

The analysis of οὐ τὸ τυχὸν καλόν is problematical. In spite of οὐ τοῦ τυχόντος . . . πόνου at 179 and similar instances (e.g. 683f, frg. 680), in which οὐχ ὁ τυχὼν goes with a noun, it may be better to assume οὐ τὸ τυχόν adverbially here than to insist that the accompanying word must have noun function 'an extraordinarily fine thing'. οὐ τὸ τυχὸν κακόν (Fraenkel, Oguse, Zuntz *et al.*) has found favour in OCT and elsewhere, but has the considerable demerit of removing irony from the mouth of Sikon; for irony is one of the characteristic turns of his colourful manner of talk (e.g. 514f, 658, 661), and is welcome here in what reads otherwise as a lively treatment of a familiar standard theme – the arrival of an animal on stage. For this, compare Nikeratos' entry with a sheep at *Sam.* 184ff; the cooks with sheep at P. *Aul.* 327ff; and the comic statuettes of men carrying animals, of which an example is Webster, *MOMC*, no. AT 56, an Attic terracotta of 375/50 B.C. in the Louvre (CA 219) = Pickard-Cambridge, *Festivals*, fig. 139. A good Aristophanic variant of the theme is the arrival of the Megarian in *Acharnians* with his daughters dressed up as pigs for market (729ff).

Sikon has tried to make progress with his sheep on his shoulders, and also tried driving it ahead of him; now he arrives 'hauling it along the road like a boat up a beach' (399).

ἄπαγ' εἰς τὸ βάραθρον: cf. 575. The 'pit' in the idiom is the rocky cleft into which Athenian criminals once used to be thrown; like ἄπαγ' ἐς κόρακας (432), it has lost its original meaning and become a well-worn expletive, to be translated accordingly.

394ff μετέωρον goes with αἰρόμενος φέρω, not with ἔχεται (ed. pr.); hence one punctuates after it. For θαλλὸς κράδης = 'fig-branch' (or 'shoot'), cf. Anon. ap. Et. Gud. 342, 36 (perhaps Alciphron), printed by Schepers (ed. *Alc.*), p. 157: μόνον οὐ ταριχεύων τοὺς θαλλοὺς τῶν κραδῶν, of a mean man all but preserving the branches as well as the fruit. ἀποσπᾷ could mean either 'pulls the branch away', or 'pulls itself off my shoulder', the latter more likely. δέ is rare connecting the second and third of three units: but cf. Ar. *Knights* 78f, and Denniston, *Particles* 164. εἰς βίαν (if right) must be taken as a variant of the normal πρὸς βίαν: note εἰς εὐτέλειαν Ar. *Birds* 805 and Antiphanes, *Akestria* 20 K, as opposed to πρὸς εὐτέλειαν Antiph. 226 K. The incident gives a glimpse of the lower part of the Phyle pass, somewhere between the notional location of Kallippides' estate and the neighbourhood of the shrine, with its ridge where Knemon's wild pears grow: cf. Introd. II.1.

[θαλλοῦ, κράδης Blake, followed by Jean Martin and Bingen[2]. ἀποσπᾷ τ' ἐς βίαν ed. pr.; ἀποσπᾷ πρὸς βίαν OCT (Lloyd-Jones); ἀποσπᾷ δ' ἐκ βίας Fraenkel, cf. *Heros* 79.]

397f '... it doesn't go ahead – quite the opposite has happened: here am I, the cook, cut to pieces by the sheep as I drag it along the road like a ship on rollers.'

Jokes with κατακόπτω (*lit.* 'chop to mincemeat'), and κόπτω are part of the stock-in-trade of cook-scenes in comedy, since they admit slang senses akin to Eng. 'to reduce someone's nerves to shreds': e.g. 410 below, *Samia* 68-70; Anaxippos, *Enkalyptomenos* 1 K.23 (ἐμὲ κατακόψεις, οὐχ ὃ θύειν μέλλομεν); Alexis, *Pannychis* 173 K.12; Sosipater, *Katapseudomenos* 1 K.20. Here the idea may be the more literal one that the cook is shredded by the rope.

[**398** P's corruption is not certainly cured, and many attempts have been made on it which will not be considered here. τοὐναντίον δ' ἀνῆγε ('il ... retourne en arrière') ed. pr.; τοὐναντίον δὴ γέγονε Barber, adopted in OCT, comparing Antiph., 233 K; τοὐναντίον ἤγαγον δέ Arnott ('Contrariwise, I dragged it'), which brings in a 'split anapaest'.]

401 τὸν Πᾶνα χαίρειν: see on 433f. The form of greeting is a normal one as between humans, perhaps more formal than χαῖρε: e.g. τὸν Ἴωνα χαίρειν Plato, *Ion* 530 a. The acc. and infin. appears to depend on a verb unexpressed, e.g. κελεύω: Gow on Theocr. 14.1, q.v.

401ff Slaves with heavy loads are yet another standard amusement of Greek comedy: see e.g. Ar. *Frogs* 1ff, M. *Poloumenoi* frg. 352. But Getas' entrance is motivated and managed with typical Menandrean skill; the παῖ Γέτα makes sure that everyone knows who he is; the reference to the 'damned women' and the load not only explains his slowness, but looks forward to their arrival soon (430), and presents the slave at once as someone who will inevitably be imposed on and resent it (see 546ff); it is no surprise either to find him a confirmed misogynist (e.g. 460ff, 568ff). συνέδησαν 'tied in a bundle (for me to carry)'; no doubt he has a carrying-pole (ἀνάφορον) *Frogs*, loc. cit. (8). On the 'four donkeys' load', see under 390; and for some illustrations, Webster, Bull. Rylands Library, 1962, p. 270 n. 1.

404f 'A big crowd coming . . .' – a matter, of course, in which the cook is professionally concerned, sometimes with amusing earnestness: see e.g. *Sam.* 68-80; Straton, *Phoenikides* 1 K (=Page, *Lit. Pap.* 57.4ff); Diphilos, *Apolipousa*, 17 K.

στρώματ' ἀδιήγηθ' ὅσα: 'an indescribable number of rugs'. Cf. the common θαυμαστὸν ὅσον, Lat. *mirum quantum*. The στρώματα are the same thing as δάπιδες 922. In a town party they would be strewn on the couches where the guests reclined to eat and drink, and possibly (if it was a luxurious one) on the floor; at this picnic in a country shrine they presumably *are* the furniture, and will do both to eat off and to lie on, spread flat, and folded to make 'divans' (στιβάδες); and eked out with any boxes, cushions or other suitable materials among the party's impedimenta. Cf. 420, 448, and 943.

406-9 Text uncertain, as usual where there are mistakes as well as gaps in P. I take the sense to be as follows: GE. But what do *I* do? SIK. Put this against the shrine here. GE. There. – Because if she sees the Pan of Paiania in a dream, I can assure you we shall march right off to sacrifice to him.

With τί δ' ἔγωγε; a verb meaning 'do' is to be understood, and the question, if right in this form, is a reaction to πολύς τις ἔρχεται ὄχλος, κτλ. (i.e. in more natural English, 'What about me?'). Cf. *Heros* 36 (ἡ Πλαγγὼν δὲ τί;), and 40; Ar. *Peace* 1116; and for similar questions without the ellipse, Ar. *Thes.* 70, 925, and *Plut.* 1197 ἐγὼ δὲ τί ποιῶ; Getas is protesting that he wants a rest: a large bundle is not only a sign of a large crowd, but a tiring thing to carry. ἐὰν ἴδῃ γάρ, κτλ. then continues the same line of thought, ignoring the interruption made by the order and assent to it in ταῦτα . . . ἰδού: cf. on 379. Since Sikon appears to have been fully preoccupied with his sheep, Getas may be presumed to have been carrying such cooking gear as he has brought with him: we know of a λοπάς (520 and n.), and can perhaps assume a meat-hook (599 n.); and, if it does not come with the main party presently, a pot of charcoal and the necessary brazier (547 and n.). It may then be that ταῦτα refers to this equipment, with which the cook is specially concerned, rather than to the whole load. One need not, perhaps, look for a more logical sequence of dialogue; the pair have been walking separately, and they continue to be somewhat out of touch with each other in the lines immediately following.

[This version of the text assumes τιδ'εγω[γε:επ]ερεισον in P, with ταῦτα misplaced, and a dicolon absent before ἰδού. τί δ' ἔγ[ωγε;] (Σικ.)

ταῦτ' ... (ed. pr.) does not account for the gap in P; Bingen differs from the version given in reading αὐτὰ for ταῦτα (hence his order is ἐπέρεισον αὐτὰ δεῦρ'); Quincey suggests τί δ' ἐγώ σοι ταῦτ'; (Σικ.) ἐπέρεισον, κτλ. – an attractive suggestion, which prompts one to think of ⟨ἀλλ'⟩ ἂν ἴδῃ γάρ ... in the following line. Other compounds of ἐρείδω are suggested: e.g. τί δ' ἐγώ; (Σικ.) προσερ. Barigazzi. τί δ' ἔγ[ωγ' οὔ]; (Σικ.) δεῦρ' ἔρεισον ταῦτ' Page; OCT adopts this treatment of the end, but does not supplement. τί δ' ἐγὼ [δρῶ; Jacques.]

407f ἐνύπνιον: adverbial, apparently; cf. Ar. *Wasps* 1218, M. *Perik.* 169f, and (better) Arrian, *Peripl. M. Eux.* 23 φαίνεσθαι ἐνύπνιον τὸν Ἀχιλλέα. [Not παρ' ἐνύπνιον (or κατ' ἐνύπνιον): see Phrynichus and Photius, s.v. κατ' ὄναρ.]

τὸν | Παιανιοῖ: for the 'run-on', see (e.g.) 264 above, *Georgos* 26, *Plokion*, frg. 333.9; for the long α (which is etymologically correct), see Philip of Macedon, *ap.* Plut., *vit. Dem.* 20, and Christodorus, *Anth. Pal.* 2.23; for the form Παιανιοῖ, cf. *IG* 2².2776 (ii A.D.), Meisterhans-Schwyzer, *Gramm. d. att. Inschriften*, p. 147, n. 1269. A few other places with neuter plural names also had singular locatives in current use, among them Megara: Ar. *Ach.* 758; Plato, *Rep.* 368 a, etc.

Visiting the Pan at Paiania would involve a jaunt to the other side of Attica, the ancient deme being located on the eastern side of Hymettus, where modern Paiania (Liopesi) has been named in its honour. The worship of Pan on the mountain is known from a story about the infant Plato in Aelian, *VH* 10.21 and Olympiodorus' *Life*; and also from a grotto on one of the southern spurs above Vari; but for the cult 'at Paiania' there seems to be no other direct evidence. [See Kirsten, quoted on 33; and Brommer, quoted Introd. II.1. P's corrupt text (in which τουπανατε may represent an original τουπανατο̄) has attracted more adventurous emendation: cf. van Groningen, *Ét. Critique*, ad loc.]

410 μή με κόπτε: 'Don't chop at me like that'; cf. on 397f. Getas is too tired and fed up, one might say, to be either coherent or ready to answer questions; but exchanges between impatient questioner and reluctant answerer are a common dramatic device to give life to what would otherwise be a narrative requiring motivation.

εἰπόν: imperative from the weak aor. εἶπα, cf. frg. 675; Plato, *Meno* 71 d; Theocr. 14.11. Schwyzer I.803 compares ἔγχεον from ἐνέχεα.

412 ἀπολεῖς: 'You'll be the death of me'. Like its Latin equivalent *enicas*, the expression occurs with an object either expressed or implied: see e.g. Ar. *Frogs* 1245 and the commentators there. [ἀπολεῖς ⟨μ'⟩ Mette.]

412-18 The first function of the dream, as narrated here, is to unite the two apparently separate lines of action by Sostratos and his mother, for Pan now appears to the audience as the cause of both. The arrival of Sikon and Getas is now fully motivated, and that of Sostratos' mother, which we are to expect, appears as likely to be relevant to the outcome: how, we cannot yet guess. See on 259ff, 556, and 570-3. Except in this very limited sense, the dream does not foreshadow future events (which is, naturally, the classic function of dreams in drama); since it refers to what the audience already knows about Sostratos, it needs, and receives, no interpretation from the stage. Hence it can more clearly fulfil its second function: further to characterize Sostratos' mother and her piety. Over-anxiety about the meaning of dreams is one of the excesses of δεισιδαιμονία (cf. Theophr., *Char.* 16); and it is echoed here in the horrified reactions of the cook to what he hears; even the slave, who finds his mistress' superstitions a nuisance, is ready to call the phenomenon alarming (418). So, as a rule, were all dreams in which Pans or similar figures appeared (save only Silenos) if we are to credit Artemidorus' *Onirocritica* (2.37); for they portended great upsets, dangers and confusions; and here the fetters, which for the audience symbolize the bonds of Sostratos' divinely-inspired passion, were no doubt particularly ominous to the characters: δεσμά are taken as a symbol of death in Chariton, *Chaireas and Callirhoe* 3.7.

The audience of course knows that all will be well; and the dramatic irony given by superior knowledge has an extra point for those who recall that Sostratos had dismissed in a petulant complaint that very quality in his mother which has brought the family along, to contribute its share to the day which brings him happiness. 'Through a god even the bad turns to good as it happens' says Agnoia in *Perik.* (49f); and Pan can evidently turn a human weakness to good use.

[Dreams, which were perenially a subject of popular interest, from time to time attracted serious scientific attention, and among those who wrote treatises on them were Aristotle, Theophrastus, and Demetrius of Phalerum. See in general, T. Hopfner, *RE* 'Traum-deutung', 2 Reihe 6.2 (1937) 2233; Dodds, *The Greeks and the Irrational*, Ch. 4; for dreams in drama (e.g.) A. *Persae* 176ff, *Cho.* 526ff; S. *El.* 410ff; E. *IT* 42ff; P. *Curc.* 253ff, *Merc.* 225ff (with discussion by Enk, *Mercator*, p. 7ff) and *Rud.* 593ff (with discussion by Marx ad loc.). For more pointed criticism of Sostratos' mother's religious activities, see Knemon's speech at 447ff; for Pan foretelling the future, see on 571f.]

414 κομψῷ νεανίσκῳ γε: evidently Sikon's services have been in demand by the family before (cf. 425f).

περικρούειν πέδας as in Plutarch, *Moralia* 499 a τὴν Τύχην . . . πέδας περικρούουσαν (Photiades).

[P's text presents two anomalies which are simultaneously removed by transposing γε: Introd. IV, p. 65f under (i). περικρούειν is not an admissible scansion since those lengthenings before mute and liquid which are optional in tragic practice are admitted by Menander only in passages of high poetic colour, as is true of Comedy generally: e.g. τέκνον is normal, but *(Δη.)* ἔχω σε, τέκνον. *(Κρ.)* ὦ ποθούμενος φανείς *Misoumenos* 16. Cf. Maas, *Gk Metre* §124. κομψῷ γε νεανίσκῳ. τί; (Jean Martin) is part of an unhappy treatment of this context in which extra changes of speaker are introduced against P.]

415 Ἄπολλον: see on 293.
διφθέραν ... δίκελλαν: see under 370.

416 ἐν τοῦ πλησίον τῷ χωρίῳ: for the position of the gen., cf. ἐν τοῦ Διονύσου τῷ ἱερῷ, Thuc. 3.81.5 (to which Dr A. P. Treweek refers me); τοῦ ἀγρογείτονος ἄφνω τὸ χωρίον διώλεσεν Theophylactus, *Ep.* 11 (p. 766 Hercher); and further Classen-Steup on Thuc. 3.70.4; Denniston, *Gk. Prose Style* 47; KG 1.617ff; *NTGramm.* §271. In this context the effect may be to emphasize the strangeness of the idea. [ἐν τῷ χωρίῳ τῷ πλησίον ed. pr.; ἐν τῷ πλησίον χωριδίῳ OCT (Lloyd-Jones); alii alia.]

417 ἄτοπον: 'strange', 'unnatural'; like καινόν, it can be a euphemism for 'bad'. Cf. 288.

419f μεμάθηκα 'I quite understand'.
ταυτί: Getas' load of rugs and other equipment, cf. on 406-9.
[P's ποιήσωμεν: cf. Introd. III, p. 51 under 'Substitution (ii)'. In spite of 943f, there is no reason to prefer ποήσω with OCT (Maas) and others. We *may* be dealing with a variant, but P's behaviour at 780 suggests that ποιησωμεν may have arisen from ποιησομεν as a clarification of πο(ι)ῶμεν.]

422 θύειν: present infin., or aorist (as is widely preferred) should probably be restored for the anomalous future given by P and retained by ed. pr. θυσίαν γ' OCT (Maas).
ἀλλ' ἀγαθῇ τύχῃ: sc. θύωμεν 'let us make the sacrifice and may all go well with it' (so taken in ed. pr.: 'que le ciel nous soit en aide'). Cf. Plato, *Laws* 625 c ἀλλ' ἴωμεν ἀγαθῇ τυχῇ; *Smp.* 177 e ἀλλὰ τύχῃ ἀγαθῇ καταρχέτω Φαῖδρος καὶ ἐγκωμιαζέτω τὸν Ἔρωτα.
This interpretation is doubtful, but perhaps not more so than the alternatives: (i) to take ἀγαθῇ τύχῃ as a phrase of agreement, as at *Epitr.* 47, *Sam.* 82 al. It should then come from Getas, to whom it is given by Jean Martin: but the ἀλλά is then odd. (ii) to take it with the following imperative, '. . . but do take that frown off your face, and good luck to you . . .' This is hardly impossible for Sikon (cf. ἀπόθνησκ' [ἀγαθῇ] τύχῃ in *CF* 36); the καί however seems to begin a new thought. (iii) to mark off the phrase by strong punctuation, as in OCT, and take it, in van Groningen's words, as 'une espèce d'interjection de portée très générale: "Que tout aille bien"' (*Ét. Crit.*, 61f).

423-4 ἄνες ποτ': cf. *Epitr.* 190 δός ποτ', ἐργαστήριον; S. *Phil.* 816 μέθες ποτέ, etc. Similarly χαλάσας ... τὸ μέτωπον of relaxing from anger, Ar. *Wasps* 655, where Schol. remarks ἔθος γὰρ τοῖς ὀργιζομένοις αἴρειν τὰς ὀφρῦς. [See further Treu, ad loc.; Post, AJP 1961.101f.]

χορτάζω is a good comic word for 'feed', 'fill with food', though a purist might object to it: see Athenaeus 3.99 e-100 b, quoting *inter alia* M. *Trophonios*, frg. 399. Properly it applied to animals, cf. Lat. *sagina*, *saginare*. This passing reference to Sikon's skill as a cook makes an interesting contrast with the effusions of his fellow professionals in some other plays: e.g. Alexis, *Ponera* 186 K; *Lebes* 124 K; *Pannychis* 172 K; Hegesippos, *Adelphoi* 1 K; Philemon, *Stratiotes* 79 K; P. *Pseud.* 790-904. See Webster, *LGC* 66, 194; and on 489-98 below.

425 οὖν: 'Well...', dismissing what has gone before with an idea rather loosely developed from it: the nearest parallel in Menander is perhaps *Epitr.* 61 ἐμμενεῖτ' οὖν, εἰπέ μοι, | οἷς ἂν δικάσω 'Well, will you accept my arbitration?'. See also S. *Phil.* 305; Plato *Apol.* 22 b ('I asked the poets what they meant, in the hope of learning something from them') αἰσχύνομαι οὖν ὑμῖν εἰπεῖν, ὦ ἄνδρες, τἀληθῆ· ὅμως δὲ ῥητέον; and cf. the remark by Menander's friend quoted in Plutarch, *Moralia* 347 E (=Koerte II, Test. 11): ἐγγὺς οὖν, Μένανδρε, τὰ Διονύσια...
[γοῦν Diano, Quincey *et al.*; μὲν OCT (Lloyd-Jones *et al.*); σοῦ τ' εἰμὶ καὶ τῆς ⟨σῆς⟩ Jacques, after Griffith (σοῦ γ').]

426 ἀεί ποτ': in later comedy, e.g. Heniochos, *Trochilos* 4 K. The sense is 'I'm an old admirer of you and your art...' For Getas' gloom, cf. 565ff.

Exeunt Getas and Sikon to the shrine. The second choral performance follows.

Act III (427-619)

Enter Knemon from his house, about to take his 'usual way' to the fields (359), as the audience realize when they see him. But his second entry, with this slight preparation for it, is in strong contrast to his first at 153; since he left the stage as long ago as 178, his sudden reappearance is calculated to start the act with an enlivening surprise.

427-9 For the situation, cf. P. *Aul.* 103f: occlude sis | foras ambobus pessulis. iam ego hic ero. It was unusual to lock up the house during the daytime (P. *Most.* 444); but Euclio and Knemon have only a young daughter and an old maidservant at home; both have compelling causes for going out, and both, though for different reasons, thoroughly mistrust their fellow men. Knemon has already met two strangers in the day: worse is to come.

σκότους ... παντελῶς: 'this (*sc.* my return) will be when it is completely dark.' For σκότους cf. ἑσπέρας (*Perik.* 33 *al.*), ὄρθρου, μεσημβρίας, illustrated with similar genitives of time by KG I.385f.

430-41 (i) The situation is the reverse of that at Ar. *Peace* 948ff. There, as Trygaios says 'We have the basket with the barley, the garland, and the knife; and here's the fire – nothing is holding us back but the sheep'. Here Sikon and Getas have brought the sheep and the furnishings for the party, and have everything ready to sacrifice when the others arrive (436f, recalling 420f), but they still need the materials to perform the preliminary rites, which the party is bringing (440). For the cook kept waiting, cf. Com. Anon., Page, *Lit. Pap.* 59 (a), and compare his actions (4ff) with the instructions of 440f here.

(ii) *The assignment of parts*: The text given is based on the following view of the action. **430**: Enter Getas from the shrine (his name is given by P) – possibly because he has heard the noise made by Knemon outside, possibly for no better reason than that given in 435ff: they are ready and hanging about waiting; for similar late (or casual) motivation, see on 233f. He immediately sees the party approaching, and calls to Plangon to hurry and Parthenis to pipe. Knemon (so P) is made to interpose a characteristic comment. **434-7** νὴ Δί' ... ἐστι: P does not give the speaker, whom ed. pr. plausibly assumes to be Sikon. His presence on stage is welcome to add to the crowd and confusion; his entry and remark are prompted by hearing the pipe tune; his tone is not unlike that of his opening words at 393ff. **437-41** ναὶ ... σύ: Getas again, continuing to nag at the women, Plangon especially, and issuing instructions. He knows all too well what has to be done, for he has suffered before from Sostratos' mother's mania for sacrifices;

his attitude to the preparations in general, and especially to the women involved, is consistent with what we have seen before and are shortly to have developed at length: see 402ff, 407ff, 425f with 568ff, noting in particular his grumbling over the forgetting of the bowl at 456ff, and the complaint that he has had to do the cook's work for him at 546ff. This view involves overriding P's change of speaker in 438.

[Ritchie (ap. Sydn.) introduces Sostratos' mother as the speaker of 430f Πλαγγών ... ἔδει; 432ff αὔλει ... προσιέναι; 436f εὐτρεπῆ ... ἐστι; (a question); and 438 τάλαν ... ἐμβρόντητέ συ. 431f τουτὶ ... κόρακας remains with Knemon, and the rest is given to Getas. Ritchie argues that the instructions to Plangon and Parthenis should come from someone in the party, and that Sostratos' mother is an appropriate speaker for them. These are points of considerable merit, as can be seen, for example, from Dikaiopolis' ordering of his 'Rural Dionysia' in Ar. *Ach.* 241ff; if the mother says these words, the entry of her party, the entry of Getas (then at 434), and, one might add, the reaction of Knemon, are all rather better motivated. On the other hand, as Ritchie also argues, the slowcoach referred to in οὐ περιμενεῖ τὴν σὴν σχολήν, κτλ. should again be Plangon, and the speaker should be the same as that of Πλαγγών, πορεύου, κτλ.: but the tone there (especially ποῖ κέχηνας ... σύ;) does not seem to suit a pious matron of the upper classes; in 438 the τάλαν obtained by correcting P's ταλαιν' certainly suggests a female speaker, but may be a single-word interjection by one of the women, as Webster has suggested, and not therefore carry any of the context with it. Moreover, there is a certain attraction, at the opening of the scene, in having strongly contrasted sets of instructions coming from the stage, as Aristophanes does much more ostentatiously at *Ach.* 1097ff. It seems doubtful whether the instructions to the party, in which Ritchie sees 'a fussy concern over religious ceremony', are 'quite out of character for Getas', and doubtful also if ed. pr.'s introduction of Sikon for 434ff can be ruled out on grounds of dramatic economy, rudeness to his employers, or the lack of an introduction (he knows them, see 414). Textually, the introduction of the mother as proposed involves the fairly easy hypothesis that P intended a division before εὐτρεπῆ, and the more disquieting one that the marginal *notae personarum* and the index of *dramatis personae* are in error: see above, pp. 124ff, and Introd. III, pp. 47ff; the problems of staging the scene with a limited cast are considered in Introd. II.2. This discussion does not by any means exhaust all the possibilities of dividing the lines between speakers: suggested variants of Ritchie's idea include (i) that of OCT, which agrees till 437, then *Getas*: ναὶ μὰ τὸν Δία. — εἴσιτε (with 438 punctuated as in this edition); *S's mother*: κανᾶ — ποιεῖτε *Getas*: ποῖ — ἐμβρόντητε σύ; (ii) that of Mette[2], which differs in assigning 434 νὴ Δί', ἀπεσώθητέ γε to 438 ... τέθνηκε γάρ wholly to Getas; (iii) that of Jean Martin, who has, 437ff, *Getas*: ναὶ μὰ τὸν Δία, τὸ γοῦν πρόβατον· μικροῦ τέθνηκε γάρ. *S's mother*: τάλαν. *Getas*: οὐ περιμενεῖ τὴν σὴν σχολήν. *S's mother*: ἀλλ' εἴσιτε — ἐμβρόντητε σύ.

(iii) *The composition of the party*: Plangon in the *Samia* (285) is the daughter of the poor Nikeratos; in the *Heros* she is the daughter of Laches and Myrrhine, but has been brought up by a freedman working as a shepherd, and when the play opens is in fact working as a servant unrecognized. It therefore seems open to us to suppose, with ed. pr., Webster and others, that Plangon is a servant here too. She has been taken to be Sostratos' sister, who will marry Gorgias; but there is no reason why the sister should be named when her mother and Knemon's daughter are not (see on 709); if Getas orders her about, as I suppose, she is more likely to be a fellow domestic than the young mistress; the mother, on the other hand, would probably have been made to address her daughter as θύγατερ. [For other instances of the name, see Kirchner, *Prosop. Att.* 11840ff (free women); Kock, *CAF* II, p. 194 on Euboulos' *Plangon* (a *hetaira* satirized in Middle Comedy, perhaps the lady of Dem. 39 *al.* = Kirchner 11840); and Chariton, 3.8 *al.* (a slave).]

Parthenis may well be a slave hired for the occasion rather than a maid who can play; if so, Menander leaves the fact to be taken for granted. Compare Elusium and Phrugia in P. *Aul.* (333); it is just worth noting that Aelian refers to an αὐλητρίς at the party in one of the letters inspired by this play (*Ep. Rust.* 15). (The male piper of 88off is the one who plays for the chorus; he could play the tune here, but the existence of Parthenis as a male name should not tempt one to identify the two.) Add then Sostratos' mother, and presumably his sister, with Donax and (?) Syros as male slaves in attendance (see 959); since the text, *passim*, presupposes a large party, Menander may well have asked for another extra or two in addition to these six.

(iv) An apt illustration of the scene, though much earlier than our text, is provided by a polychrome painted tablet of 540/20 B.C., from a cave at Pitsa near Sikyon (Athens, N.M., 16464: U. Hausmann, *Gr. Weihreliefs* (1960) Abb. 4). Ladies sacrifice to the Nymphs. A libation is poured at the altar while an attendant leads up a sheep. A piper and a lyre-player provide music. A family sacrifice in the fourth century is illustrated in a relief of about 380 B.C. in Athens, N.M. 1395 (Svoronos, *Nationalmuseum*, Taf. 59). Cf. Eitrem, Ἀρχ. Ἐφ. 1954.26; and Webster, Bull. Rylands Library, 1962, p. 270 n. 2. On the costumes and masks of members of the party, see Introd. II.3.

430f θᾶττον: 'quickly' (i.e. more quickly than you are); the comparative, like Lat. *ocius*, is often so used in exhortations.

ἤδη . . . ἔδει: not only a sign of impatience with the delay. Sacrifices should be made in the morning, and the day has already advanced some way from Pyrrhias' dawn errand (70). [For references, see Legrand and Toutain (quoted on 440) p. 964 n. 22.]

431f 'What does this confounded thing mean?' τί βούλεται; (quid sibi uult?), as e.g. at Plato, *Theaet.* 156 c.

ὄχλος τις: 'A crowd – to hell with it!': see 464f and n. [ὄχλος τίς; ed. pr.]

432f αὔλει ... Πανός: sc. μέλος, as in ᾄδων Φρυνίχου 'a lyric composed by P.', Ar. *Wasps* 269; ᾄδω ... 'Αρμοδίου 'the song about H.' (i.e. a version of the well-known scolion), *ib.* 1225. Parallels of two kinds appear to verify the assumption that the meaning is 'Pipe Pan's tune', and not 'Pipe in honour of Pan', with the gen. as in σπεῖσον ἀγαθοῦ δαίμονος Ar. *Knights* 106: (a) Similar expressions without the ellipse: καὶ τὸ τᾶς Χιτωνέας αὐλησάτω τίς μοι μέλος Epicharmus, *Sphinx*, frg. 127 Kaibel, where the 'tune of Chitonea' appears to be that mentioned by Athenaeus 14.629 e, in connection with a dance to Artemis Chitonea at Syracuse. Cf. Epikrates, *Antilais* 2 K. (b) References to 'tunes of Pan': Pausanias 8.38.11 τῆς Λυκοσούρας δέ ἐστιν ἐν δεξιᾷ Νόμια ὄρη καλούμενα καὶ Πανός τε ἱερὸν ἐν αὐτοῖς ἐστι Νομίου, καὶ τὸ χωρίον ὀνομάζουσι Μέλπειαν τὸ {ἀπὸ} τῆς σύριγγος μέλος ἐνταῦθα ⟨ὑπὸ⟩ Πανὸς εὑρεθῆναι λέγοντες (see Hitzig and Blümner ad loc.); Orphica, *Hymn.* 11.3 τάδε γὰρ μέλη ἐστὶ τὰ Πανός. The presumption is that Menander had in mind a traditional tune connected with the cult; whether, in saying αὔλει ... Πανός one thought of a tune *pertaining to* Pan or a tune *invented by* Pan is perhaps less clear: note Athena's invention of the πολυκέφαλος νομός in Pindar, *Pyth.* 12.

Παρθενί: the voc. as in Lucian, *Dial. Meretr.* 15.

433f σιωπῇ ... προσιέναι: 'One should not, they say, approach this god in silence'. Piping the Pan-tune is here presented as a musical salute equivalent to the spoken greeting proper to less festive occasions. How widespread the custom of greeting Pan was, we can only guess; but it seems to have taken Menander's fancy as a realistic detail of the cult on which dramatic variations could be played. Knemon, we learn, greets Pan in spite of himself when he passes the shrine (11ff: he does not do so in the play because the occasion never arises); Sikon duly says τὸν Πᾶνα χαίρειν at 401; here, it is possible to think that Getas, like the cook, has a feeling for what is right and proper, and is determined to keep the womenfolk up to the mark. At 571ff, it seems almost certain that Sostratos must say προσεύξομαι ἀεὶ παριών σοι to Pan, and not προσεύχομαι with P; he is not the young man to claim conscientiousness in religious matters (198ff, 259ff), and his variation of the theme is apparently a gay promise to be nice to the god when he feels somehow that everything will come right for him. One should not perhaps press the point that there are occasions when Sostratos and others might have greeted Pan but do not; for whatever might have happened in real life, the dramatist must not crowd his play with greetings. Perhaps this is why Kallippides does not greet Pan when he arrives at 775; though there may be more realistic considerations: that he

does not feel the need, since others are present; that he is too sophisticated, or too preoccupied with the thought of missing his lunch.
For what it is worth, Plato in the *Phaedrus* makes Socrates pray to Pan
and the other local gods as he leaves the scene of the dialogue (279 b),
though he does not address Pan when he arrives in conversation with
Phaedrus, near the beginning. Longus, *Daphnis and Chloe*, 2.38, brings
in the custom as part of his rustic scene-setting: τὸν Πᾶνα προσαγορεύσαντες
ὑπὸ τῇ δρυῒ καθεσθέντες ἐσύριττον. This, like the passage of Aelian
quoted on 11ff, is presumably not a piece of independent observation,
but part of the literary tradition stemming from the *Dyskolos* itself.

The dangers of disturbing Pan accidentally during his mid-day
sleep are well known (see Gow on Theocr. 1.15); the purpose of the
greeting, and of the tune when played in place of it, was presumably
apotropaic: i.e. not (or not only) to arouse the god to friendly feelings
in return, but to avert that evil possession which may show itself in
'apoplexy' or panic terror. See on 312f. A somewhat similar superstition
is that one should speak at once in the presence of a wolf, in order to
avert its power of striking a man dumb: for this and some more
recondite beliefs, see Gow's note on Theocr. 14.22.

In the learned note which appears in Schol. Ar. *Lys*.2, and in the
Suda s.v. Πανικῷ δείματι, the words we are discussing are quoted in
association with the statement that women conducted orgies to Pan
with shouting. Loud orgiastic cries are not, of course, peculiar to the
Pan-cult, any more than ceremonial pipe-music. Whether in that
cult the shouts and the piping had, or were generally thought to have,
any essential connection with the notion that one should not approach
the god in silence is a question which we need not consider here.

φασί interjected, as e.g. at *Epitr.* 264, *Perik.* 101. Ed. pr. rightly
rejects the δεῖν of the quoting sources.

434 νὴ Δί' ... γε: 'You got here right enough' – sarcastically: see
e.g. Ar. *Wasps* 1387, *Birds* 176f; further parallels will be found in
Denniston, *Particles* 128. For ἀποσωθῆναι 'arrive safely', see LSJ s.v.;
Jean Martin well compares Theocr. 15.4 μόλις ὕμμιν ἐσώθην 'I hardly
got here'.

435 ὦ Ἡράκλεις: the hiatus is normal; cf. on 963.
ἀηδίας: 'what a bore!'

435f καθήμεθα ... περιμένοντες: 'hanging about waiting'; for the
construction with χρόνον τοσοῦτον (but not the sense of κάθημαι),
cf. 210f.

436f εὐτρεπῆ ἅπαντα δ' ἡμῖν ἐστι: 'We have got everything ready'
(hardly 'We have had to prepare everything ourselves' ed. pr.).
Cf. Dion. Hal., *Ant. Rom.* 11.17 ὅταν ἀκούσητε ... τὰ πρὸς τὸν ἀγῶνα
πάντα γεγονότα ἡμῖν εὐτρεπῆ. The recall of 420f helps to mark the
lapse of dramatic time between acts.

437ff *Getas*: I should think we have! – the wretched sheep is as good as dead already: it won't wait for you to take your time. . . .'

Getas' rather grim remark is not meant to be taken literally, for to sacrifice the sheep they need the things which the party has brought (see the following note). His implication is that the animal has practically died of waiting. There is a somewhat similar joke in Plautus, *Aul.* 561-8: (566) *Megadorus*: caedundum conduxi ego illum. *Euclio*: tum tu idem optumumst | loces ecferendum; nam iam, credo, mortuost. Note also Nikeratos and his sheep at *Samia* 184ff.

μικροῦ: 'nearly' – in full, μικροῦ δεῖν. M. has it several times (e.g. 669, 681, 687 below), but not its synonym ὀλίγου.

τέθνηκε . . . τάλαν, with the text as here printed, is assumed to be a comic equivalent of (e.g.) ἐκπεραίνει τάλας βίοτον E. *HF* 428f, with τάλαν attributive, not exclamatory: for more instances, see Headlam-Knox on Herondas 3.5, and cf. 581 below. But both the interpretation and the division of parts are doubtful. Assuming, with Webster and others, that P's :ταλαιν' represents :ταλαν: the cry 'Poor thing!', as an interruption of Getas, could be given to Plangon or another of the women. A possible parallel for a single interjection by an 'extra' is P. *Pseud.* 159, where Ballio's long string of instructions to his staff is interrupted by a single brief protest from one member of it. Cf. Introd. II.2 at p. 28. Exclamatory τάλαν is only said by women in Menander (as ὦ τάλαν, 591 below), and appears from its usage elsewhere to be a characteristically feminine expression: cf. Schol. Plat. *Theaet.* 178 e (p. 32 Greene), reprinted by Koerte under *Synerosa*, frg. 392; Wilamowitz, *Schiedsgericht*, p. 74; Christina Dedoussi, quoted 188 n., pp. 1ff.

[P's ταλαιν' can probably be eliminated on metrical grounds for lack of adequate parallels. Elision between trimeters is rare, and practically confined to δέ and τε; two exceptions are τί ταῦτ' Soph. *OT* 331, and μ' Ar. *Frogs* 298. See further Jebb on S. *OT* 29; Maas, *Gk Metre* §139; Descroix, *Trim. Iambique* 292ff; Lindsay, *Early Latin Verse* 266. I assume that P's part-division came in because τάλαιν' was interpreted as the beginning of a new speaker's remark. For some other arrangements, see under 430-41 (ii) above.]

440 κανᾶ . . . χέρνιβας: only *one* basket and *one* lot of holy water are meant. For the κανοῦν, see (e.g.) *Perik.* 419, and Amyx, Hesperia 1958. 267: it may be presumed to contain barley to be consecrated and sprinkled on the victim before sacrifice, together with a garland and a sacrificial knife for use at the ceremony; the water – to be drawn, no doubt, from the spring in the shrine – will also be consecrated and used for the purification of the offering and the participants; θυλήματα, if needed at once, as it seems, will be for a burnt offering preliminary to the slaughter of the animal – either of meal (or meal cake) sprinkled with honey and wine (which, in Ar. *Peace* 1040 and elsewhere is offered later in the proceedings), or, according to another ancient explanation, of incense (=θυμιάματα); the latter view is taken by ed. pr. [For full accounts of the ritual, see Legrand and Toutain, in Daremberg-Saglio, s.v. sacrificium (with illustrations), and L. Ziehen, *RE* 'Opfer', 18.1 (1939) 579ff, esp. 598ff. Much of the detail which Menander's audience would have taken for granted is now, not surprisingly, obscure.]

The plural θυλήματα is regular (if it does not denote 'cakes', it can be compared as a collective plural with ὀλαί 'sacrificial barley', ἅλες 'salt', etc.: see, e.g. Theophr. *Char.* 10.13). The plurals κανᾶ and χέρνιβας are paralleled in high poetry (e.g. Eur. *IA* 435, 1111), but it is doubtful if any poetic effect is intended in the present context; they are rather the natural 'augmentative' plurals of the spoken language, which are liable to appear, as in English, when the speaker is angry or scornful (e.g. 'Must you leave bottles of ink on the table?'). Compare, perhaps, *Samia* 68f 'I don't know why you carry knives around', where the reference is apparently to the cook's single knife, which in drama is the badge of his profession; and in general cf. Schwyzer II.42ff. For precise sacrificial instructions, the singular would be apposite; the effect here is rather of impatient orders for action. If this is right, the view that Getas and not Sostratos' mother is the speaker may receive some confirmation; for the asyndeton εἴσιτε ... ποιεῖτε as given in this text, see on 662.

πρόχειρα ... ποιεῖτε = 'set out ready for use'; the adj. goes with all three nouns.

441 ποῖ ... σύ: since ἐμβρόντητος is a word of two terminations, this can be said to the dilatory Plangon, not necessarily to one of the male members of the party, nor yet (as some think) to Knemon. κέχηνα 'Stare with open mouth' is a colourful colloquialism used freely by Aristophanes and other comedians, but not found in formal Attic prose, nor (so far) elsewhere in Menander. Cf. Eng. 'gawp'.

442f For the sudden change of mood, cf. 177; for Knemon's reluctance to leave the house, cf. 453ff and on 427-9. The abandonment of his plan to go and work causes Sostratos to have a long bout of digging, 522ff; it leads also to the 'borrowing' comedy which immediately follows, and the 'well' comedy in the next act. See on 584f.

444f The text is disputed. ... κακὸν | ἀεὶ παροικοῦσ', if rightly read, is a representative of a fairly common type of brachylogy: 'The Nymphs are a perpetual plague living next door.' So, e.g., Ar. *Wasps* 144 καπνὸς ἔγωγ' ἐξέρχομαι 'I'm the smoke coming out'; *Ach.* 229 κοὐκ ἀνήσω πρὶν ἂν σχοῖνος αὐτοῖσιν ἀντεμπαγῶ 'I won't give up until I'm a thorn stuck in their flesh'; Theocr. 14.51 μῦς, φαντί, Θυώνιχε, γεύμεθα πίσσας 'I'm like a mouse in pitch, as they say'. Often, as in the last example, the idiom rests on a proverb; the notion of comparison ('*Like* a plague', '*like* the smoke', '*like* a thorn', etc.) is more or less strongly felt according to the nature of the expression and the context. For further examples and discussion, see on 550f, Starkie on *Wasps*, loc. cit.; Headlam-Knox on Herondas 6.14; Shorey, *Class. Phil.* 4 (1909) 433-6; Fraenkel, *Plautinisches* . . . 51 (= *Elem. Plaut.* 47). [Ed. pr., reading αταρπαροικουσ in P, gives . . . κακόν· ἀτὰρ παροικοῦσ᾽, but neither the reading nor the resultant Greek seem satisfactory. α[ἳ] γὰρ παροικοῦσ᾽ Diano *et al.* (with a stop after κακόν); but Kraus and others rightly object to αἱ γάρ as Menandrean Greek: cf. KG I.586, *NTGramm.* §§249ff. The text given here assumes that]παρπαρ — or]γαρπαρ — arises in P by dittography, and that ἀεί may have been wrongly written as αι: so also Lond. (Ha., Webster), suggesting ἀεὶ παρέχουσιν.]

445 μοι δοκῶ: see on 266f.

447-54 Elaborate sacrifices are made to please the worshipper, not the gods: true piety is expressed in a simple offering of incense and meal cake.

The conflict between sacrificial practice and common sense had long ago been exploited by Comedy: e.g. in the blockade of the gods in Ar. *Birds*, and in complaints by gods about their portions of the feast: in Old Comedy, Pherekrates, *Automoloi* 23 K (dated 428-1 by Geissler); and in Middle Comedy, Euboulos, *Semele or Dionysos* 95 K. Euboulos (who was hardly writing later than 330), makes a satirical joke about offering the tail and thighs to the gods, frg. 130 K; Menander writes in a similar comic vein in *Methe* (a very early play, almost certainly before *Dysk.*: see Webster, *SM* 104). There (frg. 264), a character contrasts the 10 drachmai spent on a sacrificial sheep with the immense expense of the feast to follow, and suggests that the gods should give a proportionate return, or insist on better treatment. Cf. also Antiphanes, *Timon* 206 K, and with it P. *Aul.* 371ff, referred to below.

The present passage tempers the tone of satire with a positive statement that simple offerings are to be preferred, in conformity with an attitude which seems fairly widespread in the fourth century, and was strikingly expressed in Theophrastus' work *On Piety*, where, *inter alia*, animal sacrifice was explicitly condemned. In support of his argument that the gods welcome the simple, sincere attentions of a pure heart, Theophrastus could adduce the moral authority of the Delphic oracle and the Asklepios-cult at Epidauros. The moral story which Theophrastus tells about Delphi is paralleled in one related by the historian Theopompos; a third variant, quoted from 'some of the historians' by Porphyry, introduces a quotation from the present passage, preceded by a closely parallel extract from Antiphanes, *Mystis* 164 K – both comic poets, according to Porphyry or his source, were inspired by the story about the oracle and its preference for simple sacrifices; but unfortunately no precise date is obtainable either for the currency of the story or for Antiphanes' play.

Coming from Knemon, the denunciation of sacrificial extravagance is naturally coloured by his own obsession that all men act from self-interest (719ff), and more immediately by the fury he has just expressed at the arrival of a crowd. Somewhat similarly, in P. *Aul.*, Euclio's purchase of incense and garlands as a wedding offering to the Lar is influenced by his own obsessive parsimony (371ff): the provision merchants wanted to overcharge him. In both plays, true piety is shown by the old men's daughters (see on 37ff). None the less, this is the clearest statement so far of a positive moral attitude in Knemon. The views expressed, if not directly influenced by those of Menander's teacher Theophrastus, are at least in harmony with them; and they conform also to the hostility to extravagance shown in the sumptuary legislation of Menander's friend and fellow pupil Demetrius of Phalerum – promulgated, according to Ferguson's dating, in the year following that of the *Dyskolos*.

Knemon's attitude, then, is neither new enough to be shocking, nor so far out of touch with contemporary thought as to be merely an old man's grumbling; it is nicely calculated by the poet both as social commentary and as a stage in the portrayal of his principal character.

[Cf. Introd. I, pp. 7ff, with notes; Pastorino in *Menandrea* (Univ. di Genova, Ist. di Fil. Class., 1960) p. 95, nn. 74-75. Theophr. περὶ εὐσεβείας is partly recoverable from Porphyry's extensive use of it in his *de abstinentia*: Bernays, *T.'s Schrift über die Frömmigkeit* (1866). Animal sacrifice, *de abst.* 2.11; Delphi and Epidauros, *ib.* 15, 19; Theopompos, *ib.* 16 (=*FGrHist* 115 F 344); 'some of the historians', *ib.* 17. See further Parke and Wormell, *The Delphic Oracle* I.384; Edelstein, *Asclepius* II.126.]

447-9 'How they sacrifice, the rogues': τοιχωρύχος 'wall-digger' is an expressive word for a burglar in a country where digging in was easier than breaking in: 'burglar' as a term of abuse, e.g. Ar. *Cl.* 1327, 588 below.

κοίτας φέρονται, σταμνία: cf. E. *Cycl.* 87ff ἀμφὶ δ' αὐχέσι | τεύχη φέρονται κενά, βορᾶς κεχρημένοι, | κρωσσούς θ' ὑδρηλούς. κοῖται here are most naturally interpreted as chests or boxes of provisions: cf. LSJ, s.v. VI, together with Hesychius κοίτη· κίστη ἐν ᾗ τὰ βρώματα ἔφερον (quoted by Kraus), and Pritchett, Hesperia 1956.225f; for the other possibility, that they are bed-frameworks to make couches, see Webster, Bull. Rylands Library 1962, p. 270 n. 3; for σταμνία 'wine-jars' cf. Amyx, Hesperia 1958.190ff. [κοῖται φέρονται (with P) Photiades, Greece & Rome 1958.119 n. 5, followed by some edd.; κοίτας φέροντες (with Athenaeus), OCT *et al.* Since φέρονται is not easy as a passive, with ἑαυτῶν to follow, the probability is that P's reading has been produced by assimilation of the endings -τας -ται to -ται -ται (cf. Introd. III, p. 51 under 'Substitution (i)'). So far as P is concerned the difference between φεροντεσσταμνι(α) and φεροντεσσταμνι(α) is minimal, but the smoother version (that of Athenaeus) is the more suspect: cf. on 433f, sub fin.]

οὐχὶ τῶν θεῶν ἕνεκ' ἀλλ' ἑαυτῶν: Antiphanes, *Mystis* 164 K (referred to above) has ὡς τἄλλα μὲν τὰ πολλὰ παραναλούμενα | δαπάνην ματαίαν οὖσαν αὐτῶν εἵνεκα | τὸ δὲ μικρὸν αὐτὸ (sc. λιβανωτός and (?) πόπανον) τοῦτ' ἀρεστὸν τοῖς θεοῖς.

449f λιβανωτός: frankincense, or gum olibanum, τᾶς χλωρᾶς λιβάνου ξανθὰ δάκρη as Pindar well describes it, frg. 107 Bowra. Cf. *Samia* frg. 1, and Page, *Sappho & Alcaeus*, p. 36.

πόπανον: a round cake, one of many forms of cereal offering.

εὐσεβές: the incense (and with it the cake) is a thing of piety, not itself pious, in spite of one of the quoting sources. Adopting εὐσεβής, as did Koerte, ed. pr. wrongly gives up Koerte's stop after πόπανον. τοῦτο refers generally to both nouns. Cf. on 122f, and for τοῦτο, on 273.

451-2 The gods only get what the worshippers cannot eat themselves! See above under 447-54. ὀσφῦς ἄκρα = ἱερὸν ὀστοῦν = os sacrum: cf. Et. Gen., s.v. ἰ.ὀ., quoted by Koerte, and Euboulos, 130 K, who calls it the 'tail'. χολή = 'gall-bladder', cf. *Samia* 186. Knemon's outburst should not be taken as literal fact; the gods could, and regularly did, get rather more. ὅτι is followed by hiatus, as elsewhere in Comedy.

454f Exit Knemon to his house. The last word in the line was almost certainly a verbal adj. in -τέον (see e.g. *Sam.* 66), and τηρητέον suits the sense well, though if normally written, it seems awkwardly long for the space. ὀρατέ]ον Page; alii alia.

456 'Forgotten the pot, have you?' Getas enters talking to someone inside the shrine – one of the maids, perhaps Plangon again. The *lebetion* was evidently intended for making a stew: when they fail to borrow anything suitable, the cook has to try other methods: cf. 519f, and on 472f; and compare P.*Aul.*390f. φής interjected, as at *Epitr.*295 and elsewhere: cf. 433 above. [Zuntz' conjecture assumes ἐπιλελη[σθ]αι in P (so Turner: 'You say you've forgotten the pot'); the correction of -ησθαι to -ησθε, given P's tendency to interchange αι/ε, is attractive and exceedingly simple. ἐπιλέλη[στ]αι OCT (Roberts); alii alia.]

457 ἀποκραιπαλᾶτε: 'You're still sleeping it off'. Cf. Com. Adesp. 946 K, in which ἀποκραιπαλισμός is quoted as τῆς κραιπάλης ἀπαλλαγὴ καὶ μέθης; and Plut., *vit. Ant.* 30, in which Antony sets out against the Parthians like a man with a hangover, ὥσπερ ἐξυπνισθεὶς καὶ ἀποκραιπαλήσας.

459-65 Getas interrupts his running commentary on the vices of the maids with calls to Knemon's (non-existent) slaves. Cf. *Perik.* 64ff, *Sam.* 145ff.

460 deferred γάρ: see on 66-68.

461ff 'Sex is all they know about... and slander if anyone sees them at it': i.e. they discredit any witness of their escapades by accusing him of complicity.

κινητιᾶν: syn. βινητιᾶν, Ar. *Lys.* 715 *al.* [It should be added, uncorrected, to LSJ: cf. Pascucci, Atene e Roma 1959.102-5, and earlier Headlam-Knox on Herondas 5.2, and van Leeuwen on Ar. *Clouds* 1102, noting also Eup. *Demoi* (Page, *Lit. Pap.* 40), 25.]

462 καλῶ: *sc.* ὑμᾶς. See on 497f. Similarly *Epitr.* 719 παῖδες, οὐχ ὑμῖν λέγω; Ar. *Clouds* 1145 παῖ, ἠμί, παῖ, παῖ (cf. *Frogs* 37). [παῖδες καλοί (P), as in 912, is retained by OCT and others, possibly rightly; but as Kraus observes, the origin of this puzzling call may be in P's ἐπισταντται, causing a corruption of καλω to καλοι which the copyist remembered in the later passage.]

464f 'What's the meaning of this – no-one at home?' οὐδὲ εἷς ἔστ᾽ ἔνδον may be a question shouted aloud, as it is taken in ed. pr., OCT, and by some others. For the word order τουτὶ τὸ κακὸν τί ἐστι, cf. Ar. *Wasps* 1136; τουτὶ τὸ κακὸν τί ποτ᾽ ἐστίν; 218 above; τουτὶ τί ἐστι τὸ κακόν; Ar. *Ach.* 156, *Peace* 181 (cf. *Birds* 1037); τί ποτ᾽ ἐστὶ τουτὶ τὸ κακόν; *Birds* 1207. [τουτὶ τί τὸ κακόν ἐστι Page, followed by OCT *et al.*]

465 ἤήν: for this cry of alarm ed. pr. compares *Perinthia* 15. Getas hears Knemon running to the door.

466f τρισάθλιε ... ἄνθρωπε together, cf. 108f, 701f. [i.e. P has omitted a dicolon after ἄνθρωπε, not a dicolon after μοι and a paragraphus under 466, as ed. pr. assumes in giving ἄνθρωπε to Getas as well as μὴ δάκῃς.]

467 μὴ δάκῃς: 'Don't bite my head off!'; cf. *Sam.* 169.

[**468** Other restorations are possible, e.g. μή, μή, πρὸς θεῶν: cf. Ar. *Wasps* 1418, Schwyzer II.597.]

469ff 'Is there a bond between you and me?'. Cf. 114f. τί interrog, is given in ed. pr. Having had his μὴ δάκῃς capped by Knemon. Getas retaliates in kind, proceeding to develop the idea of συμβόλαιον sarcastically as 'contract', 'bond of debt': for this word, cf. frg. 918.

ἔχων κλητῆρας: 'with witnesses', to serve a summons to appear at law.

471-6 There is nothing extraordinary in the word λεβήτιον or in the request: what shocks Knemon is the thought of having enough meat to need a stewpot. Sacrificing an ox for a private occasion would be a fine indication of wealth and extravagance; 'No', says Getas, 'I don't suppose you even sacrifice a snail – and a very good day to you'.

[**472f** λεβήτιον is quoted from Menander (frg. 866) as an example of a diminutive used to soften a request: i.e. 'just a little λέβης'; for this idiom, see e.g. Mnesimachos, *Dyskolos* 3 K. If however the reference is to this passage, it has been misinterpreted, for a λεβήτιον is in fact what Getas wants (456): by contrast, the request for λέβητες in 914 is deliberately grandiloquent. For the word, see e.g. *IG* 2².1541.16 (356 B.C., Eleusis); the nearest English equivalent is possibly 'cauldron' – i.e. a round bottomed pot to stand over a fire; on the shape, see Daremberg & Saglio, s.v. Lébès, and Amyx, *Hesperia* 1958.199. P's λεβοίτιον in 473 has been taken to be a rustic mispronunciation; it is much more like a copyist's error.]

474-5 On sacrificing oxen, see the Delphic stories referred to under 447-54, with Straton, *Phoenikides* 1 K. 19ff (= Page, *Lit. Pap.* 57) and Poseidippos, *Choreuousai* 26 K.19ff; for evidence of their price, see Pritchett, *Hesperia* 1956.255ff, and cf. Headlam-Knox on Herondas 4.16. For the snail, cf. Gow on Theocr. 14.17.

476 ἀλλ' εὐτύχει, βέλτιστε: cf. *Epitr.* 194; more examples of εὐτύχει 'goodbye' are given by Headlam-Knox on Herondas 1.88; for the sense of it here, cf. on 264.

476ff i.e. 'Don't storm at me – I'm just doing an errand for the womenfolk', a half-truth not unlike that of Sostratos at 171f.

478 οὐκ ἔστι: sc. λεβήτιόν σοι: cf. 917-18. For the structure of 'You haven't got one: I'll go back and tell them', see on 57ff (iii).

480 'A grizzled old viper, that's what he is': similarly Dem. 25.96 συκοφάντην ... καὶ ἔχιν τὴν φύσιν of Aristogeiton, cf. *ib.* 52. With this parting shot, Getas returns empty-handed. [ἔχις ⟨ὁ⟩ πολιὸς ... Jacques; but the article is unwanted, and gives a less probable rhythm to the verse: cf. Introd. IV, Note B, under (i) (*a*).]

481f ἀνδροφόνα θηρία: cf. ἱερόσυλα θηρία *Perik.* 176; ἀνδροφόνος 'murderous', as elsewhere, is a strong term of abuse.

εὐθὺς ... κόπτουσιν implies 'They walk straight up and knock', hence ὥσπερ πρὸς φίλον 'as if to a friend's house'. See on 174ff, and for κόπτω absolute, Ar. *Eccl.* 976.

482ff ἂν ... λάβω ... ἂν μὴ ... ποιήσω 'If I catch one of you coming to the door and then don't make an example of him ...' For ἂν and ἂν μή in threats and imprecations, see e.g. *Sam.* 173f, κατάξω τὴν κεφαλήν, ἄνθρωπέ, σου, | ἄν μοι διαλέγῃ; and *Epitr.* 704 ἂν μὴ κατάξω τὴν κεφαλήν σου, Σωφρόνη, | κάκιστ' ἀπολοίμην. Ed. pr. seems to have the text right in correcting to ὑμῶν, and in reading λάβω for λαβών in order to obtain a sentence with two protases, the second subordinate to the first: some examples are given by Goodwin, *Moods and Tenses* §510, and KG II.487 (9). The form is an old one both in Greek and in Latin: e.g. *Iliad* 2.258ff, 5.212ff (second protasis after main clause); *Leg. XII Tab.* 8.2 si membrum rupsit ni cum eo pacit, talio esto. [ὑμῶν ... λαβών τιν'ἄν, μὴ Gallavotti and others. λαβών τιν', ἂν μή, with ἄν repeated after an intervening clause, is perhaps possible: cf. KG II.367f, and compare P. Didot. I.27ff (Koerte I³, p. 144) – so Bingen² and Jacques; λαβών τιν'αὖ A. M. Dale.]

484f '. . . then take me for any Tom, Dick or Harry'.

ἕνα τινά . . . τῶν πολλῶν 'one of the crowd', 'an ordinary man': as at Dem. *Meid.* (21).96, and Isocr. 2.50, where Nikokles is reminded of his position as τὸν οὐχ ἕνα τῶν πολλῶν, ἀλλὰ πολλῶν βασιλεύοντα; Philippides, *Philadelphoi* 18 K εἶναι δ' ὑπόλαβε καὶ σὲ τῶν πολλῶν ἕνα: cf. Fraenkel, *Agamemnon*, vol. iii, p. 690 n. 1.

485f ὁ νῦν . . . οὗτος 'This man just now'; οὐκ οἶδ' ὅπως 'somehow', nescioquo modo; διευτύχηκεν idiomatically 'got away with it'. Knemon returns to his house.

487 Enter Sikon from the shrine. I assume that Getas also appeared, to witness the ensuing scene (cf. 891); but it is doubtful if he should be given any part in the dialogue, and not in fact clear that he need be seen at all, since Sikon's opening remark can be directed, in the conventional way, to Getas out of sight within, as can his reference to ὑμεῖς in 497: see further on 497-504 and 514-16, and cf. Introd. II.2.

487f ἐλοιδορεῖτό σοι: 'He was rude to you, you say?' The descriptive imperfect, matched by that of ᾔτεις, refers back to what the speaker has just been told.

καταφανῶς: 'in an obvious way', i.e. bluntly and straightforwardly: what one should do is to use a little flattery. The text is doubtful, and OCT obelizes. [σκατοφάγως (ed. pr.) is well supported; the adverb is not so far recorded, the adj. 'foul-mouthed' is found at *Sam.* 205 and elsewhere; perhaps (as Kraus and Jean Martin suggest) it had lost enough literal force for the adverb to be acceptable here and give the sense 'perhaps you were filthily rude', or something similar. For other suggestions, see van Groningen, *Ét. Crit.*, ad loc.]

489-98 εὕρηκ' ἐγὼ τούτου τέχνην: Pride in his own claims to originality is part of the comic cook's stock-in-trade, a feature which he shares with some of his modern successors; Sikon's innovation, however, is not the traditional new recipe, but a new art of borrowing, which is described with typical Menandrean neatness and restraint. See on 393 and 423-4; for some other refinements of the cook's multifarious art, cf. Anaxippos, *Enkalyptomenos* 1 K and M. *Trophonios* frg. 397 (appropriate dishes for different clients); Diphilos, *Zographos* 43 K (how to choose a client); Euphron, *Adelphoi* 1 K (culinary inventions of the old masters, contrasted with modern work in theft and fraud by the cook and his pupil); for the cook obtaining ingredients and equipment, cf. Alexis *Lebes* 127 K, *Pannychis* 174 K; P. *Aul.* 390f, 400f. [*Trophonios* frg. 397: it seems unnecessary to assume two speakers at the beginning. The structure is akin to that of the present speech, but the scale larger, as the cook deals with his traditional subject of food.]

490 Any cook worth his salt would claim an extensive clientèle in Athens, whether he had one or not; perhaps Sikon had not, since he accepts work on the remote borders of Attica. [491-2 τούτων ἐνοχλῶ . . . παρὰ πάντων ed. pr.]

493-7 Sikon gives instances of different people answering the door, and says what he calls each of them: 'Suppose an old man comes to the door, at once I call him "father" and "dad"; if an old woman, "mother"; should it be a middle-aged woman, I call her "priestess"; a slave – I call him "sir" or "my dear man".' Verbs are freely understood from one parallel clause to the next; perfect (ὑπακήκοε) and aorist (ἐκάλεσα) are acceptable variants for the present (καλῶ, restored 494 end); the construction changes from parataxis in the first two instances to the conditional form of the last two. See on 57ff (iii); for the perfect, vividly presenting the action as already accomplished, see KG I.150; for the aorist, making the action itself more vivid, ib. 160f. A good comparison for the whole passage is Anaxandrides, *Odysseus* 34 K, on Athenian nicknames, of which vv. 7-end read: ὄπισθεν ἀκολουθεῖ κόλαξ τῳ, λέμβος ἐπικέκληται· | τὰ πόλλ' ἄδειπνος περιπατεῖ, κεστρῖνός ἐστι νῆστις. | εἰς τοὺς καλοὺς δ' ἄν τις βλέπῃ, καινὸς θεατροποιός· | ὑφείλετ' ἄρνα ποιμένος παίζων, Ἀτρεὺς ἐκλήθη· | ἐὰν δὲ κριόν, Φρίξος· ἂν δὲ κωδάριον, Ἰάσων. The text adopted here agrees with OCT, except that 496 end is not there restored (and πάπα[ν is preferred in 494). The structure of the passage appears to be satisfactorily established, but within it there remains room for differences of treatment in detail, including punctuation; the following notes mention only a few of the possibilities.

494 cf. Anaxandrides, *loc. cit.*, v. 4 λαμπρός τις ἐξελήλυθ' ⟨εὐθὺς⟩ ὅλολυς οὗτός ἐστι, where the old conjecture εὐθὺς now has new support.

ὑπακούειν is 'to answer the door', of the master, as, e.g., at Ar. *Ach.* 405; usually, of course, it is said of the hall-porter, and in Theophr. *Char.* 4 it is a characteristic of the ἄγροικος to come to the door himself.

πατέρα . . . καλῶ: so commonly, e.g. 171 above; from a cook to an old man, e.g. Anaxippos, *Enkalyptomenos* 1 K.11, Diphilos, *Apolipousa* 17 K. 5. For πάππαν cf. Ar. *Peace* 120, *Eccl.* 645; and χαῖρε, πάππα φίλτατε *Misoumenos* 15, Philemon, *Metion* 42 K: see further Headlam-Knox on Herondas 1.60.

495 γραῦς, μητέρα: for μῆτερ, cf. Theocr. 15.60 and Gow's note. [γραῦν μητέρα 'I call an old woman mother' was suggested by A. M. Dale.]

τῶν διὰ μέσου τις: 'une femme entre deux ages' ed. pr., probably rightly in this context. Thierfelder, comparing Ar. *Pol.* 1296 a 8, takes it of social position, and would read γραῦς; μητέρ' ἂν τῶν διὰ μέσου· τὴν δ' εὐγενῆ | ἐκάλεσ' ἱέρειαν . . .

496 'Priestess' seems not to be known from elsewhere as a flattering form of address, but it seems doubtful, in view of his other methods of ingratiation, if we should credit Sikon with a striking novelty here. Cf. perhaps *Georgos* 42f, where Daos calls Myrrhine γεννικὴ καὶ κοσμία γύναι. Scan ἐκάλεσ' ἱερέ|-ᾱν, the line beginning with two tribrachs (◡bbCdd): cf. 113 and 388 above, *Epitr.* 721, *Perik.* 226, *Georgos* 61; and further, Descroix, *Trim. Iambique*, 148, 150f. [ἱέρειαν ed. pr., with P. This is metrically unacceptable if the penultimate syllable is scanned long (cf. Introd. IV, Note C), possibly to be accepted with the scansion -εῐ- by correption, with Diano: cf. on παιανιστάς τινας in 230 (i). The -ει- form of the word is used in the summary of Menander's play *Hiereia* (Koerte I³, 146ff), and by the authors who quote the title; so with the *Hiereia* of Apollodoros (Kock III, p. 287), and – as a rule – in our copies of dramatic texts. Its metrical behaviour, however, suggests that the short penultimate may rather reflect the well-attested Attic form with -ε- and long alpha, which I have preferred to print: for this, see Dodds on E. *Bacchae* 1114, Schwyzer I.469 n. 8, and Szemerényi, *The Greek nouns in -εύς*, in ΜΝΗΜΗΣ ΧΑΡΙΝ (Festschr. Kretschmer, 1957) II.174 n. 49. In 8 other occurrences of the word in Attic drama, the penultimate syllable is short 6 times, metrically undetermined twice, and certainly long never; the alpha is long at E. *Ba.* 1114, otherwise undetermined. Dodds, *loc. cit.*, gives the evidence from Tragedy; Comedy, apart from the present passage, contributes one instance of short penult. (Poseidippos, *Choreuousai* 26 K.21), and the two of undetermined quantity (Ar. *Thes.* 758-59). See Addenda, p. 305f below.]

496f γενναῖον ἢ βέλτιστον: i.e. ὦ γενναῖε, ὦ βέλτιστε. These are not of course normal forms of address to slaves, but Sikon's technique is one of flattery. [496 end: ἤ τις πένης Lloyd-Jones; διακόνων Winnington-Ingram; alii alia.]

497-504 Sikon's technique demonstrated. The text adopted (in agreement with OCT), assumes that he dismisses the notion of calling slaves to open the door, and addresses himself directly to the master of the house. 500: Knemon appears, with the angry cry 'You back again?' – not because he can see Getas, but because he does not distinguish one interrupter from another, as Sikon unsuccessfully tries to remind him (509): this touch of comedy may appeal in modern times to those who have had their doorbells rung by relays of ragging children. Sikon perhaps looked for moral support to Getas (παῖ, τί τοῦτ';), but finds himself seized to be 'made an example of' (see 483f); he breaks away, 504, and dodges a second attack, with a half-strangled curse.

497f For κρεμάννυσθαι, cf. 249; perhaps better ὦ κρεμάννυσθ' ἄξιοι

221

(Fraenkel). [This version of the text might be said to begin from the assumption, which is widely shared, that P's παιδιον παι[does not represent a call to the slaves, a main feature of Getas's more conventional approach: hence ὦ τῆς ἀμαθίας, 'παιδίον παῖ[δες' καλεῖν, Winnington-Ingram. 497 is certainly corrupt in P, and there are other possibilities than ν for the letter before the gap. This version gives a good run to the lines (though it has a possible weakness in φατέ): ὑμεῖς δέ γε κρεμάνν[υσθ' ἄξιοι ed. pr., alii alia; 498 παιδίον, παῖ[,παῖ καλῶ ed. pr., with some followers;'παιδίον,παῖ[δες' καλεῖς; van Groningen.]

499 The effect may be that of 'It's me – come out, old chap, I want you', but (a) the prominence of ἐγώ is a little odd; and (b) in spite of 'I want you' and Lat. *te nolo, σὲ βούλομαι* is unusual; perhaps, as is regularly the case when βούλομαι appears with acc. alone, the infinitive is to be understood; βούλει τι; (691) and other passages with neuter objects suggest that this need not be so. [ἐγώ, after Winnington-Ingram, should perhaps be read separately, and a verb of saying understood with it: 'What I say is . . .'. The letter before the gap in P is probably β rather than κ, as I now incline to think with Barrett; if κ (which was the reading of ed. pr.), we should have to consider that the letter is not normally formed; but among the possibilities is σὲ κ[αλῶ Σίκων (Lond.), for it would not be unwelcome to have the cook announce his name here. Cf. Ar. *Ach.* 406 Δικαιόπολις καλεῖ σε Χολλήδης, ἐγώ (καλῶ σ' ὁ X. Coulon, after Cobet and Brunck).]

500 παῖ, τί τοῦτ'; cf. 401f παῖ Γέτα, τοσοῦτ' ἀπολείπῃ; The restoration is no more than speculative. [π[ῶς; τί το]ῦτ'; Barigazzi; τα[ὐτὸ το]ῦτ' (Roberts *et al.*) would be a possible reaction from Sikon (Lloyd-Jones); but if it were certainly the right supplement, one would more readily override P's part-division and give the whole line to Knemon, as several have suggested; from these and other attempts on the line no wholly satisfying answer to the textual problem seems to emerge, and there seems no warrant for invoking Getas as speaker.]

502 τὸν ἱμάντα δός, γραῦ: cf. *Sam.* 106 and context; *ib.* 317f. A similar violent scene between old man and cook appears in P. *Aul.* 406-59; it shows signs of considerable elaboration by Plautus.

503 ἄφες 'let (me) go'; cf. *Synerosa*, frg. 392 (possibly ἄφες· τὸν ἄνθρωπον τί κόπτεις, ὦ μέλε;), and πάρες, 81 above; the echo of the imperative is paralleled in Com. Anon., Page, *Lit. Pap.* 65.54f. [Before βέλτιστε, a trace of ink in P is probably to be interpreted as the lower dot of a dicolon, not part of the lost σ of the second ἄφες; after βέλτιστε P has a single point. Among arrangements which assume an error in P's part division is *(Κν.)* ἄφες, βέλτιστε; Lond.; for the ironical βέλτιστε assumed, cf. the Dyskolos in Libanius, *Decl.* 26.15: ἐντυγχάνω τῷ ῥάψαντι τὸν καλὸν γάμον καὶ ὦ βέλτιστε, ἔφην, τὸν σαυτοῦ φίλον ἀπολώλεκας.]

504 ἧκε imperative 'Come back here', as in 617; for the curse, cf. 112; the dialogue is no doubt accompanied by lively action, perhaps including a swish of Knemon's whip, if he ever got it.

505 χυτρόγαυλον: the 'pot-bucket' could evidently serve as a stewpot, failing a λεβήτιον; Sikon is no doubt unwilling to ask for the same thing again. [P's error is possibly transposition, rather than the substitution of one part of the verb for another: αἰτούμενος χυτρόγαυλο[ν] OCT (Lloyd-Jones). Perhaps χ. αἰτούμενος ἐπῆλθον (Mette).]

505ff The disagreeable Knemon is as bad a neighbour as the miserly and mistrustful Euclio of P. *Aul.*: compare his instructions to Staphyla at 91ff. Theophrastus' 'Mean man' (*Char.* 10) forbids his wife to lend even the simplest things: μήτε ἅλας χρηννύειν μήτε ἐλλύχνιον μήτε κύμινον μήτε ὀρίγανον μήτε ὀλὰς μήτε στέμματα μήτε θυλήματα; the 'Mistrustful man' (*Char.* 18) will only lend cups with the greatest reluctance. Mnesimachos' Dyskolos was also miserly (φιλάργυρος according to Athenaeus), but apparently less ferociously so: Kock, vol. ii, p. 436f. For the list of kitchen requisites, see also Alexis, *Pannychis* 174 K, and M., frg. 671, discussed below. Coming from Knemon, the statement that he is without some of the obvious domestic necessities is not simply a sign of disagreeableness and fury, but indicative of the minimal way of life he has imposed on himself; that is, if an exaggeration, it is one with a good core of truth: see Introd. II.1, p. 24 n., and on 190, 584.

[Frg. 671, quoted below the text, may well be from another play with a similar scene – perhaps the *Hymnis*, as Gallavotti suggests; *Hymnis* frg. 410 οὐ πῦρ γὰρ αἰτῶν οὐδὲ λοπάδ᾽ αἰτούμενος corresponds approximately to *Dysk.* 471f, and is in fact quoted by one source as from the *Dyskolos* – wrongly, as Koerte suspected: frg. 125. If, with Lond., the quotation is held to come from this play, and ὀρίγανον preferred to P's ἀλλ᾽ οὐδέν, either a 'split anapaest' must be accepted, or ὀρίγανον held to scan with short iota: for some evidence of this, see Page, *Poetae Melici Graeci*, under 799 (Timotheus, frg. 23).]

509 ἐμοὶ μὲν ...: 'You haven't told *me*'; the antithesis 'You may have told others' is present only by implication: Denniston, *Particles* 381.

509ff 'Well, I'm telling you now' 'Yes, worse luck for you. Tell me, couldn't you say where a man could go and get one from?' σὺν κακῷ γε: 'and you'll pay for it' (Shipp, referring to LSJ s.v. σύν 6). Note also 644f 'No-one wrongs a cook and gets away with it', and cf. Lat. *cum (magno) malo*, as (e.g.) P. *As.* 412: ne tu hercle cum magno malo mihi obuiam occessisti, 'Your meeting me spells trouble for you'; and *Aul.* 425 (cook to Euclio). [For νή (P), cf. Com. Anon., Page, *Lit. Pap.* 65.72, and possibly *Georgos* 41 (Jacques).]

511f οὐκ ἐγὼ 'λεγον, κτλ. refers back to 504, the indignant καὶ λαλεῖς ἔτι; Cf. on 172.

512f χαῖρε πολλά: cf. 476.

μὴ χαῖρε δή: 'Well *bad*-bye then' (Arnott); similarly in Latin: male uale, male sit tibi, P. *Curc.* 588. For Knemon's remark, cf. P. *Truc.* 260: aegrotare malim quam esse tua salute sanior; Schmid, RhM 1959.162, compares Knemon's misanthropy here with that of [Callim.] *Epigr.* 3 μὴ χαίρειν εἴπῃς με, κακὸν κέαρ . . .

514 Knemon's cry of anguish: see on 177f. With it (as there) he returns to his house.

514-16 The piquancy of the situation is not lost on Sikon, who is prepared to turn his irony on himself. There is no sign of a second speaker in P, and it is unnecessary to give the words οἶόν ἐστ' . . . νὴ Δί' to Getas, as has been proposed (Barrett, Lond., Oguse: so OCT). If we have been right to think that he appeared on stage as a silent witness of the scene with Knemon, he may well have disappeared back into the shrine at the end of it.

βωλοκοπεῖν is lit. 'to break up clods'; tr. perhaps 'Got me under the harrow nicely, hasn't he?' Cf. P. *Amph.*183: aliquem hominem adlegent qui mihi aduenienti os ocillet probe, with Leo's note ad loc.

οἶόν ἐστ' exclamatory, as e.g. *Proenkalon*, frg. 350 οἶον τὸ γενέσθαι πατέρα παίδων ἦν ἄρα 'What a thing it is to be a father!' [The 'Aelius' to whom we owe the quotation may be Aelius Herodianus, and not, as generally assumed, Aelius Dionysius: so Pfeiffer, quoted by Treu ad loc. The ascription to Aristophanes was made by Kaehler, Hermes 1886.628f; the identification with *Dysk.* 514f was made independently by several scholars, among them Lloyd-Jones, Peek and Webster.]

516f διαφέρει, νὴ Δία: 'a lot of difference it makes'; for ironic νὴ Δία cf. on 162ff. ἑτέραν without the article is 'another'; ἔλθῃ third person deliberative subjunctive (Goodwin, *Moods and Tenses* §289). Sikon, as the following words show, is thinking of exploring the neighbourhood further. [Emendation need only correct P's spelling of ἑτέραν; then, with a stop after νὴ Δία all is in order: ed. pr., with ἐφ' ὁποίαν θύραν has prompted a series of other conjectures, which are rightly set aside by van Groningen, *Ét. Critique*.]

517-19 ἀλλ' εἰ . . . χαλεπόν: 'But it's hard if they're so ready with the gloves in this district'. σφαιρομαχεῖν, literally speaking, is to box wearing σφαῖραι: i.e. a pattern of glove more formidable (or, according to Plato, more warlike) than the soft thongs, ἱμάντες: *Laws* 830 b; see further Jüthner, *RE* 'Caestus', 3.1 (1897) 1319ff; Gardiner, *Athletics of Ancient Greece* 198f and pl. 175. [Ed. pr. puts the stop after μοι, not after χαλεπόν, and has no punctuation after πάντα.]

520 λοπάς: 'shallow casserole', cf. Sparkes and Talcott, *Pots and Pans of Classical Athens*, fig. 44; in it the meat will be baked or braised, for lack of a stewpot to boil it in, and other pieces spitted and roast. The *lopas* is presumably part of the cook's own equipment, as Webster suggests (Bull. Rylands Library 1962.256f), comparing *Samia* 150; note also P. *Aul.* 433f, 445f, and *Anth. Pal.* 6.306, a dedication of his equipment by a cook which includes a λέβης (the λεβήτιον was evidently to be provided by the employers in Sikon's case), and a κρεαγρίς (cf. *Dysk.* 599 and n.). [P's overfull line should possibly have μοι deleted rather than καί (Mette); the fact that μοι seems the more welcome word in the context may after all explain why it was added: for other possible cases of added καί, see Introd. III, p. 50.]

521 τοῖς οὖσι τούτοις: 'the things I have here'. Exit Sikon to the shrine. The echo of his ἐρρῶσθαι λέγω Φυλασίοις in the opening of Sostratos' speech is no doubt a deliberate one, as Treu well points out; it secures a degree of continuity in the action, as well as providing the audience with the amusement of a coincidence. But Sostratos' reference to hunting at Phyle is further in point to reintroduce him to the audience after his absence from the stage since 392, a consideration which is especially relevant if his appearance is now different (cf. on 370, where it is suggested that he now comes on without his *chlanis*), and if the part of Sostratos is now taken over by another actor (Introd. II.2). He enters from Gorgias' land: i.e. audience's left.

522-45 Sostratos' brief narrative of his spell in the fields can claim to be comic writing of a high order – colourful, amusing, and perceptive. We are of course expected to laugh at the elegant young man suffering the pains of unaccustomed hard work and the anxiety of evaporating hope; but we may also laugh with him, for he tells a good story against himself, and can see the situation from the outside, from the onlooker's viewpoint. A similar effect is achieved by the story of rescue at the well, 666-90.

Once again, as in Act II, the lover's mood is thrown into relief by contrast with Gorgias, kindly but detached (535ff), and with Daos, inexorably ready to take over what to him is part of the day's work. Knemon never came; but the labour was not in vain. It has served to reveal something to Sostratos of himself in relation to others, just as it does to the audience; to Gorgias, and again to the audience, his very willingness to tackle hard work is evidence of sincerity and good character (764ff); to Knemon, by a nice gradation of values, it is the sunburn that counts (754, prepared for by 535).

The speech is neatly integrated with its context. The opening theme, trouble at Phyle, is, as we have seen above, something more than a conventional introduction of the narrative; the motive for Sostratos' return is withheld till the close, when his impression that he is somehow drawn to the place reminds the audience of the presence

of Pan, from whose shrine Getas then appears. The two lines of action
which sprang from Sostratos' falling in love and from the dream sent
to his mother then move to their confluence: see on 259ff, and 555f.

523 ὦ τρισκακοδαίμων, ὡς ἔχω: cf. Antiphanes 282 K οἴμοι κακοδαίμων,
τὸν τράχηλον ὡς ἔχω (J. A. Willis), and for more examples of exclama-
tions developed by ὡς, see Fraenkel in *Festschr. G. Jachmann* (1959) 14f.
[Alternatively, . . . κυνηγέτης. ὦ τρισκακοδαίμων (Sandbach, CR 1962.
205); τρισκακοδαιμόνως ἔχω (with P) ed. pr., retaining κυνηγετήσων and
deleting the ω which P has after it, which, as Sandbach remarks, has
some claim to be genuine. In defence of ed. pr., see Kraus and van
Groningen, *Étude Critique*, ad loc.: OCT is amongst its followers.
κακοδαιμόνως is quoted from Lucian, *vit. Auct.* 7; the adverb τρισκακοδαιμόνως is not so far recorded.]

525-31 'I went hard at it at once, quite the young enthusiast;
swinging the mattock right up, just as if I were an old hand, I worked
away exceedingly industriously for a time, and then turned round a
bit, looking to see when the old man would come with the girl'.

δίκελλα, here translated by 'mattock', is given as 'two-pronged fork'
by LSJ, and that is a possible interpretation at (e.g.) Ar. *Peace* 570,
where the earth is 'tridented' (τριαινοῦν) with it. Perhaps, like English
'hoe', the word could be applied to a variety of tools of different
pattern: yet here Sostratos' manner of digging, and the fact that the
dikella can be used, *faute de mieux*, to hook up a well-bucket (576ff)
suggests something with a blade or blades at a right angle or less to
the haft; and Pritchett, Hesperia 1956.290f, noting that a *dikella* is
used in quarrying, thinks of a form 'with transverse hoe-like blades',
or blade and spike, like a quarryman's hammer: compare E. *HF*
943ff, where μοχλοί and δίκελλαι are thought of as instruments for
destroying walls. We may add, for what they are worth, the facts that
in this play the *dikella* is supposed to be heavy (390 and n.), and can be
used in shifting dung (584ff). I am not clear about the etymology, or
about the distinction between a *dikella* and its apparent relation the
makella; but perhaps an idea of the shape is to be gained from the
Chiot *skalisteri* illustrated by Argenti & Rose, *Folklore of Chios*, I.56,
in which the single transverse blade is backed by two sharp claws or
teeth (cf. Lat. *bidens*, especially at Virgil, *Geo.* 2.399f). The Chiot
dikelli (Argenti & Rose, 54), a fork with two broad flat tines, is possibly
only useful to us as a warning against pressing such identifications too
far. I am greatly indebted to Dr B. A. Sparkes for help in this matter.

From the bending and straightening, Sostratos is in pain from the
base of the spine to the back of his neck – in a word, all over (524f).

527f The text is most uncertain; OCT, adopting ὥσπερ for P's ωσαν
(Fraenkel), retains βαθύ, and prints †ειγαιπλειον†, suggesting in a foot-
note that βαθύς, | ἐπὶ πλεῖον is possible (but see on 740f).

βαθύς (if right) must be taken as 'deep' in the sense of 'experienced', 'knowing the tricks of his trade': i.e. in the present case, the trick of swinging the mattock well up to get the full advantage of its weight. Cf. Poseidippos 27 K (quoted by ed. pr.) ὁ βαθὺς τῇ φύσει στρατηγός, of a cook being compared to a good general; βαθὺς τῇ ψυχῇ Polybius 6.24.9 (what a Roman centurion should be), and *id.* 21.7.5. The quotation of βαθύς from Menander in the unexpected sense of πονηρός may perhaps derive from a misunderstanding of the present passage, but its support is slight at best: cf. on περιφθειρόμενον in 101.

ἐπὶ πλέον: as Gow points out on Theocr. 1.20, this phrase is not uncommonly used in Hellenistic Greek with little idea of comparison or progression in the comparative, and it may be right here as an approximate equivalent to σφόδρα. Cf. colloquial English 'exceedingly', 'excessively', and for examples, Stephanus-Dindorf, s.v. πολύς. For the scansion, see on 496. [Other suggestions are numerous: βαθὺ | ἔτι πλεῖον Bingen; βαθὺς | εἴ γε πλέον ed. pr., offering βαθὺ | κατέφερον in a footnote, and comparing Lucian, *Timon* 40 μᾶλλον δὲ παῖε ... σκάπτε, ὦ Τίμων, βαθείας καταφέρων; βαθὺ | ἐνέπαιον Blake; βαθὺ | ἐπὶ λῆον Lloyd-Jones; alii alia. Cf. Introd. IV, Note C. Note that P's line begins εγαι-, not ειγαι-, as ed. pr. and some others record; the φ of σφοδρα in 527 has a long descender which is confusing.]

531-4 '. . . and, by heavens, that was when I began secretly feeling the base of my spine. But when it had gone on for an absolute age, I started to unbend, but felt myself gradually going stiff as a board.'

Sostratos first feels uneasy about his lumbar muscles when he pauses and turns to look for Knemon and the girl; then, after a further spell, unbending (or 'bending back'), λορδοῦν, causes his neck muscles and the small of his back to seize up completely, so that in the end he is reduced to swinging stiffly up and down like a well-beam dipping a bucket (536ff).

τότε ... τὸ πρῶτον together, marking the first stage of the discomfort. [P's ποτε is retained by ed. pr., OCT and generally; but cf. Introd. III, p. 51 under 'Misreading'.]

δέ deferred: see on 10.

τοῦτο: the digging. Cf. 429, and for παντελῶς, note also Anaxandrides, *Odysseus* 34 K.3 μικρὸν παντελῶς ἀνθρώπιον 'absolutely tiny'.

ἀτρέμα should go with ἀπεξυλούμην: the text is punctuated accordingly, on the assumption that δέ is once again deferred, οὐδεὶς ἤρχετο following in asyndeton. The simple meaning of ἀτρέμα(ς) 'without motion', 'still', as in ἔχ' ἀτρέμα, ἀ. ἑστάναι, is very variously extended, e.g. 'quietly', 'gently', 'gradually'; sometimes, and possibly here, it seems little more than a vague 'quite': e.g. Plut. *Mor.* 1062 C, where it is used with a colour term, τὰ ἀτρέμα λευκά being contrasted with τὰ ἐπ' ἄκρον λευκά. See further Stephanus-Dindorf, s.v., and Shilleto, Mair and Headlam, CR 1902, pp. 284 and 319.

The impf. of ἔρχομαι appears in compounds in Attic Greek; in using it uncompounded here, Menander agrees with Hellenistic usage and not with that of his predecessors: cf. *NTGramm.* §101.

[ἀτρέμα δ' οὐδεὶς ἤρχετο ed. pr. ('le temps passait, personne ne venait'); ἀτρέμα. κοὐδεὶς ἤρχετο OCT (Lloyd-Jones) and ἀτρέμας for ἀτρέμα (Bingen) are methods of improving the run of the sentence (but the untidy, jerky effect may be deliberate); hardly οὐδ' εἰσήρχετο (Bingen, Gallavotti). The entry under λορδόν in Hesychius (also in the Suda) includes the definition ἀπεξυλωμένον, which may have been derived from this passage: cf. on περιφθειρόμενον in 101.]

536-8 The notion of swinging up and down like a well-beam appears earlier in Aristophanes, frg. 679 ὥστ' ἀνακύπτων καὶ κατακύπτων τοῦ σχήματος εἵνεκα τοῦδε | κηλωνείου τοῖς κηπουροῖς ... (the sense is unfortunately incomplete). Illustrations are quoted by Webster, Bull. Rylands Library 1962.256 n. 4: an Attic black-figure pelike in Berlin (inv. 3228) = Pfuhl, *Malerei u. Zeichnung* III, pl. 72, no. 276; D. von Bothmer, JHS 1951.43, no. 42; and a red-figure bell-krater in Tübingen, E. 105 (inv. 1343) = W. Zschietzschmann, *Hellas and Rome*, fig. 228.

539f ἐγὼ εὐθύς: sc. ἔφην, as ἔφη at *Sam.* 40 εὐθὺς δ' ἐκείνη "δύσμορ', ἡλίκον λαλεῖς".

541 'And there was Daos...'; for the τε, see under 39-40. [P's εασομεν is preserved by some at too great a cost in metrical probability: see Introd. IV, Note C, under (ii).]

542f ἡ πρώτη ... ἔφοδος: 'the first approach' (or 'assault'); for the use of the phrase in metaphor, Jean Martin quotes Plato, *Phaedo* 95 b πάνυ οὖν μοι ἀτόπως ἔδοξεν εὐθὺς τὴν πρώτην ἔφοδον οὐ δέξασθαι τοῦ σοῦ λόγου. [542: εἰς] ed. pr.]

543-5 See above under 522-45, and for the late motivation, compare *Epitr.* 584. 'ἕλκειν is often used of strong constraining influences...' Headlam-Knox on Herondas 2.9, with a collection of examples.

546-51 Getas appears at the door of the shrine to get the smoke out of his eyes (550), vigorously complaining that he is overworked. The real dramatic reason for his presence at this point is so that he can meet Sostratos (with 553-5 compare *Demiourgos*, frg. 100), but the list of preparations, apart from adding a touch of realism, is calculated to mark a further stage in the progress of the party (cf. Sikon at 621ff), and to add to the portrait of the disillusioned old retainer. The Greek interest in food and its preparation goes back to Homer, and is perennial in Comedy. With the present passage, compare, e.g. Com. Anon., Page, *Lit. Pap.* 59 a, and the cooks' orders in P. *Aul.* 398ff, T. *Adel.* 376ff; see further Webster, *SM* 112, 163f; and below on 946-53.

546 τί τὸ κακόν;: tr., e.g., 'What *is* this?': Ar. *Thes.* 610 *al.*

χεῖρας ἑξήκοντα: cf. Euclio's complaint in P. *Aul.* 553f: ... mi intro misti in aedis quingentos coquos | cum senis manibus, genere Geryonaceo – there, however, the implication is that they are rapacious thieves.

547 τοὺς ἄνθρακας . . . ζωπυρῶ: cf. *Arrephoros*, frg. 65. Smouldering charcoal was presumably brought to the shrine in a pot (*chytra*), for which Webster refers me to Ar. *Birds* 43 with Merry's note; braziers, grills, etc., such as one might imagine for Sikon's cookery, are illustrated by Sparkes and Talcott, *Pots and Pans of Classical Athens*, figs. 42, 44f.

548f Gaps and corruption make the text particularly doubtful, and nothing but a speculative version of it can be offered. All that seems clear is that the slave continues to describe his part in the preparations.

ἕπομαι, πελανοὺς φέρω: if this is near the truth, Getas is saying that he helps the cook to make the preliminary offerings as well as preparing entrails and cakes, serving (?), and watching someone (?); a mixture of different jobs would suit the context. Compare *Kolax*, frg. 1: (*Mageiros*) σπονδή· δίδου σὺ σπλάγχν᾽ ἀκολουθῶν· ποῖ βλέπεις; | σπονδή· φέρ᾽, ὦ παῖ Σωσία· σπονδή· καλῶς | ἔχει; Straton, *Phoenikides* 1 K. 34f (Page, *Lit. Pap.* 57), the learned cook when sacrificing calls out τὰς οὐλοχύτας φέρε δεῦρο meaning κριθαί; *Samia*, frg. 1 φέρε τὴν λιβανωτόν· σὺ δ᾽ ἐπίθες τὸ πῦρ, Τρύφη.

For πελανούς (LSJ, s.v., III), and πελανόν (which may be preferred), see Headlam-Knox on Herondas 4.91, and Fraenkel on A. *Ag.* 96.

[ἕπομαι is inconveniently short (but cf. 448-52, where supplements of a similarly damaged passage are verified by a quotation, yet do not seem to match with complete precision). Perhaps πέτο]μαι (Barber), continuing (with Turner) φέρω, πλύνω, κατατέμνω, κτλ.; but the letter after the gap may be γ or π (?) and cannot be trusted far as evidence for a verb in -μαι. Bingen[1] favours πλυνὸν φέρω 'bring the washtub'; ed. pr. (παλύνω, καὶ κατατέμνω) and Jean Martin (μολύνω καὶ κατατέμνω) discard φέρω and look for a verb in P's πολυνω. OCT and others adopt no restoration and obelize; other suggestions are legion. πολὺ νῷ φέρω Bingen[2], with Peek.]

κατατέμνω . . . μάττω 'cut up the offal', and 'make the meal cakes' – two obviously discordant operations, both a necessary part of preparing a sacrifice and feast. When the god has received his portion of roast entrails, the guests will begin their feast with them. See the works quoted in 440 n.

549 'I take *this* round, keep an eye on *him* . . .': περιφέρω possibly 'hand round' to the guests (so Barber, suggesting π. τὰ κ[ρέα).

ταῦτα . . . τουτονί if we so restore, will refer respectively to food (or utensils) and Sikon (or one of the male slaves whom Getas has to supervise). Both words – certainly τουτονί – call for accompanying gestures.

[τα[νιῶ τε το]υτονί Mette; alii alia. OCT does not restore further than το]υτονί.]

550f As at Ar. *Plut.* 821f, the smoke of the cooking gets in the slave's eyes and sends him out, providing the motivation for the speech. Getas' failure to recognize his master (552f) follows naturally from this, but may also serve to underline the unexpectedness of the meeting; Sostratos, if not now wearing his *chlanis*, will have looked odd, and may furthermore have been played by a different actor from the one who took the part at his last appearance: see on 370, and Introd. II.2, p. 29 n.

τούτοις ... ἑορτήν: 'I think my part in their celebration is that of the donkey': i.e. he does all the work and gets nothing out of it. For the attitude, compare 402f (with 426), and 565ff; the phrase ὄνος ... ἑορτήν, if that is what Menander wrote, is a variation on the proverb deployed by the sorely tried Xanthias at Ar. *Frogs* 159: νὴ τὸν Δί' ἐγὼ γοῦν ὄνος ἄγω μυστήρια 'Yes, and I'm the donkey at the Mysteries'. See the commentators, including van Leeuwen and Radermacher (p. 160) ad loc.; for the structure, see above on 444f αἱ δὲ Νύμφαι μοι κακὸν | ἀεὶ παροικοῦσ', and especially Herondas 6.13f, referred to there: κἠγὼ ... κύων ὑλακτέω ταῖς ἀνωνύμοις ταύταις. A somewhat similar, but obscurer, comparison between overworked slave and donkey seems to be made in Com. Anon., Page, *Lit. Pap.* 67; cf. perhaps *Kolax* 30ff.

[ὅλος, adopted by ed. pr., has given widespread dissatisfaction: (?) 'I think I am totally involved in their celebration'; cf. Gow on Theocr. 3.33. Possibly ὅλως (Lond. *et al.*); ὅλην and ὅλοις have also been considered. τυφλός [εἰμι πρὸ]ς τούτοις Barrett; OCT adopts ὄνος but does not supplement; [εἰμ' ὅλω]ς Jean Martin; for ὄνος, see further Kassel, Mus. Helv. 1959.172, and Taillardat, Chron. d'Égypte 35 (1960) 241f.]

552 ἐμὲ τίς;: *sc.* καλεῖ.

σὺ δ' εἶ τίς;: 'And who are *you*?', as e.g. at *Epitr.* 215.

For similar exchanges between master and slave, see *Samia* 80f; Com. Anon., Page, *Lit. Pap.* 64.17ff; and P. *Aul.* 811ff. As is suggested above, the motivation here may be complex, even though the dramatic device itself is both obvious and recurrent.

553 τί γάρ; 'What, indeed?', i.e. 'What are we doing, you ask?'. The answer begins with an echo of the question: cf. 636 τί ἐστι, Σιμίχη; Σιμ. τί γάρ; 'What is it, you ask?'; *Epitr.* 85, *Georg.* 85, *Sam.* 193 τί γὰρ ἄλλ'; For some other elliptical uses of the same phrase, see Denniston, *Particles* 82ff.

555f 'Mother here?' ... 'And father?': English readily reproduces the colloquial brachylogy of the Greek; for some parallels, see Jackson, *Marginalia Scaenica* 186.

556 προσδοκῶμεν (*sc.* αὐτόν) looks forward to Kallippides' arrival at 773.

πάραγε 'in you go', as e.g. at 780.

557 μικρὸν διαδραμών: the main verb is understood 'After I've run a little errand'; in this situation γε, though perhaps not indispensable, is probably right. Cf. *Epitr.* 286f ἤξ]ω διαδραμών· εἰς πόλιν γὰρ ἔρχομαι. [μικρὸν διαδραμὼν ἐνθαδί. τρ[ό]πον τινά OCT.]

557-62 Sostratos is quick to turn the situation to his advantage and confirm his alliance with his new friends. The usefulness of Gorgias: compare 561 with 320f; sharing in the feast, 560-2 with 613f; beneficial influence of a good lunch, 778f.

559 ὡς ἔχω, like English 'just as I am', in some contexts means 'immediately': so Hesychius, s.v., with the definition εὐθέως. Cf. Ar. *Knights* 488 with van Leeuwen and Neil ad loc., *Plut.* 1088f with Holzinger ad loc., and for more illustrations, Headlam-Knox on Herondas 7.8. It is possible, but not necessary, to assume that the phrase implies 'I will not stop to tidy up and put my cloak on': see on 370.

παραλήψομαι: here and in 563 'invite': cf. LSJ s.v., II.2.

563-70 Getas resigns himself to having two more guests to look after, not without a fine specimen of servant's grumbling. Cf. Antiphanes, *Dyspratos* 89 K (~Epikrates, *Dyspratos* 5 K): 'What could be more hateful' asks the slave 'than being ordered about at a party?', and goes on to complain of seeing half-eaten delicacies left on the table – forbidden food for slaves, ὡς φασιν αἱ γυναῖκες: if one of them takes a bite, he is called a glutton.

563 τί φής; expressing surprise and disapproval.

564f 'You can make it 3000 as far as I am concerned'. The opt. of wish seems here to express a command, analogous to that of the imperative συνάγετε and like it ironical. Cf. 175f, and for the change of construction Xen. *Anab.* 6.6.18 τούτου ἕνεκα μήτε πολεμεῖτε Λακεδαιμονίοις σώζοισθέ τε ἀσφαλῶς ὅποι θέλει ἕκαστος, quoted with other examples by KG I.229. But in the passage of Xen., P. Oxy. 463 has σώζε[σθε] in agreement with the 'deteriores', and here γένεσθε (Webster) is a simple and possibly correct emendation.

566 πόθεν γάρ; 'How could I?', 'It's impossible!' – after a negative statement, as e.g. at Eur. *Alc.* 781, Lucian, *Timon*, 8. The plural continues from γένοισθε as the slave includes the whole family in his tirade: so Knemon at 173ff ('You and your like').

568 The text is doubtful on metrical and other grounds. As we have it from P, ἄξιον ἰδεῖν τιν᾽ is 'worth someone seeing' (i.e. worth your seeing). The normal phrase is ἄξιον ἰδεῖν, to which τινα is apparently added as acc. subject to the infin. 'The allusive τις' remarks Tucker on Ar. *Frogs* 552 'is common in threats and sly or malicious references': see further KG I.662.

γύναια ταῦτα, if right, is 'the womenfolk here', said in a tone of scornful contempt, instead of αἱ γυναῖκες. This use of the deictic demonstrative without the article seems not to be paralleled in Menander (in frg. 679 νῦν δ᾽ ἔρπ᾽ ἀπ᾽ οἴκων τῶνδε is paratragic); but for ὅδε, ὁδί, οὑτοσί similarly used by Aristophanes, see Starkie on Ar. *Wasps* 1132 (τηνδὶ δὲ χλαῖναν ἀναβαλοῦ τριβωνικῶς), and cf. KG I.629. Possibly comparable is οὗτος ἀνήρ, as used when 'talking at' someone instead of addressing him directly: Plato, *Gorgias* 505 c 3 οὗτος ἀνὴρ οὐχ ὑπομένει ὠφελούμενος ..., and *ib.* 489 b 7, 467 b 1; see Dodds' note on the last passage, and J. Svennung, *Anredeformen* ... 420 (Skr. k. hum. Vetenskapssamfundet i Uppsala, 42 (1958)). The scansion is also problematical; but γύναια may have been pronounced with short penultimate by correption, as are other words in -αιος, -αιον: cf. Introd. IV, Note A, at p. 66 (*j*); and see on παιανιστάς τινας in 230 (i), and Addenda, below, p. 305f.

[Ed. pr. retains P's reading, but suggests τι for τινα, which has found favour in spite of the highly doubtful hiatus (see under 247ff). All the puzzles of the line are neatly removed by reading ἄξιον ἰδεῖν. ἀλλὰ ⟨τὰ⟩ γύναια ταῦτά μοι with Maas, Thierfelder and others: so OCT, referring to *Perik.* 272 (ἄξιον ἰδεῖν. ἀλλὰ τί φέρω νῦν εἰς μέσον). It is possible to think that P's τινα derives from τα added as a correction, then misinterpreted and misplaced; but the corruption is not easily accounted for, and the tone of the passage (so far as one can judge such matters) seems to do something to confirm P.]

569 'Nice people' ironically: γάρ as (e.g.) in 162, but for the 'anticipatory' position of the clause, cf. Denniston, *Particles* 68ff; for ἀστείως cf. *Samia* 149ff ἀστεῖον πάνυ | εἰ τὰς λοπάδας ἐν τῷ μέσῳ μοι κειμένας | ὄστρακα ποιῆσαι ('a nice thing, if he ...'); and ἀστεῖος εἶ 'Nice of you!' in Diphilos, *Synoris* 73 K.2. See also 658 below.

μεταδοῦναι with dat. (μοι), and gen. (τινος and then ἁλός), as normally. [τινι ed. pr.]

570 μὰ τὴν Δήμητρ᾽: so at *Perik.* 255 (Polemon); cf. *Epitr.* 635 (Habrotonon); not a common oath in later comedy, but I hesitate to see a special significance here.

οὐδ᾽ ... ἁλὸς πικροῦ: 'not even a lick of rough salt', i.e., in this context, not even the coarsest and cheapest of flavourings for the food. The phrase is a variant of the proverbial οὐδ᾽ ἅλα δοίης, *Odyssey* 17.455; cf. Theocr. 27.61 and Gow ad loc. Somewhat similarly *hic hodie apud me numquam delinges salem*, P. *Curc.* 562 'You won't get a scrap of welcome in my house', cf. *Persa* 430. Possibly both expressions originate from the offering of salt as a token of hospitality. ἅλς πικρός will be a variety which is naturally bitter, and not refined or flavoured: ἅλες ἡδυσμένοι are mentioned by Athenaeus 9.366 b. [For full information, see Blümner, *RE* 'Salz', 2. Reihe 1.2 (1920) 2075ff.]

570-3 The presence of his family in Phyle, and the chance to invite Gorgias to join them, have given the despairing Sostratos something positive to do; in contrast to the slave's gloom, he now feels an irrational (but understandable) surge of confidence that all will turn out well. To him, the family sacrifice at Phyle is οὐκ ἄκαιρος (558), and he addresses the recipient of it with light-hearted benevolence. The audience, knowing more than he does, enjoys the gentle irony of the situation, and is once again reminded of the pattern to which the events are moving. Cf. 545, and on 37ff, 259ff, and 412-18.

570f καλῶς ἔσται: 'all will be well', cf. Ar. *Plut.* 1188; τὸ τήμερον adverbially, as at Plato, *Smp.* 176 e.

571ff μαντεύσομαι τοῦτ' αὐτός: i.e. without aid from Pan. Pan can foretell the future by appearing in visions or dreams (as we know, 412ff); but according to a tradition represented by Apollodorus, *Bibl.* 1.4.1 and Schol. Pind., *Pyth.* (Hyp. a; II. p. 2 Drachmann) it was he who taught μαντική to Apollo; among other evidence that he was sometimes credited with oracular powers and functions is the description of his shrine on Mt. Lykaion in Arcadia as a μαντεῖον. [For further references, see Farnell, *Cults of the Greek States* V.432f, Brommer, quoted Introd. II.1 ad init., and Pastorino, in *Menandrea* (Univ. di Genova, Ist. di Fil. Class., 1960), p. 89, n. 54.]

P's series of tenses, μαντεύσομαι . . . προσεύχομαι . . . φιλανθρωπεύσομαι, is variously treated by critics. If preserved unchanged, as in OCT and elsewhere, it is best read with ἀλλὰ μὴν . . . σοι as a parenthesis; but it is hard to think that Menander intended Sostratos to say 'I always address you when I pass by' even in a light-hearted mood (see on 433f). Accordingly προσεύξομαι should be read, with φιλανθρωπεύσομαι to follow in parallel: in this context the verb need hardly mean more than 'I'll be nice to you', i.e. 'my greetings will be friendly'. Cf. 105, and for discussion cf. Schmid, RhM 1959.166f. Ed. pr. prints μαντεύομαι . . . προσεύχομαι . . . φιλανθρωπεύομαι; μαντεύομαι has found support as the more logical tense, but is not necessarily the right one: cf. KG I.172f. I am not clear how far the question of assonance at the line-endings should affect the decision.

Exit Sostratos left, to Gorgias' land.

574-611 Enter Simiche with a tale of woe: she tried to recover the lost well-bucket with Knemon's mattock, but dropped it in too. Getas stays outside to listen, a thoroughly unsympathetic bystander (575, 581, 583, 587f, 592f); then, as Knemon decides to go down the well himself, Getas relents and offers help, only to meet with a sharp rebuff, 600f. Moved to comment on the hardships of country life, he is about to return to the shrine again when Sostratos comes back with his guests, and the earlier disapproval reasserts itself (610f, cf. 563ff).

574ff The old woman as a herald of grave events within the house had played her part in Classical Tragedy (e.g. Soph. *Trach.* 871ff, Eur. *Hip.* 176ff); hence, at least in part, the comic effect of the high emotion with which her descendants in New Comedy announce or forebode their own less heroic disasters. Compare P. *Amph.* 1053ff, *Cas.* 621ff (paratragic tone); P. *Aul.* 274ff (high emotion); and on emotional language in Menander, cf. Webster *SM* 159ff. Simiche's scene here compares interestingly with what we heard from Knemon's daughter of the first stage of this chapter of accidents, 189ff. Both recollection and contrast increase the effect of the scene; the third and crowning misfortune is soon to follow, 620ff, and we shall hear of it first from a similar scene between Simiche and the cook.

574 For the threefold ὦ δυστυχής, cf. χαῖρ' ὦ Χάρων thrice repeated in Ar. *Frogs* 184 – a quotation, according to one of the ancient commentators, from Achaios, *Aithon*, a satyr play (frg. 11 N²). Aristophanes makes a comic point of the repetition, as a triple salutation to the dead; the present line has an effect akin to that of P. *Trin.* 1094, o Callicles, o Callicles, o Callicles: the gravity of the emotion seems to be relieved rather than accentuated by the neat coincidence of form and metre. For further discussion, see Treu ad loc.

[Choeroboscus *in Theod.* I.176 Hilgard illustrates the phrase ὦ δυστυχής from the *Heros* (frg. 7), then gives the words ὦ δυστυχής· τί οὐ καθεύδεις; as from the *Dyskolos*: hence the fragment in Kock (137) and Koerte (124), and the inferences based on it before the play came to light. The quotation belongs, as is now clear, in the *Misoumenos* (cf. frg. 9): it seems likely that an original list of three references (to *Heros*, *Dysk.* 574 (or 919), and *Misoumenos*) has been carelessly reduced to two, whether by Choeroboscus himself or (more likely) by one of his copyists. See Barigazzi, Riv. di. Fil. 1959.136.

In this text, as in OCT and some others, the ω is treated as exclamatory and not vocative, and accented accordingly. For evidence of the convention, see LSJ s.v. 4, and for doubts about its application and utility, see Fraenkel on A. *Ag.* 22.]

575 ἄπαγε, κτλ.: see on 393-4. Yet another woman is too much for Getas. [576: perhaps παρελήλυθεν P¹ (Rees).]

576ff '... wishing to get the bucket out of the well myself, if I could, without the master knowing ...'

τοῦ δεσπότου goes with λάθρα, not with ἐκ τοῦ φρέατος: there is no point in specifying 'the master's well'. Cf. 310, and Ar. *Plut.* 318f ἐγὼ δ' ἰὼν ἤδη λάθρα | βουλήσομαι τοῦ δεσπότου ...

[579 ἀνῆψα seems more likely than ἐνῆψα of attaching a mattock to a rope; ἐν- ed. pr., OCT and some other edd., with the original reading in P.**]**

581f ὀρθῶς, like Eng. 'good!'; or more fully, ὀρθῶς γε ποιοῦσα 'You have done well!' Cf. καὶ μάλα ὀρθῶς *Epitr.* 722f; similarly (but without the irony), Alexis, *Lebes* 127 K (B.) . . . λήψομαι γὰρ πάντ᾿ ἐγώ. (A.) ὀρθῶς. τὸ πρῶτον μὲν λάβ᾿ ἐλθὼν σήσαμα. [Ed. pr. rightly gives the remark to Getas, in spite of P.]

The perfect ἐνσέσεικα describes the state of affairs which results from the rope's breaking (aor. διερράγη); as it were 'I'm after dropping it in'; for the word, cf. 632, and for the contrast of tenses, 627f. καὶ τὴν δίκελλαν . . . μετὰ τοῦ κάδου 'the mattock too along with the bucket' implies that the rope broke under their combined weight, and that they are now together at the bottom. Cf. Ameipsias, *Sphendone* 17 K τὸ μὲν δόρυ | μετὰ τῆς ἐπιχάλκου πρὸς Πλαταιαῖς ἀπέβαλεν. For ἀθλία, see above under 437ff on τέθνηκε . . . τάλαν.

[**581**: perhaps τότ᾿ εὐθύς (cf. 236). **582**: 'Perhaps μετὰ τὸν κάδον' Lloyd-Jones: so in OCT.]

584 ὁ δέ = 'the master': cf. 207. The motivation is typically neat; Knemon, determined to live the life of the poor farmer, has only one mattock, and no spare *kados*, nor a hook to recover it when lost (see on 599); the spare rope available is weak and rotten, and his one old servant too foolish and too terrified of him to do anything more sensible. He 'happens' to be doing a job at home because he feels unable to leave the house, and must do some work: cf. 427ff, 442ff. By living as he does, he lays himself open to the misfortune which befalls him. [Not ὅδε (ed. pr.); perhaps ὁ δ᾿ ἀποτυχής 'infelix ille'.]

586 καὶ ψοφεῖ γε τὴν θύραν seems to end the sentence with a terrified whimper. τε . . . καί probably connects the three parts, as at *Georgos* 51f βουβὼν ἐπήρθη τῷ γέροντι, θέρμα τε | ἐπέλαβεν αὐτόν, καὶ κακῶς ἔσχεν πάνυ; the γε reinforcing the καί gives the effect of 'feminine underlining' (Denniston, *Particles* 157, referring in particular to Ar. *Frogs* 562ff). [Possibly, since ψοφεῖ τὴν θύραν is necessarily an unexpected development, one should mark a break in the thought before καί, with Bingen, or after it, with Jean Martin: I doubt if καὶ ψοφεῖ γε τὴν θύραν is to be attributed to Getas, with OCT (Barrett).]

587ff This final display of Knemon's *dyskolia* in full cry resembles the violent scene between Euclio and Staphyla at the beginning of P. *Aul.* (40ff). The relatively strict metre suggests that the tone may have been raised by elevated or paratragic delivery: contrast, e.g., 500ff (Knemon and Sikon), and see below on 596ff.

587 i.e. φεῦγε, φεῦγε, ὦ πονηρὰ γραῦ· ἀποκτενεῖ σε. This dislocation of word-order is unacceptable to ed. pr. and some other edd., where a stop is placed after the second φεῦγε. But compare 499, or in a higher style φεῦ τῆς βροτείας – ποῖ προβήσεται; – φρενός E. *Hip.* 936; and see further on 223ff. Dashes printed in such sentences with hyperbaton are essentially a device for the modern reader's convenience: they do not indicate real breaks in the thought.

588 τοιχωρύχος: cf. 447.

590f ἐγώ; as e.g. at *Sam.* 71: in English he would have said 'Do?'. For the threat, cf. Smikrines to Sophrone at *Epitr.* 714f: τὸ τέλμ᾽ εἶδες παριοῦσ᾽; ἐνταῦθά σε | τὴν νύκτα βαπτίζων ὅλην ἀποκτενῶ.

μὴ δῆτα: 'No, no!', cf. Denniston, *Particles* 276.

592-3 κράτιστον elliptically, sc. ἐστὶ τοῦτο ποιεῖν. Cf. 518f, and for the ellipse, βέλτιον 149. The malicious reference to the rottenness of the rope should come from Getas, and not from Knemon, to whom ed. pr. assigns both lines. It seems unnecessary to divide them, either by giving 592 to Knemon and 593 to Getas, with Zuntz, or by giving ταὐτῷ ... σχοινίῳ to Knemon and the rest to Getas, with OCT (Lloyd-Jones): P offers no warrant for this.

594 The simple Δᾶον καλῶ is made more specific, and hence more urgent, by the addition of the definite article (cf. 820), and the phrase ἐκ τῶν γειτόνων. For this, see on 24f, and cf. Ar. *Lys.* 701 τὴν ἑταίραν ἐκάλεσ᾽ ἐκ τῶν γειτόνων '... my friend from next door.' The absence of a second definite article (in contrast to Ar. *Plut.* 435; Nikostratos, *Patriotai* 22 K) presumably means that the prepositional phrase is adverbial not attributive, but the distinction is sometimes a narrow one: e.g. *Georgos* 31f προσέρχεται | [ἡμῖν] ὁ θεράπων ἐξ ἀγροῦ Δᾶος.

595 ἀνόσι᾽ ἀνειρηκυῖα γραῦ: cf. Ar. *Birds* 174 ὦ σκαιότατον εἰρηκὼς ἔπος; *Plut.* 415f ὦ θερμὸν ἔργον κἀνόσιον καὶ παράνομον | τολμῶντε δρᾶν ἀνθρωπαρίω κακοδαίμονε. [End: or σὺ from ed. pr. (so Kraus, Mette). Alternatively, ανοσι᾽ can be taken as voc. ἀνόσιε (2 terminations), and P's ανηρεικυια emended to ἀνηρηκυῖα with ed. pr.: hence, e.g., ἀνηρηκυῖά με OCT (Barber).]

596-99 With the ends of the lines lost, the possibilities for variant restorations are numerous, as may be seen from the discussion in van Groningen, *Étude Critique*; as elsewhere in this commentary, the selection of alternatives quoted is narrowly limited. OCT does not restore.

596 οὐ σοὶ λέγω; 'Do you hear me?', 'It's you I'm talking to'; cf. Herondas 4.42 and Headlam-Knox ad loc., and *Epitr.* 719, quoted above on 462.

θᾶττον βάδιζ᾽ εἴσω: 'hurry up inside'; cf. on 430f. I take it that the sense is complete at εἴσω: θᾶττον βάδιζ᾽, εἴσω [τρέχε Diano.

596ff τάλας ἐγώ, τάλας: as before (see on 177f), Knemon's outburst of fury is succeeded by an inner feeling of self pity – this time more

deeply felt, because it is more truly based, and brings him nearer to
the realization of the mistake on which his way of life is based (713ff).
Hence the assumption, on which this text is based, that τάλας is thrice
repeated, each time with a new qualification. For the resultant high
tone, cf. tragic (and paratragic) ὦ τάλας ἐγώ, τάλας (e.g. S. *OC* 847,
Ar. *Thes.* 1038); for repetition with variations, e.g. *Epitr.* 558-9,
quoted on 82. The τάλας of 596 derives some support from the word
order of ἐγὼ τάλας in 597; that at 597 end from the following ὡς οὐδὲ
εἷς, which seems unlikely to go with the colourless καταβήσομαι. Cf.
Com. Anon., Page, *Lit. Pap.* 61.21f ἐγὼ μὲν ὕβρισμαι, Λάχης, ὡς
οὐδὲ εἷς | ἄνθρωπος ἕτερος πώποθ'; similarly ὡς οὐχ ἕτερος, as Aristoph.
ap. Poll. 2. 233 (frg. 711 Edmonds) ὡς οὐχ ἕτερον ἄνδρα σάρκινον 'the
fattest man in the world'; and Lat. ut nemo, as Hor. *Sat.* 1.10.43:
forte epos acer | ut nemo Varius ducit.

ἐρημίας τῆς νῦν: word-order as, e.g., E. *Alc.* 309f τέκνοις τοῖς πρόσθε;
Andr. 979 τύχαις ταῖς οἴκοθεν; Thuc. 3.9.1 ξυμμαχίαν τὴν πρίν. To the
fourth-century ear it *may* have sounded poetic or abnormally elevated:
if so, appropriately in this context. For more examples, see Gildersleeve, *Syntax of Attic Greek* II.283f, and cf. *NTGramm.* §270 (3). τῆς
νῦν ἐρημίας (Shipp) is adopted in OCT and elsewhere.

[Ed. pr. supplies [, γύναι. 596 end; then (unwarrantably) *(Σιμ.)*
ἐγὼ τάλαιν'... νῦν. *(Γε.)* ἐγώ ... 596 [, κακόν. Kassel; 597 [ἐρῶ
Kraus, [ὅμως Mette.]

598f 'I'll go down into the well: what else is there to do?' ἔτ' ἔστιν
as (e.g.) in 583. [P's ει[followed by ειτ' in 599 suggests εἴτε ... εἴτε
(εἴ[τ' ἐπὶ τὸν κάδον | εἴτ' ἔστιν ἄλλο ed. pr.), but there is no point
in such an alternative, and a question is welcome to account for the
following remark by Getas: the clue is probably therefore false.
εἴτ' ἔστιν ἄλλο; Jean Martin (after Barigazzi and Post), with τί γάρ;
in 598; [... τί μοι | ἔξεστιν (or ἔνεστιν) ἄλλο; Barrett.]

599 The restoration assumes that Getas' offer is a realistic one.
ἁρπάγη is a hook used, as ancient grammarians tell us, for recovering
buckets from wells (cf. frg. 657, and the references given there by
Koerte) – that is to say, it is what goes under the name κρεάγρα 'meat-
hook', in Aristophanes, *Wasps* 1155f, *Eccl.* 1002ff. Getas, we may
imagine, is thinking of the rope which tied his load of στρώματα together, and a hook from Sikon's kit: cf. 402ff, and on 406-9 and 520,
with Valckenaer, *Animadv. ad Ammonium* (1739) 33-6, and Pritchett,
Hesperia 1956.295.
[OCT and some other edd. adopt no restoration. ποριού[μεθ' ἄσμενοι
ed. pr.; but the middle is not called for, and καὶ σχοινίον suggests that
a noun is lost. The suggestions made show a range of assumptions
about the nature of Getas' offer: e.g. (after ποριοῦ[μεν) σοι κάδον Lond.,
Thierfelder; σοι βρόχον Post; σοι σαπρόν van Groningen; κλίμακα
Bingen.]

600-1 This angry, blind rejection of help leads directly to disaster: cf. 626ff, 718ff.

[600: κακὸν κακ[ῶς σέ γ' οἱ θεοί ed. pr. 601: εἴ τί μ[οι δίδως ed. pr., adopted in OCT and by some others; . . . . φέρεις Gallavotti, Maas.]

602 καὶ μάλα δικαίως 'and I deserve it': see under 774f; similarly ὀρθῶς 581.

εἰσπεπήδηκεν: cf. *Sam.* 219. [καὶ μάλα δι[καίως. (Γε.) ἀπο]- ed. pr., against P.]

603ff The picture of the simple, hard-working old countryman, for all his conservative stubbornness and irascibility, was one which Attic popular tradition cherished with some affection; such, for example, were the charcoal-burners of Aristophanes, *Acharnians*, and the fellow-farmers of Chremylos who form the chorus of the *Plutus* (see esp. 223ff, 253ff). The effect of Getas' words here is to sum up what we have seen before of the 'hard-working rustic' side of Knemon's character, and so, at the moment before his critical misfortune, to add to the reasons for feeling sympathy with him. So much was anticipated from the outset: see on 3f, 127ff.

605 'Thyme and sage' are mentioned as typical of the hill-country, as heather and bracken might be in talking of an English upland farm. A farmer in Philemon (98 K) complains that his land treats him like a doctor, providing little bread and wine, but plenty of herbs from the rocks: he is afraid that this reducing diet will reduce him to a corpse. Similar is Daos' complaint in *Georgos*, that the farm grows myrtle, good ivy, and plenty of flowers, but otherwise scrupulously returns exactly what one sows in it (35ff). For illustrations and discussions of the relevant species of thyme and sage (or sage-like) plants, see S. C. Atchley, *Wild Flowers of Attica*. [Libanius, *Decl.* 27.18, appears to recall the passage, and to confirm that Menander wrote σφάκον not σκάφον, a confusion which is found elsewhere.]

606 ὀδύνας ἐπίσταται: 'he's an expert in trouble, but gains no good of it'. Menander may well have had in mind the story of the farmer of Hymettos and Peisistratos, as told by Aristotle, *Ath. Pol.* 16 (where see Sandys' note), and others: . . . ἰδὼν γάρ τινα παντελῶς πέτρας σκάπτοντα καὶ ἐργαζόμενον, διὰ τὸ θαυμάσαι τὸν παῖδα ἐκέλευσεν ἐρέσθαι τί γίγνεται ἐκ τοῦ χωρίου· ὁ δ' 'ὅσα κακὰ καὶ ὀδύναι' ἔφη. For the idea, cf. Theophylactus, *Ep.* 61 (p. 781 Hercher) ἐπιστήμην πόνων ἀσκεῖν μὴ βουλόμενος. ὀδύνας ἐπισπᾶται 'gains a crop of grief' is an attractive conjecture ('conjecture', because, although opinion is divided, επιστα[not επισπα[appears clearly to be the reading of P): so OCT (Lloyd-Jones) and others; alii alia.

608ff Fancy inviting two of the local farm-labourers! τί . . . ἢ πόθεν . . . : cf. Ar. *Plut.* 906 πῶς οὖν διέζης ἢ πόθεν μηδὲν ποιῶν; and *Perik.* 246f ποῖ φέρει γάρ; ἢ τίνα ἄξων; [νυνί ed. pr.]

611 Sostratos and Gorgias enter in conversation; Getas gets no answer to his question (he can hardly have expected one), and possibly goes back to his work in disgust without waiting to hear more. But see below.

611ff οὐκ ἄν ... ἄλλως ποῆσαι: 'I won't take "No" for an answer' – a longer form of μηδαμῶς ἄλλως ποιήσῃς (as, e.g., Ar. *Birds* 133); for οὐκ ἂν ἐπιτρέψαιμι see Com. Anon., Page, *Lit. Pap.* 65.80.

πάντ' ἔχομεν: following a suggestion of Webster's, I take this to be a form of refusal (like καλῶς ἔχει, as at 829 below); so ἔχομεν ἅπαντα in Com. Anon., Page, *Lit. Pap.* 63.24: (Demeas): 'I will tell my wife to provide what you need and pack it'. (Young man): ἔχομεν ἅπαντα (Slave): Ἄπολλον, ὡς ἄγροικος εἶ· | συσκευασάτω. Either, then, Gorgias must say the words, or (as I prefer), Sostratos must echo them from him: ' "No thank you", you say...' Ritchie, followed by OCT and others, assigns ὦ Ἡράκλεις to Getas, possibly rightly, but without warrant from P. For the δέ deferred, cf. Denniston, *Particles* 174f.

τίς ἀνθρώπων ὅλως: 'Who in the world?', analogous to οὐδεὶς ὅλως; see 860f, 865.

615f 'I assure you I've been a friend of yours since long before we met.'

ἀκριβῶς ἴσθι: cf. οἶδ' ἀκριβῶς Anaxandrides, *Odysseus* 34 K; εὖ ἴσθ' ἀκριβῶς M., frg. 532. [(Γε.) πρὶν ἰδεῖν. (Σω.) λαβών, κτλ. Jean Martin, followed by Jacques, who compares Com. Anon., Page, *Lit. Pap.* 65.59.]

616-19 Gorgias' refusal to join the party, as the enthusiastic Sostratos quite fails to see, is based on something more than the fact that he has his tools with him and is unwilling to leave his mother to lunch alone, devoted son though he is. For one thing he is shy, for another the inverted pride of the poor countryman will not let him accept what he takes as a favour. Both these points are to be made explicitly in the last act (871ff, 828ff), and they gain in effect from the brief but nicely calculated exchange here. He responds, it seems, to the appeal to friendship, but without a direct word of acceptance, and tells Daos, in effect, that he will 'only stay for a moment'. Cf. on 841.

616f Text uncertain: 'Take these things in with you, Daos, then come back' refers to the tools which the slave and Gorgias are carrying; see on 370. λαβών goes closely with the main verb, and is practically gratuitous, as, e.g., Athenion, *Samothrakes* 1 K τά τ'ἔνδον εὐτρεπῆ ποιεῖ λαβών .[P's ταυταδ', as Gallavotti observes, is probably a conflation of ταῦτα and τάδε; he adopts the latter. λαβὼν δὲ ταῦτά γ' εἰσένεγκε σύ ed. pr.; λαβὼν ταῦτ' οἴκαδ' ἐ. σ. OCT (Lloyd-Jones); alii alia: perhaps λαβὼν ταῦτ' εἰσένεγκε, δεῦρο σὺ | εἶθ' ἧκε.]

617ff Following P's arrangement of parts, Gorgias must be taken to be speaking to Daos, who now goes home, leaving his master to enter the shrine with Sostratos. Daos has no further part in the play, unless we assume that he is seen coming along to the party at 866f, or is present as a silent figure elsewhere. Ed. pr., supposing that Gorgias persists in refusing the invitation, and returns home, brings in Sostratos as speaker of ἀλλ' ἐκείνης . . . κἀγὼ παρέσομαι. A point in favour of P (which I owe to Goold) is that 635 works better if Gorgias is not in fact in his own house.

618f ἐπιμελοῦ with double construction, ἐκείνης and ὧν ἂν δέηται (=τούτων ὧν or ταῦτα ὧν).

[οἴκει Marzullo; cf. frg. 889.]

Act IV (620-783)

620 The act opens with a further woebegone excursion by Simiche, parallel to that already discussed, 574ff.

623 σπονδὰς ποῆσαι: the party is now supposed to have reached the stage where the servants remove the food, and libations of wine are poured as a preliminary to the post-prandial drinking. Cf. *Kekryphalos*, frg. 239 ... τὰς τραπέζας αἴρετε, | μύρα, στεφάνους ἑτοίμασον, σπονδὰς ποίει.
λοιδορεῖσθε, τύπτετε, οἰμώζετε i.e. Knemon abuses Getas (cf. 487), and beats *me* (503ff); now you disturb our libations with your wailing. Cf. on νενομίκατε in 173.

625 πῶς; 'How do you mean?', echoed, as normally, by ὅπως;. Cf. on 363.

627f Note the contrast of tenses: descriptive imperfect, aorist indicating single sudden action, perfect indicating result. ['Perhaps κἀπώλισθ'' Lloyd-Jones.]

628f 'Not the nasty old man? Just the right thing for him, by Heaven.' Sikon is maliciously delighted at the news: see 643ff, and for the sense of καλά γ' ἐπόησε, cf. LSJ s.v. καλῶς 5 (Shipp). [Punctuation is problematical. It is possible that Sikon's reaction to the news comes in a single crowded sentence, as ed. pr. has it: i.e. οὐ γάρ introduces a challenging rhetorical question, not a momentary doubt of news too good to be true; and ὁ χαλεπὸς γέρων ... οὗτος is interlaced with σφόδρα ... καλὰ ἐπόησε, which is then given extra emphasis by γε and the oath: for this, cf. Ar. *Plut.* 1042f, and for the position of the demonstrative, *Perik.* 198f, *Georgos* 25ff. But the sharper effect of a divided sentence seems to suit the cook's manner better, and of the possible divisions, I prefer the first remark to end after γέρων rather than after σφόδρα (Gallavotti), or οὗτος (Shipp, followed in OCT and elsewhere). Kassel and Thierfelder give οὗτος to Simiche, probably wrongly, though P has a possible trace of part-division in σφοδραῖ (=σφοδρα:?).]

630 νῦν σὸν ἔργον ἐστί: 'Now it's up to you.'

631 ὅλμον: a heavy mortar, here presumably of stone, used for pounding and crushing grain: Ar. *Wasps* 201 *al.* [See Amyx, Hesperia 1958.235; L. A. Moritz, *Grain Mills and Flour* ... (1958) 22ff. Webster remarks that the mythical Antheus was drowned in a well when the woman he had scorned induced him to go down it and then dropped a heavy stone on him – a story which may have been well enough known to lend spice to Sikon's suggestion. It was perhaps the theme of a play by the tragedian Agathon: P. Levèque, *Agathon*, 105ff.]

633 κατάβα: cf. Ar. *Wasps* 979, *Frogs* 35. This form of the intrans. aor. imperative (= βά-ε as opposed to βῆ-θι) was evidently normal in spoken Attic: so ἔμβα. From the uncompounded verb (which was not in current use), Tragedy provides the plural βᾶτε.

633f 'Good Lord – and find myself fighting a dog in the well, as they say? Not likely.'

Πόσειδον: cf. on 290ff. ἵνα ... πάθω picks up the idea 'go down' from κατάβα; ἐν ... μάχωμαι explaining the allusion, follows without connection in the same construction.

τὸ τοῦ λόγου: the phrase ἐν φρέατι κυνὶ (κυσὶ) μάχεσθαι (or ἐν φ. κυνομαχεῖν) is used generally of being at grips with an inescapable difficulty: cf. Plato's allusion to it at *Theaet.* 165 b, and the collections of proverbs quoted under the text. What is in point here is not merely the re-application of a known form of words, but the whole proverbial situation on which it rests, as embodied in the Aesopic fable κηπουρὸς καὶ κύων (192 Halm): there the gardener tried to rescue his dog from the well, only to be bitten for his pains. For examples of τὸ τοῦ λόγου and similar phrases, see Headlam-Knox on Herondas 2.45; they are used adverbially (as βαδίζεις ἴσα τοῦτο δὴ τὸ τοῦ λόγου Πυθοκλεῖ Alciphron, *Ep.* 3.56 [3.20]), or as here, as the object of a verb.

635 Simiche frantically calls Gorgias, who appears not from his own house but from the shrine: see on 617ff.

[This version of P's corrupt line assumes that τισ represents γῆς and that ποτ' ειμι is an addition originally intended to clarify the sense of the echoed question. ... ποῦ γῆς; (Γο.) ἐγώ; Shipp, (Γο.) πάρειμ' ἐγώ Winnington-Ingram; alii alia.]

636 τί γάρ; see on 553.

638 Enter Sostratos from the shrine. The double points before ἡγοῦ in P caused ed. pr. to assign the following words (implausibly) to Sostratos. They may mark the strong break in the speech as Gorgias turns to address Simiche: see Introd. III, p. 46.

639-65 Simiche leads Gorgias and Sostratos into the house to rescue Knemon; Sikon remains behind, reflecting on the disaster with vainglorious satisfaction. Presently a cry is heard from within: can the old man be dead? At this point, 648ff, damage makes the text unclear, but the cook evidently goes on to relish the prospect of his old enemy hauled up soaked and shivering; and he concludes by asking the women to pray that Knemon will be rescued a cripple, no more to trouble those whose sacrifice at the shrine – and thereby make work for cooks.

The good man, observes Aristotle, should rejoice at punishment well-merited, for example that of parricides and murderers (*Rhet.* 1386 b 28); and the audience are obviously expected to indulge, with Sikon, their natural pleasure that the unpleasant old man has had something unpleasant happen to him. But only up to a point. Being both excessive and malicious, Sikon's exultation simultaneously blackens his own character, coloured as it is with the pretentious absurdity inherent in stage cooks; and the result (perhaps more conspicuously with a modern audience than an ancient one) is to create an undercurrent of sympathy with the old man, adding one more to the series of impressions we have been given that he is not wholly and simply a comic freak of misanthropy. The same mixture of feelings, in different and possibly less successful proportions, underlies the boisterous bullying of the old man with which the play ends; and to this the present passage looks forward.

In its immediate context, the speech serves, like a fifth-century chorus, to increase the audience's appetite for news while some important event happens off stage; a report will come from Sostratos, as from a messenger (666-90), and lead climactically to the old man's appearance and the spectacle contrived for his great set speech. As elsewhere, the play gains in effect from the audience's familiarity with the patterns of Classical Tragedy: Webster appropriately refers to the sequence of events in Eur. *HF* from 875 onwards (*SM*² 229).

639 μὰ τὸν Διόνυσον strengthens a positive protesting assertion in the absence of a preparatory ναί, contrary to the accepted rule of Classical Greek usage. Cf. 151. I take it that the function of ναί is assumed by the unequivocally positive tone of the two sentences, expressed there in μέντοι and here in the emphatic εἰσίν: 'There really are gods'. Three passages quoted by LSJ show the same usage developing in Later Greek: in prose, Aristaenetus, *Ep.* 1.10 (p. 141 Hercher) μὰ τὴν Ἄρτεμιν Ἀκοντίῳ γαμοῦμαι and Achilles Tatius 8.5; in verse, δακρύω, μὰ σέ, δαῖμον from an elegiac epitaph on a monument dated saec. i-ii A.D., found at Sakkara in Egypt, and first published in *Ann. du Service* 27 (1927) 31f: see now *SEG* VIII.530, W. Peek, *Gr. Vers-Inschriften*, 1843.

[Add Libanius, *Decl.* 26.23, with Thomas Magister's remarks (quoted by Forster ad loc., vol. vi.527): he cites Liban., *ib.* 33, and Lucian, *De cal.* 14; but a longer list of instances is easily assembled. νὴ may be substituted for μὰ in 151 (Barrett, Shipp), as here (Lloyd-Jones); and this is done in OCT – but at some risk of 'improving' the author rather than correcting the copyist. An alternative approach in both passages is to read the oath in association with the neighbouring negative – very difficult in 151, less appropriate here, where a further consideration is the possibility that P's διονυσονι represents διονυσον: with a dicolon at the break in the speech, as in the preceding line. The Classical Greek rules for νή and μά have been re-examined recently by H. Thesleff, and are briefly re-stated by him in *Studies on Intensification* §288, where further references will be found; on *Dysk.* 718f (interesting in this connection, but not in my view parallel), see n. there.]

639ff 'So you won't give a stewpot to people sacrificing, you rogue, you grudge it them? Then fall in and drink your well dry.'
For the paratactic construction, see on 57ff (iii).

οὐ δίδως: 'won't give', rather than 'don't give', the present, as commonly, bearing the meaning 'I am ready to give': cf. KG I.140.

ἱερόσυλε: *lit.* 'temple-robber', a common term of abuse corresponding to *sacrilegus* in Latin Comedy.

ἔκπιθι . . . εἰσπεσών in close association, the participle being virtually timeless, as λάβ᾽ ἐλθών 'go and get' in Alexis, *Lebes* 127 K, quoted on 581f. [641 ἐμπεσών ed. pr.]

642 ἔχω with neg. and infin. 'be unable', as *Perik.* 143, *Aphrodisios* frg. 80 *al.* μεταδοῦναι with gen. and dat., as 568f and regularly. On refusing water, the supreme meanness, cf. P. *Aul.* 94 (Euclio) 'Say that the well is dry if anyone wants water'; P. *Rud.* 430ff.

643ff νυνὶ μέν is answered by no formal contrast: the speaker turns from the present fate of Knemon to the general proposition that cooks are inviolable. Cf. Denniston, *Particles* 380. The Nymphs are appropriate agencies for a watery punishment, and Sikon's reference to them and to Knemon's refusal of the stewpot is a hint to the audience that this new event is part of the divinely motivated pattern unfolding before them – a hint which can be taken in spite of the fact that Sikon is more concerned with repairing the damage to his pride than with divine retribution. See on 37ff.

644 δικαίως: 'as he deserves'; see under 774f.

645 διέφυγεν gnomic aorist.

646 '*Our* art has an aura of sanctity about it: you can do what you like to a butler.' τέχνη of the cook's art itself, which confers sanctity on its practitioners, rather than collectively of the 'profession', though the one meaning easily shades into the other. See, e.g., Sosipater, *Katapseudomenos* 1 K, 1ff; and cf. LSJ, s.v. V. Glorifying himself, sometimes at the expense of other members of the catering fraternity, is part of the comic cook's traditional stock-in-trade; and those in the audience with a taste for this kind of comedy may have been disappointed not to hear more. The brief recall of a traditional topic is however characteristic of the cook's rôle in this play. See on 393, and contrast, e.g., Athenion, *Samothrakes* 1 K (The Art's contribution to piety in civilizing mankind); Alexis, *Milesia* 149 K and Dionysios, *Thesmophoros* 2 K (cook as opposed to *opsopoios*); Antiphanes, *Metoikos* 152 K; Diphilos, *Zographos* 43 K (cook and *trapezopoios*: on whom see further Pritchett, Hesperia 1956.279.)

647 ἀλλ᾽ εἰς seems practically certain: ποιεῖν τι εἴς τινα as e.g. Philippides, 26 K; other examples in KG I.324 A.6; cf. *NTGramm.* §206(3). [OCT does not supplement; ἀδεῶ]ς ed. pr.; alii alia.]

[648f Text damaged and doubtful. The words πάππαν φίλτατον and ἀποιμώζει τις show that the girl cried out from within the house: none the less, in the absence of any signs of a change of speaker in P, it seems safest to assume that the cry was not part of the text, but simply an οἰμωγμὸς ἔνδοθεν such as might have been recorded, if at all, in a stage-direction (see on αὐλεῖ after 879). Hence, in the text given, ἀλλ' ἆρα introducing the cook's reaction and commentary (cf. *Sam.* 142), and κλαίουσ', which (unless we prefer another fem. ptcp.) is likely to be right in 649: καλοῦσ' Treu *et al.* Other suggestions include *(Κορ.)* οἴμ', ἆρα μὴ τέθνηκε; *(Σικ.)* πάππαν φίλτατον... (Lond., with οἴμ', ἆρα, a doubtful elision, from ed. pr.); *(Κορ.)* οἴμ', ἆρα μὴ τέθνηκε; πάππαν φίλτατον | πνίγουσ' (Mette); OCT does not supplement.]

649 οὐδὲν τοῦτό γε perhaps continued with ὄφελος 'That's no use'; cf. *Theophoroumene*, frg. 1.15. But it is impossible to do more than guess what came between this line and the line P gives next. [649 is the last line of the leaf on which it appears in P. The next leaf is some 30 mm. shorter than its companions, and ed. pr. accordingly allows for a loss of four complete lines here, and five after 703. The estimate is necessarily approximate, for—as Professor Victor Martin remarked when he discussed the point in London—neither the make-up of the manuscript nor the words preserved on either side of the two gaps admit of a precise calculation. Confident restoration is therefore impossible. The relevant photographs in ed. pr., plates 15-16, were printed at a different scale from the others, and give an illusory impression of uniformity.]

654f In 655, P's οὕτως, followed by some part of the fut. or aor. of ἀνιμῶ shows that the cook was speculating on the method of Knemon's rescue (and hence preparing the way for Sostratos' narrative to follow); perhaps he was prompted by a further cry from within. The preceding δηλονοθι is not very helpful: the general sense may have been on the lines of 'Someone will go down and put a rope round him, of course . . .': e.g. [. . . καταβήσεταί τις, ἐπιβαλεῖ κάλων] | δηλονότι, κᾆθ' [ἕλκοντες αὐτὸν ἀνδρικῶς] | οὕτως ἀνιμήσ[ουσιν. If κᾶθ[- after δηλονότι or δῆλον, ὅτι the next syllable must also be short. καθ[ελίξας (μέσον τῷ σχοινίῳ) Diano (but see LSJ, s.v.). OCT and others adopt no restoration until 657.

655 ὦ καλῆς θέας, given here as a stop-gap, is based on 690 and καλὴ θέα *Theophor.* 30.

656 τίνα suits the traces of letters preserved, but is uncertain: for the end of the line several alternative possibilities are open. [αὐτοῦ γ' εἰς τὸ πρόσθεν . . . (ed. pr.) does not seem to suit, nor αὐτοῦ, τοῦ κακοδαίμονος . . . Diano.]

657 βεβρεγμένου, τρέμοντος 'soaking wet and shivering', two closely related ideas put together in asyndeton: cf. 662. [Alternatively, βεβαμμένου OCT (Maas), or perhaps another ptcp. beginning βεβ-; εἰσαγομένου ed. pr., is supported by Harsh and adopted by some other edd., but does not seem to suit the traces visible in the photograph or to provide suitable sense.]

658 ἀστείαν ἐγὼ μέν: οἶμαι ἔσεσθαι is understood from the previous sentence; for ἐγὼ μέν 'ego quidem', see 509 n. [Ed. pr. and others punctuate after ἀστείαν, taking ἐγὼ μέν conveniently with what follows; but ἀστείαν is then inconveniently remote from τὴν ὄψιν. τρέμοντος; ἀστείαν. ἐγὼ μέν ... is preferred by Jacques.]

659 ἴδοιμ' ἄν: sc. αὐτήν (or αὐτόν). τουτονί refers not to Knemon, but to Apollo, present as Apollo Agyieus, the god whose emblem or altar stood at the street door of Greek houses, and will presumably have appeared on the stage set between Knemon's door and the shrine. See especially frg. 801, Ar. *Wasps* 875, *Thes.* 748; for discussion, see Fraenkel on A. *Ag.* 1081, with further references; for illustrations (a) emblem and altar, e.g. Daremberg-Saglio, s.v. Agyieus; (b) comic sets with altars, e.g. a Sicilian calyx-crater in Lentini, ca. 340-30 B.C. (Bieber, *History of the Gk and Roman Theater*[2] 488 = Trendall, *Phlyax Vases*, no. 73; Webster, *GTP*, B.67); and a relief known from several Roman terracottas (saec. i B.C./i A.D.): Bieber, *ib.* 587 = Pickard-Cambridge, *Theatre of D.*, figs. 78-79; Webster, *GTP*, C.22; *MNC*, no. IT 65.

ἄνδρες to the spectators (here and in 666: cf. on 194).

660 The cook maliciously suggests that the women in the shrine should continue the disturbed libations with a new intent. Cf. 622f.

661 σωθῆναι κακῶς together, 'to have a bad rescue', in the sense immediately made clear; for κακῶς cf. 25 n.

662 ἀνάπηρον ὄντα, χωλόν: coupled in asyndeton, the second expression 'lame' being a specific development of the first, 'maimed'. Note the similar pairs of words in this context, 657f, 660f, 676f. Sikon's calculating ill-wishes (like those of Daos, 373f) come near to fulfilment; for the old man proves to be horribly shaken: he thinks he will die and cannot rise from his bed; but the attempt to make him dance at the very end of the play (954ff) gives the actor a chance to show, with a suitable comic flourish, that no grievous and permanent harm has been done.

662f οὕτω γίνεται: i.e. 'that's the way to make him...' γίνεται vividly expressing the expected result, as e.g. 789.

ἀλυπότατος: cf. Plato, *Laws* 848 e ... ὅπου κατοικοῦντες ἀλυπότατοί τε καὶ ὠφελιμώτατοι ἔσονται τοῖσι γεωργοῦσι.

γάρ deferred: see on 66-68.

τῷδε τῷ θεῷ: Pan. [663 end: the ω of θεωι has its final stroke continued until the loop is closed, as the writer of this manuscript occasionally does. Victor Martin and Harsh (respectively) read]μοι and]ιμοι. See further van Groningen, *Étude Critique*, ad. loc.]

666-90 Sostratos' report of the rescue: a companion piece to his speech at 522-45. See n. there, and above under 639-65. Delighted at the chance which has brought him close to the girl he loves, he shares his feelings with the audience, not without realising that his own part in the rescue was less effective than it might have been.

The beginning resembles Ar. *Cl.* 627ff: μὰ τὴν Ἀναπνόην, μὰ τὸ Χάος, μὰ τὸν Ἀέρα, | οὐκ εἶδον οὕτως ἄνδρ' ἄγροικον οὐδένα | οὐδ' ἄπορον οὐδὲ σκαιὸν οὐδ' ἐπιλήσμονα ... The threefold oath recalls the triple invocation of the gods at 191f; it is a form of time-honoured significance, which seems here to have no other function than to emphasize the speaker's highly emotional state. Cf. on ὦ δυστυχής in 574, and see Radermacher on Ar. *Frogs* 305f (p. 178), and Eitrem, Symb. Osl. 1959.135. The pattern of general reflection (666-9), succeeded by narrative, ὁ Γοργίας γάρ, ὡς τάχιστ' εἰσήλθομεν, is a conventional one, well illustrated by Fraenkel, *de med. et nov. com.*, 48ff, who refers, *inter alia*, to *Perik.* 282ff, P. *Aul.* 701ff, and the long speech from Straton, *Phoenikides* (for which see Page, *Lit. Pap.* 57).

668f μικροῦ with ἀποπεπνιγμένον: 'I've never seen a man come within an ace of drowning more opportunely.'
τῆς γλυκείας διατριβῆς: 'What fun!' For διατριβή, cf. 890.

671-8 The passionate scene described resembles that at Chrysis' funeral in T. *Andria* 127ff.

672f τί γὰρ ἐμέλλομεν; sc. ποιεῖν or ποιήσειν. 'What were we to do, after all?', or, more idiomatically 'Of course not'. πλήν 'except that'; see on 304.

675 ὁ χρυσοῦς: 'precious idiot that I was'; cf. Lucian, *Laps.* 1; Aelian, *Ep. Rust.* 19 ἐγὼ μὲν ἔθυον γάμους ὁ χρυσοῦς μάτην.

676f μὴ ποεῖν ταῦθ': not to weep, etc. Cf. 335, 790 and n., and for more illustrations of this common idiom, see Radermacher on Ar. *Frogs* 358 (p. 191f).

677f ἱκέτευον ... τυχόντι, developing the idea of ἐδεόμην, follows without connection. Cf. 66of. Sostratos now imagines himself as an awestruck suppliant before a statue or a painting of a beautiful goddess, an image 'out of this world'. Szemerényi refers me to Plato, *Charmides* 154 c: οὐδεὶς ἄλλοσ' ἔβλεπεν αὐτῶν ... ἀλλὰ πάντες ὥσπερ ἄγαλμα ἐθεῶντο αὐτόν. [ἄγαλμα here may be either a painted or a sculpted representation. See frg. 126, quoted below the text, and referred here by Gallavotti. It is not clear in what sense the author intended to refer to Menander.]

678 τοῦ δὲ πεπληγμένου κάτω: apparently 'the man stricken (by misfortune) below', as opposed to the girl stricken by grief above – an odd turn of phrase which has given rise to textual doubt. [Metre: cf. Introd. IV, p. 63f and p. 66 under (c). πεπνιγμένου Page; τοῦ δὲ πεπλεγμένου κάλω Szemerényi. τοῦ δὲ πεπλεγμένου κάτω Jean Martin, after Georgoulis ('l'homme encordé'). Photius seems to quote πέπληκται from Menander in the sense ἥττηται (frg. 898, cited in defence of the text by Lloyd-Jones). There is a chance that the definition was derived from the present passage: cf. on 101, 527f, 531-4.]

679 ἔλαττον ἤ τινος: lit. '(cared for him) less than for anything': i.e. not at all; as one might say 'less than somewhat'. Cf. Dem., False Embassy (19).35 πραοτέρους . . . τινός and Meid. (21).66 ἄμεινόν . . . τινος, quoted by LSJ s.v., A.II.1. [τριχὸς olim Fraenkel.]

679f πλὴν . . . σφόδρα: 'except for pulling him the whole time – that was a great bore'. The clause ἀεὶ ἕλκειν ἐκεῖνον, immediately picked up by τοῦτ', is the subject of ἐνώχλει. [Evidence for this form of the impf. is quoted by Jean Martin, ad loc.]

681 εἰσαπολώλεκα: 'sent him in to his death'; not recorded from elsewhere, and possibly coined to suit the situation. Cf. Xenophon's unique ἐναπόλλυμαι 'to perish in a place', HG 3.1.4. ἐξαπολώλεκα (Lloyd-Jones, Morel) is adopted in OCT and elsewhere.

683 ἴσως τρίς: 'about three times'; cf. 118, 327, Epitr. 67, LSJ s.v. ἴσως, IV.

683f 'An Atlas of no common order' – a passing mythological reference like that to Odysseus at Kolax 113 (Webster). Sostratos' youthful excitement is reflected not only in his elevation of the scene to a scale larger than life – the girl like a goddess, Gorgias like the sole supporter of the earth, but in the constant and repetitive qualifying of his remarks: οὐχ ὁ τυχών twice; πλήν 673, 679; μικροῦ 669, 681, 687; σφόδρα 674, 680, 688. A more studied speech (but one less suitable to the speaker and the occasion), would have managed things differently, with ideas more precisely and variously expressed, and, for that matter, more formally connected.

684f ἀντεῖχε without connection: see on 662. Gorgias 'held firm' down below, and supported the old man when the rope slackened; then with a final struggle brought him up. ἀνενήνοχ' might be taken as first person, but ἀνείλκυκα would be more appropriate of Sostratos himself. The imperfect describes a state of affairs, the perfect a result (as in 686); contrast the aor. ἐξέβη of a single incident.

685ff The motive for Sostratos' entry is now made explicit: cf. 543ff. [685 ὡς δ' ἐκεῖνος Morel, Page: so OCT, perhaps rightly, since, as at

20 above, the speaker may have marked a new stage in his narrative
with a particle; but there can be no assurance that he did.]

688 ἐφίλουν (like ἐδυνάμην) descriptive imperfect: 'there I was, all
but going up and kissing her'.

οὕτω σφόδρα as, e.g., Eupolis, *Demoi* 117 K οὐκ ἔχω τί λέξω· | οὕτω
σφόδρ᾽ ἀλγῶ; Antiphanes, 273 K . . . ὦπτα δὲ καὶ τὰς κοιλίας· | οὕτω
σφόδρ᾽ ἦν ἀρχαῖος. Since the words preserved make complete sense, the
lost end of the line is quite uncertain, but possibly contained another
adverb: οὑτωσὶ σφόδρα | ἀπεριμερίμνως, Ar. *Clouds* 135f. For ἐνθεαστικῶς
(adopted by OCT *et al.*), cf. 44 above; ἐ[μμανῶς ἐγὼ Fraenkel,
comparing *Misoumenos* frg. 5; ε[ἴπερ τίς ποτε Webster; ἐ[ξέστηκα καὶ
Thierfelder.

689 παρασκευάζομαι δή: S. breaks off on hearing Knemon's door
open, leaving us to guess what he was preparing – presumably yet
another approach to the old man. Cf. 266f. He may even have intended to work out a suitable speech in the quiet outside: compare
Moschion at *Perik.* 300, and the young man in P. Didot. II (Koerte
I³, p. 145).

690 ὦ Ζεῦ σῶτερ: cf. on 290ff. The 'strange sight' is that of Knemon,
wheeled on to the stage on a couch or bed by Gorgias and the girl,
for all the world like a stricken tragic hero. See the following notes
(692, 701), and on 708-47, 758. The recall of a tragic situation helps
to conceal the lack of an explicit motive for the invalid's excursion,
whose purpose of holding a family meeting could equally well have
been fulfilled inside; but the audience must witness the proceedings,
and Knemon must therefore come out. He might, it is true, have felt
that he needed sun and air (like Phaedra in the *Hippolytus*, 178ff);
and understandably, after the wet and cold of the well; but such is the
force of convention that the poet can expect his audience to accept the
inevitable without this or any other explanation, unless, as is possible,
one was given or implied by the lost beginning of Knemon's long
speech. For tragic reminiscence underlined by visual means, see 189 n.

691 βούλει τι . . . τί βούλομαι; 'Is there anything you want?' 'What do
I want, you ask?' Gorgias speaks, no doubt, on completing Knemon's
instructions to take him outside; the solicitous question seems to have
provoked some of the old fractiousness. [End uncertain: τί μοι λαλεῖς;
ed. pr. τί σοι λέγω; OCT (Maas); alii alia.]

692 θάρρει — τεθάρρηκα: 'Cheer up' 'I've done with cheering up'.
Barrett compares Eur. *Hip.* 1454f (Θη.) μὴ νῦν προδῷς με, τέκνον,
ἀλλὰ καρτέρει. (Ἱπ.) κεκαρτέρηται τἄμ᾽· ὄλωλα γὰρ πάτερ – a passage
from a moving and apposite situation which Menander very probably
had in mind. Out of context τεθάρρηκα would be expected to mean 'I
am cheerful'; its force here, like that of Cicero's famous *uixerunt* of the

executed conspirators, is determined by the situation (and, no doubt, the manner) in which it is said as much as by the sharp contrast with the present. Cf. in general Schwyzer II.264. [τεθν[ηκὼς ed. pr., and similar suggestions, are hardly to be reconciled with the traces in P: τεθαρρηκὼς μὲν οὐκ Gallavotti.]

693 γὰρ in 6th place: see on 66-68. [After ἐπίλοιπον, το[ῦ χρόνου Page; γο[ῦν χρόνον Gallavotti; π[αρὰ βίον Barrett.]

694 ἐρημία: cf. 169, 222, 597; κακὸν...ἡ ἐρημία, Liban., *Decl.* 27.26. [Metre: cf. Introd. IV, p. 65 (*h*).]

695 ἀκαρής: 'within a hair's breadth', the adj. used adverbially, as in Alexis, *Mandragorizomene* 144 K, Com. Adesp. 581 K.

νῦν...ἀρτίως: 'only just now'; so νῦν...ἄρτι Pherekrates, *Cheiron* 146 K (with pres.); Plato, *Crat.* 396 c (with perf.).

696f 'A man of your advanced age should have someone to look after him': τηρούμενον passive rather than middle '... should take care of himself.'

697f χαλεπῶς μὲν...: 'I'm in a bad way, I do know...'

699-700 ὡς ἔνι μάλιστα, a strengthened form of μάλιστα, is, I take it, a reply to Knemon's request in the sense 'By all means', perhaps implying 'With all speed', as Lat. *quantum potest* commonly does, e.g. T. *Adel.* 700. So van Groningen.

τὰ κακὰ...ἔοικε: in other words πάθει μάθος. Gorgias, thinking aloud, leaves the stage to fetch his mother; this sententious reflection is in effect the answer to the dilemma he posed at 249ff. Neither force nor reasoned persuasion could change Knemon's ways; he has learnt at last (as he will presently reveal in his long speech) from the experience which misfortune has brought him. [(i) With Gallavotti, OCT *et al.*, I accept the evidence of P's paragraphus under 698 and assume that it failed to record a change of speaker after ἔοικε (rather than after μάλιστα, as van Groningen prefers). Ed. pr. *et al.* give the whole passage to Knemon; but, all else apart, it seems incredible that Gorgias' only reaction to κάλεσον τὴν μητέρα should be silent compliance, as if the old man had said something trivial. (ii) The common view (after ed. pr.) that ὡς ἔνι μάλιστα goes with what follows leaves both the sense and the function of the phrase unclear: e.g. ed. pr. takes it as 'la plupart du temps', Kraus as 'above all else'; but it is in any case otiose. The other alternative to the view taken here is to override P's paragraphus and take the phrase (like πάσῃ τέχνῃ or *quantum potest*) as a reinforcement of the imperative κάλεσον: so Page *et al.*; Maas and Zuntz would read ὡς ἔνι τάχιστα with the same function.]

700 θυγάτριον: an affectionate diminutive.

701 'Will you raise me up?' – which she will do by taking him in her arms: hence Sostratos' wistful 'Lucky man!' Compare (*a*) Phaedra in the *Hippolytus* (already mentioned above) ἄρατέ μου δέμας, ὀρθοῦτε κάρα (198); (*b*) 740 ἀλλὰ κατάκλινόν με, θύγατερ, and 914f, 928f; (*c*) the passion so feelingly expressed by Sappho in φαίνεταί μοι κῆνος ἴσος θέοισιν | ἔμμεν' ὤνηρ, ὄττις ἐνάντιός τοι | ἰσδάνει; or so angrily by the young man in P. *Most.* 265f, whose girl-friend has just kissed her mirror.

702 τί ... ἄθλιε: Knemon apparently overhears Sostratos' remark and reacts with his old exasperation at the presence of a stranger: cf. 466f τρισάθλιε ... ἄνθρωπε. The rudeness here, as from one free citizen to another, has disturbed some critics; but note 750 (Knemon to Gorgias, whom he has just adopted as his son). The misanthrope, as we shall see, has suffered a change of heart; but not a miraculous transformation into a creature of polite normality. [The letters αθλι- appear to be correctly read, but ἀθλί[ῳ (Page) demonstrates that the voc. is not inevitable. ἀσύ[νετε (?) vel sim. Lloyd-Jones, who does not restore in OCT.]

'703-7' see on 649. The loss of some text here obscures the dramatic point of Knemon's last remark and deprives us of the beginning of his speech. It is necessary for what is to come that Sostratos should remain in the background; and it seems appropriately ironical that Knemon should be so offhand with the man who helped to rescue him and will soon be his son-in-law; but the dialogue at 751ff shows that there is no place here for explanations or excuses. Anything Sostratos may have said or intended to say in reply was presumably cut short by the appearance of Gorgias and his mother. The long set speech, marked by a change of metre, can hardly have begun without them, but it would be fascinating to know precisely how the scene was set for it.

708-47 Knemon's major speech: trochaic tetrameters catalectic, which continue to the end of the act. For metrical description, see Introd. IV, pp. 59f.

(i) The core of the speech is formed by the momentous decisions which Knemon has worked out for himself and now enacts, 729-39. But he begins with a critical exposition of the views which have governed his actions, both past and proposed; and he turns at 740, when his main business is done, to asserting the virtue of his own way of life as opposed to the ways of the world, in which he has seen and still sees much evil. His closing words reflect a mood of resignation to circumstance which has been present throughout, balanced by his attempt to save what still seems valid in his own beliefs, while coming to terms with the new principles which he has been brought to recognize.

(ii) It is fitting that the climax of the play should give the fullest and most sympathetic portrait of the character about whom the action is built. A misanthrope cannot be unduly forthcoming or loquacious; up to now, though the audience have heard much about him, Knemon's appearances have been relatively brief: by holding him, as it were, in reserve, the poet concentrates interest on this one great moment, for which he has prepared with care. A striking contrast is offered by the much more substantial rôle of Euclio in P. *Aul.*; when the miser's heart was at last melted by an act of kindness amidst misfortune, what he said of himself can hardly have come with so powerful an effect. Cf. *Aul.*, Arg. II, fin.; frgg. III-IV, and Introd. I, p. 11f.

(iii) Knemon's personal crisis has an air of tragedy, and here as elsewhere it seems likely that the known patterns of classical high drama were intended to give point and depth to the more familiar affairs of the comic stage. On Menander's use of tragedy in general, see Webster, *SM* 159ff; it is worth recalling here Ajax' speech of decision at S. *Ai.* 646ff, Oedipus at *OT* 1446ff, and Iphigeneia's resolve to die, Eur. *IA* 1368ff. In contrast, Demeas' struggle between anger and self-control in the *Samia* (110-41) is much nearer the surface and more comic; Demea in T. *Adel.* weighs his life in the balance before deciding to abandon stern rusticity and affect urbane liberalism, but his situation and his decision are again of a different quality from Knemon's (855-81; cf. M. *Adel. II*, frg. 11). To see the speech in a longer perspective, it is worth comparing the scene of Strepsiades' disillusionment in the *Clouds* (1452ff), where the tragic overtones are designed to achieve a broader kind of amusement. What relief there is here to the overall seriousness comes from our superior knowledge that Knemon is not after all about to die (for this is a comedy), from our pleasure at seeing the decisions he makes resolve the dramatic problem, and from our perception of the weaknesses in his self-defence.

(iv) A predominantly serious scene in trochaic tetrameters is an accession to our knowledge of Menander, though we still know too little to say how unusual it was by his own and his contemporaries' standards. One notes, for what it is worth, that the parallel speech in *Second Adelphoi* (see above) was in iambic trimeters, and converted to the trochaic metre by Terence. In so far as it is a treatise on human behaviour, delivered by a character who transcends his ordinary dramatic rôle for the occasion, the speech can be placed in the long comic tradition which stems from the parabases of Old Comedy, persists in the speeches of self-description discussed above (57ff, 489-98), and can be illustrated further from trochaic passages such as Alexis, *Isostasion* 98 K (on the ways of *hetairai*); Philemon 213 K (on the insecurity of the idle rich); Diphilos, *Gamos* 24 K (on the evils of 'influence'); Menander, *Orge*, frg. 309 (on true and false friendship).

The clearest hint that Menander is writing with this tradition in
mind comes perhaps from the miniature diatribe at 742ff (where see n.);
as with Knemon's opening speech at 153ff, it is possible to think that
the echo of a traditional form is deliberate, and in concord with the
traditional aspects of the character. A precedent for a speech is trochaic
tetrameters at a moment of high intensity could have been claimed, if
one were needed, from Euripides, *IA* 1368ff (referred to above), at
the end of an exciting trochaic scene. But precedents apart, it seems
evident that in this play the change from iambic trimeters is intended
to underline the special nature of the occasion, just as in the last act
the change to boisterous revelling finale is marked by the movement
from trimeters to iambic tetrameters. Unfortunately, the effect of
these changes in actual performance is something which cannot now
be calculated.

709 Μυρρίνη: Knemon's wife. The name is that of a married woman
elsewhere in Menander (*Heros, Perik., Georg.*), and in P. *Cas.*, T. *Hec.*;
it is therefore unlikely to belong to Knemon's daughter, as ed. pr.
supposes; and some weight may be given to the fact that the daughter
is not given a name in the list of *dramatis personae*. If, as is imaginable,
her father was speaking to her also here, he presumably called her παῖ
or θύγατερ or something similar. In 708 μ]έσοις (ed. pr.) suggests a
remark on the lines of 'I wanted to say this with you all around me',
but we have no clear clue to Knemon's opening remarks, of which an
unknown amount is lost. Kraus calls attention to Julian, *Misopogon*
343 A κατὰ τὸν τοῦ Μενάνδρου Δύσκολον αὐτὸς ἐμαυτῷ πόνους προσετίθην as
a possible reminiscence of a lost line; another possibility is mentioned
below the text. 710-11 also leave a very wide field for conjecture, and
in common with OCT and some others, I leave them without supplement: οὐχὶ σωθ[ῆναι γ' <ἔτ'> ἐ]ῠκτ[ὸ]ν Kraus; alii alia.

711f 'Not one of you could possibly persuade me to change my
mind: (?) you will have to let me have my way.' The imperative
συγχωρήσατε (ed. pr.) is perhaps right.

713 ὅστις ... ᾠόμην: 'as one who thought', 'in that I thought';
ὅστις like Lat. *quippe qui*, cf. KG II.399, and compare ὅς at 163,
Perik. 440 and elsewhere. [For στ confused with τ cf. Introd. III,
p.51, under 'Misreading'. ὅτι τε ed. pr.; ὅτι γε plerique, adopted in
OCT; alii alia. Not ἡμάρτανον ὅτι: cf. Introd. IV, p. 70.]
    τῶν ἁπάντων: 'among all the men in the world': cf. 721, *Misoumenos*
62f νῦν ἢ μακάριον ἢ τρισάθλιον, πάτερ, | δείξεις με τῶν ζώντων ἁπάντων
γεν[όμενον.

714 αὐτάρκης τις: 'a self-contained individual'. As Solon reminded
Croesus (Hdt. 1.32) ἀνθρώπου σῶμα ἓν οὐδὲν αὔταρκές ἐστι ... σκοπέειν
δὲ χρὴ παντὸς χρήματος τὴν τελευτὴν κῇ ἀποβήσεται. Knemon's attempt
at 'self-sufficiency' was sustained, he claims, by his belief that dis-

interested kindness was impossible (719-21): so far he had planned
his life so as to be independent of other men, whose ways he despised.
Faced with a sudden death, from which no plan could have saved him,
he is doubly confuted, both by the situation and by Gorgias' example
of a nobly disinterested act in rescuing him. The earlier contrast
between their two attitudes is now underlined (see on 239f); and
Knemon, by making provision for his family, as he is about to do, at
last recognizes not only his need of others but his obligations to them.
For the claims of αὐτάρκεια balanced against those of one's fellow men,
see especially Aristotle, *Eth. Nic.* 1097 b 8ff τὸ δὲ αὔταρκες λέγομεν οὐκ
αὐτῷ μόνῳ, τῷ ζῶντι βίον μονώτην, ἀλλὰ καὶ γονεῦσι καὶ τέκνοις καὶ γυναικὶ
καὶ ὅλως τοῖς φίλοις καὶ πολίταις, ἐπειδὴ φύσει πολιτικὸν ὁ ἄνθρωπος; and
for general discussion, cf. Schmid, RhM 1959.176ff, and Webster, *SM*
207f, *SM*² 230ff.

715 ὀξεῖαν ... ἄσκοπόν τε: 'sudden and unpredictable'. Dr Treu
refers me to Ps.-Phocylides 117 ἄσκοπός ἐστι βροτῶν θάνατος, τὸ δὲ
μέλλον ἄδηλον. Cf. also Theophrastus, *ap.* Plut. *Mor.* 104 d (=frg. 73
Wimmer) ἄσκοπος γὰρ ἡ τύχη καὶ δεινὴ παρελέσθαι τὰ προπεπονημένα καὶ
μεταρρῖψαι τὴν δοκοῦσαν εὐημερίαν, οὐδένα καιρὸν ἔχουσα τακτόν. [P's
ασκαπτον may derive from ἄσκεπτον substituted, *contra metrum*, as a
synonym. ἄσκεπον 'defenceless', Gallavotti, Webster.]

717 εἶναι καὶ παρεῖναι κτλ.: there must be, as it were, a present help
in trouble. For the pairing of these two words, see e.g. *Iliad* 2.485 ὑμεῖς
γὰρ θεαί ἐστε, πάρεστέ τε, ἴστε τε πάντα; Philemon 118 K ὡς ὄντα τοῦτον
καὶ παρόντ' ἀεὶ σέβου (*sc.* τὸν θεόν). Cf. on 818.

τὸν ἐπικουρήσοντ' ἀεί: cf. Xen. *Anab.* 7.7.42 εὖ μὲν πράττων ἔχει τοὺς
συνησθησομένους, ἐὰν δέ τι σφαλῇ, οὐ σπανίζει τῶν βοηθησόντων 'people
to help him': KG I.175 (c). [Text disputed: γὰρ is probably, but not
certainly, to be read; τη[ed. pr., γγ[Turner. The collocation]ναικα-
παρειναι has suggested to ed. pr. and others some implausible versions
involving parts of the word γυνή; but see (e.g.) 684 καμολισ for καὶ μόλις.]

718-21 ἀλλὰ μὰ τὸν Ἥφαιστον looks forward to the main idea οὐδέν'
εὔνουν ᾠόμην ... ἂν γενέσθαι, the connection between protesting oath
and negative statement being remoter than usual, but not, I think,
so remote as to justify the assumption that the oath emphasizes οὕτω
σφόδρα διεφθάρμην (see on 151, 639). For οὕτω σφόδρα, see on 688; and
for the parenthesis cf. *Georgos* 65ff, aptly quoted by Oguse: ... ἀπαλλαγεὶς
δικέλλης καὶ κακῶν — | [οὕτω] τίς ἐστι σκληρὸς ὁ γέρων τῷ βίῳ — | [τοῦ μειρ]-
ακίου τὰ πράγματ' ἀνέκρινεν. διεφθάρμην in the sense of 'misguided',
'mentally unbalanced' is probably the easiest restoration. The pluperfect is used as a narrative past tense of (δι-)έφθαρμαι (cf. KG I.152);
for the sense, Oguse compares [Dem.] 48.52 διέφθαρται ... καὶ παρα-
φρονεῖ. Other compounds are possible (e.g. κατ-, παρ-); Kapsomenos
suggests οὕτω σφόδρα ⟨γὰρ⟩ ἔφθαρμην.

τοὺς βίους . . . ἔχουσιν is variously emended and interpreted, to no radical effect on the sense. Accepting P's text, with Webster *et al.*, the construction is 'seeing all their different ways of life, how they set their minds on gain'; the subject of ἔχουσιν being indefinite, and understood from the context; and the clause τοὺς λογισμοὺς . . . ἔχουσι, which develops and explains τοὺς βίους, following in parallel without connection: compare *Perik.* 38f τὰ λοιπὰ δ' αὐτὸς εἴρηχ', ὃν τρόπον | ὁ μὲν ᾤχετο, κτλ.; and Apollodoros 13 Κ δεῖ τὸν ἀκροατήν . . . πρὸ τῶν λεγομένων τὸν βίον διασκοπεῖν | ποῖός τις ὁ λέγων καὶ πόθεν ('the listener should consider the speaker's personal qualities before his speech'). οὐδένα ἂν γενέσθαι is the oblique form of the potential οὐδεὶς ἂν γένοιτο. [ἑκάστων . . . θ' ὃν τρόπον ed. pr.; ἑκάστους . . . θ' ὃν τρόπον OCT *et al.*; ἑκάστους, τοὺς λογισμούς, ὃν τρόπον Treu; ἑκάστου Gallavotti.]

722f 'One man, Gorgias, has managed to give me concrete proof (of kindness)' πεῖραν δέδωκε: cf. 770 (with gen.), πεῖραν ἔργῳ δεδωκέναι Dem. *de Cor.* (18).107. εἷς . . . Γοργίας: cf. *Perik.* 280f εἰσὶ δ' οἱ ξένοι | οἱ περιβηότοι Σωσίας εἷς οὑτοσί, and see further Schwab, in Schanz, *Beitr. z. historischen Syntax* 13 (1895) 79f.

724-9 Knemon's *dyskolía* not returned by Gorgias: cf. 247-54. The tough old man melted by generosity: cf. *Georgos* 55-74; and compare Euclio in P. *Aul.* (above, under 708-49 (ii)); see further Webster, *SM* 118f, 127.

724ff τὸν γὰρ οὐκ ἐῶντά τ' αὐτόν . . .: *sc.* ἐμέ. Similarly οὔτε . . . οὔτε . . . οὐ . . . οὐ at Eur. *Hip.* 1321ff, the change from connection to asyndeton possibly reflecting the heightened emotion of the speaker. See Denniston, *Particles* 510 (iv), with other examples; and in Comedy e.g. Alexis, *Thrason* 92 Κ οὔτε . . . οὐ . . . οὐ . . . οὔτε . . . οὐ. Here, I take it, the desire for a close association between neg. and participle – a pattern set by οὐκ ἐῶντα – has produced οὐ . . . τε (twice) instead of οὔτε. Cf. οὐ χαίρων τ' 7 above, and for single τε connecting a clause with a neg., see also *Sam.* 214f. [724: τὸν γὰρ αὐτὸν οὐκ ἐῶντα ed. pr.; τὸν γὰρ οὐκ ἐῶνθ' ἑαυτὸν . . . οὐ βοηθήσανθ' ἑαυτῷ OCT (Fraenkel). P's defective metre at the end is variously mended: ⟨γε⟩ Page *et al.*; ⟨τι⟩ Bingen, Treu; πρὸς τὴν θύραν Arnott. For the crasis τἠμῇ cf. Ar. *Birds* 815.]

725 εἰς οὐδὲν μέρος 'not in anything', 'not at all': μέρος = *res*, *negotium* ('branch, business, matter' LSJ) as at 767, *Perik.* 107 and elsewhere in Hellenistic Greek.

726 Cf. Pan's description of the old man at 9ff, and Gorgias' at 334f. He never volunteered a remark to Gorgias, and only replied with a bad grace when spoken to. ἡδέως goes with λαλήσαντα, not σέσωκε (ed. pr. *et al.*): the text is punctuated accordingly.

727 ὅπερ ἂν ἄλλος, καὶ δικαίως: 'whereas another man would have said, quite justifiably...' ὅπερ adverbial; εἶπεν understood after its subject ἄλλος; the comment καὶ δικαίως as normally (see on 774f); then the hypothetical retort is quoted. This in brief seems the best explanation of a much discussed passage: I owe it to A. M. Dale. [(i) *The adverbial neuter rel. introducing an adversative statement* ('whereas', 'although'): see LSJ s.v. ὅς A.b.iv.3, ὅσπερ II.1, quoting *inter alia* Thuc. 2.40 ('We are distinguished by our combination of audacity and calculation') ὃ τοῖς ἄλλοις ἀμαθία μὲν θράσος, λογισμὸς δὲ ὄκνον φέρει; and for ὅπερ Apollonius Dyscolus *de Pron.* 103.7, where Schneider gives more examples and a useful discussion (*Grammatici Graeci* I.ii (1912) 126f): he pertinently compares τὸ δέ, τὸ δέ γε as at Plato, *Apol.* 23 a οἴονται γάρ με ... ταῦτα αὐτὸν εἶναι σοφὸν ἃ ἂν ἄλλον ἐξελέγξω· τὸ δὲ κινδυνεύει ... τῷ ὄντι ὁ θεὸς σοφὸς εἶναι 'whereas in fact...' (ii) *Verb of saying understood with direct quotation*: see on 539f; examples could be multiplied. This is the only likely, if not the only possible ellipse. The context calls for a past potential (i.e. εἶπεν rather than εἴποι); for this ellipse with ἄν present cf. KG I.244. The easy correction ἄλλος for ἄλλως (P) has several advantages, the most obvious being that it makes better sense to contrast Gorgias' action with what another man would have said in the same case than to contrast Gorgias' action with what Gorgias would have said if the case were altered. (iii) *Alternatives*: Some critics prefer to mark a full stop after ὅμως, whereupon the ὅπερ clause can be taken purely as preparatory to what follows; but it seems unnatural and unnecessary to divorce the two remarks in this way. So, e.g., Mette, Gallavotti (retaining P's ἄλλως); Bingen also retains ἄλλως and emends to νῦν τόδ' ἐστί in 729. Other solutions aimed at the difficulty felt in the ὅπερ, the ellipse, or both, include ὅτε περ ἄλλος, κ.δ. Schwabl; ὅπερ ἂν ἄλλος κἀδικαίωσ' Szemerényi; εἶπ' ἂν ἄλλος, κ.δ. OCT (Lloyd-Jones). Thierfelder and others suppose a line to have been lost. It is wholly unsuitable for Gorgias to intervene and speak the words ὅπερ ... σοί (or ... σοὶ νῦν): the view that he does originates with ed. pr.]

728f ἡμῖν: 'my family'.

οὐδ' ἐγὼ σοὶ νῦν: sc. χρήσιμος γενήσομαι.

729 τί δ' ἐστί; 'What's the matter?', as commonly, with or without the δέ. The actor playing Gorgias presumably shows signs of strong emotion, and possibly makes as if to protest – the natural reaction of modesty to praise. μειράκιον (instead of the name) could be said with a touch of impatience. Apart from adding life and informality to the long speech, the dramatist achieves by this means a deft and sudden transition to Knemon's next point. Note the similar function of ἀλλὰ κατάκλινόν με, θύγατερ 740, and Sostratos' interruptions of Gorgias at 288, 293.

ἐάν τ': probably rightly restored, since the interjection with οἴομαι δέ (rather than οἴομαι γάρ) suggests that the expected alternative is already in mind. [So, among others, Kraus, q.v. for further justification of the text given: νῦν τί ἐστι; μειράκιον δ᾽, ἐὰν ἐγὼ ed. pr., unsatisfactorily. Cf. Introd. IV, Note D (i).]

729-39 The turning point of the whole play. Knemon gives, as from his deathbed, what amount to the terms of a last will and testament, but with the proviso that they shall be effective whether he recovers or not. His action in adopting Gorgias as his son and thereby providing for the future of his family shows simply and directly that the misanthrope has made a major concession to humanity: he is doing, in essence, what a sensible and equitable man would have been expected to do in similar circumstances.

He has no son of his own, indeed no close or trusted relations so far as we know. If he dies without making satisfactory arrangements for their future, his death will leave his daughter without a guardian and the estate without a master; both the girl, as heiress (ἐπίκληρος), and the property will fall to the claim of his nearest male relative by blood – a situation full of undesirable possibilities, and one familiar enough to be taken for granted by the poet and his audience. No father of normal feelings would wish it to arise: the degree of protection afforded by the law might well prove a poor substitute for paternal forethought.

Gorgias, as the girl's half-brother on the mother's side, cannot act as her official guardian in his own right. He is nevertheless an eminently suitable person to do so, as Knemon recognizes (737); and now (as Mr J. H. Kells remarks to me) he is appointed to that position by her father in the spirit of the law cited by [Dem.] 46.18 ἣν ἂν ἐγγυήσῃ ἐπὶ δικαίοις δάμαρτα εἶναι ἢ πατὴρ ἢ ἀδελφὸς ὁμοπάτωρ ἢ πάππος ὁ πρὸς πατρός, ἐκ ταύτης εἶναι παῖδας γνησίους. ἐὰν δὲ μηδεὶς ᾖ τούτων, ἐὰν μὲν ἐπίκληρός τις ᾖ, τὸν κύριον ἔχειν, ἐὰν δὲ μὴ ᾖ, ὅτῳ ἂν ἐπιτρέψῃ (sc. ὁ πατὴρ) τοῦτον κύριον εἶναι: 'this appears to envisage the more regular situation where the father has appointed a person to act as κύριος of his daughter after his own decease.' As to the adoption, it is worth quoting [Dem.] 59.55-58: ... ἐπείσθη δὴ τὸ παιδίον ... ποιήσασθαι υἱὸν αὐτοῦ, λογισμὸν ἀνθρώπινον καὶ εἰκότα λογιζόμενος, ὅτι πονηρῶς μὲν ἔχοι καὶ οὐ πολλὴ ἐλπὶς εἴη αὐτὸν περιγενήσεσθαι, τοῦ δὲ μὴ λαβεῖν τοὺς συγγενεῖς τὰ αὑτοῦ μηδ᾽ ἄπαις τετελευτηκέναι ἐποιήσατο τὸν παῖδα καὶ ἀνέλαβεν ὡς αὑτόν – this of a man who, it is claimed, had long ago quarrelled with his family, and (though without Knemon's additional problem of a daughter to provide for) was persuaded when gravely ill to establish a bona fide heir by recognizing a male infant as his child.

In the latter passage, the orator goes on to argue that his witness would never have acted in that way if he had been well; Knemon, however, wishes to resign his new-found responsibilities at once and end his days in peace. He recognizes that even if he recovers, his own temperament will prevent him from finding his daughter a husband, as a father should (732ff); and accordingly (with what inner feelings we are left to imagine) he relinquishes from now onward all title to the land which has been the basis of his long-cherished independence, and will have it divided – half to provide a dowry (and hence secure a good marriage) for his daughter; half to remain with Gorgias and to be his patrimony. Gorgias' mother has theoretically been in his protection since she left Knemon (see on 22); and he is now to provide both her and his adoptive father with the care and maintenance due from a son. Gorgias readily agrees; Sostratos stands by, a silent witness of the transaction.

With these arrangements, it is evident that the complications of the plot are largely solved; but not quite – there is still tidying to be done. The betrothal of Sostratos to the girl (which is imminent), and the arrival of his father (which is expected, 556) will develop the marriage theme further; Gorgias is to find further reward for his virtues (842ff), and Knemon further retribution. The right attitude which he has now adopted is tainted by his persistent and uncongenial determination to be left alone; and in the last act he is to be forcibly and farcically prised from the shell into which he is trying so hard to withdraw.

[For fuller information on the legal background to Knemon's decision, see U. E. Paoli, Mus. Helv. 1961.53-62; J.-H. Michel, Chron. d'Égypte 38 (1963) no. 76, 287-296; and A. R. W. Harrison, CR 1963.200ff, reviewing Brindesi, *La famiglia Attica*; the index to Wyse's edition of Isaeus, s.vv. Heiresses, Adopted sons, Adoption, leads to most of the relevant texts. Poets of Middle and New Comedy (not unlike modern writers of detective stories) were very ready to turn the law to the service of their plots when the situation involved was familiar or could easily be made clear. The position of heiresses provided material for several plays, among them Apollodoros, *Epidikazomenos* (= T. *Phormio*), and Menander's two plays entitled *Epikleros*, one of which (like *Epitrepontes*) had a much admired scene of debate. Among the barbed remarks about Athenian justice in Aristophanes' *Wasps* is Philokleon's unashamed assertion that the courts can be persuaded to set aside a father's will and adjudge an heiress daughter to an importunate claimant (583ff); the legal position of Athena as Zeus's daughter enters into a joke at *Birds* 1652ff.]

730 'I think I shall (*sc.* die), and I do seem to be ill.' Like Eng. 'perhaps', 'it seems', ἴσως 'is used to soften or qualify a positive assertion' (LSJ) as well as to present a mere possibility: see, e.g., 239, 775. [ἴσθ᾽ ὡς Kassel: neat but unnecessary. The οιον of P¹ might, I suppose, be a hasty misreading of a group of letters written cursively (like ιοθι for πωσ in 95); or, as οἶον, an attempt to clarify the ἴσως which it came to displace. I doubt if it conceals a variant reading: e.g. οἴομαι δὲ καὶ κακῶς, οἶόν γ᾽ ἔχω. 731: που satisfies the considerations of sense and palaeography; for the alliteration, cf. οὐχὶ πόρρω που ποιεῖ

Anaxilas, *Neottis* 22 K (end of troch. tetr.) and on 735 below. νῦν ed.
pr., δή Kraus, περισωθῶ OCT (Kassel), alii alia.]

731ff ἅ τε ... ἄνδρα τε: inelegant connection by the standards of
formal prose, but possibly what Menander wrote. Cf. on 39. Knemon
intends, though he does not use the word, that Gorgias shall be κύριος
of his estate and his daughter: see the general discussion above.
[ἅ γ' is given as the reading of P by ed. pr., and some (including OCT)
prefer it; δ' is added after ἄνδρα by ed. pr., and adopted generally, as
in OCT; ταύτῃ Gallavotti.]

733 εἰ ... καὶ σφόδρ' ὑγιαίνοιμ' ἐγώ: 'even supposing I *should* get
well ...' εἰ καὶ σφόδρα (like εἰ ὅτι μάλιστα), as (e.g.) at *Georgos* frg. 1.4,
εἰ σφόδρα 284 above, and elsewhere; but here the supposition is a
remote one: hence the opt. [Cf. KG II.478 (*b*); the present tense is
probably to be restored rather than the aorist. ὑγιεινῶς ἔχω ed. pr.;
ὑγιαίνειν δοκῶ Foss, Mette; alii alia.]

734f Knemon admits what we have already been led to believe of
him, 336ff, 355ff. Cf. 747.

735f ἐμὲ μέν answered informally by τἄλλα: cf. 509 n. (τὰ δ' ἐμὰ
van Groningen; τάδε δὲ Jean Martin). The plural ἐᾶτε presumably
includes Myrrhine: cf. 739.

ἂν ζῶ: Knemon's whole speech is coloured by his insistence that he
is likely to die soon – a good argument, in my view, for this conjecture
rather than one of several other possibilities, such as οὕτω OCT (Page,
after ed. pr.) ἤδη Kraus, μένοντα Treu: it gives an appropriate edge to
what is otherwise a commonplace idea (cf. Headlam-Knox on Herondas
2.9). The jingle of sound, which Kraus finds objectionable, may not
have been so to Menander. It is hard to say how far the apparent
sound effects in Greek authors were conspicuous or deliberate, but
note in this speech the assonance of δεῖ γὰρ εἶναι καὶ παρεῖναι 717;
repeated endings, 719; ἕτερον ἑτέρῳ τῶν ἀπάντων 721; repeated οὐ +
ptcp., 725ff; 'rhymed' line-endings, 744f; ἔστ' ἀρεστά 746; and cf.
Apollodoros, *Kitharoidos* 6 K οὐ πανταχοῦ Φρύξ εἰμι· τοῦ ζῆν ἦν ὁρῶ |
κρεῖττον τὸ μὴ ζῆν, χρήσομαι τῷ κρείττονι. ['Perhaps ἦν ζῶ' (Ha. ap.
Lond.). This may be what P had to copy, for the sequence μενηνζωζην
would easily account for the omission: but it is not clear that M.
himself ever used ἦν instead of his normal ἄν. ἦν is given by one source
in frg. 665, and there printed by Koerte; it is once or twice (possibly
wrongly) presented by MSS in quotations of other poets of later
Comedy, e.g. Apollodoros 6 K, quoted above. On sound effects, cf.
J. D. Denniston in *Oxford Class. Dict*, s.v. Assonance, and *Greek
Prose Style*, Ch. iv; and J. Defradas, REA 1958.36-49 – a brief recent
paper with some further references.]

736-7 'You are sensible, thank Heavens; and you care for your sister, as is right'. Probably rightly, ed. pr. takes νοῦν ἔχεις ... εἰκότως together as one sentence, assuming that a τε connecting its two parts is lost from P. Knemon breaks into his instructions to Gorgias with a reflection on his qualifications to carry them out. For σὺν τοῖς θεοῖς as taken here, see *Perinthia* frg. 7 and Lucian, *Hermot.* 65 σὺν θεῷ γὰρ οἶσθα νεῖν, εἰ καί τις ἄλλος; and compare Lat. *deum uirtute*, as at P. *Trin.* 355 *al.* For εἰκότως cf. P. Didot I.36f (Koerte I³, p. 144) ἤδη 'στιν, πάτερ, | ἐμὸν σκοπεῖν τοῦτ' εἰκότως. Knemon at last recognizes what Gorgias has earlier asserted – the strength of the natural bonds of οἰκειότης between children of the same mother (239ff, 318f), which persist in spite of the fact that he has (until now) had no legal claim to act in his half-sister's interests. Cf. 253ff, and the general discussion under 729-39 above; for κηδεμών, see *Georgos* 56, frg. 605, and LSJ, s.v.2. [Ed. pr. adding τε after ἐπιδίδου in 738, presents νοῦν ἔχεις ... εἰκότως as a parenthesis. Lloyd-Jones, in OCT, gives νοῦν ἔχεις in parenthesis, taking σὺν τοῖς θεοῖς with τἄλλα πρᾶττε, κτλ.; then, after a stop, κηδεμὼν εἶ τῆς ἀδελφῆς· εἰκότως, κτλ. εἰκότως has, I think, a good claim to be associated with κηδεμών; for the rest, apart from the point that Knemon seems to be intended to speak jerkily and with labour, a decision is harder to reach.]

738 ἐπιδιδόναι προῖκα is a regular phrase, as is διδόναι + ἐπί 844. By having his estate divided in half, to produce a dowry of a talent, Knemon is possibly unusually generous to his daughter; but after his own fashion he was fond of her. From the dramatist's point of view the arrangement is simple and gives an obvious impression of equity; it may therefore have to be judged by dramatic standards rather than by the typical conditions of real life. διαμετρήσας implies dividing the land with suitably inscribed boundary stones (ὅροι) of which many examples have survived. A dowry need not of course be given in cash, but might be variously made up to its stated value in land and other assets according as the parties agreed. See further on 842-4 and works quoted there. [... τό] θ' ἕτερον ed. pr. (so OCT); θήμισυ OCT (Maas) and others – possibly rightly: cf. Ar. *Lys.* 116, 132. ⟨τὴν⟩ πρ. Kraus *et al.*; but the sense 'the customary dowry' seems unwelcome here.]

739 διοίκει 'provide for', of dependents: ἀλλὰ νὴ Δία τὴν ἀδελφὴν καλῶς διῴκηκεν, Dem. 24.202. This matter-of-fact instruction is apparently as near as Knemon gets to proposing a reconciliation with his wife; cf. on ἐᾶτε 735, and on vv. 8-11 of the Hypothesis.

740f Knemon, who had never used one word where none would do, might well find congenial the virtue of economical brevity. The theme is wearisomely elaborated by Libanius' Dyskolos, *Decl.* 26. [νῦν δὲ] (ed. pr.) does not fit the space well. The gratuitous δ' in τῶν δ' ἀναγκαίων is generally accepted, but note P's behaviour at 729, 736: 'δὲ fortasse delendum' Jean Martin. 741: πλείον' is preferable to πλεῖον (ed. pr.)

in view of the doubtful authenticity of the latter form in Menander; but see Thierfelder in Koerte, vol. 2, p. 294, and note the possibility of ἐπὶ πλεῖον in 528. πλὴν ἐκεῖνο· πρόσιθι, παῖ OCT (Shipp).]

742-5 Knemon's claim to represent an ideal of conduct (however paradoxical it seems to the dispassionate observer) is reinforced by the example of an equitable decision which he has just given; his visionary picture of a city of just and contented men is moving in spite of (perhaps even because of) the lamentable failure of his own life. Once more the dramatist attempts to balance the unadmirable features of his character with a certain sympathy.

Passages of social criticism in this idealizing form are not uncommon in later Comedy: a good parallel is P. *Aul.* 478ff (Megadorus on rich men marrying poor girls, as he proposes to do himself): si idem faciant ceteri ... et multo fiat ciuitas concordior, | et inuidia nos minore utamur quam utimur, etc.; cf. Baton, *Androphonos* 3 K (quoted by Kassel) εἰ τοῦτον ἔζων πάντες ὃν ἐγὼ ζῶ βίον, | οὔτ' ἄτοπος ἦν ἂν οὔτε μοιχὸς οὐδὲ εἷς. In tracing their dramatic ancestry, Leo (*Plaut. Forsch.*², 113ff) rightly stresses the influence of Euripides (compare, e.g., *Phoen.* 1015ff with Men., frg. 543); but in metre and manner the present example seems more closely akin to the comic side of the tradition in which Menander worked. See in general under 708-47 (iv); for the 'idealizing form', Ar. *Birds* 785ff ('if men had wings like birds ...'), and *Thes.* 832ff; for the introductory βούλομ' εἰπεῖν, cf. Fraenkel, *de med. et nov. com.*, 79ff, quoting *inter alia* Ar. *Kn.* 565, 595; *Cl.* 1116; *Birds* 1076, 1101; Aristophon, *Iatros* 4 K: βούλομαι δ' αὐτῷ προσειπεῖν οἷός εἰμι τοὺς τρόπους.

[742-3 περὶ βίου, εἴπερ εὖνοι ed. pr., but β]ίου does not suit P, and εἴπερ εὖν]οι is too long. Possibly ὑπὲρ ἐ]μοῦ (Lond. ap. Sydn., OCT); several alternatives are offered for εἰ τοιοῦτ]οι, which seems very likely to be right. Comedy normally admits hiatus after περί.]

743ff The evils of the law-courts, the prisons and war are perennial, as is the self-seeking which Knemon sees as their cause; but it is possible that events of the immediate past made the lines strike the audience with particular vividness. See Introd. I, pp. 7ff and notes. An apt comparison for Knemon's visionary state of society appears at Plato, *Laws* 679 b and following, as Post and others have pointed out: cf. Webster, *SM*² 231.

αὑτοὺς 'each other', as e.g. in 49; cf. KG I.573, *NTGramm.* §287. On the 'rhymed' endings, 743-4, cf. 735 n.

746 ταῦτα = ista, 'your ways' in common with those of the rest of mankind. [Some prefer to punctuate after ἀρεστά (so ed. pr.) or οὕτω (so Kassel); OCT offers οὐ]κ ἴσως ταῦτ' ἔστ' ἀρεστά· μᾶλλον οὕτω πράττετε (]κ Roberts); for οὕτω πράττετε, see 135 n.]

748f Gorgias' ready acceptance of the arrangements is combined with an admirable eagerness to promote Sostratos' cause and to call the old man into consultation: Knemon rudely refuses.

749 σοὶ συνδοκοῦν: 'if you agree', συνδοκοῦν acc. absolute, as at Xen. *HG* 2.3.51 *al.*

750 οὗτος: 'Look here...'; impatiently, for he wants to be left alone. [αὐτός Webster.]

751 γάρ introduces an answer implying dissent: 'Don't bother me' '(Yes I will) for here is a suitor who wants to meet you'. Cf. Denniston, *Particles* 74 (2).

752 τὴν κόρην αἰτῶν τις οὗτος: αἰτεῖν as, e.g., Hdt. 3.1, E. *El.* 21, Plut. *vit Them.* 24 *al.*; οὗτος deictic (cf. οὑτοσί 167). The whole expression is defined by ὅ σε συνεκσώσας, and the pronoun emphatically repeated by οὑτοσί in the next line. [Restoration quite uncertain. Suggestions include τὴν κόρην αἰτῶν ⟨γαμεῖν⟩ τις Kraus; οὐδὲ ἓν ἔτι τούτων μοι μέλει ed. pr. τὴν κόρην αἰτῶν – (Κν.) τίς; (Γο.) ⟨ὅστις;⟩ (Κν.) οὐδὲ ἕν OCT (Lloyd-Jones and Barrett). Cf. Introd. IV, p. 60 n. 1.]

753 ὁ ποῖος; 'Who?' – having failed to recognize Sostratos as 'the man who helped to rescue you'. Cf. 146 above, *Epitr.* 216, Headlam-Knox on Herondas 6.48. 'The use of ποῖος without the article' observes Bluck on Plato, *Meno* 95 d 4, 'usually indicates surprise, indignation and/or disbelief. Normally, when asking simply for information, one uses ὁ ποῖος or ποῖός τις.' [P's dicolon after οὑτοσί may mark the break in the speech as Gorgias turns to address Sostratos: Introd. III, 45f.]

754f ἐπικέκαυται μέν: 'He's certainly sunburnt....' – the result of warm work on the land: even that hardship brings its reward. Cf. 535, and under 522-45; for the μέν (which does not demand γεωργὸς ⟨δ'⟩ ἐστί; to follow), cf. Denniston, *Particles* 380ff.

It is possible in view of this and the following lines that Sostratos is still dressed as for digging: i.e. that he has not put his *chlanis* on again: see on 370. The sunburn may well have been left to the audience's imagination, but for the possibility of representing it by a special variant of the mask, cf. Webster, *Griechische Bühnenaltertümer* (1963) 43, under 'Rhodos'.

καὶ μάλ' ὦ πάτερ: after ed. pr., Gorgias is generally assumed to have been the speaker, but Sostratos may rather have spoken for himself: for ὦ πάτερ, cf. 171. οὐ τρυφῶν ... ἡμέραν was apparently said by another character, possibly Knemon, as this text assumes; we cannot tell if he continued after ἡμέραν.

755-60 Damage to the top of the page in P obscures a few moments of the dialogue, and makes reconstruction too hazardous to be much use. Knemon apparently accepts (or does not reject) the proposed marriage, then asks to be taken in (757-8); Gorgias may say 'Take care of him' (759) to his mother or sister (or to Simiche coming from the house?); I prefer to think that it is also Gorgias who says 'It remains to betroth my sister', and that Sostratos accepts. The girl and her mother (astonishingly, by modern standards) take no part, but apparently go in after Knemon.

[756 gives no firm basis for supplementation: ἑνὸς τα[λάντου Barrett, who suggests that a verse has been lost from the top of the page, and is followed in OCT; τ]ὸ̣ γένος ψέ̣[γοις vel sim. plerique. 757 is corrupt, as the metre shows. 758 init., see below; at the end, perhaps καὶ̣ δ[ὴ Σιμίχη προσέρχεται, accepting Barrett's καὶ̣ δ[ή. 759: double points after τούτου may indicate a change of person addressed, not a change of speaker (see on 753). 760: perhaps ἐπανα̣[μεῖναι δ' οὐκ ἴσ]ως ἐ̣[μοὶ πρέπει or something of similar sense. Kassel suggests that the 'sister' mentioned is Sostratos' sister; and in OCT Lloyd-Jones accordingly ascribes τὸ λο[ιπὸν – τὴν] ἀδελφήν (without further restoration) to Sostratos, and begins Gorgias' speech from ἐπανε[(sic), in both cases doubtfully. See under 784ff.]

758 'Wheel me in.' P almost certainly had ε(ι)σκυκλειτ' whether as plural imperative or singular followed by τε.

The manner of Knemon's entry at 690 and of his exit here suggest strongly that the bed or couch on which he is lying was in fact wheeled (or rolled) out and in and not carried by the characters available to do so or by extras brought on for the purpose. His request therefore should not be taken simply as a metaphorical way of saying 'Take me in'; no more is it a plain and literal instruction; like Aristophanes on two notorious occasions, but with a less blatant comic effect, Menander is playing on the stage convention which he is using and the tragic scenes which his own dramatic situation recalls: see *Ach.* 407ff, *Thes.* 95ff, 265: (Agathon) εἴσω τις ὡς τάχιστά μ' εἰσκυκλησάτω.

The present scene does not show beyond question whether the couch itself had wheels or appeared on a movable platform, the much discussed *eccyclema* or one of its kin; but whatever machinery (if any) was available at the side doors in Menander's day, we may well think of a wheeled couch as the simplest and best device for his present purpose: the major speech can then be delivered from centre stage and not immediately outside Knemon's house. The dramatic point will still be taken even if (as is likely) scenes involving 'wheeling in' and 'wheeling out' could be staged, at least at the central door, with machinery more elaborate than a piece of furniture: for texts and discussion see Pickard-Cambridge, *Theatre of D.*, 100ff, and A. M. Dale in *Wiener Studien* 69 (1956) 96ff.

The fact that Knemon is carried out on his couch by Sikon and Getas in the last act (905ff) is interesting but independent: carrying the couch there is part of the business of moving the old man quietly

THE DYSKOLOS

while he is asleep, and whatever happened here could be ignored
without improbability.

[ἐγκ]υκλεῖτ᾽ Mette *et al.*; but the active of this compound is
not so far known, and the sense less good; – μὴ ᾽νο]χλεῖτ᾽ – (Quincey)
is ingenious but hard to reconcile with the traces of letters preserved.
Play with dramatic convention: a neat example is preserved in T. *Andria*
481-94 (483ff = M. *Andria* frgg. 36-37): the midwife gives her instructions from the street door, for the audience's benefit; but Simo finds
this so strange that he suspects a plot. The incident is however
differently interpreted by Gomme, *Essays in Gk Hist. and Lit.*, 260 n. 1.
Wheeled couch or bed: Webster refers me to the child's bed on a Caeretan
hydria of ca.530 in the Louvre (E.702; G. M. A. Richter, *Ancient
furniture*, fig. 172).]

761 ὁ πατήρ: 'her father' or 'my father'? If Sostratos is the speaker
(as I think is likely), the latter is more natural: he is then anticipating
the discussion whose concluding stages begin the next act.

761-3 Gorgias, as his sister's guardian, now betroths her to Sostratos.
The text given is far from certain; without more evidence the precise
wording of the transaction remains irrecoverable. 'Accordingly, I
betroth and give her to you in the sight of all, agreeing to pay what
is just in full, Sostratos.'

ἐγγυῶ, δίδωμι in asyndeton (ed. pr.'s δίδωμί τε is metrically unacceptable: Introd. IV, Note D (i)). πάντων ... ἐναντίον: *coram populo*.
Gorgias is apparently trying hard for a suitably official form of words;
if so, his attempt is not without its humour, since the transaction is
only public in the sense that it is witnessed by the audience; more
obvious humour of the same kind appears at P. *Ba.* 335f. ὥστε is
assumed to function in the sense of ἐφ᾽ ᾧ τε 'ea condicione ut': LSJ,
s.v., B.I.4; KG II.504f. For πλήρη cf. Xen. *Anab.* 7.5.5 φέρων πλήρη
τὸν μισθόν; and for ἐνεγκεῖν, which may literally mean '(that you
should) receive' rather than '(that I should) pay', see LSJ s.v. φέρω,
A.IV.5, A.VI.3. For parallels to the form of betrothal, see under
842-4, noting in addition Alexis, *Epikleros* 79 K ἀλλ᾽ ἔγωγ᾽, ὦ παῖ,
δίδωμι, καὶ ποιήσω πάνθ᾽ ὅσα | οὗτος αἰτεῖται παρ᾽ ἡμῶν (ἔγωγ᾽, ὦ Dobree:
ἐγὼ cod.).

[761: τήνδε γ]οῦν ed. pr., adopted in OCT and elsewhere. 762:
[μαρτύρω]ν ἐναντίον (ed. pr.) is awkward (*a*) because there are no
witnesses apart from the audience, which could hardly be referred to
in this way; (*b*) because of πάντων. Lloyd-Jones suggests, but does not
adopt, ὀμνύω]ν, to govern ἐνεγκεῖν; hardly [τῶν γ᾽ ἐμῶ]ν (Diano).
763 is desperately difficult, certainly corrupt at the beginning, where
OCT obelizes: conjectures include <προῖκ᾽> ἐνεγκεῖν Gallavotti;
ἐξενεγκεῖν ed. pr.; ὡς δίκαιόν ἐστι Roberts. Before the gap in P, what
appears as the lower part of a vertical stroke seems just possible as part
of lambda in the sequence πλ[η; after the gap, what appears in the

264

photographs as a minute speck of ink gives none but the slightest
support to]ρ; πλ[ή]ρη can only be accepted with extreme reserve.
Perhaps, among several suggestions, ἐστ' ἐπ' αὐτῇ (after Kraus and
Kamerbeek) is what Menander wrote: this assumes εστιπι[αυ]τη in
P, again not wholly satisfactory; perhaps πρ[; not πα[(i.e. not πάντη).
Ed. pr., OCT and others do not restore.]

764-71 Gorgias praises Sostratos' sincerity, shown in their first
meeting (302ff), his resolution (cf. 370, 379ff), and his willingness to
set aside his upbringing and turn his hand to hard work. These simple
virtues naturally impress the young countryman; but the praise is
tempered with a discrimination conforming to the maturity we expect
from him (28f), and in contrast with Knemon's leap to a conclusion
from superficial appearances, 754f. See further on 522-45.

764f οὐ πεπλασμένῳ ἤθει: 'not misrepresenting yourself', but ἁπλῶς
'frankly', 'unaffectedly'. Similarly πλάσασθαι τὸν τρόπον τὸν αὑτοῦ is
to dissimulate', Lys. 19.60.

765f It is best to have the stop after ἕνεκα, not after τρυφερὸς ὤν
with P, followed (e.g.) by ed. pr. and Kraus.]

766ff 'It is in this above all that the real man is revealed, if he is
prepared, although rich, to put himself on a level with the poor, for
he will bear changes of fortune sensibly.' So I should construe; for
the general sentiment (and the somewhat tangled expression of it),
cf. Gorgias above at 271-87, and frg. 634 τοῦτ' ἔστιν ἀνδρὸς νοῦν
ἔχοντος, οὐκ ἐὰν | ἀνασπάσας τις τὰς ὀφρῦς οἴμοι λαλῇ | ἀλλ' ὃς τά ‹γ'›
αὑτοῦ πράγματ' ἐγκρατῶς φέρει. The illogical correlation between main
clause and relative clause is of a kind which is familiar in sententious
reflections: e.g. Thuc. 6.14 τὸ καλῶς ἄρξαι τοῦτ' εἶναι, ὃς ἂν τὴν πατρίδα
ὠφελήσῃ . . .; cf. 4.18 σωφρόνων δὲ ἀνδρῶν (sc. ἐστιν) οἵτινες . . . ἔθεντο;
2.44 τὸ δ' εὐτυχές, οἳ ἂν . . . λάχωσιν.

ἐν τούτῳ τῷ μέρει: cf. on 725.

[768: P's reading suggests that ἐξισοῦσθαι (or ἐξισῶσαι, Jacques)
may perhaps have been a variant, but if so there is no reason to prefer
it. 769: μεταβολὴν OCT (Page). τύχ[ης being doubtfully read, Lloyd-
Jones considers μεταβολῆς . . . πλ[άνην.]

770-1 δέδωκας πεῖραν: cf. on 722f. διαμένοις μόνον τοιοῦτος 'I only
hope you will stay the same'. The wish is in effect a conditional clause,
'if only . . . etc.': cf. S. *Phil.* 527ff, Ar. *Birds* 1315, Gow on [Theocr.]
27.16: χαιρέτω ἁ Παφία· μόνον ἵλαος Ἄρτεμις εἴη. Sostratos' reply is
a modification of διαμένοις . . . τοιοῦτος, and presumably means 'I
shall be much better': i.e. understand ἔσομαι. Cf. on 829-31. [κρείττω[ν
ἐγώ Gallavotti, Lond. *et al.*; κρείττω[ν τάχ' ἄν Kraus; alii alia.]

772 Sostratos' youthful impetuosity corrects itself: cf. 75.

773f The cue for Kallippides' entry: cf. *Sam.* 65f ἀλλ' εἰς καλὸν γὰρ τοῦτον εἰσιόνθ' ὁρῶ | τὸν Παρμένοντα. . . . Gorgias is presumed to know him, at least by sight and reputation, as the owner of a neighbouring estate: cf. 39ff, 415f.

774f 'He's certainly a rich man, and deserves it: he's an indomitable farmer.' Rich, and therefore naturally suspect by Gorgias' standards, but deserving his wealth as a man who will not be worsted in 'fighting the rocks'. It is a nice point that G. has only just finished praising the son of the family for his hard work. νὴ Δία πλούσιος γ[∪ — is suspect on metrical grounds: cf. Introd. IV, Note D (i), and Addenda, below, p. 305f.

καὶ δικαίως γε: similarly δικαίως 'deservedly' 644; καὶ δίκαιως 727, *Epitr.* 73, *Sam.* 174, cf. Plato, *Theaet.* 143 d; καὶ μάλα δικαίως 602, frg. 740.13, cf. Lucian, *Timon* 25; καὶ δικαίως τοῦτό γε Amphis, *Planos* 30 K, 7; fuller forms are given by Ar. *Frogs* 584 οἶδ' οἶδ' ὅτι θυμοῖ, καὶ δικαίως αὐτὸ δρᾷς, and *Thes.* 86 καὶ δίκαιά ‹γ'› ἂν πάθοις. [Some prefer ‹καὶ› δίκαιος ‹καὶ› γεωργὸς; others καὶ δικαίως ‹γ' ὡς›; it is plain in any case that P's fault was caused by the repetition of similar or identical groups of letters as (obviously) in ἀπολέλειμμ'.]

775ff 'It seems they've abandoned me.' Kallippides may be too pre-occupied with the thought of missing his lunch to greet either Pan or his son. His late arrival is dramatically necessary, and the audience has been carefully forewarned of it (556, 761 (?)); his hunger is natural, but neatly exploited to provide a few moments' mild amusement in which the poet can motivate the characters' exit before the choral interlude, and hint at the action to follow.

777 εἰς ἀγρόν: 'to the farm'; without the art., as regularly: so ἐξ ἀγροῦ, εἰς πόλιν etc. See on 162ff.

ὀξυπείνως: the adv. was not previously recorded, the adj. known from other comic writers (e.g. Antiphanes 276 K) and elsewhere.

779 τί τοῦτο; 'What does this mean?' – surprised to see Sostratos talking outside.

781 εἰσιὼν οὕτω λαλήσεις . . .: 'Go in, then you can talk to your father alone if you wish.' Cf. *Kith.* 49ff πρὸς ἀγορὰν δ' οὕτως ἅμα | προάγων ἀκούσῃ καὶ τὰ λοίφ' ὧν μοι γενοῦ | σύμβουλος; for οὕτω see LSJ s.v., I.7; for the second person future corresponding to English 'can', and often analogous to a command, see Goodwin, *Moods and Tenses* §69 and KG I.173-6, noting P. Didot I.43f (Koerte I³, p. 144): εἰ δὲ μή, σὺ μὲν βίᾳ | πράξεις ἃ βούλει.

[αὐτῷ OCT *et al.*, with ed. pr., defended by Kraus on the ground that τῷ πατρὶ κ.μ. is an afterthought. αὐτὸς Page. λάλει is generally adopted from P, with the addition of σύ γ' (ed. pr.) or νῦν (plerique: so OCT) or another word to mend the metre.]

782f Gorgias effaces himself: he will stay with his family in Knemon's house, from which he reappears at 821. It seems clear that his mother and sister have gone in with Knemon (cf. 852f, 866-9), and there is no reason (*pace* ed. pr. *et al.*) why Gorgias should return to his own house alone, or why Sostratos should expect him to.

782 οὐ γάρ: 'Won't you?' English, lacking a phrase such as *n'est-ce pas?*, must use a variety of translations for this idiom.

783 μικρὸν διαλιπών, sc. χρόνον: one version of a common phrase illustrated by LSJ s.v. διαλείπω; διαλιπών alone, *Epitr.* 570, *Sam.* 198.

τοίνυν: fourth word, as in Alexis, *Mandragorizomene* 143 K.

Act V (784-969)

784ff A cleverly designed opening to the act. Enter Sostratos with his father from the shrine. Their first words achieve a convincing effect of realism, but are well calculated to arouse interest in the new scene, and to link it, at the appropriate interval of time, with what was happening before the choral interlude.

Sostratos is not completely satisfied. Kallippides, it appears, has accepted with reasoned enlightenment the idea that his son should marry for love, and not wait until the time comes to found a family with a wife from his own social class. But to have his daughter married to a simple farmer like Gorgias – that was too much, an idea to be rejected out of hand. As they go together to find Gorgias (for so we are to presume), the young man is seeking (somewhat resentfully, it seems) to reopen the topic. For the casual motivation of their reappearance together (783, 820), cf. on 233f; Kallippides, as Treu remarks, would naturally wish to meet the head of his future daughter-in-law's family.

This new development of the 'marriage' theme is brought forward at so late a stage partly, as is obvious, in order to round off the plot by uniting the two families in a double celebration – but also to diversify the interest of the closing scenes. It allows the poet to return to the closely related theme of riches and poverty in a manner which recalls the second act, and to make Kallippides something more than a lay figure whose sole purpose is to say 'Yes'.

An ancient audience, accustomed to arranged marriages as a phenomenon of everyday life as well as of drama, would have been less likely to react with surprise or critical condescension than many modern ones. Sudden though Sostratos' move is, it is perfectly consistent with the situation and the portrait we have been given of him; and Gorgias, who until lately has had no prospects of anything but a life of continuing hard work and misery (23ff, 341ff), is an ideal candidate for the attentions of a match-making friend now that Knemon's new dispensation has removed most of his worries. Menander has clearly left the way open for his new development: has he also prepared the audience to expect it? Sostratos' sister may well have been there to be seen in her mother's sacrifice party, even if she is not the Plangon of 430, as some suppose her to be; but her presence on that occasion would hardly create a presumption that more will be heard of her. Kassel has further suggested that she, and not Gorgias' sister, is the ἀδελφή of 760, and would have Sostratos speak of marrying her to Gorgias there. This seems doubtful, both from what can be seen of the immediate context and from Gorgias' words at 821-34: the first

ιe knows of Sostratos' proposal is apparently what he has just over-
ιeard. It seems best to conclude that what hints there have been of
:he new development were deliberately left latent, so that it can come
spontaneously and yet make dramatic sense when it does.

785-7 'But haven't I met your wishes completely?' (quid uero non
concessi?). Kallippides protests that his sincere approval of the
marriage was all that *could* be required of him; Sostratos' οὔ μοι
δοκεῖς 'I don't think so' was intended to lead to his point that approval
of his own marriage entails consent to the other (791ff), but Kallippides either cannot or will not see what he has in mind, and goes on
to justify his attitude. For τί ... οὐ ..., see, e.g., Herondas 6.74f τί δ'
οὖ, Μητροῖ, ἔπρηξα ('I did all I could'); for οὔ μοι δοκεῖς cf. 345, οὔ μοι δοκῶ
Plat. *Theaet.* 158 e, οὐ δοκεῖ Lucian, *Deorum Dial.* 20.4; for the exchange
in general, 818ff. [Punctuation: alternatively τί δέ; οὐ συγκέχωρηχ';
with OCT Gallavotti *et al.*; ed. pr. and others (less appropriately) put
the second question mark after λαμβάνειν. For τί δέ; cf. Denniston,
Particles 175. 785: προσεδοκουν P¹; cf. *NTGramm.* §90.]

788ff νὴ τοὺς θεοὺς ἔγωγε sc. βούλομαι καί φημι δεῖν, the words uppermost in the speaker's mind. For the sentiment cf. Aristaenetus, *Ep.* 2.8
καὶ τὴν συνάφειαν ἡγούμην βεβαίαν, γινώσκων ὡς ἀσφαλέστερον καθίσταται
γάμος ἐκ πόθου τινὸς τὴν πρόφασιν εὐτυχήσας: perhaps, as Marzullo
suggests, a reminiscence of the present passage. From it is constituted,
by a somewhat dubious method, Com. Adesp. 180 K ... ἀσφαλέστερος
καθίσταται | γάμος ἐκ πόθου τὴν πρόφασιν ἐξευρών τινος. [Doubt is cast
on the text by the uncertainty of ὅτι (α[or ϵ[being at least equally
likely), and by the correction in P, the intention of which remains
hard to fathom; perhaps the writer expected the recurrent phrase
τοῦτο γινώσκων ὅτι and added τοῦτο as a note from his original. If
with Lond. we assume the τοῦτο to be genuine, γινώσκων may well
be a wrong tense for γνούς; νὴ τοὺς θεούς γε τοῦτο Foss. The general
run of the dialogue and the presence of ἔγωγε (if sound) suggest an
elliptical answer rather than one with a finite verb; but Page (for
example) would read νὴ τοὺς θεοὺς ἔγωγε τοῦτ' ἔγνων ἀ[εί, and Gallavotti νὴ τούς, ἔγωγε τοῦτο γινώσκων ἔ[φην (cf. frg. 311).]

789-90 γίνεται, of an expected result: cf. 662. τοῦτο ποεῖν = γαμεῖν,
cf. 676f and n. [πο(ι)εῖν/πονεῖν is a common textual variant (e.g.
Epitr. 147): the latter, adopted by OCT *et al.*, seems to me less likely
here. οὕτω Foss, Jean Martin (-τως Blake).]

791-4 'So I am to marry the young man's sister and think him
worthy of us? But how can you now say that you will not marry my
sister to him?'

The language reflects the young man's mounting indignation, soon
to break out into an impassioned moral tirade. ἔπειτα ... ἐκεῖνον;
presents a proposition which is supposed to follow automatically from

what Kallippides has said; πῶς δὲ ... τὴν ἐμήν; raises an objection intended to destroy his position as self-inconsistent. The sentence should probably not be punctuated as a single question with ed. pr., for its parts are distinct, the ἐγὼ μέν not being in balance with πῶς δέ κτλ. Nor is a colon after ἐκεῖνον to be preferred (Gallavotti, OCT). For ἔπειτα cf. Plato, *Gorgias* 466 c, *Theaet.* 196 d, and LSJ s.v., II.3; for the future, cf. S. *Ant.* 726f οἱ τηλικοίδε καὶ διδαξόμεσθα δὴ | φρονεῖν ὑπ' ἀνδρὸς τηλικοῦδε τὴν φύσιν; [P's τοῦτο is appropriate as antecedent to οὐκ ἀντιδώσειν (see, e.g., *Epitr.* 324), and probably rightly preserved by Gallavotti, van Groningen *et al.*; others, including OCT, adopt ed. pr.'s τούτῳ; but the indirect object is easily understood. σὺ φῇς: λέγεις Lond.; ἔφης Gallavotti.]

794-6 Kallippides is driven to reveal his underlying motive: one destitute in the family is enough. πτωχός is a strong word, prompted no doubt by strong feelings; Kallippides is vastly richer than his neighbours, but would hardly have used it in a calmer mood. Cf. 836 and on 842-4. [Jean Martin, followed by Jacques, gives αἰσχρὸν λέγεις to Sostratos.]

797-812 (i) *Text*: The version of this speech preserved in Stobaeus enables us to supplement P with more than usual confidence, but must be used with great care to correct it. Passages of ancient authors culled by anthologists are liable to suffer both casual alteration and wilful 'improvement' intended to make them read more plausibly in their new isolation: the flower in the vase looks different, and sometimes *is* different, from the flower on the plant. A succinct account of this kind of textual manipulation is given by O. Hense, *RE* 'Ioannes Stobaios' 9.2 (1916) at col. 2583f; that it is present here is strongly suggested by the nature of the variants in 800-2, where, if we ask the question *utrum in alterum abiturum erat*, Stobaeus' text appears infinitely more likely to represent an 'improved' version of P's (or one very like it), than P's does to represent a corrupt or 'emended' version of what we read in Stobaeus. The extreme application of this principle may be seen in ed. pr., where (except for πάτερ in 806 and πολλῷ δὲ κρεῖττον in 811), P is followed entirely where present (its readings in 804, ταῦτα/πάντα (?), and at 809 end are too doubtful to count here). But we may say that P is intrinsically the more likely to represent what Menander wrote without conceding it so much. The opposite extreme is exemplified in OCT, where P serves only to confirm (where it does so) the text as already established from Stobaeus, and the variants it presents are regarded as *prima facie* evidence of deep corruption in P's text at large (pref., p. vi). But if our judgement of the Greek leads us to prefer this view, we may well be left with the uneasy suspicion that it agrees with the taste of the anthologist and not that of the poet. The detailed points at issue will be considered below.

(ii) *General commentary*: Sostratos argues that Kallippides has no proprietary right to his wealth: Fortune, the real owner, may dispossess him. He should not therefore hoard what he may lose to someone less worthy; but while he has control of it, he should use it to secure the permanent good of friendship. Like Gorgias in his 'serious speech' at 271ff, he begins from a form of the commonplace that human prosperity is finite and variable, but the occasion allows him to develop a more positive theory of conduct for the rich man, which is complementary to what Gorgias has said, and gains in point from the audience's recollection of the earlier scene. As there, the young man's righteous indignation gives life to the moralizing; and it comes with added piquancy from son to father: compare in general frg. 612, where a mother is angrily reproached for her insistence on the value of belonging to a good family, and T. *Adel.* 66off, where Aeschinus accuses Micio of inhumanity.

The idea that a man's worldly goods are held in trust and not owned appears in a strikingly parallel form in Euripides, *Phoen.* 555ff οὗτοι τὰ χρήματ' ἴδια κέκτηνται βροτοί, | τὰ τῶν θεῶν δ' ἔχοντες ἐπιμελούμεθα· | ὅταν δὲ χρῄζωσ' αὔτ' ἀφαιροῦνται πάλιν. | [ὁ δ' ὄλβος οὐ βέβαιος ἀλλ' ἐφήμερος]. It may be that Menander had this passage in mind. Webster, *SM* 201, notes the kindred idea that the goods given by Fortune are only a loan (*a*) in Demetrius of Phalerum, περὶ τύχης; and (*b*) in some lines which possibly derive from Menander: (*a*) Polyb. 29.21 = D., frg. 81 Wehrli; (*b*) M., frg. 598 Kock – rejected by Koerte. Demetrius also took what appears as the last line of the Euripidean passage quoted above as one of two texts for his remark that the poet was right, but should have said that human affairs can change in a moment, not in a day (Plut. *Cons. ad Apoll.* 6.104 a = D., frg. 79 Wehrli). Here as elsewhere there is something to suggest that Menander and the philosophic theories of his contemporaries are on common ground; the stress on the value of friendship is paralleled in Theophrastus, *On Marriage*, who advises the wise man to use his wealth well in his lifetime among carefully chosen friends (cf. 816), and not to leave it to the uncertain use of his heirs after death (St. Jerome, *adv. Iovianum* 315 [Migne, *Patr. Lat.* 23.290f]: see Webster, *loc cit.*, and in general on 239f above).

797f ἀβεβαίου πράγματος: cf. Alexis 281 K τῶν γὰρ ἀγαθῶν τὸν πλοῦτον ὕστατον τίθει· | ἀβεβαιότατον γάρ ἐστιν ὧν κεκτήμεθα. | τὰ δ' ἄλλ' ἐπιεικῶς τοῖς ἔχουσι παραμένει.

παραμενοῦντα 'will stay with you' is the *mot juste* by sense and by usage, as e.g. in Alexis, quoted above, and E. *El.* 942. P's περιμενοῦντα 'will be in attendance' seems more likely to be a textual confusion (perhaps prompted by περιμενεῖς 16 lines earlier) than to be a flight of fancy by Menander [περι- confused with παρα-: cf. Wyse on Isaeus 11.47.]

800 τούτου: the grammatically plural χρήματα are thought of as a

single entity (as e.g. at Thuc. 1.80 τοῖς χρήμασιν . . . τούτου): as it were
'riches . . . this (your stored wealth) you can keep and share with
no-one'. The sequence χρημάτων . . . πράγματος . . . ταῦτα . . . τούτου . . .
ὧν is considered to be 'impossible' by some critics, but seems an
acceptable inconsequence from a speaker whose thoughts are presented
as 'live' and not neatly worked out in advance; with similar ease the
Megarian's pigs in A. *Ach.* (being called χοῖροι, χοιρία and χοιρίδια)
are spoken of with a plural verb in one breath and a collective singular
in the next: 797 ἤδη δ' ἄνευ τῆς μητρὸς ἐσθίοιεν ἄν; but 799 τί δ' ἐσθίει
μάλιστα; 807 οἷον ῥοθιάζουσ' but 808 ὡς Τραγασαῖα φαίνεται; then 809
(new speaker) κατέτραγον. For repetition of the demonstrative in close
sequence, see Jackson, *Marginalia Scaenica* 220, who quotes among other
passages Ar. *Birds* 181-4. [ἄλλῳ (Stob.) I take to be an anthologist's
attempt to achieve grammatical tidiness: if Menander wrote ἄλλῳ it
is hard to see what stroke of accident or critical intent could have
produced τουτου in P. τοῦ σοῦ (Kapsomenos) is a good suggestion:
i.e. τουσου>τουτου, whence ἄλλῳ; τούτων Jacques.]

800-2 ὧν δὲ μὴ σὺ κύριος εἶ introduces the antithesis to εἰ μὲν γὰρ
οἶσθα ταῦτα . . .; neg. μή because the thought is still of a general hypothetical character. The second clause, introduced by μηδέ, explains
and amplifies the first: '. . . and which you hold not as your own
property, but entirely as that of Fortune.' πάντα acc. governed by ἔχεις,
although the leading clause had not ἅ but ὧν governed by κύριος εἶ.
σαυτοῦ, possessive gen. for possessive adj., as in αὑτοῦ ποιεῖσθαι; cf.
731f above, and σαυτοῦ νομίζεις εἶναι τὰ τῆς πόλεως Lys. 30.5. Sostratos argues here that Kallippides is not κύριος of his wealth in the
sense of being 'rightful owner'; at 805ff he shifts his ground and talks
of him being κύριος in the sense of being 'in control'. The word is a
technical term in both senses (cf. Wyse on Isaeus 8.31); as in 811f the
language takes an appropriate colour from the legal vocabulary of
property; and the suggestive power of the words is more important
to the speaker than the precision of the logic. [The version in Stob.
apparently began by seeking the antithesis to εἰ μὲν γάρ in a second εἰ
clause, the preceding line being modified accordingly, with αὐτὸς ὢν
δὲ κύριος in parallel with μηδενὶ ἄλλῳ μεταδιδούς. So far as the text of
Stob. is concerned, P confirms Meineke's εἰ μὴ δὲ σαυτοῦ for the un-
metrical εἰ δὲ μὴ σεαυτοῦ of the MSS, of which εἰ δ' οὐ σεαυτοῦ (A²) is
presumably an emendation. Since the neg. has to go closely with
σαυτοῦ, the collocation εἰ μὴ was felt, perhaps rightly, to be unfortunate. ὧν δὲ κύριος . . . (Mᵈ) happens to agree with P's ὧν; if not a
mistake, it may represent an attempt to take κύριος as 'trustee'.]

μὴ . . . φθονοίης, if sound, is a surprising alternative for the μὴ
φθόνει or μὴ φθονήσῃς which might have been expected in corres-
pondence with φύλαττε above. But the opt. of wish may on occasion
assume a jussive force analogous to that of a command: cf. 565 γένοισθε

followed by συνάγετε, and n. there; for the neg. form, cf. the phrase μὴ ὥρασι ἵκοιο (LSJ, s.v. ὥρασι; *Perik.* 131 (?), *Phasma* 43 (?)); Dem. 20.164 ἐὰν δ' ἀποψηφίσησθ', ὃ μὴ ποιήσαιτε . . .; Xen. *Oec.* 10.4 εὐφήμει . . . μὴ γένοιο σὺ τοιοῦτος.

[μήτε (P) is adopted by ed. pr. *et al.*, but I know of no adequate defence for it. μήτοι Diano: for τοι in this position, cf. Denniston, *Particles* 547. τί ἄν (Stob.) looks too like a simplification of an unusual construction to inspire trust; μηδέ, μή γε are also suggested, but seem unlikely.]

804 ἀφελομένη: cf. E. *Phoen.* 557 (quoted above), Alexis 265 K.8 ἀφείλεθ' ὅσα δεδωκὼς ἦν. παρελομένη (Stob.) may be as good, but is no better; one source or the other has substituted a synonym – presumably Stobaeus. P, though badly damaged, appears more likely to have had ταῦτα than πάντα, and I venture, with Gallavotti, to print it.

προσθήσει 'will hand over'; πάλιν 'in turn', as e.g. in 113.

805-6 σε . . . σε: for the repeated pronoun, cf. Ar. *Ach.* 383f νῦν οὖν με πρῶτον πρὶν λέγειν ἐάσατε | ἐνσκευάσασθαί μ' οἷον ἀθλιώτατον, with discussion and other examples given in KG I.660 and by Fraenkel, *Beobachtungen zu Aristophanes*, 89-91 and 216. Kraus rightly retains the text, quoting ἐμὲ . . . ἐμέ from *Samia* 206 (a different kind of repetition); the general preference is for διόπερ ἔγωγε (Tyrwhitt); so OCT. [Add, perhaps, from Epicharmus, *Odysseus Automolos* καὶ ταῦτα δή με συμβολατεύειν μ' ἔφα: frg. 100 Kaibel + P. Oxy. 2429, fr. 1 (c).]

806-7 κύριος: cf. on 800-2. τούτων is left unexpressed, as is the object of χρῆσθαι, unless the αὐτόν of Stob. is wrong. αὐτοῖς Kock, but see the following note.

807-10 Kallippides should be noble and not mean-spirited both in enjoying what he has himself and in sharing it. (The error of Knemon's life, one might say, was that he failed on both counts.) Cf. especially Aristotle, *Eth. Nic.* 1169 a 11ff τὸν μὲν ἀγαθὸν δεῖ φίλαυτον εἶναι (καὶ γὰρ αὐτὸς ὀνήσεται τὰ καλὰ πράττων καὶ τοὺς ἄλλους ὠφελήσει). The whole analysis of generosity in this and the preceding chapter of *Eth. Nic.* is worth reading as a commentary on Sostratos' attempt at an argument for enlightened self-interest. See further Alexis 265 K τοὺς εὐτυχοῦντας ἐπιφανῶς | δεῖ ζῆν φανεράν τε τὴν δόσιν τὴν τοῦ θεοῦ | ποιεῖν – the theory there being that if wealth is hidden away the god who gave it will suspect ingratitude and take it back; and earlier, Thuc. 2.40.4 with Gomme's note (οὐ γὰρ πάσχοντες εὖ ἀλλὰ δρῶντες κτώμεθα τοὺς φίλους. βεβαιότερος δὲ ὁ δράσας τὴν χάριν ὥστε ὀφειλομένην δι' εὐνοίας ᾧ δέδωκε σῴζειν); and Pindar, *Nem.* 1.31ff οὐκ ἔραμαι πολὺν ἐν μεγάρῳ πλοῦτον κατακρύψαις ἔχειν, | ἀλλ' ἐόντων εὖ τε παθεῖν καὶ ἀκοῦσαι φίλοις ἐξαρκέων.

808ff τοῦτο refers collectively to χρῆσθαι γενναίως, ἐπικουρεῖν κτλ.

ἀθάνατον: 'undying' – the idea is not that the good men do lives after them, but rather that unlike money it lasts: friends whom you have secured by generosity will make good a misfortune by repaying their debt of gratitude. [809: P presumably had ἐστιν, ἐστι being too short. What stood at the end of the line is unclear: ed. pr. transcribes as πταισασтηχη[; it may well be, however, that the writer of P was in difficulty with his original, and has produced a nonsensical misreading, as in 98.]

811-12 An appropriate *gnome* to end the speech. 'Hidden wealth' appears to make a somewhat forced contrast with a 'visible' or 'real' friend, but Sostratos is using the words partly for the sake of their technical connotations, ἀφανής being applied to personal property (such as money), which is or may be private in the sense that ἐμφανὴς or φανερὸς οὐσία (e.g. land) is not. Cf. Ar. *Eccl.* 601f (quoted by Waddell); LSJ s.v. ἀφανής 5, and for more examples, Wyse on Isaeus 6.30. For the sentiment, Dr J. R. Green refers me to E. *Or.* 1155ff: οὐκ ἔστιν οὐδὲν κρεῖττον ἢ φίλος σαφής, | οὐ πλοῦτος, οὐ τυραννίς.

κατορύξας ἔχεις: 'keep buried'; cf. κατακρύψαις ἔχειν in Pindar, quoted under 807-10.

813-19 Kallippides' generosity reasserts itself. By being based on reasoned consent, and not mere amenability to persuasion, it emerges as a positive quality, something better than the mechanical liberality of an over-fond father.

813 οἶσθ' οἷόν ἐστι: cf. τοιοῦτόν ἐστιν *Heros* 6; οἶσθας] οἷ[όν ἐ]στιν, οἶμαι *Perik.* 152 (suppl. Wilamowitz). [οἶσθ' οἷός ἐστι (P) is preserved by some, and referred to πλοῦτος; but neither this nor ed. pr.'s οἶσθ' οἷός εἰμι (so OCT) seems as likely to be right.]

814 'I shan't take it to my grave with me. How could I?' Sostratos will inherit the fortune: he may as well use it sensibly in his father's lifetime. Cf. under 797-812 (ii).

816 δοκιμάσας: rightly taken with πρᾶττε τοῦτ' by ed. pr.; the text is punctuated accordingly; sc. αὐτόν. [φίλον δοκιμάσας; OCT et al.] ἀγαθῇ τύχῃ: cf. on 422.

817 'Why moralize to me?' – a gentle reproof which helps the audience to see Sostratos' outburst in proportion.

The end of the line is wholly uncertain. πόριζε and βάδιζε appear to be alternative readings, one of which has driven out some word or words of the text. Assuming the latter to be genuine, in the sense 'Carry on', 'Get on with it', we may perhaps supply νοῦν ἔχεις: cf. 736, 884; and for the tone of the remark, compare T. *Adel.* 564: abi, uirum te iudico (Demea, of Ctesipho). [Alternatives proposed and possible are very many: e.g. βάδιζε· ταῦτα νῦν Lond. (providing an object); πόριζε πόριζε δή ed. pr. (introducing a 'split anapaest': cf. Introd. IV, p. 66 (k)); πόριζ' ὅτῳ θέλεις van Groningen ('θέλεις if so?); πόρισον· βάδιζε καὶ Kraus (assuming πόριζε to be a wrong form). OCT and others obelize.]

818 δίδου, μεταδίδου: for the repetition, cf. Alexis, *Asotodidaskalos* 25 K πίνωμεν, ἐμπινῶμεν. [Arnott, CQ 1955 at p. 214.]

819 ἑκών; κτλ. Kallippides agrees by the light of his better judgement, not in spite of it. The exchange neatly underlines a major point of the scene (see under 813-19), but it is entirely natural, after what has happened, that Sostratos should be anxious for complete reassurance, and that Kallippides should emphasize his sincerity. Cf. T. *Adel.* 699f *Micio*: abi domum ac deos conprecare ut uxorem accersas: abi. | *Aeschinus*: quid? iam uxorem? M. iam. A. iam? M. iam quantum potest. [Arrangement of speakers: Gallavotti and Page prefer ... ἑκών. (Σω.) ἑκών; (Καλλ.) εὖ ἴσθι ..., assuming that P has failed to mark a change after the second ἑκών (double point), rather than after σοι in 818 (paragraphus and double point).]

820 'Then I'll call Gorgias.' Content with the ground he has won, Sostratos does what he had set out to do. See under 784ff.

821f Menander takes a short cut to the next stage of the action by having Gorgias overhear the whole discussion. He was 'coming out'; we should perhaps not stop to wonder why, but if we do we can think that he was anxious at the delay: μικρὸν διαλιπὼν παρακαλῶ σε Sostratos had said, 783. He was πρὸς τῇ θύρᾳ 'at the door' and behind it, like Charisios in *Epitrepontes* (cf. 563ff). He may have been seen peering out, but should not, one feels, do anything to lay stress on the eavesdropping and distract attention from the scene on stage. His remark might be accepted by an ancient audience either as confirmation of what they have seen or as a substitute for what they have not; it is both necessary to the dramatic situation and consistent with the straightforwardness which is one of Gorgias' characteristics. It was, no doubt, a venial fault to stay and listen to what so obviously concerned his sister's future and his own; but he declares himself at once. [Overhearing: see Webster, *SM*, index s.v.; Duckworth, *Nature of Roman Comedy* 109ff, with further references.]

823 τί οὖν; 'What follows?' 'So what?', leading to the main point. Cf. τί οὖν λέγω; 284. [(Σω.) τί οὖν; Thierfelder, followed by van Groningen and others. σ' ὦ Σώστρατ' OCT (Page).]

823-34 Gorgias, like Kallippides, has his pride – that of the poor man who will not accept favours. It momentarily triumphs over his respect and friendship for Sostratos. Compare Euclio in P. *Aul.*, unwilling to have his daughter marry the wealthy Megadorus (220ff, cf. 244ff). Sostratos simply does not understand; his father is surprised, but admiring, 835f.

828f Tr. perhaps '. . . as to marrying your sister, I'd like to, but . . .'
'What do you mean, "like to, but . . ."?'

καλῶς ἔχει ('I am content', 'It suits me') can express both genuine
enthusiasm and polite reluctance (as here), according to the tone and
context in which the words are said. For the former sense, cf. Isaeus 2.11
ἔφη δοκεῖν αὐτῷ καλῶς ἔχειν . . . ἐκ ταύτης τῆς οἰκίας υἱὸν αὐτῷ ποιήσασθαι
'said it seemed a good idea to adopt a son from the family'; for the
latter, cf. *Perik.* 266f, Antiphanes, *Mystis* 165 K (A.) βούλει καὶ σύ, φιλτάτη,
πιεῖν; (B.) καλῶς ἔχει μοι 'Will you join me, dear?' 'I'm quite happy'
(= 'No, thank you'). Further examples and discussion of such phrases
will be found in Gow's note to Theocr. 15.3 and the commentators on
Ar. *Frogs* 508; cf. also LSJ s.v. ἐπαινέω III. The antithetical shape of
the sentence suggests that the speaker was about to say something
more directly negative, like οὐ βούλομαι or οὐκ ἂν δυναίμην; hence it
might be better, with OCT, to print a dash after λαβεῖν.

829-31 'I think it's unsatisfactory to live in luxury by others' hard
work: one should have one's own resources': i.e. he will not marry
money.

τρυφαίνειν (for τρυφᾶν) is not so far recorded, but should not therefore be altered: closely parallel formations are λυσσαίνειν (for λυσσᾶν),
and ὀργαίνειν (for ὀργᾶν): cf. Schwyzer I.733; we know χλιδαίνεσθαι in
the sense of χλιδᾶν only from Xen. *Smp.* 8.8, and χηραίνειν in the sense
of χηρεύειν only from Herondas 1.21; some other denominative verbs
in Menander are relatively rare: e.g. ἀλεαίνειν frg. 806, παθαίνεσθαι
Epitr. 769. [τρυφᾶν ἐν plerique, adopted in OCT and by some others.]

συλλεξάμενον δ' αὐτόν: understand not ἡδύ μοι δοκεῖ τρυφαίνειν but
supply from τρυφαίνειν a neutral or contrasting idea like that of διάγειν
or φείδεσθαι. As often in Greek the second member of the antithesis
is left to be completed from the first: KG II.566f. [δοκῶ (P) preserved
by ed. pr. *et al.*, seems indefensible.]

833f κέκρικα answering κρίνεις: 'I do indeed consider myself personally worthy of her – but I do not think it right that I, a man with
little, should receive much.' [P's word-order, which has found defenders, seems only capable of giving a sense impossible in the context.]

[**836-41** The loss of the beginnings of these lines in P makes it hopeless
to do more than imagine ways in which Menander might have written
them. As usual in such places, the text given here must be viewed by
the reader with appropriate scepticism. Several widely differing
versions are set out and discussed by van Groningen, *Ét. Critique*; and
I have thought full illustration unnecessary: OCT adopts no supplements.]

836 περίεργος: an attractive and plausible supplement. Tr. perhaps
'Your excess of conscience does you credit.' The remark is of the same
kind as Sostratos' ἐλευθερίως γέ πως ἄγροικός ἐστιν of Knemon's

daughter, 201f. Gorgias could have said nothing, and simply accepted what was bound to come – an offer of marriage with a handsome dowry. By intervening gratuitously to his own material disadvantage, he shows at the same time what Kallippides regards as an excess of conscientious zeal and a kind of honest independence which is the mark of the true gentleman. For περίεργος, cf. esp. *Epitr.* 86 and Theophr., *Char.* 13 *ad init.*; for the comment on Gorgias' character, cf. 321 above. [The line in P begins with traces best suited to be π, but interpreted by some, after ed. pr., as a paragraphus under 835 – an erroneous one if so. The next letter could have been ε or α; that before the ο was joined to it by a horizontal stroke which suggests γ or τ, possibly π. Alternatives proposed include παράκοπος Barigazzi; ἄγροικος Merkelbach (quoted but not adopted in OCT); ἀπόπληκτος Mette.]

836f 'You have no money and you want to appear to have.' Kallippides presumably developed the paradox implied by his last remark. See above and on 838. [Bingen and Mette take the sense to be complete at δοκεῖν; Barigazzi completes it with φρονεῖν; others otherwise. Quincey would emend and read οὐχ ἑκὼν βούλει δοκεῖν | πείθεσθ']: this is the suggestion quoted in OCT.]

837-40 'You can see I'm persuaded, and your attitude has persuaded me twice over, so don't be senseless as well as poor: don't run away from the prospect of security which this marriage offers you.'

[The provisional text given is based on these considerations: (i) It seems likely that Kallippides continues to σωτηρίαν, where P has a dicolon. It is true that other signs of change of speaker may have been given in the lost portion of P, and/or omitted, but the echo of συμπεπεισμένον μ' in τούτῳ μ' ἀναπέπεικας διπλασίως is, I believe, a strong argument *against* introducing Gorgias, as do ed. pr. *et al.*: μικρὰ λαβ]έ. *(Γο.)* τούτῳ ... ed. pr.; λαβέ. *(Γο.)* εὖγ]ε ... Mette; alii alia. (ii) If Kallippides does continue, it may well be that 838 is parenthetic; Merkelbach, however, suggests ἀρνεῖ δ]έ, ... We have also to accept that Gorgias' objections collapse with startling (but not, I think, incomprehensible) suddenness, 841. (iii) 839-40 should mean 'It would be mad to refuse', but remain very difficult. 839 must be considered corrupt as well as mutilated, since the scansion ἀπόπληκτος is irreconcilable with what we know of Menander's practice (see 414 n.); in 840]ς seems possible, but not typically formed, and therefore doubtful. For comparison with the version given, I quote *(a)* ed. pr. *(Γο.)* ... μὴ γὰρ λαβ]ὼν πένης ἀπόπληκτός θ' ἅμα | ἦν — ὄφελο]ς (πένης ⟨ἂν⟩ Kraus, Mette); *(b)* ἀεὶ δ' ἅμ'] ὢν πένης ⟨τις⟩ ἀποπληκτός θ' ἅμα | τίν' ἐλπί]δ', suggested *exempli gratia* in OCT (τίν' ἐλπί]δ' Barrett).]

838 αὐτῷ δὲ τούτῳ, on the view taken here, refers to οὐκ ἔχων βούλει δοκεῖν ἔχειν. ['fort. αὐτῷ δ]έ' OCT.]

839 τις: cf. LSJ s.v. A.II.7; ἀπόπληκτος 'senseless' as e.g. *Epitr.* 385, *Perik.* 246. It is a strong word; for its literal meaning cf. 312 above.

841 νικᾷς, cf. *Perik.* 162 ὁμολογῶ νικᾶν σε; perhaps κρατεῖς, cf. 958. The sudden change of heart which this version postulates is, perhaps, psychologically plausible in view of Gorgias' affection for Sostratos and his long-standing respect for Kallippides (cf. 773ff); but one suspects also that the poet has extracted all he wishes from the situation, and sees no cause to develop it with a further display of reluctance or a more fulsome assent. Note also Gorgias' behaviour at the end of Act III, and see n. there on 616-19. [(Σω.) οὐκοῦν τ]ὸ λοιπὸν ed. pr.; ὑπ]όλοιπον Gallavotti, Shipp. The scansion ἡμῖν is unjustifiable in Menander.]

842-4 The formula of betrothal; cf. *Perik.* 435ff, 761-3 above, and frg. 682 with Koerte's note.

The dowry of three talents (18,000 drachmas) is of course a vast amount in Gorgias' eyes. From being the owner of a χωρίδιον which barely supported two people and a slave (23ff), he now finds himself in charge of Knemon's estate 'worth about two talents' as he told Sostratos (327f); even so, the talent which he proudly claims to have for his sister's dowry (representing half its value), is outclassed by what the rich man can give, and even waved aside in a lordly gesture of generosity and trust. To Kallippides, Gorgias is a 'have-not' (836), 'a poor man', even (in the heat of the moment) a 'destitute' (795).

By real life standards (in so far as we know them), it seems probable that these figures are high; but Menander is concerned to make points in a drama, not to present economic statistics. He chooses large round sums, presenting a generous and unmistakable scale of status between the three households. Kallippides' dowry is vast to show, apart from all other indications, how very wealthy he is – the common condition of a comic hero's father-in-law; Knemon's estate is given a value which makes it manifestly much larger than that of Gorgias, and far too large for a normal Attic farmer to work alone (of course, even Knemon can only work part of it, 163ff) – a value, moreover, which will divide simply and equitably by two to yield an impressive dowry for his daughter and the prospect of a respectable living for the rest of the family once Gorgias takes it in hand (739-49). At the same time, the old man can be characterized as 'a poor farmer' because he chooses to live, work and behave like one – quite unnecessarily, as the audience must realize (30ff, 129ff, 603ff and elsewhere).

For the economic historian, the mixture of truth and 'lies like the truth' in the lives of comic characters presents some diverting problems; for the translator, the choice of equivalents in modern coinage is a matter of taste as much as calculation: for this play Webster (*The Birth of Modern Comedy*, 5) and Arnott, in his English version, reasonably equate the talent with £5,000.

[See in general Webster, 'First Things First', in Proc. Class. Ass. 57 (1960) at pp. 18ff; for an attempt to work out the values of the *Dyskolos* in terms of fourth-century reality, see E. Cavaignac, Bull. Ass. Budé 1960.367ff; on marriage contracts, T. Williams, Wiener Studien 1961. 43ff; on dowries, H. J. Wolff, *RE* προίξ 32.1 (1957) at col. 139ff and M. I. Finley, *Studies in Land and Credit* . . . (1951) 79, 266ff, both with further references. Finley, rightly discounting the vast dowries of Comedy as factual evidence, concludes that 'Roughly, 3,000-6,000 drachmas seems to have been the accepted standard for the wealthiest people': among the exceptions is a dowry of 14,000 drachmas in the third-century register from Mykonos (Dittenberger, *Syll.*³ 1215). *Sizes and values of estates*: Finley, *op. cit.*, esp. 57ff; Pritchett, Hesperia 1956.269ff; A. H. M. Jones, *Athenian Democracy* (1957) IV (= Econ. Hist. Review 8 (1955) 141-55). Two farms at Eleusis and Thria involved in the lawsuits of Isaeus 11 and [Dem.] 43 are said to have been worth 2 and 2½ talents respectively; but these appear to be exceptionally high values for single holdings.]

845f ἔχεις μηδ' αὖ σὺ λίαν; 'Surely you're not too well off yourself?' It is a characteristic of the 'overzealous' man in Theophrastus 13 to commit himself to more than he can perform, and Kallippides, who seems to have thought of Gorgias as εὐγενῶς περίεργος (835f) is tactfully solicitous for the young man's own finances if he gives as much as a talent for his sister's dowry.

The text and interpretation are much disputed. I prefer to accept what P gives and punctuate as a question – which, containing the neg. μή, expects (though it does not in fact receive) a negative answer. On this view, ἔχεις is first word because it takes up Gorgias' ἔχω – a phenomenon of word-order well described and illustrated by G. Thomson, CQ 1939 at p. 148, in discussing deferred interrogatives. The negatives when used in interrogative sentences may be similarly placed, as the following three examples show. (*a*) Plato, *Smp.* 202 c εὐδαίμονας δὲ δὴ λέγεις οὐ τοὺς τἀγαθὰ καὶ τὰ καλὰ κεκτημένους; (taking up φῂς εὐδαίμονας εἶναι and φάναι . . . εὐδαίμονα εἶναι from the previous question); (*b*) E. *Hip.* 799 (Theseus) οἴμοι· τέκνων μοι μή τι συλᾶται βίος; (takes up from νέοι θανόντες ἀλγυνοῦσί σε); (*c*) Plat. *Prot.* 332 c τούτῳ μὴ ἔστι τι ἐναντίον ἄλλο πλὴν τὸ βαρύ; (takes up from the previous question ἔστι τι ὀξὺ ἐν φωνῇ;). ἔχεις, being used without an object, is 'have' in the sense 'be wealthy', and hence can be qualified by λίαν rather than constructed with e.g. περιττά.

[*Alternatives*: If, with ed. pr., the remark is taken as a statement, the only likely force of the neg. is that of tentative suggestion (see, e.g., Goodwin, *MT* §269). That would be inappropriate: hence Flacelière proposes to substitute οὐδ' αὖ. If, with OCT (Fraenkel) *et al.*, ἔχεις is taken as a separate question, μή . . . λίαν can be thought of as an elliptical expression meaning something like 'Don't say too much' or

'Don't be too ambitious' (see, e.g., Schwyzer II.707); but then the force of αὖ is hard to see: hence μηδὲν σὺ λίαν Barigazzi, μὴ δῶς σι λίαν Arnott.]

ἀλλ' ἔχω: probably understand τάλαντον προῖκα τῆς ἑτέρας 'I have it, all the same'; otherwise the remark is simply a negative to Kallip pides' question: 'On the contrary . . .' One might insist on providing a dowry for several reasons, among them family pride, and the desire to give the girl a kind of security from her financial stake in the mar riage; Gorgias has further accepted Knemon's arrangement that the girl shall have half the estate: but Kallippides' warm generosity sweep Gorgias into assent (849). [Ed. pr. rightly gives τὸ δὲ χωρίον to Kallip pides. ἀλλ' ἔχω τόδε χωρίον (Gallavotti) introduces an anomalous use of the demonstrative without the article; if we suppose that the change of speaker comes after χωρίον, it may be right, with OCT, to read τό γε (Quincey et al.).]

846f 'Le domaine, garde-le tout entier pour toi' (ed. pr.). Kallip pides need not be supposed to know of Knemon's instructions, 737f anyone would guess what the provision of a large dowry by a smal farmer would involve.

849 τὰς παρ' ἡμῖν: 'our' womenfolk, the party in the shrine; cf. τὴ παρ' ἐμοῦ, 375; and compare in general T. *Adel.* 910.

ἀλλὰ χρή: 'Very well', given by Hesychius (quoted below the text and by others as an equivalent of ἔστω. Cf. Denniston, *Particles* 18f.

850-1 The lines are too badly damaged for anything more than a sketch of their possible sense to be offered, and OCT does not restore Compare in general *Epitr.* 202f νῦν γὰρ μενοῦμεν ἐνθάδε | εἰς αὔριον δ ἐπ' ἔργον ἐξορμήσομεν | τὴν ἀποφορὰν ἀποδόντες; and for εὐφρανούμεθα here preferred to ed. pr.'s ἑστιάσομεν, cf. Ar. *Eccl.* 1123 εὐφρανεῖ τὴ νύχθ' ὅλην. The sacrifice and feast originally arranged by Sostratos mother to propitiate Pan is now to become an all-night party, the firs stage of the wedding celebrations.

851f τοὺς γάμους ποιήσομεν perhaps refers to both weddings, althoug the plural in this phrase is normal of a single celebration: *Sam.* 328 *Georg.*, frg. 4, *Koneiaz.* 5, etc.: see Headlam-Knox on Herondas 7.86-88 Anything as long as ἀμφοτέρους δὲ το]ὺς γάμους makes the line hard t restore.

853 κομίσατε refers collectively to Gorgias and his family, the plura suggesting what is later confirmed – that his mother and sister returne with Knemon to his house at 759 or soon after; Gorgias is about t fetch them from there. See on 867ff.

856-9 The distinction between a drinking party for the men and a all-night revel for the women is here one of name rather than nature

ιs may be seen from the description at 935ff; they sit separately, but
share the same celebration. Kallippides' reply is an urbane version
of the traditional joke that women and wine are firm friends: cf.
Athenaeus 10.440 e, and Oeri, *Typ der komischen Alten*, 13ff, 39ff.

859-65 Exit Kallippides to the shrine 'to get things ready'. This
move adds a little to the atmosphere of bustle and festivity which is
being created; it leaves the stage clear for Sostratos' brief monologue,
which writes *finis* to his romantic adventure; and it also gives the actor
who played Kallippides time to change and reappear as Simiche (see
Introd. II.2). The dramatic situation is similar to that at T. *Adel.* 706ff;
cf. also Chairea's brief monologue at *Eun.* 1044-9. [860-3: Another
brief comparison between Stobaeus and P is possible: see under 797-
812 (i). P reduces χρὴ πράγματος to χρήματος by its typical fault of
haplography; in Stob. φρονοῦνθ' has apparently been replaced by
τονοῦνθ' in an attempt to underline the point. ποιοῦνθ' Stob. codd.
was rightly recognized as an error by Grotius: cf. on 790.]

860ff πόει τοῦτ': 'Do'; cf. on 676f. οὐδενὸς ... ὅλως together (cf. 865).
τὸν εὖ φρονοῦνθ': cf. Gorgias at 380f εἴπερ λέγεις | ἃ φρονεῖς, ἐπιτύχοις.
Successive sentences follow each other without connection; the
speaker is represented as following an unpremeditated line of thought
where it leads him.

862f ἐπιμελείᾳ καὶ πόνῳ: cf. Gorgias at 764ff. The idea is a commonplace.

864 ἐν ἡμέρᾳ μιᾷ: cf. 187f πόλλ' ἂν ἡμέρᾳ μιᾷ γένοιτ' ἄν. The recall is
surely deliberate; but the stress on 'one day' (as e.g. at T. *Eun.* 1047)
perhaps has as much to do with the notion that change in human
affairs is swift as with stressing the 'Unity of Time' in the action: see
under 797-812 (ii); and on realism of time in Menander, cf. Webster,
SM 178ff, and Bull. Rylands Library 1962.235ff.

866 Enter Gorgias with his mother and sister – a little flustered (as
well they might be), and not quite knowing what is expected of them.
προάγετε δή: cf. on 905f.
δεῦτε δή: 'Do come this way'; cf. Ar. *Eccl.* 952ff δεῦρο δή, δεῦρο δή, |
φίλον ἐμόν, δεῦρό μοι | πρόσελθε ... δεῦτε, the plural form of δεῦρο,
survives from Homer in Classical, post-Classical and Modern Greek;
surprisingly enough, this seems to be the first instance of it known from
ancient Comedy, and Shipp and others would therefore replace it by
δεῦρο. [Cf. Schwyzer I.804, Headlam-Knox on Herondas 4.11. The
second ε of δεῦτε is clumsily rewritten in P; but I see no sign that
δεῦρο was intended.]

867ff μῆτερ, δέχου ταύτας: Sostratos speaks into the shrine, and
continues (to Gorgias) 'Knemon not here yet?' Cf. 555f ἐνθάδ' ἡ

μήτηρ; . . . ὁ πατὴρ δέ; and van Leeuwen on Ar. *Thes.* 846. The ellip
tical phrase is wrongly taken as a statement by ed. pr., and attributec
to Gorgias, against P.

ὅς . . . καθ' αὑτόν; I prefer, with OCT (Lloyd-Jones) *et al.* to reac
this remark as a question 'What, when he begged . . .?'; so also
perhaps at *Perik.* 221f; hardly at *Sam.* 197ff and 162ff above, where
ὅς is similarly used.

ἱκέτευεν with object understood, as at 677: ἱκέτευέ μ' OCT (Lloyd-
Jones). 'Begged me to take the old woman as well, so that he could be
completely alone' is, I think, enough to show that Myrrhine and her
daughter were with the old man. Gorgias does not need to call in both
houses, and distract attention from Sostratos' monologue by dashing
from one to the other.

Knemon persists in his determination to be left alone, even refusing
to take part in the celebration of his daughter's wedding in Pan's
shrine. 'We may doubt whether Menander sympathized', as Webster
remarks (*SM* 200). What Gorgias, Sostratos and Simiche say of him
is said as much in sorrow as in anger; but the close of the scene, and
especially Simiche's speech of foreboding, is calculated to lay stress
on his refusal, and hence to give some dramatic justification to the
comic scene of ragging to which it looks forward. See under 880-958.

870 τοιοῦτος: 'Yes, he's like that', assenting to Sostratos' ὦ τρόπου
ἀμάχου. The neuter τοιαῦτα is similarly used at E. *Hec.* 776, *El.* 645.
Thierfelder compares T. *Andria* 919: sic, Crito, est hic: mitte. [Ed. pr.
attributes ὦ τρόπου . . . ἴωμεν entirely to Sostratos; perhaps, with
Kraus, the division should be *(Γο.)* τοιοῦτος, ἀλλὰ πολλὰ χαιρέτω.]

871f As a countryman, Gorgias has something of Knemon's instinctive unsociability. A party of this kind, with ladies present, is
something outside his experience, and in his rustic *diphthera* he will
look out of place too. Webster (*SM*² 232) aptly compares frg. 761 :
εὐκαταφρόνητος τῇ στολῇ | εἴσειμι, καὶ τοῦτ' εἰς γυναῖκας. Sostratos' up-
bringing naturally makes him more self-assured, and he gaily sweeps
the objections aside – a neat final touch of character contrast between
the two young men. See on 932f (ii).

872 γυναιξὶν ἐν ταὐτῷ: cf. 933, LSJ s.v. αὐτός III. [873: οἰκεῖα: a
simple and admirable correction by ed. pr., almost universally adopted.]

874 Sostratos and Gorgias go into the shrine; enter Simiche, talking
back into Knemon's house in words which blend pity with disapproval
and foreboding. Cf. on 574ff.

κἀγώ = I, as well as the others. See under 867ff.

[**875** τάλαν τοῦ σοῦ τρόπου Lond.]

876f πρὸς τὸν θεόν possibly implies that the refusal was not only unreasonable to the family, but insulting to the god.

77f μέγα κακὸν 'a heap of trouble': cf. on 91.

νὴ τὼ θεώ: see on 201f.

εὖ πάθοις: 'may all go well'; similarly εὖ πάθωμεν, Lucian, *Dial. Mort.* 10.10. [877: λέγω, ed. pr. – a stop-gap; 878 μεῖζον πότ᾽ ed. pr.; ͅεῖζόν ποτ᾽ ἢ νῦν εὐπα[θεῖν Webster; alii alia.]

879 Enter Getas from the shrine, speaking back into it in reply to ͅ remark which we are left to assume: e.g. 'I wonder how Knemon is?' ͅompare *Perik.* 61 (Enter Doris) ἐγὼ προ[ελ]θ[οῦσ]᾽ ὄψομαι, κεκτημένη. ͅoris is genuinely trying to be helpful; Getas (who will assert in a ͅoment that 'They're sending me to the invalid here') has apparently ͅeen a good chance for an excuse to escape from the party. He wants ͅo get Knemon alone and take some kind of revenge, but does not yet ͅee how (884ff).

What stood at the end of the line is wholly uncertain; for ὡς ἔχω ͅf. 559. I assume that the piper plays, as P indicates, immediately ͅfter Getas has spoken his entrance line; the change of metre then ͅomes when he continues with the musical accompaniment. [ὡς ἔχει comment il va᾽ ed. pr. OCT prints δεῦρ᾽ ạ[∪ _ ∪ _ ͅ with the com-ͅent '879 tetrametrum fuisse suspicatur Barrett.' I am not clear from ͅhe photographs whether anything can be said about the letter follow-ͅing δευρ-.]

αὐλεῖ sc. ὁ αὐλητής: a stage-direction written into the text, as in Ar. *Birds*, after 222 (so RVM; αὐλεῖ τις B Ald.); αὐλεῖ τις ἔνδοθεν *Frogs*, after 311 (RVM); διαύλιον προσαυλεῖ τις *Frogs*, after 1263 (RVMU, with minor variants). It could well go back to Menander himself: see Introd. III, p. 48 and n. 2. The piper seems to take Getas' appearance as a cue to play for a musical scene, and is amusingly rebuked: 880 n.

880-958 Finale: Knemon forced to join the party. Iambic tetra-meters catalectic; for metrical description, see Introd. IV.

(i) The opening by-play with the piper confirms one's expectation from the metre that the scene is to be performed to musical accom-paniment. Getas' command to the piper to stop in 881 may have been in vain; but it is possible to think of the accompaniment suspended or muted for the conspiracy between him and the cook; if so, it will presumably resume at full strength for the ragging of Knemon which follows, on the cue ἐγὼ προάξω πρότερος, κτλ. in 910; it is also possible, if we think of the style in general as recitative, to imagine it rising to a kind of song as the language rises to poetry in the description of the party, 946ff. What little is known about the delivery of words to music on the ancient stage is set out and discussed by Pickard-Cam-bridge, *Festivals*, 153ff. We may also plausibly suppose that the action was enlivened by exaggerated movements and gestures *ad lib.*, some of them possibly dance-steps or burlesques of dance-steps (e.g. at 910ff, 954.)

(ii) Until this play came to light, Menander was not known to have written in this metre, nor was there any good evidence that he allowed himself to end a comedy with a riotous scene of this kind – a descendant of the lively and varied *exodos*-scenes which we know in Old Comedy. As with the serious speech in trochaics in Act IV, we cannot say how exceptional the scene was by the standards of the later fourth century, but the new discovery materially increases the probability that the revels at the end of Plautus' *Stichus* were based on a similar finale in its original, Menander's *First Adelphoi*. See Webster, *SM²* 233, *SM* 141f. and works quoted there. (We are concerned here only to note a possible Menandrean parallel; to consider the implications of the end of the *Dyskolos* for Roman Comedy and its musical scenes in general would take us too far afield: for some discussion of the matter, see D'Anna and Paratore in Riv. di cultura class. e medioevale 1959, 298ff and 310ff, and Fraenkel, *Elem. Plautini*, 268ff, 434, 443.)

Iambic tetrameter is a traditional comic metre, known from fragments of the fifth and fourth centuries as well as from Aristophanes (see White, *Verse of Greek Comedy*, 62ff). Webster (op. cit.) compares in particular the scene of 45 lines near the end of the *Clouds*, where Pheidippides turns the New Learning against his father and asserts his right to beat him (1399ff); note also, for the convivial tone of the latter part of our scene, the descriptions of parties in this metre preserved from Plato, *Lakones* (69 K, quoted in part on 950ff) and Philyllios, *Auge* (3-4 K); and in New Comedy, Diphilos, *Agnoia* 1 K.

(iii) The dramatic justification for this ending to the comedy must be in part that it is an ending of a traditional kind, less surprising to an ancient audience than it is in performance nowadays. Continuity with the earlier action is secured by the persistent theme of celebration, by the comic reprise of the scenes of asking at the door from Act III, and by the fulfilment of the audience's expectation that there will be more trouble for Knemon, which he has (once again) done something to deserve; it is typical of Menander that the emergence of Getas as a schemer of ingenious improvisation – a trait which might have been taken for granted in a comic slave – was unostentatiously forecast at the moment when we first heard of him (181ff). The change of mood from high comedy to revel is marked for the audience by the notes of the pipe and the transition from ordinary dialogue metre which it heralds; the breaking of the dramatic illusion when Getas addresses the piper directly is possibly a further sign that seriousness has departed. (See the following note.) It remains a little difficult to accept Knemon as a figure of fun after what we have seen of him before – the more so the more we have been engaged by the sympathetic aspects of the carefully developed character portrait. But to leave Knemon alone in his self-imposed isolation and let him fade from the play would scarcely have been possible; to have him abandon the

ast vestige of his principles and join the party without protest would
1ave been tame or worse; he might, like Demea in T. *Adel.*, have been
made to reverse his previous behaviour and join in the festivities all
too enthusiastically; but – all else apart – he has no Micio to outdo in
complaisance. Accordingly, he is bullied and teased into consent – a
comic relief, we may say, after the seriousness of his last great scene,
but one which comes dangerously near to compromising the subtle
blend of amusement and serious feeling on which the best of this kind
of high comedy is built. See under 932f (ii), and cf. Thierfelder in
Menandrea (Univ. di Genova, Ist. di Fil. Class., 1960) 107-12.

880 τί μοι προσαυλεῖς; 'Why are you piping for me?' – in the strictest
sense of the words 'Why are you playing me an accompaniment?'
Where the papyrus has αὐλεῖ the piper is presumably intended to
produce a trill or a snatch of tune to warm up his pipe and lead in the
scene. Anything more elaborate would be superfluous.

ἄθλι' οὗτος: the combination of οὗτος with a voc. in this order is
paralleled by βέντισθ' οὗτος at Theocr. 5.76 (where see Gow's note);
it should not therefore be removed by writing οὕτως with ed. pr., or
punctuating so as to separate the words with van Groningen *et al.*

The reference to the accompanist (for no other piper can be meant)
is interesting in that it breaks the dramatic illusion, which Menander,
like Terence, and unlike Aristophanes and Plautus, is normally careful
to preserve; though he follows convention in allowing the speakers of
prologues and epilogues to address the audience directly (see on 1f,
965-9); he admits ἄνδρες and the like both in soliloquies and asides
(194 n.); and he seems sometimes to have extracted a certain recherché
amusement from playing on the conventions of the theatre (see under
758).

Here, one suspects, a traditional kind of scene has brought with it
a traditional kind of joke, and it may be no more; but it could (as was
suggested above) help to make the point that the ending of the play
is not going to be serious, and it might have had a twist of novelty in
the fact that the piper is not asked to do his best, but to stop – and dis-
respectfully at that. Compare (i) Ar. *Eccl.* 884ff, an old woman and a
young woman preparing to sing rival love-songs ('There is something
pleasantly comic about this, even if it bores the audience', 888f). The
old woman says, 890, σὺ δέ, | φιλοττάριον αὐλητά, τοὺς αὐλοὺς λαβὼν |
ἄξιον ἐμοῦ καὶ σοῦ προσαύλησον μέλος. Her song follows. (ii) P. *Stichus*
715ff: the piper is invited to stop for a drink, and does so, while the
characters carry on without him; *ib.* 768ff, he is called on, as in Ar.
Eccl., for a special effort – a new tune in return for the old wine. This
of course must refer to what happened in Plautus' production, but
may have had a basis in Menander's *First Adelphoi*. See above under
880-958 (ii). (iii) P. *Pseud.* 573 a: Pseudolus tells the audience that the
piper will entertain them with an interlude. This, however, may well

be an idea devised for the occasion by Plautus; there is nothing to prove an extended pipe-solo in the *Dyskolos*, and the only analogy lie in the extra-dramatic allusion.

Apart from what he does here, the accompanist has to play for the chorus when they enter and on the other occasions when they perform he may also have provided the 'tune of Pan' which is supposed to come from Parthenis at 432ff. There should be no confusion between the two. The accompanist is, and remains, a person outside the play he wears the traditional piper's costume, a long decorated robe with sleeves, the badge of his office; his natural place is in the orchestra (If we assume that he mounted the stage platform for scenes like the present one, we shall not expect him, *pace* OCT, to come out from the shrine after Getas, but to appear discreetly at the side.) Parthenis, a figure in the play, arrived with the sacrifice-party, went into the shrine with them, and is now supposed to be playing for the dances of which we shall hear (950ff). She (there is no good reason to make her male) was seen wearing the feminine costume appropriate to her status, whether as a servant or as a hired music girl (430-41 (iii)). Her dramatic rôle could, if thought fit, be taken by the accompanist, but only if he can desert his post after the interlude before Act III and change costumes very rapidly before she has to appear. This is hardly likely. Still less should we attempt to eliminate the reference to the accompanist in the present context by postulating a male piper, otherwise unknown, who can be spared from the party to come out and play on the stage.

[*Costumes*: (i) *The piper as accompanist*: (*a*) Attic rf. oenochoe, *ca.* 400 B.C., in Leningrad; children dressing up as if to perform a Comedy, one of them as piper: Trendall, *Phlyax Vases*, no. 6; Bieber, *HT²*, fig. 184; drawing in Pickard-Cambridge, *Festivals*, fig. 80. (*b*) Campanian bell-krater, 350/325, in Princeton (Univ. Art Museum 50-64); piper accompanies a comic reveller with garland and torch: Trendall, *PV* 52; Bieber, *HT²* 531. Beazley in Hesperia 1955.305ff discusses these and other illustrations of dramatic accompanists in vase paintings. Cf. also the fragments of a marble relief from the Agora, 350/25 (?), with a comic chorus apparently led by its piper: Agora Museum, S.1026, 1586; Webster, *MOMC*, no. AS 3, and Hesperia 1960.263ff (with plate); Bieber *HT²* 181.

(ii) *Female pipers in dramatic scenes*: (*a*) Apulian bell-krater in Leningrad, 375/350 B.C.: Trendall, *PV* 32; Bieber *HT²* 511. (*b*) Mosaic by Dioskourides, saec. II B.C., from original 300/275 B.C., in Naples (9985): Webster, *MNC*, no. NM 2; Bieber, *HT²*, fig. 346; colour plate in Maiuri, *Roman Painting* (Geneva, Skira, 1953), p. 96. See also Introd. II.3 (iii) under (*m*), p. 39.]

881 πέμπουσ' need not imply that Getas is in fact acting under orders: he may simply be making an excuse: 879 n.

ἐπίσχες: perhaps ἔπισχε Arnott *et al.*, cf. 255; ἐπίστω ed. pr. The piper may (*a*) ignore the command and carry on; (*b*) obey it so far as to reduce his accompaniment; or (*c*) obey it literally and stop. See under 880-958 (i).

882 καὶ . . . γε: 'Yes, and . . .'; cf. on 586. Simiche is made to ignore Getas' remark to the piper, and carry on her train of thought in the new metre from where she left off, this time speaking into the shrine.

883 'Now that I'm losing Young Mistress . . .' ἀποστέλλουσα is lit. 'sending away' from home as a bride; cf. ἀποστολαί at E. *IA* 688. The old woman's feelings are understandably motherly; the girl's affection for her was brought out at 189ff.

τροφίμην, familiarly, without the article, as sometimes happens with other terms of relationship, e.g. ἐπαινῶ διαφόρως κεκτημένην *Perik.* 72; παιδίου 'στιν, οὐκ ἐμά 'They're Baby's, not mine', *Epitr.* 227. The common noun, habitually used with a particular reference, in effect becomes a proper name.

884 βάδιζε: 'carry on'; cf. on 817. [ταύτῃ: αὐτῇ OCT (Kassel).]

885-6 Damage makes the text uncertain. After πάλαι, most likely ϙ[or λ[; δέδοκται makes good sense and may well be right. The beginning of 886 can be accepted with moderate confidence; at the end ἀλλὰ διαπορ[ῶ τί χρὴ δρᾶν OCT (Maas); but ρ[looks unlikely; διαπον[εῖν ἔχρην με Barigazzi: alii alia.

887-8 leave a wide field for invention, since we do not know what part of the verb δυνησ[may have been. μάγειρε Σίκων probably, but not certainly, began a new sentence.

889 The cook's name: this is the first we hear of it from the text (unless it has been lost earlier: see 499 n.), and the choice was hardly a matter of great moment for the poet. Σίκων is known as a name both of free citizens and slaves, and presumably would not of itself imply anything definite about the status or profession of its owner. But there is some reason, apart from the present passage, to believe that the name may have been particularly appropriate for a stage cook. (i) Sosipater, *Katapseudomenos* 1 K, makes a cook claim to be one of three true surviving representatives of the school of the great master cook Sikon. The play is undated, and we can only guess at the basis of fact behind the comic tall tale; but it is possible that both Menander's cook and Sosipater's derive their name from some *maître de cuisine* of the past, whether real or fictional. (ii) Was this figure the Sikon of Aristophanes, *Aiolosikon I-II*? *Aiolosikon II*, apparently a revised version, was produced at the very end of Aristophanes' dramatic career, *ca.* 386 B.C. It was recognized in antiquity as a myth-parody of a type which became common later in the century; in the general modern view, the leading character was a compound of the Euripidean

Aiolos with a Sikon who was (or was portrayed as), a cook. If so, he was in some sense a forbear of the μάγειροι who appear as a stock figure in Middle Comedy (cf. 393 n.); and his name, as well as his nature, may have passed into the tradition. Unfortunately, what we know of this play is too tenuous to support anything more than speculation on the matter. See Meineke, *FCG* II.940ff; Kock, *CAF* I.392ff; Schmid-Stählin, *Gesch. d. gr. Lit.* I.4.221; Webster, *LGC* 18; Zwicker, *RE Σίκων* 2. Reihe 2.2 (1923) 2527f.

σὺ θᾶττον: a plausible, not a certain restoration; for θᾶττον cf. on 430f. κἄκουσ]ον OCT (Post).

890 'What a bit of fun I propose to have.' οἶμαι, cf. LSJ s.v., VI.3; διατριβήν as e.g. in 669, not 'delay' as ed. pr. takes it, printing οἴαν ἔχεις, οἴμοι, διατριβήν.

892 'Went through it just now, did I? Go and chase yourself, you and your damned nonsense.' The affray of 500ff is still a sore point with the cook. For 'indignant' δέ in questions, cf. Denniston, *Particles* 173ff. οὐ λαικάσει; is a colloquial obscenity which had no doubt lost some of its force through constant use, but would bear a stronger equivalent than the one given. Cf. Straton, *Phoenikides* 1 K (Page, *Lit. Pap.* 57.36f), where a man exasperated by a learned cook says οὐχὶ λαικάσει, ἐρεῖς σαφέστερόν θ' ὃ βούλει μοι λέγειν; For the exchange in general, cf. the opening of the cook-and-slave scene at P. *Aul.* 280-6, with its play on *diuidere*. [λαικάζειν is lit. *fellare* according to Housman, Hermes 1931.408 n. 2. (Fraenkel).]

893 ἔχει δὲ δὴ πῶς;: 'Well, how *is* he?' The inversion suggests a tone of impatient animation: cf. Thomson, *CQ* 1939 at p. 150, quoting, *inter alia*, Ar. *Plut.* 264 ἔστιν δὲ δὴ τί καὶ πόθεν τὸ πρᾶγμα τοῦθ' ὅ φησιν; [Beginning:]ων not]ον P; [γέρ]ων suits the space and seems certain: alii alia. The end is also variously restored: e.g. ἔχει δὲ πῶς νῦν; Page *et al.*; but πῶς was probably (not certainly) the last word in P's line.]

894ff Several arrangements of speakers have been suggested; with that of ed. pr., adopted here, we assume a division at the end of 893 (it cannot be said whether P had one there or not), and suppose that αἰτήσομ' εἰσιών τι has been wrongly divided, by paragraphos and double point, from ἔξω γὰρ ἔσται τῶν φρενῶν. OCT, assuming either no division or a wrong one at 893 end, arranges with P as follows: (Sikon) ... οὐ παντάπασιν ἀθλίως; (Getas) οὐκ ἄν ... ἀναστάς. (Sik.) οὐδ' ἀναστῆναι ... ἐγῷμαι. (G.) ὡς ἡδὺ ... εἰσιών τι. (S.) ἔξω ... τῶν φρενῶν, then on with Getas. But ὡς ἡδὺ πρᾶγμά μοι λέγεις seems odd in the mouth of Getas, and it might be better, if we begin in this way, to go on (G.) οὐκ ἄν ... ἐγῷμαι. (S.) ὡς ἡδὺ ... τῶν φρενῶν.

894-5 οὐ παντάπασιν ἀθλίως (here taken as a statement) = 'He's not completely down and out' – implying that there is still something they can do to vex him. Getas, I take it, is egging Sikon on, making sure of his man by leading up to the plan in easy stages and implicating him in the evolution of it; the cook, not surprisingly, would rather not let himself in for another beating. ('Couldn't he get up and hit us?': cf. 900f.) A simpler version of the same manoeuvre appears in the slave-comedy of Ar. *Knights* 20ff. [895 οὐδ' ἀναστῆναι ⟨γάρ⟩ ed. pr., followed by OCT and others. On the abnormal metrical pattern, see Introd. IV, Note E.]

897ff τί δ' ἄν, τὸ δεῖνα, κτλ. 'I say, what if we drag him out first . . .? There'll be some fun, I tell you.' The text given is based on Ar. *Wasps* 524 τί δ' ἦν, τὸ δεῖνα, τῇ διαίτῃ μὴ 'μμένῃς; τὸ δεῖνα is used as 'an inter-jection to express an idea which suddenly strikes one' (LSJ); on its formation, cf. Schwyzer I.612 (ε). [Alternatively, supplement ὦ τᾶν after πρῶτον (ed. pr., comparing *Sam.* 202), and – possibly – punctuate τὸ δεῖνα· πρῶτον, ὦ τ. with OCT. P's omission, whatever it was, is likely to have arisen from its recurrent fault of skipping one of two similar groups of letters, but certain restoration by these or other means is hardly possible: ⟨εἴσει⟩ τὸ δεῖνα Blake, from *Perik.*145. Cf. Moorhouse, CQ 1963.19ff. 898: προσελκύσωμεν is retained by ed. pr. *et al.*, and αὐτόν by van Groningen *et al.* – I believe wrongly, but cf. Jackson, *Marginalia Scaenica* 220ff.]

899 οὕτω: cf. on 781.

901 καθαίρῃ: 'beat', see on 114.

902ff 'Above all, we must teach the man his manners.' Knemon's *dyskolia*, if unchecked, will make him an intolerable in-law. Getas, as an old servant, speaks as one of the family, and ingratiatingly includes the cook in the circle.

With the punctuation given, τὸ δ' ὅλον is taken adverbially (lit. 'in general'), marking the transition from subsidiary considerations to the main point. Cf. LSJ s.v., I.4; Philemon 119 K; Com. Adesp. 339 K; Lucian, *Vit. Auct.* 8. But perhaps there should be a strong stop after ἡμῖν; then with ἐστὶν ἡ. (or better ἔστ' ἐφ' ἡ.), the meaning might be 'It's all ours', 'We have the whole situation in our power'.

ἡμερωτέος: an admirable conjecture, which seems indispensable if the passage is to make satisfactory sense. Kraus compares Aelian, *Ep. Rust.* 15, where Knemon is told δεῖ δέ σε καὶ ὅμως μὴ βουλόμενον ἥμερον ἡμῖν γενέσθαι – a slight but not insignificant support. [Nothing good seems to come of P's ἡμερώτερος, retained by ed. pr. and others: any suspicion that it makes sense to say 'the man is more polite to us' of Knemon (or of Gorgias, as Stoessl would have it), is banished by the difficulty of interpreting εἰ δ' ἔσται τοιοῦτος ἀεί, which can hardly be referred to οἰκεῖος, nor taken, without further qualification, to mean 'if he stays as he previously was'. αἰεί ed. pr., from P; but Menander's normal form is ἀεί (ᾱ̆), and we should not assume an anomaly here. P has αιϵ[ι in 31.]

905 ἔργον ὑπενεγκεῖν might have been more fully expressed as ἔργον ἔσται ὑπενεγκεῖν αὐτόν 'It'll be a job to put up with him'; but cf. *Karchedonios*, frg. 228; Diphilos 100 K; Poseidippos, *Homoioi* 20 K. [Metre: for this treatment of the first metron, cf. Ar. *Kn.* 422 ὥσπερ ἀκαλήφας (Introd. IV, p. 69).]

905-10 P's distribution of speakers seems wrong at least twice here (906, 909), and may be more seriously so, for more than one view can be taken of the dialogue and the action supposed to accompany it. See under 910ff.

905f λαθεῖν μόνον ἐπιθύμει i.e. 'do be quiet, above all'; noise would spoil the unpleasant surprise and possibly bring out someone from the shrine. The imperative ἐπιθύμει seems odd, but cf. βουλήθητε 46; the rhythm of the line-ending is also a possible sign that the text is corrupt: see Introd. IV, p. 69.

πρόαγε δὴ σύ: 'lead on then', 'come along'. This is a conventional courtesy between people who are going somewhere together, as for instance between Socrates and Phaedrus in Plato, *Phaedr.* 227 c, 229 a; cf. 228 b. At 866 above, Gorgias escorts his mother and sister from Knemon's house to the shrine with the words πρόαγετε δὴ θᾶττόν ποθ' ὑμεῖς – the θᾶττόν ποτε adding a touch of impatience. One should, no doubt, stand aside, or wait for the other person to move first; but here, it seems, there is no standing on ceremony: no sooner has Getas spoken the words than he makes a dash for the door, leaving Sikon protesting in the rear. [Cf. also Krobylos, *Pseudhypobolimaios* 5 K, where the defective first line might be read as A. Λάχης. Λα. ἐγὼ δὲ πρὸς σέ. A. πρόαγε ⟨δὴ σύ.⟩ Λα. ποῖ; With the second remark, a verb like ἔρχομαι is to be understood; see Gow on Theocr. 1.116f.]

906f μικρὸν πρόσμεινον: 'wait a bit', cf. *Epitr.* 538; *ib.* 188f βραχὺ | πρόσμεινον, ἱκετεύω σε. [It seems clear that P, as well as inverting δὴ σύ, has also put the dicolon the wrong side of μικρόν: the word is as appropriate with πρόσμεινον as it is out of place with what precedes. 907: ἐγκαταλιπὼν Turner.]

908 'Don't make a noise' is possibly said for fear that an exuberant opening of the door will make enough noise to bring Gorgias out. Cf. 900f, and on the noise of ancient doors, 188 n., with references there given. Getas swears he is not being noisy, and both go in, leaving the stage momentarily empty. We may assume, if we prefer, that Getas bundled the cook in and waited at the door, leaving him to struggle with the burden of Knemon and his couch alone; but in any case the way in which the orders are issued suggests that Sikon will have the heavy end, and his companion's part will be more supervisory than energetic. He has complained before of doing all the donkey-work (402ff, 550f), and there is good comic amusement in seeing him now with the rôles reversed.

909 εἰς δεξιάν 'to the right', means, on the view taken in this edition, to the actors' right: if we assume, as is reasonable, that the old man is to be deposited at the centre of the stage starting from his house, on the audience's left, it must be that one or both of his tormentors is facing the stage-building when this is said. See 5 n.

ἰδού is said, as at 406 and commonly, on complying with an order; θὲς αὐτοῦ is a further order which (in spite of P), clearly belongs to the speaker of εἰς δεξιάν, whom we presume to be Getas.

νῦν ὁ καιρός: cf. Ar. *Knights* 242; Nikostratos, *Tokistes* 25 K εἶεν· καλὸς ὁ καιρός (Marzullo).

910ff Having stationed their victim, the cook and the slave take it in turns to batter at the door with calls to Knemon's non-existent slaves, and ambitious requests to borrow party equipment. Given the liability of P to errors in marking changes of speaker, and given words which of themselves admit several possible arrangements, it is impossible to say with confidence how Menander intended the scene to be played. As above, I give what I hope is a plausible version, and attempt to explain and justify it; some of the many variations suggested will be found tabulated in van Groningen, *Ét. Critique*, 105f, 159f.

910 'I'll lead off – there! – and you keep in step.' (i) The general view (followed here) is that Getas is the speaker. This is consistent (for what that is worth) with the order of events in Act III, and with the leading rôle we have supposed him to take so far. But if we think that Sikon should now come to the fore, we may suppose without grave injustice to P that it omitted a double point after ειεν (so ed. pr.) – or, indeed, before it. (ii) The language is probably figurative. For προάξω, cf. Plato, *Phaedr.* 228 b (the context referred to on 905f): Socrates says of Phaedrus ... ἰδὼν μὲν ἰδὼν ἥσθη ὅτι ἕξει τὸν συγκορυβαντιῶντα, καὶ προάγειν ἐκέλευε. There, I take it, προάγειν implies 'lead the revel', and plays on Phaedrus' use of the phrase πρόαγε δὴ a little earlier. ἤν (if right) implies a caper or lively gesture as the speaker suits action to words and moves towards the door; τὸν ῥυθμὸν σὺ τήρει (again figuratively rather than literally) is then a command to his partner to tread the same measure when his turn comes. For the general sense of the remark, compare Ar. *Eccl.* 633f; at P. *Sti.* 719, as the piper pauses for a drink, we have: ubi illic biberit, uel seruato meum modum uel tu dato. If, guided by 880f, we assume that the accompaniment was suspended or muted for the scene of plotting, the line could also be the piper's cue to resume (880-958 (i)); Gallavotti suggests that the piper is being addressed directly again, and asked (literally) for strict tempo – but if so the aside would probably have been more clearly re-

flected in the language. Ed. pr. postulates a series of rhythmic raps on
the door by Sikon (who calls to the slaves, 911); Getas then copies him
and in turn calls to the slaves, 912. This hypothesis, even if we retain
both 911 and 912, seems to account for the Greek less satisfactorily.
(iii) 911 must either be radically rewritten or deleted. Page and Barrett
(followed by OCT) would see in it a botched attempt to write 912
which the copyist failed to cancel; Goold (Phoenix 1959.154) suspects
interpolation by someone who wished to explain 910 on the same lines
as ed. pr. There is however no reason in principle why a scene which
gains part of its point by repetitions should not begin with a double
sequence of calls and groans as Knemon wakes up; and P's general
carelessness in this context leaves little to choose between possible
diagnoses of its errors: I therefore prefer to print the line as it is most
plausibly remodelled. οἴχομ' οἴμοι must be a cry of distress by Knemon,
in spite of P's failure to indicate the fact: see e.g. *Epitr.* 585. In this
context (*pace* Stoessl *et al.*) it is perverse to take the verb literally and
think of the cook or the slave as speaker. [On the metrical difficulty
of παῖ, παιδίον (Κν.) οἴχομ' οἴμοι (ed. pr.), see Introd. IV, Note D (ii).
καλοί (P) is retained by OCT and others: see on 462.]

913 'Who's this? Do you belong to this house?' Cf. *Perik.* 184. Getas
devilishly pretends never to have seen the old man in his life before.
δηλονότι as an answer 'Of course', as e.g. Alexis, *Pannychis* 173 K.14.
[Ed. pr. (less satisfactorily) gives the whole line to Knemon: . . . ἐντεῦθέν
τις εἶ δηλονότι. σὺ δὲ τί βούλει; P's odd behaviour in leaving a blank
space in the line suggests that the δη of δηλονότι was already absent or
illegible in the original. A similar blank appears again 18 lines later,
μὴ ⟨∪⟩ γρύζων 931.]

914 λέβητας . . . καὶ σκάφας (if the reading is right) should possibly
be taken as 'augmentative' plurals (440 n.); but the request for
'cauldrons and bowls' is in any case deliberately pretentious, like
those which follow. What was originally asked for, and refused, was a
λεβήτιον: see on 472f, and on the vessels in question, Amyx, Hesperia
1958, at pp. 199f, 231f, and Obst, *RE* 'Skaphe' 2. Reihe 3.1 (1927)
439ff.

αἰτοῦμαι παρ' ὑμῶν, the plural referring to the household or family;
for the construction, see e.g. Alexis, *Epikleros* 79 K, quoted on 761-3.

[(i) Ed. pr. *et al.* make Sikon the speaker: cf. under 910 (i). (ii)
σφακον P; but 'sage' will not do here. Having observed the confusion
σκαφ-/σφακ- already in 605, one is ready to abandon it in favour of a
word for 'vessel(s)': σκάφος (ed. pr., followed by OCT *et al.*) might
conceivably have been used by Menander to mean a large bowl, but
given that P's termination is misread or confused, σκάφην (Marzullo)
or the plural σκάφας is preferable as the normal word. (iii) λέβητά σ'
αἰτοῦμαι παρ' ὑμῶν is adopted by OCT from Page, with the explanation

'rogo te uasculum ex aedibus uestris'; but the possible advantage of
the singular is offset by the clash of pronouns.]

914f τίς ἄν ... ὀρθόν; (and again 928f): cf. 701.

916 καὶ ... καί continues the list. Both τρίποδες and τραπέζαι are here
small tables for the guests. To ask for seven of the one and twelve of
the other is indeed a refinement of high living, for in common parlance
a small table might be called either, whether it was a 'three-leg' or not:
hence the somewhat frigid jokes retailed by Athenaeus 2.49. See
Pritchett, Hesperia 1956.241ff and Webster, Bull. Rylands Library
1962.271 with further references and discussion. [917 αὖτ' ἀγγείλατε
ed. pr.; ἄγετ', ἀγγείλατε Thierfelder. 918: not οὔκ, ἀκήκοας μυριάκις
(ed. pr.); cf. 172, 511; ἀλλ' ἀκήκοας Mette.]

918-20 On ἀποτρέχω δή Getas presumably skips off a step or two,
leaving Knemon a brief moment to puzzle on his situation before
Sikon takes up the game. The end of 920 admits several arrangements
and interpretations. As printed here, ἄπαγε δὴ σύ is taken as a remark
of Sikon's: 'Off you go then' (and let me have my turn); καὶ δή, although
not separated by P, seems unsatisfactory as an appendage to the
imperative phrase, and most likely as a preface to the calling and
knocking at the door (compare, perhaps CF 68ff); it can be taken as an
elliptical answer by Getas ('I've already gone' or 'I'm going') if the
verb, which (if not part of the verb 'to be') is normally present in this
idiom, is assumed to be understood from ἄπαγε. [919 ὦ δυστυχὴς ἐγώ:
cf. on 574. 920 τίς εἰς τὸ πρόσθε με κατέθηκεν; ἄπαγε δὴ σύ (Σικ.) καὶ
δή ed. pr.; τίς μ' ... κατατέθηκεν; (Σικ.) ἄπαγε δὴ σὺ καὶ δή OCT;
... κατατέθηκεν; ἄπαγε καὶ σύ. (Σικ.) κ.δ. Kraus; alii alia. I doubt if
Knemon is supposed to have seen Sikon yet; if we think he says
ἄπαγε δὴ σύ to speed the departing Getas, we may compare 926 and
regard P's double point before ἄπαγε either as a mark of change of
direction in the speech or as an error (Introd. III, pp. 45f). On καὶ
δή =ἤδη (so Jacques) cf. Starkie on Ar. Wasps 492.]

921f cf. 466f. I prefer, with Gallavotti and OCT, to read μαίνει,
ἄνθρωπε as a question.

922f δάπιδας: 'rugs' or 'covers', called στρώματα in 405. Cf. Pritchett,
Hesperia 1956.246f.

χρήσατε seems better suited to the space available than δίδοτε (van
Groningen; cf. Sam. 86), but other alternatives are available. πάρεχε
ed. pr.; but the letter before ε was probably not χ. A strong break at
this point in the tetrameter after resolution is unusual: cf. Introd. IV,
p. 69.

923-5 The text is variously supplemented and arranged; without
better evidence much must remain uncertain. The 'Oriental curtain'
is large enough to hang as a surround for a fair-sized banquet; one

might be able to borrow it, like the rest of the equipment, from a wealthy man's house in town, but not, of course, from Knemon's. One of the affectations of the ἄρεσκος in Theophrastus *Char.* 5 is to own αὐλαίαν ἔχουσαν Πέρσας ἐνυφασμένους.

βαρβαρικόν suggests, but does not of course prove, a fabric of Persian origin: textiles and carpets were in fact available to the Greek world from several Eastern centres, and Menander has no reason to be precise. Cf. especially Ar. *Frogs* 937f (παραπετάσματα Μηδικά decorated with strange Oriental animals), P. *Sti.* 378f (Epignomus brings home *Babylonica et peristroma tonsilia et tappetia*); and for further references, discussion and examples, see Pritchett, Hesperia 1956.248ff, and Webster, Bull. Rylands Library 1962.263ff.

ὑφαντόν probably 'brocaded' or with a fancy weave of some kind, as opposed to λεῖον 'smooth', 'plain' (LSJ, s.vv.). *Exodus* 38.23 distinguishes τὰ ὑφαντὰ καὶ τὰ ῥαφιδευτὰ καὶ ποικιλτικά 'woven and embroidered work' (F. von Lorenz, *ΒΑΡΒΑΡΩΝ ΥΦΑΣΜΑΤΑ*, in Römische Mitteilungen 52 (1937) 220).

λινοῦν is a guess based on the expectation of another adj. describing the curtain (therefore possibly its material, as in κρατῆρα . . . χαλκοῦν μέγαν below); some evidence for linen decorative fabrics is given by Pritchett, loc. cit. [ἐρεοῦν might seem equally or more attractive (cf. the παραπέτασμα ἐρεοῦν described by Pausanias 5.12.4), but is open to metrical objection, as is Barrett's brilliant but adventurous . . . ἑκατὸν] ποδῶν τὸ μῆκος. *(Κν.)* ἑκατόν; εἴθε μοι γένοιτο | ἐ]ν[ός] π[ο]θεν, adopted by OCT. Cf. Introd. IV, Note D (ii). μακρὸν ed. pr. (superfluous); λεπτὸν Diano, Foss; alii alia.]

924ff ἱμάς ποθεν: again an uncertain supplement, but cf. 502. The objection raised by van Groningen and Kraus that Knemon is now in no condition to use a strap is not one which would occur readily to an irascible old man in Knemon's situation, nor (I suspect) to a dramatist writing this scene.

[*(Σικ.)* ἔστιν. *(Κν.)* πόθεν; ed. pr. τίς ἔνδοθεν; Webster (not . . . τις ἔνδοθεν as in BICS 1959.71); ἑνός ποθεν Barrett: see above. A hanging one foot long is a brave notion, possibly too brave for the context and speaker. The irregularities of P's margin on this page make it hard to guess how long a supplement we need; for τίς ἔνδοθεν cf. τοῖς ἔνδον 917.]

ἐφ' ἑτέραν . . . θύραν: cf. 516f. Possibly, as there, to be taken as a deliberative question (so Winnington-Ingram, and Lloyd-Jones in OCT), but I prefer the parallel with ἀποτρέχω δή 918. Sikon presumably pretends to give up and moves towards Getas; Getas comes forward to ask for the mixing-bowl, and provokes Knemon's curse. [926f: alternatively, κακὸν δὲ κακῶς σ' ἅπαντες . . . (ed. pr.). The curse comes ill from Sikon or Getas, to whom some give it; for the double points before κακόν and after θεοί, cf. Introd. III, p. 45f).]

928f τίς ἄν ... ὀρθόν; request and reaction echo 914f. On the mixing-bowl, cf. Amyx, Hesperia 1958.198f.

929f Back comes Sikon to repeat his request for the curtain. The end of 930 is variously emended and interpreted. Adopting μὰ τὸν Δί᾽, I prefer, with Kraus, to take οὐδ᾽ ὁ κρατήρ as an elliptical question from Getas, rather than a continuation of Knemon's reply with OCT, as Fraenkel and Quincey originally suggested. See e.g. Perik. 254 οὐδ᾽ ἄρα νῦν; 'Not even now?', and Ar. Thes. II, 318 K (A.) ... ἢ νῆστις ἑπτᾶτ᾽ ἢ γαλεὸς ἢ τευθίδες; (B.) μὰ τὸν Δί᾽ οὐ δῆτ᾽. (A.) οὐδὲ βατίς; P's παιδιον is metrically anomalous (cf. Introd. IV, Note D (ii)), as well as puzzling in itself: why a slave at this point? If not a complete mental aberration induced by the writer's unfortunate experience with 911f, it could imaginably arise from an original with ματονουδ᾽ and δι added over the line. Neither the lack of a double point after παιδιον nor the presence of one after κρατηρ is decisive for the arrangement of speakers. Cf. 926f. *(Γε.)* πατρίδιον, οὐδ᾽ ὁ κρατήρ; Barigazzi, followed by Diano, Mette et al.; ed. pr. offers *(Κν.)* ποῦ παιδίον; *(Σικ.)* οὐδ᾽ ὁ κρατήρ; – a version with fatal objections.]

931-53 *Distribution of parts*: P's indications of speaker continue to be inadequate, as they are till the end of the tetrameters, but the damage to 935ff makes the situation here particularly difficult. 931-4: Knemon is told that he deserves his fate and that fuss is useless; 935-53: a glowing account of the proceedings at the party in the shrine, with at least two interruptions, 941f, 945. Sikon must speak 942 (after οἴμοι) to 945 μάγειρος ... μέμνησο, and there are reasonably good general grounds of content and style for crediting him with the concluding section, 946-53. Working back, the words ηὐτρέπιζον συμπόσιον κτλ. in 940f appear *prima facie* to be the preface to the action described in 943, and the ἄκουε κτλ. of 935 to be the same speaker's preface to his whole account. Since P's paragraphos under ἄκουε (if not erroneous) could indicate a brief intervention by Getas or Knemon (which need not have outlasted the line), there is no theoretical objection to the view that the whole section (less interruptions) belongs to Sikon, and the text is set out accordingly. True, one might expect Getas to take a more prominent part, but the words preserved give no secure ground for supposing that he did. In particular, the κάθευδε of 931 does not necessarily indicate a different speaker from that of πρῖε σαυτόν 934 and μὴ κάθευδε 941 (see nn.); nor does the emphatic ἐγώ in 940 have to be said by another speaker than ἔγωγε ... ἐμοί in 944: the vainglorious cook could be emphasizing his own part throughout. I quote three alternative arrangements: (i) ed. pr.: Getas, 931 κάθευδε ... 935; Knemon, 936-7; Getas, 938-41 μὴ κάθευδε; Knemon, μὴ γάρ, οἴμοι 941f, then Sikon to 953. (ii) Lond.: Sikon, 931 κάθευδε ... 935; Getas, 936-41 μὴ κάθευδε; Knemon, μ.γ.ο. 941f, then Sikon to 953, with μαλακὸς ἀνήρ 945 as an interruption by Getas. (iii) OCT: Sikon,

931 κάθευδε ... γρύζων; Getas, 931-5; Sikon, 936-41 μὴ κάθευδε, then
as Lond., but with doubt about the speaker of 946-53 (?Σικ.).

931-4 'Pipe down and go to sleep. If you can't face a crowd, hate
women, and won't have yourself taken to join people at a sacrifice
you must put up with all this. There's no-one to help you, so lie there
and keep your temper.'

931 κάθευδε: cf. *Perik.* 219f κάθευδ' ἀπελθών, ὦ μακάριε, τὰς μάχας
ταύτας ἐάσας – the tone of taunting sarcasm is evident. When the
wretched Knemon does lie still and say nothing at a point where his
tormentor would like a reaction, he is bullied in the opposite direction
941f μὴ κάθευδε. (Κν.) μὴ γάρ; οἴμοι. The humour of the situation is
underlined by the verbal echo, and emerges more clearly if (as I
assume) the speaker of both commands is the same.

μή τι γρύζων: i.e. 'don't go on muttering and grumbling'. Some
prefer μηδέ: so OCT (Lloyd-Jones).

932f (i) On the paratactic structure, see under 57ff (iii); the future
ἀνέξει expresses the inevitable consequence of the situation described
by the three presents: cf. κατακείσει 875. πάντα ταῦτα, like Eng. 'all
this' can refer generally to one's present situation or surroundings, and
should be so taken here, not referred to ὄχλον, γυναῖκας etc. Cf. Ar.
Κn. 99f πάντα ταυτὶ καταπάσω | βουλευματίων 'I'll spatter bright ideas
all over the place.' (173 n.)

(ii) Reading μισεῖς γυναῖκας, one takes the three parallel statements
all to refer to the last manifestation of Knemon's *dyskolia* – his refusal
to join the party, which, as Simiche foretold, has brought him more
trouble. The point is not only that the cook and the slave are trying
to teach Knemon a lesson; the lines serve to remind the audience that
the scene of ragging, however amusing for its own sake, has a place in
the design of the plot (880-958 (iii)). Gorgias was able to overcome
the countryman's natural unsociability, which he shares in some
degree with Knemon (note especially 871f ὑπεραισχύνομαι γυναιξὶν ἐ
ταὐτῷ); but Knemon's unsociability is ancient, ingrained, and still
(in spite of all) excessive.

With γυναῖκα μισεῖς (Kassel, Ad. Mette), adopted by OCT, the
lines become a general condemnation of the old man's conduct
– more pointed, it is true, but less apt to this context, where there is
no need to bring in Knemon's old estrangement from his wife.

(iii) οὐκ ἐᾷς κομίζειν ... σαυτόν: cf. *Methe*, frg. 264 οὐκ εἴασα τὴν
ὀσφῦν ἂν ἐπὶ τὸν βωμὸν ἐπιθεῖναί ποτε | εἰ μὴ καθήγιζέν τις ἅμα τὴν ἔγχελυν
English naturally uses the passive in sentences of this kind; Greek
strongly prefers the active (or middle) infin. Similarly, e.g., παρέχω
(ἐμαυτὸν) κομίζειν (τινί) 'I let myself be taken': cf. Starkie on Ar. *Cl*
422, KG II.15f.

εἰς ταὐτὸ τοῖς θύουσι: 872 n.

934 πρῖε σαυτόν: the meaning here seems to be 'set your teeth' or 'bite your lip' (i.e. 'keep your rage in control'), not 'gnash your teeth' (i.e. 'go on raging'), although the middle means 'rage' in frg. 695 and elsewhere. But cf. ὀδόντι πρῖε τὸ στόμα Soph. frg. 897 P, with Pearson's note; δακὼν δ' ἀνάσχου Sam. 141, and similar phrases with δάκνειν. Hence αὐτοῦ (i.e. 'lie there and . . .') is preferable to αὐτός (Mette et al.) or αὐτῶς. αὐτός in this collocation would surely intensify the reflexive, giving it an unwelcome emphasis.

935-7 The damage is too serious for restoration to be useful.

[935: If γὰρ (or γὰ[ρ]) is right after πάντα, we should probably punctuate after ἄκουε δ', and not after ἑξῆς with Bingen, OCT et al., for ἑξῆς πάντα are words which naturally go together. Cf. Philemon 89 K.5 with Kock's note, and ἐφεξῆς πάντας 34 above. But for other possible readings, see Turner, BICS 1959.63; τα[λ]λω might also be read, though if so there is no diastole for τἄλλ'. 936: ἀν]άγκας (printed by Mette) is obvious but not inevitable; at the end μὴ γά]ρ (Stoessl) would fit, but it is not easy to accommodate a repetition of 941f. On the metre, cf. Introd. IV, Note E. 937: αἱ] παρ' ὑμῶν is likely; cf. on 375, 849. The sense required might be given by καλῶς διῆγ]ον (or ἤδη παρῆλθ]ον) αἱ γυναῖκες ἐ[νθάδ' αἱ] παρ' ὑμῶν: what is lost is unfortunately the vital part of the line. On the distribution of parts, see above under 931-53.]

938-9 Restoration doubtful. περιβολαὶ . . καὶ δεξιώματα (if right) means 'embraces and welcoming handclasps'. μῆτερ, δέχου ταύτας Sostratos had said (867), and a warm greeting for the future in-laws is exactly what we should expect. Now, it seems, they are enjoying themselves. [περιβολαί is the most attractive among the words which might have been in P, and if right strongly suggests that the missing word in -ματ' belonged to the same sphere. For δεξιώματα cf. Jebb on S. OC 619, adding Dio Cassius 58.5. A very rare word of poetic background should not lightly be ascribed to Menander, but seems well suited to the style of this particular narrative, which is markedly poetic from 946 onwards. OCT adopts περιβολαὶ alone; μεταβολαὶ . . . εἰς εὐτυχήματ' ed. pr.; συμβολαὶ . . . εἶτα τὰ τραγήματ' (Diano) gives an antithesis for τὸ πρῶτον but otherwise seems improbable.]

940 μικρὸν δ' ἄνωθεν requires a verb of saying to be understood: μικρόν γ' ἄνωθεν, Epitr. 64; τί οὖν δὴ λέγω; νυνὶ ἐρῶ ἄνωθεν ἀρξάμενος, Plato, Ep. ii, 310 e. Such a verb may have been present or implied at the start of the narrative; but the text is uncertain and variously treated. ηὐτρέπιζον, like ἐστρώννυον etc. below, is narrative imperfect ('. . . there I was, preparing . . .'). [ἐγένετ' ἄνωθεν (ed. pr.) cannot be read, nor is ἄνωθεν likely to mean 'up there' in reference to the shrine. Lloyd-Jones, followed by Kraus, suggests κα]ὶ [μὴν ἄ]νωθεν . . . , but does not restore in OCT; alii alia.]

941 τοῖς ἀνδράσιν τούτοις said, no doubt, with a gesture. Men and women sit separately (cf. 948), as is normal on such occasions: see e.g. *Sam.* 72 f; Euangelos, *Anakalyptomene* 1 K.

μὴ γάρ; ('Not sleep?') must be taken as an echo of μὴ κάθευδε, as Oguse and Quincey saw: they are followed by Kraus, Jean Martin and others.

In view of 931 (where see n.) the old man's protest is both under-standable and amusing. If the verb had been repeated, we should by the normal rule have had μὴ (γὰρ) καθεύδω; delib. subjunctive: KG I.222. [μὴ γάρ as a statement, ed. pr., followed among others by OCT. I do not know why this punctuation is so popular, nor why such efforts are made to defend it: see, e.g., van Groningen, *Ét. Crit.*, ad loc.].

942 With τί φῇς; βούλει παρεῖναι one assumes deliberate, and ap-propriately cruel, misunderstanding of the οἴμοι. But no-one can say what is missing from P. ⟨πότῳ⟩ ed. pr. ⟨σὺ δ' οὐ⟩ Page: alii alia. OCT *et al.* leave a gap. For παρεῖναι 'to be at the party', see e.g. Ar. *Birds* 131.

943 Text exceedingly doubtful: 'There was a great to-do; I set out places on the ground.' Cf. P. *Sti.* 677f, quoted by D'Anna and others: ibi festinamus omnes; | lectis sternendis studuimus munditiisque apparandis.

σπουδὴ γὰρ ἦν is probably sound, and refers to the atmosphere of enthusiasm and bustle which ensued from the decisions of 850ff. Sikon was involved when Kallippides went in to arrange for the party at 860, and now plays up his own part to the limit. For the phrase σπουδή ἐστι (γίγνεται), cf. Stephanus-Dindorf, s.v.; γάρ resumes the narrative after the prefatory πρόσεχε: cf. 117 n. The brevity is no surprise in lively narrative: e.g. Xenarchos, *Porphyra* 7 K.9ff μάχην | ἐποίησ' ἐν αὐτοῖς ἐξεπίτηδες εὖ πάνυ, | ἦσαν δὲ πληγαί, κτλ.

The end is variously treated, but remains beyond certain solution: OCT accordingly obelizes. I give what seems a good but unverifiable guess. χαμαιστιβής is unknown, but cf. πεδοστιβής and the compounds of χάμαι listed in LSJ, p. 1975; a coined word (if it is a coinage) would not be unthinkable in the style of the present context; if the acc. denotes the object effected by the verb, as it commonly does with στρώννυμι, the literal sense may be 'I spread rugs so as to make places that-walked-the-ground' – perhaps not more far-fetched for a party where rugs are essentially the furniture than it is to call old wine εὔιον γέροντα πολιὸν ἤδη, 946. For the acc. in this use, cf. KG I.323 and *NTGramm.* §158, noting νόμισμα κόπτειν 'strike a coin'; ὤρυττον εὐνάς 'dug themselves beds', Ar. *Kn.* 605; Lat. *lectum sternere*; Eng. 'cut bread and butter'. For τράπεζαι as 'places', cf. τραπέζας ποιεῖν *Sam.* 72f *al.* [σπονδὴ γὰρ ἦν is suggested to me by Lloyd-Jones; σπονδὴ παρῆν might also be considered if it were clear that the beginning is corrupt; so Kassel, followed by Jacques. σπονδῇ γὰρ ἦν ἐστρωμένη χαμαὶ στιβάς Gallavotti. Those who take τραπέζας ἔγωγε as a separate statement (as

lo Gallavotti, van Groningen *et al.*) postulate a difficult ellipse, or else assume that the sentence is incomplete when ἀκούεις; interrupts it Bingen²). ἐστρώννυον χαμαὶ στιβάδας, τραπέζας (ed. pr.) is metrically anomalous, as are a number of other proposals: e.g. the ἐστρώννυόν τι ·αμαί, κτλ. of Bingen¹: cf. Introd. IV, Note D (ii). There is in any case hardly room for τι[χα]μαι or -γ[ε]χ[α]μαι in P; perhaps for -τ[ο]χ[α]μαι.
.. στιβάδα, τραπέζας (Maas) introduces a very difficult singular;
.. στιβάσι, τραπέζαις 'laid out the party with divans and tables' may be worth considering, but the dative is unwelcome. Kraus considers that a line may have been lost between στιβάδας and τραπέζας; Jacques, assuming transposition, prints ἐστρώννυτ[ο] στιβὰς χαμαί; these and other possibilities of severe corruption must naturally be borne in mind.]

944f It was no doubt amusing to hear Sikon claim as the proper duty of a skilled caterer the work which should fall to the τραπεζοποιός, of whom he elsewhere speaks with scorn (see 646-7 and nn.). But for his party no τραπεζοποιός was hired, and he must make what capital he can of having arranged things for the men's side of the party, while leaving 'others' to look after the women and take round the wine.

μαλακὸς ἀνήρ must be Getas' comment, as many have seen. I take it to refer jokingly to the spreading of rugs which S. has just mentioned: an excessive liking for soft furnishings at a party was, by Greek standards, a sign of that effeminate luxury which they associated with the East – as it were, μαλακῶς ὑποστρωννύει, μαλακὸς οὖν ἐστιν. See, e.g., Hdt. 9.82; Xen. *Cyrop.* 8.8.16; Athenaeus 2.48, 11.474 c-d; Menander, *Halieus*, frg. 24 and frg. 858; and cf. on 923-5 above. The same atmosphere is present in a description by Aelian of a luxurious party for performing elephants, *NA* 2.11: τὰ δὲ ἐπὶ τούτοις καὶ ἐκμῆναι τὸν θεατὴν ἱκανά· χαμαιζήλων κλινῶν στιβάδες ἐν τῇ ψάμμῳ τοῦ θεάτρου τεθεῖσαι, εἶτα ἐδέξαντο τυλεῖα καὶ ἐπὶ τούτοις στρωμνὴν ποικίλην, οἰκίας μέγα εὐδαίμονος καὶ παλαιοπλούτου σαφῆ μαρτύρια· καὶ κυλίκια ἦν πολυτελῆ παρακείμενα ... τράπεζαί τε παρέκειντο θύου τε καὶ ἐλέφαντος ...

Another possibility, raised by Dr Christina Dedoussi, is that μαλακὸς ἀνὴρ is a comment on an effeminate gesture or dance step (cf. P. *Sti.* 760f, 769ff); if so, there is no direct cue for it in the text. Webster further refers me to *MG* 668: tum ad saltandum non cinaedus malacus aequest atque ego.

946-53 As the description reaches its climax, the language takes on a marked poetic colour, and the metre is noticeably strict and smooth; the actor's delivery may have risen correspondingly towards song: see on 880-958 (i) and Introd. IV, pp. 61f.

No closely comparable passage of Menander is so far known, but a similar use of elevated style to heighten the description of a festive occasion is recognizable (in spite of textual uncertainties), in Parmeno's words at *Sam.* 328f ποοῦσι γάρ σοι τοὺς γάμους· κεράννυται, |

θυμίαμ' ἀνάπτεταί τι θῦμά θ' 'Ηφαίστου φλογί ('fire' = 'flame of Hephaistos';
more ostentatiously ῥιπὶς δ' ἐγείρει σκύλακας 'Ηφαίστου κύνας Euboulos,
Orthanes 75 K; ἤδη πυκνοὶ δ' ᾄσσουσιν 'Η. κ. Alexis, Milesia 149 K).

In parallel situations, earlier comic poets draw freely on the poetic
manner of tragedy and dithyrambic lyric: in calling old wine εὔιον
γέροντα πολιὸν ἤδη, and water νᾶμα Νυμφῶν (for example), Menander
can be said to be indulging himself and his audience in a piece of
traditional comic *panache*; but he stops short of the more elaborate
excesses of this allusive poetic style, and achieves at the end of the
brief narrative an attractive word-picture of the maidservants dancing,
gay with wine but girlishly shy. [Feasts, parties and the things which
go with them are ancient and perennial topics for comic description,
lending themselves to a wide variety of treatment. See in general
Herter, Wiener Studien 1956.33ff; Süss, RhM 1910.450ff; Fraenkel,
de med. et nov. com. 13ff; Webster, *LGC* 22, 65f, 155. I mention some
particularly relevant passages, some of which will be quoted in part
in following notes. (i) *Iambic tetrameters in similar contexts*: see under
880-958 (ii). (ii) *Elevated style*: e.g. Plato 189 K, Antiphanes 237 K,
Alexis, *Kyknos* 119 K (paratragic); Antiphanes, *Homoioi* 174 K (pseudo-
dithyrambic, presumably sung, perhaps recalling in particular the
Deipnon of Philoxenos: Page, *PMG* no. 836. (iii) *Elaborate excesses*:
cf. esp. Euboulos, *Orthanes* 75 K (contrasted above with *Sam.* 328f);
Antiphanes, *Aphrodisios* 52 K; Timokles, *Heroes* 13 K (a table described
as βίου τιθήνη, πολεμία λιμοῦ, φύλαξ | φιλίας, ἰατρὸς ἐκλύτου βουλιμίας).
Cooks are to be recognized as speakers at least in some of these passages;
poetizing diction is part of their stock-in-trade. On the allusive poetic
style ('figuratum dicendi genus') as characteristic of Middle Comedy,
see Meineke, *FCG* i.290ff.]

946-8 Mixing and serving the wine.

946f εὔιον γέροντα πολιόν 'old wine': εὔιον, although glossed in P
with τὸν Διόνυσον (misplaced at the end of 944), should be taken as an
adj. 'the Bacchic elder': similarly γέροντα Θάσιον Epinikos, *Mnesipto-
lemos* 1 K; Λέσβιον γέροντα νεκταροσταγῆ Euboulos 124 K; (οἶνος) ἡδύς
γ', ὀδόντας οὐκ ἔχων, ἤδη σαπρός, | ...γέρων γε δαιμονίως Alexis,
Orchestris 167 K; Antiphanes, *Aphrodisios* 52 K has Βρομιάδος...
ἰδρῶτα πηγῆς for 'wine'.

ἔκλινε prob. 'tilted', metaphorically for 'poured'; but could be 'put
to rest'.

κοῖλον κύτος is here perhaps said of a *krater*, perhaps of a large cup
in which the wine is both mixed and served. Cf. Plato 189 K ... στάμνον
εὐώδους ποτοῦ | ἵησιν εὐθὺς κύλικος εἰς κοῖλον κύτος, | ἔπειτ' ἄκρατον κοὔ
τεταργανωμένον | ἔπινε ... The guests here, unlike the man in Plato,
do not do anything so outlandish as to take their wine neat.

'Water' is 'the Nymphs' stream', as, for example, wine is Βάκχιον νᾶμα in the elevated style of Ar. *Eccl.* 14; the fact that the party was held in a shrine of the Nymphs need hardly have crossed Menander's mind.

948 δεξιοῦσθαι in a context of drinking is to pledge someone – to offer him a cup with the right hand to drink a toast, a gesture of formal politeness and friendship: see Headlam-Knox on Herondas 1.82 and cf. E. *Rhes.* 419. The use of the dat. with this verb to indicate the recipient of the gesture is paralleled at A. *Ag.* 852 θεοῖσι . . . δεξιώσομαι where however the sense is something like 'hail with honour'.

κύκλῳ: as it were 'went round' to each guest in turn.

949 'It was just as if you were carrying sand – do you understand that?' Text and interpretation are disputed. On the view taken here, the comparison – a rather far-fetched one – is between going backwards and forwards with wine from the bowl to the guests, and the apparently endless cycle of moving a heap of sand basketful at a time, perhaps with the additional point that the cup or jug may run short by being diverted on the way, just as the sand may be blown away or sift through the wicker. Menander may have had in mind some such scene as that described by Hdt. 8.71 οἰκοδόμεον διὰ τοῦ Ἰσθμοῦ τεῖχος. ἅτε δὲ ἐουσέων μυριάδων πολλέων καὶ παντὸς ἀνδρὸς ἐργαζομένου ἤνετο τὸ ἔργον· καὶ γὰρ λίθοι καὶ πλίνθοι καὶ ξύλα καὶ φορμοὶ ψάμμου πλήρεες ἐσεφορέοντο, καὶ ἐλίννον οὐδένα χρόνον οἱ βοηθήσαντες ἐργαζόμενοι, οὔτε νυκτὸς οὔτε ἡμέρης. A Philemon would probably have exploited the idea at length: cf. the cook's elaborate comparison in *Stratiotes*, 79 K, discussed by Webster, *LGC* 128f. [The reading ὥσπερ εἰς ἄμμον φοροίης (so OCT) involves no alteration of P, but is perhaps only to be defended on Thierfelder's assumption that ὥσπερ εἰς stands for ὥσπερ εἰ εἰς by haplology (Schwyzer I.264); the sense would be 'as if you were carrying it to sand' = 'as if you were watering a beach' *vel sim.* ὥσπερ εἰ 's (Diano, Sydn., *et al.*) assumes both the anomalous form ἐς (see on 112) and prodelision of it; ed. pr. prints ὥσπερ ἂν εἰς to the detriment of the metre; alii alia.]

ταῦτα μανθάνεις σύ; is here punctuated to go together as an expanded form of the common μανθάνεις; (see e.g. Antiphanes, *Hautou Eron* 49 K; Damoxenos, *Syntrophoi* 2 K. 23, 53). ταῦτα could however belong with the preceding words, as given by ed. pr., OCT *et al.* Perhaps ἦν δ' ὥσπερ εἰ ψάμμον φοροίης, ταῦτά.

950ff Cf. Plato, *Lakones* 69 K.10ff:

σπονδὴ μὲν ἤδη γέγονε, καὶ πίνοντές εἰσι πόρρω.
καὶ σκόλιον ᾖσται, κότταβος δ' ἐξοίχεται θύραζε.
αὐλοὺς δ' ἔχουσά τις κορίσκη Καρικὸν μέλος τι
μελίζεται τοῖς συμπόταις, κἄλλην τρίγωνον εἶδον
ἔχουσαν, εἶτ' ᾖδεν πρὸς αὐτὸ μέλος Ἰωνικόν τι.

950f βραχεῖσα 'tipsy'. [βρεχεῖσα from ἐβρέχην (P) is printed by ed. pr., OCT *et al.* This form of the aor. is recorded from Greco-Egyptian sources from saec. ii B.C. onwards (where it has a special reference to the Nile flood); on the available evidence it is markedly more likely to have been introduced by a copyist than written by Menander. Cf. LSJ and Preisigke-Kiessling, *Wörterbuch d. gr. Papyrusurkunden* IV.2 (1958), s.v.]

εὐήλικος ... κατεσκιασμένη: the girl appears 'with the bloom of her fair young face shaded' because she is going to dance; though βραχεῖσα, she still behaves μετ' αἰσχύνης. We may imagine her wearing a veil or head-scarf, possibly with a garland of leaves and flowers, and with her hair flowing over her cheeks. See especially E. *IT* 1143-51, to which Webster refers me, and *Phoen.* 1485ff with Schol.; *Iliad* 18.597 with Lorimer, *Homer and the Monuments* 387; Simonides 148 B = *Anth. Pal.* 13.28, and Semonides 7 D, 65f; for κατασκιάζειν specifically of hair, cf. Archilochus 25 D. ἄνθος in this sense is familiar from poetry: ed. pr. notes also Plato, *Rep.* 501 b. εὐῆλιξ seems to make its first appearance here.

951-3 χορεῖον εἰσέβαινε ῥυθμὸν: 'began to dance'. Once one girl had found the charms of the music stronger than her shyness, another felt daring enough to take her hand and dance too. Compare Ar. *Thes.* 953ff.

συγκαθῆπτε: a compound not previously recorded. [εἰσέβαινε, ῥυθμὸν ...μέλπουσα κ.τ. ed. pr.; κἀχόρευον Maas. No alteration seems desirable.]

954 πρᾶγμα πάνδεινον: cf. *Sam.* 212. [(Κν.) ὢ ... παθών Lond.]

συνεπίβαινε: 'join in'. I imagine (no stronger word can be used) that Getas suits action to Sikon's description, dancing up to the couch with hand extended and inviting Knemon to partner him. Perhaps the pair attempt to pull him to his feet. He has the awful choice of being forced to agree, or being carried to the party, and chooses the latter (958). 'Agrestem quandam saltationem exhibet Cnemo' remarks Lloyd-Jones in OCT; but the text does not make it clear whether the old man was supposed to get up and totter a step or two before being carried in on his couch, or whether he merely kicked and gesticulated as he lay there: in either case the actor would have a welcome chance to show (appropriately for the end of a comedy) that the invalid still had some life and spirit in him, and was not permanently crippled. Webster recalls to me two broadly analogous scenes: (*a*) on an Apulian bell-krater of 380/370, where two slaves attempt to push the elderly Centaur Chiron upstairs while Nymphs look on from their grotto: British Museum F.151 = Trendall, *Phlyax Vases*, No. 35; Bieber, *HT*², fig. 491; (*b*) on a Paestan calyx-krater by Assteas (ca. 350 B.C.) where two men attempt to dislodge 'Charinos' from a chest on which he is lying: Berlin, F.3044 = Trendall, 70; Bieber, 508.

955 τί ποτε, τί βούλεσθ᾽ ('What *do* you want with me?'; cf. 913, 927) is probably the best way to remove P's corruption. For the double interrogative, cf. ποῖ σύ, ποῖ Sam. 109, 225 and Ar. *Eccl.* 1065; πῶς δῆτα, πῶς *Knights* 82; τίς ... τίς ποτε *Peace* 877; τίνα τρόπον ... τίνα *Frogs* 460; τί δαὶ σύ, τί λέγεις ib. 1454. The last two are commonly printed with two question marks, as Koerte does at *Sam.* 109 but not 225.

ἄθλιοι = *importuni* (Kraus); cf. 702.

μᾶλλον here is apparently a weak adversative ('rather', 'instead'), implying 'join in rather than protest and call us names' – not an intensitive ('join in more'). Cf. [Theocritus] 27.2 and Gow ad loc. P continues not to identify the parts: I assume, with OCT, that Getas now takes up: ed. pr. and others bring in Sikon again. [τί ποτ᾽ ἔτι Householder, Marzullo: if so, perhaps continue with Knemon to μᾶλλον. τύπτετε Fraenkel, adopted by OCT *et al.*; alii alia. For the assumed τιποτε > τιπτε > τυπτε cf. οικεια > ουκ᾽ εια 873.]

956 ἄγροικος εἶ: 'you are rude', 'your manners!' – a mocking reference to the old man's refusal to dance. Cf. Com. Anon., Page, *Lit. Pap.* 63.24, quoted on 611ff.

μὴ πρὸς θεῶν: cf. 751.

957f 'Take me: perhaps it's better to put up with the party in there.' τἀκεῖ seems to give the best point in this context. [P has probably either incorporated κακά as an explanation of the expression, or conflated the alternatives > τἀκεῖ and τὰ κακά – the latter preferred by OCT. ἔστ᾽ ἐκεῖ κακά or ἐστὶ κεῖ κακά would be metrically anomalous. At the end, κρατοῦμεν fits well with ὦ καλλίνικοι, and is to be preferred to κρατοῦ γε (ed. pr.) *vel sim.*]

959 ὦ καλλίνικοι: a vestige of the victory revel which is a traditional form of comic ending: see e.g. Ar. *Ach.* 1227ff, *Birds* 1764.

Σύρε is far from certain, but a list of three names is probable enough (cf. Ar. *Frogs* 608), and P's σύ γε, adopted by ed. pr. *et al.*, seems indefensible. Donax and Syros (if we believe in him) are Getas' fellow-slaves whom we have seen in Sostratos' mother's procession at 430ff; the point that two men *could* carry Knemon is immaterial. Perhaps Σίκων σύ τε; better σύ τ᾽ ὦ Σίκων OCT (Lloyd-Jones). The idea that the accompanist is a slave called Donax (Gallavotti and others) is, I think, an extravagant one.

961 παρακινοῦντα: 'giving trouble'; so, e.g., Dem. 15.12.

962 οὐδὲ μετρίως: cf. 314.

963f τὸ τηνικαῦτα (if right, as seems most likely) belongs naturally with what precedes, not with what follows as taken by ed. pr.: the text is punctuated accordingly.

For garlands and torch, see e.g. Antiphanes 272 K, and *Skythai* 199 K; an illustration is quoted under the heading 'Costumes (i) (*b*)' in 880 n. They go together as natural accompaniments of a κῶμος and (like Aristophanes in the *Plutus*, 1194f), Menander will have his hero taken off in the traditionally appropriate way: ἀλλ' ἐκδότω τις δεῦρο δᾷδας ἡμμένας | ἵν' ἔχων προηγῇ τῷ θεῷ σύ. The pair of closely associated words stand in asyndeton, separated by the interlaced τις ἡμῖν; for the coupling, cf. e.g. *Kekryphalos* frg. 239 μύρα, στεφάνους ἑτοίμασον, and for the separation, e.g. ἀνάπηρον ὄντα, χωλὸν 662 above.

[P's corrupt text is variously treated: τὸ τηνίκ' ἀλλ' ἔξω δότω Page; cf. Antiphanes, *Ganymedes* 74 K.7. τὸ τηνικαῦτ'· ὦ ἐκδότω is perhaps worth considering, if we assume τηνικαδ(ε) as an error for τηνικαῦτ(α); for ὦ (ὥ) preceding an imperative, cf. Fraenkel on A. *Ag.* 22. But without better parallels, it seems unwise to introduce the hiatus involved: for instances in trimeters, see Descroix, *Trim. Iambique* 26-9. τὸ τηνικάδ'. ἰώ, ἐκδότω (Gallavotti, followed by Jean Martin and Jacques) brings in both hiatus and – whether we scan ἰω or ἰω – an anomalous metrical break (Introd. IV, Notes A and B). ὡς ἐκδότω at the end, with the imperative analogous to an expression of wishing, would have the doubtful support of Ar. *Peace* 320: see the commentators there and on *Frogs* 955, *Plut.* 891.]

964 τουτονὶ λαβέ: 'take this one'. The garland opportunely seized by Sikon was perhaps hanging at the door of the shrine, or, as I prefer to suppose, lay on the altar of Apollo Agyieus close by. Polemon seizes a garland similarly at *Perik.* 421 f: cf. Capps ad loc. (his line 880), and on 659 above. [νὴ τὸν Ἀπόλλω τουτονί is not however to be read in *Perik.* 172 (241 Capps) without departing from the MS: cf. Jensen and Koerte ad loc.]

965-9 Before the actors leave, Getas calls on the audience to applaud, and expresses the hope that Victory may attend the company's efforts. In spite of P, εἶέν should very probably come from Getas, and not from the speaker of τουτονὶ λαβέ: cf. *Perik.* 144, *Phasma* 48. OCT continues with Sikon.

κατηγωνισμένοις . . . γέροντα is literally 'triumphed over the troublesome old man'; but in their context, the words no doubt play on the sense 'performed the *Dyskolos* to the end'. See LSJ s.v. ἀγωνίζομαι A.3, and compare Aristophanes' word-play with the title *Knights* at *Ach.* 300f. A more obvious flight of fancy transforms the dramatic victory which the cast hope for (and in fact were to win for their author) into the personified 'noble, laughter-loving maiden'.

967 μειράκια, παῖδες, ἄνδρες: for similar series, cf. Headlam-Knox on Herondas 2.68. The audience, as at Ar. *Peace* 50ff, is deemed to consist of its male members of various ages; it was perhaps not the done thing to appeal to the ladies present. The evidence for their presence at performances of plays is admirably dealt with by Pickard-Cambridge, *Festivals*, 268ff.

ἐπικρότησατε: compare frg. 771, presumably also from the end of a comedy; otherwise δότε κρότον; Lat. plaudite, plausum date.

968f The closing lines are formulaic, like the introduction of the chorus at 230ff. They were already known from a quotation which Wilamowitz tentatively assigned to the end of the *Epitrepontes* (=*Epitr.* frg. 11 Kö.); Turner reports them from an unpublished papyrus of another play by Menander (now recognized as the *Misoumenos*, under an alternative title) and Bataille from the *Sikyonios*. P. Heid. 183 gives the ending of Poseidippos, *Apokleiomene* as [ἡ] δὲ φιλόγελως θεὰ | [Νίκη με]θ' ἡμῶν εὐμενὴς ἔπ[οι]τ' ἀεί, perhaps a conscious recall of Menander: although we do not know that he invented the formula, the fact that he uses it repeatedly suggests so. Cf. Maas, Glotta 1956.301; Vogt, RhM 1959.192.

Euripides provides a precedent (*Orestes, Phoenissae*; cf. *IT*); an interesting comparison and contrast is offered by Ar. *Knights* 586ff. Both these poets speak through their choruses; the writers of New Comedy naturally entrust their prayers for victory to actors.

Nike is φιλόγελως as the Victory of Comedy (Euripides addresses her as ὦ μέγα σεμνὴ Νίκη); in calling her εὐπάτειρα, Menander does not reveal who he thought her father was, and, according to Wilamowitz (*Schiedsgericht*, 116), this is something only a pedant will ask: he might begin by consulting Hesiod, *Theogony* 383ff, Bacchylides, *Epinikoi* 11 init., and Bernert, *RE* 'Nike' 17.1 (1936) 285ff.

ADDENDA

New fragments of *Misoumenos* and *Sikyonios*: see above on 968f, and pp. 16 n.3, 48 n.2, 60 n.2. Information about these important new texts came too late for me to make more than the slightest of references to them, and I take a welcome opportunity to add a very little more.

(*i*) *Misoumenos*: fragments of a papyrus codex from Oxyrhynchus, to be dated to the later third or early fourth century A.D., give some 300 partly preserved lines, overlapping at several places with fragments of the play already known. The title which this copy gives was formerly believed to be *Thratta*; it is now recognized (in spite of damage) as *Thrasonides*. The new fragments are to be published by Professor E. G. Turner – during 1965, it is hoped – and have already been discussed by him in a paper read at the IVth International Congress of Classical Studies in Philadelphia on 25 August 1964.

(*ii*) *Sikyonios*: see now the *editio princeps* by A. Blanchard and A. Bataille, in Recherches de Papyrologie, tome III, pp. 103-176 and planches VI-XIII [= Publications de la Faculté des Lettres et Sciences humaines de Paris, Série 'Recherches', tome XIX, 1964]. These fragments are substantial new pieces of the roll which was first published as P. Ghoran 1 by Jouguet, Bull. Corr. Hellénique 1906. 103ff [= Page, *Lit. Pap.* 66]. The title is given as *Sikyonioi* (frg. XXI); from the script and other evidence, the editors suggest a date in the last third of the third century B.C. I am very grateful to Professor Bataille for showing me the papyrus and discussing a number of points. There is still much work to be done on the text, and I note here only a few small points which affect *Dyskolos* and can be put briefly:

45-6: cf. *Sik.* frg. IV/A, 4f.

496 The word for 'priestess' appears three times in *Sik.*: frg. VI/B, 7; frg. VI/C, 1 and 22. At the first two places, the spelling is -ει-; at the third, where B.-B. read παρὰ τῆς ἱερεί[ας, I prefer παρὰ τῆς ἱερέα[ς. So far as the metre is concerned, the penultimate syllable could scan long or short in all three; the length of the alpha is undetermined. The figures I give should be modified accordingly.

568 γύναῖα: in suggesting this scansion, I have referred to the discussion of παιανιστάς τινας in the note on 230 (i). Add now ὦ γεραιέ, *Sik.* frg. X/C, 15.

774f (cf. Introd. IV, Note D): add to the evidence for 'dactyls' in trochaic tetrameters the line-ending Στρατοφάνη κατὰ σύμβολα, *Sik.* frg. X/B, 3. I doubt, however, if the text of the papyrus should stand, and am clear that it should not in the previous line, which begins ὤφελεν ὁ πατήρ, nor in 14, where for ἦ ῥά γε (B.-B.) πραγε (i.e. πάραγε) seems probable.

INDEX

References are to page-numbers throughout. Occasionally there is an extra reference to a particular note in the commentary, as '161 (173 n.)'.

Two economies made in selecting entries for the index perhaps deserve special mention. (*i*) Certain sections of the Introduction contain a high proportion of detail set out under headings – namely II.3, on costumes and masks (pp. 30-39), III on the text (pp. 40-55), and IV on metre (pp. 56-73); I hope that the layout of these may make their content accessible, and have therefore not itemized it rigorously in the index. (*ii*) Where notes in the commentary provide their own further references, I have often shortened the index accordingly, especially in listing Greek words and phrases.